THE BODY AND SOCIETY

LECTURES ON THE HISTORY OF RELIGIONS

Sponsored by the American Council of Learned Societies
New Series, Number Thirteen

PETER BROWN

THE BODY AND SOCIETY

Men, Women and Sexual Renunciation in Early Christianity

COLUMBIA UNIVERSITY PRESS

New York *1988*

Library of Congress Cataloging-in-Publication Data

Brown, Peter Robert Lamont.
The body and society.

(Lectures on the history of religions; new ser., no. 13)
Bibliography: p.
Includes index.
1. Celibacy—Christianity—History of doctrines—Early
church, ca. 30–600. 2. Virginity—Religious aspects—
Christianity—History of doctrines—Early church, ca.
30–600. 3. Sex—Religious aspects—Christianity—
History of doctrines—Early church, ca. 30–600.
4. Asceticism—History—Early church, ca. 30–600.
I. Title. II. Series.
BT708.B77   1988   253'.2   87-30941

Columbia University Press
New York   Guildford, Surrey

Book design by Ken Venezio

This volume is the thirteenth to be published in the series of Lectures on the History of Religions for which the American Council of Learned Societies, through its Committee on the History of Religions, assumed responsibility in 1936.

Under the program the Committee from time to time enlists the services of scholars to lecture in colleges, universities, and seminaries on topics in need of expert elucidation. Subsequently, when possible and appropriate, the Committee arranges for the publication of the lectures. Other volumes in the series are Martin P. Nilsson, *Greek Popular Religion* (1940), Henri Frankfort, *Ancient Egyptian Religion* (1948), Wing-tsit Chan, *Religious Trends in Modern China* (1953), Joachim Wach, *The Comparative Study of Religions*, edited by Joseph M. Kitagawa (1958), R. M. Grant, *Gnosticism and Early Christianity* (1959), Robert Lawson Slater, *World Religions and World Community* (1963), Joseph M. Kitagawa, *Religion in Japanese History* (1966), Joseph L. Blau, *Modern Varieties of Judaism* (1966), Morton Smith, *Palestinian Parties and Politics That Shaped the Old Testament* (1971), Philip H. Ashby, *Modern Trends in Hinduism* (1974), Victor Turner and Edith Turner, *Image and Pilgrimage in Christian Culture* (1978), and Annemarie Schimmel, *As Through a Veil: Mystical Poetry in Islam* (1982).

IRELAND

BRITAIN

Rhine

Trier

Danube

GAUL

Moselle

Nantes

Tours

Aquileia

Lyons

LIGURIA

Vercelli

Milan

DALMATIA

Clermont

Vienne

Rhône

Ravenna

Thessalonica

Bordeaux

Arles

Lérins

Rome

Beneventum

Eclanum

Tarragona

Nola

CAMPANIA

Messina

Carthage

SICILY

Syracuse

Elvira

Hippo Regius

Cirta

Thagaste

Arbitina

Mediterranean Sea

NUMIDIA

Theveste

AFRICA

N

E

W

S

C. Carlson

100 A.D.   200 A.D.

Marcus Aurelius 161–180   Decius 249–251

Philo of Alexandria
±25 B.C.–50A.D.

Plotinus 205–270

Porphyry 225– ±305

270* ? *Against the Christians*

Origen 185–254

Clement of Alexandria ±150– ±215

Plutarch ±50–120

Jesus ±30   ±225* *Peri Archôn*

±90* *Gospels* collected   229/30* Moves to Caesarea

248* *Against Celsus* 296–373

Paul of Tarsus → ±67   Athanasius ±296–373

54* *Letter to Corinthians*   Anthony ±250–356

Marcion ±140–180   Anthony Pachomius ±290–347

±120* *Shepherd* of Hermas

Eusebius of Caesarea 260–339

Legend of Paul and Thecla ±140*

±220* *Acts of Judas Thomas*

Soranus 98–138   ±200* *Letter on Virginity*

Galen 140–199   Mani 216–277

Valentinus 130–165   172* Tatian leaves Rome for Syria

Justin Martyr 130–165

±165* Martyrdom of Polycarp

Cyprian of Carthage 248–258

Tertullian 160–220

203* Martyrdom of Perpetua

177* Martyrs of Lyon

Irenaeus ±130– ±200

100 A.D.   200 A.D.

300 A.D.   Julian   400 A.D.   500 A.D.

Constantine 306–337   361/3   Justinian 527–565

Constantius II 337–361   Theodosius I

303* Great Persecution   379–395   Romanao Melodes ±490–±554

312* Conversion of Constantine

312* Methodius of Olympus martyred   Dorotheus of Gaza ±500–580

±330* Amun at Nitria

Ephraim 306–373

John Chrysostom 347–407   Barsanuphius ±470–543

Theodoret of Cyrrhus 399–466

325* Council of Nicaea   ±450* *Saying of the Fathers* collected

303* Council of Elvira   Symeon Stylites 396–459   451* Council of Chalcedon

Evagrius of Pontus 346–399

Olympias of Constantinople 361–408   John Climacus 575–650

Macrina ±325–380   419* Palladius, *Lausiac History*

Basil of Caesarea ±330–379

Gregory of Nyssa ±335–395   Philoxenus of Mabbug 440–523

Eusthathius of Sebaste ±300–377

Basil of Ancyra 336–360   390* Messalians condemned

Gregory Nazianzen 323–389

Ambrose of Milan 339–397

Jerome ±342–420

386* Priscillian executed   Gregory of Tours 538–594

Melania the Elder 342–411   393* Condemnation of Jovinian

Marcella 330–410

Paula 347–404   410* Sack of Rome

Rufinus of Aquileia 345–410

Melania the Younger 380–434   Pope Gregory I 590–604

Paulinus of Nola 356–431

418* Pelagius condemned

Julian of Eclanum ±386–454

Augustine of Hippo 354–430

396* *Confessions*

401→* *On Genesis*

413→* *City of God*

419* *On Marriage and Concupiscence*

John Cassian 360–435

300 A.D.   400 A.D.   500 A.D.

Contents

Preface

In this book, I study the practice of permanent sexual renunciation—continence, celibacy, life-long virginity as opposed to observance of temporary periods of sexual abstinence—that developed among men and women in Christian circles in the period from a little before the missionary journeys of Saint Paul, in the 40s and 50s A.D., to a little after the death of Saint Augustine, in 430 A.D. My principal concern has been to make clear the notions of the human person and of society implied in such renunciations, and to follow in detail the reflection and controversy which these notions generated, among Christian writers, on such topics as the nature of sexuality, the relation of men and women, and the structure and meaning of society.

My account begins in the second century A.D., in a pagan world where Christianity had begun to achieve a certain measure of public visibility. The second chapter returns in time to the Palestine of Jesus, to Saint Paul and to the role of continence in the obscure and stormy first century of the Christian movement. By around the year 150, sexual renunciation had come to mean many things to many Christian groups. For this reason, chapters 3 through 6 will move around the Mediterranean and the Near East, from Lyon and Carthage to Edessa.

I hope to do justice, in this way, to the range of options faced by Christians in the remarkable fifty years that stretched from the generation of Marcion, Valentinus, and Tatian to that of Tertullian and Clement of Alexandria.

The towering genius of Origen dominates all accounts of the further development of notions on sexuality and the human person in the Greek world. But the fascination that came to be exercised by Origen's peculiarly majestic ideal of virginity is difficult to understand if we do not risk an opinion on the role of continence in the relations between men and women within the changing structures of the churches of his generation. Chapter 7, devoted to this topic, precedes our account of the thought of Origen. Chapter 9 delineates the parting of the ways between pagan notions of abstinence and the Christian ideal of virginity in the later third century. The first part of the book closes, in chapter 10, with a survey that presents some of the varied meanings taken on by the practice of sexual renunciation in the different regions of the Christian world, and then considers the relations established between continent and married members of the churches in the age of Saint Anthony and Constantine.

The second part of the book opens with the traditions of spiritual guidance associated with the Desert Fathers, who came to flank the churches of the settled land, in Egypt and elsewhere, from the reign of Constantine to the last days of the Roman Empire in the East. The next chapters take up in detail, topic by topic and region by region, the impact of ascetic ideals on the thought and practice of the churches of the Eastern Empire throughout the fourth and early fifth centuries.

Part III deals with the Latin world, which is closer in many ways to the traditions with which many modern Western readers can identify themselves. I set the attitudes of three outstanding authors—Ambrose, Jerome and Augustine—against the dilemmas peculiar to their place and generation, and measure the degree to which the Catholic tradition, to which they contributed so decisively, differed from the traditions that we have met in the eastern Christian world. The Epilogue forms a doublet to the first chapter: it sums up the changes in the notion of the human person and of society that had taken place between the age of the Antonines and the beginning of the Middle Ages.

A book of this size and span demands some explanation and, above all, a frank statement of the limitations and renunciations that came to be imposed upon it in the course of writing. It is a book about Early

Christianity. I have been concerned with recapturing the distinctive flavor of that period in the history of Christianity which distinguished it from all subsequent centuries. It will soon become apparent, to any reader, that the notions of sexual renunciation it considers are profoundly different from those to which we have become accustomed from our acquaintance with medieval Catholicism and with the Christianity of modern times. This is a book where the cult of the Virgin Mary emerges only toward the end. Clerical celibacy, though finally advocated by some, was practiced in a manner totally unlike that now current in the Catholic Church. The ascetic movement, though a constant, fascinating presence for much of this period, lacked the clear and orderly profile later associated with the Benedictine monasticism of the Latin West. Even the notion of perpetual virginity, though it dazzled many writers in the late third and fourth centuries, came into clear focus only in fits and starts: above all, it never acquired the unambiguous association with specifically female chastity that it achieved in other ages, both in the pagan world and in later forms of Catholic Christianity. The Early Church remains a period still charged with more than academic interest for many readers. Stereotypes, alternately placid and histrionic, gravitate around it with remarkable ease. If my book gives back to the Christian men and women of the first five centuries a little of the disturbing strangeness of their most central preoccupations, I will consider that I have achieved my purpose in writing it.

But the reader must be aware of the limitations of this book. It became a book about Early Christianity in particular, and not about late antiquity in general. This was a hard renunciation for me to have made. It was due not only to my own, frank predilection for Early Christian texts, from Paul to Augustine, but in part also to my own perception of the state of scholarship on sexuality and the family in the ancient world. Acutely aware of my own lack of competence in Jewish studies and in the history of the Greek and Roman family, I thought that it was wiser not to venture too deep into terrain which, I gradually learned from my reading, had remained largely unexplored even by the experts. I have done my best to indicate, in my footnotes and in the bibliography, those studies on which I depended with gratitude. Readers should treat them as doors, left deliberately ajar, in order to tempt them to wander from room to room, far beyond the self-imposed limits of this book. Nothing would distress me more than if the reader were to receive the impression that my deliberate and regretful prudence countenanced the belief that the experience of Christians was somehow different (in a privileged manner) from that of their Jewish and pagan neighbors. To be frank: I have frequently observed that the sharp and dangerous flavor of many Christian notions of sexual renunciation, both in their personal and their social consequences, have been rendered tame and insipid, through being explained away as no more than inert borrowings from a supposed pagan or Jewish "background." But an effort to do justice to the particularity of certain strains of Christian thought and practice should not be held to justify the systematic dismissal of the complex and resilient ecology of moral notions that characterized the Mediterranean cultures of the age; still less should it encourage us to ignore the profound changes in the structure of ancient society in this period. If renewed study of the actual sexual practices and attitudes of Judaism, in Palestine and the Diaspora, and of the changes in the family structure and moral tone of pagans, in the long centuries that stretch from Trajan to Theodosius II, were to correct this book, render parts of it out of date, or set my narrative in a more cogent social framework, no one would be more delighted than myself.

Only a hundred years ago, I would have had to begin any study that dealt with sexuality and its renunciation with an apology. When he wrote his *History of European Morals from Augustus to Charlemagne,* William Lecky found himself obliged to warn his readers that parts of it dealt with the notion of chastity, and so with its presumed antithesis—experience of sex:

It will be necessary for me in the course of the present work to dwell at greater length than I should desire upon questions connected with this virtue. . . . I am sorry to bring such subjects before the reader, but it is impossible to write a history of morals without doing so.[1]

It is more appropriate, to a humane person of the modern age, rather, to make plain to the reader how little can be said on these important subjects. The necessary word of caution is briefly stated: from one end of this book to the other, we shall be dealing with evidence of an overwhelmingly prescriptive and theoretical nature, written exclusively by male authors. How, and indeed whether, such evidence can be used is a matter of prolonged academic debate. It is important to make one point clear. Given the harsh values of the Greco-Roman world, it is a

---

1. William Lecky, *History of European Morals from Augustus to Charlemagne* 1:51 and note 1 on p. 52.

comfortable and dangerous illusion to assume that, in much of the evidence, the presence of women is even sensed by its male authors, as might well be the case in later periods of European history. To pass from a reading of the Fathers of the Church to a book such as Caroline Walker Bynum's study of a crucial aspect of the piety of late medieval women,[2] is to realize that the Christianity of the High and Later Middle Ages—to say nothing of the Christianity of our own times—is separated from the Christianity of the Roman world by a chasm almost as vast as that which still appears to separate us from the moral horizons of a Mediterranean Islamic country. Despite the continued fascination, for the Western reader, of the Roman Empire and the origins of Christianity, we must respect their irreducible particularity, and nowhere more than in the stark limitations that silently and insistently delimited the relations of men and women in a late Roman society. Bynum's model study has revealed a world of surprising richness, in which significant differences of viewpoint existed between men and women on central issues of Christian faith and practice. Able to draw on the abundant evidence of late medieval Catholic Europe, a book of such subtlety serves to remind us, scholars of the Early Church, that it is both our privilege and our accursed lot to work the flinty soil of a long-extinct and deeply reticent world. We shall be dealing with a Christianity whose back is firmly turned toward us, untroubled by our own most urgent, and legitimate, questions.

These cautions are not merely perfunctory. They were learned on the job. I would not have written this book ten years ago, and if I had I would not have written it with so persistent a sense of salutary vertigo. I have begun to benefit, slowly, from the gains of a remarkable recent development in the study of the religious world of women, most especially from the chastening sophistication of viewpoint that this study can now offer. At a crucial moment in my own work, I was fortunate to have had the opportunity to take heart from the humbling serenity and unaffected craftsmanship of Michel Foucault, in what I was not to know were his last years. To readers, for whom, I suspect, sexuality has come to wear a more comfortable face than it did for William Lecky and his Victorian audience, I would use Foucault's words, to warn them, as he would have done, and with a clearer voice than I, that they must not sink into the cozy, even arch, familiarity with

---

2. Caroline Walker Bynum, *Holy Feast and Holy Fast: The Religious Significance of Food to Medieval Women.*

which a modern person often feels entitled to approach the sexual concerns of men and women in a distant age:

After all, what would be the value of the passion for knowledge if it resulted only in a certain knowingness . . . and not, in one way or another, . . . in the knower's straying afield from himself? There are times in life when the question of knowing if one can think differently than one thinks, and perceive differently than one sees, is absolutely necessary if one is to go on thinking and reflecting at all.[3]

This brings me to the last, and perhaps the most serious, caution. For all the creaking rigidities of our ancient sources, and for all the intellectual skills demanded of a modern scholar in rendering them intelligible, it would be deeply inhumane to deny that, in these centuries, real men and women faced desperate choices, endured privation and physical pain, courted breakdown and bitter disillusionment, and frequently experienced themselves, and addressed others, with a searing violence of language. It is disturbing to read of Saint Eupraxia, a noble girl, and so better fed and more vigorous than her fellow-nuns in a great Egyptian monastery, sleeping on hard ashes to tame her body at the time when her periods first began. The very matter-of-fact manner in which monastic sources report bloody, botched attempts at self-castration by desperate monks shocks us by its lack of surprise. Reading even measured and well-known utterances, such as the sermons of Augustine on the daily martyrdom of the Christian life, we are touched, for a moment, by the chill of "a melancholy day of late September."[4] The texts bring us up against pains and sadnesses that lie as close to us as our own flesh. The historian's obligation to the truth forces us to strive to make these texts intelligible, with all the cunning and serenity that we would wish to associate with a living, modern culture. But the reader must remain aware that understanding is no substitute for compassion. This book will have failed in its deepest purpose if the elaborate, and strictly necessary, strategies involved in the recovery of a distant age were considered to have explained away, to have diminished or, worse still, to have stared through the brutal cost of commitment in any age, that of the Early Church included.

The present text grew from the series of Lectures in the History of Religions, sponsored by the American Council of Learned Societies, delivered in 1982–1983. It was from the American Council of Learned

3. Michel Foucault, *The Use of Pleasure*, R. Hurley, trans. p. 8.
4. C. P. Cavafy, *Manuel Comnenus*, line 2.

Societies and the History Department of the University of California at Berkeley that I received funds for the year's leave during which I made my first start on this project, in 1980–1981. In 1982, the John D. and Catherine T. MacArthur Foundation gave me the unforeseen possibility for leisure, and with it the responsibility, to bring this book to a conclusion on a scale, and with a rapidity, that would have been inconceivable in any other circumstances. I have been more than fortunate in the different environments in which this book was written. An ambitious undertaking, it was got under way with a sense of joy and quiet purpose that I will always associate with the University of California at Berkeley. I completed it at the History Department of Princeton University, among new friends, chastened by the resources of new libraries, and instructed by regular contacts with visiting scholars to the neighboring Institute for Advanced Study. Throughout these years, I knew that I could rely on the quiet and apposite riches of the Biblioteca Marciana at Venice, and on the unfailing courtesy and interest of Marino Zorzi. As a visiting professor and colleague to Giorgio Cracco, at the Istituto di Storia Medioevale e Moderna, at the University of Padua, in 1986, I gave the near-final version of part of this book, in the form of lectures and profoundly helpful seminars. In all this period, I have learned the meaning of intellectual friendship as never before. The names that I now mention, ranged facelessly enough in alphabetical order on the printed page, have, each one, been a reminder to me of the inextricable bonds of companionship, candor, and shared concern that have brought the breath of life to the slow, and largely unpredictable, growth of this book: Caroline Bynum, Han Drijvers, Elizabeth Gilliam, Susan Harvey, Tom Laqueur, Glenn Most, Elaine Pagels, Carol Quillen, Susan Watkins, Michael Williams, and Froma Zeitlin. The two bibliographies (of primary sources and of secondary literature), the index and the chronological table—all, that is, that makes a text of use to scholars and navigable by its readers—are the work of one person: Catherine Peyroux. I trust that all who use this book will also come to feel a little of my own deep gratitude for her alert enthusiasm and unremitting precision. They must, however, bear in mind that the bibliographies, though large, were not intended to be comprehensive: the list of primary sources, especially, registers only the editions and translations that I myself happened to use, or happened to find worthy of recommendation to students, when preparing this study. My use of Biblical citations has been equally flexible.

No one known to me has maintained with such unremitting vigor the necessity for truth in historical studies than has Arnaldo Momigliano. It is to his sense of truth, as well as to the magnificently unconstricted range and human warmth of his concern for the role of Judaism and Christianity in the history of the ancient world, that I have turned, for all of thirty years now, as a model and an inspiration. It is an honor for me to make clear, through the dedication of this book to him, the fact that he has been my teacher and my friend.

Arnaldo Momigliano died between the time of his reading the near-final draft of this book and its preparation for the printer. There is little consolation for such a loss. One can, at least, pour one's feelings into the mold provided by his own words, when he wrote of another, amazing scholar of the ancient world—Michael Rostovtzeff: "Those who have known him have known greatness. They will always cherish the memory of a courageous and honest historian for whom civilization meant creative liberty."[5]

Nor would it be out of place to cite in his memory a saying of the rabbis, which, for all its ancient solemnity, still has its place, as Arnaldo Momigliano knew so well, in the very different circumstances of our own times: "Every judge who judges a judgement of truth, true to the truth of the matter, causes the glory of God to dwell in Israel."[6]

Peter Brown

PRINCETON,
MARCH 25, 1987

5. A. D. Momigliano, "M. I. Rostovtzeff." *The Cambridge Journal* (1954) 7:346.
6. *Babylonian Talmud: Sanhedrin* 7a.

THE BODY AND SOCIETY

PART ONE

FROM PAUL TO ANTHONY

ONE

Body and City

On the southern coast of Turkey, in the middle of the fifth century
A.D., a Christian priest of the shrine of Saint Thecla at Seleucia (now
Meryemlik, near Silifke) decided to write an improved version of the
legend of the virgin saint. He presented Thamyris, the rejected fiancé
of Thecla, arraigning Saint Paul before the local governor for having
preached perpetual virginity in the city, and, with virginity, the abandonment of marriage:

This man has introduced a new teaching, bizarre and disruptive of the human
race. He denigrates marriage: yes, marriage, which you might say is the beginning, root and fountainhead of our nature. From it spring fathers, mothers, children and families. Cities, villages and cultivation have appeared
because of it. Agriculture, the sailing of the seas and all the skills of this state—
courts, the army, the High Command, philosophy, rhetoric, the whole hum-
ming swarm of rhetors—depend on it. What is more, from marriage come
the temples and sanctuaries of our land, sacrifice, rituals, initiations, prayers
and solemn days of intercession.[1]

---

1. *Vita Theclae* 16, in G. Dagron, ed. *Vie et Miracles de Sainte Thècle*, pp. 190–192.

We should not dismiss Thamyris' speech out of hand, as no more than a magniloquent glimpse of the obvious. Our book is set in a society that was more helplessly exposed to death than is even the most afflicted underdeveloped country in the modern world. Citizens of the Roman Empire at its height, in the second century A.D., were born into the world with an average life expectancy of less than twenty-five years. Death fell savagely on the young. Those who survived childhood remained at risk. Only four out of every hundred men, and fewer women, lived beyond the age of fifty.[2] It was a population "grazed thin by death."[3] In such a situation, only the privileged or the eccentric few could enjoy the freedom to do what they pleased with their sexual drives. Unexacting in so many ways in sexual matters, the ancient city expected its citizens to expend a requisite proportion of their energy begetting and rearing legitimate children to replace the dead.[4] Whether through conscious legislation, such as that of Emperor Augustus, which penalized bachelors and rewarded families for producing children, or simply through the unquestioned weight of habit, young men and women were discreetly mobilized to use their bodies for reproduction. The pressure on the young women was inexorable. For the population of the Roman Empire to remain even stationary, it appears that each woman would have had to have produced an average of five children.[5] Young girls were recruited early for their task. The median age of Roman girls at marriage may have been as low as fourteen.[6] In North Africa, nearly 95 percent of the women recorded on gravestones had been married, over half of those before the age of twenty-three.[7]

2. A. R. Burn, "Hic Breve Vivitur," pp. 1–31. Keith Hopkins, "On the Probable Age Structure of the Roman Population," pp. 245–264 urges caution; see also Bruce W. Frier, "Roman Life Expectancy: Ulpian's Evidence," pp. 213–251.

3. John Chrysostom, *de virginitate* 14.1, in H. Musurillo and B. Grillet, eds., *Jean Chrysostome: La Virginité*, p. 138.

4. See esp. P. A. Brunt, *Italian Manpower*, pp. 558–566; and B. Rawson, "The Roman Family," in Rawson, ed., *The Family in Ancient Rome: New Perspectives*, pp. 9–10 on Augustan legislation; P. Veyne, "Rome devant la prétendue fuite de l'or," pp. 231–234 is perceptive on the attitudes behind such legislation. See now Peter Garnsey and Richard Saller, *The Roman Empire*, pp. 126–147.

5. Frier, "Roman Life Expectancy," p. 248, cites E. A. Wrigley in C. Tilly, ed., p. 148. Such a society could "hardly allow private choice since it must mobilize maximum fertility if it is to survive at all."

6. Keith Hopkins, "The Age of Roman Girls at Marriage," pp. 309–327. But now see Brent Shaw, "The Age of Roman Girls at Marriage: Some Reconsiderations."

7. The conclusions of B. W. Frier, "The Demography of the Early Roman Empire," to appear in the relevant volume of the new edition of *The Cambridge Ancient History*. I am indebted to the author for having shown this manuscript to me.

The inhabitants of an ancient Mediterranean community, such as the little town of Seleucia or the inland city of Iconium (modern Konya), where Thecla had been so infelicitously espoused to Thamyris, knew very well that a fertile Mediterranean landscape, dotted with ancient towns and immemorial temples, could die for lack of men. They knew that they had few resources for continuity and cohesion more dependable, and for which they were more directly responsible, than their own bodies.[8] If their little world was not to come to an end for lack of citizens, they must reproduce it, every generation, by marriage, intercourse and the begetting and rearing of children. As the opponents of Paul and Thecla pointed out, procreation, and not the chilling doctrine introduced by Saint Paul, was the only way to ensure a "resurrection of the dead." The true resurrection was

That which takes place through the nature of the human body itself, and which, through human means, is accomplished every day . . . the succession of children born from us, by which the image of those who begot them is renewed in their offspring, so that it seems as if those who have passed away a long time ago still move again among the living, as if risen from the dead.[9]

Outside the city, the inscriptions on the graves spoke incessantly to the living, that the chain of human life had not been snapped by death. The dead remained "exemplars of virtue" to the living. They had been "decked out with the virtues of their ancestors." Their *eutaxia*—the faultless deportment of the well-to-do men and women who effectively controlled the cities of the Empire—would be replicated exactly by the living, and would be passed down, yet once again, to their children.[10] It was a world determined to admit no break in the easy flow of civilized life from generation to generation.

Bachelors continued to exist in upper-class circles, even though they were occasionally rebuked by public-minded Emperors. Philosophers, professional individualists, had been allowed to parade their notorious eccentricity by remaining without legitimate heirs, even by practicing life-long continence. Yet even a philosopher could be challenged to "bequeath a copy of himself" to posterity:[11] he was urged to marry,

8. Polybius, *History* 36.17.5–10, on the depopulation of Greece: "About this there was no use at all to ask the gods to suggest a means of deliverance from such an evil. For any ordinary man will tell you that the most effectual cure has to be men's actions."
9. *Vita Theclae* 5, p. 188.
10. Louis Robert, *Hellenica*, pp. 226–227 and Jeanne and Louis Robert, *La Carie*, inscription nos. 70, 71, p. 177.
11. Lucian, *Demonax* 55.

"to take thought for his own city, and to make of his home a rampart for its protection."[12]

Virgin women, however, had been part of the timeless religious landscape of the classical world. Soranus, a Greek doctor writing in Rome in the second century, assured his readers that the strange chastity of these women did no harm to their health: some "have menstrual difficulties and become fat and ill-proportioned," but this was due to lack of exercise, as a result of their confined life in the shrines where they lived as perpetual guardians.[13]

There is no denying the wealth of associations that had gathered throughout the centuries around such figures. Many of these associations later clustered around Christian virgins. We should be careful, however, not to overlook some decisive differences between pagan virgin priestesses and, later, Christian nuns. The message conveyed by such women as the Vestal Virgins at Rome and the virgin priestesses and prophetesses of the classical Greek world was that their state was of crucial importance for the community precisely because it was anomalous.[14] They fitted into a clearly demarcated space in civic society.[15] Though eminent and admired, they were not thought to stand for human nature at its peak. Their virginity did not speak to the community as a whole of a long-lost perfection. It did not represent the primal state of humankind, that could, and should, be recaptured by men quite as much as by women. Chastity did not announce the dawning light of the end of time, after millennia of misplaced skirmishing with death through married intercourse—as the Paul of our legend had preached in no uncertain terms to Thecla. The chastity of many virgin priestesses was not a matter of free choice for them. No heroic freedom of the individual will was made plain by their decision not to marry. The city recruited its virgins, by dedicating them to the service of the gods. Many virgin priestesses, such as the Vestals at Rome, were free to marry later in life. What had mattered, in their

12. Musonius Rufus, *Fragment* 14, Cora E. Lutz, ed., pp. 33–36.

13. Soranus, *Gynaecia* 1.7.32.1, J. Ilberg, ed. p. 21; *Soranus' Gynaecology*, O. Temkin, ed., p. 29.

14. Mary Beard, "The Sexual Status of the Vestal Virgins," pp. 12–27 is a model study, and Giulia Sissa, *Le corps virginal*, opens up new perspectives on the meaning of virginity in ancient Greece. By contrast, E. Fehrle, *Die kultische Keuschheit im Altertum* assembles much evidence, is dutifully cited, and is out of date; see now Han J. W. Drijvers, s.v. Virginity, *The Encyclopedia of Religion*, vol. 15, M. Eliade, ed.

15. Robin Lane Fox, *Pagans and Christians*, pp. 347–348 discusses examples of virgin priestesses in the second century A.D.

case, was an elaborately contrived suspension of the normal process, by which a girl moved with little interruption from puberty to child-bearing. By not marrying until they were thirty, the Vestal Virgins stood out as glaring anomalies. They were the exceptions that rein-forced the rule. The presence in some cities of a handful of young girls, chosen by others to forgo marriage, heightened the awareness of contemporaries that marriage and childbirth were the unquestioned destiny of all other women:

Immediately after they are fourteen, women are called "ladies" by men. And so when they see that they have nothing else but only to be the bedfellows of men, they begin to beautify themselves and put all their hopes in that.[16]

To bring a young girl into the household, and to beget children with her, raised problems for well-to-do males on which their more literate peers and mentors chose to linger at considerable length.[17] Let us look at the world of upper-class marriage and sexuality—unfortunately, the only one that it is possible to glimpse from our evidence—along the narrow beam of this large body of prescriptive writings. We must use evidence of this kind with extreme caution in reconstructing the real-ities of marriage and of sexual behavior in the Roman world. It does, however, reveal what passed as desirable, even as commonsense, among the well-to-do: it enables us to map out the horizons beyond which the majority of educated males in this and later centuries were un-willing to think. Like long-familiar music, the *idées reçues* of the ancient world filled the minds of educated Christians when they, in their turn, came to write on marriage and on sexual desire.

In the second century A.D., a young man of the privileged classes of the Roman Empire grew up looking at the world from a position of unchallenged dominance. Women, slaves, and barbarians were un-alterably different from him and inferior to him.[18] The most obtrusive polarity of all, that between himself and women, was explained to him in terms of a hierarchy based upon nature itself. Biologically, the doc-tors said, males were those fetuses who had realized their full poten-

16. Epictetus, *Enchiridion* 40, W. A. Oldfather, ed. and trans. *Epictetus*, 2:525.

17. On this literature, Michel Foucault, *Le Souci de Soi*, pp. 90–100; 173–216. English trans. R. Hurley, *The Care of the Self*, pp. 72–80; 147–185, contains reflections to which I owe a particular debt.

18. Galatians 3:18 and Colossians 3:10; Wayne A. Meeks, "The Image of the Andro-gyne," pp. 167–168, 180, provides further examples of this threefold division. See now Peter Brown, "Antiquité tardive," in P. Veyne, ed., *Histoire de la Vie Privée*, pp. 226–240; English trans. A. Goldhammer, *A History of Private Life*, pp. 239–250.

tial. They had amassed a decisive surplus of "heat" and fervent "vital spirit" in the early stages of their coagulation in the womb. The hot ejaculation of male seed proved this: "For it is the semen, when possessed of vitality, which makes us men, hot, well-braced in limbs, heavy, well-voiced, spirited, strong to think and act."[19]

Women, by contrast, were failed males. The precious vital heat had not come to them in sufficient quantities in the womb. Their lack of heat made them more soft, more liquid, more clammy-cold, altogether more formless than were men. Periodic menstruation showed that their bodies could not burn up the heavy surpluses that coagulated within them. Yet precisely such surpluses were needed to nurture and contain the hot male seed, thus producing children. Were this not so, the doctor Galen added, men might think that "the Creator had purposely made one half of the whole race imperfect, and, as it were, mutilated."[20]

The sensibilities of a modern reader are understandably bruised by such assertions. We must remember that they had already been made for over half a millennium by this time, and they would continue to be made until this century. They effectively confined women to a lower place than men in an irrefutable, "natural" hierarchy. In the second century, however, the notion was also exploited to subject men themselves to an unremitting process of fine-tuning. Even men could not be entirely certain of themselves. Their superiority to women was not based on a "physiology of incommensurability," such as was elaborated in the nineteenth century, to declare men irrevocably different from women.[21] The medical entities of heat and vital spirit were imponderable elements in the makeup of the male. It could be assumed that men always had more of that precious heat than did women. But this heat, unless actively mobilized, might cool, leading even a man to approach the state of a woman. In the Roman world, the physical appearance and the reputed character of eunuchs acted as constant reminders that the male body was a fearsomely plastic thing. As Galen suggested, in his treatise *On the Seed*, lack of heat from childhood on

19. Aretaeus, *Causes and Symptoms of Chronic Diseases* 2.5, in F. Adams, trans., *The Extant Works of Aretaeus the Cappadocian*, pp. 346–347.

20. Galen, *de usu partium* 14.6, in C. G. Kühn, ed., *Galeni Opera* 4:162; M. T. May, trans., *Galen: On the Usefulness of the Parts of the Body*, 2:620. Ian Maclean, *The Renaissance Notion of Woman*, pp. 8–27 is a convenient summary of the ancient tradition and its legacy; Thomas Laqueur, "Orgasm, Generation and the Politics of Reproductive Biology," esp. pp. 4–7 is learned and perceptive.

21. Laqueur, "Orgasm," p. 3.

could cause the male body to collapse back into a state of primary undifferentiation.[22] No normal man might actually become a woman; but each man trembled forever on the brink of becoming "womanish." His flickering heat was an uncertain force. If it was to remain effective, its momentum had to be consciously maintained. It was never enough to be male: a man had to strive to remain "virile." He had to learn to exclude from his character and from the poise and temper of his body all telltale traces of "softness" that might betray, in him, the half-formed state of a woman. The small-town notables of the second century watched each other with hard, clear eyes. They noted a man's walk.[23] They reacted to the rhythms of his speech.[24] They listened attentively to the telltale resonance of his voice.[25] Any of these might betray the ominous loss of a hot, high-spirited momentum, a flagging of the clear-cut self-restraint, and a relaxing of the taut elegance of voice and gesture that made a man a man, the unruffled master of a subject world.

The maintenance of exacting codes of deportment was no trivial issue for the men of the second century. Entrusted by the formidable Roman government with the task of controlling their own cities, the elites of the Greek world (for whom and by whom the bulk of our evidence was written) learned rapidly and well how to bring upon their peers and their inferiors the "gentle violence" of a studiously self-controlled and benevolent style of rule: "avoidance of discord, gentle but firm control of the populace" were their principal political and social aims.[26] They praised in each other qualities of gentleness, accessibility, self-control, and compassionate feeling. They expected to be treated in this courteous manner by the Emperor and by his representatives, and they were prepared to extend these gentle virtues to their loyal dependents: a man was to be "fair-minded and humane" to his slaves, "a father" to his household servants, and, always, "at his ease" with his fellow-townsmen.[27] Even their wetnurses must have

22. Galen, *de semine* 1.16, in C. G. Kühn, ed., *Galeni Opera* 4:586.
23. Polemo, *Physiognomica*, R. Förster, ed., *Physiognomici Graeci* 1:260.
24. Lucian, *Demonax* 12.
25. Aline Rousselle, "Parole et Inspiration: le travail de la voix dans le monde romain," pp. 129–157.
26. C. P. Jones, *Plutarch and Rome*, p. 119.
27. Two splendid examples are published by P. Hermann, *Anzeiger der österreichischen Akademie der Wissenschaften* (1974) 111: pp. 439–444 and Paavo Roos and P. Herrmann, *Opuscula Atheniensia* (1971) 10:36–39. On the treatment of slaves, see Miriam Griffin, *Seneca: A Philosopher in Politics*, pp. 256–285, with the perceptive remarks of B. D. Shaw, "The Divine Economy: Stoicism as Ideology," pp. 38–39.

such qualities: they must swaddle the little men meticulously, "as Grecian women do," so that they already learned to hold themselves correctly at the age of one.[28]

Any disruption of the even tenor of their style of command over others caused acute anxiety. Anger, and not sexual passion, preoccupied the mentors of the upper classes. Men who patronized without a qualm the virile carnage of the gladiatorial games and who collaborated with the Roman government in imposing upon the lower classes an increasingly savage and peremptory penal system,[29] were concerned lest outbursts of rage and irrational cruelty should enter into their own dealings with dependents. The slave system of the ancient world rested on force and cruelty. Yet direct physical violence by masters on slaves was frequently criticized. The doctor Galen's father chided men who "had bruised a tendon while striking their slaves on the teeth. . . . I have seen a man [Galen added] strike a slave in the eye with a reed pen."[30]

Galen knew of a landowner in Crete, "in other respects an estimable person," who would fall upon his servants "with his hands, and even sometimes with his feet, but far more frequently with a whip or any piece of wood that happened to be handy."[31]

Galen learned early from his own family not to be surprised by the time-worn polarity between "male" self-control and its opposite, a convulsive violence, associated with a "womanish" lack of self-restraint: his father had been "the most just, the most devoted and the kindest of men. My mother, however, was so very prone to anger that sometimes she bit her handmaids."[32]

Relations to slaves were almost invariably abrasive. With women, however, matters could be different. To set up household with a young wife was presented as a peculiarly reassuring exercise in the gentle control and eventual absorption into one's world of an inferior "other." Greeks disapproved of the child marriages of the Romans. Girls were usually married in their later teens, to young men who had completed

28. Soranus, *Gynaecia* 2.12(32).19(88).1 and 2.20(40).44(113).1, pp. 66, 116; Temkin, trans., pp. 90, 116.

29. Louis Robert, *Les gladiateurs dans l'Orient grec* and Peter Garnsey, *Social Status and Legal Privilege in the Roman Empire*.

30. Galen, *de cognoscendis animi morbis* 1.4, in C. G. Kühn, ed., *Galeni Opera* 5:17; English translation: P. W. Harkins, *On the Passions and Errors of the Soul*, pp. 38–39.

31. Ibid. 1.4, Kühn, p. 18; Harkins, pp. 38–39.

32. Ibid. 1.8, Kühn, pp. 40–41; Harkins, p. 57; compare Aristotle, *Historia Animalium* 608AB.

their studies, and were some five years older than themselves. In the Latin world, men appear to have married even later: they could treat their young wives almost as daughters.[33] It was to a Greek couple, Pollianus and Eurydice, that Plutarch wrote his *Advice on Marriage*, ca. 100 A.D. He solved the problems of hierarchy and bonding between a man and a woman by the expedient of turning the husband into the philosophical mentor of his bride. Plutarch warned Pollianus that women were intractable creatures. Left to themselves, they "conceive many untoward ideas, low designs and emotions."[34]

But he urged the conscientious young man not to give up. Pollianus could absorb Eurydice into his own, grave world. She must eat with him and his friends. Otherwise she would learn to "stuff herself when alone."[35] She must share the same gods with him, rather than withdraw to the rustling powers that ruled the women's quarters.[36] Her property would silently vanish into the common fund, along with all other aspects of her life that she might call her own.[37] In the meantime, Pollianus would already have practiced finesse and studied good nature in his public dealings with his male peers and his inferiors. A relationship with a woman was a greater challenge to him, precisely because it did not take place in the hard, clearly signposted world of public life. It gave him the nearest that he might ever come in his life to an unmotivated friendship, based on his own talent as the moral guide of his wife. As a result of his tact and quiet authority, Eurydice would be "knit in goodwill to him," as the pliant body hung upon the all-controlling, discreet soul.[38]

We meet such women on the sarcophagi of Italy and Asia Minor in the second and third centuries. In them, the wife was shown standing attentively, or sitting, in front of her husband, as he raised his right hand to make a point, while in his left hand he displayed the scroll which represented the superior literary culture on which he based his claim to outright dominance, in society at large as in his marriage.[39] The woman shown on such sarcophagi had ceased to be the little creature that a hot young man deflowered abruptly for the sake of heirs,

33. Hopkins, "Age of Roman Girls," p. 314; see now Garnsey and Saller, *The Roman Empire*, pp. 131, 138, 140.

34. Plutarch, *Praecepta Conjugalia* 48.145E, in F. C. Babbitt, ed. and trans. *Plutarch's Moralia*, 2:341.

35. 15.140A, p. 308.   36. 19.140D, p. 310.   37. 20.140E, p. 312.

38. 33.142E, p. 318.

39. For an Italian example and its meaning, see now Richard Brilliant, "Una statua ritratto femminile dal territorio di Tarquinia," pp. 1–12.

earning from his young wife "the timorous hate that follows unnatural compulsion."[40] She would not be left to her own devices, free to run to seed unnoticed in the women's quarters. She had been swept, by her cultivated husband, into the charmed circle of a shared excellence.

Peculiarly beautiful examples of such sarcophagi now stand in the Archaeological Museum at Konya, the home town of the legendary Thecla. Had Paul not intervened dramatically, as in the legend of Paul and Thecla, to usurp the role of male mentor to the young woman, Thecla might have come to sit in this manner in front of Thamyris. Their married concord would have radiated, to those who set up such costly monuments, a message of benign order that spilled, quite naturally, from its domestic setting into the public sphere. A man who had "harmonized" his domestic life with such elegance and authority could be trusted to "harmonize state, forum and friends."[41]

Plutarch's *Advice on Marriage* was a stilted tract, destined to enjoy a long future in Christian sermonizing. But second-century reality was on its side. We are dealing with close-knit regional oligarchies. The girls came from the same class as did the boys; some might even have been their cousins, and many were the daughters or sisters of friends and allies.[42] They would have grown up together in great households, in the relatively free years that preceded the onset of puberty. Girls might occasionally have enjoyed discreet love affairs with their future betrothed.[43]

The novels of the age explored with a new respect the theme of love at first sight among the young. Both hero and heroine were presented as passing through dramatic trials in order to preserve their chastity for a predestinate marriage. The clearest message of these novels was that, among the upper classes, noble souls were made for each other: it was not a *genre* where princes marry beggar-girls.[44]

40. Plutarch, *Comparison of Lycurgus and Numa* 4.1, in B. Perrin, ed. and trans. *Plutarch's Lives*, 1:395.

41. Plutarch, *Praecept. Conjug.* 43.144C, p. 333.

42. Apuleius, *Metamorphoses* 4.26.2; E. Patlagean, *Pauvreté économique et pauvreté sociale à Byzance*, pp. 122–123; but see Brent D. Shaw and Richard P. Saller, "Close Kin Marriage in Roman Society?" pp. 435–437. See now the excellent and suggestive synthesis of Aline Rousselle, "Gestes et signes de la famille dans l'Empire romain," pp. 263–264.

43. Elaine Fantham, "Sex, Status and Survival in Hellenistic Athens: A Study of Women in New Comedy," pp. 53–56 is revealing for a somewhat different social situation; see Aristaenetus, *Letters on Love* 1.6, in J. Bernous, trans. *Aristénète: Lettres d'Amour*, pp. 18–19.

44. M. M. Bakhtin, *The Dialogic Imagination*, Michael Holquist, ed., C. Emerson and M. Holquist, trans. pp. 86–110.

Once married, the couple would appear in public. The city needed the wealth of its leading women, and was prepared to lavish public honors on those women who acted as benefactresses to the community.[45] In his *Dreambook*, Artemidorus of Daldis wrote "that it is good for women and maidens who are both rich and free to [dream that they] drive a chariot through a city, since it means that they will receive respected priesthoods." For poor women, he added, such exposure to the public gaze could only foretell prostitution.[46]

Later in life, a man would expect to find in his wife the one thing that he could not expect to find among his peers—honesty. *Parrhésia*, unflinching frankness with one's fellows and superiors, was an infinitely rare and precious commodity. It could be had only from the only two authoritative figures who stood to one side of political life—from a philosopher and from one's wife. We should not underestimate how heavily the need for intimacy of this kind weighed upon ancient men.[47] A fourth-century pagan, Praetextatus, wrote of his wife Paulina:

To you I could entrust the fast-closed depths of my own mind . . .
And so as friends we have been joined in trust,
By long acquaintance, by shared initiations of the gods,
All in one bond of faith, one single heart, united in one mind.[48]

When, in the sixth century, Theodora berated Emperor Justinian for his loss of nerve during the Nika Riot, her decisive phrase—"The purple is a glorious winding-sheet"—was delivered before the full council of state. On that occasion, Theodora used the *parrhésia*, the privileged freedom of speech, of a Roman wife to her husband.[49] There would have been many such women among the busy oligarchies of the second century. Married to husbands for whom political and cultural activity involved endless travel to the centers of power, these women were left by their husbands to manage the miniature empire of an aristocrat's estates:

the wife of Diognetos [possibly, the tutor of Marcus Aurelius] dreamt that she had a beard on the right side of her face. . . . For a long time while her

---

45. Ramsay MacMullen, "Woman in Public in the Roman Empire," pp. 212–216 and Riet Van Bremen, "Women and Wealth," pp. 227–234.
46. Artemidorus, *Oneirocritica* 1.56, R. A. Pack, ed. p. 56; R. White, trans. *The Interpretation of Dreams*, p. 46.
47. Galen, *de cognosc. anim. morb.* 1.3, Kühn, pp. 8–9; Harkins, pp. 32–33.
48. H. Dessau, *Inscriptiones Latinae Selectae* 1259.4–5 and 10–11, 1:278.
49. Procopius, *History of the Wars* 1.24.37.

husband was travelling abroad, she was left behind in her native country and took care of his household.[50]

It appears that the nuclear family, and with it a tendency to lay stress on the affective bonds between husband and wife and parents and children, was already a well-established feature of Roman society, at least in the West.[51] What makes the second century significant is the frequency with which the domestic concord associated with the nuclear family was played up symbolically, as part of a public desire to emphasize the effortless harmony of the Roman order. Emperor Marcus Aurelius placed his wife, Faustina the Younger, on coins bearing the motto *concordia*. Young married couples were expected to assemble to offer sacrifice in honor of "the exceptional concord" of the Imperial spouses. Sarcophagi show the careers of eminent Romans, presented through scenes that illustrated the specific traditional virtues manifested on different occasions in the life of their heroes—scenes of sacrifice represented his *pietas*, scenes of battle and the submission of barbarians represented his *virtus* and his *clementia*. It was the moment of marriage that was now chosen to represent the all-important social and political virtue of *concordia*.[52]

The Emperor himself was expected to radiate marital propriety. In model speeches for Imperial occasions, the rhetor was advised to add:

Because of the Emperor, marriages are chaste and fathers have legitimate offspring. . . . The lady he has admired and loved, he has also made the sharer of his throne. As for the rest of womenkind, he does not so much as know that they exist.[53]

The Roman view of marriage, as a free consensus of man and wife, has been acclaimed as a "notion of remarkable theoretical potential [for the] expression of a whole and satisfying love."[54] By the beginning of the late antique period, however, the vast weight of Empire had ensured that the Roman ideal of marital concord had taken on a crys-

50. Artemidorus, *Oneirocritica* 4.83, Pack, p. 298; White, p. 217.

51. Richard P. Saller and Brent D. Shaw, "Tombstones and Roman Family Relations in the Principate," pp. 134–135; though corrected by this article on important points, Paul Veyne, "La famille et l'amour sous le haut empire romain," pp. 33–63 is an exceptionally thought-provoking study, to which I remain indebted.

52. G. Rodenwaldt, "Über den Stilwandel in der antoninischen Kunst," pp. 14–15.

53. Menander, *Epideictica* 2.1.396, D. A. Russell and N. G. Wilson eds. and trans., pp. 90–91.

54. R. O. A. M. Lyne, *The Latin Love Poets* p. 17.

talline hardness: the married couple were presented less as a pair of equal lovers than as a reassuring microcosm of the social order.

(II) "A SCHOOL OF ORDERLY BEHAVIOR"

Whatever they did in practice, it was not easy for such men to articulate their experiences of women in writing. It was difficult to express how the act of intercourse, on which they based their hopes of well-born children, fitted into their well-groomed world. Galen admitted that it was strange that the gods should have decided to maintain the human species by means of a pleasure so sharp and so potentially anti-social, for "a very great pleasure is coupled with the exercise of the generative parts, and a raging desire precedes their use."[55]

Nor could this pleasure be bypassed. The learned treatises of the age collaborated with ancient commonsense notions to endow the men and women of late antiquity with bodies totally unlike those of modern persons. Here were little fiery universes, through whose heart, brain, and veins there pulsed the same heat and vital spirit as glowed in the stars. To make love was to bring one's blood to the boil, as the fiery vital spirit swept through the veins, turning the blood into the whitened foam of semen. It was a process in which the body as a whole—the brain cavity, the marrow of the backbone, the kidneys, and the lower bowel region—was brought into play, "as in a mighty choir."[56] The genital regions were mere points of passage.[57] They were the outlets of a human Espresso machine. It was the body as a whole, and not merely the genitals, that made orgasm possible. "In a single impact of both parts," wrote the somber but well-read Christian, Tertullian,

the whole human frame is shaken and foams with semen, as the damp humor of the body is joined to the hot substance of the spirit. And then, (I speak of this at the risk of seeming improper, but I do not wish to forego my chance of proving my case) [that body and soul were created at the same moment] in that last breaking wave of delight, do we not feel something of our very soul go out from us?[58]

55. Galen, *de usu partium* 14.9, Kühn, p. 179; May, p. 640.
56. Galen, *de semine* 1.8, Kühn, p. 569.
57. Danielle Jacquart and Claude Thomasset, *Sexualité et savoir médical au Moyen-Âge*, p. 16; Laqueur, "Orgasm," pp. 7–16, sums up this tradition and its long afterlife.
58. Tertullian, *de anima* 27.5, in J. H. Waszink, ed., *Corpus Christianorum* 2:823.

Though a clammier creature, through whom damp mists swirled, even the wife must give all of herself if her seed was to be released into the womb so as to embrace that of her husband. She also must feel, a little after the moment of the man's ejaculation, "an unaccustomed, shivering sensation."[59] Well-born children, preferably a male heir who resembled both parents (so deep had been their bonding in the act of love) might come from such a union.[60] It was deemed altogether appropriate that Venus, Aphrodite, should have taken her name from the hot froth—the *aphros*—that beat in this manner on the shores of love.[61] Altogether, the young couple were positively encouraged by their learned elders to go to bed with their minds well-stocked with fantasies of considerable warmth.

But the doctors hastened to add a significant note of caution for the male.[62] Successful intercourse was a convulsive act, little different in its causes and physical effects from a sudden burst of rage. It bore a dread resemblance to the falling sickness: orgasm was a "minor epilepsy." Did not the very mouth of the epileptic also froth with the same bubbling, whitened blood as did the penis?[63] We are dealing with gentlemen whose gait must be measured, whose gestures were controlled, and who were advised by Plutarch in his *Advice on Keeping Well* to maintain their health by reading aloud from harmoniously composed declamations, and to avoid "passionate and convulsive vociferations" of any kind.[64] It is hardly surprising that the young couple were encouraged to approach this, "the most sacred of all sowings," with due circumspection.[65]

Concern for deportment and medical science converged on the issue of intercourse. The fiery body was a fragile reservoir from which vital energy might leak away. Its fires had to be carefully banked up if they were to last. Frequent sexual activity was frowned upon. It decreased the fertility of the male seed and hence the father's chance of children. Ejaculation brought about an appreciable diminution of the heat that

---

59. Soranus, *Gynaecia* 1.12.44, Ilberg, p. 31; Temkin, p. 43.

60. Menander, *Epideictica* 2.7.407, pp. 180–181.

61. Cornutus, *Theologiae Graecae Compendium* 24, C. Lang, ed., p. 45.

62. See esp. Foucault, *Souci de Soi*, p. 132, *Care of the Self*, p. 110. On these matters, Aline Rousselle, *Porneia: de la maîtrise du corps à la privation sensorielle*, pp. 23–27 is a groundbreaking study.

63. Clement of Alexandria, *Paidagogos* 2.10.94.3; Aretaeus, *Causes and Symptoms of Acute Diseases* 1.5, p. 246.

64. Plutarch, *de sanitate tuenda* 16.130A, in F. C. Babbitt, ed., *Plutarch's Moralia*, 2:251.

65. Plutarch, *Praecept. Conjug.* 41.144B, p. 331.

maintained the momentum of a virile man. The "obsessively virile morality"[66] long current in the Graeco-Roman world was validated by the medical handbooks. The lover and the uxorious did not merely sink into a suspect state of emotional dependence on a woman; physiologically, their progressive loss of heat threatened to make them "womanish."

A powerful "fantasy of the loss of vital spirit" lay at the root of many late classical attitudes to the male body. It is one of the many notions that gave male continence a firm foothold in the folk wisdom of the world in which Christian celibacy would soon be preached.[67] The most virile man was the man who had kept most of his vital spirit—the one, that is, who lost little or no seed. Hence the ambivalence that surrounded the figure of the postpubertal eunuch, such as the self-castrated devotee of Attis. Far from crumbling into a presexual formlessness, as was the case with those castrated when young, the full-grown man who made himself a eunuch, by carefully tying his testicles, became an *asporos*, a man who wasted no vital fire on others.[68] Galen thought that if Olympic athletes could be castrated in such a way that their reserves of heat would not be disrupted by the operation, they would be stronger.[69] Soranus agreed: "Men who remain chaste are stronger and better than others and pass their lives in better health."[70]

To preserve the male voice that Quintillian loved to hear resounding in the courtrooms around the forum, "strong, rich, flexible and firm," the busy lawyer must practice, among other things, "abstinence from sex."[71] Artemidorus wrote of an athlete:

he dreamed that he cut off his genitals, bound his head and was crowned [as a victor]. . . . As long as he remained a virgin [*aphthoros*], his athletic career was brilliant and distinguished. But once he began to have sexual intercourse, he ended his career ingloriously.[72]

We should be careful not to conclude from these cautions that second-century men were haunted by a fear of sex. Far from it: they viewed the act of intercourse as one of the many aspects of their lives that they could bring under their control through good sense and breeding. Comfortable, well-exercised, and well-fed, they knew how

66. Veyne, "Amour et famille," p. 54.   67. Rousselle, *Porneia*, p. 26.
68. Ibid. pp. 157–164.   69. Galen, *de semine* 1.8, Kühn, p. 571.
70. Soranus, *Gynaecia* 17.30.2, Ilberg, p. 20; Temkin, p. 27.
71. Quintilian, *Institutio oratoria* 11.3.19.4, H. E. Butler, ed. and trans. 4:253.
72. Artemidorus, *Oneirocritica* 5.95, Pack, p. 324; White, pp. 242–243.

to counteract the dangers that might accompany their periodic and distinctly pleasurable outlays of vital spirit by means of a judiciously chosen regimen of diet and exercise. At times, doctors might even counsel ejaculation, so as to relieve the body of the excessive deposits of seed that caused headaches and torpor: health-conscious gentlemen made love, wrote Galen, even when the act gave them no particular pleasure.[73]

Intercourse was a matter which the alert gentleman felt that he could control. The married couple were encouraged to believe that the act of intercourse itself, if conducted in the right frame of mind—in effect, with correct decorum—would have a positive effect on the character and the sex of the ensuing child, and certainly that the neglect of such decorum might produce offspring worthy of shame and pity. The myth of eugenic sex circulated widely, although evidence for it has surfaced largely in Jewish sources. The myth provided the young couple with a fearsomely two-edged sexual charter. It implied that the young bride had to be consciously enlisted as a willing partner in the act of intercourse. Her spirit had to be, if not exactly elated, at least tranquil at the moment of conception.[74] This belief protected the girl from the worst effects of brutal and insensitive love-making: only the uneducated, the rabbis said, would neglect to "cherish" a woman before attempting to beget a child with her.[75] But the eugenic myth also imposed a peculiarly intimate and insinuating discipline upon her. As the more fluid and labile party, whose seed provided the damp nurture for the child, it was the particular duty of the wife to concentrate her mind during intercourse. Inappropriate images and feelings at that time might affect the temperament of her husband's child: for

Frequently, if a woman sleeps with her husband out of necessity, while her heart is with the adulterer with whom she usually has intercourse, the child she will bear is born resembling the adulterer.[76]

73. Galen, *de locis affectis* 6.5, in C. G. Kühn, ed. *Galeni Opera* 8:417–420; see esp. Rousselle, *Porneia*, pp. 29–31, Foucault, *Souci de Soi*, pp. 167–168, *Care of the Self*, pp. 142–143, and Lane Fox, *Pagans and Christians*, pp. 348–349.

74. Soranus, *Gynaecia* 1.10.39.2, Ilberg, p. 27; Temkin, pp. 37–38.

75. See esp. *Babylonian Talmud: Niddah* 31b, in I. Epstein, trans., p. 217 and *Babylonian Talmud: ʿErubin* 100b, in ibid, pp. 696–698.

76. *Gospel of Philip: N.H.C.II.3* 78, in W. W. Isenberg, trans., *The Nag Hammadi Library*, p. 147. Similar restraints could rest on a man: see *Babylonian Talmud: Nedarim* 20a, I. Epstein, trans., p. 57.

The fact that this peculiarly unpleasant piece of learned folklore should occur in a Gnostic treatise of spiritual guidance shows how pervasive and how controlling such beliefs might be.

The notion of eugenic sex committed both the man and the woman to codes of decorum in bed that were continuous with the public self. The Stoic insistence that intercourse should happen only "according to nature" converged on this potent fantasy.[77] For the Stoics, intercourse was supposed to take place only so as to produce children. The couple must not make love for the sake of pleasure alone; even the positions that they adopted should only be those that enabled the seed to be "sown" to best effect. All other forms of lovemaking were a *tolméma*: they were "gratuitous acts."[78] The philosophers regarded them as chilling assertions of an arbitrary freedom on the part of human beings to do what they pleased with their own bodies. The adoption of a variety of sexual positions was a form of playing around in the face of mankind's great Mother, "Nature": "men invented other positions as a result of wantonness, licentiousness and intoxication."[79]

Stoic attitudes to marital intercourse deliberately stared past the possibility of erotic satisfaction to the grave and purposive gestures of the public man. Even the marriage chamber was to be "a school of orderly behavior."[80] At the moment of intercourse, the bodies of the elite must not be allowed to set up so much as a single, random eddy in the solemn stream that flowed from generation to generation through the marriage bed.

Despite its obvious limitations, the evidence that we have considered so far gives little support to the widespread romantic notion that the pre-Christian Roman world was a sunny "Eden of the unrepressed."[81] Still less is it possible to explain, and by implication to excuse, the austerity of Christian sexual ethics, and the novelty of the Christian emphasis on total sexual renunciation, as if it were no more than an understandable, if excessive, reaction to the debauchery that

77. John T. Noonan, *Contraception*, pp. 46, 75 provides a clear account of this doctrine.
78. Musonius Rufus, *Fragment* 12, Lutz, p. 86.10.
79. Artemidorus, *Oneirocritica* 1.79, Pack, p. 94; White, p. 63.
80. Plutarch, *Praecept. Conjug.* 47.144F, p. 334.
81. Paul Veyne, "L'Empire romain," *Histoire de la vie privée*, p. 196, *History of Private Life*, p. 202. This essay is the most vivid and provocative evocation of the moral tone of the High Empire: see esp. pp. 179–199, *Private Life*, pp. 183–205.

prevailed among the cultivated classes of the Empire.[82] What we have, instead, is an Empire whose tone had long been set by somber and careful persons. Their mentors wrote at such length on the topics of women and marriage, even on sexual intercourse, so as to find a way to enable members of the upper class to think aloud, among themselves, about the weighty issues of power, due order, and untroubled continuity.

The governing classes had no intention of loosening their grip on a world that they viewed with such inflexible certainty. The instability of the third century changed little in this respect: it merely hardened their resolve to hold on to the self-discipline and to maintain the symbols of public order that had come to the fore in more peaceful days. A *severitas,* a hard-bitten, manly austerity, that made few concessions to women or to pleasure, was the current coin of public utterance in the third century. The conversion of Constantine to Christianity merely made the hardening of the public mood irrevocable. Pagan and Christian alike, the upper classes of the Roman Empire in its last centuries lived by codes of sexual restraint and public decorum that they liked to think of as continuous with the virile austerity of archaic Rome. Sexual tolerance was out of place in the public realm. In the middle of the fourth century A.D., the Emperor Jovian, though a demonstrative Christian, had been unduly fond of drinking and women; but these were faults, a contemporary pagan observed, "which he would certainly have corrected [had he lived longer] out of regard for the Imperial dignity."[83]

A Latin school exercise of the same time, from Gaul, gives the speech of a father whose son had disgraced himself by misbehaving at a banquet:

what would people say when they saw you behaving like that? . . . One who gives counsel to others must know how to rule himself. . . . You have incurred deep shame.[84]

82. Two examples can suffice: W. Rordorf, "Marriage in the New Testament and in the Early Church," p. 208—"We know well that the mistrust of the Church Fathers in regard to sexuality was a reaction against the debauchery of the later Roman Empire"; B. Grillet and G. H. Ettlinger, eds. *Jean Chrysostome: À une jeune veuve sur le mariage unique,* Sources chrétiennes 138:40—"cette sage conduite de vie qui prévalut sans doute dans les milieux chrétiens, tranchant sur la corruption et la "débauche legalisée" de la société païenne."

83. Ammianus Marcellinus, *Res Gestae* 25.10.15.

84. A. C. Dionisotti, "From Ausonius' Schooldays," p. 103, lines 66–67.

The young man's father did not need to be a Christian to insist that his son behave in public with a puritanical rectitude, which was closer to that subscribed to by men in a modern fundamentalist Muslim country than to our modern, romantic fantasies of a "decadent" Roman Empire.

These codes, however, did not apply to everyone. Even among the elites, they were a matter of choice. It was, after all, quite possible to dominate one's region, to beget well-formed sons, and to enter one's grave with a reputation for stolid marital concord without filling one's head with so many learned cobwebs. Certain restraints that came to be advocated in Christian circles rested lightly on upper-class males. The well-to-do Greek or Roman was a slave-owner. Men owned the bodies of their male and female servants. Within the walls of a great rambling house, filled with young servants, over whom the master ruled supreme, fidelity to one's wife remained a personal option. Despite harsh laws punishing married women for adultery, infidelity by their husbands incurred no legal punishment and very little moral disapprobation. It was thought sufficient to limit fidelity "to the walls around the house, not to tie it down to the marriage bed itself."[85] The husband was not encouraged to live in the brothels, to set up a separate *ménage*, or to introduce new women into the house. But infidelity with servants was "a thing which some people consider quite without blame, since every master is held to have it in his power to use his slave as he wishes."[86]

The leaders of the Christian church in late antiquity followed the philosophers in condemning the anomaly of the Roman "double standard," which had punished the wife for adultery while accepting unfaithfulness in a husband. But the clergy showed themselves as little prepared as the philosophers had been to overturn the institution of household slavery. By their hesitation on that issue, they doomed themselves from the outset to an honorable ineffectiveness on the issue of marital fidelity. Most infidelity took the form of sleeping with one's own slaves: it was simply one assertion, among so many others, of the master's power over the bodies of his dependents. Half a millennium after Musonius Rufus had condemned unfaithful husbands, the courtyards of the church at Arles still rang with the guffaws of the

85. Lactantius, *Divine Institutes* 6.23: *Patrologia Latina* 6: 719A; Veyne, "L'Empire romain," *Vie privée*, pp. 82–83, *Private Life*, pp. 72–73 describes such households.
86. Musonius Rufus, *Fragment* 12, Lutz, p. 86.30.

sons of a Christian gentry, boasting of their sexual exploits with serving girls.[87]

The writers of the second century A.D. couched their precepts in universal terms. In reality they wrote for the privileged few. The codes of sexual deportment that we have described were valued by the recipients of moral advice because they were regarded as congruent with the refinement and self-control that distinguished the well-born from their unruly inferiors. Such elevated rules for excellence, in marriage as in everything else, did not have to be shared with others.[88] Hence, the glaring inconsistencies of the age, to which Christian polemists and preachers constantly drew attention. Men who wished to draw around themselves and their womenfolk a carapace of moral rigor were quite prepared to establish their position in the towns by means of great remissive moments at the public games, in which cruelty and erotic delight were considered quite normal. Here again, the conversion of Constantine meant nothing. As late as the sixth century A.D., the notables of Gerasa (Jerash in Jordan) were proud to have maintained a water festival in which teams of nude girls sported in front of what was, by that time, a totally Christian populace: it was, they said, "a most delightful spectacle."[89] The bodies of such women counted for little. While the wives of the owners of taverns were deemed to be sufficiently honorable to be liable to accusations of adultery on the part of their husbands if they had sex with passing clients, this was not the case for barmaids:

for from those women to whom the law applies, chastity should be expected; but those girls are free from the severity of legal process whose worthless life puts them beneath observance of the law.[90]

It is the public voice of Constantine, the first Christian Emperor.

All this is a world known to us from a resolutely male viewpoint. There was much in the world around them that educated Greeks and Romans did not wish to see or to articulate. The exquisite ideal of marital concord deliberately stared past the grief, pain and illness associated with childbirth. It aimed to absorb marriage into the greater order of the city. Yet, in the city's dogged battle with death, women

---

87. Caesarius of Arles, *Sermon* 42.3, G. Morin, ed. *Corpus Christianorum*, 103:187.
88. Veyne, "L'Empire romain," *Vie privée*, pp. 215–222, *Private Life*, pp. 224–233.
89. C. H. Kraeling, *Gerasa: City of the Decapolis*, inscription no. 279, p. 471.
90. *Codex Theodosianus* 9.7.1 of 326 A.D.

in their twenties fought in the first line.[91] Many men learned to grieve early:

What use to you, Probina, was your fertile womb?
You conceived affection; but dread is your only child.[92]

The great Roman teacher of rhetoric, Quintillian, lost his wife when she was eighteen. She had already borne him two sons: "her death was like the loss not merely of a wife, but of a daughter."[93]

It was left to Christian treatises on virginity to speak in public on the physical state of the married woman—on their danger in childbirth, on the pain in their breasts during suckling, on their exposure to children's infections, on the terrible shame of infertility, and on the humiliation of being replaced by servants in their husbands' affections: "and all this they endure, seeing no end to their labors."[94] Had they not married "they would be blessed, even if there were no Kingdom of Heaven for them to receive."[95]

It is a glimpse of the huge pain that any underdeveloped society places on the bodies of its fertile women. Even though they possessed a sophisticated medical tradition and were willing to practice contraception and abortion, the ruling classes of the Roman Empire could do little to alleviate pain and death in their wives.[96] As for the Christian clergy, the majority were as unwilling to disrupt the institution of marriage as they had been to contemplate the abolition of household slavery. Like the pagan moralists, whose ideas they echoed, Christian writers were mainly content to smooth away the more abrasive features of married life. When they spoke most fervently on the ills of marriage, it was not to wives but to the unmarried young. Christian exhortations to virginity did little to reduce the suffering of those already committed, by marriage, to the bearing of children.

91. Burn, "Hic Breve Vivitur," pp. 11–12; but see Hopkins, "Age Structure of the Roman Population," pp. 260–263.

92. E. Diehl, *Inscriptiones latinae christianae veteres* 3330, line 18; 2:179.

93. Quintilian, *Institutio Oratoria* 6, Praef. 5, in Butler, trans., *Quintilian*, 2:375.

94. Ps.-Athanasius, *Vita Sanctae Syncleticae* 42: *Patrologia Graeca* 28: 1512CD.

95. Eusebius of Emesa, *Sermon* 6.5, E. M. Buytaert, ed. *Eusèbe d'Émèse: Discours conservés en latin*, 1:155.

96. Keith Hopkins, "Contraception in the Roman Empire," pp. 124–151; E. Eyben, "Family Planning in Antiquity," pp. 5–82; note Rousselle, *Porneia*, p. 63 on the absence of mention of diseases caused by frequent childbirth in doctors dealing with Roman upper-class women.

(III) "CLAY CUNNINGLY COMPOUNDED"

It is impossible to sum up in so short a survey, and from such documents, the moral tone of a society as extensive, as diverse, and as
little known to us in its day-to-day life as was the Roman Empire at
its height. We are dealing with a society among whose upper classes
areas of extreme rigidity coexisted with areas which immediately strike
a modern reader as marked by a graciousness, a tolerance, and a mat-
ter-of-factness that vanished in medieval Byzantium and in the Catholic West. This peculiar juxtapostion of severity and tolerance made
sense to thinking pagans in terms of an image of the human person
based on what may best be called a "benevolent dualism." The soul
met the body as the inferior "other" to the self. The body was as different from the soul, and as intractable, as were women, slaves, and
the opaque and restless populace of the cities. Not even the gods could
change that fact.

What says Zeus? "Epictetus, had it been possible, I should have made this
paltry body, this small estate of thine, free and unhampered. But, as it is—
let it not escape thee—this body is not thine own, but is only clay cunningly
compounded."[97]

It was a clay on which age, disease, and death fastened inexorably.
At the end of so much long pain, it was best for the soul to go away—
perhaps to the stars—"clean of a body," the diseased flesh melted at
last from the mind.[98]
   Yet the soul had been sent down from heaven for a time to act as
an administrator to the murmurous and fertile province of the body.
A wise man's relation to his body was one of benevolent concern. Its
government demanded a refined *sprezzatura*. The body's observed
physical needs could not be overruled in a tyrannical manner by
"overmeticulous and rigid control."[99] The soul must learn to exercise

---

97. Epictetus, *Discourses* 1.1.11, Oldfather, ed. *Epictetus*, 1:8–10.
98. *Studia Pontica* 3, J. G. C. Anderson, F. Cumont and H. Grégoire, eds., inscription
no. 86, p. 102; compare Aretaeus, *Causes and Symptoms of Acute Diseases* 2.4, pp. 272–
273.
99. Plutarch, *de san. tuenda* 17.131B, p. 260.

gentle violence on the body, much as the husband groomed his young bride, "entering into its feelings, being knit to it by good will."[100]

An unaffected symbiosis of body and soul was the aim both of medicine and of philosophical exhortation. The body must not be permitted to force its needs upon the tranquil mind: it was to be kept well-tuned according to its own, intrinsic laws. The mind, in turn, must constantly refine itself, lest, through weakness and uncertainty, it come to participate in the lability of the flesh.[101] A man unduly preoccupied with his body was an undignified sight. To spend one's time "in much exercise, in much eating, drinking, much evacuating the bowels and much copulating" was, quite simply, "a mark of lack of refinement."[102] From a well-born Greek, no judgment could have been more crushing. But the ostentatious ascetic was equally distasteful. A young man might opt not to have love affairs before marriage: "but do not make yourself offensive or censorious to those who so indulge, and do not make frequent mentions of the fact that you yourself do not indulge."[103]

The body had its rightful place in a great chain of being that linked man both to the gods and to the beasts. It had risen toward the soul, like the highest crest of a dancing wave, from the mighty ocean of an eternal Nature. Even the dull earth, which both gave and reclaimed the body, was not neutral: it could be addressed as divine, a majestic presence forever stirring with new life.[104] The men we meet in the literature of the second century still belonged to the rustling universe of late classical polytheism. They knew that they had been knit, by the cunning of the gods, to the animal world. They felt pulsing in their own bodies the same fiery spirit that covered the hills every year with newborn lambs and that ripened the crops, in seasonal love-play, as the spring winds embraced the fertile ears.[105] Above them, the same

---

100. Plutarch, *Praecept. Conjug.* 33.142E, p. 323.

101. Well seen by Foucault, *Souci de Soi*, pp. 72–73 and 157–158, *Care of the Self*, pp. 56–57 and 133–134.

102. Epictetus, *Enchiridion* 41, Oldfather, p. 527.   103. Ibid. 33.8, p. 519.

104. *Corpus Inscriptionum Latinarum* 6.4, fasc. 2. 35887, C. Huelsen, ed., 3681—all the more poignant as the tomb is that of a thirteen-year-old virgin girl. For the background, see Sabine G. MacCormack, "Roma, Constantinopolis, the Emperor and his Genius," pp. 133–134.

105. Ephraim the Syrian, *de Paradiso* 9.10–13 and 10.5–8, R. Lavenant, trans. *Éphrem de Nisibe: Hymnes sur le Paradis*, Sources chrétiennes 137:125–126; 137–138 is an exceptionally beautiful rendering of this theme.

fire glowed in the twinkling stars.[106] Their bodies, and their sexual drives, shared directly in the unshakable perpetuity of an immense universe, through which the gods played exuberantly.[107]

A thing of the natural world, the body was expected to speak of its own needs in an ancient, authoritative voice. It was only prudent to listen at times. The tolerance that was extended to the body in late classical times was based on a sense that the antithesis to the animal world, the city, was so strong that, once made, the claims of the city were inexorable. The family and the city determined the degree to which the results of the body's connection with the natural world was acceptable in organized society. The mere fact of physical birth, for instance, did not make a Roman child a person. Its father must lift it from the floor. If not, the little bundle of ensouled matter, as much a fetus as if it were still in its mother's womb, must wait for others to collect it from a place outside the father's house. The fetus could be aborted in the womb; and it might yet die, if no one picked it up and made it part of their own family, when left out in a public place to be claimed by passers-by.[108]

Young men found themselves in an analogous, if less perilous, situation. Nature made their bodies different from those of children long before they were useful to the city. The boy's first ejaculation was celebrated by his family at the feast of the Liberalia, on March 17.[109] For a few years, he was free to "sprout rank growth."[110] The unsteadying heats of adolescence (or, on another account, the lingering damp humors that were betrayed in a boy's wavering voice) must be burned off a little before the young man could take on the hard-baked role of a civic dignitary.[111] This was the time of the *ludus.*

Nature itself develops a young man's desire. If these desires break out in such a way that they disrupt no one's life and undermine no household [by adultery], they are generally regarded as unproblematic: we tolerate them.[112]

---

106. Cicero, *de natura deorum* 2.10.28.

107. Lane Fox, *Pagans and Christians*, pp. 41–46, 110–133 is an impressive evocation of this mentality.

108. Veyne, "L'Empire romain," *Vie privée*, pp. 23–27, *Private Life*, pp. 9–14; W. V. Harris, "The Roman Father's Power of Life and Death," in R. S. Bagnall and W. V. Harris, eds., *Studies in Roman Law in Memory of A. Arthur Schiller.*

109. Rousselle, *Porneia*, p. 79.

110. Augustine, *Confessions* 2.1.1, describing himself at the age of sixteen.

111. Quintilian, *Institutio oratoria* 11.3.28.

112. Cicero, *Pro Caelio* 28, from the translation of Lyne, *Latin Love Poets*, pp. 1–2.

The call of the city would come soon enough; only "soft" men—among them, the great erotic poets of Augustan Rome![113]—were slow to answer the summons of duty, by abandoning the life of the lover:

Finally, when he has hearkened to pleasure . . . let him, at last, recall himself to action, to the business of the household, to the forum, to the service of the state.[114]

Even Marcus Aurelius, a paragon of public sobriety, had "given way to amatory passions" for a requisite, short time.[115] Though a man of great austerity, he by no means considered himself to be bound to perpetual sexual abstinence. Rather than remarrying, he spent his old age with a concubine, the daughter of an estate-manager of his former wife, so as not to burden his children with a stepmother.[116]

The young woman was often treated in a similar, matter-of-fact manner. Too labile a creature to be allowed the periods of sexual freedom granted to young men, and tolerated even in husbands, her family must guard her carefully. But the physical integrity of her body had not yet become the charged symbol that we now associate with Mediterranean Christian societies.[117] The girl's loss of her virginity was, simply, a bad omen for her future conduct. A girl who had already enjoyed furtive love affairs might do the same when married. She was not a "well brought up" girl.[118] From a second-century author, no harsher judgment was necessary.

The effect of such benevolent dualism was to make late classical attitudes toward the body seem deeply alien to later, Christian eyes, and hence to modern observers of the ancient world. In the pagan world of the second century A.D., a marked degree of tolerance was accorded to men, both on the matter of homosexuality and in their love affairs before and outside marriage. But to emphasize this fact alone is to trivialize the meaning of the changes that occurred in later centuries. It is not sufficient to talk of the rise of Christianity in the Roman world simply in terms of a shift from a less to a more repressive society.

113. Jasper Griffin, "Augustan Poetry and the Life of Luxury;" Lyne, *Latin Love Poets,* pp. 65–81; Paul Veyne, *L'Élégie érotique romaine,* pp. 170–183.

114. Cicero, *Pro Caelio* 42.   115. Marcus Aurelius, *Meditations* 1.17.6.

116. *Scriptores Historiae Augustae: Marcus Aurelius* 29.10.

117. G. Sissa, "Une virginité sans hymen: le corps féminin en Grèce ancienne," p. 1132, and *Le corps virginal,* pp. 97–143 and 189–198.

118. Soranus, *Gynaecia* 1.8.33.4, Ilberg, p. 22; Temkin, p. 31—on the precocious sexual desires of "ill-bred" girls.

What was at stake was a subtle change in the perception of the body itself. The men and women of later centuries were not only hedged around with a different and more exacting set of prohibitions. They had also come to see their own bodies in a different light.

Seen through the lens of the fully elaborated Christianity of the early middle ages, the body image of second-century persons seemed strangely blurred. A diffused sensuality flickered through it. Sexual desire lacked the distinctive flavor that it soon acquired in Christian circles. No one need for sensual gratification was brought into sharper focus than any other. None was considered peculiarly deeply rooted, or exceptionally revealing of human frailty. Nor was any one desire singled out as uniquely worthy of reprobation. Sexual desire itself was unproblematic: it was a predictable response to physical beauty; its satisfaction was accepted as an occasion that brought intense physical pleasure. The city could be safely left to judge the further consequences of having yielded to the sweet delight of "the things of Venus." That men might wish to caress and penetrate other beautiful men caused the Greeks, at least, little surprise.[119] What was judged harshly was the fact that the pursuit of pleasure might lead some men to wish to play the female role, by offering themselves to be penetrated by their lovers: such behavior was puzzling to the doctors and shocking to most people.[120] No free man should allow himself to be so weakened by desire as to allow himself to step out of the ferociously maintained hierarchy that placed all free men, in all their dealings, above women and slaves.[121]

What might appear at first sight as tolerance reveals, in fact, the comprehensiveness of the codes adopted by the elites. They lay across the whole body of the public man. As well they might. Wealthy, perpetually in the public gaze, exercising the power of life and limb over others, and close to figures who could exercise such power over themselves, the civic notables found anger, irrational cruelty, the exuberant and menacing physicality of the greedy eater, and the erratic savagery

119. Ramsay MacMullen, "Roman Attitudes to Greek Love," would wish to contrast Greek and Roman attitudes; but see T. Wade Richardson, "Homosexuality in the *Satyricon*."

120. P. H. Schrijvers, *Eine medizinische Erklärung der männlichen Homosexualität aus der Antike*, p. 7—the desires of the active partner were "medically of no interest."

121. Paul Veyne, "Amour et famille," pp. 50–55 and "L'homosexualité à Rome," pp. 26–33, now translated in P. Ariès and A. Béjin, eds., *Western Sexuality: Practise and Precept in Past Times*, pp. 26–35; Rousselle, "Gestes et signes de la famille," pp. 257–261 now offers important nuances.

of the tippler subjects far more worthy of concern than was the soft passion of desire. It was to those passions that moralists devoted their most serious attention.

Where second-century pagans differed most profoundly from the views that had already begun to circulate in Christian circles was in their estimate of the horizons of the possible for the body itself. Potentially formless and eternal matter, the body was barely held together, for a short lifetime, by the vivid soul of the well-born man. Its solid matter could change as little as the crystalline marble of a sharply cut and exquisitely polished statue might blossom magically in its depths, into a more refined and malleable substance. Like society, the body was there to be administered, not to be changed. Others had begun to disagree with this view. Writing at the end of the second century, Clement of Alexandria, a Christian who knew his pagan authors well, summed up with admirable clarity and fairness the essence of the expectations of the body that we have described. Pagan philosophers, he knew, subscribed to an austere image of the person:

The human ideal of continence, I mean that which is set forth by the Greek philosophers, teaches one to resist passion, so as not to be made subservient to it, and to train the instincts to pursue rational goals.

But Christians, he added, went further: "our ideal is not to experience desire at all."

Moses had stood on Sinai for forty days, a man transfigured by the close presence of God. The needs of the body were stilled in him for all that time.[122] Through the Incarnation of Christ, the Highest God had reached down to make even the body capable of transformation. In admitting this possibility, Clement implied that the stable environment posited by pagan thought, an intractable body and a social order adjusted to its unchanging needs, might burst from its ancient bounds. Sexual renunciation might lead the Christian to transform the body and, in transforming the body, to break with the discreet discipline of the ancient city.

Clement was a moderate among Christians. He stood closer to Plutarch, Musonius Rufus, and the doctors of his age than he did to many of his fellow-believers. In little groups scattered throughout the eastern Mediterranean, other Christians had seized upon the body. They

122. Clement, *Stromateis* 3.7.57, in Henry Chadwick, trans., *Alexandrian Christianity*, p. 66.

had set it up as a palpable blazon of the end of the "present age." They believed that the universe itself had shattered with the rising of Christ from the grave. By renouncing all sexual activity the human body could join in Christ's victory: it could turn back the inexorable. The body could wrench itself free from the grip of the animal world. By refusing to act upon the youthful stirrings of desire, Christians could bring marriage and childbirth to an end. With marriage at an end, the huge fabric of organized society would crumble like a sandcastle, touched by the "ocean-flood of the Messiah."[123]

These were the views of exact contemporaries of Galen and Marcus Aurelius. Their implications could hardly have been more appalling to the pagan elites of Rome and the Aegean, and more calculated to upset the average married householder in any Mediterranean or Near Eastern community. In the century that followed the death of Jesus of Nazareth, the issue of sexual renunciation came to be elaborated in Christian circles as a drastic alternative to the moral and social order that seemed so secure, so prepared to expatiate upon its fundamental values in treatises, in works of medicine and on the warm stones of so many monuments in so many little cities. If we are to understand the emergence of this alternative, we must now turn to the very different world of Judaism, to the Palestine of Jesus, and to the dilemmas of the communities founded by Saint Paul in many of the major cities of the Greco-Roman world.

123. *Acts of Judas Thomas* 31, A. F. J. Klijn, trans. *The Acts of Judas Thomas*, Supplements to Novum Testamentum 5:80.

TWO

From Apostle to Apologist: Sexual Order and Sexual Renunciation in the Early Church

---

(I) "WALK IN SINGLENESS OF HEART"

At some time in the later half of the second century, the doctor Galen referred in passing to Christians:

Their contempt for death is patent to us every day, and likewise their restraint from intercourse. For they include not only men but also women who refrain from intercourse all through their lives.[1]

Galen had arrived in Rome from Ephesus in 162, around the time that Justin, a Christian teacher, was executed. Justin, who had been established in the city since 140 A.D., was a pagan convert from a Greek settlement in Samaria. An impenitent intellectual, he always made a point of wearing the *pallium*, the somber robe of the professional philospher.[2] It was as one philosopher appealing to another that he wrote his *Apology* for the Christian faith, in the form of a petition to the Emperor Antoninus Pius, "guardian of justice, philosopher . . . and lover

---

1. Cited in Richard Walzer, *Galen on Jews and Christians*, p. 15. One cannot, however, entirely exclude the possibility that this remark is a later, Christian interpolation in the Arabic tradition.

2. Jerome, *de viris illustribus* 23: *Patrologia Latina* 23:641.

of learning.''[3] Justin knew how to elicit the respect of that small but articulate circle of notables and Imperial servants whose preoccupation with moral grooming had come to include a measure of respect for sexual restraint. He presented Christianity to them as a religion distinguished from all others by the stringency of the sexual codes observed by its married believers. More than that:

Many, both men and women of the age of sixty or seventy years, who have been disciples of Christ from their youth continue in immaculate purity. . . . It is our boast to be able to display such persons before the human race.[4]

By emphasizing in Christianity the sexual discipline of the many and the heroic self-denial of the few, Justin attempted to find common ground with a "philosophical" emperor. In reality, the Christian notion of sexual renunciation had emerged from a world profoundly different from that of an emperor such as Antoninus Pius and a Greek doctor such as Galen. It carried with it the distinctive flavor of its radical Jewish origins.

We must begin with a different image of the human person and, with it, a very different view of society from that which prevailed among the civic elites of the Empire. There had been little room in Judaism for the benevolent dualism that summed up so appositely the moral commonsense of the governing classes of the pagan world. In the pagan notion of the person, the soul had been thought of as ruling the body with the same alert, if occasionally tolerant, authority as the wellborn male ruled those inferior and alien to himself—his wife, his slaves, and the populace of his city. To many upright and well-to-do Jews, aristocrats in their own right, similar dualistic attitudes came naturally. The body was palpably weaker than the soul. The soul would be separated from it at death; and this could be hailed as a blessing.[5] The body had physical needs that troubled the pious. Upright Jews and early Christians alike expected sexual temptation to bulk large in the life of young males. They did not approve of the "love of pleasure" associated with "the power of procreation," for it "leadeth the young as a blind man to a pit and as a beast to a precipice."[6]

Yet, for Jews, the daily conflict of body and mind was overshadowed

---

3. Justin, *Apology* 1 2.   4. Ibid. 15.1–5.

5. R. H. Gunday, *Sôma in Biblical Theology: with Emphasis on Pauline Anthropology*, pp. 136–140 and E. Stiegman, "Rabbinic Anthropology."

6. *Testaments of the Twelve Patriarchs: Reuben* 2.8–9, in R. H. Charles, *The Apocrypha and Pseudepigrapha of the Old Testament* 2: *Pseudepigrapha*, p. 297; see now James H.

by a mightier and more significant dualism. All mankind stood before the majesty of God as other and inferior to Him. Body and soul faced Him together: He had created both and would judge both. Every believer confronted God not as a soul committed, for a time, to the necessary if thankless task of bringing order to an alien body, but rather as the possessor of a "heart," that is, of a hidden core of the self, that could respond to or reject the will of its Creator. The human heart might harden: it could become a *heart of stone*, clenched in a state of mute rebellion to God's will. Or it might open itself fully to receive His commands and to respond without reluctance to His fatherly love. The pain of the pious was precisely that—while a "good inclination" urged them to obey God, an "evil inclination," a deep-set tendency to hold back from following His will, also lay so very close to their own hearts.[7] The evil inclination appeared to suffuse the human person as a whole, like an "evil yeast" working deep within the dough of human nature:

Sovereign of the universe, it is known full well to Thee that our will is to perform Thy will, and what prevents us? The yeast in the dough of our nature. . . . May it be Thy will to deliver us . . . so that we may return to perform the statutes of Thy will with a perfect heart.[8]

True peace would come to the faithful, not when the soul slipped off the alien clay of the body, but when a faceless reluctance had finally melted away within the heart: *"A new heart will I give you, and a new spirit will I put within you; and I will take out of your flesh the heart of stone."*[9]

Charlesworth, ed. *The Old Testament Pseudepigrapha.* On the nature of the Testaments, a document of Jewish origin that circulated among Christians, see now M. de Jonge. "The Pre-Mosaic Servants of God in the Testaments of the Twelve Patriarchs and in the Writings of Justin and Irenaeus," and G. Vermes, "Methodology in the Study of Jewish Literature in the Greco-Roman Period," pp. 152–156.

7. See esp. H. Strack and P. Billerbeck, *Kommentar zum Neuen Testament aus Talmud und Midrasch,* 4, pp. 466–483, Jean Hadot, *Penchant Mauvais et Volonté Libre dans la Sagesse de Ben Sira (Ecclésiastique);* and E. E. Urbach, *The Sages: Their Concepts and Beliefs,* pp. 471–483. The reader must always bear in mind the composite nature of any overall presentation of Judaism, drawn as it is largely from the Palestinian and Babylonian Talmud—that is, from writings of widely differing periods and regions. Such sources may serve to delineate certain general horizons and to emphasize certain options taken among the rabbis of Palestine and Babylonia in the course of the late antique period; but they can be used only with great caution.

8. M. Simon, trans., *Babylonian Talmud: Berakhoth* 17a, p. 100.

9. *Ezechiel* 36:6, cited in *Midrash Rabba: Numbers* 17.6, J. J. Slotki, trans. 2:707.

The religious notion of the "perfect heart" carried with it unmistakable social overtones. All too many Jews showed to each other the same reluctance to open themselves wholeheartedly to the demands placed upon them by their fellows as they showed when confronted by the demands of God. Such persons were branded as the "double hearted." They bore a heart within their heart: at the very back of the self there lurked a shadowy enclave that nurtured guile, rebelliousness, resentment and hidden lust. The religious ideal of the "perfect heart" was intimately connected with hopes for an ideal society that were poignantly reiterated in Jewish and early Christian texts. The true believer should learn to "walk in singleness of heart."[10]

The heart should be all of one piece. No hidden motives should lurk within it. The believer should face others with a heart as transparent to their needs as it was to the will of God. "Singleness of heart" condensed a warm and eminently sociable ideal. It summed up the moral horizons of the average man. It formed the basis of a morality of solidarity, which stressed unaffected straight dealing and ungrudging loyalty to kin and neighbors. It was a virtue peculiarly appropriate to the self-reliant and abrasive householders of the small towns and villages of the eastern Mediterranean. The emphasis on the control of violence toward inferiors and on the need to hold in check the physical desires that might infect wielders of power with a "womanish" sensuality, which bulked so large in the moral grooming of the pagan ruling classes of the Empire, was irrelevant to them. These men did not need to discipline their bodies by meticulous codes of public deportment and by repeated reminders of the superiority of spirit over matter. Their most bitter struggle was to control cunning and resentment in their relations with their modest peers.

Guile arose not in my heart;
A lie passed not through my lips.
If any man were in distress, I joined my sighs with him.
And I shared my bread with the poor.[11]

In Palestine, however, the ideal of singleness of heart carried with it a more urgent message. Many pious Jews looked out on an Israel alienated from God and torn by inner strife:

10. *Testaments of the Twelve Patriarchs: Simeon* 4.5, Charles, p. 302; see O. J. Seitz, "Antecedents and Significance of the Term δίψυχος," p. 213 and H. C. Kee, "The Ethical Dimensions of the Testaments of the XII Patriarchs as a clue to Provenance."
11. *Testaments: Issachar* 7.4–5, Charles, *Apocrypha*, pp. 327–328.

Every man has chosen the stubborness of his heart. . . . They have taken revenge and borne malice . . . and every man has hated his fellow, and every man has sinned against his near kin, and has approached [women] for unchastity, and has acted arrogantly for the sake of riches and gain.[12]

Documents discovered in 1947 in a cave in the Wadi Qumran, in the Judaean desert beside the Dead Sea (and hence named "The Dead Sea Scrolls"), reveal a self-styled "Community" of devout males who wished to establish among themselves a "house of perfection and truth in Israel."[13] Whether this "house of perfection and truth" was actually located in a desert monastery (as some scholars deduced from the fact that the ruins of a settlement of some kind were discovered at Khirbet Qumran, close to the caves) or whether we are dealing with a less physically enclosed association of pious persons, scattered throughout the towns and villages of Judaea, we do not know.[14] Whichever may be the case, the documents reveal the manner in which, within the narrow confines of a beleaguered religious group, the yearning for singleness of heart led to nothing less than a demand for total transparency to the will of God, gained by the transparency of the will of each member to his fellows within the Community. Each member of the Community had vowed "that they should seek God with a whole heart and soul . . . and no longer stubbornly follow a sinful heart."[15]

The members of the Community believed that, at the end of the troubled age in which they lived, God would deliver Israel. He would re-create His people as they should be. The Community would stand before Him in a new Israel: "He will refine for himself the human frame, by rooting out the spirit of falsehood from the bounds of the flesh."[16]

This was no distant prospect. Every year, the quality of each member's "spirits and deeds" was assessed by a skilled adviser.[17] It was a searching examination of the precise and intimate alloy of the heart, which brought with it a foretaste of a future where the dark shadows

---

12. *Damascus Rule* 8, in G. Vermes, trans. *The Dead Sea Scrolls in English,* p. 105 (hereafter cited as *Dead Sea Scrolls*).

13. *Community Rule* 5, in *Dead Sea Scrolls,* p. 85.

14. The scholarly consensus that tends to link the Dead Sea Scrolls to the Essenes and to a precise community, settled at Khirbet Qumran, is ably summarized in E. Schürer, *The History of the Jewish People in the Age of Jesus Christ.* Serious objections have been raised by N. Golb, "The Problem of the Origin and Identification of the Dead Sea Scrolls," and "Les manuscrits de la Mer Morte."

15. *Community Rule* 1, in *Dead Sea Scrolls,* p. 72.

16. *Community Rule* 4, in ibid., p. 77.   17. *Community Rule* 5, in ibid., p. 80.

of falsehood and self-will would vanish forever from the heart: "all the glory of Adam shall be theirs. There shall be no more lies."[18]

Many Jewish groups reacted to the situation in which they found themselves by fostering a "radicalization" of sexual codes among their adherents.[19] The community revealed in the Dead Sea Scrolls appears to have demanded that a number of its male members should live under a vow of celibacy for an indefinite period. It seems that they considered themselves to be warriors of Israel, subject to the vows of abstinence that bound men for the duration of a holy war. The celibate state of these few stood for the embattled character of the Community as a whole. They were the true "Camp" of the children of Israel, established, once again, in the Promised Land. In the Camp, male devotees thought of themselves as standing beside the "holy angels."[20] These angels were not thought of primarily as sexless beings. They were imagined, rather, as the serried ranks of an expectant army, which must not be allowed to crumble into the disordered state of mere civilians, whose seed flowed freely when they slept at ease with their wives.[21]

We do not know whether other groups of continent males saw their own abstinence in these drastic terms. We do know that Roman observers were struck by the presence of colonies of celibates in Palestine. A younger contemporary of Jesus of Nazareth, Pliny the Elder, had heard of the well-known sect of the Essenes, settled at Engeddi near the Dead Sea. Here was a startling suspension of the relentless rhythm of procreation that had covered the Greco-Roman Mediterranean with settled communities: "remarkable among all other tribes in the whole world, as it has no women and has renounced all sexual desire . . . a race in which no one is born [nevertheless] lives on forever."[22]

Two Jewish writers, Philo in Alexandria and Josephus in Palestine, found it easy to justify such exotic behavior. They presented the celibacy of the Essenes to pagans as no more than the consequential up-

18. *Community Rule* 4, in ibid., p. 78.

19. Kurt Niederwimmer, *Askese und Mysterium*, pp. 13–33.

20. *War Rule* 7, *Dead Sea Scrolls*, p. 133.

21. Matthew Black, "The Tradition of Hasidaean-Essene Asceticism: Its Origin and Influence," and *The Scrolls and Christian Origins*, pp. 27–32, with Paul Beauchamp, *Création et Séparation*, p. 275. See now Steven D. Fraade, "Ascetical Aspects of Ancient Judaism," p. 267.

22. Pliny, *Natural History* 5.15.73, in Rackham, ed., *Pliny: Natural History*, 2:277.

shot of a long tradition of misogyny with which Greeks were expected to sympathize. The Essenes, they said, had created an all-male utopia. Jewish folk wisdom, like that of the pagans, stressed the seductive wiles of women and the disruptive effect of the claims that women made upon men as the bearers of their children and the sharers of their bed.[23]

Singleness of heart, we must remember, was a profoundly male virtue: upright men tended to regard women as the causes, *par excellence*, of "double-hearted" behavior. Women were thought to stir up the lust and jealousy that pitted males against each other. To ensure the *philallélia*, the precious loyalty of male Companions to one another, the Essenes, so Philo assured his readers, had abandoned both women and the ownership of slaves. Slaves were the second inferior other in the world of the free male; their presence in a free community encouraged arrogance on the part of their masters and introduced a note of manipulative servility into the relations between unfree and free members of the group.[24] Only outside Alexandria did one community, that of the Therapeutae, include elderly continent women.[25]

In Palestine proper, Josephus spoke lovingly of the awesome silence of the communal meals of the Essenes, and of the solemn little groups that processed from one lodge to another in the towns and villages, all dressed in white, walking sedately "like well-disciplined schoolboys."[26] These vignettes were intended to appeal to the sharp "appetite for order"[27] that well-to-do Jews such as Philo and Josephus shared with the ceremonious and self-disciplined elites of the Greek world.

It is, however, misleading to concentrate attention exclusively on the small groups of professed male celibates. In hailing the Essenes and the mysterious authors of the Dead Sea Scrolls as direct predecessors of the Christian monks, we risk losing the precise flavor of their contribution to the life of Jewish Palestine in the age of Jesus. We know very little about why Jewish male militants adopted lives of permanent continence.[28] What we do know is that the continent were fellow-

---

23. E.g., *Testaments: Reuben* 5.1–4, Charles, *Apocrypha*, p. 299.
24. Philo, *Hypothetica* in Eusebius, *Praeparatio Evangelica* 8.11: *Patrologia Graeca* 21: 644B.
25. Philo, *de vita contemplativa* 8.68, in F. H. Colson, ed., *Philo*, 9:155: see Schürer, *History of the Jewish People*, 2:591–597.
26. Josephus, *Jewish War* 2.124 and 133.
27. Michael Carrithers, *The Forest Monks of Sri Lanka*, p. 20.
28. A. Marx, "Les racines du célibat essénien," and Fraade, "Ascetical Aspects of Ancient Judaism," pp. 266–269.

members of associations largely made up of married householders. They did not form isolated communities. The reform of Israel as a whole was at stake. For this reason, the militants had no intention of challenging Jewish married life. Far from it: the structures of the household were strengthened by being brought back to their original, imagined purity.[29] Sexual codes were made to bear a heavy weight of meaning. The prohibition of marriage to non-Jews;[30] the condemnation of close-kin marriages;[31] the insistence of the careful observance of the codes of purity that governed the woman's menstrual cycle and the man's emission of seed;[32] a carefully nurtured disgust for the promiscuity, public nudity, and homosexual love allowed to the young male in pagan cities:[33] all these points of difference heightened the sense of the separation of Israel from the pagan world. The writers of the Dead Sea Scrolls even took the significant step of presenting the reform of marriage in terms of a return to the single-hearted solidarity of the first couple, Adam and Eve. Those who took another wife while the other was alive (possibly by practicing polygamy) sinned against "the principle of Creation . . . *Male and female created He them.*"[34]

All radical groups believed that the new Israel of the future would be a community of the married, "fruitful in seed," an Israel renowned for its disciplined sexuality, from which the abnormalities associated with the present age had been removed.[35]

When Jesus of Nazareth preached in Galilee and Judaea after 30 A.D., the options open to him and to his followers were already clearly mapped out on the landscape of Palestine. Toward the Dead Sea, the wilderness of Judaea harbored sizable settlements of disaffected males. Ascetic figures whose prophetic calling had long been associated, in Jewish folklore, with sexual abstinence, continued to emerge from the desert to preach repentance to the nearby cities. One such, John the

29. See esp. E. P. Sanders, *Jesus and Judaism*, pp. 230–232, 256–260 and J. M. Baumgarten, "4Q502, Marriage or Golden Age Ritual?"

30. Jubilees 25.7–9, Charles, *Apocrypha*, p. 51; see esp. Geza Vermes, "Leviticus 18:21 in Ancient Jewish Bible Exegesis."

31. *Damascus Rule* 5, *Dead Sea Scrolls*, pp. 101–102.

32. *Damascus Rule* 4, *Dead Sea Scrolls*, p. 101; *Psalms of Solomon* 8.13, Charles, *Apocrypha*.

33. I Maccabees 1:14–15; Josephus, *Against Apion* 2.24.1–5.

34. *Damascus Rule* 4, *Dead Sea Scrolls*, p. 101.

35. *Community Rule* 4 and *Messianic Rule* 1, *Dead Sea Scrolls*, pp. 76 and 118—"fruitfulness" and "women and children"; see esp. B. Janowski and H. Lichtenberg, "Enderwartung und Reinheitsidee," esp. pp. 34–40, 59.

Baptist, was reputedly a cousin of Jesus. The fact that Jesus himself had not married by the age of thirty occasioned no comment. It was almost a century before any of his followers claimed to base their own celibacy on his example.[36] At the time, the prophetic role of Jesus held the center of attention, not his continence. His celibacy was an unremarkable adjunct of his prophet's calling.[37]

We know singularly little about Jesus' own hopes for the coming of what he called "the kingdom of heaven," except that he identified this kingdom with the renewal of Israel and that he expected this renewal to be imminent.[38] He seems not to have envisioned the total disappearance of family structures. Rather, like the writers in the Dead Sea Scrolls, he insisted on monogamous marriage as a renewal of the undivided union of Adam and Eve. In one of his very few breaches with Jewish custom, he even went so far as to rule out the possibility of divorce. The "hardness of heart" that had rendered divorce necessary in the laws of Moses would simply no longer prevail in the renewed Israel of the future.[39] The "yoke" that he laid on his hearers rested on the usual recipients of Jewish exhortation—on married males, good Jews, and decent heads of households, who strove as best they could to walk in singleness of heart:

I say to you that every one who looks at a woman lustfully has already committed adultery with her in his heart.[40]

For from within, out of the heart of man, come evil thoughts, fornication, theft, murder . . .[41]

Jesus was crucified around 30 A.D. By the time that his sayings and the story of his death and resurrection were collected in what later became the Gospels, Jewish Palestine had changed profoundly. Jerusalem had been stormed by the Romans in 70 A.D. The Temple lay in ruins. Judaea was devastated. The eccentric settlements by the Dead Sea lay deserted. In the Gospels we meet, not the world of Jesus, but the very different, more tense world of his disciples. The stories in them had been collected in that terrible period, to meet the needs and to validate the activities of a group of wandering preachers, who claimed to be his true followers.[42]

---

36. Ignatius, *Letter to Polycarp* 5.2.   37. Geza Vermes, *Jesus the Jew*, pp. 99–102.
38. Sanders, *Jesus*, p. 75.
39. Mark 10:5–9; Sanders, *Jesus*, pp. 230–232 and 256–260.
40. Matthew 5:28.   41. Mark 7:21.

To that particular small group, Jesus had not preached singleness of heart within a married household. He had said, "Follow me . . ." His abrupt call had involved a break with the normal patterns of settled life. Even the strongest ties of Jewish piety were set aside: sons must no longer linger to bury their fathers.[43] Married persons, such as Peter, could claim, "Lo, we have left our homes and followed you."[44]

Many had "left home or wife or brothers or parents or children for the sake of the kingdom of God."[45]

There were even some young males who "have made themselves eunuchs for the sake of the kingdom of heaven." The intensity of their mission rendered them ineligible for marriage.[46] Such persons had been sent out along the roads of Galilee and Judaea:

preach as you go, saying, "The kingdom of heaven is at hand" . . . for truly, I say to you, you will not have gone through all the towns of Israel, before the Son of Man comes.[47]

By 70 A.D., wandering preachers ministered to groups of married believers scattered in a wide arc from Jerusalem and Judaea, through Syria, and as far as Antioch. Their continence was no more than one aspect, and by no means the most prominent aspect, of a drastic dislocation of the normal course of their lives. The wanderers found a clearly demarcated place for themselves in the social landscape of Palestine. This was a world where the enterprising male had always faced stark alternatives. A few could give up "house or wife or brothers or parents or children." But those who had not received such a call remained in the villages as married persons. In that fixed environment, they battled with the wayward heart according to the traditional norms of Jewish life. The approach of the kingdom meant for them that these norms were, if anything, heightened rather than relaxed: it was a time of stern resolve, a time for a "righteousness that exceeds that of the Pharisees."[48] By contrast, those who preached that "the kingdom of heaven is at hand" moved in a different world. They had followed the

---

42. In this interpretation, I am particularly indebted to G. Kretschmar, "Ein Beitrag zur Frage nach dem Ursprung frühchristlicher Askese." See also Gerd Theissen, *Sociology of Early Palestinian Christianity*, pp. 24–30.

43. Matthew 8:21, Luke 9:59; see also Sanders, *Jesus*, pp. 253–255.

44. Luke 18:28.   45. Luke 18:29.

46. Matthew 19:12; see esp. H. Baltensweiler, *Die Ehe im Neuen Testament*, pp. 102–111.

47. Matthew 10:7, 23.   48. Matthew 5:20; Sanders, *Jesus*, p. 260.

open road. The same roads led from the villages to the brigands in the hills, and were already crowded with the vagrant poor.[49] Women might even join the roving bands, ministering to those who had "followed" Jesus, as they had once ministered to Jesus himself.[50] The relatively prosperous countryside of Galilee and Syria, and the village-like poor quarters of a great city such as Antioch, had enough agrarian surplus to support small numbers of persons thrown clear, by their religious vocation, from their family and their fields.[51]

Christian communities soon had to lay down rules as to how to treat prestigious wanderers endowed with prophetic gifts. A visiting preacher of the kingdom must be welcomed "as if he were the Lord himself"; but he could be fed and lodged by the local householders for only three days. If he so much as ordered a special meal for himself, he was to be shown the road: he was a false prophet![52] It was a world of modest men, in which those who wished to change their lives could do so only by breaking irreparably with the iron disciplines of the settled land. Even to put aside enough money to give alms to the poor and to support their wandering guides, the householders had to fast for days on end.[53] When the Emperor Domitian, around 90 A.D., examined the surviving kin of Jesus of Nazareth, he found two grandchildren of the brother of Jesus: their only property consisted of

a piece of land which contained only thirty nine acres, and from which they raised their taxes and supported themselves by their labors.

Then they showed their hands . . . and the callousness produced upon their hands as evidence of their own labor. . . . Domitian . . . despising them as of no account . . . let them go.[54]

Sixty years after the death of Jesus, little was clear about the profile of the Christian groups in Palestine and Syria. It was far from certain who would take the lead in preaching the kingdom and who would most effectively represent the "churches of Christ" before an increasingly angered Jewish population and a suspicious Roman government. On the one hand, there were those who had "followed" Jesus. His more radical sayings provided them with a clear charter for their own

---

49. Theissen, *Sociology*, pp. 8–16.   50. Luke 8:2 and I Corinthians 9:4.

51. S. Appelbaum, "Economic Life in Palestine," p. 657; G. E. M. de Ste. Croix, *The Class Struggle in the Ancient World*, p. 431 is exceptionally illuminating; see now Martin Goodman, *State and Society in Roman Galilee, A.D. 132–212*, pp. 28–40.

52. *Didache* 11.4.   53. Ibid. 1.3.

54. Eusebius, *Ecclesiastical History* 3.20.1–3 and 5, trans. A. C. McGiffert, *Library of Nicene and Post-Nicene Fathers* (Grand Rapids, Mich.: Eerdmans 1979), 1:149.

breach with the settled world. The story of his resurrection from the dead and ascension into heaven became indissolubly linked with the shaking of the grip of death on all human beings, and, so, with a stunning suspension of the inflexible laws of the normal.

The proclamation of the resurrection of Jesus had coincided with decades of growing estrangement between his supporters and their fellow Jews. Many followers lost the sense that there would be a natural, undisrupted continuity between the present social structures of Israel and those of the new kingdom. Rather than a miraculous return to married stability, with all "hardness of heart" banished from society, many disciples now saw a stark contrast between "that [coming] age" and the life of the "sons of this age," who "marry and are given in marriage."[55] The frankly extraordinary lives of the few preachers of the kingdom came to be thought of as standing for the nature of life itself within the kingdom: in such a kingdom, even the accustomed landmark of marriage was absent.

On the other hand, the silent majority of those who awaited the coming of the kingdom were careworn and decent householders, long used to the punctilious rhythms of Jewish life. Secure in their moral horizons, they were in no position to allow the painfully assembled fabric of their social person—their wives, their children, their kinfolk, and the few ancestral fields that they would inherit when they buried their father—to evaporate at the call of the wandering few. Christian communities where such men came to the fore would look at the world around them in a very different manner from those who imagined that, on the open road, they already breathed the heady air of the kingdom.

(II) "A NEW CREATION"

The most startlingly idiosyncratic of all the followers of Jesus known to us came from a world that barely touched at any point on the experiences of those who preached in the cramped and explosive countryside of Palestine. Paul of Tarsus was a Greek-speaking Jew of the Diaspora. He was even, apparently, a Roman citizen. His missionary journeys took him to cities deep in the hinterland of western Asia Minor. In the early 50s, he lingered, for periods of years at a time, in the

---

55. Luke 20:34–36.

great pagan cities of the Aegean—Ephesus, Thessalonica, Philippi, and Corinth. He was executed at Rome, in the faraway capital of the Empire, around 60 A.D.[56] His mission had been to bring pagans into the kingdom:

to win obedience from the gentiles, by word and deed, by the power of signs and wonders, by the power of the Holy Spirit, so that from Jerusalem and as far round as Illyricum [the Balkan frontier of the Greek and Latin-speaking worlds] I have fully preached the Gospel of Christ. *They shall see who have never been told of him; And they shall understand who have never heard of him.*[57]

In a letter to the Galatians, written around 54 A.D., Paul made abundantly clear how little he owed to the "churches of Christ in Judaea."[58] Jesus had appeared to him long after he had appeared to the other disciples.[59] Paul had received a mandate of his own: he was

an apostle—not from men nor through man, but through Jesus Christ and God the Father, who raised him from the dead. . . . the gospel which is preached by me . . . came through a revelation of Jesus Christ . . . who had set me apart before I was born . . . in order that I might preach him among the gentiles.[60]

On the strength of this direct, personal revelation and the consequent gift of the Holy Spirit, Paul declared the kingdom available to total pagans, that is to "the gentiles," to persons who had received no circumcision and had taken on no obligations to observe distinctions of clean and unclean foods, as would those who had entered Israel in the normal manner. Many such pagans may have been recruited from among those already attracted to the impressive Jewish synagogues of their cities. Judaism and its demands may not have been entirely unknown to them. Paul, however, took no notice of that fact. To him, they were, quite simply, "gentiles." As a result of his preaching, they had

56. In what follows, I have limited myself strictly to the letters that can be unquestionably ascribed to Paul: see G. Bornkamm, *Paul*, pp. 241–247. Faced by the abundant literature available on the career and teaching of Paul, I have cited only those works that have helped me to reach the conclusions given in the text. For the sake of clarity, I cite the Revised Standard Version, rather than the Authorized (King James') Version, for the passages of Paul that follow.

57. Romans 15:18–19, 21, citing Isaiah 52:15.   58. Galatians 1:22.
59. I Corinthians 15:8.   60. Galatians 1:1, 11–12, 15–16.

turned to God from idols to serve a living and true God, and to await for his Son from heaven, whom he raised from the dead, Jesus, who delivers us from the wrath to come.[61]

The possession of the Holy Spirit, palpably expressed in ecstatic cries of "Abba, Father," assured them that they were now children of God. Along with the Jews, they were the heirs of God's promises to Abraham and the recipients of his inexhaustible love.[62] They were "the Israel of God."[63]

"For neither circumcision counts for anything nor does the intact foreskin [of the gentile], but a new creation."[64]

Paul claimed that by converting the pagans he had saved Israel. For only when the gentiles turned to God would the terrible hardness that Paul, like many other radical Jews, tended to see lingering in the heart of Israel, be taken away. With the gentiles gathered in, Israel would lose its *heart of stone* and the kingdom would come:[65]

For the Lord himself will descend from heaven with a cry of command, with the archangel's call, and with the sound of the trumpet of God. And the dead in Christ will rise first. . . . Then we who are alive, who are left, shall be caught up together with them in the clouds to meet the Lord in the air. . . . Comfort one another with these words.[66]

In Paul, we meet a man whose whole body ached for the great change that might soon come upon it. He lived his life poised between revelation and resurrection. Describing his first, decisive vision of the risen Jesus, he wrote:

I know a man in Christ who fourteen years ago was caught up into the third heaven—whether in the body or out of the body I do not know. . . . I know this man was caught up into Paradise.[67]

In an equally near future, so Paul hoped, Christ would come again. The bodies of those who had been gathered into his kingdom would then share in the glory of his risen body. The dead would rise from the numbness of the grave, and the living also would be clothed with the power of God. Huge forces of opposition to the will of God, which lurked throughout the universe—only glimpsed in Paul's letters, as if at the corner of his intently focussed field of vision—would surrender.

---

61. I Thessalonians 1:9–10. 62. Galatians 3:29, 4:6.
63. Galatians 5:16. 64. Galatians 5:15.
65. See most recently Paula Fredriksen, "Paul and Augustine." pp. 28–31.
66. I Thessalonians 4:16–18. 67. II Corinthians 12:2–3.

Jesus "will change our lowly body to be like his glorious body, by the power which enables him even to subject all things unto himself."[68]

In Paul's letters, we are presented with the human body as in a photograph taken against the sun: it is a jet-black shape whose edges are suffused with light. Perishable, weak, "sown in dishonor,"[69] "always carrying the death of Jesus" in its vulnerability to physical risk and to bitter frustration,[70] Paul's body was very much an "earthen vessel." Yet it already glowed with a measure of the same spirit that had raised the inert body of Jesus from the grave: "so that the life of Jesus may be manifested in our mortal flesh."[71]

The approach of that bright light threw dramatic shadows. No Jewish writer had ever shown such an agonized sense as did Paul, in the famous seventh chapter of his Letter to the Romans, of the sheer force of pent-up resistance to the will of God that lingered in the heart. He presented the human heart as hardened to a degree and to a depth unheard of in contemporary Judaism.[72] The giving of the Law had had no other effect but to make the dark forces of rebellion stir yet more vigorously at every level of the self.[73] As for the glad obedience to the Law shown by many pious Jews: the spontaneous obedience of the upright mind served only to highlight the extent to which deep-set enmity to God lay diffused throughout the human person as a whole, blocking the wishes of the pious with a weight of spiritual impotence as terrible as the heaviness with which the mortal body weighed down the soul:

For I know that nothing good dwells in me, that is, in my flesh. . . . I see in my members another Law at war with the Law in my mind. . . . Wretched man that I am! Who will deliver me from this body of death?[74]

Paul's use of so brutally dualistic an image is the sharpest expression that he ever gave, in any of his letters, to his sense of a terrible darkness that had gathered in the heart before the blaze of Christ's resurrection.

The notion of an antithesis between *the spirit* and *the flesh* was a pe-

---

68. Philippians 3:21.   69. I Corinthians 15:43.
70. II Corinthians 4:10.   71. II Corinthians 4:11.
72. Urbach, *The Sages*, pp. 422–430 is a clear statement of the manner in which Paul differed from later rabbinic opinion; see now E. P. Sanders, *Paul, the Law and the Jewish People*, pp. 72–81.
73. Romans 7:7–10.   74. Romans 7:18, 23–24; see Sanders, *Paul*, pp. 76–81.

culiarly fateful "theological abbreviation."[75] Paul crammed into the notion of the flesh a superabundance of overlapping notions. The charged opacity of his language faced all later ages like a Rohrschach test: it is possible to measure, in the repeated exegesis of a mere hundred words of Paul's letters, the future course of Christian thought on the human person. At the time, Paul had slid together associations that a less urgent thinker might have kept apart. The war of the spirit against the flesh and of the flesh against the spirit was a desperate image of human resistance to the will of God. He did not view the human body as in itself the sole cause of so terrible an evil. Yet we must remember that Paul was an educated Jew with a culture similar to that of Philo and Josephus. Whatever its cause, the painful conflict of body and soul was a fact of life: many of the sins most distasteful to him—notably lust and drunkenness—obviously arose from surrender to the promptings of the body.[76] Such sins did not exhaust his notion of the flesh. Yet we should not overlook the half-conscious momentum of Paul's phrases. A weak thing in itself, the body was presented as lying in the shadow of a mighty force, the power of *the flesh:* the body's physical frailty, its liability to death and the undeniable penchant of its instincts toward sin served Paul as a synecdoche for the state of humankind pitted against the spirit of God.[77] Those somber resonances lingered disquietingly upon it. "The flesh" was not simply the body, an inferior other to the self, whose undisciplined stirrings might even at times receive a certain indulgent tolerance, as representing the natural claims of a physical being. In all later Christian writing, the notion of "the flesh" suffused the body with disturbing associations: somehow, as "flesh," the body's weaknesses and temptations echoed a state of helplessness, even of rebellion against God, that was larger than the body itself.

The hierarchy of body and soul, which linked man both to the gods above and to the animal world below in the benign and differentiated order of an eternal universe, concerned Paul not in the slightest. The universe itself was about to be transformed by the power of God. Paul spoke of the "sting" of death,[78] of the stubborn war of the flesh, of the dark counter-Law "of sin which dwells in my members."[79] These

---

75. H. D. Betz, *Galatians,* p. 8.   76. E.g., Galatians 5:19, 21.
77. W. G. Kümmel, *Römer 7 und das Bild des Menschen im Neuen Testament,* pp. 24–25.
78. I Corinthians 15:26, 55.   79. Romans 7:23.

were towering forces for him; but by giving them a palpable face, he could present them as so many "enemies," who had been definitively conquered by Jesus when he rose from the grave. Their defeat would soon be made manifest, when Jesus gave back to God the kingdom of a universe from which every force of evil had been banished.[80] Thus, the human person, divided between *the spirit* and *the flesh*, was not primarily a being torn between body and soul. Rather, with Paul, we see human beings caught in a hurried instant, as they passed dramatically from a life lived *in the flesh*, tensed against the Law because subject to the tyranny of half-seen powers reared in rebellion to God, to a life of glorious freedom lived *in Christ, in the spirit:* "The Spirit of Him who raised Jesus from the dead dwells in you, he will . . . give life to your mortal bodies also."[81]

The problem that faced Paul was how exactly the pagans, whom he had gathered into the "Israel of God" in this abrupt and high-hearted manner, should live their lives in the indefinite period before "the coming of our Lord Jesus with all his saints." These were people who had been made separate from their neighbors by dramatic ecstatic experiences and by the speaking of unintelligible tongues.[82] In their assemblies, they experienced a foretaste of the new age that the coming of Jesus would soon bring to them. At the high moment of prophecy, the screens that separated the seen from the unseen world and that kept each heart hidden from the other were swept aside: "if all prophesy and an unbeliever or an outsider enters . . . the secrets of the heart are disclosed, and so, falling on his face, he will worship God and declare that God is really among you."[83]

Nor was the newly formed group a closed association of free males, as the Essenes had been. Jews and former pagans, men and women, slaves and free, came together in its assemblies. If the group was to be a "new creation" in any real sense, the problems posed by traditional social barriers, and not only the burning issue of the religious boundary between Jews and non-Jews, had to be faced.[84] The rite of entry into the church, baptism, was apparently already connected with rituals that acted out an explicit stripping off of the distinguishing marks on which the hierarchy of ancient society depended. Divested of these

---

80. I Corinthians 15:24–26.   81. Romans 8:11.
82. I Corinthians 14:2, 22; see esp. Gerd Theissen, *Psychologische Aspekte paulinischer Theologie*, pp. 294–296.
83. I Corinthians 14:24–25; cf. I Corinthians 4:5.   84. Sanders, *Paul*, pp. 172–177.

features, the believers were considered to have recaptured a primal, undifferentiated unity:

For as many of you who were baptised into Christ have put on Christ. There is neither Jew nor Greek, there is neither slave nor free, there is neither male nor female; for you are all one in Christ Jesus.[85]

Had Paul moved around the villages of Palestine and Syria, such views might not have stirred up such acute anxieties. In that less differentiated environment, a few broke from the village in order to live a life "in the spirit" that was quite as boundless as any that Paul envisioned. The remainder were unambiguously committed to a married life, lived in accordance with ancestral Jewish norms. Paul, by contrast, had let into the "Israel of God" pagans with little or no knowledge of Judaism. Furthermore, the householders he addressed were far from poor. Some owned slaves.[86] Some women were heads of households in their own right and effective protectresses of the new churches. Men and women in cities such as Ephesus and Corinth had traveled as widely as had Paul. They were as cultivated and quite as argumentative. Their households could harbor any number of rival teachers, each as eccentric as was Paul himself.[87] For them freedom did not mean simply the stark call of the open road for a spirit-filled few. Leisured and sufficiently wealthy, they were in a position to change the tenor of their lives from top to bottom. Neither the permafrost of rural poverty nor the discreet disciplines of long Jewish practice held them back from daring experiments in social living.

Paul wanted none of this. In his letters to the churches, we meet a man hurriedly placing sandbags along the bank of a potentially devastating torrent whose impetus, he knew only too well, owed much to his own previous message and example. Paul had gathered pagans into Israel, and had reassured them that they had become children of God, by encouraging extraordinary, spirit-filled behavior. His notion of the resurrection was as high-pitched as that of any Palestinian militant. The new life of the risen Jesus stood for a challenging discontinuity between the old and the new. It was no longer a resurrection

85. Galatians 3:27–28; see esp. Wayne A. Meeks, "The Image of the Androgyne," and Betz, *Galatians*, pp. 190–200.

86. Philemon 1–2; see esp. G. Feeley-Harnick, "The Case of the Runaway Slave."

87. See esp. Wayne A. Meeks, *The First Urban Christians: The Social World of the Apostle Paul*, pp. 51–73, 75–77.

envisioned simply as the miraculous reintegration of a strife-ridden social order: "the old has passed away, behold the new has come."[88]

But once pagans entered the "Israel of God," Paul had every intention of subjecting them to what he evidently considered to be the ordinary decencies of Jewish life: "Do not be deceived, neither the immoral, nor idolaters, nor adulterers, nor homosexuals, passive or active . . . will inherit the kingdom of God."[89]

Paul was a Jew, burning to make pagans into children of the true God. He looked out with undisguised disgust at the tedious prospect of the sins of the gentile world. In that dark landscape, sexual sins cluttered the foreground. By committing the supreme anomaly of worshipping created things rather than their Creator, pagans had brought upon themselves every kind of sexual anomaly. All boundaries had collapsed before their ignorant pride and lust:

God gave them up in the lusts of their hearts to impurity, to the dishonoring of their bodies among themselves. . . .
Their women exchanged natural relations for unnatural, and the men gave up natural relations with women and were consumed with passion one for another.[90]

In the communities that Paul had founded, the body—and most especially the body of the young male—was to enjoy none of the carefree moments of indeterminacy allowed to it by pagans. The body was not a neutral thing, placed between nature and the city. Paul set it firmly in place as a "temple of the Holy Spirit."[91] It was a clearly visible locus of order, subject to limits that it was sacrilegious to overstep. It belonged to the Lord. It was, indeed, a physical object as totally infused by his spirit as the limb of a body: "Do you not know that your bodies are members of Christ?"[92]

To sleep with a prostitute was natural enough for a young man in Corinth. Jews admitted that a bachelor who remained chaste in a great city must be an outstandingly pious man.[93] For Paul, to sleep with a prostitute involved nothing less than becoming "one flesh" with her, as surely as Adam had become one flesh with Eve. It was a startling

---

88. II Corinthians 5:17.
89. I Corinthians 6:9–10; see David F. Wright, "Homosexuals or Prostitutes?"
90. Romans 1:24–27.   91. I Corinthians 6:19.   92. I Corinthians 6:15.
93. *Babylonian Talmud: Pesaḥim* 113a, I. Epstein, trans., p. 52.

use of an image of physical joining usually applied only to husband and wife.[94]

Altogether, when Paul wrote on the exact manner in which he wished his communities to show themselves to be a holy people, separated from the pagan world, codes of sexual behavior, taken directly from the practice of the Jewish married household, were made to bear the main weight of his notion of "sanctification": "For God has not called us for uncleanness, but in holiness."[95] For those about to join Christ "in the air," it was a bleakly down-to-earth message.

In the spring of 54 A.D., Paul wrote from Ephesus to answer a series of letters from his supporters in Corinth. This letter came to be known as Paul's famous First Letter to the Corinthians. In it, we can glimpse a church where issues of sexual control and sexual renunciation condensed anxieties about the entire structure of the communities that Paul had wished to found.

The "church of the saints" in Corinth was a sociological beargarden. Differences between rich and poor, masters and slaves, men and women had exploded in the form of strife between the various households that made up the community. The ritual unity of the Lord's supper had been fissured by competitive displays of family eating. The wealthy had maintained contacts with their pagan friends to the extent of attending civic banquets in which sacrificial meat was served.[96] The women refused to wear veils at the solemn sessions in which prophets and prophetesses spoke to the faithful, drawing from Paul a disquisition on hair and on the natural hierarchy that made men superior to women, so contorted and so heavy with unspoken anxieties, that modern scholars remain at a loss as to how to unravel it.[97] Either Paul himself (or a follower so close to him as to be able to place the passage in the text of Paul's letter at a very early stage in its circulation), attempted to solve the dilemma by brusquely ordering married women to remain silent in church: "For they are not permitted to speak, but should be subordinate, as even the Law says. . . . For God is not a God of confusion but of peace."[98]

94. I Corinthians 6:16.   95. I Thessalonians 4:7.

96. I Corinthians 8:4–13; 10:14–33; 11:17–34; see esp. Gerd Theissen, *The Social Setting of Pauline Christianity: Essays on Corinth*, pp. 121–174.

97. I Corinthians 11:4–16; see Theissen, *Psychologische Aspekte*, pp. 163–180.

98. I Corinthians 14:34–35 and 33; see Meeks, *First Urban Christians*, p. 71 and note 108 on p. 220.

Afflicted by so much disorder, a group of devout householders appear to have sought a trenchant solution. Their entry into the church had been extraordinary. They saw no reason why the newly founded community should be content to replicate, within itself, the tension-laden compromises of the ordinary world. They would undo the elementary building blocks of conventional society. They would renounce marriage. Some would separate from pagan spouses;[99] others would commit themselves to perpetual abstinence from sexual relations. The growing children for whose marriages they were responsible would remain virgins.[100] As consequential as the Essenes, they would also free their slaves. Somewhat like the little groups described by Philo outside Alexandria, men and women together would await the coming of Jesus "holy in body and spirit."[101] Only by dissolving the household was it possible to achieve the priceless transparency associated with a new creation. It is the great hope which, in all future centuries, would continue to flicker disquietingly along the edges of the Christian church.

In 54 A.D., Paul wanted no part in such a hope. The forty highly condensed verses that made up the seventh chapter of his First Letter to the Corinthians have been justly acclaimed as "the most important in the entire Bible for the question of marriage and related subjects."[102] Yet it is impossible to resist the impression that "the chapter is wholly intelligible as a rearguard action."[103] In his other letters, sexual renunciation played no part in Paul's message or in his presentation of his apostolic mission. No Saint Thecla would have heard words "on continence and the resurrection" floating up to her through the open window from a neighboring courtyard, when the real Paul (and not Paul as he was imagined only a century later) preached in Iconium. If anything, it is striking how little weight Paul placed on the fact that he was, apparently, unmarried or had left a wife. An active man of learning, his principal claim on his followers was that he had set aside the palpable social advantages associated with a public career. Resources of birth, of rhetorical skill, of wisdom that enabled a man to cut a figure in his community were, for Paul, mere "strength according to

---

99. I. Corinthians 7:12–16.   100. I Corinthians 7:36–37.   101. I Corinthians 7:34.
102. J. Héring, *The First Epistle of Saint Paul to the Corinthians,* p. 147.
103. H. E. Chadwick, "All Things to All Men," p. 264: I am particularly indebted to this article.

the flesh": they had been "crucified" in him as a result of the call of Jesus.[104] Only a Galilaean peasant would have given prominence to the relatively unimportant, because domestic, decision to leave "wife and children." When challenged by the Corinthians, Paul agreed with them that "It is good for a man not to touch a woman."[105] He even went as far as to state that "I wish all men were as I myself am." Yet he immediately qualified that remark by implying that not all had received from God his own, specific gift of continence.[106]

Paul was, indeed, determined that his own state of celibacy should not be adopted by the church of Corinth as a whole. To have done so would have been to sweep away the structures of the pious household. And to abolish the household would have undermined Paul's own authority in the distant city. It would have broken the subtle chain of command by which his own teachings were passed on to each local community through the authority of local householders.[107] A community of total celibates, and especially if it were a community in which women and slaves realized a little of the equality promised them, in ritual terms, at their baptism, would have been a community effectively sealed off against the outside world. But Paul had hoped to gather the gentiles into Israel in large numbers before Jesus returned from heaven. A community rendered starkly separate from its neighbors by group-celibacy would hardly have attracted many pagans into its midst. In coming down firmly on the side of allowing marriage to continue within the Church, Paul acted as he usually did whenever his converts were tempted to erect excessively rigid barriers between themselves and the outside world. As in his tolerant attitude to the eating of "polluted" pagan foods, so in his attitude to marriage, Paul sided with the well-to-do householders who had most to lose from total separation from the pagan world.[108] For it was they who would support his ambitious mission to the gentiles most effectively.

Paul, therefore, needed to deter his correspondents from so radical a remedy for their ills. Hence the distinctly lopsided quality of the one chapter that was to determine all Christian thought on marriage and celibacy for well over a millennium. It had not been Paul's concern to praise marriage; he strove, rather, to point out that marriage was safer

---

104. I Corinthians 1:20–21 and II Corinthians 11:22 with Galatians 2:20.
105. I Corinthians 7:1.   106. I Corinthians 7:7.
107. Feeley-Harnick, "The Case of the Runaway Slave," pp. 120–126.
108. Theissen, Social Setting, pp. 125–132.

than unconsidered celibacy. Much of the letter, therefore, consisted of blocking moves. Married couples should not renounce intercourse for fear that worse might happen—"because of the temptation of immorality" that abstinence might provoke.[109] After protracted bouts of abstinence, like those with which contemporary Jewish prophets prepared themselves to receive their visions, husbands and wives must resume intercourse, "lest Satan tempt you through lack of self-control."[110] It was no sin for the hot young to marry: "for it is better to marry than to be aflame with passion."[111] These remarks were supposed to carry the leaden weight of the obvious. Parallels to every one of them recur in the plentiful folklore invoked by the rabbis in favor of early marriage.[112] What was notably lacking, in Paul's letter, was the warm faith shown by contemporary pagans and Jews that the sexual urge, although disorderly, was capable of socialization and of ordered, even warm, expression within marriage. The dangers of *porneia*, of potential immorality brought about by sexual frustration, were allowed to hold the center of the stage. By this essentially negative, even alarmist, strategy, Paul left a fatal legacy to future ages. An argument against abandoning sexual intercourse within marriage and in favor of allowing the younger generation to continue to have children slid imperceptibly into an attitude that viewed marriage itself as no more than a defense against desire. In the future, a sense of the presence of "Satan," in the form of a constant and ill-defined risk of lust, lay like a heavy shadow in the corner of every Christian church.

At the time, however, fornication and its avoidance did not preoccupy Paul greatly. He was concerned to emphasize, rather, the continuing validity of all social bonds. The structure of the household as a whole was at stake. This included the institution of domestic slavery. On this, Paul was adamant: slaves, like wives, must remain in their place:

let everyone lead the life which the Lord has assigned to him, and in which God has called him. This is my rule in all the churches. . . . Were you a slave when called? Never mind.[113]

109. I Corinthians 7:2.
110. I Corinthians 7:5; see also Fraade, "Ascetical Aspects of Ancient Judaism," p. 263.
111. I Corinthians 7:9.
112. Strack and Billerbeck, *Kommentar zum Neuen Testament aus Talmud und Midrasch,* 3:368–373 provides the standard collection.
113. I Corinthians 7:17, 21.

Most important of all for the future fortune of his views, Paul tended to solve the issue of the precise position of celibacy in the Christian church by sweeping it into the high trajectory of his own apostolic calling. He accepted the views of his correspondents with gusto: "It is good for a man not to touch a woman." But this was because Paul had received from God the prophetic gift of continence. Not all could expect this gift, for not all had been called as Paul had been called. We simply do not know how many others were considered by him to be engaged in roles in which continence was one element. There were probably more of them in Corinth than in the average Christian community in Palestine. Certainly, in Corinth, Paul accepted the possibility of groups that included mature continent women. He even envisioned some young, virgin children, committed to a future of perpetual chastity. These continent persons shared a gift on which he was prepared to speak with transparent enthusiasm:

The appointed time has grown very short. . . . For the form of this world is passing away. . . . The unmarried man is anxious [only] about the affairs of the Lord . . . And the unmarried woman or virgin girl is anxious about the affairs of the Lord, how to be holy in body and spirit.[114]

They lived better prepared than were the married for the great travail that would precede the coming of Jesus.[115] By contrast, marriage was not a "gift." Rather, the fact of being married betrayed an absence of God's call to continence. The married lacked the supreme quality of the undivided heart: "the married person is anxious about worldly affairs, how to please his wife, and he is divided."[116]

Kai memeristai: for Paul, a man to whom the highest ideal of life was to be "united to the Lord," to "become one spirit with him,"[117] this was a crushing disqualification. The married person, whose heart was inevitably divided, was almost of necessity a "half-Christian."[118] Ascetic readers of Paul in late antiquity did not mis-hear the tone of his voice. The apostolic gift of celibacy was too precious a thing to extend to the Church as a whole. Paul made that clear. But he had not been greatly concerned to defend marriage. He left the world of the married householder a long way behind, bobbing in the stormy wake of his own urgent call to live a life of "undistracted" service before the com-

---

114. I Corinthians 7:29–30, 32, 34.   115. I Corinthians 7:26.
116. I Corinthians 7:33–34.
117. I Corinthians 6:17; see esp. E. P. Sanders, *Paul and Palestinian Judaism,* p. 553.
118. Niederwimmer, *Askese und Mysterium,* p. 114.

ing of the Lord. Marriage, like household slavery, was a "calling" devoid of glamor. It did not attract close attention as the present age slipped silently toward its end. The "shortening of the time" itself would soon sweep it away.

(III) "A LAW OVER AGAINST A LAW"

By approximately 60 A.D., Paul was dead. There were many, even among his most loyal followers, who came to think that his spirit-filled journeys had scattered the Mediterranean, in a manner cheerful and improvident, with unworkable communities. Many letters ascribed to Saint Paul were, in reality, assembled by his followers in the two generations after his death. In them, we can sense the strength of the undertow that had gathered beneath the mighty wave of his gentile mission. It is striking how many of these wished to present Paul, an apostle notably fired by the ideal of an "undistracted" life in Christ, as a man concerned to validate the structures of the married household. The Letter to the Ephesians handsomely corrected the chill tone of Paul's answer to the Corinthians. It presented the relations of husband and wife as a reflection of the primal solidarity brought back by Christ to the universe and to the church:

Husbands, love your wives, as Christ loved the church and gave himself for her, that he might sanctify her . . . that she might be holy and without blemish. . . .
   Even so husbands should love their wives as their own bodies. . . . For no man ever hates his own flesh, but nourishes and cherishes it, as Christ does the church, because we are members of his body.[119]

Taken in conjunction with Christ's unusual rejection of divorce, this daring extension of the myth of Adam and Eve provided Christians with an image of unbreakable order that the pagan world could understand. In the church, as in the city, the concord of a married couple was made to bear the heavy weight of expressing the ideal harmony of a whole society.

   Other pseudo-Pauline writings made clear that this order, though gentle, was to be quite as hierarchical as that praised in his *Advice on*

119. Ephesians 5:25, 28–30; see esp. Niederwimmer, *Askese und Mysterium*, pp. 125–134 with Meeks, *First Urban Christians*, p. 90.

Marriage by Plutarch, the exact contemporary, we should remember, of Paul's later followers.

Let a woman learn in silence with all submissiveness. I permit no woman to teach or to have authority over men. . . . For Adam was formed first, then Eve. . . . Yet a women will be saved through bearing children.[120]

By the time the books that we now read as the New Testament began to circulate, in roughly the same years as Justin wrote his *Apology*, readers would have met in many of the letters ascribed to Paul a thoroughly "domesticated Apostle."[121]

The contrasts that modern scholars have revealed between the authentic letters of Paul and the pseudo-Pauline writings hint at a muffled dialogue between a militant, "apostolic" view of the church and an increasingly secure local leadership. The *episkopoi*, the bishops, and the *presbyteroi*, the priests or elders, came from the local Christian communities. Many were recruited from among the married householders, and most were more sensitive to the needs of the married and the respectable than were the spirit-filled wanderers of the previous generation.[122] "Continence" and "chastity," *enkrateia* and *hagneia*, appear in the letters of Christian leaders in the generation after Paul; but they appear to be referred to only with a distinct coolness. When Ignatius, the Bishop of Antioch, passed through Asia Minor on his way to execution in Rome, between 110 and 117 A.D., his letters were magnificent statements of the ideal unity of each local Christian church: "Give thought to unity, than which nothing is more sweet."[123]

Saint Ignatius had no intention of allowing this unity to be disrupted by virtuoso practitioners of continence. Members of a congregation might live in chastity, "in honor of the flesh of the Lord," but those who boasted of doing so would surely perish.[124] When Ignatius gave practical advice to the churches, the world he wished for was one based on an ordered sexuality. It was a church made up of generous householders, well-disciplined children, submissive wives, and reliable slaves. These last were even forbidden to ask their fellow-believers to make charitable contributions toward the sum they required to buy their

---

120. I Timothy 2:11–13, 15.
121. J. M. Gager, *The Origins of Anti-Semitism*, p. 191; W. Munro, *Authority in Paul and Peter*, pp. 134–140 is a clear statement of this view.
122. Kretschmar, "Ursprung christlicher Askese," pp. 37–38.
123. Ignatius, *Letter to Polycarp* 1.2.
124. Ignatius, *Letter to Polycarp* 1.2 and *I Clement* 38.2.

freedom. Marriages were to be arranged by the bishop himself, "so that the marriage might be according to the Lord and not according to lust."[125] The mystical end of an undivided church was to be acheived by singularly prosaic family arrangements.

Paul's apostolic mission had left the Christian communities with one, decisive *lacuna*. He had imposed strict moral codes on all pagan converts; but he had bitterly resisted any attempt to encourage pagans to adopt the clear badges of a separate identity provided to those who converted to Judaism. They were to bear no physical mark on their bodies—no circumcision. They were to engage in no careful discrimination of clean and unclean foods—that would have involved a clear choice of dining companions and even separate marketing facilities (no *kashrut*). They were to observe no clear distinctions between profane and holy days—no Sabbaths and new moons. Many other Christians felt that they could not afford to be so off-hand with the venerable Law of Moses.[126] In the cities of the Diaspora, Judaism continued to appeal to pagans precisely because it was an ancient religion as punctilious as their own. Jews observed the solemn rhythms of high festival. They held to codes of purity. They gave men and women an opportunity to approach, in a disciplined and thoughtful manner, the "things that lie between nature and culture, half-wild, half-civilised."[127]

In the ancient world, ceremonious persons had always regarded intercourse, childbirth, and death as proper subjects for taboo. Far from being repugnant to pagans, much of Jewish observance on such matters (circumcision apart) earned the respect due to the upholders of a solemn and long-established religion.[128] It was pagan converts, and not the local Jews, who put pressure on Paul to adopt Jewish customs. They wished to become like Jews, rather than creatures condemned to ritual invisibility.[129] Paul's notion of a "new creation," of a community formed abruptly without the palpable, physical attributes of a distinctive religious observance, struck many as a bleak and homeless prospect. Time had passed. Jesus had not come to snatch their bodies away from the world in which they lived. By the end of the first cen-

---

125. Ignatius, *Letter to Polycarp* 5.2.

126. Meeks, *First Urban Christians*, p. 81.

127. Greg Dening, *Islands and Beaches*, p. 150.

128. Josephus, *Against Apion* 2.198; see W. Dittenberger, *Sylloge Inscriptionum Graecarum*, no. 983, 3:112 for similar taboos observed in a pagan temple.

129. Gager, *Origins of Anti-Semitism*, pp. 132 and 206.

tury, Christians found that they were forced to create for themselves the equivalent of the Jewish Law, if they were to survive as a recognizable group, separate from pagans and Jews. As Justin claimed, Jesus had brought them "a Law over against a Law, [that] has made the one before it to cease."[130]

This was the situation that Justin found at the time of his conversion, in the first decades of the second century. As his *Apology* made plain, strict codes of sexual discipline were made to bear much of the weight of providing the Christian Church with a distinctive code of behavior. Sexual prohibitions had always distinguished Jews, in their own eyes at least, from the sinister indeterminacy of the gentiles. These were now asserted with exceptional vigor. Christian marital codes were rendered yet more idiosyncratic by a few novel features, such as the relinquishment of divorce and a growing prejudice against the remarriage of widows and widowers. Above the solid conglomerate of ancient, Jewish notions there now rose the peak of total chastity. Whatever exotic associations the gesture of continence might have had for the Christians themselves, outsiders could admire it as a form of physical heroism equivalent to the observed capacity of Christians to face down the chill fear of death. Celibacy already appealed to "the faith that a person who is an exception on this point will be an exception on all others as well."[131]

By concentrating in a single-minded manner on sexual restraint and on sexual heroism, the Christians of the age of Justin had found their way to presenting themselves as the bearers of a truly universal religion: in stressing the vulnerability of all human beings to sexual desire they had been able "to discover or invent a common human condition which underlay . . . complexity . . . [thereby] deriving simplicity out of confusion."[132]

The sense of a common human condition, defined by sexual desire, was very necessary in the churches of the second century. The Christian communities were heterogeneous groups. Men and women, and persons of widely different social and religious backgrounds, faced each other awkwardly in the tiny assembly rooms of the churches. A sexual nature was the one thing that they had in common. It is not altogether

130. Justin, *Dialogue with Trypho* 11.2.
131. F. Nietzsche, *Die fröhliche Wissenschaft* 358, p. 267.
132. Carrithers, *Forest Monks of Sri Lanka*, p. 11, on the Buddhist notion of a universal human condition of "suffering."

surprising that, at just this time, we hear shocked rumors that esoteric Christian groups had turned to free love. Their enemies claimed that these explored, through promiscuity, the nature of "true communion." The rumor was apposite enough. It is not altogether unthinkable that some believers, baffled by so much diversity, should have used the common bedrock of their shared sexuality to explore the potent ideal of an utterly undivided and truly universal religious community.[133] The less enterprising majority simply opted for codes of sexual discipline that they knew everyone could share, independent of their sex and of their levels of culture and social status.

Continence, in particular, carried with it associations of an elemental simplicity. Sexual renunciation was a *carrière ouverte aux talents*. As Christians, women and the uneducated could achieve reputations for sexual abstinence as stunning as those achieved by any cultivated male. Total chastity was a gesture that cut through the silken web of decorum that swathed the public man: here was "philosophical" restraint at its most drastic, now made open to all. In the years that Justin taught in Rome, the first version of the legend of Saint Thecla had begun to circulate in Asia Minor. The legend showed that a sheltered girl, quite as much as any active male, could rally to the appeal of an imagined Apostle: "Blessed are they who have kept the flesh pure, for they shall become a temple of God. . . . Blessed are the continent, for to them will God speak."[134]

By 150 A.D., we stand at the beginning of an irreparable parting of the ways. The nature of the leadership acceptable in Judaism and that current in the Christian churches had begun to diverge precisely on the issue of marriage and continence. With the destruction of the Temple and the strengthening of the synagogue and the house of study, Judaism was fast on its way to becoming a religion of the book and of the sanctified, married household.[135] Passed on by learned males to devoted adolescent boys, in houses of learning not so very different

133. Examined in detail in the cases of Epiphanes, Carpocrates and the Nicolaitans by Clement of Alexandria, *Stromateis* 3.2.5–11 and 4.25–28, in Henry Chadwick, trans. *Alexandrian Christianity*, pp. 42–45, 51–53, with an excellent introduction at pp. 24–29. One cannot rule out the existence of such groups within second-century Christianity: they were not merely figments of a polemist's imagination.

134. *Acts of Paul and Thecla* 4, trans. in E. Hennecke and W. Schneemelcher, *New Testament Apocrypha*, 2:354.

135. See esp. A. D. Momigliano, "Ciò che Flavio Giuseppe non vide," pp. 567–568 with Schürer, *History of the Jewish People*, 2:415–463, and now Alan F. Segal, *Rebecca's Children: Judaism and Christianity in the Roman World*, pp. 163–181.

from the neighboring schools of pagan philosophers, the Law still spoke
to the world with an ancient solemnity:

For we are all one celebrated people,
Who have received one Law from the One:
And the Law which is amongst us will aid us,
And the surpassing wisdom which is in our midst will help us.[136]

In Judaism, the Law rested equally on every aspect of the human
person. It required reverent attention to those things which all human
beings were held to share—food, time, and marriage. These kept God's
world in being, while providing the abiding materials from which the
pious Jew made those distinctions and faced out those renunciations
that marked off Israel as "holy" in the midst of a blind and formless
world. For that reason alone, no single aspect of normal life could be
renounced. Each must be given form according to the declared will of
God.[137] A later legend speaks of how the Sages of Palestine once cap-
tured the sexual drive. Fully aware of its disorderly nature, they were
at first inclined to execute it. But they relented. They maimed it, so
that it could never force an Israelite, against his will, to commit incest
or sins against nature. But the impulse itself must be allowed to continue in Israel: "for if you kill it, the world itself goes down."[138] The
near-contemporary legend of Paul and Thecla could not have received
a more definitive rebuttal.

When they first trickled into Galilee, after 132 A.D., as refugees from
the last and most terrible Roman devastation of Judaea, the early rabbis were figures quite as uprooted, as eccentric, and as peripheral to
the settled population as the wandering preachers of the kingdom of
Jesus of Nazareth had once been.[139] But even at that time they had
opted doggedly for the continuity of Israel. They had no intention of
bringing the end of the world into the present by breaking with marriage, the normal means with which a community ensured its survival.
Throughout the second century, they were exceptional persons, embattled and good haters of the ignorant.[140] But they did not give up

---

136. *Il Baruch* 48.24, Charles, *Apocrypha* p. 506; see the excellent translation and commentary of P. Bogaert, *L'Apocalypse de Baruch*, p. 391.
137. J. Neusner, *Judaism: The Evidence of the Mishnah*, p. 272 is the clearest statement
of this crucial notion, among that author's many important works on the period.
138. *Babylonian Talmud: Yoma* 69b, I. Epstein, trans. p. 328.
139. Goodman, *State and Society in Roman Galilee*, pp. 93–94.
140. See esp. A. Oppenheimer, *The ʿAm Ha-Aretz*, pp. 172–183.

the one institution that they shared with all other Jews. They firmly maintained that the life of the married householder, the father of children, was the only life appropriate to a spiritual guide in Israel:

He who does not engage in procreation of the race is as though he sheds human blood.[141] When Adam saw that his offspring were fated [through his fall] to be consigned to Gehenna, he refrained from procreation. But when he saw that . . . Israel would accept the Law, he applied himself to producing descendants.[142]

The rabbis were well aware of the radical asceticism that had characterized many movements in Judaism in their immediate past. They were prepared to sympathize with the view that a catastrophe as terrible as the destruction of the Temple might drive some pious Jews to embrace a life of perpetual abstinence and mourning. Yet they avoided that dire option. They stressed, instead, the solidarity of Israel. "Leave Israel in peace." It was better that all the people should abstain for some of the time than that only a few of the people should fast and withold from their wives for all of the time.[143]

Self-disciplined, capable of enduring considerable privation in the pursuit of learning, and legendary in their abruptness with women, the rabbis of Palestine came to wield influence in Judaism largely because they stood for a world that had no intention of vanishing. They maintained themselves as a learned class by marrying the daughters of their teachers and their colleagues.[144] Their blessing rested warmly on married persons:

Concerning the man who loves his wife as himself, who honors her more than himself, who guides his sons and daughters in the right path, and arranges for them to be married around the period of puberty, of him it is written: *Thou shalt know that thy tent is at peace.*[145]

The self-appointed leaders of Judaism, and their less scholarly patrons, the local Jewish notables and the patrons of synagogues throughout the Diaspora, came to take for granted that they lived in a world that would not vanish. Much of this world was disorderly; but all aspects

---

141. *Babylonian Talmud: Yebamoth* 63b, W. Slotki, trans., p. 426.
142. *Midrash Rabba: Genesis* 21.9, H. Freedman, trans., p. 179.
143. *Babylonian Talmud: Baba Bathra* 60b, M. Simon, trans., 1:245–246; see Bogaert, *L'Apocalypse de Baruch,* pp. 136–138.
144. *Babylonian Talmud: Pesaḥim* 49ab, I. Epstein, trans., p. 236; see Oppenheimer, *ᶜAm Ha-Aretz,* pp. 171–173 and Goodman, *State and Society,* p. 78.
145. *Babylonian Talmud: Yebamoth* 62B, W. Slotki, trans., p. 419.

of it could be controlled, and so none must be rejected: "Human [sexual] desire, a child and a woman—the left hand should repulse them but the right hand bring them back."[146]

For good or ill, this was not a decision that the leaders of the new religion were prepared to take. A small number of prominent Christian men and women used their bodies to mock continuity, through the drastic gesture of perpetual chastity. They believed that time was running short. Their lives radiated a message different from that of the emergent leaders of Judaism. They did not speak of the faith of a society that it could harness and discipline the unbroken flow of a human sexual nature that caused life to continue from generation to generation. Far from it: for them the continent body stood for a principle of reversibility; the flow of life itself could be halted. The renunciation of marriage laid bare the fragility of a seemingly changeless order. The means by which society was continued could be abandoned. Chastity announced the imminent approach of a "new creation."

Nothing, however, is more striking to an observer of the Christian churches of the second century than is the variety of meanings that had already come to cluster around the mute fact of sexual renunciation. By this time, Christian communities lay scattered all over the Roman world, as far apart as Lyons in the West and the frontier town of Dura Europos, overlooking the Euphrates, in the East.[147] These communities were separated by at least eighty days of travel. Variants of Christianity that now lie so neatly, side by side, in books on the shelves of a modern library were often unknown to each other at the time. Each betrayed the silent presence of a distinctive religious and social landscape. It is to the wide variety of meanings attached to continence in early Christian circles that we must now turn, in order to measure the novelty of the ideas that had come to gather behind the somewhat bland praise of Christian chastity, with which Justin, the eccentric intellectual, had thought it prudent to approach a philosophical Emperor.

---

146. *Babylonian Talmud: Sanhedrin* 107b, I. Epstein, trans., p. 736.
147. See now Robin Lane Fox, *Pagans and Christians*, pp. 267–335.

THREE

Martydom, Prophecy and Continence: Hermas to Tertullian

Prophecy was a fact of life in the Early Church. In the age of Paul, the presence of the Spirit of God among pagan converts had declared that the return of Christ was imminent.[1] By the time that Justin wrote, a century later, the existence of prophets in the Christian churches was taken to prove conclusively that God had deserted Israel. His mighty Spirit now dwelt in the "New Israel" of the Church:

And it shall come to pass afterward,
that I will pour out my spirit on all flesh;
your sons and your daughters shall prophesy,
your old men shall dream dreams,
and your young men shall see visions.[2]

The day-to-day culture of a Christian community—its prayers, its psalms, its songs, its reconciliation of personal differences, and its vi-

---

1. Among many studies, I am particularly indebted to Marie E. Isaacs, *The Concept of Spirit. A Study of Pneuma in Hellenistic Judaism and Its Bearing on the New Testament*, pp. 82–112.

2. *Joel* 2:28 cited in Justin, *Dialogue with Trypho* 87.6, see also 82.1 and 88.1 and Isaacs, *Concept of Spirit*, pp. 144–145.

sion of itself in a troubled future—flowered under the breath of the Spirit of God:

Let each person be diligent to go to the church, the place where the Spirit blossoms . . . and you shall hear there what had not come into your own mind, and you shall make progress in those things which the Spirit shall give you, by means of the prophet who offers instruction to the people.[3]

The active presence among them of the Spirit of a high God was a crushing weight for any group composed of human flesh and blood to bear, and especially a group like the Christians, who considered themselves to be the heirs of Judaism's sense of the exclusive majesty and transcendance of the God of Israel. Christians of the second century lived in a world populated by invisible, lying spirits. They had a clear sense—in their enemies, at least—of the power of trickery and self-delusion.[4] To carry authority, prophecy had to be seen as a wrenching, almost necessarily a spasmodic experience—one that escaped the conscious control of the prophet. Those who, like Paul himself, prayed in strange "angelic" tongues, prayed "in the Spirit," while their conscious mind "lay fallow."[5] In tense situations, the truthful prophet spoke most effectively when he uttered a great unpremeditated shout.[6] God's Spirit was not an occasional visitor to the Church. It was always available to believers as a sign of His exclusive presence in their midst. But in each community, some Christians distinguished themselves as outstandingly reliable vehicles of God's messages. Their lives were expected to bear the mark of exceptional closeness to the Spirit of God. Sexual abstinence was one such mark. It played an important role in establishing the authority of prophets in many second-century churches. As the apologist Athenagoras wrote:

you would find many among us, both men and women, growing old unmarried, in the hope of living in closer communion with God. [For] remaining in virginity and in the state of a eunuch brings one nearer to God.[7]

3. Hippolytus, *The Apostolic Tradition* 35.3, p. 62.
4. J. Reiling, *Hermas and Christian Prophecy: A Study in the Eleventh Mandate*, remains the best single collection of material on the criteria of true prophecy in Christian communities.
5. I Corinthians 14:14; Isaacs, *Concept of Spirit*, pp. 49–50, 75.
6. Ignatius, *Letter to the Philadelphians* 7.
7. Athenagoras, *A Plea for the Christians* 33, in B. P. Pratten, trans., *The Ante-Nicene Fathers*, 2:146.

Such a remark would have been instantly intelligible to contemporary Jews and pagans. Both believed that abstinence from sexual activity, and especially virginity, made the human body a more appropriate vehicle to receive divine inspiration. Possession was an intimate and dramatically physical experience. It involved a flooding of the body with an alien, divine Spirit. Hardly surprisingly, such an experience was thought to exclude the warm rush of vital spirits through the same body, traditionally associated with intercourse.[8] Philo of Alexandria had presented Moses in that light: after his encounter with God on Sinai, he had come to disdain sex,

for many a day, and almost from the time when, possessed by the Spirit, he entered on his work as a prophet, since he held it fitting to hold himself always in readiness to receive oracular messages.[9]

Later Jewish legends ratified this view. After forty days spent in the presence of God, Moses had lost interest in "the deed"; his wife felt neglected, and when she learned that the Spirit of God had fallen also on others, all that she could say was, "Woe to the wives of these men!"[10] While this much is certain, we know very little about what continence meant in the lives of the prophets themselves and of the congregations to which they ministered. Some second-century Christians considered themselves called to be prophets "from their mother's womb," and so maintained a perpetual unmarried state. The strong emphasis on the virgin birth of Christ in the Gospel of Luke points to a mentality where virginity and the gift of prophecy were closely linked.[11] A man could be spoken of with esteem as "a eunuch."[12] Virgin girls appear as prophets.[13] Yet, striking though such virgin figures may have been, they were exceptional. It was more usual for prophets to enter into their calling as elderly persons. They were known to the Christian community. They had begotten children whom they had raised as Christians. They maintained households and personal wealth, from

8. Irenaeus, *Against the Heresies* 1.13.2, on the false (and blatantly sexual) heat induced by magic in false prophetesses.
9. Philo, *Life of Moses* 2. 68–69, in F. H. Colson, ed., *Philo*, 6:483.
10. *Sifre on Numbers* 12.1 (99), cited by Geza Vermes, *Jesus the Jew*, p. 101.
11. Luke 1:34–35; see Isaacs, *Concept of Spirit*, pp. 119–121.
12. Eusebius, *Ecclesiastical History* (hereafter *Eccles. Hist.*) 5.24.5; for a later example, see W. M. Calder, "The Epigraphy of the Anatolian Heresies," in W. H. Buckler and W. M. Calder, eds., *Anatolian Studies presented to Sir William Mitchell Ramsay*, p. 90.
13. Acts 21:8; cf. Eusebius, *Eccles. Hist.* 3.31.3.

which they supported the Church. Unlike the wilder "followers" of Jesus, or even Saint Paul, they had not become spirit-filled wanderers. Nor were they recluses, greatly tempted to retire to the desert.

The men and women whom we will meet in this chapter remained securely rooted in the cities of the Mediterranean. Many retained the social and sexual prejudices of elderly, once-married persons. Although they had come to abandon sexual activity and considered themselves relatively immune from sexual desire, they still expected the young to marry and (as the case of Tertullian made abundantly plain, at the end of the century) they reacted stridently to the sexual dangers associated with the presence of women in the assemblies of the saints. They did not believe that the coming of the Spirit would abruptly deliver their body from sexual activity and from sexual desire, as other Christians did. Writing in the latter part of the second century, men like Irenaeus, at Lyon, and Tertullian, at Carthage, tended, rather, to think of the body as undergoing a slow but sure preparation to take upon itself the awesome weight of the Spirit of God. Irenaeus, for instance, firmly believed that the state that he occasionally witnessed in a Christian prophet was that to which all Christians would come at the resurrection. The Spirit of God would come to rest securely on the frail clay of the body, as it might have done had Adam not fallen away from God.[14]

Prophecy came only to a chosen few, in this age, because the human person had been deprived of the Spirit by Adam's fall and was now exposed to the enmity of death. Irenaeus' contemporary, Melito of Sardis, was spoken of with great respect as "a [continent] eunuch, who lived altogether in the Holy Spirit."[15] For him, as for Irenaeus, death was the sign of a tragic disruption of the original, Spirit-filled unity of the human person:

there was separation of what once fitted beautifully,
and the beautiful body was split apart,
for man was divided by death.[16]

How the frail, mortal body might become a reliable container for the Spirit of God was the center of the concerns of Christians such as Mel-

14. See esp. W. D. Hauschild, *Gottes Geist und der Mensch*, pp. 206–220.
15. Eusebius, *Eccles. Hist.* 5.24.5.
16. Melito, *On Pascha* 55.390–392, in S. G. Hall, ed., *Melito of Sardis: On Pascha and Fragments*, p. 31.

ito and Irenaeus. The gradual waning of married sexual activity was a recognized part of this process. But the abandonment of intercourse followed the normal rhythms of life: it was usually associated with widowhood and with the onset of old age. Not every believer, however, could wait to become a widow or a widower. The call to a violent death was as much a reality for Christians of the second century as was the coming of the Spirit. It was a matter of vital importance for the believer that a body capable of bearing the Spirit of God within the Christian assemblies, in times of peace, should be enabled, also, through Christ and His Spirit, to endure the devastating negative possession associated with the torments of a martyr's fate. Only Christ and His Spirit dwelling deep within them could enable men and women to resist the invasion of their souls and bodies by the overwhelming pain of torture and by the chill fear of death.

Thus, continence, though a marked feature of Christian prophecy, remained a secondary feature; it was a preoccupation that tended to rise to the fore in Christian literature at times when the prospect of violent death was less immediate. Only slowly, in certain circles, did prophecy and sexual renunciation come to be linked in an unambiguous manner, as if the one depended on the other. We can best appreciate the complexity of the situation by considering the one Christian prophet whose visionary life is known to us—Hermas, the author of a collection of visions that he had experienced in Rome around 120 A.D. Circulated widely under the name of *The Shepherd*, the visions of Hermas enable us to look at a prophet who, if continent himself, never moved far from the life and from the values of the married householder.[17]

Few figures in the Early Church are as delightful or as open-hearted as Hermas (or, to be more cautious, as the *persona* which Hermas chose to adopt when addressing the Roman community). He carried conviction because he so transparently described the tensions of his own heart. He was a prophet of "singleness of heart" in a sophisticated urban community. He knew the cares that could divide the heart. He had few illusions that such cares were there to stay in Rome. The community enjoyed the financial support and protection of rich believers. *Dipsychia*, anxious "doubleness of soul," was the besetting sin of rich patrons, torn between trust in God and the need to preserve their fam-

17. R. Joly, Introduction, *Hermas: Le Pasteur*, pp. 11–21, 55–57; see now Robin Lane Fox, *Pagans and Christians*, pp. 381–390.

ily fortunes and to maintain contacts with pagan friends.[18] Hermas was no exception. He fussed constantly about his family, and he was convinced that the good favor of God would be shown in the worldly success of his household.[19]

Before he became a Christian prophet, Hermas had been an upwardly mobile freedman. His master had sold him to the Christian lady, Rhode. "Patient, not given to indignation, always with a smile," Hermas, "the continent," knew what it meant to struggle to control the unruly heart.[20] The fact that his Christian owner, when bathing in the Tiber, had once asked Hermas (a mere slave, at that time, whose sexual feelings counted for little) to help her, stark naked, out of the river, had not been calculated to increase our prophet's peace of mind. "I would be a blessed man," he had thought, "if I had a woman of such beauty and stylishness to be my wife."[21] The incident, of which he was later reminded in a vision by Rhode herself, was a reminder of sexual temptations that threatened to flaw his prophetic gift, and to bring upon him the anger of God. Lust and private longings were out of place in a man whose heart was to become transparent to the Spirit.[22]

Yet, this was the flaw of a married man, living among married households. Hermas was careful to advise those who, like himself, had been tempted to lust for another woman to try to think, on such occasions, of the charms of their own wives.[23] He and his wife intended to live in continence as a result of the renewed call to vision that had led to the composition of *The Shepherd*; but the time when his wife would be a "sister" to him still lay in the future.[24] His deepest moral striving had not been to overcome sexual temptation. It had been to achieve, and exhort others to achieve, a precious state of childlike simplicity—of *népiotés*.[25] This was the keystone of a whole complex of moral notions that were plainly of great importance within the confederation of Christian households that made up the Roman church. Hermas lingered lovingly upon it. The child before puberty was "blameless." He enjoyed without disruption the precious gift of "sin-

18. Hermas, *Shepherd*, Vision 3.14(6).3; Mandate 10.40(1).4 and Similitude 8.75(9).1, Joly, pp. 114, 186 and 282.
19. Vis. 1.3 and 2.7(3).1–2, Joly, pp. 84 and 94.
20. Vis. 1(1).1, 1.2.3 and Mand. 3.28.3, Joly, pp. 76, 82 and 150.
21. Vis. 1(1).1, Joly, p. 76.   22. Vis. 1(1).3–7, Joly, p. 78.
23. Mand. 4.29(1).1, Joly, p. 152.   24. Vis. 2.2(6).3, Joly, p. 90.
25. Mand. 2.27.1, Simil. 9.101(24).3 and 106(29).1–3, Joly, pp. 146, 340 and 348.

gleness of heart," of "absence of malice."[26] Sexual urges and sexual imaginings had not yet come to divide his "face" from his "heart." The world of adult cunning, of adult self-interest, and of adult hypocrisy—of which the rise of sexual feeling at puberty was a first, premonitory symptom—had not yet closed in upon him. He could trust wholeheartedly, and had not learned to frame evil in his heart. Hermas wanted the Christian church to be made up of "childlike" plain dealers.[27] "A man of shining countenance," transparent to his neighbors and trusting in God, was what Hermas dearly wished himself and others to be.[28] Only into a group composed of such persons would the word of God drop from Heaven, heavy with authority because unflawed by personal self-interest.[29]

Hermas did not expect many of his readers to be unmarried persons, continent "eunuchs," or virgins. When he wrote of virginity, he had in mind the abiding loyalty of the Church to her Lord, and not the chastity of individual believers. Virginity, indeed, was too serious a matter for mere humans. For Hermas, a man of Jewish background, virginity was associated less with a state of physical intactness prior to marriage than it was with a dangerous hiatus in the life of a marriageable girl—one that started with the onset of the girl's puberty and continued until the "opening of the womb" by the birth of the first child.[30] It was an image that conjured up the notion of risk, not of integrity. Thus, Paul presented the Church at Corinth as like the virgin Eve, trembling on the edge of yet another potential seduction by the cunning serpent, in the form of Paul's enemies.[31] Later, Hegesippus wrote with a sigh: "They used to call the church a virgin, for she had not yet been seduced."[32] Not all virgins fell in those perilous, flighty years of a young woman's life. The good virgin remained loyal to her betrothed and husband. He was her only Lord. It was with these overtones that the term "virgins" was used by the prophet of the Book of Revelation: the term was applied there not to individuals, but to whole

26. On Hermas himself: *Shepherd*, Vis. 1.2.4 and Mand. 2.27.1, Joly, pp. 82 and 146.
27. Simil. 9.101(24).3, Joly, p. 340.   28. Mand. 10.42(3).1, Joly, p. 190.
29. Mand. 11.43.20, Joly, p. 198.
30. See G. J. Wenham, "Betûlāh: 'A Girl of Marriageable Age' "; Elena Cassin, "Le Proche-Orient ancien: Virginité et stratégie de sexe," pp. 253–255; and C. Locher, *Die Ehre einer Frau in Israel*, pp. 176–192.
31. II Corinthians 11:2–3; see esp. R. A. Batey, *New Testament Nuptial Imagery*, pp. 13, 68; A Orbe, "El pecado de Eva, signo de división," pp. 303–305.
32. Cited in Eusebius, *Eccles. Hist.* 4.22.4.

bodies of believers who had not been seduced away from their loyalty to Christ.[33]

For Hermas, the only virgin at Rome worthy of consideration was the Church itself. Under her were gathered the "virginal" powers of the soul.[34] The sweet influence of these virgin spirits on his heart enabled Hermas to communicate to his community the humble, workaday virtues appropriate to married persons—childlike lack of affectation, trust, and candor. They rustled in his capacious mind, light-footed girls, dancing on the green meadows of a Christian Arcadia.[35] They kissed and embraced our prophet. He danced with them, "as cheerfully as a little boy."[36] As evening faded, they took off their linen robes, and spread them on the ground to lie down to sleep in his company, while Hermas, "the continent," dutifully prayed through the night at their side.[37]

Hermas was a prophet formed *À l'Ombre de Jeunes Filles en Fleur*. The touch of the virgin spirits helped him to live in continence with his wife; but it did not make him a preacher of virginity. What he offered, rather, on the strength of his visions, was a last chance for Roman Christians to gain forgiveness for their sins. These were the sins of a sophisticated community that needed not continence but the more sociable and elementary virtue of singleness of heart. We meet in Hermas' pages successful businessmen investing in landed property,[38] competitive and status-conscious priests,[39] self-appointed teachers,[40] and professional rivals to Hermas himself in the high art of prophecy.[41] It is a vivid glimpse of what a Christian community could become in any major Roman city. The urban Christians addressed by Hermas are already similar to those to whom Tertullian would react with studied disapproval, in Carthage, and for whose complex needs Clement of Alexandria would write with gentle circumstantiality, at the very end of the century.

A generation after Hermas, in western Asia Minor and, later still, at Lyon, the shadow of death fell on the spokesmen of the churches. As a boy, Irenaeus had remembered the elderly Bishop of Smyrna,

33. Revelation 14:3–5; see G. B. Caird, *A Commentary on the Revelation of Saint John the Divine*, pp. 178–179.
34. Hermas, *Shepherd*, Simil. 9.78(1).2 and 91(14).2, Joly, pp. 288 and 322.
35. Simil. 9.78(1).4, Joly, pp. 288–290.   36. Simil. 9.88(11).4, Joly, p. 314.
37. Simil. 9.88(11).3–8, Joly, p. 314.   38. Simil. 1.50.1, Joly, p. 210.
39. Simil. 8.73(7).4 and 87(10)6–7, Joly, pp. 278 and 312.
40. Simil. 9.99.2, Joly, p. 338.   41. Mand. 11.43.1–9, Joly, pp. 192–198.

Polycarp.[42] When Polycarp was executed, in around 156–157, at the age of eighty-six, those who recorded his martyrdom stressed the indestructible beauty of his "holy flesh."[43] In the terrible scene in which Polycarp was lynched by burning, the author of the *Martyrdom* described only the sweet perfume that rose from his charred body as he stood up in the fire, "not as burning flesh, but rather like bread being baked, or like gold and silver being purified in a smelting furnace."[44]

A generation later, Irenaeus wrote of the future glory of all Christians, placed in a world re-created by God for their physical enjoyment, as a just reward for having endured so much torment on earth. The uncanny beauty that had superimposed itself over Polycarp's horrendous death was a glimpse of that future. The new body, no longer divided from the Spirit, would live in a fully material world that was as heavy with goodness as the intoxicating breath of a field in full flower.[45]

It may have been Irenaeus who described the deaths of the martyrs of Lyon in 177–178 A.D.[46] The slave girl Blandina had been tortured with a group of her fellows. She had hung from a post with arms outstretched, so that "in their agony [her companions] saw with their outward eyes in the person of their sister, the One who was crucified for them."[46] Blandina died, at last, after renewed torments, insensitive to goring by a wild bull, "rapt in communion with Christ."[47]

For Irenaeus, such a person stood for nothing less than human nature at its highest. Blandina the martyr was the culmination of those long ages, since the first creation of Adam and his fall, in which the human race had been "accustomed, little by little, to receive and to bear the mighty weight of God."[48] Only a very trivial man, indeed, would have asked, at such a time, whether Blandina had prepared herself for the presence of the Spirit by practicing sexual abstinence. Irenaeus was not such a man.

Vibia Perpetua was a young married woman from a good provincial family. The gift of the Spirit enabled her to emerge as the spokesman and moral leader of the martyrs in prison in Carthage in 203 A.D. Her

42. Eusebius, *Eccles. Hist.* 5.20.4.
43. *Martyrdom of Polycarp* 13, in H. Musurillo, ed., *The Acts of the Christian Martyrs*, p. 13.
44. Ibid. 15, Musurillo, p. 15.   45. Irenaeus, *Against the Heresies* 5.32.1 and 33.1.
46. Eusebius, *Eccles. Hist.* 5.1.41.   47. Ibid. 5.1.56.
48. Irenaeus, *Against the Heresies* 8.1, in A. Roberts and W. H. Rambaut, trans., *Ante-Nicene Library: The Writings of Irenaeus*, 2:72.

visions and her account of her feelings at that time have a gripping freshness and personal authority. A well-educated and courageous woman, Perpetua was enabled by the Spirit to step into a new, high calling, confident that a "superabundance of grace" had been granted to her church, with which to face the grim conditions of "modern times."[49]

Perpetua was not a woman vowed to continence. She was already the head of a household in a small North African town. She may have been the mistress and the protector of the group of Christians who had been arrested with her. A twenty-two-year-old mother, a fully adult *matrona* by Roman standards,[50] she was happy to suckle her child in prison, before it was taken away from her:

At once I recovered my health, relieved as I was of my worry and anxiety over the child. My prison had suddenly become a palace, so that I would be there rather than anywhere else.[51]

Her entry into the prison-house at Carthage was an entry into the world of the Holy Spirit:

During those few days I was baptized, and I was inspired by the Spirit not to ask for any other favour after the water but simply to endure the torment of the flesh.[52]

These were terrifying weeks:

I had never before been in such a dark hole. . . . With the crowd the heat was stifling; then there was the extortion by the soldiers; and . . . I was tortured by worry for my baby.[53]

But Perpetua was now a woman on whom the huge favor of God had come to rest.[54] In a series of great visions of the other world, Perpetua led her followers, with open eyes, into their terrible death.

In her first great dream, it was the dragon's head of sheer physical terror that she trod underfoot, making her way to the sweet garden of Paradise up a ladder of tearing swords.[55] She later dreamed that she was "made a male" in order to wrestle with a towering Egyptian. Such

49. *Martyrdom of Saints Perpetua and Felicitas* 1.3, Musurillo, *Acts*, 106.

50. *Martyrdom of Saints Perpetua and Felicitas* 2.3, Musurillo, p. 108. See Peter Dronke, *Women Writers of the Middle Ages*, pp. 1–16.

51. *Martyrdom of Perpetua* 3.9, p. 110.

52. 3.5, p. 108.   53. 3.5–6, p. 108.   54. 4.1, p. 110.

55. 4.6–7, p. 110. Dronke, *Women Writers*, p. 8; see also Jacqueline Amat, *Songes et visions. L'au-delà dans la littérature latine tardive*, pp. 68–76.

a dream came as a deep comfort to her.[56] The poor wretches condemned to the beasts could not hope even for a human antagonist. The surreal horror of the *damnatio ad bestias*, condemnation to the wild beasts, was that the human was allowed to succumb totally to the animal.

A man dreamt that he underwent a transformation and that he had bear's paws for hands. Sentenced to death, he was given to the wild beasts. He was bound to a wooden post and devoured by a bear. [Hence the dream of the hand:] For whenever a bear hibernates in its den, it puts its paw in its mouth and sucks [it for nourishment].[57]

The priest Saturus, Perpetua's companion, had remained terrified up to the last moment at the prospect of such a death; but

when he was bound in the stocks awaiting the bear, the animal refused to come out of the cage.[58]

To sense behind the faceless nightmare that lay ahead of her, the firm shape of a struggle with the Devil, man to man, in the form of a human athlete familiar to the crowds of Carthage,[59] was a triumph of Perpetua's will: "I knew that I would win the victory."[60]

A *matrona* to the last, "with shining face and quiet poise," "beating back the gaze of the crowd with the power of her eyes,"[61] Perpetua even turned to ask for a pin with which to keep up her hair, which had tumbled at the first shock of the wild cow that was sent against her. She would not be seen with her hair flowing loose, as if she were a woman "dissolved" by mourning.[62] For this was the day of her own high good cheer, the day of her triumph in the Lord. Hers was a *munus*,[63] a public display. Her spirit-filled courage enabled her to outdo the mood of solemn celebration, in which the citizens of Carthage had gathered, on the birthday of the heir apparent, to humiliate and annihilate their enemies, with a playful exuberance that was a peculiarly chilling aspect of the Roman order.[64]

56. *Martyrdom of Perpetua* 10.7, p. 118.
57. Artemidorus, *Oneirocritica* 5.49, in R. White, trans., Noyes Classical Studies, pp. 235–236.
58. *Martyrdom of Perpetua* 19.4, p. 127.
59. Louis Robert, "Une vision de Perpétue."
60. *Martyrdom of Perpetua* 10.14, p. 118.   61. 18.2, p. 126.
62. 20.5, p. 128.   63. 12.7, 16.1; pp. 120, 124.
64. See esp. Georges Ville, "Religion et politique: comment ont pris fin les combats de gladiateurs," esp. pp. 664–665; and Keith Hopkins, "Murderous Games," esp. pp. 27–30.

It is possible, but not certain, that Perpetua had taken part in the revival of faith in the abiding presence of the Spirit in the Church that had begun with the emergence of the "New Prophecy" of Montanus.[65] Montanism arose in faraway Phrygia, in the 150s and 160s. It involved dramatic manifestations of Christian prophecy. It became one of the first grass-roots movements in the history of the Church.[66] Roman Carthage, however, was a long way from the upland valleys of western Anatolia. At the same time as Perpetua suffered martyrdom in the city, the prophetic authority claimed by the Montanists was espoused, for reasons very much his own, by the gifted and magnificently articulate Tertullian. A man of robust idiosyncrasy, Tertullian was also one of the most skilled *rhetors* of his age.[67] He knew exactly how to create an audience for his own, admittedly extremist, views by appealing to the unquestioned prejudices and the shared anxieties of literate Christians. Thus, far from representing the morose outpourings of a lonely genius, Tertullian's writings enable us to glimpse the conglomerate of conflicting notions on sexuality, and on the meanings that might be attached to its renunciation, that circulated in a major Latin church at the beginning of the third century.[68]

If the "New Prophecy" had not existed, one suspects that Tertullian would have had to invent it. By 205 he was convinced that the *disciplina* of God, the precise and unbending code of behavior expected of serious Christians, needed to be brought up to date by direct, new mandates, conveyed to the faithful by visions and ecstatic prophecies. Renewed commands from Heaven would check the growing self-satisfaction, the immorality, and the cowardice of the majority of Tertullian's fellow-Christians. Only Christians perpetually open to the breath of the Spirit, as Montanus and his followers had been, would know how to live their lives in such a way that the fate meted out to Perpetua could become, for them also, a moment of high triumph.[69]

The problem, however, was that martyrdom was slow to come. Tertullian's model Christians were austere, private philosophers, culti-

65. T. D. Barnes, *Tertullian*, pp. 77–80.

66. See now Lane Fox, *Pagans and Christians*, pp. 404–410, with A. Strobel, *Das Heilige Land der Montanisten*.

67. Barnes, *Tertullian*, pp. 210–232.

68. C. Rambaux, *Tertullien face aux morales des trois premiers siècles* is a sobering survey of Tertullian's moral attitudes.

69. Barnes, *Tertullian*, pp. 130–142.

vated and comparatively well-placed in Carthaginian society. For just that reason, the Roman authorities tended to pass them by.[70] While the martyr's cell might be the true "desert," to which the Christian must aspire, in order to speak face to face with God,[71] Tertullian and his readers were spared the fate of Perpetua. Tertullian had to look elsewhere for a criterion of true prophecy that could apply to those who had not yet come to live under the majestic shadow of a martyr's death. His answer was magnificently, insistently simple. Continence, the suspension of all future sexual activity, brought down the gift of the Spirit: "By continence you will buy up a great stock of sanctity, by making savings on the flesh, you will be able to invest in the Spirit."[72]

"Look to the body." This was Tertullian's brilliantly, deceptively simple formula. The body was a "unified organism."[73] Tertullian was a Stoic, and like so many of his contemporaries a voracious reader of medical literature. He was not a "dualist" in any way. Indeed, his insistence on the control of the body was so rigorous precisely because he believed that it was directly through the body and its sensations that the soul was tuned to the high pitch required for it to vibrate to the Spirit of God. The soul was a subtle, invisible, but concrete "body," "set in the mould" of the outer body.[74] Hence the gripping immediacy with which the soul experienced the other world. At the moment of vision, this other world impinged upon it with full, palpable force. As a prophetess assured him, on one occasion: she herself had just seen a soul; "it was not something empty and spaceless, but, indeed, it was something you could almost reach out and touch."[75] Waking from her first vision in the prison in Carthage, Perpetua had felt herself still "chewing on some sweet substance" that Christ Himself had given her to eat when she had risen, in her vision, to Paradise.[76] For those who faced a cruel death, Tertullian's view of the soul accounted for the gripping immediacy of their visions, as the inner person pressed up

70. G. Schöllgen, *Ecclesia sordida? Zur Frage der sozialen Schichtung frühchristlicher Gemeinden am Beispiel Karthagos zur Zeit Tertullians*, pp. 155–224.

71. Tertullian, *ad martyras* 2.8, *Corpus Christianorum* 1, p. 4.

72. Tertullian, *de exhortatione castitatis* 10.1–2, in A. Kroymann, ed., *Corpus Christianorum*, 2:1029.

73. Tertullian, *de ieiunio* 1.1, *Corpus Christianorum* 2:1262.

74. Tertullian, *de anima* 9.4, *Corpus Christianorum* 2:793; see esp. Amat, *Songes et Visions*, pp. 93–104. H. A. Armstrong, "Gnosis and Greek Philosophy," p. 94 is revealing on the implications of Stoicism.

75. *De anima* 9.4, pp. 792–793.   76. *Martyrdom of Perpetua*, 4, Musurillo, *Acts*, 112.

against the firm, real comfort of God's presence. It was a doctrine for the times, bizarre though it might appear in later ages.[77]

Yet the doctrine had its shadow-side. The instinctual life of the body, the random, distressing fantasies of the heart, made themselves felt in the soul with unbuffered, gripping intensity. The heart was a seismograph that jarred instantly at the minutest sexual stirring, at the most fleeting sexual image. Mounting sexual desire registered the tiniest portion of food consumed beyond the prescribed norm. Tertullian spoke for the New Prophecy, advocating long fasts and continence with unrelenting, medical precision. Fasting was necessary, otherwise

the whole dwelling-place of the inner person becomes blocked up with food . . . a thought-flow panting to burn off its load of excrement becomes no more than an obsession with the lavatory. Nothing else remains but to pass on from this to thoughts of lust.[78]

It was the voice of an inimitable master of Latin rhetoric, whom Jerome would read, two centuries later, with delight and, one fears, with all too great profit. With Tertullian, we have the first consequential statement, written for educated Christians and destined to enjoy a long future in the Latin world, of the belief that abstinence from sex was the most effective technique with which to achieve clarity of soul:

Let us look at our own inner world. Think of how a man feels in himself when he abstains from a woman. He thinks spiritual thoughts. If he prays to the Lord, he is next door to heaven; if he turns to the Scriptures, he is all of him present to them; if he sings a psalm, it fills his whole being with enjoyment; if he exorcises a demon, he does so confident in his own strength.[79]

Tertullian's recipe for clear vision was austere; but it was, at the same time, deeply conservative. He isolated the body with medical precision. He subjected it to a series of harsh abstinences that clarified the soul for vision. Yet he did not allow the practice of continence to weaken in any way the basic structures of the household: even when the master and mistress of the house lived in chastity, in order to receive clear guidance from the Spirit, their household would retain its wealth and slaves; women would obey their menfolk, and children their elders. The Christian community that Tertullian addressed in Carthage differed little from that of Rome, as revealed to us in the *Shepherd* of

---

77. Augustine, *de Genesi ad litteram* 10.26.45.
78. Tertullian, *de ieiunio* 5.1, *Corpus Christianorum* 2:1261.
79. *De exhortatione castitatis* 10.1, p. 1029.

Hermas. It was a confederation of believing households, in which married persons predominated.

Tertullian's view of the ideal leadership of the Church was a Spirit-filled gerontocracy. Those who sat on the benches reserved for the clergy and the leaders of the community were elderly widows and widowers. They had long experience of life.[80] This experience had included the begetting and the rearing of children, in the distant, hot years of youth, before the sexual urge had "fizzled out" with the approach of age.[81] The addressee of his *Exhortation to Chastity* was one such widower. He was to be no charismatic wanderer. He needed to be warned against temptations no more lurid than a hankering for remarriage. Without a hint of anxiety, Tertullian set about advising him to take in a Christian "sister," to live with him, as a companion, to keep house for him. Sexual urges that had to be sternly repressed in the young were unlikely, in Tertullian's opinion, to afflict an elderly gentleman of prophetic inclinations.[82]

Powerful though its breath might be, the Spirit respected the domestic structures without which Christianity would have found it impossible to survive in a city such as Carthage. It was the same in the little towns of upland Asia Minor. One prophetess in Cotyaion in Phrygia, Nanas, was described as a woman of long, powerful prayer. She was noted for "the visitations of angels, mighty in the gift of tongues." But Nanas remained known as a married woman, plainly respected by the neighborhood: it was her husband who crowded her simple gravestone with line after line of florid Greek. Though not necessarily a Montanist, Nanas, one suspects, would have been a prophetess after Tertullian's heart.[83]

Tertullian's writings sum up one current of Christian opinion on the human person and on the links between individual and society. For Christians of his persuasion, the normal restraints of society were not to be shaken by the wind of the Spirit. Tertullian still thought instinctively in terms of a fixed hierarchy of age groups, and of a church grouped around the Christian household. Sexuality was to be rigidly controlled among the marriageable and married young. But age would soon cool its heat. It was to be repressed at the end of life, so that the

80. *De virginibus velandis* 9.3, *Corpus Christianorum* 2:1219.

81. *De monogamia* 3.1, *Corpus Christianorum* 2:1230.   82. *Exhort. cast.* 12.2, p. 1032.

83. C. H. Emilie Haspels, *The Highlands of Phrygia: Sites and Monuments*, 1:338–339, no. 107, plate 630.

Spirit might flood unimpeded into the hearts of widows and widow-ers. As for sexual desire, this might diminish in the old; but it could never be abolished altogether. Sexual drives were an irremoveable and perilous component of the human person. Those who thought that the grace conferred on Christians by the coming of the Holy Spirit might enable them to transcend the dangers associated with sexual attraction were, in his opinion, profoundly mistaken.

Tertullian's angry tract, *On the Veiling of Virgins,* was written in the same years of his *Exhortation to Chastity.*[84] It made plain profound divergences in Christian attitudes to sexuality and to the possible meanings that might cluster around the act of sexual renunciation. A group of young girls in the Carthaginian church had decided to remain unmarried. Because of this decision, their fellow-believers encouraged them to stand in church with their heads unveiled and their faces uncovered. They may even have done so in a specially designated, prominent position.[85] By renouncing sexual activity, they were thought to have broken the "sound barrier" of sexual shame on which the traditional veiling of women was supposed to be based. Though fully adult women, they considered themselves free to abandon the veil that was held to externalize the sexual shame associated with women old enough to undergo the "common slur" of the marriage bed.[86] Far from being shocked by this gesture, many members of the Carthaginian church positively relished it. The uncanny, non-normal state of dedicated virgin girls, raised above shame and splendidly unveiled, stood for a fleck of divine glory in a dark world.

Tertullian's reaction to this situation reveals a view of the nature of the Christian Church that clearly foreshadowed the future development of Latin Christendom. In other Christian communities, particularly in Syria, high hopes gathered around the gesture of sexual renunciation: to have renounced sexual activity meant something more than to have brought sexual urges under control by rigorous self-discipline. Renunciation and baptism into the Church declared the power of sex null and void. Possession of the Holy Spirit conferred by baptism was thought to lift men and women above the vast "shame" of the human condition. To stand unveiled among the believers was to declare the fullness of the redemption brought by Christ. These were symbolic gestures, limited to the assembly of the believers, and per-

84. See Christoph Stücklin, *Tertullian: de virginibus velandis.*
85. *De virg. vel.* 9.2, p. 1219.   86. Ibid., 10.3, p. 1220.

mitted only to continent women. They may not have had any appreciable effect on the day-to-day behavior of the average Christian man and woman. Yet, in the church at least, an unveiled, continent woman was a stunning sight. Her open face and free hair summed up the hope of all believers: "I am not veiled because the veil of corruption is taken from me; . . . I am not ashamed, because the deed of shame has been removed far from me."[87]

Tertullian flatly denied that such hopes could be entertained by Christians. For him, the Church was a somber assembly. No person in it, and much less a woman, could dare to claim to be exceptional. "Grace," for Tertullian, fell from the hand of God alone. And it fell in order to flatten the frail show of human initiative.[88] To pass into the Church was to have weakened a little the grip of the demonic powers that ruled the pagan world outside its walls. But it was not to find oneself shot free, if even for one, highly stylized moment, of the huge gravitational pull of human nature. This meant, in practice, that no Christian could claim to be free from the social conventions that human frailty demanded.[89] A girl above sexual shame was, quite bluntly, a "sport of nature, a third sex."[90]

Tertullian was the first, but by no means the last, Latin writer to create, with a rhetor's mastery of the *ad hominem* argument, the cunning artefact of an unchanging and unchangeable human nature, forever subject to the facts of sex. He sunk sexuality deep into the human body. *Mulieritas*, the state of a woman aware of her own sexual feelings and capable of inspiring sexual feelings in others, was a state that began, ineluctably, with puberty.[91] It was not possible for a mature girl to "virginify herself" simply by leaving her head bare in church.[92] Social convention, therefore, was the same inside as it was outside the church. It was based on a commonsense reaction, shared by pagans and Christians alike, to the palpable menace of sexual desire among all human beings, and, most especially, to the known seductiveness of women. The misogyny to which Tertullian appealed so insistently was, in his opinion, based on unalterable facts of nature: women were seductive, and Christian baptism did nothing to change this fact. The

---

87. *Acts of Judas Thomas* 10, in A. F. J. Klijn, trans., *The Acts of [Judas] Thomas*, p. 69.
88. Tertullian, *de oratione* 22.9, Corpus Christianorum 1, p. 271 and *de virg. vel.* 13.3, p. 1223.
89. *De virg. vel.* 11.6, p. 1221.
90. 7.6, p. 1216.   91. 11.1, p. 1220.   92. 12.2, p. 1222.

precautions that had been taken to enforce modesty on women, in the pagan world, were merely maximized among the saints. The veiling of women addressed a shared human nature which no drastic baptismal rite could claim to slough off.[93]

The Spirit might grant the human body the supreme gift of endurance in the face of death. But the grace of God would not remove from men and women the permanent weaknesses associated with their sexual nature. It was a clear message, written in compelling Latin. It would not be lost on the churches that later produced Cyprian, Ambrose, Jerome and the great Augustine. We must go, now, to the other end of the Christian world, to the eastern provinces of the Roman Empire, to the area between Antioch and northern Mesopotamia, in order to trace the emergence, in the course of the second century, of Christian groups based upon attitudes to sexuality, to its renunciation, and to the human person that diverged significantly from those of Tertullian and of his future readers in the Latin West.

93. *De oratione* 22.10, p. 271.

FOUR

"To Undo the Works of Women": Marcion, Tatian, and the Encratites

The question which had preoccupied many Christian groups in the second century was embarrassingly simple:

What new thing did the Lord bring by coming down to earth?[1]

The answer was clear:

One mighty deed alone was sufficient for our God—to bring freedom to the human person.[2]

It was as to how this had happened, and, above all, as to how it could be seen to have happened, in their own community, in their own time, that many Christian teachers and their disciples came to startlingly radical conclusions.

It was believed that the coming of Christ to earth had brought "the present age" to an end. The duty of every Christian was to make His victory plain and to hasten the collapse of the power of the "Rulers

---

1. Irenaeus, *Against the Heresies* 4.34.1.   2. Tertullian, *Adversus Marcionem* 1.17.

of the present age." The "present age" was the product of an over-riding demonic tyranny, to which human beings and, indeed, the universe as a whole, had come to be subjected. Christ's victory over death had brought about a stunning reversal of the crushing flow of irreversible negative processes that made the tyranny of the demons seemingly irresistible on earth. The problem, then, was where precisely to locate the outward visible sign of the huge, inward mutation that had brought freedom to a humanity locked in the grip of gigantic forces of evil. Tertullian put the question to the radicals with his accustomed brutal clarity. How could ordinary human beings, men and women "subject still to doctors and to debt,"[3] dare to claim to have achieved, in the narrow compass of their cramped lives, the new freedom which, so they said, had become available to them with the coming of Christ? "How can you possibly think that you are freed from the Ruler of this Age, when even his flies still crawl all over you?"[4]

Yet there was one potentially reversible process shared by all human beings. Sexuality was based on a drive that was widely spoken of as irresistible—a current Greek euphemism for the penis was "The Necessity."[5] This drive, furthermore, was the known cause of the one irrefutably unidirectional process to which human beings freely contributed—procreation. Without human collaboration, that layer, at least, of the somber landslip of the "present age" would not continue. If sexual activity could cease among human beings, the tumultuous cascade of the human race from copulation, through birth to the grave, would come to a halt: "Jordan" would "roll backwards."[6] To give up sexual joining (even, some thought, to transcend the sexual urge) was known to be humanly possible. Given the manner in which freedom from the "present age" was posed—in terms of the halting of one-way processes—to halt sexual activity could be regarded as a symbolically stunning gesture.

It was the perfect answer to Tertullian's question. The "present age" might be a vast engine, too large to be seen. Its faceless energy was too dangerously impalpable to the average person, its tyranny too intricate to trace in all its ramifications. But at least one part of that mighty

3. Tertullian, *de pudicitia* 22.3.   4. Tertullian, *Adv. Marc.* 1.24.6.
5. Artemidorus, *Oneirocritica* 1.79: and for that reason, it stands for any kind of inescapable necessity, such as debt.
6. *The Testimony of Truth*, NHC IX,3, 30.19 ff., B. A. Pearson and S. Giversen, trans., in James M. Robinson, eds., *The Nag Hammadi Library in English*, p. 407; Hippolytus, *Refutatio* 5.2.

current could be symbolically condensed in the sexual urge and in its manifest consequences, the endlessly repeated cycle of birth and death. In a world seemingly governed by iron constraints, the human body could stand out as a clearly marked locus of free choice. To renounce sexual intercourse was to throw a switch located in the human person; and, by throwing that precise switch, it was believed possible to cut the current that sustained the sinister *perpetuum mobile* of life in "the present age."

From the second century onward, and almost certainly from an earlier, less well-documented period, little groups of men and women, scattered among the Christian communities throughout the eastern Mediterranean and in the Near East, as far as the foothills of Iran, strove to render almost audible, by their "singleness," their studied isolation from marriage, the vast hush of the imminent end of the age. It was for this reason, they claimed, that Christ had come to earth. He came to

deliver us from error and from this use of the generative organs.[7]

When Salome asked the Lord: "How long shall death hold sway?" He answered: "As long as you women bear children. . . ."

They say that the Savior himself said: "I came to undo the works of women," meaning by this "female," sexual desire, and by "work," birth and the corruption of death.[8]

Up to the second century, Christians, like other ancient persons, pagan and Jewish, had tended to regard the fact of death as the privileged landmark against which to measure the extent of human frailty. By contrast, the vulnerability of the human person to sexual urges, though blatant and a matter of concern to the upright, had remained a subject of relatively parochial interest. It seemed to offer no viewing point from which to scan what was truly universal in the human condition. Talk of its dangers referred always to particular groups and occasions. Sexual desire was thought to affect the "hot" young rather than the old. When men worried about it, they tended to see it in terms of the peril presented to them by the perpetual seductiveness

7. Clement, *Strom.* 3.12.92, citing Julius Cassianus, *Concerning Continence and Celibacy.* The third book of the *Stromateis*, which deals with sexuality and marriage, was left largely in a Latin translation by the prudent A. Cleveland Coxe, in *The Ante-Nicene Fathers*, vol. 2; it is now excellently translated with a preface by H. E. Chadwick in J. E. L. Oulton and H. E. Chadwick, *Alexandrian Christianity.*

8. Clement, *Strom.* 3.6.45 and 3.6.63.

of women. Death, by contrast, fell on all. It was a truly inescapable reminder to both sexes and to all ages of mankind's most universal, intimate, and enduring weakness.

Because it was closely associated with the urge to overcome death through the begetting of children, sexual intercourse had always carried with it a tinge of sadness. For many ancient Greeks and Romans, their very need to sleep with women so as to obtain offspring was, in itself, a somber reminder of transience and the grave.[9] But the new way of thinking that emerged in Christian circles in the course of the second century shifted the center of gravity of thought on the nature of human frailty from death to sexuality. For sexual desire was no longer presented as a benign remedy for death. Some Christian thinkers presented it as the first cause of death. Others, less drastic, saw it as the first, most blatant manifestation of Adam and Eve's loss of the immortality conferred on them by possession of God's Spirit. For all, sexuality edged itself into the center of attention, as a privileged symptom of humanity's fall into bondage. Consequently, the renunciation of sexual intercourse came to be linked on a deep symbolic level with the reestablishment of a lost human freedom, with a regaining of the Spirit of God, and, so, with man's ability to undo the power of death.

It is, however, important to stress the great diversity of the radical groups that had emerged in the course of the second century. Nor should we treat them as innovations that owed little to the original spirit of Christianity. Far from it: to subscribe to that view would be to entertain a singularly placid image of the life of the Early Church. Many Christians already took for granted habits of rigorous sexual abstinence and had long practiced rites of baptismal initiation that linked the beginning of the true life of Christians with the perpetual renunciation of sexual activity.[10] Behind even the most extreme statements of many of the leaders of the second and third centuries—highly articulate men, for the most part—we can usually sense the mute assent of whole churches, even of whole Christian regions.

The careers of Marcion and Tatian illustrate the tenacity of the links between figures whom we first meet as isolated teachers in Rome, and

---

9. Ton H. J. Van Eijk, "Marriage and Virginity, Death and Immortality," in C. Kannengiesser, ed., *Epektasis: Mélanges J. Daniélou.*

10. The point has been well made on the relations of Encratites and Gnostics by F. Beatrice, "Continenza e matrimonio nel Cristianesimo primitivo," in R. Cantalamessa, *Etica sessuale e matrimonio nel Cristianesimo delle origini*, pp. 43–47.

their spiritual "constituency" in faraway regions of the Empire. Marcion was the son of a bishop from Pontus. He arrived in Rome in 140. He could claim to be the authentic exponent of the message of Paul to the gentile world, *Behold all things have become new.*[11] The attitude that he expected his followers to adopt to the Creator-God, the misguided inferior of the true God of love—an attitude of bleak noncollaboration with all the Creator's purposes—was an emotional *calque* upon the attitude of earlier Christian groups to "the present age."

Around the year 80, the Christians of Antioch put together the Gospel of Saint Luke. This Gospel contained some of the most uncompromising sayings of Jesus on the role of his disciples in the "present age." In such sayings, it was "the poor," *tout court*—the homeless, the rootless, the oppressed—who had been called "blessed."[12] The "Beatitudes" of the Sermon on the Mount, as reported in this extreme form in the Gospel of Luke, acted as a charter for the wandering followers of Jesus who had first preached the coming of his kingdom in Palestine, Syria, and southern Asia Minor. They were read by Marcion and his followers as having asserted that those disciples who "neither married nor were given in marriage" might become "*already* equal to the angels," and had already "attained the world beyond and the resurrection."[13]

Such a state of opinion among many local churches explains why the Marcionites could claim to represent "true" Christianity in many parts of Syria.[14] Similarly, while Tatian's break with the Church in Rome, in 172, was long remembered in the Graeco-Roman Mediterranean, he merged back without remark into a Syrian Christianity that may always have been as radical as himself.[15] His greatest achievement was the composition of a single Gospel, in Greek and Syriac, that harmonized the four Gospels—his *Diatessaron*. Although this Gospel betrayed throughout his own, sharp views in favor of sexual abstinence,[16] it was taken for granted in the Syrian world. As late as the

11. H. Koester in J. M. Robinson and H. Koester, eds., *Trajectories through Early Christianity*, p. 155.

12. S. P. Brock, "Early Syrian Asceticism," pp. 3–4.

13. D. E. Aune, *The Cultic Setting of Realized Eschatology in Early Christianity*, pp. 195–212.

14. A. von Harnack, *Marcion: das Evangelium vom fremden Gott*, pp. 341–344 and A. Vööbus, *A History of Asceticism in the Syrian Orient*, pp. 45–54.

15. M. Elze, *Tatian und seine Theologie*, p. 121.

16. A. Vööbus, *Celibacy, a Requirement for Admission to Baptism in the Early Syriac Church*, pp. 18 ff.

fifth century, at least two hundred copies were circulating in one diocese alone.[17]

Altogether, views and attitudes that are made to appear, in the surviving polemical literature, as if they were the work of strikingly idiosyncratic innovators circulated in many churches of Palestine, Syria, and in parts of Asia Minor, as no more than so many variants of a well-established "radical consensus." In much the same manner as revivals swept at regular intervals through the "Burned Over" regions of the State of New York, in the nineteenth century—each producing distinctive variants of a shared sectarian religiosity—so we must imagine the Christian communities of the hinterland of the eastern Mediterranean as sharing, throughout the second and third centuries, in a common tendency for Christian militancy to find its most clear expression in the renunciation of married life.

We are dealing with a very different world from that of Polycarp in Smyrna, Hermas in Rome, Irenaeus in Lyon, and Tertullian in Carthage. The huge, stridently pagan cities of the Mediterranean were less in evidence. Further away from the Mediterranean, east of Antioch, persecution was a relatively unimportant issue for Christians: martyrdom at the hands of the Imperial authorities did not become a reality until after 300 A.D. Instead, Syrian Christians "lived at the door of the Jews, like poor relations not on speaking terms."[18] The mobility of the early phases of the "Jesus Movement" in Palestine continued in this eastern Christianity. In a landscape of villages and of smaller, less cohesive towns, the idea that possession of the Holy Spirit might bring about a dramatic break with the believer's entire social identity flickered alluringly at the very center of the Christian imagination, in a manner that would have shocked the rigid Tertullian.

Though they may have spread against a common background and have imposed their own meanings upon a common religious sensibility, the teachings of Marcion and Tatian differed greatly. Both demanded full sexual abstinence from all baptized Christians; but the meaning of this abstinence was not the same in each group.

For Marcion, the "present age" was the visible world, subject in its entirety to the rule of a Creator-God, to whom the true God of love was unknown. A chasm separated the present world from the heaven

---

17. Theodoret, *Haer. fabul.* 1.20: *Patrologia Graeca* 83: 372A.
18. Robert Murray, *Symbols of Church and Kingdom: A Study in Early Syriac Tradition*, p. 19; see now Han J. W. Drijvers, "Jews and Christians at Edessa."

from which Christ came to save mankind. The cosmic dimension of Marcion's thought was explicit. It was stressed by his opponents in the second as in later centuries. The present universe, in his opinion, had been brought about by a forming power that was far removed from the radiant tranquility of the highest God.[19] Human life was lived out under the shadow of an unreliable and oppressive force that maintained and guided the material world. Yet, unlike many of his equally bleak contemporaries, Marcion gave this harsh dualism of spirit and matter a marked social dimension. The Creator-God was the God of the Jewish Law. His sinister power was shown less in the tension of body and spirit than in the dire constraints of conventional society. He had imposed on the human race dull rules and cramping compartmentalizations that cut human beings off from each other. Mankind as a whole, and not merely the Jews, lived "under the Law." It was to unlock those heavy bars that Christ had suddenly appeared, as a total stranger, in a cramped and outmoded world. His person radiated a new, disturbing openness. Where the Creator had ordered men to shun lepers, Christ had touched them.[20] Where the Creator had decreed menstruating women to be a source of impurity, Christ had let the woman with an issue of blood lay her hand upon him.[21] "This is the basic and most absolute goodness of Christ, that such goodness should be poured out to total strangers, to those to whom we owe no debt of kinship, as a free act of will."[22]

The Christian message was *unfamiliar* in both senses of the word: it was a message of which those caught in the narrow confines of the family could have no inkling. Only by rendering men and women utterly unfamiliar to each other, by demanding that they should renounce the marriages that had previously held them together,[23] and even by dissolving the ties that bound children to their parents,[24] could true Christians come together in a freely chosen communion, undetermined by preexisting family bonds, loyalties, and habits.

This was a peculiarly unsettling message to the average Christian

---

19. See Barbara Aland, "Marcion. Versuch einer neuen Interpretation." I am indebted to the forthcoming study of Han J. W. Drijvers, "Marcionism in Syria: Principles, Problems and Polemics," which makes plain the relationship of Marcion's Creator-God to Middle Platonic speculations on the Demiurge.

20. Tertullian, *Adv. Marc.* 4.9.3.   21. Ibid. 4.20.9.

22. Ibid. 1.23.3: see Aland, Marcion, pp. 426–428.

23. Tertullian, *Adv. Marc.* 1.29.1.

24. Epiphanius, *Panarion* 1.3.42.11.70: *P.G.* 41: 720A.

church. Up to the middle of the second century, the Christian communities had tended to expand hesitantly, in the manner of most religious groups in the ancient world. Ties of family, marriages, and loyalties to heads of households had been the most effective means of recruiting members of the church, and had maintained the continued adherence of the average Christian to the new cult.[25] In many regions, the leadership of the church lay in the hands of dynasties of Old Believers. In the 190s, bishop Polycrates of Ephesus could claim that seven of his kinsmen had already been bishops of the city![26] To abandon marriage was to erode the household-based core of the church. A group that defined the Christian community as a company of baptized celibates had to commit itself, in fact, to different forms of leadership, linked to an aggressive missionary strategy, that was quite unusual in the ancient world.

Rather than building outward slowly from a core of established Old Christian families, the Marcionite churches deliberately wrenched the individual out of the familiar structures of society. Tertullian warned his readers: Marcion's view of Christ's coming into the world, to "snatch" His own away from the established rule of the Creator God, threatened to "snatch" sons from their fathers, pupils from their teachers, slaves from their masters.[27] Small though such groups might have been, they spread with unusual rapidity. Marcionite churches competed as equals with the other Christian communities in Asia Minor and Syria. Beyond the Roman frontiers, in Iraq and in the foothills of Iran, the Marcionites successfully monopolized the term "Christian" up to the end of the sixth century.[28]

Tatian's concerns bring us into a different thought-world. Marcion had scanned society from a "horizontal" perspective. To abandon the Creator-God was to step out of the narrow confines of a family-based society into the unexpected openness of a missionary, celibate church. Tatian, by contrast, stressed the "vertical" dimension of the human person. The joining of the existing, insufficient human being to the Holy Spirit formed the center of gravity of his thought. His insistence on sexual abstinence flowed from this overriding preoccupation.[29]

25. Ramsay MacMullen, *Christianizing the Roman Empire*, pp. 34, 65, 148 *n*17.

26. Eusebius, *Ecclesiastical History* 5.24.6.   27. Tertullian, *Adv. Marc.* 1.23.8.

28. J. M. Fiey, "Les Marcionites dans les textes historiques de l'Église de Perse," pp. 183–188; Michael G. Morony, *Iraq after the Muslim Conquest*, p. 426.

29. Elze, *Tatian*, p. 92 ff; W. Cramer, *Der Geist Gottes und des Menschen in frühsyrischer Theologie*, pp. 48–55, with H. D. Hauschild, *Gottes Geist und der Mensch*, pp. 196–206.

Man, in the "present age," was a headless torso.[30] Ever since Adam had "separated" from God in Paradise, a layer of the soul that made the person truly human had been lacking. For

Man is not, as the croaking philosophers say, merely a rational animal. . . . Man alone is in the image and likeness of God; but by "man" I mean not one who performs actions similar to those of animals, but one who has advanced beyond such mere humanity—to God Himself.

[For] the Spirit of God is not with all, but it takes up its abode with those who love righteousness, and intimately combines with the soul . . . [Such ones] have attached themselves to that cognate Spirit.[31]

In itself, the human soul was nothing. It existed to be "married" to the Spirit. Souls that did not "cleave" to the Spirit must fall into an equally intimate and all-engulfing state of possession by the spirits of evil.[32] Unbaptized human beings lived in the grip of "ten thousand tyrants."[33]

A suffusion of the person by the Holy Spirit, based on a union as permanent and as intense as was the inextricable mingling of two lives that was admired by contemporary pagan writers in an ideal human marriage, formed the essence of the life of the Christian.[34] Such "marriage" to the Spirit differed from the mighty inspiration that fell, infrequently, upon the individual prophets that we described in our last chapter. Rather, what Tatian had in mind was a benign state of permanent possession gained by the Christian at the moment of baptism. It involved a notion of the working of the Spirit deep within the soul of the baptized believer, which expressed itself most appositely in the measured ecstasy of chant and poetry:

As the wind moves through the harp
And the strings speak,
So the Spirit of the Lord speaks through my members
And I speak through His love.[35]

---

30. Cramer, *Geist Gottes*, p. 52.

31. Tatian, *Oratio* 15 and 13, in J. E. Ryland, trans. *The Ante-Nicene Fathers* 2:71.

32. Ibid. 13.   33. Ibid. 29.

34. Musonius, *Reliquiae* 13B, in Cora E. Lutz, ed., *Yale Classical Studies* 10:90–91: see M. Foucault, *Le Souci de Soi*, pp. 189–190; English edition: R. Hurley, trans., *The Care of the Self*, pp. 161–162.

35. *The Odes of Solomon* 6.1. J. H. Charlesworth, ed., p. 29; for the date, now see L. Abramowski, "Sprache und Abfassungszeit der Oden Salomos."

What Christ had brought to the world was the possibility of marriage to His Spirit.

Like the arm of the bridegroom over the bride
So is my yoke over those who know Me.[36]

The Holy Spirit was a source of unfailing nurture. In Syriac, the word for Spirit was feminine. The Spirit was the mother of the soul:

I fashioned their members,
And my own breasts I prepared for them,
That they might drink my holy milk and live by it.[37]

In the thought of Tatian, images of marital bonding and of nurture were so powerful that they blocked out the possibility of sexual joining in ordinary marriage. So huge an inner reality permitted no rival. In his *Diatessaron*, Tatian subtly reinterpreted the passage of Genesis to which Christ had appealed as the basis of his demand for monogamous marriage. For Tatian, once Adam had willfully decided to "leave" his Father and Mother, God and His Spirit, he became subject to death, and so was forced to "cleave," through physical intercourse, to a woman, by marrying Eve.[38] To regain the Spirit of God that had once raised Adam above death, and so above the need for marriage, human beings must abandon married intercourse, the most clear symptom of Adam's frailty and the most decisive obstacle to the indwelling of the Spirit.

Contemporaries assigned to the views of Tatian, and of the many groups loosely associated with him, the general term of "Encratite"—from *enkrateia*, continence.[39] The Encratites declared that the Christian church had to consist of men and women who were "continent" in the strict sense: they had "contained" the urge to have sexual intercourse with each other. To this basic continence, the Encratites added dietary restraints, abstention from meat and from the drinking of wine. These abstentions were intimately linked to the constitutive act of sex-

36. *Odes of Solomon* 42.8, p. 145.

37. Ibid. 8.14, p. 42; see esp. Cramer, *Geist Gottes*, p. 37 and Robert Murray, *Symbols of Church and Kingdom*, pp. 312–320.

38. Vööbus, *Celibacy*, p. 18; Aphrahat, *Demonstratio* 18.10–11, in J. Neusner, trans. *Aphrahat and Judaism*, pp. 79–80, continues this exegesis in the early fourth century.

39. See esp. H. Chadwick, s.v. Enkrateia, *Reallexikon für Antike und Christentum*, 5:343–365, and now G. Sfameni Gasparro, "Le motivazioni protologiche dell'*Enkrateia* nel cristianesimo dei primi secoli e nello Gnosticismo," pp. 149–184 and 228–231.

ual renunciation: for the eating of meat was held to link human beings to the wild, carnivorous nature of animals, as intercourse linked them to the sexual nature of brute beasts. Furthermore, wine was a known source of sexual energy—"for wine imparts warmth to the nerves, soothes the soul, recalls pleasure, engenders semen, and provokes to venery."[40]

It made little difference whether baptized believers had remained virgins from birth, or whether they had decided to abstain from intercourse when already married. What mattered was that the rule of the demons over the human person had been replaced, at baptism, by the exclusive, intimate nurture of the Holy Spirit, which would henceforth admit no further sexual joining.

The Encratites expounded their view of the cause of the universal bondage of mankind through exegesis of the story of the Fall of Adam and Eve, as this was recounted in the opening chapters of the book of Genesis. Obsessed as he had been with Christ's victory over death in the Resurrection, Paul had already "roused the Adam myth from its lethargy."[41] From the second century onward, the myth was destined to remain very wide awake indeed. For Tatian and his followers, Adam and Eve stood for humanity as it had first been created by God. They had been "holy" beings in the strict sense: they were beings who belonged exclusively to the one category, that of the non-animal, as possessors of the Spirit of God and destined to live forever.[42] The basic anomaly of human existence, by which human beings, though once endowed with spirit, now die like the non-human beasts, had begun when Adam and Eve abandoned their marriage to the Spirit of God and found themselves forced, by mortality, to enter into relations with each other in a manner not originally intended for them by God. By this action, they further excluded the Spirit and blurred the clear boundary that kept the human person in a category distinct from that of animals.

There were even radical disciples of Tatian who ascribed Adam and Eve's original loss of the Spirit directly to a sexual act. They asserted

40. Aretaeus, *Therapeutics of Acute Diseases* 2.11, in F. Adams, trans., *The Extant Works of Aretaeus the Cappadocian* p. 453; see now Robert McL. Wilson, "Alimentary and Sexual Encratism in the Nag Hammadi Texts."

41. Paul Ricoeur, *The Symbolism of Evil*, E. Buchanan, trans., p. 238.

42. Mary Douglas, *Purity and Danger*, p. 53: "Holiness is exemplified by completeness. Holiness requires that individuals should conform to the class to which they belong. And holiness requires that different classes of things shall not be confused."

that Eve had met the serpent, who represented the animal world, and that the serpent had taught Eve to do what animals do—to have intercourse.[43] Joined to the animal kingdom, therefore, by being "sexualised," Adam and Eve found themselves on a slippery slope that led, through sexuality, to the animal kingdom, and, hence, to the grave.

Man being in honor did not abide; he has become comparable to the mindless beasts and has taken on a resemblance to them.[44] For that which befalleth the sons of man befalleth the beasts: as the one dieth, so dieth the other; yea, they have all one breath: so that a man has no preeminence above a beast.[45]

In either view, man's loss of his preeminence over the beasts was shown with brutal clarity by the fact that human beings, in becoming mortal, had come to share with the animal world the facts of sex.

It was a bleak vision. In it, the ancient continuity of man and the natural world was broken and, with it, the assumption that human society grew organically from natural urges. By sexual joining Adam and Eve did not found and continue society; they fell into a false society. Human society, as it was now constituted and kept in being through marriage, did not develop naturally; it was, rather, a society created by a tacit "sexual social contract." To maintain it, human beings surrendered and must continue to surrender those inalienable, original qualities that had originally distinguished them from animals, as beings rendered immortal by the presence of God's Spirit. By continuing to contribute to a society built up through marriage arrangements, associated with physical intercourse, humans condemned themselves to sharing in the other aspect of the life of animals—they remained mortal creatures, untouched by the live-giving Spirit of God. To initiate sex by entering into marriage, therefore, was to contribute directly to the cycle of mortality: "And marriage followed the woman, and reproduction followed marriage, and death followed reproduction.[46]

It was a view designed to flatten the social landscape of the Roman world. A society which sunnier contemporaries had liked to portray as flowering, generation after generation, through the natural urge of

43. Clement, *Strom.* 3.17.102, referring to Julius Cassianus. Such views are tacitly combatted by later Jewish exegesis: it was Adam and Eve who taught the animals how to have intercourse by initiating the act: *Midrash Rabba: Genesis* 18.2, H. Freedman and M. Simon, trans., p. 180.

44. Psalms 48:13, 31.   45. Ecclesiastes 3:19.

46. *Origin of the World: NHC II,5* 109, H. G. Bethge and O. S. Wintermute, trans. *Nag Hammadi*, p. 168.

young men and women to procreate, was now presented as slipping irrevocably into the grave: "The world is created, cities are adorned, and the dead continue to be carried out."[47]

At a stroke, sexuality was detached from society. Pagan and Jewish societies had shared a robust faith in the ability of man to socialize those physical drives that men and women shared with the animal world. They believed that sexuality could be swept into the charmed circle of society. No matter how much anxiety disorderly sexual feelings might cause to the pious, this anxiety was held in check by the certainty that there was such a thing as "good" sex, that is, socially useful sex: only the antisocial aspects of sexuality had to be renounced. The Encratites dismissed such optimism as a selective and arbitrary compartmentalization. Sex was sex, wherever, whenever, with whomever, and however it happened: in any form, licit or illicit, it made plain humanity's present separation from the Spirit of God.

Jewish exegetes had suggested that Adam and Eve had allowed themselves to be penetrated by the serpent in order to explain, by such a myth, what struck them as peculiarly bizarre and aberrant variants of sexual behavior, such as bestiality and sodomy. Encratite exegesis presented sexuality itself, as such, as the abiding sign of an unnatural kinship with the animal world that the serpent had forced upon Adam and Eve.[48]

Sexuality was an unmodified outcrop of the alien, "animal" world into which the serpent had first led Adam and Eve. *Wild horses were they become, each man whinnied after his neighbor's wife*—Jeremiah's denunciation of adultery in ancient Israel was read by Encratite writers to refer to married intercourse of any sort.[49] The elaborate system of disciplined sexuality that the Christian communities had inherited from Judaism, and on whose observance they had based their claim to admiration in the pagan world, was rendered irrelevant. Sexuality was not there to be used in a disciplined manner: it was there only to be renounced.

Yet within this terrible symphony, it is possible to catch a high-pitched refrain of joy and freedom. It is to this refrain that the adherents of

---

47. *Gospel of Philip*: NHC II,*3* 52.18, W. Isenberg, trans., *Nag Hammadi*, p. 132.

48. *Babylonian Talmud: ʿAbodah Zarah* 22b, in A. Mishcon, trans., *The Talmud*, p. 114 and *Babylonian Talmud: Yebamoth* 103B, in W. Slotki, trans., *The Talmud*, 2:771; see A. Orbe, "El pecado original y el matrimonio en la teologia del s. II," pp. 449–450.

49. Jeremiah 5:8 in Clement, *Strom.* 3.17.102.

the Encratite movement appear to have listened. It is important that we should do the same. Intercourse and the chill contagion of the grave summed up human frailty. But intercourse could be halted, as death could not be. The sinister continuum that linked the human race to the animal kingdom and to the grave had once been put together by a series of free choices. Adam and Eve's fatal step could be undone by the free will. Each person had it within his or her power to regain the original unconfused "holiness" that possession of the Spirit had conferred on Adam and Eve: "For it is ordained that everyone should correct his own fall."[50]

Young men and women could decide to remain virgins: by passing through puberty without intercourse, they could overcome the sexual temptations to which Adam and Eve had finally succumbed. Young married women could initiate nothing less than a "boycott of the womb"; they could withhold their bodies from sexual intercourse, thereby cheating death of further prey.[51] Husbands and wives could withdraw from the marriage bed after baptism; by so doing, they regained a state of "holiness"—the term became virtually coextensive with "continence," in the Syriac church, when referring to continent married couples.[52] Furthermore, baptism was presented as a rite of effective desexualization. The initiates stepped naked into the baptismal pool. They were thought to have put off the sexualized "garments" of their old body.[53] They stood beside the pool like little children.

Children were regarded as untouched by adult sexual shame and so by an adult need for garments; they were not yet fully recruited into the structures of adult society, and hence subjected to an adult's obligation to marry.[54] The cold water cancelled out the hot fire that had

50. *Acts of Andrew* 5 in E. Hennecke and W. Schneemelcher, *New Testament Apocrypha*, 2:410.

51. Peterson, "Einige Beobachtungen zu den Anfängen der christlichen Askese," p. 219.

52. See esp. R. Murray, "The Exhortation to Candidates for Ascetical Vows at Baptism in the Ancient Syrian Church," and S. P. Brock, "Jewish Traditions in Syriac Sources," pp. 217–218.

53. J. Z. Smith, "The Garments of Shame," in *Map Is Not Territory*. Both initiate and priest would stand naked: Hippolytus, *Apostolic Traditions* 21.5 and 11.

54. For nakedness as the absence of social status—as in the case of children—and not exclusively as a sign of absence of sexual shame, see W. Helcke and W. Westerdorf, eds., *Lexikon der Ägyptologie*, p. 292. To accept "nakedness" was also to accept poverty and detachment from the world; that is, to be "stripped." *Gospel of Thomas: N.H.C. II,2,* 21 and 37, *Nag Hammadi*, pp. 120, 122.

given them birth.[55] Into this water, the Holy Spirit descended, wrapping the person in a robe of glory, as subtly as did the translucent streams of liquid that sheathed the naked body as it rose from the pool.[56] Abstention from meat and wine further marked off the members of the baptized group as unambiguously "holy" persons. Anyone confronted by such a group knew in no uncertain manner what it stood for. Standing in a pagan temple in faraway Ctesiphon around 214, Mani's father had heard the mysterious cry: "Oh, Futtuq, do not eat meat! Do not drink wine! Do not marry a human being!" Very often, it was in that form that the inhabitants of the Near East (and, for all we know, elsewhere) made their first acquaintance with Christianity.[57]

The legendary *Acts of Judas Thomas* enable us to enter into the imaginative world of Encratite Christianity in Syria. They were written in Syriac, in Edessa, around 220. The problems that concerned Hermas, Irenaeus, and Tertullian in the cities of the Roman West seem very far away from this remarkable account of the impact of an ideal missionary in the Encratite tradition on the society around him.[58] We are made to look at "the present age" through the silent eyes of Christ. This Christ had reached down into the abyss of a world dominated by demonic powers.[59] Thomas was the "Twin" of Christ. He continued Christ's mission on earth, as the ideal militant in the Syrian tradition.[60] He moved as a challenging stranger in a society that had to be turned on its head to be the right way up at last. He reached into

55. Pseudo-Clement, *Homilies* 9.15.4.

56. Aphrahat, *Demonstratio* 4.14; on the significance of the "robe of glory" see esp. S. P. Brock, "Jewish Traditions in Syriac Sources," pp. 221–223, with the same author's "Clothing Metaphors as a Means of Theological Expression in Syriac Tradition," in M. Schmidt and C. F. Geyer, eds., *Typus, Symbol und Allegorie bei den östlichen Vätern*, pp. 11–40 and P. F. Beatrice, "Le tuniche di pelle," pp. 473–474.

57. al-Nadim, *Fihrist* 9.1, B. Dodge, trans. 2:773–774. Similar communities may have existed in the Mediterranean world; see the case of Pinytus of Knossos in Eusebius, *Eccles. Hist.* 4.23.7–8, with P. Nautin, *Lettres et écrivains chrétiens du iie et iiie siècles*, pp. 13–31. But we know nothing of their theological rationale nor of the behavior of the believers in them.

58. Notably the best treatments of this area and of its Early Christian culture are those of H. J. W. Drijvers, now collected as *East of Antioch*; see also J. Gribomont, "Le monachisme au sein de l'Église," pp. 14–17. I am indebted to Professor Drijvers for reminding me of this judicious article.

59. A. F. J. Klijn, *The Acts of Thomas*, Supplements to Novum Testamentum 5, esp. pp. 14–15 and 34.

60. Klijn, *Acts of Thomas*, p. 37 and Drijvers, "Hellenistic and Oriental Origins," in S. Hackel, ed., *The Byzantine Saint*, pp. 25–33 and "Die Legende des heiligen Alexius und der Typus des Gottesmannes im syrischen Christentum," pp. 187–217.

the bedroom, to halt the landslip of sexuality at its source. In no other legendary *Acts* do we meet in such vivid form the classic ascetic scenario of sexual renunciation on the wedding night:

And our Lord [looking like Thomas] sat down on the bed, and let the young people sit down on the chairs . . . [and so] they were preserved from filthy lust, and passed the night in their [separate] places.[61]

Women who were already married were urged to reject their husbands:

[Prince Karish] came and stood over her, and took off his clothes. And she perceived him and saith to him: There is no place for thee beside me, because my Lord Jesus, with whom I am united, is better than thee.[62]

Karish ended the night trussed up by his sturdy wife, Mygdonia, who fled from him wrapped in nothing but the veil that hung across the marriage-bed.[63] Poor Prince Karish! In his humiliation in the bedroom the swaggering pride of the "present age" could be seen to crumble:

I am Karish, the husband of thy youth and I am thy true husband, whom the whole country honoureth and whom they fear. . . . lift up thy eyes and look upon me, for I am far better than that wizard, and I am handsomer than he, and I have wealth and honour, and everyone knoweth that none hath a lineage like to mine.[64]

Hence the lasting importance of the view of sexuality presented in the *Acts of Thomas*. Married intercourse was treated as the linchpin of the towering structure of the "present age." To break the spell of the bed was to break the spell of the world. This was a world whose social structures stood condemned. We are looking not only at sexuality, but also at a society whose values were upside down—a society where the poor went hungry in winter while kings planned huge palaces;[65] where servants carried great ladies in towering palanquins, trampling their fellow-creatures underfoot to make way for their mistresses.[66] It was a society without word of a heaven where everything would be turned the right way up again, for those who abandoned riches and family in this present life, and who sank the money usually amassed for display in the care of the nameless poor.[67] Thomas' heaven was a

---

61. *Acts of Thomas* 11 and 13, trans. Klijn, pp. 70 and 71. 62. 98, p. 115.
63. 98, p. 115. 64. 115–116, pp. 126–127.
65. 18–19, pp. 72–74; see commentary, p. 201. 66. 82–83, p. 108
67. 22–23, pp. 75–76

place where there would no longer be "any who are proud and uplifted over those who are humble."[68]

Thomas was presented as preaching to an uncomprehending world,

a new doctrine of purity . . . that a man cannot live unless he separates himself from all that belongeth to him, and becometh an ascetic and a wandering mendicant like unto himself, and lo he wishes to make companions for himself.[69]

In the Encratite tradition, the end of the present age was to be brought about by the boycott of the womb. And the boycott of the womb was crucial because sexuality was presented less as a drive than as the symbol of ineluctable processes, the clearest token of human bondage. Thomas' call, therefore, was to the women to reject their men, and no longer simply to men to resist seduction by women. This marked a significant shift in emphasis. The other Christian traditions had been quite content to look at sexuality only as a man might experience it. It was a dangerous, hidden drive, frequently stirred up in men by women. By drawing attention to the generalized frailty of the human race as a whole, the Encratites introduced a more poignant, muted note to all future Christian presentations of sexuality. Something like "binocular vision," an attempt to join male and female perceptions of what sexuality could mean, in the full life cycle of members of each sex, flickers behind the high rhetoric of the *Acts of Thomas*. We are never far from a sense of the vulnerability of all humanity to the catastrophe of social life as conventionally organized in the "present age." This was a catastrophe most clearly revealed in the huge pressure with which society weighed down upon the body of the married woman.

Concretely, marriage and childbirth were presented as committing families to continuing the pride and violence on which the stability of society depended.[70] But the *Acts of Thomas* said more than that. The continuance of society was achieved by breaking the life of the woman into transitory fragments. Seen from the woman's viewpoint, the change from virginity to childbearing revealed most blatantly the chasm that separated eternity from a humanity now caught in the cruel flux of time. The stilled tranquillity of the girl's former state, symbolized by her untouched body, was turned, through the high ceremonials of her marriage-day, into a series of short acts that flashed past rapidly. Each action emphasized a poignant moment of loss and discontinuity. The

68. 129, p. 134.   69. 100, p. 116.   70. 12 and 126, pp. 71 and 133.

veil was put on as a sign of new sexual shame.[71] The opulent cloth of gold of the wedding tent was set up, only to be taken down again. The end of all that splendor was decay, the premonition of long years of enslavement to the body, as the bearer and nurturer of children.[72] In this way, the woman's condemnation to the marriage bed was made to stand for all human bondage in the present age, and the rejection of married intercourse, as a window that had suddenly been thrown open on to eternity, for "marriage passeth away with much contempt, Jesus alone abideth."[73]

For all the stirring rhetoric of their imagined heroes, the average practitioners of continence in Syria strike us as remarkably serene persons. The followers of Tatian included austere wandering preachers, for whom the deeds of Apostles such as Thomas continued to act as a model. By their "apostolic" journeys from town to town and village to village, they linked quiet little groups of men and women. To these men and women, Christian baptism had brought an ability to live at ease with each other. The presence of the Holy Spirit ensured that the fearsome current of sexuality that had once flowed through their bodies was safely disconnected. No treacherous spark now jumped between the once-charged poles of male and female.[74]

Men and women missionaries even traveled together—the most grueling test of all of sexual good faith in a society used to the sedentary seclusion of most of its womenfolk.[75] Possessed by the Holy Spirit, as Adam and Eve had once been, men and women could once again stand together as couples, linked in a chaste communion that astonished and appalled observers in this and in all future centuries.[76] When, for instance, in the late fourth century, Jerome arrived from Italy to live for a time in a Syrian village, he came to know of an elderly, unmarried couple, a man and a woman, who would walk to church every day and return home together. The phenomenon intrigued him and greatly titillated his imagination. The villagers, however, referred to

---

71. 13–14, pp. 71–72.   72. 14, p. 72.   73. 88, p. 111.

74. Beatrice, "Continenza e matrimonio," pp. 51, 59.

75. *Babylonian Talmud: Sukka* 52a, in W. Slotki, trans., *The Talmud*, pp. 248–249. In the *Acts of Philip*, the holy woman Mariamne was denounced for traveling with the Apostles. "She travels about with these magicians and no doubt commits adultery with them." *Acts of Philip* 125, in M. Bonnet, ed., *Acta Apostolorum Apocrypha* 3:54; trans. A. Walker, *The Ante-Nicene Fathers*, 8:499.

76. G. Flecker, *Amphilochiana*, p. 69 and Epiphanius, *Panarion* 46.3, with A. Guillaumont, "Le nom des 'Agapètes.'"

the couple, without any to-do, as the "Holy Ones."[77] The incident is a reminder that sexual renunciation, as practiced in one region, could look very different to Christians from another part of the Roman world.

The celibacy of the Encratites was a group celibacy, and not one that favored isolated recluses. The individual gained a sense of security, which supported his or her renunciation, through the sense of belonging to a clearly defined holy group. There was a tendency, built into the Near Eastern landscape itself, for Encratite communities and for the churches of the Marcionites to settle down into tight-knit sectarian villages. These communities may have resembled the Shaker "Families" of nineteenth-century America. They survived for very long periods by attracting converts and by acting as substitutes for foundling hospitals among the neighboring peasantry. They throve in the mountainous areas of Syria and Asia Minor, where the population always exceeded the scarce resources of the highlands, and where there were many children to be taken.[78]

But this was not the only solution adopted by the continent. By the end of the third century, little groups of continent men and women— called "The Sons and Daughters of the Covenant"—stood at the core of the married Christian communities in the Syriac-speaking regions of the Near East.[79] These were not settlements of wild ascetics, but pools of quiet confidence that the Spirit rested on those who had regained, through baptism and continence, the full humanity of Adam and Eve. Their presence bathed the Christian community as a whole with a sense of being a group marked out by inviolate holiness. Crowded into the little churches of Syria and Northern Iraq, they stood like the animals in Noah's Ark, their sexual urges marvelously stilled by the presence of God. The Holy Spirit bubbled up within them in the chanting of the Psalms and the self-composed hymns that are the glory of the Syriac church.[80] Unjoined in bodies, young men and women were truly joined by the ethereal harmony of their voices, kept sweet by the

---

77. Jerome, *Life of Malchus* 2: *Patrologia Latina* 23: 56A.

78. See the later example of the community of the Abelonii, reported near Hippo— presumably in the mountains—by Augustine, *de haeresibus* 87: *Patrologia Latina* 42:47. For Marcionite villages that survived in the hills near Cyrrhus into the middle of the fifth century, see Theodoret, *Historia Religiosa* 21: *P.G.* 82: 1439D–1449B and *Letter* 81: *P.G.* 83: 1261C.

79. G. Nedungatt, "The Covenanters in the Early Syriac-Speaking Church": F. Burkitt, *Early Christianity Outside the Roman Empire*, p. 139—"quiet, dignified and temperate."

80. Murray, *Symbols of Church and Kingdom*, pp. 28–29 is exceptionally fine on this.

absence of sexual activity, which ancient people knew to affect the voice adversely,[81] in the spiritual chants that gave density and human warmth to the austere doctrines that we have described:

Outside the Ark were fearsome waves,
but inside, lovely voices;
tongues all in pairs,
uttered together in chaste fashion,
foreshadowing our festival day,
when unmarried girls and boys
sing together in innocence
praise to the Lord of the Ark.[82]

We must now return to Rome and Alexandria, to Valentinus and the other Gnostic teachers of the second century, to examine yet another, significantly different way in which, in different Christian circles, the cessation of sexual activity was held to signal redemption from the "present age."

81. Nemesianus, *Eclogue* 4.11—loss of virginity is betrayed by a change in the girl's voice; Soranus, *Gynaecia* 3.1.7—on professional woman singers.
82. Ephrem the Syrian, *Hymns on the Resurrection* 2.4, S. P. Brock, trans. *The Harp of the Spirit*, p. 74; compare Philo, *de vita contemplativa* 88.

FIVE

"When You Make the Two One": Valentinus and Gnostic Spiritual Guidance

At some time between 161 and 168, the Christian apologist Justin (whose views on the moral heroism of the Christians we have already encountered) found himself on trial before Rusticus, the Prefect of the City of Rome. Appropriately enough, Rusticus himself was a philosopher. It had been he, indeed, who had taught the Emperor Marcus Aurelius "not to pose ostentatiously as an ascetic."[1] In Rusticus and Justin, two very different representatives of the wide class of spiritual guides came face to face. Justin was only one of the many eccentric sages who had set themselves up as teachers in the sprawling, all-absorbing capital of the Empire:

I have been living above the baths of a certain Martinus . . . And for the entire period of my sojourn in Rome . . . I have known no other meeting place but there. Anyone who wished could come to my abode and I would impart to him the word of truth.[2]

1. Marcus Aurelius, *Meditations* 1.7.
2. *Martyrdom of Justin and Companions*, Recension B3, in H. Musurillo, ed. *The Acts of the Christian Martyrs*, pp. 49–51.

It is difficult for a modern reader to enter into the intensity of the *didaskaleion*, of the small study-circle of male and female disciples that would gather for years on end around a single spiritual guide.[3] Yet well-to-do Christians of the second century took it for granted that their spiritual growth depended on close, face-to-face consultation with beloved teachers. A Christian bishop traveled regularly all the way from Cappadocia, in Anatolia, to Palestine "in order to deepen his spiritual life," by sitting at the feet of the great Origen.[4] There were many serious Christians who were convinced that only through prolonged, intimate contact with a spiritual guide, and not through the somewhat jejune preaching of the clergy in church, would "the dead coals of sacred learning come to glow again in the heart."[5]

Small study-circles were the powerhouses of the Christian culture of the second and third century. The extraordinary intellectual ferment of the period is unthinkable without them. The shadow side of this creativity was a growing sense of polarization. The notion of "heresy" developed early among Christians. It was, indeed, Justin, a man accustomed to the intellectual infighting of pagan schools of philosophy, who may well have been the first to introduce the notion into Christian literature. His model for the rise of heresy assumed that it was a deviation from the original truths of Christianity, brought about by a process of degeneration and proliferation. The competitive spirit of individual teachers allied with pre-existing pagan and Jewish sects to introduce alien doctrines into the Church.[6]

A modern reader should not be misled by this potent stereotype. It was evolved so as to give an acceptable explanation for the painful fact that Christians had disagreed profoundly with each other since the days of Saint Paul. But its acceptance by many second-century Christians reflects a hardening of the boundaries between rival traditions of Christian teaching. One group, connected with the bishops

---

3. The best studies concern pagan philosophers; see esp. G. Fowden, "The Platonist Philosopher and his Circle in Late Antiquity," and M.-O. Goulet-Cazé, in L. Brisson, ed., *Porphyre: La Vie de Plotin. Travaux Préliminaires*, pp. 231–236; now see the masterly presentation of G. Fowden, *The Egyptian Hermes: A historical approach to the late pagan mind*, pp. 190–191. For an earlier period, see particularly B. Frischer, *The Sculpted Word: Epicureanism and Philosophical Recruitment in Ancient Greece* and I. Hadot, "The Spiritual Guide."

4. Eusebius, *Ecclesiastical History* 6.27.   5. Clement, *Stromateis* 6.15.116.2.

6. See now the important study of Alain Le Boulluec, *La notion d'hérésie dans la littérature grecque: iie-iiie siècles* 1:36–91.

and clergy, wished to present itself as representing the "Great Church." They claimed not only that they alone had preserved the authentic teachings of Christ—every group claimed to do that—but also that they represented the views of an overwhelming majority of right-thinking believers.

The *didaskaleia*, being small study-groups led by individual teachers, were made to bear the brunt of the clergy's claim to stand for the mainstream of Christian belief. They were the minority that had to suffer if the "Great Church" was to think of itself as speaking for the majority. There were few Christian study-groups whose leaders were not, at one time or other, condemned as heretical by the local clergy. Yet spiritual guides and teachers remained indispensable. In the early third century, a bishop of Alexandria had to rule that those who attended study-circles could not be said to have seceded from the church for "they were still regarded as members of the congregation even when they were reported as the regular pupils of some heterodox teacher."[7]

In the following chapters, we will never move far from the intense, inward-looking and relatively cultivated world of Christian teachers and their pupils.

Valentinus came to Rome from Alexandria in 138 and taught there until 166. He emerged as one of the greatest spiritual guides in the Christian community, in a generation that produced teachers of the caliber of Marcion, Justin, and Tatian.[8] He was believed to have been considered a possible candidate for the office of Bishop of Rome.[9] Like many of his Christian contemporaries, he was proud of the title "Gnostic." At the time, the term did not have the exotic overtones that have come to cluster around it. It referred to those who possessed "Gnosis," true knowledge: they knew more than did other Christians about the teachings that Jesus had first intimated to the innermost circle of his disciples.

A Gnostic study-circle of the second century was a group of men and women who relived, at the feet of their guide, the first moment of liberating precision, when the Savior Himself had spoken to a cho-

---

7. Eusebius, *Ecclés. Hist.* 7.7.4.

8. The best single exposition of the thought of Valentinus remains that of F. M. M. Sagnard, *La Gnose valentinienne et le témoignage de Saint Irénée.* For a convenient collection of recent studies, see B. Layton, ed., *The Rediscovery of Gnosticism, Vol. 1: The School of Valentinus.*

9. Tertullian, *Adversus Valentinianos* 4.1.

sen few. Serious souls, they had come together disquieted by a world that had lost contact with God:

Ignorance brought about anguish and horror.
And the anguish grew solid like a fog.

The teacher relived among them the role of Christ with His disciples. Here was "a guide, restful and leisurely."[10] Like Christ, he unfolded an account of the origins of the world and of the nature of the soul that brought intellectual certainty and moral purpose to all who heard it.

What distinguished Gnostics, in the eyes of their enemies, was their use of myth as a chosen vehicle of religious instruction. Their teaching consisted of what a modern reader would regard as mythical accounts of the origins of the material universe and of the processes by which mythical figures had found redemption. Polemists for the Great Church took pleasure in unveiling Gnostic myths as if they were grandiose and pseudo-scientific speculations, totally unrelated to the stern simplicity of the Gospel. They presented the Gnostics as creatures from a "fabulous bestiary," whose teachings represented bizarre and frequently immoral deviations from orthodox truth.[11] In doing this, they deliberately wrenched the Gnostic myths from the original context that had given them a specifically Christian meaning. Gnostic myths, in fact, followed the same rhythm as the Gospels and the teachings of Paul: the redemption brought to the world by Christ was central to them.[12] Where they differed was in the scope of that redemption. They presented redemption in cosmic terms: the whole human person and the whole universe had been transformed by the coming of Christ.

This was not surprising, given the intellectual climate of the time. Second-century thinkers invariably regarded the human person as a microcosm of the universe. Only a doctrine of redemption that explained the salvation of the human soul in terms of the origin and purpose of the created world of which it was a part would satisfy them. It was this urgent need to explain the origin of things that a Gnostic teacher, such as Valentinus, addressed.

Valentinus was the least esoteric of the many Gnostic spiritual guides

---

10. *The Gospel of Truth: N.H.C. I,3* 17.11 and 19.16, G. W. MacCrae, trans., *The Nag Hammadi Library in English*, pp. 38, 39.

11. H. Savon, *Saint Ambroise devant l'exégèse de Philon le Juif* 1:32.

12. Le Boulluec, *La notion d'hérésie,* 1:240–241 and 2:329–332.

who appeared in the second century. He claimed to be a privileged
exegete of the existing Christian tradition. The letters of Paul and the
Gospel of Saint John were central to his teaching and that of his followers.[13] He claimed that only he and his disciples had understood
the extent of the invisible transformation of the entire creation, which
had been announced to mankind by the brief ministry of Christ on
earth. Ordinary believers were content to live according to the deceptively simple anecdotes, homely parables, and banal ethical injunctions contained in the Gospels. The Valentinian initiate, by contrast,
had ears to hear, in these humble signs, the faint but unmistakable
echo of the news of a universe brought to rest.

To many Gnostics, the bishop and his clergy were "canals without
water."[14] Under their guidance, the believer plodded conscientiously
round and round, getting nowhere, like a blindfolded donkey hitched
to a mill-wheel.[15] Valentinus and his disciples made no secret of the
fact that they thought the committed believer was entitled to more.
Valentinus' *didaskaleion* addressed men and women touched by the
metaphysical ferocity that was a feature of all second-century intellectuals. For them, doubt and moral uncertainty were spiritual perils. Lack
of knowledge of the divine world and of the destiny of the soul were
presented in contemporary literature (and doubtless experienced by
many) as a source of shame and intense restlessness. Such persons
wanted from a Christian spiritual guide what any educated pagan might
expect—an end to the ache of doubt and the hope of personal transformation.[16]

This explains the deliberate choice of myth as the preferred vehicle
of Valentinus' teaching. The Gnostic movement has been acclaimed as
one of the great moments of the recovery of the power of myth in the
ancient world.[17] Deeply alien though such mythical narratives might
appear to us, the Gnostic myths addressed a pain and expressed an

13. See esp. Elaine Pagels, *The Johannine Gospel in Gnostic Exegesis*, and *The Gnostic
Paul*.

14. *Apocalypse of Peter*: N.H.C. VII,*2* 79, R. A. Bullard, trans. p. 343. See esp. Klaus
Koschorke, *Die Polemik der Gnostiker gegen das kirchliche Christentum*, pp. 64–65; Elaine
Pagels, *The Gnostic Gospels*, pp. 28–47; 102–118 is a humane synthesis; Alan E. Samuel,
"How Many Gnostics?" is a necessary critical reassessment.

15. *Gospel of Philip*: N.H.C. II,*3* 63.12, W. W. Isenberg, trans., p. 138.

16. A. J. Festugière, *La Révélation d'Hermès Trismégiste*, 1:45–66 is a vivid evocation of
this mood, to which we can now add Fowden, *The Egyptian Hermes*, pp. 104–115.

17. This aspect has been particularly well studied, with reference to a system of myths
strikingly different from those of Valentinus, by Gedaliahu A. G. Stroumsa, *Another*

urgency too deep for the stale words of philosophical demonstration.[18] By unfolding, with majestic precision, an account of the distant origins of the physical world and of the dire sequence of events that had led to the present misery of the soul within it, Gnostic teachers enabled their disciples to pass through the equivalent of a healing séance: as in a ritual of healing, their myths presented "a system of interpretations that structure[d] phases of the illness from the diagnosis to the cure [in terms of a] fabulation of a reality unknown in itself."[19] The Gnostic myth, that is, mapped out the future trajectory of a process that would bring spiritual health to its hearers. Their story was the story of a cure.

For this reason, the myth of the fall, the repentance and the return of Sophia was central to the Valentinian system. In this myth, the mighty, all-embracing principle of God's Wisdom, personified in the nurturing, intimate, ever-fertile Sophia, had once stood before God in the "Place of Fullness," the *Plérôma*. She had been one of a multitude of eternal, unshakeable forces that gave order to a purely spiritual universe. This had been a universe without division, where base matter was unheard of. Sophia had wished to know God as He knew Himself, and to replace Him as the creator of other beings in her own right. As a result, the former, effortless abundance with which she had once transmitted the glory of God's wisdom to all other beings became a false creativity. Rebellious Wisdom became a frenetic power of mere proliferation. Driven to create out of despair at her separation from God, Sophia formed a redundant universe. Matter came into being, and, with matter, the sad sense, which many second-century thinkers shared with Valentinus, that the material world was an abortive attempt to imitate an infinitely distant, invisible, and ever-elusive model. The world created by Sophia spoke only of the chasm that separated what was from what should be. The physical world was, at best, a grotesquely distorted mirror of the spiritual riches of the "Place of Fullness"; at worst, it was a meaningless excrescence that must be severed from the spirit.

The present human person mirrored, with terrible precision, the confusion that lay at the root of the physical universe. The body was

---

Seed: Studies in Gnostic Mythology; see esp. pp. 1–4; see also the careful analysis of M. Tardieu, *Trois Mythes Gnostiques.*

18. A. J. Festugière, *La Révélation d'Hermès Trismégiste* 3:25–26.

19. Claude Lévi-Strauss, "The Sorcerer and his Magic," p. 179.

deeply alien to the true self. It was not simply an inferior other that might be brought to order by the vigorous soul. It came from matter, from *hylé*, a substance that would not have existed at all, if it had not been for the tragic "bubbling over" of Sophia. Even the soul, the *psyché*, the conscious self, had occurred as an afterthought. It swathed the lucid spirit in a thick fog of doubt, anxiety, and passion. The unredeemed lived as in a waking nightmare. All human thought, even the most profound religious quest, was riven with uncertainty and misplaced amibition. Only the spirit had a right to exist. It stirred in the depths of the initiate with a blind, insistent "ferment," which betrayed its distant origin in the Place of Fullness. The spirit, the *pneuma*, was the true person. It was the enduring bone and marrow around which the body and soul had come to cluster, as labile, tragically vulnerable "flesh," condemned to waste away with the passing of time.

The process of disintegration had been brought to a halt by the coming of Christ. Sophia had "repented." She had returned to God by submitting to the embrace of her Savior. Following her example, the human person would be progressively healed of the aching divisions between spirit and soul, soul and body. The believer whose spirit, like Sophia, had been reestablished in its rightful preeminence, would enter "the Kingdom which is in Christ . . . liberated from all multiplicity of moods, and from disharmony and change."[20]

Precisely because his view of the physical world was so bleak, Valentinus offered his Christian charges a hope of redemption that was more drastic than that of any of his pagan contemporaries. The physical universe would not remain eternally harmonious, schooled by the gentle play of the spirit. It was a mistake that must be rectified. Parts of the universe, the human body among them, would eventually be cast off as abortive and misconceived creations. All that remained, however, would sink back into the spirit. The visible world would be swallowed up again into the perfect spiritual order from which it had flickered uneasily in a short moment of confusion. The redeemed person was a tiny microcosm of a universe that had begun to undergo a gigantic mutation. No longer divided between conflicting layers of the self, whose unresolved tensions betrayed a confusion as ancient and as tenacious as the disastrous origin of the world, Gnostic initiates enjoyed, in the present life, a touch of *Anapausis*, of *the peace of God*

---

20. *The Tripartite Tractate: N.H.C.I,5* 132, M. L. Peel, trans., p. 95.

which passeth all understanding.[21] Their spirits were linked again to their true source, their anxious souls were stilled; even their bodies were hushed, soon to pass from them forever. The redeemed had "passed to within the Fullness of Being"; they had stepped back into the first moment of balanced rapture, when Wisdom rejoiced untroubled in the presence of God.[22] In the same way, Christ had breathed on His disciples, as a man breathes on the dying embers of a fire. He had scattered from their spirits the loose ash of confusion, causing the whole self to glow throughout with a single radiance.[23]

Valentinus' drastic notion of redemption added yet a further variant to the practice of sexual renunciation among Christians. The adherents of Valentinus did not live in a world closed off from the other exponents of the radical consensus in second-century Christianity. They had ample opportunity to contrast their own experience of continence with those current among their fellows. A continence resolved upon at the moment of baptism, as was the case among the Encratites, struck them as a somewhat external matter: it was quite possible to "go down into the water without having received anything."[24]

The fierce sense of a group identity, visibly declared through the renunciation of marriage, which pitted Marcionites and Encratites against the "present age," was lacking in Valentinian circles. The Valentinian redeemed person does not seem to have moved in a "holy" group, protected from the outside world by firm boundaries, such as celibacy and abstention from specific forbidden foods. The tragedy of human bondage to the present age could not be so easily concretized. Liberation could not be made manifest solely by the peremptory denial of conventional social ties, such as marriage. The huge agony of the universe dwarfed these hasty gestures. The body, indeed, was of little value as a declaratory agent. An unnecessary and deceptive covering compared with the spirit hidden deep within it, the body's visible stance to society counted for little.[25] It did not have to take upon itself the

21. See now esp. Jan Helderman, *Die Anapausis im Evangelium Veritatis*, pp. 198–199, 230.

22. Irenaeus, *Against the Heresies* 3.15.2.

23. Clement, *Excerpta ex Theodoto* 3.2, pp. 56–58.

24. *Gospel of Philip* 64.22, p. 139.

25. See the excellent characterization of Michael Allen Williams, *The Immovable Race. A Gnostic Designation and the Theory of Stability in Late Antiquity*, pp. 186–209, a study to which I am particularly indebted, as to many papers which the author has kindly allowed me to see before their publication.

weight of a public renunciation of marriage; nor did it have to bear the public agony of martyrdom.[26]

The universe itself had fallen, and must be restored, by intricate labor at the very root of the soul. Hence the Gnostic tendency to link redemption with nothing less than a definitive modification of the sexual drive. The men and women who had been redeemed by Valentinian teaching and initiation looked toward the stilling of sexual feeling as the outward visible sign of a mighty subsidence that had first taken place in the spiritual reaches of the universe. The individual could rise again from the dead, like Christ, as the hidden depths of the self became suffused with power of their spirit: "While we are still in the world it is fitting for us to acquire this resurrection for ourselves."[27]

The Gnostic teachers of the second century offered their charges a wide variety of mythical systems, in which imagery taken from the relations between the sexes and perceptions of the sexual drive always played an important part; but the imagery varied greatly from group to group.[28] Those images which were most frequently used in the Valentinian tradition have a quite distinctive flavor. Valentinus drew upon the polarity of male and female so as to preach a process of redemption that took place in two stages. The spiritual principles whose confusion had brought about all that was unnecessary in the universe would regain their stability. They were the fluid female that would be given form by the dominant male. But this was not all. All that was other to the spirit must be absorbed back into it: the polarity of male and female itself would be abolished. The female would become male. Hence the distinctive manner in which Valentinus adapted the conjugal imagery current in his age.

We begin with straightforward echoes of the second-century themes of hierarchy and control within the ideal marriage. Plutarch had urged the husband to exercise unceasing vigilance in forming the mind and actions of his bride:

It is said that no woman ever produced a child without the cooperation of a man, yet there are misshapen, fleshlike uterine growths . . . which develop themselves and acquire firmness and solidity. . . . Great care must be taken

---

26. See esp. Elaine Pagels, "Gnostic and Orthodox Views of Christ's Passion: Paradigms of the Christian Response to Persecution?"

27. *Gospel of Philip* 66.17, p. 140.

28. This is made particularly plain by Michael A. Williams, "Uses of Gender Imagery in Ancient Gnostic Texts."

that this sort of thing does not take place in women's minds. For if they do not receive the seed of good doctrines and share with their husbands in intellectual advancement, they, left to themselves, conceive many untoward ideas and low designs and emotions.[29]

For Valentinus, as for Plutarch, the female stood for all that was open, aimless, lacking in shape and direction. It stood for all that needed to be formed by being made subject to the hard, clear outlines of the male. In the very act of conception, it was the male seed that had brought shape and solidity to the labile, unstructured emission of the female.[30] Thus, both the learned myths of contemporary medicine and contemporary attitudes to marriage provided Valentinus with entirely apposite language for his own myth of the origin and eventual redemption of disorder in the universe. The universe as a whole was a "misshapen, fleshlike growth," that had developed in Wisdom when she deprived herself, by her own wilfullness, of the forming seed of God.[31]

The relations of male and female conjured up strong associations of the bringing of form and discipline to the disorderly and the inferior. But this was not all. Conjugal imagery had also spoken to contemporaries of a rare event—the concord achieved between two potentially alien and ill-matched beings, a man and a woman. For Valentinus, the universe would be redeemed when Wisdom recovered the conjugal harmony of her own, original relations to God. She would come to rest in the formative embrace of Christ, her male Redeemer.[32] The soul of any believer could do the same:

This marriage has brought them back together again and the soul has been joined to her true love, her real master, as it is written, *For the master of the woman is her husband.*[33]

Yet the imagery of conjugal unity took on a more urgent note in Valentinus' thought. It had been enough for Plutarch that potentially intractable matter should cling lovingly to her husband, the forming spirit:

29. Plutarch, *Praecepta conjugalia* 48. 145E, F. C. Babbitt, ed. and trans., 2:339–341.
30. Clement, *Excerpta ex Theodoto* 2.1, p. 56 and Irenaeus, *Against the Heresies* 1.30.1.
31. Clement, *Excerpta ex Theodoto* 32.1 and 68, pp. 132, 192.
32. Ibid. 19.5 and 21.1, pp. 94 and 98.
33. *Exegesis of the Soul: N.H.C. II,6*, W. C. Robinson, trans., p. 184.

She has an innate love for the first and most dominant of all things . . . and inclines towards the better and offers to it opportunity to create from her . . . and is glad that she is made pregnant [by the organizing soul.][34]

With Valentinus, by contrast, the very element of otherness condensed in the polarity of male and female, as in that between spirit and its opposites, matter and mere soul, must vanish. The otherness of matter was not an eternal aspect of the universe, as pagan philosophers tended to think. Matter was an ephemeral accident: it had resulted from a tragic dislocation of the spiritual world. The otherness of all that was not pure spirit would be healed: the female would be swallowed up in the male. It would not simply be disciplined by the male; it would become male. In pagan thought, the intimacy of husband and wife had always been valued as a relationship through which two originally unequal persons might slowly come to share a common excellence. It was considered good for a woman to dream that she had grown a beard: for then she "will have a very sympathetic husband, so that their faces will seem to merge into one."[35]

Gnostic circles treasured those incidents in the Gospels that had described the close relations of Christ with the women of His circle, and most especially those with Mary Magdalen. For a second-century writer, such anecdotes were an image of the sweet and irresistible absorption of the woman, the perpetual inferior other, into her guiding principle, the male:

Simon Peter said to them, "Let Mary leave us, for women are not worthy of life." Jesus said, "I myself shall lead her and make her male."[36]

Nothing less than the hope of redemption hung on that moment. Once rejoined to its male forming principles and no longer excluded from the untouchable purity of the world of the spirit, the universe would enjoy the disciplined stability of a restored conjugal bond. More than that: it would become transparent to the spirit. The last streak of otherness implied in the notion of the female would vanish. The *Plérôma* would come together again, having made the female male, through

34. Plutarch, *de Iside* 53. 372EF, F. C. Babbitt, ed. and trans., 5:128–130.

35. Artemidorus, *Oneirocritica* 1.30, R. White, trans., 31.

36. *Gospel of Thomas*: N.H.C. II,2 114, T. O. Lambdin, trans., p. 130; see now M. W. Meyer, "Making Mary Male: The Categories 'Male' and 'Female' in the Gospel of Thomas."

absorbing it into its perfect order. Eve, the troubled soul, would sink back into the hard, sure bone of Adam, the spirit:

Enter through the rib whence you came and
hide yourself from the beasts.[37]

Ultimately, Valentinian Gnostics, unlike their pagan contemporaries, wished to be faced by no inferior other to persuade and discipline: "Separation is the problem, reunification the solution. Separation is death, reunification life."[38]

Ideally all things would rise back into the spiritual world from which they had fallen. Only *hylé*, the last, most restless enemy of the spirit, would be left. A mistake from the beginning, it would sink from view. Spirit and soul, "male" and "female," would be reunited in a single radiant whole. All the phenomena that the notion of the "female" evoked in the minds of a male thinker of the ancient world, that is, all that stood for the antithesis of the "male"—"female" lability associated with time and process, "female" weakness of the will, "female" formlessness that led to doubt and ignorance—would come to an end. The tragedy of a fallen universe would cease.

A yearning to overcome "otherness" of any kind runs through the thought of Valentinus. The very existence of two distinct and opposed sexes condensed, with an intensity largely lacking in contemporary pagan and Jewish thought,[39] the sense that a tragic and unnecessary division was the cause of the misery under which all creation labored:

On the day when you were one you became two. But when you have become two, what will you do?[40]

It was awareness of that primal moment of division that had caused Christ to cry on the Cross:

My God, my God, why, O Lord, have you forsaken me? It was on the Cross that he said these words, for it was there that he was divided.[41]

37. *The Interpretation of Knowledge: N.H.C. XI* 10.34, J. D. Turner, trans., p. 430.
38. Williams, "Use of Gender Imagery," p. 210.
39. See esp. J. P. Mahé, "Le sens des symboles sexuels dans quelques textes hermétiques et gnostiques," pp. 123–145, esp. pp. 130 and 135, and M. Harl, "Adam et les deux arbres du Paradis,"—a model study.
40. *Gospel of Thomas* 11, p. 119.   41. *Gospel of Philip* 68.26, p. 141.

The transcendance of all divisions, even of a division as seemingly irremovable as that between male and female, was the surest sign that the redemption offered by Christ had come to the believer:

They said to Him: "Shall we then, as children, enter the Kingdom?" Jesus said to them: "When you make the two one . . . and when you make the male and the female into one and the same, so that the male shall not be male nor the female female . . . then you will enter the Kingdom."[42]

Hence the importance of his doctrine of the *syzygies* for Valentinus' notion of the redemption of the individual person. In its present un-redeemed state, the self was a fallen cosmos in miniature. It had sep-arated out into layers that had originally coinhered in a series of con-jugal pairs. The spirit of each individual was male to the random, female soul. But even the spirit was female to the dominant guardian angel that hovered, as yet undiscovered, close to it. Redemption took the form of a reunion with that guardian angel. Gnostic baptism reestab-lished the severed link between the conscious person and its angel, a being that stood for the latent, truest self. When once this happened, the divisions within the soul gave way to a new unity. The many lay-ers of the self would no longer conflict as they did in the unredeemed. Even the heavy flesh itself would rest more lightly on the "spiritual" person. Like an undone cloak, the body would come to hang gently on the spirit, ready to slip off forever at death.[43] For Valentinus and his followers, the only baptism that was decisive was baptism "into the angels." It linked the individual back to a long-hidden, unshakable identity: "For, by this, the female is said to be transformed into a male, and the church on earth becomes a company of angels."[44]

With his habitual caustic humor, Tertullian made great play with the Valentinian notion of redemption. Think of Marcus and Caius, he wrote, "solid, well-bearded" men, coming into the Bridal Chamber to receive the hot embrace of those all-male angels![45] What Tertullian deliberately ignored was that, for Valentinus, baptism into the angels was held to mark the final disappearance of all otherness. The aching sense of di-vision that had separated the spirit from its angelic self and the soul

---

42. *Gospel of Thomas* 22, p. 121.
43. *Gospel of Philip* 66.15, p. 140; *Gospel of Thomas* 21, p. 120.
44. Clement, *Excerpta ex Theodoto* 21.3, p. 98.   45. Tertullian, *Adv. Val.* 32.4.

from the spirit vanished, as a shadow slips away in the rising sun. It was a process that could take place within any man or woman.[46]

It is not easy to know what the Gnostic notion of redemption meant for the initiates' perception of their own sexual drives. Many layers of attitudes overlap in Gnostic texts. Gnostic literature of exhortation, for instance, demanded that the believers should first wrench their spirit free from a fallen universe. Man was a microcosm in a truly fearsome sense: body and soul partook of the qualities of a universe sustained by the frenetic energies of fallen powers. The vivid fire that Cicero had once sensed with pleasure, flickering through the veins of lovers as it shimmered in the distant stars, was presented by the Gnostics as a sinister, all-devouring, mindless flame.[47] To have intercourse was to open the human body to the firestorm that raged through the universe. Sexual desire was made to stand out in sharp relief as an enduring feature of the unredeemed human person: it stood for the headlong energy of a universe that was opposed to the cool tranquillity of the realm of unmoving spirit. Those who indulged in sexual passion "show that they are assisting the world."[48] No process could be more antithetical to the ethereal bonds that linked spirit to spirit than was physical procreation: sex was "the unclean rubbing that is from the fearful fire that came from the fleshly part."[49]

But the Gnostics, and most particularly the Valentinians, usually wrote for the redeemed. In the texts that deal with the state of the redeemed, the guttering out of the fire of sexual desire was treated as a sign of a profound mutation that might come slowly to the believer. By presenting sexual temptation as no more than a symbol of more deep-seated ills, and by acclaiming the transcendance of sexual desire as nothing less than a "resurrection" of the self, Gnostic spiritual guidance in the school of Valentinus looked forward directly to the wisdom of the Desert Fathers. The rise and fall of sexual desire enabled the spiritual guide to plumb the vast inner spaces of the initiate's soul.

For Valentinus, the human soul was peopled by a host of unruly spirits, of *pneumata*. These were incomplete, needy creatures, who used

---

46. See esp. A. F. J. Klijn, "The 'Single One' in the Gospel of Thomas."

47. Compare Cicero, *de natura deorum* 2.10.28 with Clement, *Excerpta ex Theodoto* 48.4, pp. 160–162.

48. *Testimony of Truth*: N.H.C. IX,3, 30, S. Giversen and B. A. Pearson, trans., p. 407; cf. M. Roberge, "Anthropologie et Anthropogonie dans la Paraphrase de Sem," pp. 245–246.

49. *Sophia of Jesus Christ*: N.H.C. II,4 108, D. M. Parrott, trans. p. 220.

the person to seek their own fulfillment, in the manner of a permanent, half-conscious state of possession. The *pneumata* were, as it were,
false *syzygies*. Like the syzygies, they also strained toward a primal
undividedness. But this was a unity achieved not through intimate
bonding with the spirit, but through the reverse: they bound the soul
ever more closely to the flesh. The restless presence of these *pneumata*,
each one perpetually seeking fulfillment in an invisible mate, accounted for the strength of the inverted urge toward unity that sought
expression in sexual love. Sexual desire betrayed the yearning of parts
of the soul itself for completion.[50]

Not all hearers of Valentinus could hope that they could bring unity
to the vortices that swirled in the labile regions of the soul. The Valentinians appear to have accepted the fact that many believers still
lived trapped in the lower life of the soul: they were called *psychikoi*,
as distinct from the *pneumatikoi*, persons already firmly ruled by their
commanding spirit. Mere renunciation of sexual activity was not, in
itself, enough to bring about the transformation that produced the
spiritual person: the problem lay deeper. "Let each of us dig down
after the root of evil that is within one, and let one pluck it out of
one's heart from the root."[51]

In the apocryphal Acts of John, a young man dramatically castrated
himself with a sickle, declaring, "There you have the pattern and cause
of all this!" He was warned by the Apostle that he should have reached
down yet further to eradicate "the unseen spring through which every
shameful emotion is stirred up and comes to light."[52]

It was thought prudent to respect the long, half-conscious labor of
the spirit in the soul rather than to commit oneself to premature continence. Married believers were tolerated by the Valentinians. They
provided the physical continuity that was necessary if the human race
were to offer to Christ the full harvest of its spiritual "seed," in the
form of many generations of believers, which would be gathered, in
due time, into the Place of Fullness.[53] Far from being an embattled
group of baptized continents, as were even the most discreet and sedentary among the Encratites, the Valentinians were a shadow image
of the normal urban church of the late second century. Married per-

50. *Gospel of Philip* 65.2ff., p. 139; see esp. J. E. Ménard, *L'Évangile selon Philippe*, p.
16.
51. *Gospel of Philip* 83.18–21, p. 149.   52. *Acts of John* 53–54, 2:241.
53. Clement, *Excerpta ex Theodoto* 67.3, p. 192.

sons received appropriate guidance. In a contemporary Gnostic group, we catch a glimpse of the realities of a situation in which many Christian initiates must have found themselves: when a young man was "too poor, too young or suffered from weak health," and could not for that reason get a bride, he was advised to approach his spiritual guide and say, "Brother, lay your hands upon me lest I sin."[54] The Valentinians solved the problem of married members, and of those who dearly wished to become married, by allowing a hierarchy of "spiritual" and "psychic" persons to develop within their own community.[55]

Yet within this loose and differentiated group, the authority of the inner core of leaders remained unshakable. It was rooted in nothing less than the stability of a universe restored to its first order. The Gnostic redeemed person radiated a vast serenity in which sexual desire had been swallowed up along with all other signs of inner division. Even their bodies lay gently on them: the flesh needed neither to be feared nor loved; it would soon drop from them.[56] Such persons could reenact, indifferently to male and female disciples, the absorbing intimacy by which Christ had "possessed" the soul of Mary Magdalen.[57] The accusations of sexual immorality made against almost all Gnostic teachers made plain that this was a matter of no small importance in the second-century Christian church.

The Valentinian study-circles stand out as consisting of intimate gatherings where spiritual men and women could mingle at the feet of a sage, in the ancient and authoritative manner of a philosopher's study-circle. In Judaism, rabbis were remembered to have declared that women had no place in the intense and intimate atmosphere in which male students studied the Law: to teach Torah to one's daughter was tantamount to teaching her immorality.[58] In Carthage, Tertullian was prepared to expatiate on the perils of an unveiled girl in church:

There she is patted all over by the roving eyes of total strangers, is tickled by the fingers of those who point her out, and, the darling of us all, she warms to it amid assiduous hugs and kisses.[59]

54. Clement, *Strom.* 3.1.2, Henry Chadwick, trans., p. 41.
55. H. A. Green, "Ritual in Valentinian Gnosticism: A Sociological Interpretation," pp. 118–123.
56. *Gospel of Philip* 66.1, p. 139.   57. Irenaeus, *Against the Heresies* 1.6.3.
58. *Babylonian Talmud: Soṭah* 21b, A. Cohen, trans., p. 108.
59. Tertullian, *de virginibus velandis* 14.5, E. Dekkers, ed., *Corpus Christianorum*, 2:1224.

The Valentinians were the exact contemporaries of Tertullian and the rabbis. By claiming that the redeemed had overcome sexual desire, Gnostics were able to accept women as equal partners in the intense group-life of a Christian intelligentsia.

The Valentinian study-circles raised in an acute form the issues of spiritual friendship and of spiritual continuity that had been addressed in other Christian groups. For their initiates, the filaments of teacher-pupil relations and the invisible bond of like-minded souls, established by shared spiritual guidance, constituted the true unity of the church. All other bonds seemed flaccid to them.[60] Theirs was an unbreakable "unity of perfect thought," as light but as pervasive as the mingled scents of a rose garden.[61] "Spiritual" persons moved with ease in a system of thought where everything in the material world referred inward to the vivid reality of the spiritual Place of Fullness. For the redeemed, the body was no longer a place of danger, where the restless fire lurked: it was, rather, a translucent screen on which shadows played. The most intense relationships of this world—marriage, love and parenthood—were not shocking or repugnant to them. Such things were mere empty "names." The believer read them as signs, mercifully distributed throughout the visible world. They referred back to processes and sensations that happened with true intensity at their "root," in the vibrant life of a purely spiritual world.[62] Love "For ever warm and still to be enjoyed,"[63] the happy merging of two beings, an exuberant fertility: these were not disowned by the believer. They were sought, instead, at the undivided core of the universe, in the Place of Fullness. They were not to be found through the body, nor along the shattered fringes of the physical world.

This strongly symbolic mentality made the physical world transparent to mighty spiritual events. Because of this, the Valentinians contributed directly to the spinning of one fine strand in the sensibility of continent Christians of all shades of opinion. Along with the Christians of the Great Church, they presented the intimate passing on of an irreplaceable, saving wisdom as the truest form of procreation. Teaching and baptism, and not the begetting of children, made the best provision for the future. Natural, social man gained continuity through physical intercourse; but such intercourse produced only fod-

---

60. *Apocalypse of Peter* 78, p. 343.   61. *Gospel of Truth* 34.25, p. 45.
62. *Gospel of Philip* 53.20–54, pp. 132–133.   63. William Keats, *Ode to a Grecian Urn*.

der for death. Truly lasting continuity came through spiritual birth, due to spiritual intercourse.[64]

In order to be born again, the initiate hung on the lips of an inspired guide: "Whoever will drink from my mouth [Christ had said] will become like me."[65] Hence the charged associations of the act of kissing in Christian teaching circles. Valentinians gave their own interpretation to the traditional Christian kiss of fellowship: it was by the light touch of mouth and breath, and not through the hot genitals, that the firmest links in the chain of true humanity were formed: "For it is by a kiss that the perfect conceive and give birth."[66]

Precisely for that reason, sexual intercourse could be abandoned. Physical marriage, the *gamos*, was drained of significance by its mighty spiritual archetype. The *pastos*, the secret, tapestry-hung bridal tent, blazing with light, now overshadowed the social and physical joining of mere marriage. Marriage was a dark and shadowy affair compared with the intimate and insubstantial moment when, through initiation after long teaching, the initiate joined his or her spirit to the angel guide on the spiritual marriage bed of baptism.[67] Through teaching and through solemn baptismal initiation, the Christian church as a whole—and not only the sheltered study-groups within it—had found a strange, high-arched means of continuity that could look past both marriage and the grave. It had discovered the sources of its own continuity. Unlike the ancient city, where generation replaced generation through intercourse, the Church enjoyed a continuity that "belongs not to desire but to the will."[68]

There was a certain symbolic truth in the bizarre pagan slur against Christians, that "They actually revere the genitals of their director . . . and adore his sexual organs as parents of their being."[69]

Through the efforts of a generation of great teachers, the Christian church had become, in effect, an institution possessed of the ethereal secret of perpetual self-reproduction. This secret was made all the more plain once the public leaders of the church, the bishops and clergy, came to abandon the normal demographic duties appropriate to married householders. The continence of its clergy and of its spiritual guides

64. Clement, *Strom.* 3.6.45; *Gospel of Philip* 58.28, p. 135.
65. *Gospel of Thomas* 108, p. 129.   66. *Gospel of Philip* 59, p. 135.
67. *Gospel of Philip* 86, p. 151; on the *pastos*, see C. Vatin, *Recherches sur le mariage et la condition de la femme mariée a l'époque hellénistique*, pp. 211–228.
68. *Gospel of Philip* 86, p. 151.
69. Minucius Felix, *Octavius* 9.4, G. H. Rendall ed. and trans., p. 337.

announced to the Roman world of the late second century that the church was a new form of public body, confident that it possessed its own means of securing a perpetual existence.

Sing, o barren, that didst not bear: break forth into singing and cry aloud, thou that dost not travail with child: for more are the children of the desolate one than the children of the married wife, saith the Lord.[70]

It is to a younger generation of teachers that we must now turn, to Clement of Alexandria and then, a generation later, to the great Origen. In their works we can see what alternatives, if any, other segments of the Christian church were prepared to offer to the views canvassed by the Encratites and by the disciples of Valentinus.

70. Isaiah 54:1.

SIX

"A Faint Image of Divine Providence": Clement of Alexandria

Clement arrived in Alexandria around 180, still in search of a spiritual guide. He had already passed through the hands of many Christian teachers, drawn from as far apart as Sicily and Syria. Tatian may even have been among them.[1] An air of mystery and of far-ranging "apostolic" horizons hung around the man to whom he finally attached himself. Pantaenus was a philosopher known as an "ornament of the Stoic school." A devoted Christian, he had been appointed "to preach the Gospel of Christ to the peoples of the East and travelled as far as

---

1. Clement, *Stromateis* 1.1.1.11:2, p. 8. On Clement in general, I have received most help from Walter Völker, *Der wahre Gnostiker nach Clemens Alexandrinus*, Texte und Untersuchungen 57; André Méhat, *Étude sur les "Stromates" de Clément d'Alexandrie*, Patristica Sorbonensia; and Salvatore R. C. Lilla, *Clement of Alexandria: A Study in Christian Platonism and Gnosticism*. See also Dietmar Wyrwa, *Die christliche Platonaneignung in den Stromateis des Clemens von Alexandrien*. I have cited the respective volume and page numbers of the three volumes of the works of Clement edited by O. Stählin, as follows: *Protrepticus* and *Paedagogus*, Clemens Alexandrinus 1, Griechische christliche Schriftsteller 12; *Stromateis* 1–6, Clemens Alexandrinus 2, Griechische christliche Schriftsteller 52 (15); *Stromateis* 7 and 8, Clemens Alexandrinus 3, Griechische christliche Schriftsteller 17*.

India"—possibly, to make contact with Christian groups among the trading communities established in the Persian Gulf and along the Malabar Coast.[2] Settled in Alexandria as a presbyter and as head of a school for the instruction of converts—the so-called "Catechetical School"—Pantaenus was succeeded by Clement, to whom he had first passed on his teaching in the expected manner.[3] That is, he "begot" his disciple "through the mouth"—through intensive verbal communication, of which not a word survives, or was intended to survive, in written form.[4] For Clement, his own extensive written works were tinged with a studied sadness. They were weak, Clement wrote, "when compared with that spirit full of grace, whom I was privileged to hear."[5] Dry river beds down which a torrent of life-giving words had once poured from the lips of Pantaenus, Clement's own works now lie heavy on the shelves of modern libraries. For Clement, they were "a remedy against forgetfulness, a mere image and outline of the vigorous and soul-shaking discourses of that man."[6]

Despite his principal role as an intimate guide of souls, Clement was one of the most extensive writers in the pre-Constantinian Church. He is surely the one we think we know best. The unflagging, gentle precision of his vignettes of Christian deportment charm us into believing that we can be with him in the Alexandria of the second century— dining, holding *conversazioni*,[7] walking with sprightly steps across the well-clipped lawns of a Hellenistic suburban villa,[8] even, on occasions, retiring discreetly to bed with his spouse—where, among other things, he declares himself in favor of the "natural gymnasium" of a hard bed, a sovereign cure for backache.[9]

---

2. Eusebius, *Ecclesiastical History* 5.10. On the trade between Egypt and India, see now H. Harrauer and P. J. Sijpesteijn, "Ein neues Dokument zu Roms Indienhandel."

3. On this school, see most recently Annick Martin, "Aux origines de l'église copte," pp. 35–36, and on the relation of Pantaenus to it, see Colin H. Roberts, *Manuscript and Belief in Early Christian Egypt*, p. 54. One must be careful never to exaggerate the institutional formality of the catechetical school, nor of any other "school" in late antiquity: see John Dillon, "The Academy in the Middle Platonic Period."

4. The same is true of Plotinus' master, Ammonius: Plotinus himself did not begin to commit his teachings to writing until after some twenty-two years—Porphyry, *Life of Plotinus* 3.

5. *Strom.* 1.14.1.1: 2, p. 10.

6. Ibid. 1.1.11. 1: 2, p. 86: See Méhat, *Étude*, pp. 287–290.

7. *Paedagogus* 2.1.4.4: 1, p. 156.

8. Ibid. 2.10.104.3.2: 1, p. 219. See the delightful and perceptive introduction of H. I. Marrou to *Clément d'Alexandrie: Le Pédagogue*, pp. 41–53 and 89.

9. *Paed.* 1.9.77.3: 1, p. 135.

Yet this is merely the Clement who survives: it is the impression we derive from his *Exhortation to the Pagans*, his *Paidagôgos*, his *Stromateis*, or *Miscellanies*, and his homily on *The Rich Man's Salvation*. The other Clement is almost entirely lost to us: Clement the churchman; Clement the author of lost works *On Easter*, of *Against Judaizers;* Clement the compiler of the *Hypotyposes*, the first complete Biblical commentary in the history of the church.[10] What later generations delighted in, and preserved by copying the writings that we now possess, was the huge cultural serenity of the man. He presented himself as Christ's gardener. He would cut twigs from the rank, dried-back and brittle bushes of pagan literature, and graft them on to the succulent root-stock of Christ's truth. Thus engrafted, they would grow richer, more robust fruit in the orchard of the Church.[11] In Clement's gentle hands, the graft took with amazing ease.

For all this, we must never forget that other Christians, and not pagans, were the true pace setters of Clement's delightful classicism. A teacher in Alexandria, who had traveled widely, Clement knew that his charges were exposed to interpretations of Christianity far more radical than were his own. In all likelihood, they had passed through the hands of austere spiritual guides—the Encratite followers of Tatian, Gnostics of the school of Valentinus. The close links between Alexandria and Palestine brought the piety of Encratite circles in Syria to Clement's doorstep.[12] The role of Gnostic teachers within the Catechetical School of Alexandria placed the views of Valentinus and his followers in the foreground of his concerns.[13]

These groups, if each in a very different manner, appeared to Clement to preach a Christianity of discontinuity—a Christianity of the "born-again." They had claimed to be able to tear "reborn" believers clear of the fabric of normal life. The Encratites claimed that they could bring to an instant halt the natural processes out of which God, in His providence, had woven, through married intercourse, the humble and necessary fabric of the human race. The Gnostics claimed to be able to

10. Eusebius, *Ecclesiastical History* 16.13.2–3; see F. di Benedetto, "Un nuovo frammento delle Ipotiposi di Clemente Alessandrino," and C. Duckworth and E. Osborn, "Clement of Alexandria's *Hypotyposeis:* a French Eighteenth-Century Sighting," pp. 74–83.

11. *Strom.* 6.1.2.1–4 and 7.18.111.1–2: 2, pp. 422–423 and 3, pp. 78–79: see Méhat, *Étude*, pp. 524–528.

12. Roberts, *Manuscript and Belief*, p. 54–60.   13. Ibid., pp. 49–54.

bypass, through a moment of instant "redemption," the long moral and intellectual discipline required of every Christian.

Here we are dealing with a head-on confrontation. Contemptuous of the Encratites, Clement always took the Valentinian image of the "redeemed" person very seriously indeed.[14] He passionately believed that the slow and patient labor of Christ on the soul produced men and women quite as profoundly changed as were any who had undergone the "mutation" associated with a Gnostic conversion. To him, these were the "true Gnostics." It is a term that Clement took for granted: for him, as for his opponents, such a term summed up humanity at its highest. Perfect Christian "Sages" (and I shall use this, less value-laden term throughout), such persons looked at the world from the far side of a huge mutation of their inner being. But, unlike the converts of more radical groups, Clement's Christian sages gazed more serenely at their past life, and at the society and culture in which they had lived. Their past spread out beneath them like a pleasant landscape, its once-accustomed landmarks now shrunk to miniature proportions from their high viewing-point. Though dwindled by distance, they had not been wished away. The absorption of a conventional culture in the pagan schools, the solemn duties of the marriage-bed, the microcosmic "providence" involved in the care of children and of a household: all these had played a necessary role in the earlier stages of the development of the spiritually mature Christian. Far from constituting an unsurmountable bar to spiritual perfection, the cares of an active life, even the act of married intercourse itself, had served to tune the strings that would, in old age, produce the well-tempered sound of a perfected sage.

Clement's extensive use of pagan, Greek sources was the result of a carefully considered alliance. He drew on the rules for disciplined deportment, commended by philosophers to the Greek elites of his age, in order to wrap the believer in a web of minute, seemingly insignificant patterns of daily living. But every detail of these codes unobtrusively communicated a view of the world, of the human person and of society that was soundproof to the shrill claims of the "born-again." An instinctive sense of form, an alert sensitivity to others, and a deep belief that the body could convey messages as precisely as any words could do had lain at the heart of the pagan notion of moral

14. Alain Le Boulluec, *La notion d'hérésie dans la littérature grecque: iie–iiie siecles*, 2:329–332.

refinement. The codes taught by philosophers, and applied to the needs of the public man by a cultivated urban aristocracy, were appropriated and transformed by Clement. They were taken back from the tense and power-conscious world of civic notables and applied to the more sheltered needs of the believing household. The result was to provide the Christian believer with an equivalent (in its effects if not in its underlying assumptions) of the *halakha* that the rabbis had begun to elaborate for conscientious Jews. Clement's writings communicated a sense of the God-given importance of every moment of daily life, and especially of the life of the household. By free acts of conscious moral craftsmanship, the believer could create, within the home, a pool of circumstantial order in the midst of an untidy world.

The *Paidagôgos* was written, "To say how each of us ought to conduct himself in respect to the body, or rather how to regulate the body itself."[15]

The book was a triumph of "paedagogic reason." Clement, the gifted teacher, "extorts the essential while seeming to demand the insignificant."[16] At first sight, the *Paidogôgos* strikes us as egregiously fussy. We are spared few details. We meet the Christian at table: "Keeping the hand and couch and chin free of grease-stains; possessing the grace of the countenance undisturbed, and committing no indecorum in the act of swallowing."[17]

He must burp gently,[18] sit correctly,[19] and refrain from scratching his ears.[20] The perfect tuning of body and soul must be reflected in the most delicate instrument of all—in the voice. Greek and Near Eastern ears had a sensitivity to the human voice that takes some mental effort if the modern Anglo-Saxon imagination is to recapture it.[21] Clement shrank from the coarse explosion of the laugh. Its sudden, instinctive release seemed like a deliberate attempt to sabotage the measured flow of conscious human words, that echoed, in controlled, intelligible sounds, the still, abiding order of the divine Word, of Christ, within

15. *Paed.* 2.1.1.2: 1, p. 154.
16. Pierre Bourdieu, *Outline of a Theory of Practice*, p. 94.
17. *Paed.* 2.1.13.1: 1, p. 163.　　18. 2.2.33.4 and 2.7.60.2: 1, pp. 176 and 193.
19. 2.7.54.3: 1, p. 190.　　20. 2.7.60.4: 1, p. 193.
21. Note the attempt of the soldier-Emperor Macrinus to imitate Marcus Aurelius: "speaking to people at audiences very slowly and laboriously so that frequently he could not be heard because of his low voice"—a brave attempt by a military man at "philosophical" serenity of tone! Herodian, *History* 5.2.3.

the soul.[22] He wrote with genuine anger of those who summoned slaves
by snapping their fingers: to deny slaves contact through the gentle
harmonies of the human voice was to deny them their humanity.[23]

Seated round the table, their great, silvery beards "blossoming with
the solemnity of long experience,"[24] the tranquil patriarchs whom
Clement loved so dearly must learn, among other things, how to set
tongue-tied boys and girls at their ease with an appropriate, gentle
joke (Clement, of course, could suggest one such joke).[25] They must
learn not to speak in a pious mumble to deaf persons: "for that would
show extreme insensitivity."[26] Their character well-anchored in old age,
they could afford to take the occasional nip of mulled wine against the
winter's cold.[27] Their ordered mirth would bubble up among them in
harmonious chuckles.[28]

Let the look be steady, and the turning and movement of the neck and the
motions of the hands in conversation be decorous. In a word, the Christian
is characterised by composure, tranquillity, calmness and peace.[29]

Altogether, if genius can be defined as an infinite capacity for taking
pains, the *Paidagôgos* reveals Clement as a moral genius. For such detail carried the weight of his message: the human person "attains its
destined end through the body, the soul's consort and ally."[30] For, "In
us it is not only the spirit which ought to be sanctified, but also our
behavior, manner of life and our body."[31]

The end product of such grooming was, in many ways, a reassur-
ingly old-fashioned figure. Beneath the charming Attic guise of Clement's refined Christian lay the "single-hearted" believer of the Early
Christian communities. "Virgin speech, tender and free of fraud," was
what Clement yearned for in his gentle householders, much as Hermas had done, two generations previously, in Rome.[32] Copies of *The
Shepherd* of Hermas circulated among the provincial churches of Egypt.[33]
The Christians who read *The Shepherd* probably lived a life close to such
ancient, unpretentious notions. They meant more to them than they
did to the ferocious intellectuals of Alexandria.[34] *Népiotés*, the artless
simplicity, candor and lack of affectation of the child, were qualities

22. *Paed.* 2.5.46.2: 1, p. 185.   23. 2.7.60.5: 1, p. 193.   24. 3.3.18.3: 1, p. 247.
25. 2.7.57.1: 1, p. 191.   26. 2.7.59.1: 1, p. 192.   27. 2.2.22.4: 1, p. 169.
28. 2.5.46.2: 1, p. 185.   29. 2.7.60.5: 1, p. 193.   30. 1.13.102.3: 1, p. 151.
31. *Strom.* 3.6.47.1: 2, p. 217.   32. *Paed.* 1.5.19.3: 1, p. 101.
33. Roberts, *Manuscript and Belief*, pp. 21–22.   34. Ibid. pp. 71–72.

dear to Clement's heart.[35] For Clement, the notion condensed a whole moral and social program. It assumed that the Christian believer had remained a full member of society. Married or unmarried, male or female, young or old, those who had remained children at heart brought into the midst of a cunning and abrasive world a touch of the original, unaffected courtesy of Adam, "nature's gentleman," and of Christ, the new Adam, who had walked among men with a childlike gentleness.

Clement's ideal of the Christian life was permeated by a deep sense of the service of God, as Creator of the universe, combined with an awareness of the presence, in the soul of the believer, of His Word, Christ—an intimate companion, to Whom every detail of the believer's life must be referred:

The pure, pellucid Jesus, the eye that watches in the flesh, the translucent Word . . .[36] sharing one house with us, sharing our deepest counsels, speaking within the soul, sitting at table within it, sharing in the moral effort of our life.[37]

To do justice to this notion, and to the program of lifelong moral grooming that it implied, Clement fell back instinctively on the Stoic views which, along with Platonic metaphysics, were part and parcel of the intellectual *koiné* of the age.[38] Stoicism provided Clement with precisely the language that he needed. The Stoic Sage had also been presented as a person committed to the unquestioning service of a higher power, made possible by a vivid sense of intimacy with that power. The Sage was free to collaborate, joyfully and ungrudgingly, with the hidden action of the Supreme Mind, as it triumphantly summoned beauty and order out of the apparent flux of the material world.[39] Far from being a philosophy that had encouraged inactivity, the Stoic showed his virtues in an active life. The monarch who accepted the

---

35. Marrou, *Le Pédagogue*, p. 25. R. B. Tollinton, *Clement of Alexandria*, 1:288–289— "lingering on the phraseology with a sort of affection for its associations."

36. *Paed.* 2.12.118.5: 1, p. 228.   37. *Protrepticus* 59.2: 1, p. 46.

38. See esp. Lilla, *Clement, passim,* on the Platonic elements in Clement's thought, which can never be reduced to simple Stoicism.

39. A. A. Long, *Hellenistic Philosophy*, pp. 118–209, is an exceptionally lucid statement of the "classical" Stoic system; A. J. Festugière, *La Révélation d'Hermès Trismégiste*, 2:260–309 is a fine evocation of the human qualities associated with such a system; Pierre Hadot, *Exercices spirituels et philosophie antique*, pp. 27–41, is an unequaled account of the therapy involved in Stoic moral grooming.

40. Festugière, *Hermès Trismégiste*, 2:299.

cares of ordering the state as a "noble slavery";[40] the athlete, whose nimble, fine-tuned body danced and swayed in the perpetual boxing match between the mind and the erratic blows of fortune;[41] the volunteer soldier, always ready to take on yet another dangerous mission, to respond to yet another call to face the manifold experiences of this world, and to treat as equally "heaven-sent" the opportunity to experience joy, grief, triumph, or death—these were the images that summed up the life of the conscientious Stoic.[42]

To achieve a state of high-hearted readiness, the individual *ego* had to undergo "a total transformation of its way of perceiving the world"; the "inner climate" of the mind itself must change.[43] Every situation was to be perceived for exactly what it was—not as an occasion to experience fear, frustration, or inappropriate hope, but as an opportunity for joyful service.[44]

What stood in the way of such a state of lucid and alert availability were what are misleadingly called, in modern summaries of Stoicism, "the passions." The "passions" are best seen as tendencies built up within the *ego*, which could force the sage to overreact to any situation, to cathect it with a charge of personal, egotistic significance that distorted its true meaning. The "passions" colored perceptions of the outside world with nonexistent sources of fear, anxiety, and hope; or else they bathed it in a false glow of pleasure and potential satisfaction.[45]

This was an austerely introspective doctrine. The passions might have their distant origin in the body; but it was only when they had brought about a change in the inner climate of the mind that they were to be eradicated. As physical creatures, human beings could not avoid "urges"—*orexeis*. Hunger, dumb fear of extinction, the sensations necessarily associated with sexual desire: these were the unavoidable, muted creakings of the biological self. They could never be abandoned. Consciousness of them rose in the mind like thin vapors.[46] If undispersed by vigilant reflection, such vapors could mist over the entire inner climate of the mind, wrapping it in a thick fog of "passions." Only a meticulous rhythm of life, in which the body's stirrings were minutely assessed in terms of what were legitimate and what were illegitimate

41. Ibid. p. 300.   42. Ibid. pp. 285, 297 and 328–330.
43. Hadot, *Exercices*, p. 22.   44. Ibid. pp. 129–130.
45. Well defined in *Strom.* 2.13.59.6: 2, p. 145; see Lilla, *Clement*, p. 85.
46. Völker, *Der wahre Gnostiker*, p. 129.

expressions of its instinctual needs, would enable the sage to maintain the infinitely precious lucidity and serenity of vision associated with the "passionless state."

Clement identified himself wholeheartedly with the Stoic notion of *apatheia*, with the ideal of a life freed of the passions. Faced by so austere a doctrine, with such a long future ahead of it in the Christian Church, we must be careful to define exactly what Clement envisioned in such a life. It was not as drastic as it might seem at first sight. Clement's language, like that of his pagan contemporaries, was consciously aesthetic. The sage was an artist, working with loving care on mind and body. To "form" a life, in Clement's circles, involved no harsh buffeting of the body. It was, rather, a process as meticulous, as exacting, and as loving as was the attention that a literary man (such as Clement himself) must give to the right placing of every word, to the correct tone and balance of every phrase.[47] It was a polishing away of those ugly excrescences that blurred the true, sharp form of the person.[48] Clement had little doubt that this was an exacting process. But it was very definitely not a process that demanded the repression of feeling. Passions were not what we tend to call feelings: they were, rather, complexes which hindered the true expression of feelings. Clement's most tender images of the Christian life were images of unswerving, eager activity set loose to love and serve the Lord:

Bridle of colts untamed
Over our wills presiding;
Wing of unwavering birds
Our flight securely guiding.
Rudder of youth unbending,
Firm against every shock.[49]

Nothing, therefore, could be more misleading than to treat Clement's view of the final goal of the Christian as if it were a state in which feeling, and even activity, would be suspended. To call Clement "almost the caricature of a puritan" is to caricature both Clement and his Stoic sources.[50] What Clement envisioned, in the ideal of *apatheia*, was

47. *Strom.* 7.11.71.6: 2, p. 51.   48. Hadot, *Exercices*, p. 48–49.

49. *Paedagogus*, 3.12.101.3 (*Concluding Hymn* 1–4): 1, p. 291, in the poetic translation of A. Cleveland Coxe, *Ante-Nicene Fathers*, 2:295.

50. Raoul Wortley, *Connaissance religieuse et herméneutique chez Clément d'Alexandrie*, pp. 126–127.

a state of final serenity of purpose. No longer held back by the fears and uncertainties engendered by the passions, good actions might spring from right knowledge as gently as a shadow fell from a body.[51] Christ loved to bend His ear to hear such serene "sporting" among His saints on earth: "to sport and to be glad in the endurance of what is good, and in the administration of what is good, holding high festival with God. . . . For *such a sport Jove sports.*"[52]

The last citation, from Heraclitus, dropped off Clement's pen without a quiver of doubt. To become like God was to share in the huge good nature of an Olympian Zeus, playing merrily within a beautiful universe.

Clement's serene Christian sage was to be no recluse. He was an active teacher, even an "administrator." His "sport" was the care of souls, even the government of the church. Like Moses, the sage bore a "kingly soul."[53] Nor was the Christian sage a fleshless abstraction, a mere pious ideal. In pagan thought, the serene state of *apatheia* was enumerated as a "canon of excellence" by which to judge the perfected sage, "if any candidate were forthcoming."[54] For Christians, the candidate for excellence was already present in the figure of Christ. Christ's servants, the succession of apostles, teachers, and martyrs up to Clement's own days, made clear that the abiding presence of Christ within the soul could, indeed, polish the life of the believer into a clear reflection of His own life. To suggest otherwise angered Clement greatly.[55]

Nowhere is the overriding concern of Clement to produce the perfect Christian sage more obvious than in his views on sexuality and marriage. His *Paidagôgos,* and the discussion of marriage and sexuality in the third book of the *Miscellanies,* were written for the "moderate" Christian, for the *metriopathés*—that is, for believers who had not yet reached the huge serenity associated with the sage, whose passions were no longer in need of anxious control.[56]

It was to such moderate married Christians—probably young married men and women and children approaching marriageable age— that the Encratite image of sexuality presented the greatest peril. The Encratites had charged sexuality with heavy associations. They had presented it as a privileged indicator of the fallen state of mankind,

51. *Strom.* 7.13.82.7: 3, p. 59.   52. *Paed.* 1.5.22.1: 1, p. 103.
53. *Strom.* 6.15.115.3: 2, p. 490; see Méhat, *Étude,* p. 376.
54. Long, *Hellenistic Philosophy,* p. 207.   55. *Strom.* 6.9.71–72: 2, pp. 467–468.
56. Lilla, *Clement,* pp. 104–113; Méhat, *Étude,* pp. 506–510.

and had advocated *enkrateia*—in effect, an abrupt renunciation of marriage—as the privileged instrument by which Christians could bring to an end the terrible necessity of the grave. No attitude could have been more deeply repugnant to Clement: "They set their hopes on their private parts."[57] A man of the ancient world through and through, death, not sexuality, still stood for Clement as the most abiding affliction of the human race. *All flesh is grass and all the glory of man is as the flower of the grass* did not mean for him that intercourse was a waste of time: it meant the exact opposite—that the frail flesh, so easily withered by death, must be renewed in every generation by procreation; otherwise the *word of the Lord* would not *abide*. "Without the body, how could the divine plan for us in the church achieve its end?"[58]

Clement, our master of "paedagogic reason," was only too willing to tell Christian couples exactly how to conduct their married intercourse. Modern readers, understandably enough, wish that he had not done so. At the beginning of the century, our paedagogue was held to have said far too much:

He takes his readers at times into the most intimate details of the relationship of the sexes, which we should only feel it natural to discuss in a medical treatise. . . . Perhaps what he felt it right to attempt in the lecture room and the published book is best done under modern conditions in the consulting room of the doctor.[59]

Today, by contrast, he is more usually berated for having admitted too little.[60] We have already noticed the tendency of the Greek writers under the Roman Empire to invest married intercourse with portentous overtones of ideal order. They tended to speak of the sexual joining of the couples as if it were an act from which erotic satisfaction must be excluded. Clement reached out to such writings, and, in so doing, he caricatured them. The late classical tendency to demand order even in the act of love reached its peak in Clement's discussion of marriage in the *Paidagôgos*. Moses, he wrote, had been prudent to forbid the children of Israel to eat the flesh of the hyaena. For the sexual habits of the hyaena left much to be desired: the disreputable beast, he pointed out, had intercourse frequently, in a variety of po-

57. *Strom.* 3.18.109.3: 2, p. 247.   58. 3.17.103.3: 2, pp. 343–344.
59. Tollinton, *Clement*, 1:272, 274.
60. C. Mondésert–H. I. Marrou, *Clément d'Alexandrie: Le Pédagogue*, Sources chrétiennes 108:164 *n* 1 and 184 *n* 5: "Perspective étroite."

sitions, and even at times when the female was pregnant.[61] His married Christians were not to allow themselves such liberties in bed.

What mattered for Clement was that married intercourse should be approached in the Stoic manner, as a conscious action, undertaken in the service of God. For that reason, it could not be set apart from the harmonious ordering of the Christian life. The marriage bed must not be like Penelope's loom. The silken threads of Christian deportment, woven so carefully around the person in the daylight hours, must not be torn apart at night.[62] With Clement, the disciplined sexuality of Judaism and of the Early Christian communities was subtly hardened by its infusion with the sharp aesthetic sensibility of a Greek. The maximization of "pleasure" in the sexual act, through the choice of differing positions and through the continuance of sexual activity beyond the periods strictly necessary for the conception of a child, were deemed "vulgar and plebeian."[63] Untidy tumblings were incongruous in the finely tuned figures of potential sages, for whom even a word or a gesture should not be out of place.[64] As for the *charis*, the "graciousness" created by intercourse—that indefinable quality of mutual trust and affection gained through the pleasure of the bed itself—which even the dignified Plutarch took for granted: Clement's stark insistence that intercourse should take place only for the begetting of children caused the delicate bloom of such a notion to vanish forever from late antique Christian thought.[65]

Clement had allowed himself to be maneuvered into a stance which pagan moralists had had the good sense to avoid. The norms of sexual conduct had remained somewhat peripheral matters for them. But Clement could not afford to imitate their reticence. He was a Christian writing for Christians faced by attacks on married intercourse of quite unprecedented circumstantiality. Encratite arguments against sex demanded answers taken from the very heart of the marriage bed. Clement told his readers, in a concrete and fastidious manner, that a well-ordered sexuality was not, in itself, a "bestial" act. Yet in so doing, he moved the center of gravity of ancient attitudes to the grooming and control of the body out of their accustomed, daytime setting. They came to rest on the Christian couple in bed.

61. *Paed.* 2.10.83.3: 1, p. 208.   62. 2.10.97.2: 1, p. 215.
63. 2.10.93.1: 1, p. 213.   64. *Strom.* 7.11.71.6: 3, p. 51.
65. Plutarch, *Dialogue on Love* 769AB: see Michel Foucault, *Le Souci de Soi*, pp. 238–239; R. Hurley, trans. *The Care of the Self*, pp. 206–207.

It was a heavy weight for anyone to bear in such a situation. In pagan circles, the tests of the refined person had been extremely public. Contemporaries watched individuals in their public *personae*, speaking, standing, at the table, reacting, usually in public, to grief, fear and anger. In such contexts, it had been legitimate to expect that the sage should not move so much as a finger without reasoned deliberation. Such deportment, however, could hardly be expected of his penis.[66] Yet Clement took that fatal step. The supreme test of the "well-tuned" soul shifted from its ancient setting—the banquet, the tribunal, the highly public deathbed—into a more intimate, more strictly sexual, scenario. It was in the bed itself that the ancient contest of reason and the passions came to be fought out most clearly and with the greatest circumstantiality.

Clement, however, did not expect his charges to suffer as exquisitely on such topics as later Christian moralists, in certain Christian regions, came to insist that they should. His sense of the solemn service of God overrode his casuistry. We simply do not know with what rituals—with what prayers, with what gestures, with what occult precautions—the Christian couple of the second century settled down to collaborate with their Creator. Fragments of Jewish lore of this and later times suggest that Christian intercourse was not the antiseptic act of reason that it might appear to be in cold print.[67] The "agreement of a controlled marriage"[68] need not have been an entirely pallid matter. We know what Clement thought about that other point where mind and physical reflex met in the human body—the voice. This may provide an analogy with which to approach his attitude to the experience of physical release in intercourse. The uncontrolled guffaw appalled him. But he liked to dwell on the slow, melodious chuckle of the saints: "harmoniously relaxing the austerity and over-tension of our serious pursuits."[69] For all we know, Clement may have taken for granted that the young Christian couple would come together in bed in a similar relaxed mood.

As for Clement's grey-haired sages, nothing whatever prevented such persons from having once performed their marital duties in this measured manner. Sexual activity, in itself, carried with it no stigma that

---

66. *Paed.* 2.10.90.2: 1, p. 211.

67. See, e.g., *Babylonian Talmud: Niddah* 16b, trans. I. Epstein, p. 11 on the angel of conception; note the prayer in *Tobit* 8:5–8.

68. *Strom.* 3.12.82.3: 2, p. 233.   69. *Paed.* 2.5.46.2: 1, p. 185.

might debar the Christian from achieving perfection in Christ. Whether such a person, once perfected, would continue to be sexually active was another point, and a somewhat academic one. Clement's "moderate" Christians were the sexually active younger members of the community. As the final serenity of the sage was not the result of some instant mutation, this serenity would usually have come to the believer late in life. And intercourse was not a matter for old men. Clement was robustly insensitive to the emphasis placed by many of his contemporaries on the permanent, menacing ache of sexual desire. Sexual desire was not, for him, a palpable symbol, within the human body, of the sinister *perpetuum mobile* of a fallen world. He did not think in terms of "the bitterness of the fire that burns in the bodies of men, burning them night and day."[70]

Sexual differentiation, and the growth in young persons of a charged sexual awareness of others, were mere crevasses that opened, for a time, between the delicious indeterminacy of the prepubertal young and the serenity of an old age, "all passion spent."[71] There was no reason why the sage who, in middle age, had transcended the need to have children might not have begotten them, as a baptized Christian, in his youth.

What mattered far more for Clement was that the spiritually mature Christian might often find himself or herself at the head of a large family. Like a Hellenistic monarch in miniature, to preside over a household was to be "a faint image of the Divine Providence."[72]

This was a point of some importance in the conditions of the late second century. Clement's church, like the community addressed by Hermas in Rome, had remained a loose confederation of believing households. Clement tended to view the world from the perspective of these householders. Many must have been his pupils, many more would have entrusted their children to him. Unlike other, more radical spiritual fathers, Clement seems notably untouched by fear of the family. *When two or three are gathered in My name* meant, for Clement, father, mother, and child praying in a Christian home.[73] Clement insisted that husband and wife could serve Christ together "without

70. *The Book of Thomas the Contender: N.H.C.II,7* 139, *The Nag Hammadi Library*, p. 190.
71. *Paed.* 1.4.10.3: 1, p. 96; *Strom.* 6.12.99–100: 2, pp. 481–482.
72. *Strom.* 7.11.70.7: 3, p. 51.   73. 3.10.68.1: 2, p. 226.

distraction." In citing Paul in this way, Clement showed sublime indifference to the original intention of the Apostle's words.[74]

By accepting marriage, and, with marriage, the enduring structures of the Christian household, Clement was well aware that he was also advocating a peculiar and necessary brand of Christian courage. Should God demand it, the Christian sage was to become the Christian martyr. For Clement, the martyr was "the true human being in our race."[75] This meant, in practice, that the sage must face death—as many an ancient pagan had faced it—unshaken by the most terrible wrench of all: by fear for the fate of his wife and children. Peter had seen his wife led to execution and had cried out to her: "Remember the Lord."[76] This was no distant legend. The year that Clement left Alexandria, Leonides, the father of seven children from a provincial town in Egypt, had been executed by the Augustal Prefect. His own child, the young Origen, had written to him not to be swayed by anxiety for his family. Leonides had been in the habit of kissing his son every night on the breast as he lay asleep.[77]

The married Christian had to learn to live not only *ahédonôs*, untouched by undisciplined pleasure, but *alupétôs*, unshaken by grief.[78] Only those of us who live in a very sheltered world indeed, among our books, can afford to concentrate on Clement the forbidding controller of sexual pleasure, and ignore Clement's somber corollary—the quiet courage demanded of ordinary married men and women who, under the conditions of the late second century, might yet be called upon to become martyrs. This was a courage that was all the greater because it could be shown despite the ties of spouses and children, "the dearest relations of our life."[79]

Clement became a priest. In 202–203, he left Alexandria to serve the bishop of Jerusalem, and may have died around 215. His place in Alexandria was taken by the amazing young Origen—a soul already steeled by his father's execution. Clement may have sought, in the clergy, the more active role of the sage, called upon to confront, to charm, and even to educate his persecutors. We meet such persons in the Acts of many martyr-bishops in the Greek world of the coming century: some were married, many were well-to-do, all appealed to

---

74. 7.14.88.2: 3, p. 62.
75. 7.3.18.1: 3, p. 13; see Völker, *Der wahre Gnostiker*, p. 536.
76. *Strom.* 7.11.63.3: 3, p. 46.   77. Eusebius, *Ecclesiastical History* 6.1.6.
78. *Strom.* 7.11.64.2: 3, p. 46.   79. 7.11.64.1: 3, p. 46.

the image of Socrates to justify their own heroic stance and that of Christ, their model.[80] Yet there is no *Martyrdom of Clement*. Only Clement *ho Stromateus*, Clement "of the *Miscellanies*," has survived.[81]

Clement's work raised questions that had scarcely been resolved a century after his death. His Christian sage was a figure of awesome serenity. Yet he was inconceivable outside the conventional structures of society. The ideal proposed by Clement has been likened, by one of his most sensitive expositors, to that of a Hesychast monk.[82] But it is a monk without a monastery, and without a desert. He could taunt his opponents:

They proudly say that they are imitating the Lord, who neither married nor had any possessions in this world, boasting that they understand the Gospel better than anyone else. . . .
Which of them goes about like Elijah, clad in a sheepskin and a leather girdle? Which like Isaiah, naked except for a piece of sacking and without shoes? Which of them will imitate John the Baptist's awesome way of life?[83]

Yet, a century later, the life of Saint Anthony made Clement's taunt irrevocably out of date. Anthony had understood the Gospel in just that drastic way, and, by so doing, he had become, by his old age, "a doctor to all Egypt."[84]

Clement's writings take us, for a welcome moment, out of the narrow confines of the radical groups that we have described in the last two chapters. His work owed its human texture to the skill with which he grafted the shimmering twigs of Greek *paideia* on to a humble rootstock of married Christian morality. Behind this elegant façade, we can glimpse Christians whose codes for daily living may have differed little from those of their Jewish neighbors. Clement's most daring act, in a time of increasingly vocal radicalism, was to have spoken up, in this ingenious and elegant manner, for the married Christian laity. His erudite disquisitions did not reach all members of the Christian congregation; but, at least, his writings implicitly validated the role, within the Church, of the well-to-do married householders who protected and

---

80. *Martyrdom of Pionius* 5.4 and 17.2, in H. Musurillo, *The Acts of the Christian Martyrs*, pp. 142–144 and 158; *Acts of Phileas* (Latin Manuscript) 4.2 and 6.1, Musurillo, pp. 348 and 360: Phileas was married with children. See esp. V. Saxer, "Le 'juste crucifié' de Platon à Théodoret."
81. Palladius, *Lausiac History* 60 and Cassiodorus, *Institutes* 1.8.4.
82. Marrou, *Le Pédagogue*, p. 61.   83. *Strom.* 3.6.49.1 and 653.5: 2, p. 218 and 221.
84. Athanasius, *Life of Anthony* 14: *Patrologia Graeca* 26: 865A.

endowed the Christian community. It is they whom the radicals had wished to push aside, in a bid to create a very different form of leadership within the churches.

It may even be possible to glimpse the outlines of a social struggle in Clement's Alexandrian milieu, fought on the issue of marriage and continence within the Church. Insistence on continence would have opened the leadership of the Church to very different figures from those for whom Clement wrote. In certain circumstances, the rejection of marriage would have made the clergy a *carrière ouverte aux talents*, in which the ambitious and poorer members of the Christain community could rise, through chastity, at the expense of more established figures, rich and cultivated heads of families, who were tarnished by the mere fact of wedlock. In different conditions, it might have encouraged small groups of continent "spiritual" persons, of higher class and culture than their neighbors, to look down on the humdrum married clergy of their city. Both situations must have existed in the third century. Clement wrote, in part, to block the rise of a dangerous mystique of continence. He reassured married householders that they did not need to feel ashamed to have married leaders, nor, as married persons, need they feel unable to aspire to Christian perfection. They also could aspire to leadership within the Christian communities. Even Paul had been a married man, so Clement surmised, rather ingeniously.[85] Certainly, Peter had been married.[86]

We should never forget the presence of a "silent majority" of married persons in the large churches of the East. By 300 A.D. there may have been as many as five million Christians scattered throughout the Roman world.[87] Yet they are shadowy figures, hardly visible on the edge of the bright limelight in which the vivid and articulate few argued so vehemently and with such deadly consequentiality. In the upper echelons of the Church, Clement's voice was soon drowned. The copious works written by the bishops and clergy of the third and fourth centuries pass for the history of late antique Christianity. It is they that now line the shelves of our libraries. These writings tacitly abandoned Clement's mission. A younger generation of leaders were simply not interested in rethinking the issue of the sanctification of the married, as Clement plainly felt himself obliged to do. Their slogan was "vir-

85. *Strom.* 3.6.52.4 and 53.1: 2, p. 220.
86. 7.11.64.2 and 4.21.130.5: 3, p. 46 and 2, pp. 305–306.
87. Ramsay MacMullen, *Christianizing the Roman Empire*, p. 32, pp. 135–136, n 26.

ginity." The rise to prominence of the Christian Church in Roman society in the course of the third century was a process that gathered
momentum at a surprising rate. It was accompanied by the emergence
of what can best be called a "sensibility," almost an "aesthetic," of
virginity. The ideal of the untouched human body came to the fore.
In the imagination of the time, it acted as a charged joining point of
heaven and earth and, on earth itself, as the symbolic rallying point
for a rapidly expanding church. We must look around us, for a moment, at the relations of men and women in the Christian churches
of the late second and early third centuries, in order to understand
the conditions under which this crucial change took place.

SEVEN

"A Promiscuous Brotherhood and Sisterhood": Men and Women in The Early Churches

To its pagan critics, Christianity was a religion notorious for close association with women:

They recognize each other by secret signs and marks; they fall in love almost before they are acquainted; everywhere they introduce a kind of religious lust, a promiscuous "brotherhood" and "sisterhood."[1]

Pagan conviction that Christians met in order to indulge in sexual promiscuity died hard. This was hardly surprising: by the year 200, every Christian group had accused its own Christian rivals of bizarre sexual practices.[2] In the time of Justin, a young man in Alexandria even petitioned the Augustal Prefect for permission to have himself castrated. Only by undergoing this drastic operation could he hope to persuade pagans that indiscriminate intercourse was not what Christian men sought in their "sisters."[3] As late as the 320s, the Emperor

1. Minucius Felix, *Octavius* 9, G. H. Rendall, trans., p. 337.
2. W. Speyer, "Zu den Vorwürfen der Heiden gegen die Christen."
3. Justin, *I Apologia* 29.2.

Licinius harassed the churches in the eastern provinces, by a law that "enjoined that men should not appear in company with women in the houses of prayer, and forbade women to attend the sacred schools of virtue or to receive instruction from the bishops."[4]

Such reactions tell us more about traditional Mediterranean fantasies of the world turned upside down than they do about the actual relations of men and women in the Christian communities. The accounts of the martyrs, however, offer grim statistics. At Lyon, in 177, twenty-four men died and twenty-three women;[5] at Scilli, in 180, seven men and five women;[6] at Abitina, in 303, the authorities entered a Christian assembly, arresting thirty-one men and seventeen women.[7]

The most clear and disturbing voice that has come down to us from the Roman world is the voice of a Christian woman, Vibia Perpetua. Not only did the Acts of her martyrdom begin with a long autobiographical account of Perpetua's experiences at her trial and in prison; the author who completed her account presented himself as no more than the executor of Perpetua's will, by bringing to its chilling conclusion the description of a fully public display of heroism, which Perpetua, *generosa illa*, "that noble woman," had bequeathed to the Christian Church.[8]

Perpetua was not the only woman to suffer in Carthage. In 259, Quartillosa awaited martyrdom. Her husband and son had already been executed. She and her friends were starving:

I saw my son who had suffered come to the prison . . . After him there entered a young man, carrying in each of his hands two drinking cups full of milk . . . And he gave everyone to drink from the cups which he carried, and they were never empty.

Suddenly the stone which divided the window was removed and the window became light, and we saw the fullness of the sky.[9]

Many were denied even the dignity of a public death. Four women were among a group of thirteen in Rome in 250: "all by God's will

4. Eusebius, *Life of Constantine* 1.53, E. C. Richardson, trans., *Library of the Nicene Fathers,* 1:497.

5. Eusebius, *Ecclesiastical History* 5.1.3–61 and *Martyrologium Hieronymianum* analyzed by P. Nautin, *Lettres et écrivains des iième et iiième siècles,* pp. 49–50.

6. *The Acts of the Scillitan Martyrs* 16, ed. Musurillo, *Acts of the Martyrs,* p. 88.

7. *Acta Saturnini* 2: *Patrologia Latina* 8: 705–706.

8. *The Martyrdom of Saints Perpetua and Felicitas* 16.1, Musurillo, p. 124.

9. *The Martyrdom of Saints Montanus and Lucius* 8.3–7, Musurillo, p. 221.

starved to death in prison."[10] In the legacy of courage, at least, men and women were remembered as equal within the Christian Church.

Between the slurs of pagans and fellow-Christians and the Spirit-filled heroism of the martyrs, we know surprisingly little about the relations of men and women in the Christian communities of the second and early third centuries.[11] The day-to-day life of Christians is a darkened landscape, intermittently lit up for us by the flashes of polemical fireworks that crackled far overhead. Most of the evidence that has survived comes from the leaders of the Church, as they argued furiously among themselves. It was never intended to answer the sort of questions that a modern person would wish to ask of an early Christian community.

One fact, however, is certain: the second and third centuries witnessed two silent revolutions that would determine the future development of religion in Europe and the Near East—the rise to dominance of the rabbis within Judaism,[12] and the creation of a strict division between clergy and laity in the Christian Church.[13] Both revolutions posed acutely the problems of the relations between the rank and file of a religious community and its elite. The rabbis, for instance, had no doubt as to their unique importance in Israel: it was they and their disciples who "all their days engage in upbuilding the world."[14]

Yet the ethereal strand of words woven by the Sages depended, for its continuance, on the solid flesh and blood of normal married relationships. Synagogues and scholars were supported by Jews of high social status, who were wealthy and married benefactors. The Sages themselves were married men, and were greatly interested in regulating the marriages of others.[15] Women frequently consulted them on sexual issues.[16] They resisted a strong temptation to deny their dependence on the less observant rank and file, on the *ʿam ha-aretz.* Israel

10. Cyprian, *Letter* 22.2.2.

11. For a short survey see Robin Lane Fox, *Pagans and Christians*, pp. 308–311; Jo Ann McNamara, *A New Song: Celibate Women in the First Three Christian Centuries* covers much of the material in this chapter from another perspective.

12. Martin Goodman, *State and Society in Roman Galilee*, pp. 175–181.

13. A. Faivre, *Naissance d'une hiérarchie*, pp. 37–171 is fundamental.

14. *Babylonian Talmud: Shabbat* 114a, I. Epstein, trans., 2:558.

15. See esp. J. Neusner, *The History of the Mishnaic Law of Woman, Part 5: The Mishnaic System of Women*, pp. 213–216.

16. *Midrash Rabba: Song of Songs* 3.7, M. Simon, trans., *The Midrash: Song of Songs*, p. 162 and *Babylonian Talmud: Nedarim* 20a, I. Epstein, trans., *The Talmud*, p. 58.

was a single, undivided community, in which learned and unlearned must collaborate: "Let the clusters on the vine pray for the leaves, for were it not for the leaves, the clusters would not exist."[17]

The leaders of the Christian churches found themselves in a similar position. Every Sunday, the laity piled up against the altar wealth that was known to come from activities that had brought them into daily contact with a tainted, pagan world.[18] Although many of their clergy, prophets, and spiritual guides were continent, the average Christian congregation maintained its numbers through children begotten by the laity. The dividing line between the upholders of the Christianity of the "Great Church" and those groups branded as "heretics" was made plain on this eminently practical issue. In the Great Church, as in Judaism, the rank and file were considered capable of gaining merit by providing support for the chosen few. They did so by offering the Christian community many of the things that the elite had pointedly renounced for themselves: they provided the wealth and the children. One suspects that the orthodox doctrine of God as the Creator of the material world would not have been so hotly debated, in the course of the second century, if this doctrine had not also played a part in validating the discreet flow of "the goods of this world" into the Church. As in any well-endowed synagogue, personal wealth was considered, by wealthy Christians, to be one of the many "gifts" that a benign Creator had lavished on His world: it could be offered up to Him, in gratitude, by being spent on the Church.[19]

In more radical groups the exchange of merit between elite and rank and file was short-circuited. In a church where all baptized members were continent, the distinction between continent clergy and reproductive laity was blurred. Nor could wealth be used in quite the same, prudent manner. Criticizing Marcion, Irenaeus pointed out that if all wealth belonged to the evil Creator God of the present age, it could not be offered up to the Church in gratitude, as part of a good Creation. It could not be redistributed by the bishop in the form of alms and similar pious works. To accept wealth as a gift of God was to accept, by implication, the structures of the society that enabled wealth

---

17. *Babylonian Talmud: Ḥullin* 92a, E. Cashdan, trans., *The Talmud*, 2:516.

18. *Didascalia Apostolorum* 4.6.1–2, F. X. Funk, ed., *Didascalia et Constitutiones Apostolorum*, p. 224 and R. H. Connolly, *Didascalia Apostolorum*, p. 158.

19. L. Robert, *Nouvelles inscriptions de Sardes* p. 49 *n* 1.

to be accumulated. It meant, in fact, to accept the peace of the pagan Roman Empire as itself one of the many gifts of God to His creatures.[20] It was a telling point to have made. Marcion was known by his critics to have bought himself into the Church at Rome by offering a princely sum (as large as any that a small-town notable was expected to lavish on his city). This sum represented the fruits of his family business as a shipowner, trading between the Black Sea and Italy.[21] The orthodox could accept such wealth with a clear conscience. The slow rise of the Christianity of the Great Church at the expense of more radical groups was made possible by that elementary decision. If wealth, like marriage, was deemed to be part of an evil "present age," which must be abruptly renounced rather than carefully husbanded as a gift of God's providence, then there would have been no possibility of accumulating resources for the Church and of producing generations of children reared in Christian families. By the third century, the Church was securely established in the Roman cities precisely because it was wealthy enough to take care of its own poor and could count on the loyal support of the kind of well-to-do, married householders for whom Clement of Alexandria had written.

What made the history of the Christian Church notably different from that of other religious groups was the constant anxiety of its clergy to define their own position against the principal benefactors of the Christian community. Early Christians came to expect that their leaders should possess recognizable and perpetual tokens of superiority to the laity: they might be expected to give evidence of a charismatic calling; they were encouraged, if possible, to practice perpetual continence; even when both these criteria were lacking, only they had received due ordination through the "laying on of hands." This, in turn, gave them an exclusive role in the celebration of the Eucharist that was the central rite of the Christian community. By these precautions, the clergy ensured that leadership of the Church would not gravitate unthinkingly into the hands of its wealthiest and most powerful lay benefactors.[22]

The Christian clergy, therefore, defended their privileged position

---

20. Irenaeus, *Against the Heresies* 3.30.3.

21. Tertullian, *de praescriptione haereticorum* 30.2; R. Duncan-Jones, *The Economy of the Roman Empire*, pp. 147–155.

22. L. W. Countryman, *The Rich Christian in the Church of the Early Empire: Contradictions and Accomodations*, pp. 157–182.

over the laity. They also took a step that separated them from the rabbis of Palestine and (for all we know) from the Jewish leadership of the Diaspora: they welcomed women as patrons and even offered women roles in which they could act as collaborators. By 200 A.D., the role of women in the Christian churches was quite unmistakable.

The crucial factor here was that women had been encouraged to be continent and had been urged to remain widows after the death of their first husband. It is highly unlikely that their prominence would have been achieved in a community where every woman was expected to marry. In Judaism, by contrast, women were excluded from the central activity of the rabbis: with a few, outstanding exceptions, women took no part in the passing down of the tradition through the intensive study of Torah.[23] In return, the married woman provided for the biological continuity of Israel. She maintained the home from which the scholars and the sons of the scholars set out.[24] It was a role unambiguously blessed by the rabbis as part of the goodness of God's creation. But it formed a crushing bar to further religious service. The study of Torah assumed the precious privilege of free males in an ancient society—the freedom to dispose of their time. For a woman, the duties of childbearing occurred in precisely those years when their spouses, as late adolescent males, were free to serve their long apprenticeship at the feet of the Sages. The biological fact of menstruation incurred disqualifications from participation in so many rituals that it was all but impossible for a mature woman to adjust the timetable of her life so as to keep pace with that of the leisured men.[25] In Palestine, at least, if not in the Diaspora, the role of women as patrons of the community was kept to a minimum.[26] The notorious remark that it was better to burn Torah than to allow a woman to handle it was a snub addressed by a rabbi to a rich *matrona*. If the Sages were forced to be dependent on unscholarly patrons, they would at least avoid the humiliation of appearing to be dependent on a woman.[27]

23. This did not in any way mean that a well-to-do Jewish woman could not live an active life outside the narrow circle of the scholars: see G. W. Bowersock, *Roman Arabia*, pp. 76–79, 87–90, on the litigation of Babata, a Jewish woman whose documents were found in Masada.

24. *Babylonian Talmud: Soṭah* 21a, A. Cohen, trans., *The Talmud*, p. 105.

25. L. J. Archer, "The Role of Jewish Women in Graeco-Roman Palestine," pp. 277–280.

26. But see the evidence for the Diaspora, as marshalled and interpreted by B. J. Brooten, *Woman Leaders in the Ancient Synagogue*.

27. *Palestinian Talmud: Soṭah* 3.4, in M. Schwab, trans., *Le Talmud de Jérusalem*, 4:261.

Much though they may have wished, at times, to snub their own protectresses in the same abrupt manner, the Christian clergy of late antiquity found that, in their community, influential women were there to stay. This was not a development which we should take for granted. The pseudo-Pauline letters show us Christian communities that had been quite content with the solution upheld by the rabbis.

Let women learn in silence with all subjection. But I suffer not a woman to teach, nor to usurp authority over the man, but to be in silence. . . . Notwithstanding, she shall be saved through child-bearing if they [her children] continue in faith and charity and holiness with sobriety.[28]

By the year 200, however, this dismissive attitude was no longer possible. Continence had been actively encouraged for women as well as for men. Less merit was attached to motherhood. The sense of pollution by blood, which had tended to exclude women as a source of menstrual impurity, was not entirely abandoned in Christian circles. An unknown author in Syria, in the mid-third century, set aside many pages to persuade both men and women to pay no attention to the disqualifications contained in the Jewish laws of purity. The fact of having menstruated, of having had intercourse, or of having experienced a night-emission, was still considered by them as a reason for not approaching the Eucharist, for not praying, for not touching holy books.[29] A bishop of Alexandria could assume that no Christian woman would approach the Eucharist during her period.[30] But these mercifully precise taboos had been swamped by a general sense that intercourse in itself (and not merely the formless products of the human body, blood and semen) excluded the Holy Spirit. It was to men that Clement of Alexandria wrote at length, in order to reassure them that sexual intercourse in marriage did not automatically debar the Christian from perfection. In Christian circles, the vocal advocacy, for well over a century, of extreme views on continence had brought about a situation unheard of in Judaism. Married men trembled on the brink of being demoted to the position of women: their physiological involvement in sex made them ineligible for roles of leadership in the community. Some women, however, edged closer to the clergy: continence or widowhood set them free from the disqualifications associated with sexual activity.

28. I Timothy 2:12 and 15.
29. *Didascalia* 6.21.1–8, Funk, ed. pp. 368–372; Connolly, pp. 242–250.
30. Dionysius of Alexandria, *Canonical Letter* 2: P. G. 10: 1281a.

We only have a few, vivid glimpses of what it was like to be a woman in the Christian communities of the time. They suggest that in reality continence was often the only option that a young person could take. In a small group, where marriage with pagans was severely discouraged and yet where considerations of social status had by no means been suspended among the saints, it would have been extremely difficult for many heads of households to find suitable husbands and wives for their children. Many believers simply avoided *mésalliances* by encouraging their children to grow up as virgins. Clement had heard of the deacon Nicholas: "of his children, his daughters all remained virgins to their old age and his son has also remained uncorrupted."[31]

It is possible that some of the more exotic Gnostic teachings, which seemed to advocate "Communion" through free love, may have served as a way of encouraging Christian parents to allow their girls to circulate more freely among the brethren, as brides:

The story goes that one of them came to a virgin of our church who had a lovely face and said to her: "Scripture says, *Give to every one that asks of you.*" She, however . . . gave the dignified reply: "On the subject of marriage, talk to my mother."[32]

At the beginning of the third century, Pope Callistus earned the scorn of his rival, Hippolytus, by allowing the upper-class women of the Roman Church to live in concubinage with lower-class believers. Women from a resolutely pagan nobility, they would consent to marry husbands within the Church only if these commoners did not count as fully legal spouses.[33] It is hardly surprising, given these difficulties, that many Christians preferred continence to the complexities of finding a partner, and that men and women alike were strongly urged not to add to these complexities by attempting to marry again once widowed.

An "order" of widows sprang up in all churches from an early time.[34] Most of these were helpless creatures, destitute old ladies only too glad to receive food and clothing from the hands of the clergy. What

31. Clement, *Strom.* 3.4.25, H. E. Chadwick, trans., *Alexandrian Christianity*, p. 52.
32. Ibid. 3.4.27, Chadwick, trans. p. 52.
33. Hippolytus, *Refutation of All Heresies* 9.7, in J. H. MacMahon, trans. *The Ante-Nicene Fathers*, 5:131. For upper-class women in Carthage, see G. Schöllgen, *Ecclesia sordida? Zur Frage der sozialen Schichtung frühchristlicher Gemeinden am Beispiel Karthagos zur Zeit Tertullians*, pp. 204–215.
34. R. Gryson, *The Ministry of Women in the Early Church* is a clear survey.

we know of other groups where remarriage is discouraged indicates that widowed women would have become a numerically important element in any Christian church. In the mid-third century, the Roman church supported 1500 widows and destitute persons.[35] In one African church, at Cirta, in 303, the pagan authorities confiscated thirty-eight veils, eighty-two ladies' tunics, forty-seven pairs of female slippers, and only sixteen pieces of male clothing.[36] By the end of the fourth century, the church of Antioch supported three thousand widows and virgins.[37] Not all of these widows, however, were of low social status. It was, after all, women of high status who would have experienced the greatest difficulty in finding husbands within the church. Many wealthy and cultivated young women would have found themselves, on the death of their husbands, with the prospect of spending the rest of their lives in the service of the church. Jerome knew of three ladies in Gaul, who had already spent widowhoods of forty, twenty, and twelve years.[38] John Chrysostom's mother had been widowed at the age of twenty. His future soul mate, the remarkable Olympias, had been widowed in her mid-twenties, and spent the remaining twenty years of her life supporting the church at Constantinople.[39]

Influential and devout widows were disturbingly amphibious creatures. They were neither unambiguously disqualified as married, sexually active persons, nor were they fully at home in the ranks of the clergy. They were the only lay persons who had accumulated all the attributes of effective members of the clergy, barring the crucial prerogative of ordained service at the altar. The influential widow stood for lay persons of either sex at their most active in the church. The role that members of the clergy were prepared to allow such a widow to play was a clear omen of much or how little they valued the active participation of lay persons of either sex.

In 200, we are still dealing with a Christianity dominated by married householders. All discussion of sexual renunication took place in the light of an unspoken timetable, laid down, within the household, by the old for the young. Sexuality was not regarded as a problem for the young. It was, rather, a problem for their parents: the parents would

35. Eusebius, *Eccles. Hist.* 6.43.11.

36. *Gesta apud Zenophilum, P. L.* 8: 731B, ingeniously adduced by Lane Fox, *Pagans and Christians*, p. 310.

37. John Chrysostom, *Hom. 66 in Matt.* 3: *Patrologia Graeca* 57:630.

38. Jerome, *Letter* 123.1: *P. L.* 22:1047.

39. See esp. E. A. Clark, *Jerome, Chrysostom and Friends*, pp. 107–144.

be held responsible on the Day of Judgment if their children lapsed into fornication because they had not provided marriage-partners for them at an appropriate, early age.[40] The marriage that followed, in the early teens, was held to be indissoluble and exclusive. It was therefore only on the death of a spouse that any Christian man or woman could contemplate continence as a personal choice. Unlike the Roman *univira*, who was praised by her husband for having been loyal to him alone, in a society where she was free to abandon him by divorce or by adultery, the Christian widow was free to choose virtue only after the death of her husband. At that time, the *fides* that Romans occasionally expected a woman to show even to her dead husband, by refusing to remarry, was tranformed into a perpetual loyalty to Christ, which good Christian widows were expected to show for the rest of their lives.[41]

Continence therefore grew out of marriage for both men and women. Indeed, for a rigorist such as Tertullian, marriage itself was no more than a school of continence. It was a somber preparation for long years of widowhood. When Tertullian spoke of *castitas* he did not mean virginity; he meant sexual activity whittled away to a minimum in marriage and abandoned totally after marriage.[42] Nor was such a view unrealistic. Those men and women who were the most likely to decide not to remarry were those who were already committed members of the church. Leonides, for instance, the father of Origen, was executed when Origen, his eldest son, was barely seventeen. He had begotten six other children in fewer than seventeen years. If Leonides had observed the prolonged periods of abstinence that a man like Clement of Alexandria took for granted, witholding from his wife during the period of her pregnancy and during lactation, he may well have slept with her only every second year of their marriage.[43] He must have felt reassured that he had, indeed, enjoyed intercourse with his wife only for the sake of begetting the six children who had emerged from such solemnly spaced encounters. It was from this austere reservoir of postmarital celibates, widowed men and women, and not from those

---

40. *Didascalia Apostolorum* 4.11.5–6, Funk, ed. pp. 232–234 and Connolly, p. 194.

41. B. Kötting, "Univira in Inschriften," in W. van den Boer, et al., eds., *Romanitas et Christianitas. Studia I. H. Waszink oblata*, pp. 195–206.

42. Tertullian, *de monogamia* 3.1 and 17.5.

43. Eusebius, *Eccles. Hist.* 6.2.12. The restraints are spelled out in Clement, *Paedagogus* 2.92.3–93.2 and *Strom.* 2.144.1 and 3.72.1.

who had committed themselves to a distinctive, virginal life from adolescence onward, that the Christian churches tended to draw their leaders.

As a result, men and women found themselves on the same footing as to the nature of the continence that they had embraced. The normal continent woman was not a virgin girl, dedicated to a pious seclusion from childhood up. Rather, she was a woman who had been the head of a Christian household and the mother of Christian children. She frequently controlled property. Her wealth enabled her to impinge on the local church as a benefactress, in a manner that was normal in pagan and Jewish circles.[44] She was no demure creature, who would sink back into her parents' house. "Passing around the houses," continent adult women, as widows, enjoyed some of the enviable mobility associated with the apostolic calling.[45] Mature, financially independent, and already influential, the Christian widow had made a decision to embrace continence that was as formal and as heroic as that of her fellow widowers, the average members of the clergy.

Not surprisingly, the descriptions of the proper ordering of a church that were put together in the course of the third century betray a growing tension on the position of the widow. Widows frequently exercised "paraclerical" roles. They would receive requests for advice and instruction. One church order even arranged for the support of two widows, "for the sake of their prayers and revelations."[46] Though prophecy was excluded from the solemn, clerical assembly of the Eucharist in most churches outside the Montanist communities of Phrygia, female prophecy continued in more private settings.[47] In the imaginative economy of most Christian groups, the prophetic gift of the woman was virtually ineradicable. Male perceptions of women as more "open" to the unknown ensured that they continued to attract male clients and admirers throughout the second and third centuries.[48] Prophet-

44. R. MacMullen, "Woman in Public in the Roman Empire," pp. 208–218 with R. Van Bremen, "Women and Wealth," esp. pp. 233–237. Brooten, *Woman Leaders*, pp. 157–165, gives an impressive list of women donors and founders of synagogues.

45. I Timothy 5:13.

46. *Allgemeine Kirchenordnung* 21.1, T. Schermann, ed. p. 29.

47. Even among the Montanists in Carthage, a woman prophetess would experience her visions during the main assembly of the church, but would not make them public until after the service: Tertullian, *de anima* 9.4.

48. R. Padel, "Women: Model for Possession by Greek Daemons," p. 7, and now Giulia Sissa, *Le corps virginal*, pp. 66–75.

esses emerged dramatically in times of crisis. In 234, after earthquakes and renewed persecutions in Cappadocia,

on a sudden, a certain woman . . . in a state of ecstacy announced herself as a prophetess, and acted as if filled with the Holy Ghost. . . . [she] would walk in the keen winter with bare feet over frozen snow . . . [and] deceived many . . . [by pretending] that with a powerful invocation she could sanctify bread and celebrate the Eucharist . . . and also to baptize many, making use of the usual and lawful words of the rite.[49]

Remembered twenty-two years later by the Bishop of Caesarea in a letter to Cyprian, Bishop of Carthage, the incident was a chilling reminder of how easily the clergy's hold on their flocks, based upon the male prerogative of ordination, could be brushed aside.

Nor did the clergy enjoy exclusive control over the intellectual life of the churches. In any Christian community that boasted upper-class members and well-wishers, women were prominent. The world of the great Christian teachers was close to that of the upper-class study circles of pagan philosophers. Like the philosophers, Christian teachers assumed that women might be present at their gatherings, that they would raise questions, and that they were entitled to receive careful answers. In the early third century, the *didaskaleion* presided over by Hippolytus at Rome set up in his memory a re-used statue of a seated figure. Among the list of his works written on the side of the throne was one treatise dedicated to a woman.[50] Women recipients of Christian teaching were often well placed in Roman society: Hippolytus himself may once have written to an Empress, and Origen was later consulted by one.[51] Such women could influence their husbands to protect the Church. Hippolytus' *bête noire*, the future Pope Callistus, had been recalled from hard labor in the mines of Sardinia through the good offices of Marcia, the concubine of the Emperor Commodus:

a God-loving female, and desirous of performing some good work, [Marcia had] invited into her presence the blessed Victor [the Bishop of Rome] . . . and enquired of him what martyrs were in Sardinia. . . . Obtaining her request from Commodus, she had sent the letter granting their freedom to Hy-

49. Cyprian, *Letter* 75.10 in E. Wallis, trans. *The Ante-Nicene Fathers*, 5:393.

50. The list is in *Patrologia Graeca* 10: 287.

51. Theodoret of Cyrrhus, *Dialogus* 3: P. G. 83: 284D; Eusebius, *Eccles. Hist.* 6.21.3, on Origen and Julia Mammaea, "a woman as pious as any." See esp. A. D. Momigliano, "The Life of Saint Macrina by Gregory of Nyssa," in J. W. Eadie and J. Ober, eds., *The Craft of the Ancient Historian, Essays in Honor of C. G. Starr*, pp. 443–444.

acinthus, a eunuch [possibly meaning a "celibate"] priest. He, on receiving it, sailed away to Sardinia.[52]

At much the same time, in Alexandria, the young Origen grew up under the protection of Christian ladies. After his father's death, "he found welcome and rest with a woman of great wealth and distinguished in her manner of life." His protectress also patronized a famous Gnostic teacher, to whom "a great multitude would come, not only of heretics but also of our people."[53]

Origen's later patron, Ambrosius, was a former Valentinian. He may have begun to live in continence with his wife when a follower of Valentinus. Marcella, "his pious companion," and Ambrosius' sister, Tatiana, were very much part of the household without whose support Origen's prodigious exegetical labor would have been impossible.[54] Altogether, the Christian intelligentsia of the age took the presence of women, as disciples and patronesses, absolutely for granted.

Even in more simple communities, it was difficult to maintain a strict segregation of roles. In an ideal church order, whose rulings applied to Northern Syria, the widow was expected to offer only moral exhortation, presumably to younger women, on domestic duties. The pseudo-Pauline Letter to Titus had been clear on that point: elderly widows were to be

teachers of good things. That they may teach the young women to be sober, to love their husbands, to love their children, to be discreet, chaste, keepers at home, good, obedient to their own husbands, that the word of God be not blasphemed.[55]

Yet a pagan of around 250 might well have heard a member of the Christian "order" of widows positively encouraged by a mixed audience to discourse on the great themes of salvation, "on the end of the idols, the rest of the saints, the order of Christ's coming." These were topics on which "neither a widow nor [the writer adds, significantly]

52. Hippolytus, *Refutation* 9.7, MacMahon, trans. pp. 129–130.

53. Eusebius, *Eccles. Hist.* 6.2.13–14.

54. P. Nautin, *Origène*, p. 181; Origen also received a text of Symmachus' translation of the Bible from a certain Juliana: Eusebius, *Eccles. Hist.* 6.17; see Nautin, *Origène*, pp. 219–221.

55. Titus 2.3–5; cf. *Didascalia Apostolorum* 3.5.3, Funk, ed., p. 188 and Connolly, p. 132. This was a local church order, whose rulings did not apply to other regions of the Greek East: A. G. Martimort, *Les Diaconesses: essai historique*, pp. 40–41; 126–137. Yet the problems addressed were common to other parts of the Christian world, even if the solutions arrived at in the *Didascalia Apostolorum* were peculiar to Syria.

a layman should hold forth." As the author added with engaging self-esteem: the Gospel was like a mustard seed; it tasted very hot indeed if not competently prepared by a member of the clergy![56] It is the voice of a clergyman within only two generations of the triumph of his church in the Roman Empire.

The circumstances of Christianity in the late second and third centuries threw up a remarkable literary genre, that of the Apocryphal Acts of the Apostles. Continent women play a central role in these narratives. Yet the Apocryphal Acts should not be read as evidence for the actual role of women in Christianity. Rather, they reflect the manner in which Christian males of that period partook in the deeply ingrained tendency of all men in the ancient world, to use women "to think with."[57] There is no doubt that women played an important role in the imaginative economy of the Church. Their presence condensed the deep preoccupation of male Christians with their own relations with the "world," with the ever present reality of a tainted and seductive pagan society that pressed up against the doors of their houses and abutted the closed spaces of their new meeting places.[58]

Throughout this period, Christian men used women "to think with" in order to verbalize their own nagging concern with the stance that the Church should take to the world. For ancient men tended to regard women as creatures less clearly defined and less securely bounded by the structures that held men in place in society. The woman was a "gateway." She was both a weak link and a bridgehead. Women allowed in what men did not permit to enter. For the morose Tertullian, women needed to be reminded that they might be Eve, "the Devil's gateway."[59]

With their alluring hairstyles and disturbingly unveiled faces, the women of the church of Carthage were regarded by Tertullian as a breach in the defenses of the Church, by which the world might gain an entry into the somber assemblies of the male saints.[60] Yet women

---

56. *Didascalia Apostolorum* 3.5.4, Funk, ed,. p. 188 and Connolly, pp. 132–133.

57. Sally Humphreys, *The Family, Women and Death*, p. 33; the term is that of C. Lévi-Strauss, *Structural Anthropology*, pp. 61–62, and implies considerably more than the creation and manipulation of stereotypes.

58. See esp. T. D. Barnes, *Tertullian*, pp. 87–88; 93–102 and Ramsay MacMullen, *Christianizing the Roman Empire*, pp. 39–40.

59. Tertullian, *de cultu feminarum* 1.1.2; see M. Z. Rosaldo, "Woman, Culture and Society: A Theoretical Overview," p. 29 and *n* 8.

60. Tertullian, *de cultu feminarum* 2.11.1.

were as often a "gateway" in a positive sense. They could enter pagan families without being tainted as a man would be. They were the wives, servants, and nurses of unbelievers.[61] Male slaves could play the same role, but the bonding between women and children, as mother, nurse, or wetnurse, made the woman more responsible than a male slave would have been for the health of children and, hence, for the supernatural remedies that might be applied when they fell ill. Tertullian could even speak of an Emperor as "reared on the milk of a Christian."[62]

The immediacy of the bonds of which women were considered capable was valued by a community that desperately needed loyalty. It was as a woman, responsible for her own flesh and blood, and not simply as a Spirit-filled visionary, that Perpetua had been able to reach into the other world, to deliver her brother from torment.[63] In Carthage, it appears that the women in the Christian community were the leaders of the intense, physical reverence for the martyrs that anticipated the later cult of saints. As women, they could pass more easily into the terrible prison-house than could the Christian men. Kissing the chains of the martyrs, weeping at their feet, the women brought back the blessing of the heroes of the Church to their cowed menfolk, who dared not show their faces in the public spaces of a pagan city in times of persecution.[64]

Women, therefore, could be used "to think with" by Christians who faced the crucial issue of loyalty in a pagan environment. They were also central to a concern that Christian writers shared with their pagan contemporaries. Women could fall in love; and the bodies of women, exposed to innumerable misfortunes in the pursuit of their love, were potentially the most vulnerable of all bodies, and their resilience, for that reason, was the most impressive. The Apocryphal Acts began to circulate in the province of Asia (on the Aegean coast of Turkey) in the middle of the second century. They dealt obsessively with this theme. They spoke to the Christian churches as a whole. The Acts of

61. The most complete collection of evidence remains that of A. von Harnack, *Mission und Ausbreitung des Christentums*, 2:51–67.

62. Tertullian, *Ad Scapulam* 4.4.2.

63. *Passio Perpetuae* 7–8, in Musurillo ed., pp. 114–116; see Peter Dronke, *Medieval Women Writers*, pp. 11–12; see now C. Mertens, "Les premiers martyrs et leurs rêves," p. 24. I have learned much from Nancy Chodorow, "Family Structure and Female Personality," *Woman, Culture and Society*, pp. 43–66, esp. pp. 54–62.

64. Tertullian, *ad uxorem* 2.4.2 and *de pudicitia* 22.1.

Thomas came to serve the needs of Encratite groups in Syria, in the early third century. But not all Acts belong to an identifiable radical milieu. Their loose texture made them as open as a Rorschach blot to widely differing interpretations. Generation after generation of Christians read them with pleasure and reworked them with gusto.[65]

These Acts reveal to us a Christianity very different from that either of a Tertullian or of a Clement of Alexandria. It is an epic Christianity, a Christianity of impact. Wandering Apostles pass through proud cities wreaking havoc with the established pagan order—altars explode, temples collapse, storms bring to an ignominious halt the evil roar of the circus.[66] They were regularly portrayed drawing unmarried girls out of staid seclusion, and wives out of the beds of their husbands: "And many other women besides fell in love with the doctrine of purity . . . and men too ceased to sleep with their wives. . . . So there was the greatest dismay in Rome."[67]

The Apocryphal Acts explored with zest and attentiveness the issues of vocation, of vulnerability and of survival in a dramatically hostile environment. For this reason, the choice of the late classical Romance as a model for so many Acts was a stroke of genius. For the pagan Romances had already developed a narrative form that overlapped with the central concerns of a Christianity of impact and vocation. They had frequently begun with a moment of love a first sight. Time stood still as two souls, destined for each other, met for the first time.[68] The remainder of the Romance was an ingeniously spun out delaying action.[69] The manifest destiny of the young lovers was postponed, over and again, by adventures that emphasized the vulnerability of all humans to the caprice of fortune, and, more particularly, the vulnerability of the young and the beautiful to the sexual lusts of the pow-

---

65. Y. Tissot, "Encratisme et Actes Apocryphes," in *Les Actes Apocryphes des Apôtres*, F. Bovon, ed., pp. 109–119 and E. Junod and J. D. Kaestli, *L'Histoire des Actes Apocryphes du iiième au ixème siècle: le cas des Actes de Jean*. See now *Acta Iohannis*, E. Junod and J.-D. Kaestli, eds,. *Corpus christianorum: Series Apocryphorum* 1.

66. *Acts of John* 38–42, in Edgar Hennecke, *New Testament Apocrypha*; English. trans. R. McL. Wilson, ed., 2:236–237; *Acts of Paul* p. 5, 2:373.

67. *Acts of Peter* 34, 2:317.

68. Heliodorus, *Ethiopica* 3.5.4. The most perceptive study of this aspect of the ancient novel is that of Mikhail Bakhtin, *Voprosy literatury i estetiki*, pp. 236–261, now available in English: M. M. Bakhtin, *The Dialogic Imagination*, M. Holquist ed., C. Emerson and M. Holquist, trans., pp. 86–108; see also Graham Anderson, *Ancient Fiction: The Novel in the Graeco-Roman World*, pp. 114–115.

69. Bakhtin, *Dialogic Imagination*, pp. 89–97.

erful, the brutal, and the seductive. Throughout their trials, the girl, and sometimes even the boy, had preserved their virginity in circumstances where such preservation was considered so unlikely as to be miraculous.[70] Love and the loyalty engendered by love were presented as the only abiding force in a chaotic and menacing world.

The Christian authors of the Apocryphal Acts had only to replace a manifest destiny to the wedding bed, with which every pagan novel had ended, by the Apostle's call to continence. As in the Romances, danger followed from that first moment. For after the moment of conversion, the readers of the Acts were treated to a dramatic evocation of the towering force of the world, as it bore down on their heroes and heroines. The impression of its brutal power was heightened by being seen from the viewpoint of the most vulnerable of all of its potential victims, the unprotected virgin woman.[71]

In the Acts of Paul and Thecla, charged relations between the sexes stood in the foreground. Looking out on the house of a neighbor from the modest seclusion of her window in Iconium, the betrothed girl, Thecla, saw "many women and virgins going into Paul, she desired to be considered worthy herself to stand in Paul's presence."[72] Entranced by Paul's words on virginity and the resurrection, as they floated up to her from a neighboring garden,[73] Thecla was swept out of the household into the entourage of Paul. She became the model Christian supplicant at the cells of the martyrs. She spent the night in the cell, watching the untroubled figure of Paul: "her faith also was increased as she kissed his fetters."[74] She "rolled herself" in the place where he had taught.[75]

Later, the bond between Thecla and Paul became yet more poignant: "she sought for Paul as a lamb in the wilderness."[76] In the same way, a real woman, in third-century Smyrna, would not be parted from her spiritual father, the priest Pionius: Sabina "held on to his clothing be-

---

70. Heliodorus, *Ethiopica* 10.7.8; Achilles Tatius, *Leucippe and Clitophon* 5.20: the young man promises to remain a virgin "if there be a virginity in men"—he had only lapsed once by the end of the book!

71. R. Söder, *Die apokryphen Apostelakten und die romanhafte Literatur der Antike* is much-cited, conscientious and, basically, misleading. See C. Milovanović, "Apokrpypha Dela Pavlova i njihov odnos prema antičkom grčkom romanu," esp. pp. 329–331. Judith Perkins, "The Apocryphal Acts and the Early Christian Martyrdom," is a valuable contribution.

72. *Acts of Paul and Thecla* 7, *New Testament Apocrypha* 2:355.

73. 6, p. 355.   74. 18, p. 358.   75. 20, p. 358; 42, p. 364.   76. 20, p. 358.

cause of the jostling of the crowd, so that some said in jest, 'Why, how terrified she is that she may be weaned.'"[77]

Thecla was even prepared to dress as a man in order to accompany Paul on his journeys.[78] Her pagan parents had no doubt as to what all that must mean. They instantly "sexualized" Thecla's behavior. The ancient scenario of supernatural violence exercised through love-spells was a device exploited with gusto by all writers in the second century.[79]

I wonder how a maiden of such modesty as she can be so strangely troubled . . . like a spider at the window bound by his words [she] is dominated by a new desire and a fearful passion. . . . Turn to thy Thamyris and be ashamed.[80]
Away with the sorcerer, for he has corrupted all our women.[81]

Yet, behind the unabashedly sexual scenarios of the Acts, there looms the more terrible presence of the "world." In Asia this took the form of a self-confident Roman order, exuberantly loyal to its local gods.[82] The little circles who clustered round to hear readings of the Acts of Paul and Thecla may well have found the scenes of persecution triumphantly confronted to be the narrative's most gripping portions. Thecla, the exposed, virgin traveler, did not merely resist the advances of the noble Alexander of Antioch; she boxed his ears with such force that the great golden crown of a priest of the Imperial cult, heavy with images of the Emperors themselves, toppled from his head.[83] "The stranger, the desolate" Thecla,[84] a virgin girl exposed in a strange city, and so totally vulnerable, was more than an object of sexual violence; she was paraded before the people of Antioch as a "destroyer of holy things."[85] To the Christian reader, Thecla at her most exposed was the privileged vehicle of the indestructible power of Christ. At Iconium, "she was brought in naked, [and] the governor wept and marvelled at the power that was in her."[86] In the amphitheater of Antioch, she

77. *Martyrdom of Pionius* 10.2, in Musurillo, p. 149.

78. Acts of Paul and Thecla 40, p. 364.

79. G. Poupon, "L'accusation de magie dans les Actes Apocryphes," In F. Bovon et al., eds., *Les Actes Apocryphes*, pp. 71–93; see Brown, *The Making of Late Antiquity*, p. 24.

80. *Acts of Paul and Thecla* 10, p. 356.   81. 5, p. 357.

82. Now made plain in the masterly study of S. R. F. Price, *Rituals and Power: The Roman imperial cult in Asia Minor*, pp. 122–126.

83. The meaning of the incident is made plain by Price, *Rituals*, p. 170 note 1, appealing to the Syriac version of the *Acts*.

84. *Acts of Paul and Thecla* 26, p. 361.   85. 28, p. 361.   86. 22, p. 359.

leapt into a pool full of sharks with the cry, "now is the time for me to wash."[87] She received, in this way, the great rite of baptism. A cloud of fire surrounded her, "so that neither could the beasts touch her nor could she be seen naked."[88]

This triumphant scene was to be taken to convey more than a victory over sexual shame. For the author of the Acts, baptism was a "seal"; it gave Thecla the protection that the believer needed to live through the most terrible "temptation" of all—helpless passivity to the ritualized humiliation of a martyr's death.[89] Thecla was the ideal Christian in an age of persecution. Her story summed up

a vision of human integrity imprisoned in a world that it is in but not of . . . always managing to avoid the one fate that is worse than death, the annihilation of one's identity.[90]

As the rapid growth of her cult shows, Thecla, the imagined inviolate virgin, and not Vibia Perpetua, a real woman, *matronaliter nupta* and the mother of a child, was destined to become the female saint of the future.[91] The circulation of a legend such as that of Thecla added yet another, more high-pitched note to the conglomerate of notions associated with the ideal of chastity in Christian circles. Tertullian and Clement of Alexandria would have found the courage of Perpetua more intelligible.[92] Men entering middle age in 200, Tertullian and Clement stood for forms of Christianity that already belonged to an earlier age. However much they differed from each other, both had viewed the human person as essentially part of society as normally constituted. For both, sexual activity was to be disciplined and eventually suspended in such a way as to leave the human body still tied to its immediate environment. Neither Clement's Christian Sages nor Tertullian's elderly prophets were expected to abandon the stable household, as Thecla was imagined to have done. Nor did Thecla sink her identity into that of a holy group, as the Encratites tended to do.

Thecla's young body stood stunningly alone. To preserve her virginity meant to preserve an individual identity rooted in her physical

87. 34, p. 362.   88. 34, p. 362.   89. 25, p. 360.

90. Northrop Frye, *The Secular Scripture: A Study of the Structure of Romance*, p. 86.

91. See esp. M. Aubineau, "Le Panégyrique de Thècle attribué à Jean Chrysostome," pp. 359–362, G. Dagron, *Vie et Miracles de Sainte Thècle*, pp. 31–54, C. Nauerth and R. Warns, *Thekla: ihre Bilder in der frühchristlichen Kunst*, and Ruth Albrecht, *Das Leben der heiligen Makrina auf dem Hintergrund der Thekla-Traditionen*, pp. 239–319.

92. Dronke, *Medieval Women Writers*, p. 282, shows how medieval legends made Perpetua look as much like Thecla as possible.

body, because expressed in the state of physical intactness that she had carried with her from her birth. Thecla was not a role model that only Christian women were expected to follow. Her intact body spoke to both men and women. It was a condensed image of the individual, always threatened with annihilation, poised from birth above the menacing pressures of the world.

That it should have been this particular form of heroism, linked to a particular form of sexual renunciation—the preservation of a virgin state in the strict sense—which increasingly caught the imagination of all Christians, is a development we should not take for granted simply because it happened with seemingly unquestioned rapidity. The next chapters will attempt to trace aspects of the emergence of a fully fledged notion of virginity in the crucial century that stretched between the youth of Origen and the emergence from the desert of Saint Anthony.

EIGHT

"I Beseech You: Be Transformed":
Origen

Between May 200 and the middle of 203, Laetus, the Augustal Prefect of Egypt, rounded up a group of Christians from Alexandria and from Egypt proper. The father of Origen had been among them. Origen was sixteen or seventeen at the time, the eldest son of a family of seven. His mother hid his clothes, lest he should rush out to join his father by presenting himself to the authorities. "It was," wrote Eusebius of Caesarea a century later, "an ambition extraordinary in one so young."[1] Origen entered adulthood steeled by closeness to death. For him, the charged antithesis of "true" and "false" paternity, the contrast between continuities created by spiritual guidance and mere physical re-

---

1. Eusebius, *Ecclesiastical History* 6.2.6. On the life of Origen, Pierre Nautin, *Origène: sa vie et son oeuvre* is essential, Henry Chadwick, *Early Christian Thought and the Classical Tradition*, pp. 66–94 is judicious. For Eusebius' presentation of the youth of Origen, see Patricia Cox, *Biography in Late Antiquity: A Quest for the Holy Man*, pp. 69–101. Like all modern scholars, I am particularly indebted to the patient work of F. Crouzel, most especially his *Origène et la "connaissance mystique"* and *Virginité et mariage chez Origène*, and to W. Völker, *Das Vollkommenheitsideal des Origenes*. See also J. W. Trigg, *Origen: the Bible and Philosophy in the Third-Century Church*.

production, which had been so current in Christian teaching circles in the second century, had become a bitter fact of life. The young man's loyalty to a father who had expected so much from him had been wrenched out of its normal course by the brutal blow of execution. All the continuity, all the loyalty that Origen now wished for lay in the finer, more enduring links of soul to soul, created between a teacher and his disciples within the Christian church.

Settled in Alexandria, Origen became a spiritual guide at a precociously early age. A nucleus of committed young Christians and of recent converts gravitated around the brilliant young teacher and "son of a martyr." When persecution flared up again, between 206 and 210, the group around Origen showed surprising resilience. The Alexandrian clergy discreetly vanished, leaving Origen to maintain the morale of his spiritual charges.[2] Daring the hostile crowd—no small act of courage in a city notorious for its lynch law—the young teacher would step forward to bestow on his spiritual "children" the solemn kiss that declared they had become worthy of their martyr's death.[3]

We know surprisingly little, from Origen's own works, of the texture of the remaining forty years of his life in Alexandria and elsewhere. His career as a teacher in Alexandria ended in 234 with virtual exile and the transfer of his school to Caesarea, on the seacoast of Palestine.[4] He taught there and preached regularly as a priest, expounding the Scriptures in church, until his death some time around 253–254, as a result of the tortures inflicted on him in the previous year in the prison-house of Caesarea.[5]

With Clement, we had been encouraged to look around us, at every detail of the life of a Christian in a great city; with Origen that busy world has vanished: we already breathe the changeless air of the desert.[6] Time stands still in a spiritual Sinai where, for forty years, Origen, the exegete, had gathered from the Scriptures the sweet bread of the angels.[7] Origen thought of himself, above all, as an exegete. Facing

---

2. Eusebius, *Ecclesiastical History* 6.3.13–4.3.   3. Ibid. 6.3.4. and 41.1–23.

4. See Nautin, *Origène*, pp. 69–101 and 421–432 and Trigg, *Origen*, pp. 130–146.

5. See Nautin, *Origène*, pp. 433–441 and Trigg, *Origen*, pp. 241–243. G. W. Clarke, *The Letters of Saint Cyprian of Carthage*, Ancient Christian Writers 43, pp. 22–39, esp. pp. 35–36, gives a masterly account of the pressure put on leading Christians to sacrifice and the consequent discreet release of those who proved too difficult to frighten into conformity.

6. This aspect of Origen is beautifully evoked by Marguerite Harl, *Origène et la fonction révélatrice du Verbe incarné*, pp. 360–363.

7. *In Num.* 17.4, *Griechische christliche Schriftsteller: Origenes Werke* 7, p. 163.

the unchanging Word of God, he strove to achieve an icon-like tranquillity, *to make* his *countenance firm before the people.*[8] A man whose heart burned with the hidden fire of the Scriptures,[9] Origen's unhurried, timeless scholarship brought a breath of changelessness into the Christian communities of Alexandria and Caesarea, at the very moment when these communities had begun to hurry headlong into a new age of prosperity, fraught with occasions for compromise with the world and marked by intellectual recrimination and the flagrant quest for power among the clergy.[10] What earned him the admiration of Christian intellectuals in all later centuries was not so much what Origen had taught, exciting and frequently disturbing though that might be; it was the manner in which, as an exegete and spiritual guide, Origen had presented the life of a Christian teacher as suspended above time and space. It was this that made him a role model, a "saint" of Christian culture, a man who could be hailed over a century later as "the whetstone of us all."[11]

From the start, Origen's message had been stark and confident: "I beseech you, therefore, be transformed. Resolve to know that in you there is a capacity to be transformed."[12] (In this phrase we can actually hear Origen speaking: it is taken from a shorthand record of a discussion between Origen and a group of somewhat puzzled bishops, which has survived on a papyrus discovered in Tura, south of Cairo, in 1941.)[13]

By the year 229/230, Origen felt free to commit himself to his most remarkable book, the *Peri Archôn, On First Principles.* He was then in his late forties, an age when a serious philosopher could be thought to be sufficiently anchored in decades of meditation and direct experience of oral spiritual guidance (and had stirred up enough criticism

8. *In Ezech.* 3.1, *Origenes Werke* 8, p. 349.

9. *In Joh.* 10.18.105, ed. Cécile Blanc, *Origène: Commentaire sur Saint Jean,* Sources chrétiennes 157, p. 444 and *Hom. in Cant. Cant.* 2.8, in O. Rousseau, ed., *Origène: Homélies sur le Cantique des Cantiques,* p. 95. See esp. Marguerite Harl, "Le langage de l'expérience religieuse chez les pères grecs."

10. Origen's view of contemporary bishops was distinctly unflattering: *in Matt.* 16.6, *Origenes Werke* 10, pp. 493–497.

11. Gregory Nazianzen cited in Suidas, *Lexicon,* A. Adler, ed., 3:619.

12. *Dialogue with Heraclides* 150, in H. E. Chadwick, trans., *Alexandrian Christianity,* p. 446.

13. Chadwick, *Alexandrian Christianity,* pp. 430–436, provides a quite exceptionally good introduction to the incident.

among his colleagues) to make it worth his time to commit his thoughts to writing. In this book, he took the opportunity to lay bare the assumptions about the position of human beings in the universe that had underlain his personal alchemy as an exegete and guide of souls.

The problem that Origen posed was simple: "In what way has there come to be so great and various a diversity among created beings?"[14]

It was the old Platonic problem—how did the diversity observed in the material world emerge out of the original unity of the world of the Ideas? His answer to the question, however, was magnificently idiosyncratic. In his opinion, each created being had freely chosen to be different from its fellows; and each difference reflected a precise degree of decline from or progress toward an original, common perfection. Originally created equal, as "angelic" spirits, intended by God to stand forever in rapt contemplation of His wisdom, each spirit had "fallen" by choosing of its own free will to neglect, if ever so slightly— and even, in the case of the demons, to reject—the life-giving warmth of the presence of God.[15]

What we now call the "soul," the subjective self, was merely the result of a subtle cooling off of the original ardor of the primal, deepest self: the "spirit." As Origen pointed out, the word *psyché*, for "soul," derived from *psychros*, "cold." Compared with the fiery spirit that flickered upward, always straining to sink back into the primal fire of God, the conscious self was a dull thing, numbed by the cold absence of love.[16] The baffling diversity of the present universe, divided as it was between ranks of invisible angels and demons, and marked on earth by an apparently infinite variety of human destinies, was the end product of countless particular choices, by which each spirit had freely chosen to be what it now was.

The most obvious feature of such a view was an unrelieved feeling of "divine discontent" with the present limitations of the human person. A vast impatience ran through the universe. Each being—angelic, human, or demonic—had in some way fallen away from God, through the insidious, fatal sin of self-satisfaction. Each mighty spirit had made, and could still make, a dire choice to remain content with its present condition, and to neglect the opportunity to expose itself to the con-

---

14. *De Principiis.* 2.9.7.245, in F. Crouzel and M. Simonetti, eds., *Origène: Traité des Principes*, Sources chrétiennes 252, p. 368.
15. Ibid. 1.3.8.323, p. 164.   16. Ibid. 2.8.3.120, p. 344.

suming fire of God's love.[17] For Origen, Christ had been the only being whose original deepest self had remained "uncooled" by inertia. Christ's mighty spirit alone had remained inseparably joined to God, much as the white heat of an iron merged with the blaze of the furnace in which it rested.[18] All other beings must experience an unremitting sense of sadness and frustration: the primal, truest, most expansive definition of their self inevitably reached beyond the cramped circumstances of their present mode of existence. A shadow of regret always fell on the body. Whether this "body" was the ethereal frame of an angel or the heavy flesh of a human being, the body was always a limit and a source of frustration. But it was also a challenge; it was a frontier that demanded to be crossed. "Tents," Origen pointed out, were invariably spoken of with favor in the Old Testament. They stood for the limitless horizons of each created spirit, always ready to be struck and to be pitched ever further on. "Houses," by contrast, stood as symbols of dread satiety, "rooted, settled, defined by fixed limits."[19] Even the most resplendent beings were touched by this sadness: Origen believed that the huge soul of the Sun pressed ceaselessly against its radiant disc, and that its spirit sighed, as Saint Paul had sighed: *I could desire to be dissolved and to be with Christ: for it is far better.*[20]

If the tension to transcend the present limits of the self was the most vivid aspect of Origen's view of the human person, it was the least original. What concerned him most was how to reconcile a drive for transformation, shared by many Platonists and Christian Gnostics of the school of Valentinus, with whom he remained in constant dialogue,[21] with a sense of the unfathomable subtlety of God's justice in placing the "fallen" spirit within the temporary limits of a particular material body. The material universe as a whole, in his opinion, had been *subjected to frustration, not of its will;* but it had been *subjected in hope.*[22] For Origen, the fall of each individual spirit into a particular body had not been in any way a cataclysm; to be placed in a body was to experience a positive act of divine mercy. He distanced himself from many of his contemporaries by insisting that the body was nec-

---

17. See esp. Marguerite Harl, "Recherches sur l'origénisme d'Origène: la 'satiété' (kóros) de la contemplation comme motif de la chute des âmes."

18. *De Princip.* 2.6.5–6.159–192, pp. 318–320.   19. *In Num.* 17.4, p. 160.

20. *De Princip.* 1.7.5.180, pp. 218–220.

21. See esp. Elaine Pagels, *The Johannine Gospel in Gnostic Exegesis.*

22. Ibid. 1.7.5.156, p. 216, citing Romans 8:19.

essary for the slow healing of the soul.[23] It was only by pressing against the limitations imposed by a specific material environment that the spirit would learn to recover its earliest yearning to stretch beyond itself, to open itself "ever more fully and more warmly" to the love of God.[24] The body posed a challenge that counteracted the numb sin of self-satisfaction. For this reason, "The world before our eyes became a material world for the sake of those spirits who are in need of a life lived in physical matter."[25] If anything, Origen thought, it was the demons who were to be pitied: turned by their immense self-satisfaction away from the love of God, their bodies had been left perfectly within the control of their proud wills; their eerie flesh was as supple as a chill north wind.[26] "They are regarded as unworthy of this instruction and training whereby, through the flesh, the human race . . . aided by the heavenly powers, is being instructed and trained."[27]

Hence, Origen's profound ambivalence about the human body. Looking at the body at close quarters, as a source of temptation and frustration, Origen offered little comfort to his readers:

You have coals of fire, you will sit upon them, and they will be of help to you.[28]

Yet, in the eyes of God, each particular human spirit had been allotted a particular physical constitution as its appropriate sparring partner. Each person's *flesh and blood* was particular to that person, and had been exquisitely calibrated by God, "who alone is the searcher of hearts," to challenge the potentially mighty spirit of each to stretch beyond itself.[29] Thus, far from regarding the body as a prison of the soul, Origen arrived at an unexpected familiarity with the body. It always seemed to him that each person's spirit must be as vividly distinctive as were the features of his or her face. The gentle precision of God's mercy ensured that each body was adjusted to the peculiar needs of its soul

---

23. This has been made plain in general by Hal Koch, *Pronoia und Paideusis. Studien über Origenes und sein Verhältnis zum Platonismus*, esp. pp. 28–30; see now Trigg, *Origen*, pp. 103–120 and Margaret R. Miles, *Fullness of Life*, pp. 49–61.

24. *De Princip.* 1.3.8.319–320, p. 164.

25. *In Joh.* 19.20.132, Sources chrétiennes 292, p. 126.

26. *De Princip.* 1.8.165, p. 86 and 2.8.3.150, p. 346.

27. Ibid. 1.6.3.111, p. 111; in G. W. Butterworth, trans., *Origen: On First Principles*, p. 56.

28. *In Ezech.* 1.3, *Origenes Werke* 8, 324–325.

29. *De Princip.* 3.2.3.157, Sources chrétiennes 268, p. 164.

down to the finest details, much as the lines of each person's handwriting remained unmistakably their own. Each person's relations with the body, therefore, had its own, unfathomably particular story: to the eye of God, the "chastity" of a Peter was as different from the "chastity" of a Paul as was each Apostle's signature.[30] Confronted with their own, irreducibly particular *flesh and blood,* all believers struggled to maintain, in themselves, the huge momentum of their spirit's longing for God.

Origen's view of the spiritual struggle entered the bloodstream of all future traditions of ascetic guidance in the Greek and Near Eastern worlds. It involved the human person in a solemn and continuous dialogue with the intangible powers that brushed against the mind. For "if we are possessed of free will, some spiritual beings may be very likely to be able to urge us on to sin and others to assist us to salvation."[31]

Angels and demons were as close to the Christian of the third century as were adjacent rooms. The free soul expanded in love or slipped back into numbed satiety in as far as it chose to "seek counsellors" in the mighty, unseen spirits that stood so close to every person.[32] At the moment of intense prayer, for instance, the believer could sense, in the undisturbed serenity of the mind, a touch of the stilled silence of the angelic spirits who stood beside all Christians, lovingly concerned that humans should join with them in their own untrammeled worship of God.[33]

Surrounded on every side by invisible helpers and invisible seducers, the thought flow of the Christian could rarely be treated as neutral. Piety and firm resolves rose into consciousness through the soul's willingness to cooperate with its angelic guides. These protecting presences drew the healthful properties of the person to the fore, as mysteriously and as intimately as the contact of healing poultices mobilized the energies of humors that lay far beneath the skin.[34] The themes of a Christian's meditations rose within the "heart" with a power that frequently betrayed resources deeper than those of the isolated, conscious mind:

Blessed is the man whose acceptance is in Thee, O Lord: Thy ascents are in his heart.[35]

---

30. *In Num.* 2.2, p. 11.   31. *De Princip.* Praef. 5.111, p. 84.
32. *In Num.* 20.3, p. 195.   33. Ibid. 11.9, p. 93.
34. *In Jerem.* (Latin version) 2.12, *Origenes Werke* 8:301.
35. *De Princip.* 3.2.4.250, Sources chrétiennes 268: p. 168.

It was the same with temptation. Consent to <u>evil thoughts</u>, many of which were occasioned, in the <u>first instance</u>, by the dull creakings of the body—<u>by its need for food and its organic, sexual drives</u>[36]—implied a decision to <u>collaborate with other invisible spirits, the demons,</u> whose pervasive presence, close to the human person, was <u>registered</u> in the <u>"heart"</u> in the form of inappropriate images, fantasies, and obsessions. For these demonic promptings also had a dynamism that could not be explained by the normal stream of conscious thought. Hence, for Origen, as for all later ascetic writers, the "heart" was a place where momentous, faceless options were mercifully condensed in the form of conscious trains of thought—*logismoi*. Little wonder, then, that the wise Solomon had said: *Keep thy heart with all diligence.*[37] For to <u>consent</u> to such *logismoi* was to "<u>consecrate oneself</u>" to <u>demonic partners.</u>[38] It was to give oneself over, on many more levels of the self than the conscious person, to an alternative identity: it was to lose oneself to the powers of numbness that still lurked in the hidden reaches of the universe, and to take on the character of chill demonic spirits who had been content to exist without the ardent search for God.

Origen bequeathed to his successors a view of the human person that continued to inspire, to fascinate, and to dismay all later generations. He <u>conveyed, above all, a profound sense of the fluidity of the</u> body. Basic aspects of human beings, such as sexuality, sexual differences, and other seemingly indestructible attributes of the person associated with the physical body, struck Origen as no more than provisional. The <u>present human body reflected the needs of a single,</u> somewhat <u>cramped moment in the spirit's progress back to a former,</u> limitless identity.

A <u>body, in the</u> sense of <u>a limiting frame for the spirit,</u> would remain with all created beings throughout their long period of healing. But Origen was careful to point out that this body was not necessarily continuous with the present physical organism. It also would become transformed, along with the spirit, "throughout diverse and immeasurable ages," of which the present life was one short interlude.[39] The transformation of the body in the future ages of its existence involved

36. Ibid. 3.2.2.89 and 96, p. 158.
37. Ibid. 3.2.4.292, Sources chrétiennes 268: p. 172, citing *Proverbs* 4:23.
38. *In Num.* 20.3, p. 193.
39. *De Princip.* 3.1.23.1025 [Latin of Rufinus], Sources chrétiennes 268, p. 146; Butterworth trans., p. 209.

a long, mysterious process, as splendid in its final outcome as was the the pure, "healed" matter that emerged from the alchemist's crucible as gold.[40] The body itself would become less "thick," less "coagulated," less "hardened," as the numbing inertia of the spirit thawed in the growing heat of its yearning for the Wisdom of God.[41] As under the delicious working of fresh wine, the barriers that cramped the person would be dissolved.[42] The "vessel of clay" of the present self would be shattered, to be remolded, ever again, into containers of ever wider capacity, in stages of life that stretched far beyond the grave.[43]

This was a view of the bodies of actual men and women taken from a disturbingly distant vantage point. It meant that Origen was prepared to look at sexuality in the human person as if it were a mere passing phase. It was a dispensable adjunct of the personality that played no role in defining the essence of the human spirit. Men and women could do without it even in this present existence. Human life, lived in a body endowed with sexual characteristics, was but the last dark hour of a long night that would vanish with the dawn. The body was poised on the edge of a transformation so enormous as to make all present notions of identity tied to sexual differences, and all social roles based upon marriage, procreation, and childbirth, seem as fragile as dust dancing in a sunbeam.

Origen was widely believed to have practiced what he preached. It was always said of him that, as a young man of about twenty, around 206, he had discreetly gone to a doctor to have himself castrated.[44] At the time, castration was a routine operation.[45] Origen's supporters were prepared to believe that he had undergone the operation so as to avoid slanderous rumors about the intimacy that he enjoyed with women who were his spiritual charges.[46] Two generations previously, a young

---

40. Ibid. 1.6.4.104, p. 204: On gold as "healed" matter, see esp. S. Averincev, "L'or dans le système des symboles de la culture protobyzantine," esp. p. 63.

42. *In Joh.* 1.30.205–206, pp. 160–162.   43. *In Num.* 9.6–7, pp. 62–64.

44. Eusebius, *Eccles. Hist.* 6.8.2–3: see Pierre Nautin, *Lettres et écrivains des iième et iiième siècles,* pp. 121–126. The reader should know that Chadwick, *Early Christian Thought,* p. 67 is unconvinced that such an incident ever happened. I think that the sources for it are sufficiently reliable, that there was nothing impossible about such an action in the third century, and, hence, that—at the very least—Origen could certainly have been viewed as someone who had had himself castrated.

45. Aline Rousselle, *Porneia: de la maîtrise du corps à la privation sensorielle,* pp. 158–164 takes us into a world little dreamed of by most commentators.

46. Eusebius, *Eccles. Hist.* 6.8.2.

[handwritten marginalia at top: body: a grace partner in the adventure of redemption — + transformation]

Alexandrian had been prepared to undergo the same operation, for the same reason.[47]

When, as a priest at Caesarea, Origen preached against those who took too literally the words of Christ, when He had blessed those who had *made themselves eunuchs for the sake of the kingdom of heaven*, he treated the matter in a manner so unruffled as to reveal a chasm between a third-century audience and ourselves.[48] Given the vivid fantasies that surrounded the adult eunuch, it was far from certain that everyone would have believed that Origen had gained immunity from sexual temptation by such an operation. Postpubertal castration merely made the man infertile; it was, in itself, no guarantee of chastity.[49] What Origen may have sought, at that time, was something more deeply unsettling. The eunuch was notorious (and repulsive to many) because he had dared to shift the massive boundary between the sexes. He had opted out of being male. By losing the sexual "heat" that was held to cause his facial hair to grow, the eunuch was no longer recognizable as a man.[50] He was a human being "exiled from either gender."[51] De- *[marginalia: ≠ gender?]* prived of the standard professional credential of a philosopher in late antique circles—a flowing beard—Origen would have appeared in public with a smooth face, like a women or like a boy frozen into a state of prepubertal innocence. He was a walking lesson in the basic indeterminacy of the body.

This body did not have to be defined by its sexual components, still less by the social roles that were conventionally derived from those components. Rather, the body should act as a blazon of the freedom of the spirit. John the Baptist's soul had been so huge as to have caused his tiny body to leap in his mother's womb. The body of so great a spirit must necessarily have remained a virgin.[52] To reject marriage and sexual activity of any kind was to make plain the fiery spirit's "manifest destiny." Virginity preserved an identity already formed in a former, more splendid existence and destined for yet further glory.

---

47. Justin, *I Apology* 29.2; Henry Chadwick, *The Sentences of Sextus*, p. 111 provides full evidence on the prevalence of castration in third- and fourth-century Christian circles.

48. *In Matt.* 15.1, pp. 347–353.

49. See Basil of Ancyra, *de virginitate tuenda* 61, *Patrologia Graeca* 30: 769C for the misdeeds of eunuchs in Christian circles.

50. *In Matt.* 15.3, p. 356.   51. Claudius Mamertinus, *Panegyrici latini* 11.19.4.

52. *In Joh.* 1.31.183 and 187, pp. 330 and 334.

At a stroke, continence ceased to be what it had largely been in the Early Church—a postmarital matter for the middle-aged. Origen, indeed, had been unusual in his early commitment as a Christian, and in the fascination that he had exercised on young persons in Alexandria in the first years of his career. His first years in Alexandria give us a rare glimpse of something like the radicalism of a "youth culture" at work in a church more usually dominated by sober greybeards.[53]

In middle age, Origen tended to present virginity as a state that declared the joining of an "immaculate" spirit with its well-tempered, material frame. As a result of this shift in perspective, virginity could no longer be regarded simply as a perilous state of suspended sexuality, imposed upon the frisky young by their elders in the relatively short period between puberty and marriage. Nor was it an anomaly, made plain by the suspension of a natural destiny to marriage, undergone, in the pagan world, by a few prophetesses and priestesses. Virginity stood for the original state in which every body and soul had joined. It was a physical concretization, through the untouched body, of the pre-existing purity of the soul. In the words of an author appreciated by Origen, the continent body was a waxen seal that bore the exact "imprint" of the untarnished soul.[54] Identified in this intimate manner with the pristine soul, the intact flesh of a virgin of either sex stood out also as a fragile oasis of human freedom. Refusal to marry mirrored the right of a human being, the possessor of a preexistent, utterly free soul, not to surrender its liberty to the pressures placed upon the person by society.

Origen was quite prepared to draw this consequence. Social and physical mingled inextricably in his thought. Behind the definition imposed upon the spirit by the body, there lay the definition imposed upon the person, through the body, by society. Origen always thought of a body as more than the physical body, seen in isolation. The body was a "microclimate." It was a vehicle through which the spirit adjusted to its present material environment as a whole.[55] Innumerable subtle filaments led the spirit through the body, into involvement with others, and so into involvement with society. When he spoke of sex-

53. Eusebius, *Eccles. Hist.* 6.3.13–4.3 and *in Jud.* 9.1. *Origenes Werke* 7, p. 518.

54. *Sentences of Sextus* 346, Chadwick ed., p. 5; see pp. 114–115 on Origen and "Sextus."

55. Thus fish have a scaly body suited to their watery environment and angels shimmering bodies suited to their life in etherial fire: Origen apud Methodius, *de Resurrectione* 1.22.4–5: see H. Chadwick, "Origen, Celsus and the Resurrection of the Body."

ually active married persons, Origen took Paul's words on *the present necessity* (or *constraint*) not to refer to the pressure exercised on the soul by the sexual drives of the body. He understood *constraint* in a far wider sense. He thought that Paul had referred to the social bonds that tied the believer to marriage, and, through marriage, to the *frame of this world*—to the great, extended body of society, into which the Christian became inextricably grafted through marriage.[56] To reject sexuality, therefore, did not mean, for Origen, simply to suppress the sexual drives. It meant the assertion of a basic freedom so intense, a sense of identity so deeply rooted, as to cause to evaporate the normal social and physical constraints that tied the Christian to his or her gender. Society might see the Christian virgin, the continent boy, or the young Christian widow as persons defined by their sexual physical nature, and so as potential householders and bearers of children. Origen was less certain: the human spirit did not necessarily need to acquiesce to so self-limiting a definition.

Not to belong to married society was to belong more intensely to others. The invisible world was magnificently sociable. It was a "great city" crowded with angelic spirits. The sense of an invisible, alternative society, of a great communion of human and angelic beings, was central to Origen's notion of the virgin state. Bonds based on physical paternity, on physical love, and on social roles derived from the physical person seemed peculiarly evanescent when compared with the resonant unity of a universe that strained toward the embrace of Christ. In the light of such future intimacy, the humble, physical bonds of human marriage, based as they were on a momentary adjustment of the spirit to the heavy climate of earth, appeared peculiarly insubstantial.[57] A time would come when all relations based upon physical kinship would vanish. His huge identity no longer definable within such narrow limits, even Abraham—so Origen, the son of Leonides the martyr, "dared" to suggest—would no longer be called "father of Isaac," but by some other, deeper name:

Remember ye not the former things, neither consider the things of old. Behold I will do a new thing.[58]

In thinking in this way, Origen had appropriated, in a characteristically idiosyncratic manner, a distinctive feature of the Platonism of

---

56. *Fragments on I Corinthians*, 42 C. Jenkins, ed., p. 512.
57. *In Matt.* 14.22, p. 338.　　58. Ibid., 17.33, pp. 690–691.

his age, which he may have first encountered through the disciples of Valentinus.[59] The Platonic doctrine of the Ideas was an essential ingredient of Origen's view of the person. The notion that all beauty and order in the visible world was a distant echo of a yet more majestic, unseen harmony haunted contemporaries. For Origen, everything perceived with senses could be thought of as existing in undimmed intensity in God, the source of all being. The spiritual realm was alive with joys whose sensuous delight was veiled from the pious only by the present numbness of their spirits. Those who could thaw their frozen hearts would once again experience the sharp, precise impression of a wealth of spiritual sensations. The prophets and Evangelists had "felt" the original joy of God's Wisdom. In a manner that escaped normal experience, they had actually "tasted," "smelled," and "drunk" it, savoring the sweet taste of the Wisdom of God with a sensibility undulled by long negligence.[60]

It had been Origen's life's labor, as an exegete and guide of souls, to make the "spiritual senses" of his charges come alive again in their original intensity. By withdrawing from the dull anaesthesia of common, physical sensation, the soul of the "spiritual" person might recapture the sharp delights of another, more intensely joyful world. The believer's spirit would stand totally exposed before the Bridegroom, stripped of all sensual joys, to receive on a "naked" sensibility the exquisite touch of His darts.[61]

Origen wrote *Homilies on the Song of Songs*, around 240, as a peculiarly consequential exponent of what has been aptly called the "wild" Platonism of his generation.[62] In such a Platonism, sensuality could not simply be abandoned or repressed. Rather, the sharpness of sensual experience was brought back to its primordial intensity: it was

---

59. On this topic, see the excellent introduction of O. Rousseau, *Origène: Homélies sur le Cantique des Cantiques*, pp. 21–25. I am indebted to John Dillon, "Aesthésis Noété: a doctrine of spiritual senses in Origen and in Plotinus," who makes plain that the final formulation of the notion takes place only in Origen's later years. Patricia Cox, "Origen and the Bestial Soul," and now "Pleasure of the Text, Text of Pleasure: Eros and Language in Origen's *Commentary on the Song of Songs*" are suggestive treatments.

60. *Contra Celsum* 1.48: see the translation and notes of Henry Chadwick, *Origen: Contra Celsum*, p. 44; cf. *in Num.* 21.1, p. 200—the Levites are those of "undulled" sensibility.

61. *Hom. in Cant. Cant.* 2.8, p. 132.

62. The phrase is that of A. H. Armstrong, "Neoplatonic Valuations of Nature, Body and Intellect," at p. 41.

reawakened, in the mystic's heart, at its true level—the level of the
spirit. By contrast, physical pleasure was a stale and bland displace-
ment of true feeling, a deflection of the spirit's huge capacity for delight into the dulled sensations of the body. The spirit must learn to
"burn" in its deepest self, to yearn for the indefinable precision of the
scent of God, to hope for the delicious particularity of the taste of Christ
deep in the mouth, and to prepare itself for the final embrace of the
Bridegroom. This meant, in effect—for Origen and for his successors—a discipline of the senses that was all the more searching because what was at stake was no longer simply continence, but the
hesitant, fragile growth of a spiritual sense of preternatural sharpness.
Physical indulgence, undue eating, undue enjoyment of sight and
sound, the physical joys of sexual bonding in marriage: these became
subjects of vigilance. Sensual experiences nurtured a counter sensibility. They led to a dulling of the spirit's true capacity for joy. They were
a "cushion," which deadened the impact of those deeper, more vivid
pleasures that might fall like kisses on the bared spirit.[63]

Origen's attitude to marriage was so much sharper than that of
Clement mainly because of the streak of "wild" Platonism that ran
through his thought. A refined suspicion came to rest on the joys and
duties of the married state for which Clement had still been prepared
to praise the providence of God. The pleasures of the marriage bed,
the intimacy and loyalty of married life, were slurred echoes of the
more clear delights reserved for spirits unnumbed and uncushioned
by sensual experience. The refined soul was well advised to shun them:
they might bring about a degradation of the spiritual sense that was
all the more subtle and anxiety-producing because it could not be pinned
down with any great precision. Origen, and many like him in later
centuries, felt, with the intangible certainty of a refined, almost an
aesthetic, spiritual sensibility, that married intercourse actually coarsened the spirit. The spirit was destined for a moment of startling,
unimaginably precise "knowledge" of Christ, of which the subtle
"knowledge" of a partner gained through physical love was but a blurred
and—so Origen was convinced—a distracting and inapposite echo.[64]

63. *Hom. in Cant. Cant.* 2.9, p. 134. By the same token, the pains of Hell will be more
excruciating for the spirit, just as blows fall more sharply on a naked than on a clothed
body: see the citation in Pamphilus, *Apologia for Origen* 8: *Patrologia Graeca* 8: 602D–
603B; trans. Nautin, *Origène*, p. 274.

64. *In Joh.* 19.4.1, Sources chrétiennes 290, pp. 22–25.

The kisses of the Bridegroom would come only in the empty study-room:

> We find there a certain sensation of an embrace by the Spirit . . . and, oh, that I could be the one who yet might say: *His left hand is beneath my head, and his right arm reaches around me.*[65]

Such a view cast a chill shadow over the marriage bed. As a social institution, the partnership of the married couple—their intimacy, their loyalty to each other, the ordered and benevolent hierarchy of husband and wife (topics on which the author of the pseudo-Pauline Letter to the Ephesians had written with such warmth)—struck Origen as valid symbols of the invisible concord of a redeemed creation. But even they were transient symbols.[66] As for the facts of the marriage-bed, there was something pointedly "inapposite" about them.[67] No amount of decorum in the sexual act could smooth away the incongruities associated with it. Origen did not share Clement's optimism on that score. Rather, seen with high Platonic eyes, married intercourse could be evoked only in terms of what it lacked. It made painfully clear the extent of the hiatus between itself and "true" spiritual joining. In this, Origen's thought resembled that of the Valentinian Gnostics. Married intercourse took place in a "chamber," that is, "in darkness." An undispelled suspicion of "wantonness" lingered over it. Knowledge of married love could not be a stepping stone, by which the soul might rise, through physical experience, to a higher, more spiritual sense of partnership with God. Rather, the experience of sexuality, even in marriage, was delineated with bleak precision, as a darkened antithesis to the blazing, light-filled embrace of Christ in the spirit.[68]

Yet, with Origen, the same "wild" Platonism that would lead him to cast a dark shadow on the physical concomitants of marriage led him to fasten with complete satisfaction on the isolated virgin body. Here, at last, was a physical symbol that reflected without distortion the purity of the spiritual world. Solemnly set apart from married so-

---

65. *Hom. in Cant. Cant.* 1.2, p. 65. By contrast, the bedroom is not regarded as a proper place for prayer: *de orat.* 31.4; see esp. Giulia Sfameni Gasparro, *Origene: studi di antropologia*, pp. 234–242.

66. *Fragments on Ephesians*, 29, J. A. Gregg, ed. p. 566.

67. *Hom. in Cant. Cant.* 2.1, p. 80.

68. *Fragments on I Corinthians*, 39, p. 510, citing Romans 13:13.

ciety, the bodies of the continent—men and women alike—stood out as privileged material objects: they were "temples of God:"

Do not think that just as *the belly* is made *for food and food for the belly*, that in the same way the body is made for intercourse. If you wish to understand the Apostle's train of reasoning, for what reason the body was made, then listen: it was made that it should be a *temple to the Lord*; that the soul, being holy and blessed, should act in it as if it were a priest serving before the Holy Spirit that dwells in you. In this manner, Adam had a body in Paradise; but in Paradise he did not "know" Eve.[69]

Such statements had practical implications. By 248, it was plain that a general persecution was imminent. The onset of persecution had been associated, in many cities, with a positive revival of a sense of the sacred in pagan communities: mobs had rioted at the instigation of pagan priests, angered by insults to the temples; and the Emperor Decius had come to believe that neglect of the visible gestures of sacrifice had jeopardized the safety of the Empire.[70] It was a time when a Christian teacher, such as Origen, had to make clear to pagan critics where exactly the "holy" might be found on earth. In order to reassure his devoted patron and disciple, Ambrosius, Origen began to rebut in great detail an attack on Christianity made by Celsus, a pagan Platonist, written some eighty years previously.

The long work contained quite remarkable statements on the "declaratory" role of the Christian virgin in the Roman world of the mid-third century. A sense of history comes to run through Origen's presentation of virginity. Virginity was presented as a privileged link between heaven and earth. For it was only through the "holy" body of a virgin woman that God had been able to join Himself to humanity, thus enabling the human race to speak, at last, of Immanuel, "God among us."[71] Christ's Incarnation, through His descent into a virgin body, marked the beginning of a historic mutation: "human and divine began to be woven together, so that by prolonged fellowship with divinity, human nature might become divine."[72]

And the "human nature" that was on its slow way to the divine

---

69. *Fragments on I Corinthians*, 29, p. 370.

70. Eusebius, *Eccles. Hist.* 6.41.1: mobs stirred up in Alexandria by pagan priests; on Decius, see Clarke, *Letters of Saint Cyprian*, pp. 21–25, and now Robin Lane Fox, *Pagans and Christians*, pp. 451–454.

71. *Contra Celsum* 1.35, Chadwick, trans., p. 34.   72. Ibid. 3.28, p. 146.

the body could be
holy — if it
does not on[...] its[...]
[...]

was a nature most clearly revealed in bodies untouched by sexual experience. In Origen's view, perpetual continence, now upheld, for a wide variety of reasons, by little groups of Christian men and women all over the Mediterranean, made of such persons clearly privileged representatives of God's deepest purposes for the transformation of the human race.

What was at stake, between Celsus, the pagan, and Origen, the Christian, both of them Platonists, was where to find the holy in the visible world, and consequently from what source to derive the authority that the holy might come to exercise among men. A good Platonist, Celsus had looked to the material universe as a whole. Here was a refulgent "body," palpably worthy of the mighty Creator-soul that embraced it.[73] The blazing Sun, the heavy clusters of the Milky Way: these were "bodies" set on fire by the touch of the Ideas. The quiet radiance of the One God, delegated to "angelic" ministers, better known to men in their traditional guise as the ancient gods, filtered down yet further beneath the Moon, to touch the dull earth, bathing with an untroubled light the immemorial holy places of pagan worship. Statues, temples, ancestral rites—these were the symbols that echoed most appositely on earth the blazing holiness of the heavens. Compared with these, the individual human body was too frail a thing to carry so much majesty: it was no more than a needy beggar that had sidled up to the soul, demanding with disagreeable insistence a small share of its attention.[74] Celsus was deeply angry because Jews, and now Christians, were claiming that they stood above all temples— even above the stars themselves. They claimed that they enjoyed direct communion with the One God of the universe. Celsus, and later Plotinus, Origen's younger contemporary (both of them Platonic philosophers steeped in the same culture as Origen), showed deep religious anger that such an overvaluation of their persons should have led Christians to overturn the established hierarchy of the universe. Mere human beings were to know their place, far below the stars; they must not claim that they could brush aside the gods who ministered to them from the distant heavens. Christians, Celsus had said, were like

73. This has been particularly well stated, in the case of Plotinus, by A. H. Armstrong, *Saint Augustine and Christian Platonism*. Now in R. A. Markus, *Augustine: A Collection of Critical Essays*, p. 13.

74. Plotinus, *Enneads* 1.8.14.

frogs holding counsel round a marsh, or worms assembling in some filthy corner, saying "God has even deserted the whole world and the motions of the heavens and disregarded the vast earth to give attention to us alone." They are like worms that say, "There is God first, and we are next after Him in rank . . . and all things exist for our benefit."[75]

Faced by such withering indignation, Origen, the Christian Platonist, made the *gran rifiuto* that separated him forever from the "Ancient Wisdom" of his pagan colleagues. Christians, he replied, "have already learned . . . that the body of a rational being that is devoted to the God of the Universe is a temple of the God they worship."[76]

The human body could be "offered up"; it could be "made holy" for God. The humble "ass" of the body could become the "resplendent" vehicle of the soul.[77] Each Christian man or woman could build their body into a "holy tabernacle of the Lord."[78]

Look now at how you have progressed from being a tiny little human creature on the face of this earth. You have progressed to become a *temple of God*, and you who were mere flesh and blood have reached so far that you are a *limb of Christ's body.*[79]

Let us now follow the fortunes of these "temples of God" in the Christian churches in the Mediterranean and the Near East through the decisive half century that stretched from the death of Origen, through further pagan reaction in the Great Persecution, to the conversion of Constantine and the first public appearance of Saint Anthony.

75. *C. Cels.* 4.23, pp. 199–200; compare Plotinus, *Enneads* 2.9: *Against the Gnostics.*
76. Ibid. 4.26, pp. 201–202.   77. *in Jud.* 6.5, *Origenes Werke* 7:503.
78. *In Exod.* 13.5, pp. 277–278.   79. *in Jes. Nave* 5.5, *Origenes Werke* 7:319.

NINE

"Walking on Earth, Touching High Heaven's Vault": Porphyry and Methodius

In 253, the same year Origen died in Caesarea, worn out by torture and the fetid heat of the prison-house,[1] Plotinus, a man some twenty years his junior, began to commit to writing the philosophical instruction that he himself had given over the past decade, in Rome, to a quiet study-circle of well-connected pagans. Origen and Plotinus were fellow-countrymen. Both men were Platonists. In their contrasting attitudes to sexuality, we can see very clearly the parting of the ways between Christianity and paganism in late antiquity.

Quite as much as Origen, Plotinus was haunted by spiritual longing for the gracious beauty of The One. A sweet touch of the fullness of life, startlingly sensuous in its soft and gentle exuberance, frequently flooded his soul, stilling all thoughts of mere physical love: "This is no affirmation of an excited body, but of a soul become again what she was in the time of her early joy."[2]

---

1. Eusebius, *Ecclesiastical History* 6.39.5. Peter of Alexandria, *Canonical Epistle* 2: *Patrologia Graeca* 18: 469C, speaks of the "nauseous odors" of prison as a particular affliction to the martyrs.

2. Plotinus, *Enneads* 6.7.34, S. MacKenna, trans., *The Enneads*, p. 588. P. Hadot, *Plotin*, pp. 105–135 is unequalled on the tone of Plotinus' circle; see now L. Brisson, eds. *Porphyre: La Vie de Plotin 1: Travaux Préliminaires*, pp. 55–140, 231–280.

Yet the difference between the two men is equally significant. Origen's anxious sense of the threat of a "counter-sensibility," his fear that the soul's capacity for spiritual delight might be subtly and irreparably coarsened by the experience of physical intercourse, was notably lacking in Plotinus. For Plotinus, the physical embraces of the married couple were a very distant mirror, indeed, of that primal joining; but he never treated them as a tarnished and distorting mirror. The mystical union of the soul with the One "is the explanation of even copulative love . . . [although] those that have not obtained to that memory do not understand what is happening inside them."[3]

Searching for an image with which to convey the undeliberating yet utterly apposite joining of each soul to its appropriate body, in an instantaneous, unthinking "leap" into the flesh, the image of a loving couple fell from his pen with magnificent unconcern: such a moment "is more like an instinctively right leap, like the couple who move to fulfill their desire for sexual union . . . like is destined unfailingly to like."[4]

More like Clement in his attitude to sexuality than Origen, Plotinus looked at the body from a huge height: "His attitude is one of austere detached tolerance."[5] His own ascetic regimen included total chastity, yet he moved with ease among patrons and disciples whose married state he took for granted.[6] A fine-tuned body, as vibrant as a well-used lyre, was his ideal.[7]

The pagan spiritual guides of late antiquity, and their disciples, were capable of imposing on their bodies restraints that bruise a modern sensibility, and that were regarded as extraordinary even by their contemporaries. They held to these, and to the social isolation that such restraints imposed upon them, with impressive courage.[8] Yet the renunciations that carried the heaviest symbolic weight in their eyes did not coincide with those that had come to be most valued by their Christian contemporaries. The pagan sages were often members of the

3. *Ennead* 3.5.1, p. 191: see Hadot, *Plotin*, pp. 65 and 73–75.
4. *Ennead* 4.3.13, p. 272.
5. A. H. Armstrong, *The Cambridge History of Later Greek and Early Medieval Philosophy*, p. 229.
6. Porphyry, *Life of Plotinus* 9: Hadot, *Plotin*, pp. 71–72.
7. *Ennead* 1.4.16, see esp. E. R. Dodds, *Pagan and Christian in an Age of Anxiety*, pp. 24–26—the statement of a master.
8. Garth Fowden, "The Pagan Holy Man in Late Antique Society," pp. 33–59, esp. pp. 33–38; 51–59.

urban governing classes of the Empire. They drew their disciples almost exclusively from that class. They wished to snatch their charges away from the bustle of the forum, not from the marriage bed.

Within Plotinus' circle, the touch of the terrible beauty of the One still fell upon active members of the Roman Senate. Their families were already established. It was the public life of Rome, and not their sexual life, that was drained of all meaning for them, by the approach of their soul's true love.⁹ Rogatianus had been an active member of the "managerial aristocracy" of Rome.¹⁰ Under the guidance of Plotinus, he learned to blot out his former public self. He even moved out of his family *palazzo*, lodging undemandingly with friends. Eating only every second day, his punctilious abstinence was rewarded by the cure of a nobleman's affliction—Rogatianus' strict diet cured him of a severe state of the gout. His most spectacular renunciation involved the turning down of an official dignity: "on the point of taking up the praetorship, the lictors already at the door, [he] refused to come out, or to have anything to do with the office."¹¹

Rogatianus, we must remember, was a contemporary of the author of the Acts of Judas Thomas. The scenario that delighted those who remembered him was that of public office rejected on the very day of its inauguration; it was not sexual renunciation proclaimed on the wedding-night. Wandering through Rome, Rogatianus had made himself a ghost of his public self: he was not what many Christians would soon wish to see in their own heroes—a sexual being poised between the bed and the desert.

Nothing shows more clearly the divergence between pagan and Christian notions of renunciation than do the writings of Plotinus' disciple, editor, and biographer, the philosopher Porphyry. A native of Tyre, Porphyry knew Origen at Caesarea and thoroughly disapproved of him. At some time around 270, he composed a devastatingly learned attack on Christianity.¹² He was well aware of the options taken by

9. *Ennead* 6.7.34.

10. *Porphyre: Vie de Plotin: Travaux Préliminaires*, p. 109.

11. Porphyry, *Life of Plotinus* 7, p. 6.

12. Eusebius, *Ecclesiastical History* 6.19.5–8. The fragments of Poprhyry's *Against the Christians* are edited by A. von Harnack, "Porphyrius, 'Gegen die Christen'." For the date, see now Brian Croke, "The Era of Porphyry's Anti-Christian Polemic." The reader should know that strong arguments for a considerably later date, around 303 A.D., and hence for a very different context, have been advanced by T. D. Barnes, "Porphyry *Against the Christians*: Date and the Attribution of Fragments."

his Christian contemporaries, and his rejection of them was all the more crushing because he shared with so many Christians of the educated classes an inherited conglomerate of exceedingly demanding moral notions.

The sexual ideals fostered in Porphyry's world, and that of his pagan successors, differed little from the austerely disciplined sexual codes upheld by Clement of Alexandria for his Christian sages. The life of a married household might be marked by "a struggle for continence"; but this meant not the absolute rejection of sexual activity, but merely its severe control; and with the passing of time its abandonment.[13] The more drastic alternatives to such an ideal—demonstrative conversions to perpetual virginity among young Christian women—annoyed Porphyry greatly. There are now Christian women, he wrote, in his *Against the Christians*, who have ignored Saint Paul, when he warned that *some shall depart from the faith . . . forbidding to marry*. They had forgotten the Apostle's admission that *concerning virgins I have no commandment from the Lord*:

It being clear that a girl does not do well by remaining a virgin, or a married person by renouncing marriage . . . how can it be that some who practise the virgin state make so great an ado about it, and say that they are "Filled with the Holy Spirit," for all the world like she who gave birth to Jesus?[14]

It is a devastating rejection of the most cherished ideal of Origen and his circle.

Altogether, Porphyry and his pagan colleagues took sexual austerity for granted. They saw no peculiar symbolic value in sexual renunciation when practiced by their male peers; and they thought that it was positively inappropriate, if not impious, that young women of marriageable age should renounce their duty to society and to the "gods that preside over generation," by vowing their bodies to perpetual virginity. Porphyry's own image of the body condensed subtly different anxieties. Food, not sexuality, was the topic on which he felt most

13. The precept is taken from Henry Chadwick, ed., *Sextus*, no. 239, p. 38. As Chadwick has shown, this collection of Neo-Pythagorean maxims was used both by Christians and by Porphyry: Chadwick, *Sentences of Sextus*, pp. 107–116 and 141–143. It was later translated into Latin by Rufinus of Aquileia, to serve as a guide for a couple who had come to practice continence after the birth of two children. Though austere, the precepts envision restraint in sexual intercourse of the same kind as that exercised in eating (cf. no. 240, Chadwick, p. 38), and not total renunciation.

14. Porphyry, *Against the Christians*, fragment 33, Harnack, p. 60: see J. M. Démarolle, "Les femmes chrétiennes vues par Porphyre," p. 45.

strongly: he was a strict vegetarian, the author of the pamphlet "On Abstinence from Animal Foods."[15]

The ingestion of animal meat summed up for Porphyry far more appropriately than did the hot passions of the bed the vulnerability of the human spirit to the cloying materiality that weighed in upon it on every side. Like Origen, Porphyry believed that a world of invisible spirits pressed up against the person. But they did so in their most sinister manner at the dinner table, hovering over the quivering red meat. Their presence was sensed less (as with Origen) in the disturbing, partly sexual, fantasies that rose into the "heart" of the believer, than in the raucous hiccups and unruly farts of those whose very bodies had been made permeable to matter at its most disorderly, through their lax diet.[16]

Hagneia, a notion of ritual purity—a visceral reflex of avoidance, by which the pious strove to preserve charged boundaries between their bodies and all forms of polluting, anomalous mixture—was still a force to be reckoned with among late-third-century pagans.[17] In Christian circles, the sense of purity weighed most heavily upon the state of the continent virgin: a strong charge of sacred awe surrounded the bodies of men and women whose flesh had not been "corrupted" by sexual intercourse. With Porphyry, the sense of holy horror lay, rather, on the mouth. He made his own the cry of Empedocles: would that his pure soul had ceased to be,

Before those lips began the guilty deed,
On the dire nutriment of flesh to feed.[18]

To fall greedily upon the gross, blood-filled food of meat was to reenact the fall of the pure soul into matter. To adopt a sparse diet from which all meat was excluded—by no means a starvation diet—was to halt the fall of the soul, by means of a gesture of perpetual renunci-

---

15. Porphyry, *On Abstinence from Animal Foods*, Thomas Taylor, trans.; J. Bouffartigue and M. Patillon, eds., *Porphyre: De l'Abstinence*.

16. Porphyry, *On Philosophy from Oracles* in Eusebius, *Preparation for the Gospel* 4.23: *Patrologia Graeca* 21: 305B.

17. Porphyry, *On Abstinence* 1.57.2–4 and 2.46.2, Bouffartigue, pp. 89–90 and 112; Taylor, pp. 61 and 98. See the temple inscription at Lindos: F. Sokolowski, *Les lois sacrées des cités grecques: Supplément* no. 91.1–5, at p. 159.

18. *On Abstinence* 2.31.3, p. 98; Taylor, p. 85.

ation that was as cogent, in its own way, as was the cessation of sexual activity in Christian, Encratite circles.[19]

Yet Porphyry's motive in refusing to eat meat was subtly different from what had been at stake for Christians in the gesture of sexual renunciation. Porphyry thought only in terms of the individual soul. By abstaining from meat, his soul escaped identification with matter: he had furthered the escape of his eternal mind from the "blood-drenched surge" of the body.[20] He did not think that his renunciation would have any immediate social repercussions, beyond a certain distancing from the normal habits of public life. Porphyry did not claim that his decision to abstain from meat would bring a collective social process to a stunning halt, as the renunciation of marriage and the bearing of children was thought to do, in Encratite Christian circles. Porphyry's concern concentrated on the descent and return of the soul. He was not in any way inclined to break the cycle of birth, copulation, and death that swept organized society, in its blind and swaggering pride, into the grave. Such thoughts lay outside his horizon. For him, as for most pagan philosophers, human society was a mere sliver in the huge, godlike organism of the universe.

In this universe, a few vigilant souls might swim to shore, out of the swaying ocean of matter, to join their bodiless peers in their true homeland, beyond the stars. They would return to a world of the spirit where the inconvenience of possessing a body would be forgotten, as if it had never been.[21] But the *cosmos* as a whole, and with it the human race, would continue forever: "misty and dim" to humans caught in the flesh, it was also "sacred and pleasing" in its harmonious immensity.[22] In that cosmos, souls were destined to descend into matter ceaselessly, as the gods of "generative love" continued to weave the "sea purple garments" of new human bodies upon the ancient loom of the marriage bed.[23]

It would not have pleased Porphyry to know that, at the same time as he was writing in Italy, Methodius, a Christian teacher in Olympus in Lycia, on the Aegean coast of southwest Turkey, had composed a

19. See esp. A. Smith, *Porphyry's Place in the Neoplatonic Tradition*, pp. 20–80.
20. Porphyry, *Life of Plotinus* 22; MacKenna, p. 16.
21. Porphyry, *The Cave of the Nymphs* 35, ed. and trans., Arethusa Monographs, p. 35; and now Robert Lamberton, trans., *Porphyry: On the Cave of the Nymphs*, p. 40.
22. Porphyry, *The Cave of the Nymphs* 6, p. 12; Lamberton, p. 24.
23. Porphyry, *The Cave of the Nymphs* 14, p. 17; Lamberton, p. 29.

dialogue in praise of virginity, entitled *The Symposium*.[24] It was a bare-faced pastiche of Plato's great work. Instead of portraying a gathering of sexually active Athenian gentlemen, however, Methodius' banquet brought together ten young girls to celebrate the beauty of their virginal resolve. Writing at the behest of a mysterious "Lady of Termessus," Methodius, the male teacher, remained a discreet presence. It was Saint Thecla who replaced Socrates; it was she who evoked the homing flight of a young girl's soul, as it thrilled with an innate love for spiritual beauty. But this eternal beauty was no longer to be found in the abstract realm of the Ideas; it was most present in the radiant purity of the virgin state.[25]

Seated around a clear fountain, "flowing smooth as heavy oil," the little group was shaded by the *agnus castus* tree—by the tree, that is, on whose branches young Athenian girls would sleep, to lull their sexual urges at the time of abstinence imposed upon them by the festival of the Thesmophoria.[26] In this *Symposium*, we can glimpse a study-circle more like that of Origen than that of Plotinus: it was an inward-looking assembly of "domestic precursors of the monks."[27]

The *Symposium* of Methodius has not inspired enthusiasm in modern readers: "The book is stilted, its outlook narrow."[28] Yet we can easily understand its importance to a third-century reader. In the first place, Methodius reconciled the highly personal perspective of Origen with the older traditions of Asia Minor. He followed Irenaeus of Lyon in presenting the process of salvation in terms of the slow but sure return of the human race to the state of Adam. That state had been renewed in the person of Christ, and would be regained, in its entirety, by the saints, at the time of the Resurrection.[29]

The limitless horizons of Origen were more narrowly delimited by Methodius; but the sense of historical momentum that had emerged so clearly in Origen's last great work, *Against Celsus*, was made more present in Methodius' *Symposium*.[30] Christ had brought back to earth the original virginal flesh of Adam. In defeating the devil in that flesh, He had shown that a human being could become once again, in this life, what Adam had first been—a well-tuned instrument for the praise

---

24. See the introduction of H. Musurillo to *Méthode d'Olympe: Le Banquet*.
25. Methodius, *Symposium* 8.2.173–175, Sources chrétiennes, pp. 204–206.
26. *Ibid*. Prelude 8, pp. 48–50.
27. K. E. Kirk, *The Vision of God*, p. 187.   28. Ibid.
29. Musurillo, *Méthode d'Olympe*, pp. 14–23.
30. See above, ch. 8, pp. 175–176.

of God.[31] Settled married society did not tumble at such a message, as in the Acts of Judas Thomas; rather, it was allowed to fade into the background. Marriage was a matter for the faceless multitude of the faithful.[32] It was permitted to continue as a concession to human frailty, much as invalids were excused from taking part in the solemn collective fast that preceded the festival of Easter.[33]

The process of reproduction, the solemn "shudder" of intercourse[34] and the hot male "thirst" for progeny[35]—topics which our virgins discussed, in the Platonic manner, with studied good nature and surprising circumstantiality—had become transparent to the higher reality that they represented. They were passing shadows, which pointed to the only truly fecund union, that of Christ and the Church. True progeny came, not through physical intercourse, but through the preaching of the Gospel. The joys of physical parenthood were a pallid reflection of the truly fertile life of the virgin girls, gathered around their spiritual father, a discreet and learned priest.[36]

In this development, Methodius sensed a slow but sure change for the better in the human race. His view of the history of mankind was of civilization gently shedding its discontents. He presented human history as the story of the slow but sure taming of the raw sexual drive. Humanity had begun with brutish incest and had slowly progressed to polygamy. But now that the earth was fully populated, even stolid marital restraint—the *sophrosyné* praised in good wives on so many epitaphs of the contemporary Greek world—had given way to the *aphtharsia*, the uncorrupted stability of the virgin state.[37] It was a vision of humanity quietly come to rest, its pony-frisking adolescence long past, facing the end of time "all passion spent." The culmination of history was to be seen in Methodius' little group of consecrated girls,

Where the green swell is in the havens dumb,
And out of the swing of the sea.[38]

Behind this muted idyll we can appreciate the power of a structure of thought destined for a long future in the Greek-speaking world.

31. Methodius, *Symposium* 3.7.69, p. 106.   32. 1.5.27, p. 66.
33. 3.10.78–13.89, pp. 112–122.   34. 2.2.31–32, p. 70.   35. 2.5.41, p. 80.
36. 1.1.14, p. 56.   37. 9.1.236, p. 264 and 10.1.259, p. 286.
38. Gerard Manley Hopkins, *Heaven-haven: a nun takes the veil*, in *Poems and Prose*, W. H. Gardiner, ed., p. 5; Methodius, *Symposium* 1.2.18, p. 58: *eudion choron*.

Seen "horizontally," as it were, virginity represented the slow dawning of a spiritual millennium among the saints.[39] Seen "vertically," however, the virgin state—that is, the concrete fact of a perpetually untouched body—fitted into a singularly potent structure of mediation.

Methodius might have agreed wholeheartedly with the modern anthropologist, that

> The central "problem" of religion is . . . to reestablish some kind of bridge between God and Man. . . . "Mediation" (in this sense) . . . is always achieved by introducing a third category which is "abnormal" in terms of ordinary, "rational" categories. . . . The middle ground is abnormal, non-natural, holy. It is typically the focus of all taboos and ritual observances.[40]

In creating Adam, God had joined the antithetical spheres of incorruptible spirit and the crumbling clay of earth. Only by keeping his body intact, through the renunciation of a sexuality normally associated with the physical person—that is, with mortal and corruptible "clay"—had Adam been able to stand in Paradise, singing the praises of his Creator, as a creature of the earth joined in solemn antiphony to the fleshless hosts of the angels.[41]

Hence it was essential for Methodius to deny what he took to be the suggestion of Origen—that human flesh might one day "evaporate" entirely into that of an angelic being. At no time had humans ever existed as entirely angelic beings, devoid of the solid flesh and bone of Adam and Eve.[42] Such a notion unstrung the high tension of Methodius' universe. Virginal human flesh, physical clay that could at any moment crumble into sexuality, and that must lie broken in the grave before it was reformed by the Creator at the resurrection of the dead, was the highly charged point of mediation between two irreconcilable poles. Those who had learned, through a constant effort of the will, to maintain their "abnormal" state, as the possessors of an earthy body denied the sexual expression habitually associated with earthly beings, could stand between heaven and earth. They bridged the huge divide which all late antique thinkers, pagan, Jewish, and

---

39. Musurillo, pp. 15–16.　　40. E. Leach, *Genesis as Myth*, p. 10.
41. Methodius, *Symposium* 3.6.63–64, p. 100.
42. Methodius, *On the Resurrection*, fragment 1.2 and 10: *P.G.* 18: 268AB and 277BC; W. R. Clark, trans., *The Ante-Nicene Fathers*, 6:364, 366.

Christian alike, saw between the "upper" and the "lower" world.[43] Virginity, *parthenia*, Thecla reminded the group, was derived from *para to theion*: the physical state of virginity caused the human being to "stand next to the divine."[44] In the imagination of Methodius, the bridge across the chasm between God and man passed through the bodies of his virgin girls.

It is precisely in his most Hellenic phrases that we can see, in Methodius, the difference between his view of the position of human beings in the cosmos and that upheld by Plotinus and Porphyry. For Plotinus, the disembodied soul itself was the mediator that joined the antithetical poles of the universe. The soul was a joyful being that reached out from the One to touch the cold surface of matter. Like the towering figure of Athena seen beside the walls of Troy, it was the vivid soul alone that bound earth to heaven: for "though her feet still walk the ground, she has struck high heaven with her head."[45]

With Methodius, it is the frail clay of the virgin body, and not the soul, that is spoken of as towering like Athena, "walking on earth, touching high heaven's vault."[46] For Porphyry, the sleepless mind of Plotinus had remained forever poised safe above the surge of his body;[47] with Methodius, it is the virgin body itself that is lifted up above the common clay of the world. In its virgin state, the body enjoyed a superiority once ascribed only to the mind. The bodies of Methodius' virgins hung, like well-strung harps, from the cool and fruitless willow-tree, far above the sucking swirl of the waters of Babylon.[48]

We can sense, in these small hints, a further turning of the age. In the second century, sexuality had pushed mortality to one side, in the eyes of many radical Christians, as the privileged symptom of the frailty of humankind. From Origen and Methodius onward, the absence of sexuality in the chosen few provided the human race with new mediators. The shimmering, ethereal figures of *daimones*, of heroes and of the souls of the wise, that had linked heaven to earth, towering above the human race in the middle regions of the late Platonic uni-

43. Peter Brown, *The Making of Late Antiquity*, pp. 16–18; *The Cult of the Saints*, pp. 2–3; and "The Notion of Virginity in the Early Church," pp. 427–433, esp. pp. 432–434.
44. Methodius, *Symposium* 8.1.171, p. 200.
45. Homer, *Iliad* 4.443 in Plotinus, *Ennead* 4.3.12, MacKenna, p. 270–271.
46. Methodius, *Symposium* 1.1.11, p. 54.
47. Porphyry, *Life of Plotinus* 22, MacKenna, p. 16.
48. Methodius, *Symposium* 4.3.99, p. 134. citing *Psalm* 136:1.

verse, were eclipsed, in the Christian imagination, by the bodies of the virgin young on earth. Tranquil lamps of pure, filtered oil in a darkened world,[49] they glowed through the long night watches of childhood, adolescence, and old age until the dawn light of Christ's coming.[50]

Methodius' own days were numbered. The quiet guide of virgin souls moved from Olympus to Patara. Patara was a seaport close to Caria, a province that still boasted a stridently revivalist pagan cult site, the great shrine of Zeus at Panamara. In 312, the pagan Emperor Maximin Daia visted Caria. His "divine presence . . . blazed forth" in the province, causing banditry to cease in the uplands.[51] Law and order returned to the area. Then the Emperor may have moved to the coast of Lycia. Methodius, the Christian bishop and mentor of well-born ladies, was executed.[52]

In that same, last bout of persecution, a figure had appeared in Alexandria. He did exactly what Origen had done, a little over a century earlier:

he rendered service to the confessors, both in the mines and in the prisons. In the lawcourt he showed great enthusiasm, stirring to readiness those who were called forth as contestants and receiving them [presumably with the kiss of peace] as they underwent martyrdom and remaining with them until they were perfected.[53]

Yet one could not imagine a spiritual guide more different from the young Origen. He was a middle-aged Egyptian, who had grown up in a village in the Fayum. He wore a countryman's garb: "a tunic without sleeves like that with which Egyptians are covered." He took care to launder it, before standing in a prominent position among the Christian hecklers at the governor's court.[54] The tunic alone marked him as an outsider in the city. In Origen's days, the Emperor Caracalla had driven similar Egyptian countryfolk from Alexandria. They would stay to idle in the city, after having streamed in from the countryside

---

49. 6.4.141, p. 172.　50. 5.2.113, p. 146.
51. *Bulletin de correspondance hellénique* 12 (1888): 101–103.
52. T. D. Barnes, "Methodius, Maximus and Valentinus," pp. 54–55.
53. Athanasius, *Life of Anthony* 46, R. C. Gregg, trans., p. 66.
54. The full detail is in the Syriac version: R. Draguet, ed., *La Vie primitive de Saint Antoine*, p. 48.

to the great festival of Serapis.[55] Now, the "great festival" was the spectacle provided for the churches of the Nile Delta by the trial of Christian martyrs. Many of these fervent visitors to Alexandria were men already called, it appears, even at that time, "monks," *monachoi*—"lonely ones."[56]

The strange man was Anthony. He had come to Alexandria after some twenty years spent in a ruined fort on the confines of the desert, across the Nile from Arsinoe. Let us take a brief *tour d'horizon* in our next chapter, in order to survey the wide range of meanings that had come to be attached to sexual renunciation in varying Christian regions, before the churches of the settled land came to be challenged, in the course of the fourth century, by the novel horizons opened to them by the immensity of the desert.

55. Pap. Giessen 40, col. 2, lines 16–29, in A. S. Hunt and C. C. Edgar, *Select Papyri*, 2:90–92.

56. Athanasius, *Life of Anthony* 46.

TEN

Church and Body: Cyprian, Mani and Eusebius

While Porphyry and Methodius wrote, in Italy and in Lycia, a Christian family of the Upper Tembris Valley, in Anatolia, had been forced to face a domestic tragedy. Aurelius Telesphorus and Aurelia Ammia, members of the austere church of the Novatians, buried Ammia, their unmarried daughter. The epitaph began with ancient phrases:

How is it that you die already . . . before the bridal crown . . . snatched out of due time, deprived of the marriage-bed?

It ended with a vision. On the eighth day, Ammia had appeared in a dream:

Weep not, afflicted father, nor thou, mother; to die is common . . . But my Savior Jesus Christ has joined me to the righteous; . . . at the Presbyter's hand I received baptism, virginity's lawful prerogative; I came to heaven a pure virgin . . . having life eternal among the holy ones. . . . My slothful father and sluggard mother sought to frighten me . . . For by espousing my virginity to Christ I brought them sorrow insufferable.[1]

---

1. W. H. Buckler, W. M. Calder and C. W. M. Cox, "A Monument from the Upper Tembris Valley," at pp. 51–57,

The high notions of Origen and Methodius did not occur in a vacuum. They reflected a new situation. For the first time in its history, Christianity had become a religion for the young. No longer did every Christian household take for granted that it was the duty of God-fearing parents to save their children from falling into fornication by marrying them off at an early age. Many children, mostly girls, now wished to remain unmarried. No longer was the father, the head of the family, regarded as the only person responsible for "keeping" his daughters as virgins for future marriage. The pre-pubertal child came to be presented, in theory at least, as the "keeper" of his or her own body: like little Ammia, some chose to "keep their own flesh," as virgins, through vows of perpetual continence.[2] It is even possible (though far from certain) that Christian families were a little less willing, than were traditionalist pagans, to subject their girls to brutally early marriages.[3]

Nor would the girl's decision to remain a virgin always be unwelcome to her family. Frequently, it relieved the parents of the difficult task of finding a husband for her. The Christian communities had grown rapidly in the course of the third century; but they remained suspicious of the outside world. Christian families were not encouraged to marry their children to Jews, pagans, or heretics. As a result, many communities found themselves having to deal with a *copia puellarum*, a pool of Catholic girls for whom no suitable husbands could be found.[4] These women often opted for a life of voluntary continence, protected and esteemed by the clergy. In much the same way, young men who found it difficult to marry now gravitated in increasing numbers toward the clergy or to more radical forms of Christian militancy. The *Acts of John the Evangelist*, which circulated widely at this time, offered a model of perpetual male celibacy very different from the postmarital continence that had prevailed in a former age: John could pray to Christ,

2. Methodius, *Symposium* 3.14.90, in H. Musurillo, ed., *Méthode d'Olympe: Le Banquet*, p. 124, expounding *I Corinthians* 7:37 *to keep his virgin*.

3. K. M. Hopkins, "The Age of Roman Girls at Marriage," pp. 309–327, esp. pp. 319–320 and Charles Pietri, "Le mariage chrétien à Rome," in J. Delumeau, ed., *Histoire vécue du peuple chrétien*, pp. 105–131. But now see Brent Shaw, "The Age of Roman Girls at Marriage: Some Reconsiderations"—Christian practice may simply have reflected the habits of different classes in areas where early marriage was not as common as in Rome itself. In Africa, it was said that Victoria threw herself over a cliff rather than be married—*Acta Saturnini* 16: *Patrologia Latina* 8: 714A—but this may be a later legend.

4. Council of Elvira, *Canon 15.*, in E. F. Jonkers, ed., *Acta et symbola conciliorum quae saeculo quarto habita sunt*, pp. 8–9.

Thou who hast kept me also till this present hour pure for Thyself and untouched by union with a woman; Who, when I wished to marry in my youth,
didst appear to me and say: . . . "John, if thou wert not mine, I should have
allowed thee to marry."[5]

All over the Mediterranean, a discreet pressure of numbers caused
groups of young persons, demonstratively committed to the virgin state,
to pile up, like pack-ice, around the Christian communities. The virgins of the Church caught the attention of their neighbors: by the end
of the third century, attempts at sexual violence against dedicated
women and threats of condemnation to the brothels (and no longer,
simply, the threat of shameful execution) came to feature as a regular
aspect of pagan persecutions of the Christians.[6]

This slow change coincided with a rapid shift in the leadership of
the Christian Church. Within a decade of the death of Origen, men
accustomed to public life and skilled in the exercise of power emerged
as Christian bishops in all the major cities of the Roman world. Paul
of Samosata, Bishop of Antioch from around 260 to 269, used to parade
through the *agora*, reading aloud to his clients from his official correspondence. Surrounded by chanting choirs of virgins, he took his place
in a great new church, on a high throne veiled with curtains, like a
governor's judgment seat. Though his rivals claimed to be shocked by
all this, Paul was the Christian bishop of the future.[7] At the same time,
the Bishop of Rome controlled a staff of 154 persons, and was responsible for the support of 1500 widows and distressed persons. Quite
apart from the ordinary congregations, such numbers made the Christian Church in Rome a body larger than any other voluntary group in
the city.[8] Only a man who could be thought to have shown "virginal
continence" in his personal life could be entrusted with so much power.[9]

The career of Cyprian, Bishop of Carthage from 248 to 258, shows

5. *Acts of John* 113, in E. Hennecke, ed., *New Testament Apocrypha*, 2:257.
6. Eusebius, *Ecclesiastical History* 6.5.1; *Martyrs of Palestine*, in H. J. Lawlor and J. E.
L. Oulton, trans., *Eusebius: The Ecclesiastical History and the Martyrs of Palestine*, p. 353—
the longer Syriac version; Pio Franchi de' Cavalieri, ed., *Martyrdom of Saint Theodotus*
13–19, pp. 69–73.
7. Eusebius, *Ecclesiastical History* 7.30.8–9.
8. Eusebius, *Eccles. Hist.* 6.43.11–12: see A. Duncan-Jones, *The Economy of the Roman
Empire*, p. 283—the largest single association of craftsmen in Rome was between 1200
and 1500.
9. Cyprian, *Letter* 55.8, in W. Hartel, ed., *Corpus Scriptorum Ecclesiasticorum Latinorum*,
3:629.

very clearly the extent to which, in a major city of the Latin world, virginity was harnessed to the needs of the Catholic clergy. Cyprian was a converted *rhetor*. He had grown up in the all-male atmosphere of the forum. The delicious indeterminacy of Origen's *didaskaleion*, where "spiritual" men and women had mingled as equals, was unimaginable in his tense world. Accustomed to treating his own male clergy as a *grand seigneur*, Cyprian was the last person who would have treated continent women as partners.[10] He praised the virgins of the Church in the current heady language of admiration;[11] but he wrote to them, largely, about discipline—"discipline, the guardian of all hope, the anchor-cable of the faith . . . the teacher of all virtue, to neglect which is certain death."[12]

The virgins whom he warned in this peremptory manner came from well-to-do families.[13] It was a matter of crucial importance to Cyprian that their considerable personal wealth should be used only to support the Christian poor; it must not be brought to bear in any way to put pressure on the clergy.[14]

In the writings of Cyprian, virginity never achieved the exalted position that was given to it in the Greek-speaking world. The powerful imaginative logic that placed the virgin body in a category apart, joining heaven and earth, was notably absent from the thought of Cyprian and from that of his Latin successors. Cyprian's religious sensibility, rather, was dominated by the presence of the *saeculum*. He faced a deeply conservative Roman society, still tenaciously devoted to its ancient gods, behind whose brutal face he sensed the abiding presence of the Devil and his angels. It was from that *saeculum*, a crooked, blood-drenched world, that he had wrenched his heart at the moment of his baptism, passing from it into the tight "bond of brotherhood" of the Christian church.[15] For ten years, until his execution in 258, the discipline of an embattled community lay in his hands. It is of that discipline that all later Latin Catholics would read, in his surviving works.[16]

10. G. W. Clarke, trans., *The Letters of Saint Cyprian*, Ancient Christian Writers 43 and 44 is a memorable study of Cyprian in action.

11. Cyprian, *de habitu virginum* 3, Hartel, ed., p. 189.

12. 1, p. 187.

13. 8, 9, 10 and 11, pp. 193–195: repeats the phrase *Locupletem te dicis et divitem*.

14. 11, p. 195.   15. Cyprian, *de bono patientiae* 15, p. 407.

16. Clarke, *Letters of Saint Cyprian*, Ancient Christian Writers, 43:17–21, rightly stresses that only a small portion of the writings and preaching of Cyprian has survived, and offers, in conclusion, an exceptionally precise and humane judgement on the man.

Cyprian wrote of the Christians of Carthage and Rome as a group that faced the *saeculum* "in the fighting line"[17] of what was the six thousandth year of the Devil's war against the human race.[18] So much as a hint of "effeminate weakening of the hard resolve of the Christian" could prove disastrous to the Church.[19] The view of the body that Cyprian bequeathed, with decisive effect, to Ambrose, Jerome, and Augustine was determined by this overriding preoccupation. The "flesh" of the Christian was a bulwark against the *saeculum*. This "flesh" might be "dedicated to Christ," as was the case with a virgin girl or man. The preservation of the body's integrity was a matter of the greatest importance.[20] But the body could never be set apart in a state of uncanny purity, in which the weakness of mortal clay was thought to have been suspended, as among the quiet charges of Methodius of Olympus. "Flesh" marked, for Cyprian, a point of perpetual danger, an outpost of the self tensed to receive the myriad blows of the world. Though frail in and of itself, and notoriously exposed to sexual temptation, the body was undermined less by the hidden "fire" of sexuality that smoldered within it than it was in danger of being swayed, from the outside, by the sinister attractive force of the world.[21] A man of power, Cyprian knew only too well, in himself and in his obstreperous colleagues, what it was for the Christian to be besieged not only by sensuality, but by the heavier and more devastating "worldly" lusts of anger, jealousy, and ecclesiastical pride.[22]

It was upon the flesh of the martyrs and the *confessores* that the *saeculum* rained down its most terrible blows. There is a physicality in the writings of Cyprian that crackles with the sense of the flesh as a charged boundary, under constant threat of violation. The "glory" of martydom unfolds like a dark red flower in his pages.[23] The red wine of the Eucharist strengthened the members of his flock.[24] It prepared

17. Cyprian, *Letter* 13.2.1, p. 505, trans. Clarke 43:83.

18. Cyprian, *Ad Fortunatum* 2, p. 317.

19. Cyprian, *de zelo et livore* 2, p. 420: it is hard to render in English the full weight of each word for a Roman reader—*ut molliat Christianam vigorem*.

20. Cyprian, *Letter* 62.3, p. 699: *membra Christo dicata et ad aeternum continentiae honorem pudica virtute devota*.

21. Cyprian, *de dominica oratione* 16 and 31, pp. 276 and 289.

22. Cyprian, *de zelo et livore* 2, p. 420.

23. Cyprian, *Letter* 10.5, p. 495—the phrase is that of a *confessor*; cf. *Letter* 21.1, p. 530 and Clarke, 43:324 at note 21.

24. Cyprian, *Letter* 57.2, p. 652.

them to endure the sight of their own blood, as it gushed forth "to quiet with its glorious flood the flames and fires of Hell."[25] The fear of death and of physical pain, and not the subtle sting of sexual temptation, was the most pressing enemy that the Christian must learn to overcome. The control of sexuality was merely one example—and not a very prominent one—of the Christian's need to control a body subjected to the huge pain of the world. For Cyprian, to "follow Christ" was nothing less than a daily martyrdom.[26]

In the writings of Cyprian, the body of the Christian emerged as a microcosm of the threatened state of the Church, which itself was a compact body, held in firm restraint by the unshakable, God-given will of its head and guiding mind, the Bishop.[27] Like a great organism, it was to reject, with a visceral "intolerance," the lethal taint of pagan sacrifice.[28] It must not let into itself the polluting waters of heresy.[29] The great collective body of the Church had to exert constant discipline, lest it be disrupted by the "blind, uncontrolled urges" of its own unruly members.[30] Church and body alike were both presented in terms of ever-vigilant control, from which the relentless pressure of the *saeculum* gave no respite. It was a somber message, whose implications were not lost on Cyprian's successors in the Latin world, Ambrose and Augustine.

To pass from Carthage to the eastern Mediterranean is to enter a different world. As can only be expected from a region that had already produced the *Acts of Judas Thomas*, Syria was a "'seismic zone." Distinctive forms of radical Christianity radiated from the region between Antioch and the Tigris. Around 200 A.D., a bishop led the inhabitants of a whole village up into the mountains to seek the coming of the Lord. Arrested as brigands by the local governor, they were released through the good offices of the governor's pious Christian wife.[31] It is a glimpse straight into the future, when the highlands of

25. Ibid. 10.2, p. 491, trans. Clarke 43:72.
26. S. Deléani, *Christum Sequi. Étude d'un thème dans l'oeuvre de saint Cyprien*, pp. 89–95.
27. Cyprian, *Letter* 59.5, p. 672; see now Joyce E. Salisbury, " 'The Bond of a Common Mind': A Study of Collective Salvation from Cyprian to Augustine," pp. 236–240.
28. Cyprian, *de lapsis* 25, p. 255.   29. Cyprian, *Letter* 73.6, p. 783.
30. Ibid. 45.2, p. 601.
31. Hippolytus, *Commentary on Daniel* 4.18, in N. Bonwetsch and H. Achelis, eds., *Griechische christliche Schriftsteller* 1:230–232.

Syria would be traversed by bands of wandering holy men and dotted with the pillars of Stylite monks.

In Syria, the continent body was not, as it was for Cyprian, an image of the compact, unflinching discipline of a beleaguered church. Nor was it a haunting anomaly, poised between heaven and earth, as in the *Symposium* of Methodius. It was a living sign of the imminent end of the present age, a pocket of "anti-matter," threatening to dissolve the solid foundations of the social order. Such views placed considerable strain on the settled community. The *Letter on Virginity*, ascribed to Clement of Rome, may have been written in the third century.[32] It shows a church accustomed to the notion of the continent household, but not so well equipped to deal with an abrupt rise in the number of young bachelors of apostolic leanings.

These were called the "walking men." They were committed to a life of holy vagrancy "for the kingdom."[33] Unattached males endowed with more "love and leisure" than was good for them,[34] they formed a colorful crowd as they wandered from village to village. Their long exorcistic invocations, like the great prayers of the *Apocryphal Acts*, were a poor man's rhetoric.[35] They brought with them the arts of psalm-singing and of Scriptural recitation that filled the roads of Syria with the sound of spiritual shanties.[36] When no Christians were present in a village, they were to remain silent—lest they be taken for traveling musicians![37] When they came to the houses of believers, the women must gather at the back, filing up modestly to receive from them the "peace of the Lord":

the women and the maidens will wrap their hands in their garments; and we also, with circumspection and with our eyes looking upwards, shall wrap our right hands in our garments; and they will come and give us the salutation on our right hand, wrapped as it is in our garments. Then we go where God permits.[38]

---

32. A. Adam, "Erwägungen zur Herkunft der Didache," p. 24 suggests 170 A.D.; I would prefer a third-century date. The text itself poses problems: see A. Guillaumont, *Annuaire du Collège de France* 1981–1982: 432–433. I cite the Syriac text with Latin translation in *Patrologia Graeca* 1. H. Duensing, "Die dem Klemens von Rom zugeschriebenen Briefe über die Jungfräulichkeit," provides a German translation.

33. Pseudo-Clement, *Ad Virgines* 1.2, *Patrologia Graeca* 1: 379B and 3, 385C.

34. Ibid. 1.3: 385B.   35. Ibid. 1.12: 409A.

36. Robert Murray, *Symbols of Church and Kingdom*, pp. 28–29.

37. *Ad Virgines* 2.6: 433A

38. Ibid. 2.2: 421BC, M. P. Pratten, trans. *The Ante-Nicene Fathers*, 8:61.

These men were so strictly controlled because they had to be more than irreproachable. Like Judas Thomas, they bore in their own bodies the person of Jesus Christ. It was through their virgin, rootless state that His presence was felt in the villages and towns of Syria: "The body which our Lord bore, and in which he carried out His conflict in this world, He put on from a holy virgin. . . . Doest thou wish to be a Christian? Imitate Christ in everything."[39]

Further to the East, in the self-contained environment of a sectarian village near the new Sassanian capital at Ctesiphon, on the Tigris, the young man Mani grew up in contact with a Christianity for which the apostles of the *Apocryphal Acts* provided the unquestioned paradigms for Christian action.[40] At the age of twelve, in the year 228/9, Mani received the first of a series of visions that made of him the founder of the only independent universal religion to emerge directly from the Christian tradition.[41] In 276, he was horribly martyred by the Persian king of kings. By 300 A.D., Manichaean missionaries had established the new church of their founder in Edessa, Antioch, Alexandria, and Carthage.[42] The sudden appearance of yet another new "church," represented by the pale Manichaean "Elect," revealed the strength of the Syrian Christian tradition. The idea of the wandering stranger, his continent body charged with the power to shake the kingdoms of the earth,[43] had lost none of its appeal in the Christian Near East of the late third century.

Mani had grown up among the followers of Elchasai, a Judaeo-Christian leader of the second century. They lived in a settlement perched on the edge of the Tigris. It was a village of grave householders, careful to eat only bread that had been baked in their own, "pure" ovens, and to feed themselves only from their own "pure"

39. *Ad Virgines* 1.6: 391A.

40. The common background is made particularly plain by H. J. W. Drijvers, "Odes of Solomon and Psalms of Mani: Christians and Manichaeans in Third-Century Syria," in R. van den Broek and M. J. Vermaseren, eds., *Studies in Gnosticism and Hellenistic Religions presented to Gilles Quispel*, pp. 117–130, now in *East of Antioch*.

41. This is no place for a full bibliography of modern studies of Manichaeism. S. N. C. Lieu, *Manichaeism in the Later Roman Empire and Medieval China*, mobilizes much erudition and an up-to-date bibliography. For the pages that follow, my principal debt is to H. J. W. Drijvers, "Conflict and Alliance in Manichaeism."

42. Peter Brown, "The Diffusion of Manichaeism in the Roman Empire," in *Religion and Society in the Age of Saint Augustine*, esp. pp. 97–105.

43. *Kephalaia* 76, in H. J. Polotsky, ed., *Manichäische Handschriften der staatlichen Museen Berlins 1: Kephalaia* 181.21–25, and 77, p. 189.23–26.

fields. They would frequently cleanse their bodies from the stains of a polluted world by ritual washings.[44] Mani freed himself from the self-limiting punctilio of his fellow-villagers through emphasizing the utter bankruptcy of the body. How could such "blood and bile and flatulence and excrement of shame,"[45] such a "mould of defilement,"[46] ever hope to be made clean by mere external washings? In itself, the body was a lost cause. Mani's first vision was of his true self, his Spirit—Twin. From this Twin he learned of a message entrusted to his soul before it had entered his body "before I clothed myself in this instrument, and before I was led to this detestable flesh, and before I clothed myself with its drunkeness."[47]

Yet Mani's view of the body was not entirely dismissive. The bodies of the believers, if kept holy by continence, could play a role in nothing less than the redemption of the universe. The cosmic drama that had been revealed to Mani was more optimistic than had been that of any previous Gnostic system.[48] The physical world was deeply polluted; but it was not irrevocably fallen. Just beneath its surface there shimmered the hope of a great deliverance, which would be brought about, on earth, through the true church of Mani.

In the Manichaean myth, only a small portion of the Kingdom of Light, a place of untarnished purity, the distant homeland for which the soul longed, had been devoured by the Kingdom of Darkness. At first sight, the visible universe might seem a chaotic mixture of Light and Darkness, in which the Darkness held the Light in a suffocating embrace. But this universe held within itself the hope of its redemption. It had been subtly reconstructed, by the Father of Light, after the first catastrophic impact of the powers of Darkness. All the "Light," that is, the pure spirit, that lay trapped in its depths was capable of salvation. Manichaeans saw the physical world around them less as a

44. We know of this from a remarkable new discovery of a papyrus containing a biography of Mani: first reported by A. Henrichs and L. Koenen, "Ein griechischer Mani Codex," (P. Colon. inv.no.4780), *Zeitschrift für Papyrologie und Epigraphik* (1970) 5:27–216 and subsequently edited, translated and commented in the same journal, (1975) 19:1–85; (1978) 32:87–199; (1981) 44:201–318 and (1982) 48:319–377. The document has been translated into English up to p. 99 by R. Cameron and A. J. Dewey, *The Cologne Mani Codex; "Concerning the Origin of His Body"* (Missoula, Mont.: Scholars Press 1979).

45. *Mani Codex* 81.8ff, Cameron and Dewey, trans. p. 65, cf. 84.lff, p. 67.

46. 81.lff, p. 65.   47. 22.8ff, p. 23.

48. This was already clear to S. Petrément, *Le Dualisme chez Platon, les Gnostiques et les Manichéens*, pp. 196–197, and is now stressed by Drijvers, "Conflict and Alliance," pp. 102–105.

prison than as a lovingly constructed crucible. By means of mysterious and infallible processes, the Father of Light distilled out of the physical world the precious, spiritual essences that had become wrapped, for a short time only, in alien matter.[49]

Manichaeans, therefore, were first taught to look up to the heavens, to worship "the Luminaries," the Sun and the Moon.[50] They saw in these the salvation of their own souls played out with reassuring constancy far above their heads. Each month the Moon swelled with the particles of light that rose from the world, passing on their way to a final resting place in the Kingdom of Light, which lay a little beyond the blazing purity of the Sun.[51] To look up at the Sun was to see a door into the Kingdom of Light swing open; it was to contemplate one's own eventual escape from matter. To smell the perfume rising from the frail flowers and incense-bearing bushes of Iraq was to be made poignantly aware of the huge love of the Sun, as it wooed the souls of the righteous back to their ancient home.[52]

The human body was a microcosm of that universe. A deep dungeon to the unillumined, it became an active agent of salvation, a crucible in miniature, once the power of Mani's message had descended upon it. Hence the vital importance to the Manichaean church of the "Elect": "the Elect have I chosen and [through them] a path to the height."[53]

The bodies of the Elect were far from being treated as loathsome detritus, whose physical fate was of no importance to their owners. The exact opposite was the case. They were the Sun and Moon come down to earth.[54] The solemn prayers of the Elect forwarded the liberation of the world. Their cultic meals set free the entrapped light that shimmered so palpably beneath the bright peels of fruits and vegetables: they were solemn reenactments, through the primal processes of eating and digestion, of the liberation of all souls from the husk of matter. The rigidly controlled eating of the Elect reversed the indiscriminate, devouring greed of the Kingdom of Darkness.[55]

The Manichaean rank and file, the catechumens or *auditors*, were

---

49. The image is taken from a Chinese text: A. Chavannes and P. Pelliot, "Un traité manichéen retrouvé en Chine," *Journal asiatique* (1911) ser. 10: 18, p. 155; but it is implied throughout Western sources; see C. R. C. Allberry, ed., *Manichaean Psalmbook*, *Psalm* 223, 11:3–10.

50. *Psalm* 265, p. 83.19ff.   51. *Kephalaia* 65, p. 158.26–159.4.   52. Ibid. p. 160.1–3.
53. *Mani Codex* 67.8, p. 53.   54. *Kephalaia* 87, p. 218.15–21.
55. Augustine, *Confessions* 4.1.1.

bound to the Elect by the most intimate of possible ties. They fed them.[56] The food the *auditors* brought to these pale wanderers passed through their holy bodies into the Kingdom of Light. This highly ritualized relationship enabled the Manichaean laity to play a part in bringing about the victory of good over evil. Elect and catechumens collaborated in performing "the righteousness that a man can do in his body."[57] In the most concrete sense, the pure bodies of the Elect were essential to the great distilling process that led to the salvation of the light imprisoned in the universe. Slowly but surely they would pump back to its source

the sweet water that lies beneath the Sons of Matter.[58]
The Light shall go to the Light,
the fragrance shall go to the fragrance . . .
The Light shall return to its place,
the Darkness shall fall and not rise again.[59]

Hence the double attitude to sexuality that made Manichaeism distinctive in the following centuries. On the one hand, sexuality was a mighty force. It summed up, for Mani, the perpetual, greedy, and excited drive that had first caused the Kingdom of Darkness to spread, like a polluting oilslick, over the face of the Kingdom of Light. Sexual desire and procreation stood for the horrendous opposite of true creation. Sexuality was a principle of mindless proliferation:

a nature of which there is no builder nor creater nor maker. . . . The intercourse of men with wives comes from that sort of happening. When you are satiated with fleshly food your concupiscence is excited. The fruits of generation are in this way multiplied.[60]

On the other hand, the Manichees believed that the sexual urge could be totally transcended: it could be banished forever from the self. The Elect were able to take on their cosmic role because sexual desire had

---

56. Brown, "Diffusion of Manichaeism," *Religion and Society*, pp. 108–110. See esp. *Pap. Rylands* 469.25–26 in A. Adam, *Texte zum Manichäismus* p. 53 and the fragments of a Manichaean document found in Theveste, North Africa: *Patrologia Latina: Supplementum* 2:1378–1380.

57. *Kephalaia* 80, p. 192.14.   58. *Psalm* 246, p. 54.29.

59. *Psalmbook: Psalms of Thomas* 8, p. 215.2.

60. Hegemonius, *Acta Archelaei* 166–8, in C. H. Beeson, ed., *Griechische christliche Schriftsteller*, 16:26–27; compare *Psalm* 139, p. 40.29–30: "The fire that dwells in the body, its affair is eating and drinking."

already been excluded from their inmost self as surely as normal, polluted food was kept away from their holy mouths. The power of sin
might occasionally stir in their bodies. But this was held to be due
largely to remissness in diet;[61] it did not affect the light-filled soul,

but you must know that the powers of Light are good. The Beginning and
the End [the first and last states of unsullied purity before Darkness came
upon the Kingdom of Light] stand clear before you.[62]

It is extremely difficult to know what Manichaeism meant to the average supporters of the church of Mani. It is easy to exaggerate the
extent of the impact upon them of Mani's powerful myths. They were
not expected to view themselves or to attempt to behave in the same
manner as did the austere Elect. Unlike the Elect, the *auditors* were
married men and women. They had not undergone a definitive mutation of the self. They had to be prepared to wait, fasting and ob-
serving sexual abstinence for at least fifty days in the year,[63] until the
slow turning of the universe set their souls free to join those of the
Elect in the Kingdom of Light. Somber though Mani's vision of the
human condition might be, Manichaeism maintained the high-pitched
hope of its Encratite and Gnostic background. The total cessation of
desire was possible for the few. Among the Elect, there was no room
for the anxious attention to the frailty of the will and to the sexual
fantasies that crowded unbidden into the heart that characterized the
thought of the Desert Fathers and of Augustine. A sexual drive whose
force was limited to the transient "outer garment" of the body did not
speak to the continent Elect of any weakness in their own untarnished
and incorruptible souls. These souls were already suffused with light.

For their married clients, the Elect were windows that let in the sun-
light of a distant world. We know of the musings of only one Manichaean *auditor*—the young Augustine, at Carthage, in the 370s. All the
time that he attended the ceremonies of the Elect, he was living, punc-
tiliously, with a concubine. There is no reason to assume that, as an
auditor, he had internalized the bleak attitudes to sexuality current among
the Elect, the guardians of the esoteric myths of Mani. The great mutation, associated with full redemption in every Gnostic system, had
plainly not yet come upon him. The solemn hymns of the Elect spoke
of a perfect state that lay safely out of reach for him, to one side of

61. *Kephalaia* 86, p. 216.22–23.   62. Ibid. 33, p. 94.28.   63. Ibid. 91, p. 233.3–7.

his own experience. He found himself praying fervently for "chastity and continence . . . but not quite yet!"[64]

The Christian communities of the eastern Mediterranean soon came to realize that the Manichaean Elect were disturbingly like the apostolic wanderers of their own tradition. The heroes and heroines of the *Apocryphal Acts* were the heroes and heroines also of the Manichaean church.[65] But the Manichees were real men and women: throughout the late third and fourth centuries, Paul and Thecla walked the roads of Syria together, in the form of the little groups of "Elect" men and women, moving from city to city. As members of the "Elect," Manichaean women traveled on long missionary journeys with their male peers. Christian bishops believed that Manichaean women were capable of acting as spokesmen in public debates.[66] These austere and widely traveled figures drifted into the heart of the Christian communities. They came with the unsettling ease of total strangers. They brought a touch of the terrible, high freedom, associated with the radical Christianity of Syria, out of its distant homeland and into the streets of Antioch, Carthage and Alexandria.

[They] took up the cross upon them, they went from village to village.
[They] went into the roads hungry, with no bread in their hands.
They walked in the heat thirsty, they took no water to drink.
They went in to the villages not knowing a single person,
They were welcomed for His sake.[67]

We need to remind ourselves that Mani, Cyprian and Plotinus were near contemporaries, and that Constantine was born at roughly the same time that Anthony had moved to the outskirts of his village, as a young man of around eighteen to twenty. By the year 300, Christian asceticism, invariably associated with some form or other of perpetual sexual renunciation, was a well-established feature of most regions of the Christian world.

The forms that such renunciation took varied greatly. In each area, sexual renunciation carried a significantly different message, and led to the formation of different patterns of life within the local churches.

64. Augustine, *Confessions* 8.7.17.
65. *Psalmbook: Psalmoi Sarakotôn*, p. 143.4–16.
66. *Marc le Diacre: Vie de Porphyre* 85 and 87–90, in H. Grégoire and A. Kugener, eds., *Collection Budé* pp. 66–70. But this encounter may be fictional.
67. *Psalmbook: Psalms of Heraclides*, p. 195.8–12.

In the Latin West, "holiness of continence of the flesh"[68] tended to gravitate around the clergy of the Catholic church. It defined them as a "holy" priesthood, subject to a state of perpetual ritual abstinence. A little before 303, the Council of Elvira, in southern Spain, declared that "bishops, priests, deacons and all members of the clergy connected with the liturgy must abstain from their wives and must not beget sons."[69] Such clergymen might have been married and raised families: but the notion that they would continue to have intercourse with their wives while serving at the altar was increasingly regarded as shocking.

In Asia Minor, inscriptions and stray references hint at a forgotten world of ascetic Christian groups. It was possible for a young boy, Theodotus of Ancyra, to be brought up "in asceticism," against the will of his parents, by an elderly virgin, Tekousa, and for seven virgins of his church—and not the clergy—to be singled out as leaders of the Christians in a time of persecution. Theodotus and his fellows may have been Montanists. But they were not alone: a local sect of *apotactitae*, of "Renouncers," claimed the virgins for themselves.[70]

Encratite villages were scattered all over Asia Minor and Northern Syria. Protected from the attentions of the more orthodox bishops of the cities by the great stretches of the Anatolian plateau and by the mountains of Northern Syria, these little groups maintained celibacy, at least for their widows and widowers, and distinguished themselves from their laxer neighbors by means of strict taboos on meat, wine, and styles of dress.[71] Men and women whose views we know of from their solid gravestones were plainly not the wandering strangers that we meet, on descending the foothills of the Anatolian plateau, into the plains of Syria and the Upper Tigris. The "Walking Men," now joined by the Manichaean "Elect," continued to blow in sudden gusts between Iran and Antioch.

68. *Martyrdom of Saints Marian and James* 3.1, in H. Musurillo, ed., *The Acts of the Christian Martyrs*, p. 196.
69. Council of Elvira, *Canon* 33, Jonkers, ed., pp. 12–13.
70. *Martyrdom of Saint Theodotus* 13–19, ed. de' Cavalieri, pp. 69–73: see now Stephen Mitchell, "The Life of Saint Theodotus of Ancyra," pp. 102–103.
71. See esp. W. M. Calder, "The Epigraphy of the Anatolian Heresies," in W. H. Buckler and W. M. Calder, eds., *Anatolian Studies: Presented to W. M. Ramsay* and the evidence, collected from a wide variety of sources, by G. Blond, "L' 'hérésie' encratite vers la fin du quatrième siècle."

All over northern Mesopotamia, the "Sons and Daughters of the Covenant" remained the declaratory center of the church.[72] Grave, urban, and basically comfortable persons, frequently ensconced in their own family houses, the members of the Covenant were not wild vagrants. The man who exhorted them, Aphrahat, "the Persian Sage," a bishop and teacher from near Mosul, was an advertisement for their tranquil way of life: "a serene, sweet-natured man."[73] In a region with large Jewish communities, placed on the edge of the confident Zoroastrian Empire of Iran, these dignified celibates posed a direct challenge to their married neighbors: "You have received a curse," the Jews complained to Aphrahat, "and have multiplied barrenness."[74]

In the memoir which Eusebius, Bishop of Caesarea, drew up on the martyrs of Palestine in the time of the Great Persecution, we meet members of the clergy, in cities and in villages, who already enjoyed personal reputations for extreme asceticism: Procopius of Eleutheropolis, for instance,

was in truth a man of God; for even before his martyrdom, he had dedicated his life to philosophy, and from a child had embraced chastity and a most rigorous mode of living. . . . His meat was bread and his drink water, and these would be his only food every two or three days . . . from his meditation on the divine words he ceased not day or night.

Through exceptionally impolitic heckling at the governor's court in Caesarea, Procopius gained the martyrdom that Anthony had sought in vain, at much the same time, in Alexandria.[75]

In Egypt, Anthony himself was no innovator. In the very next village he found "an old man who had practised from his youth the solitary life." As a young man, Anthony had traveled around the Fayum to seek advice from ascetics who were already established on the fringes of the desert.[76] The deep desert, the *Panerémos*, to which he retired later in his life created the asceticism of the fourth-century monks as

72. Aphrahat, *Demonstratio* 6: "On the Sons of the Convenant," in J. Parisot, ed., *Patrologia Syriaca*, 1:243–312. This combines magnificent exhortations with notably moderate rulings.

73. Murray, *Symbols of Church and Kingdom*, p. 29.

74. Aphrahat, *Demonstratio* 18.1, Parisot, p. 817; see J. Neusner, *Aphrahat and Judaism: the Jewish-Christian Argument in fourth-century Iran*, for a translation and helpful commentary.

75. Eusebius, *Martyrs of Palestine* 1.1, Lawlor and Oulton, trans., pp. 332–333.

76. Athanasius, *Life of Anthony* 3–4.

little as the inhospitable woods of the New World created the Puritanism of the Pilgrim Fathers. It only gave ascetics a new freedom with which to follow ideals and practices that they had taken with them into the desert from the churches of their villages.

By the time that the Great Persecution had come to an end in the East, in 313, Eusebius of Caesarea, the admirer of Origen, recently the author of the triumphant *History of the Church*, and the future panegyrist of Constantine, found himself free to begin on a detailed rebuttal of the learned Porphyry's *Against the Christians*. His *Preparation* and his *Proof of the Gospel* were to be definitive annihilations of the great philosopher: they were "the most majestic and disdainful of all polemics."[77]

For Eusebius, the victory of Christianity in the Roman world implied, also, the victory of an elite within the Christian church. In a memorable passage in the opening book of his *Proof of the Gospel*, Eusebius sketched out the upshot of the revolution that we have followed so far:

Two ways of life were thus given by the Lord to His Church. The one is above nature, and beyond common human living; it admits not marriage, childbearing, property nor the possession of wealth. . . . Like some celestial beings, these gaze down upon human life, performing the duty of a priesthood to Almighty God for the whole race. . . .

And the more humble, more human way prompts men to join in pure nuptials, and to produce children, to undertake government, to give orders to soldiers fighting for right; it allows them to have minds for farming, for trade and for the other more secular interests as well as for religion.[78]

The clear structuring of Christianity as a religion of two "ways" became so commonplace, and endured for so long in East and West,[79] that it is important to step back a little to measure the meaning of Eusebius' words.

It had been far from inevitable, in the first and second centuries, that so clear-cut a division would come to characterize the Christian church. A Christianity based exclusively on the married household,

77. T. D. Barnes, *Constantine and Eusebius*, p. 175.
78. Eusebius, *Demonstratio Evangelica* 1.8, *Patrologia Graeca* 22: 76C, in W. J. Ferrar, trans., *Eusebius: The Proof of the Gospel*, 1:48.
79. The characterization of N. H. Baynes, "The Thought World of East Rome," pp. 26–27 remains unequaled.

such as was implied in the pseudo-Pauline letters and defended with resolute grace by a man such as Clement of Alexandria, might have gained unchallenged preeminence throughout the Mediterranean basin. This would have been a Christianity associated with rigorous sexual discipline, and marked by fear of women; but it would not necessarily have been a Christianity committed to the total renunciation of all sexual activity, except, perhaps, in a few postmarital continent persons—widows and clergymen. Had such a Christianity prevailed, the sexual codes current in the Mediterranean world in late antiquity would certainly have hardened. A highly disciplined, monogamous sexuality, accompanied by strict control exercised by men over women, and by the old over the young, would have become the norm.

The councils and church orders of the third century show that the silent majority of the five million or so Christians living in the Roman Empire, around the year 300, were prepared to settle for little more than a morality of sexual discipline that was as intensely puritanical as that which still prevails along the Islamic shores of the Mediterranean. The bishops assembled at Elvira devoted thirty-four out of their eight-one rulings to matters regarding marriage and sexual misdeeds; one quarter of all their decisions involved imposing greater control than heretofore on the women of the Christian community.[80]

In many regions, the Christian churches remained on the defensive against the radical claims of the Encratites and took little interest in other forms of asceticism. Time-honored concerns—fornication by the unmarried young, the shame brought upon the family by daughters who had lost their virginity before marriage, and, as always, the lurking fear of adultery—were regarded as sufficient objects of clerical concern. The chaste married woman faithful to her husband, rather than the brittle virgin girl, was the figure who was held up for admiration. She filled the local church with the "sweet perfume" of her good name: such a woman, "never assuredly remains alone with young men and suspects even the old."[81] Veiled in public and careful to show their Christian faith by "shame and meekness," the married women held

80. See Remo Cacitti, "L'etica sessuale nella canonistica del iiio secolo," in R. Cantalamassa, ed., *Etica sessuale e matrimonio nel cristianesimo delle origini*, pp. 101–102 and S. Laeuchli, *Power and Sexuality: The Emergence of Canon Law at the Synod of Elvira*, pp. 89, 82.

81. Pseudo-Clement, *Homilies* 13.14–18: *P. G.* 2: 339A–341C.

up as exemplars by the clergy of many churches of the late third century have not yet vanished from the shores of the Mediterranean.[82]

These highly restrictive codes were applied with zest in the Christian churches. But they were the creation of moral forces that had never been limited to Christianity. Pagans and Jews also liked to see their womenfolk reduced to order in the same manner. The victory of a puritanical conjugal morality in the later Empire was the most predictable development in the history of the moral evolution of the Roman world. There can be no doubt as to the harshness with which it was imposed. A middle-aged man by the time that he declared himself a Christian, the Emperor Constantine knew exactly what many of his subjects, pagans quite as much as Christians, wanted of him. In 320, he issued a law of quite horrendous brutality. Any young girl who eloped with her suitor would be executed along with him. The female servant responsible for the girl would be held to have encouraged her charge to assert her freedom in this improper manner: she would have molten lead poured down her throat. The fact that the girl might have given her consent to the boy, by a formal promise of marriage, was brushed aside, "by reason of the invalidity associated with the flightiness and inconsequentiality of the female sex."[83]

Fulsomely praised, by a pagan orator, for being immune to the charms of attractive women petitioners, Constantine gave his upper-class contemporaries what they looked for in an Emperor in the tradition of Augustus: "new laws to control morals and to crush vice. . . . Chastity made safe, marriage protected and property secure."[84]

Yet although the tightening of sexual discipline is a peculiarly blatant aspect of the society of the later Roman Empire, it was not its only feature. Late antique and early medieval Christianity gave pride of place, not to the sexual discipline of the married, but to those who, in Eusebius' words, rose "above nature and beyond common human living."[85] The spread of sexual renunciation in the churches of the Mediterranean and the Near East ensured that a Roman society, whose disciplined conjugal morality might have resembled that current in re-

---

82. *Didascalia Apostolorum* 1.10.3 in F. X. Funk, ed., *Didascalia et Constitutiones Apostolorum*, p. 28.
83. *Codex Theodosianus* 9.24.1; see Denise Grodzynski, "Ravies et coupables: un essai d'interprétation de la loi ix.24.1 du Codex Théodosien."
84. Nazarius, *Panegyric* 34 and 38: *P. L.* 8: 605B and 608B.
85. Eusebius, *Demonstratio Evangelica* 1.8.

gions where Islam or Judaism now predominate, had come, by the beginning of the fourth century, to accept a clear distinction between the life of the married householder and the life of the "world renouncer" that was closer to that which prevailed in the India of the *sanyasi* and in Buddhist Asia.[86]

The reverent chasm that had opened up between married persons "in the world" and the "angelic life" of their ascetic heroes and heroines reflected a tacit truce between two wings within the Christian movement. In the second and third centuries, Christian conjugal morality was most frequently presented by its defenders as a reaction to the supposed immorality of the pagan world. In reality, Christian marital codes were asserted, for the most part, so as to defend the views of moderate Christians against their more radical co-religionists. Without the challenge of the Encratite attack on married intercourse, for instance, the meticulous advice to married couples, offered by Clement of Alexandria, would never have been written.

The clergy and apologists presented the pagan world, in a potent if inaccurate stereotype, as a society where sexual disorder luxuriated. Strict codes of marital morality maintained the identity of the Christian group. They separated believing families from the imagined dissoluteness of their pagan neighbors. But the insistence of many vocal Christians that marriage itself might be totally renounced, chilled the average Christian householder. The *quid pro quo* that a married laity exacted from their leaders was that they and their families should be sheltered from such disturbingly radical views. A Christian head of a family might have enjoyed listening to readings from the Apocryphal Acts; but he had no intention of allowing his daughter to become a Thecla, and even less did he wish his wife to play Mygdonia to his own pathetic Prince Karish.

Anthony and the monks of the fourth century inherited a revolution; they did not initiate one. In the century that had elapsed between the youth of Origen and the conversion of Constantine, the horizons of the possible had already been determined, silently and decisively, in a slow folding of the moral landscape of the Christian world. Total sexual renunciation had become a widely acclaimed feature of the Christian life. This renunciation carried with it implications of incal-

86. See esp. L. Dumont, "World Renunciation in Indian Religions," and I. F. Silber, "Dissent through Holiness: the Case of the Radical Renouncer in Theravada Buddhist Countries."

culable significance for current notions of the human person and for conventional attitudes to society. But it was a renunciation safely confined to the admired few. What the presence of these new heroes and heroines might mean for the moral tone and the social attitudes of the Christian church within the Roman Empire was as yet unclear. The spirited dialogue between the new society of the desert and the churches of the settled world, on the nature of sexuality, on the relation between marriage and continence, and on the possible relations between men and women within the ascetic movement, ensured that the century that stretched between the triumph of Constantine and the last writings of Augustine of Hippo was one of the most magnificently articulate periods in the entire history of the ancient world. It is to this golden century that we must now turn.

PART TWO

ASCETICISM AND SOCIETY IN THE EASTERN EMPIRE

ELEVEN

The Desert Fathers: Anthony to John Climacus

(I) "THE LIKENESS OF THE GLORY OF ADAM"

In the years after 270, the inhabitants of a village in the Fayum in Egypt could have seen a young man, the son of a well-to-do landowner, sitting outside his farm on the outskirts of the village. He was wrestling with the Devil to renounce his sexual desires: "even those who watched were aware of the struggle within him."[1] This was hardly surprising. Anthony was about twenty. He was at an age when, as the *Talmud*

---

1. Athanasius, *Life of Anthony* 5: *Patrologia Graeca* 26: 848B; Robert Gregg, *Athanasius: The Life of Anthony and the Letter to Marcellinus* provides a clear translation. G. J. M. Bartelink, *Vita di Antonio*, edits the earliest Latin translation with notes. The reader should know that a strong case has been made against direct authorship by Athanasius of the *Life of Anthony*: see R. Draguet, *La vie primitive de S. Antoine conservée en syriaque*. I have cited many of the small turns of phrase that occur only in the Syriac version in the belief that they may reflect attitudes current in monastic circles in Anthony's own lifetime. See now T. D. Barnes, "Angel of Light or Mystic Initiate? The Problem of the *Life* of Anthony." I do not expect all scholars to share this view: see e.g., M. Tetz, "Athanasius und die Vita Antonii," and Brian Brennan, "Athanasius' *Vita Antonii*: A Sociological Interpretation," for different interpretations.

put it, a young man "is like a neighing horse, adorning his person and longing for a wife."[2] Anthony was facing out the consequences, in a young man, of having refused to take the natural, next step into adulthood. Looking back almost a century later, the *Life of Anthony* devoted singularly little space to the description of specifically sexual temptations. Anthony's battle with the "demon of fornication" was presented as a mere preliminary. To overcome the "itch of youth"[3] involved, for Anthony, a drastic but mercifully shortlived struggle: it was part of a far greater effort to sever the umbilical cord that linked him to his village. In the normal course of events, the villagers would have expected to retain Anthony, by providing him with a bride. The struggle to overcome his sexual needs, therefore, was a necessary by-product of the self-imposed annihilation of Anthony's social status as a whole, which had come about after he had abandoned his wealth, given his money to the local poor, settled his sister as a dedicated virgin, and taken up his position on the edge of the desert, in places "preserved from the tread of human feet."[4]

In the ascetic literature of the fourth and fifth centuries, the immensity of the Egyptian desert dwarfed the facts of sex. The *Life of Anthony* went on, after its short opening chapters, to present a life that seems to have stood still for a further eighty years. The desert alone, and Anthony's journeys within it, provided the map against which the *Life* plotted the profound changes in Anthony's person.[5] Fifteen years spent on the edge of the village culminated in the eerie darkness of the tombs that marked the boundary between desert and settled land. After 285, Anthony moved to a deserted fortress across the Nile, emerging around 305 to gather disciples. After 313, he made his way, by tracks traveled only by nomads (whose language he, as an Egyptian of the settled land, would not have shared), to the eastern desert, near the Red Sea. It was the place of his heart's desire. He settled there until his death in 356, "in full magnificence, like a king in his palace."[6] The silence of the "Mountain of Saint Anthony" mirrored, at last, the huge serenity that had descended on his heart.

Anthony was the hero of the *Panerémos*, of the Deep Desert, the

---

2. *Midrash Rabba: Ecclesiastes* 1.2.1, trans. A. Cohen, p. 5.
3. Draguet, *Vie primitive*, p. 10, line 18.   4. Ibid, p. 16, line 16; *Life* 3: 844B.
5. Derwas Chitty, *The Desert a City*, pp. 3–6 is, as always, learned and humane on Anthony's evolution.
6. *Life* 50: 916A: Draguet, p. 50, line 23.

Outer Space of the ascetic world. But the stark boundary between the rich land of the Nile Delta and the rolling dunes of dead sand, which rose in gentle ridges from the very edge of Lake Mareotis (Maryût), immediately to the south of Alexandria, had only to be crossed to register, with equal clarity, a new departure in ascetic piety for many other Egyptian Christians. Christian "renouncers" were already a common sight in the towns and villages of Egypt. Amun, a farmer of the Nile Delta, married off at an early age by his kinsfolk, had persuaded his wife to live with him in continence as early as 297. It had been an old-fashioned gesture of renunciation, similar to those long current in Syria, and celebrated in the Acts of Judas Thomas.[7]

Eighteen years later, however, new ways were open for the couple. His wife told Amun that he should "go public" by leaving the settled land for its awesome antithesis, the neighboring desert: "It is inappropriate that you should hide such virtue as yours."[8] Little colonies of renouncers first settled around Amun in Nitria and a little further into the desert, at Kellia, "the Cells." They burrowed into the depressions among the dunes, to form a series of tiny man-made oases, each with its own well, dug into the brackish water that seeped erratically beneath the sands from Lake Mareotis.

A day and a night's further journey into the desert led to Scetis (the modern Wadi Natrûn), a place where springs could be found on the edge of a nitrate-laden marshland. Scetis was the heroic outpost of Egyptian asceticism. It formed the backdrop of much of the literature associated, in all later ages, with the Desert Fathers. By the year 400, nearly five thousand monks were said to be settled at Nitria alone, and many thousands were scattered up and down the length of the Nile and even in the bleak, waterless mountains beside the Red Sea.[9]

The settlements of the fourth-century Egyptian ascetics combined geographical proximity to the settled land with a sense of measureless imaginative distance. Amun and his successors lived only a day and a half away from Alexandria, separated from the rich land of the Nile Delta by a mere strip of sand. Despite their physical closeness to the

7. See above chapter 4, pp. 97–101.   8. Palladius, *Historia Lausiaca* 8.4.
9. Chitty, *The Desert*, pp. 11–13; 29–35. H. Evelyn-White, *The Monasteries of the Wadî'n Natrûn 2: The History of the Monasteries of Nitria and Scetis* remains fundamental; see now R. Kasser, *Kellia: Recherches suisses d'archéologie copte 1: Kellia 1965*. L. A. Tregenza, *The Red Sea Mountains of Egypt*, pp. 177–178 is a vivid description of the hermitages of the Red Sea.

settled land, the monks of Egypt towered in the imagination of contemporaries because they stood against an ocean of sand that was thought to stretch from Nitria to the furthest edges of the known world.[10] They were a new humanity, settled where no human beings should be found. In the well-known words of the *Life of Anthony*, Anthony and his emulators had "made the desert a city."[11]

The myth of the desert was one of the most abiding creations of late antiquity. It was, above all, a myth of liberating precision. It delimited the towering presence of "the world," from which the Christian must be set free, by emphasizing a clear ecological frontier. It identified the process of disengagement from the world with a move from one ecological zone to another, from the settled land of Egypt to the desert. It was a brutally clear boundary, already heavy with immemorial associations.[12]

The "world," the "present age" of previous Christian radicals had been almost too big to be seen. Its measureless demonic structures had engulfed the very stars. There was no outside viewing-point from which to take the measure of its faceless immensity, and no hope of disengagement from its clutches other than through drastic rituals that promised total transformation, through the formation of small, inward-looking groups of the redeemed; or, as we have seen in third-century Syria, through adopting the disturbing rootlessness of the religious vagabond.

Seen from the slight eminence of the desert of Egypt, however, the "world" was no more and no less than the green valley below. This was a valley of crowded villages, condemned to ceaseless labor by the ever-present fear of famine. These villages were presided over by ancient temples. Throughout the fourth and much of the fifth centuries, the temples still resounded with oracles that foretold the rising of the Nile: seductive, demonic rumors, as insistent as the excited honking of the bullfrogs along the stagnant canals in the tense nights before

---

10. Palladius, *Hist. Laus.* 7.2.

11. *Life of Anthony* 14: 865AB; cf. Athanasius, *Festal Epistle* 10 (for 338), transl. W. H. Burgess, *Historical Tracts of Athanasius*, p. 74, on the people of Israel in the wilderness of Sinai.

12. A. Guillaumont, "La conception du désert chez les moines d'Égypte." For the tradition of retreat in ancient Egypt, see F. Daumas, Introduction, *Philo: De vita contemplativa*, *Oeuvres de Philon d'Alexandrie*, R. Arnaldez, ed., 29:60–62 and A. D. Nock, "A Vision of Mandulis Aion," *Essays on Religion and the Ancient World*, 1:362–363, 368–374.

the great river once again stirred to life, to flood the dry fields.[13] Seen from the desert, this timeless landscape gave to the notion of "the world" a concreteness and a precision that it had lacked in all earlier Christian sensibility.

To flee "the world" was to leave a precise social structure for an equally precise and, as we shall see, an equally social alternative. The desert was a "counter-world," a place where an alternative "city" could grow. Thus, Pachomius, the founder of the first great monasteries of Egypt, who died in 346, was able to create a chain of man-made "deserts" in among the rural slums of the middle Nile. The great Pachomian monasteries at Tabennisi, Phbow, and their dependencies, rapidly emerged as alternative villages in miniature, ringed by defensive walls.[14]

Among the monks of Egypt, the problems of sexual temptation were most often seen in terms of the massive antithesis of "desert" and "world." Sexual temptation was frequently treated in a somewhat offhand manner, presented as if it were no more than a drive toward women, toward matrimony, and hence toward fateful conscription, through marriage, into the structures of the settled land.

There was at Scetis with Apa Paphnutios a brother who had to fight against fornication, and he said, "Even if I take ten wives, I shall not satisfy my desire." . . . He left for Egypt to take a wife. After a time it happened that the old man went up to Egypt and met him carrying baskets of broken pots. He did not even recognise him. . . . Seeing him in such misery, the old man wept and said: "How have you lost your sense of dignity and come on such bad times? No doubt you have taken ten wives?" And, groaning, the disciple said: "Truly, I have taken only one, and I have a great deal of trouble satisfying her with food." The old man said, "Come back with me." He said, "Is it possible to repent, Apa?" . . . Leaving everything the brother followed him and returned to Scetis, and thanks to his experience, he became a famous monk.[15]

13. Shenute of Atripe, *Letter* 18, in J. Leipoldt and W. E. Crum, eds., *Corpus Scriptorum Christianorum Orientalium 43: Scriptores Coptici* 3:49, H. Wiesmann, trans. *C.S.C.O.* 96: *Script. Copt.* 8:25.

14. See esp. H. Torp, "Les murs d'enceinte des monastères coptes primitifs," and now Philip Rousseau, *Pachomius: The Making of a Community in Fourth-Century Egypt*, pp. 9–13 with J. E. Goehring, *The Letter of Ammon and Pachomian Monasticism*, and "New Frontiers in Pachomian Studies," in *The Roots of Egyptian Christianity*, Birger A. Pearson and James E. Goehring, eds.

15. *Apophthegmata Patrum*, Paphnutius 4: *Patrologia Graeca* 65: 380D; in Benedicta Ward, trans., *The Sayings of the Desert Fathers*, pp. 170–171.

The serene inconsequentiality of such anecdotes showed that sexual needs could be regarded as affecting only a superficial layer of the person. By moving to the desert, the ascetic mobilized his physical person as a whole; and in the image of the person current in ascetic circles, food and the unending battle with the ache of fasting always counted for more than did the sexual drive.

Whatever his social status, no Egyptian of the fourth century could have had any doubt that his was a land whose population lived under a pall of perpetual fear of starvation.[16] It was not for nothing that "poverty" and "famine," "the poor" and "the starving" shared the same root in Coptic.[17] While the Nile valley was a zone of food, braced against the threat of famine, the desert was thought of as the zone deprived of human food: it was a zone of the nonhuman. For this reason, the most bitter struggle of the desert ascetic was presented not so much as a struggle with his sexuality as with his belly. It was his triumph in the struggle with hunger that released, in the popular imagination, the most majestic and the most haunting images of a new humanity. Nothing less than the hope of Paradise regained flickered, spasmodically but recognizably, around the figures who had dared to create a human "city" in a landscape void of human food.[18]

The ascetic brought with him into the desert fragile tokens of an enduring humanity that he had to defend tenaciously if he was to survive at all and maintain his sanity. He could not sink like an animal into its alluring immensity. His cell was most often a product of anxious human care: its walls stood between him and the wild beasts that roamed the desert in far greater numbers than they do today.[19] He

16. Aline Rousselle, *Porneia: De la maîtrise du corps à la privation sensorielle*, pp. 205–206; see, in general, Evelyne Patlagean, *Pauvreté économique et pauvreté sociale à Byzance*, pp. 78–84.

17. W. E. Crum, *A Coptic Dictionary*, pp. 663–664.

18. Peter Brown, "Response to R. M. Grant," *The Problem of Miraculous Feedings in the Graeco-Roman World*, pp. 19–24. In what follows, I am particularly indebted to the suggestions of R. Flusin, *Miracle et Histoire dans l'oeuvre de Cyrille de Scythopolis*, pp. 125–126. A. Arbesmann, "Fasting and Prophecy in Pagan and Christian Antiquity," and H. Musurillo, "The Problem of Ascetical Fasting in the Greek Patristic Writers," assemble much evidence. The reader is strongly advised to consult Caroline Bynum, *Holy Feast and Holy Fast: The Religious Significance of Food to Medieval Women*. This is an account of the meaning of fasting and of self-mortification that is conducted on a level of empathy and sophistication unusual in Early Church or medieval history; see esp. pp. 31–40 for the late antique period.

19. *Sentences des Pères du Désert: Nouveau Recueil*, 17, L. Regnault, trans., pp. 17–18; S. Sauneron and J. Jacquet, "Les ermitages chrétiens du désert d'Esna," pp. 25–26.

was committed to that cell. He had to learn to savor its "sweetness"; it was both his fiery furnace and the place where he spoke to God.[20] It was the deep grave in which he lay, "dead" to the world, in the desert.[21] In his long vigils, only his unbroken human will stood between his body and the vast insensitivity of sleep.[22]

Throughout his life in the desert, the monk's body remained irrevocably tied to human food. This tie was condensed in the little pile of dried loaves, stacked in a corner of his cell. Bread meant a continued tie to human social life. It was usually acquired by constant manual labor. Its purchase necessitated occasional journeys back to the edge of the Nile, to sell his wares at the village market and to earn yet more money by stints of back-breaking labor as a migrant harvester in the fields of the valley.[23] The need for human food, earned by hard work, tied the monk indissolubly to the shared weaknesses of a starving humanity. He could expect to be besieged by thoughts

of lengthy old age, inability to perform manual labor, fear of the starvation that will ensue, of the sickness that follows undernourishment, and the deep shame of having to accept the necessities of life from the hands of others.[24]

The titillating whispers of the "demon of fornication," much though they appear to fascinate modern readers, seemed trivial compared with such dire obsessions.

The most terrible temptation of all that pressed in continuously upon

20. The sweetness of the cell: *Apophthegmata Patrum*, Theodore of Pherme 14: 189D–192A; furnace: *Anonymous Apophth. M. S. Coislin 126*, 206, in F. Nau, ed., *Revue de l'Orient chrétien* (1908) 13:279.

21. The cells at Bawit were built like tomb houses: H. Torp, "Le monastère copte de Baouit," p. 8.

22. *Apophthegmata Patrum*, Poimen 185: 368AB; *Bohairic Life of Pachomius* 10, *First Greek Life* 6, A. Veilleux, trans., *Pachomian Koinonia 1: The Life of Saint Pachomius and his Disciples*, pp. 33, 301–302; Palladius, *Lausiac History* 18.3

23. *Apophthegmata Patrum*, Lucius: 253C—earned 16 coins a day, of which he used 14 for food and the remainder for alms; Megethios 1: 300D—three baskets a day makes a monk independent; Amun 3: 128D—disciple sent to the village for food; Agatho 16: 113D—monk sells his pots at market; Esaias 5: 181B, Macarius the Egyptian 7: 265AB, John Colobos 6: 205B and *Anon. Copt. Apophth.* 166, in M. Chaine, ed., *Institut français d'archéologie orientale: Bibliothèque des études coptes* (1960) 6:115—harvest labor.

24. Evagrius, *Praktikos* 9, ed. A. and C. Guillaumont, *Évagre le Pontique: Traité Pratique ou le Moine*, p. 512; J. E. Bamberger, trans., *Evagrius Ponticus: The Praktikos and Chapters on Prayer*, p. 17. Such cases happened: see the appeal to Epiphanius of Thebes on behalf of a monk—"for he is unable to reap, neither hath he any other craft, nor can he go South by reason of the sickness that is on him:" W. E. Crum and H. G. Evelyn-White, *The Monastery of Epiphanius of Thebes, Part 2: Coptic Ostraca and Papyri*, p. 198.

men perched, in this way, on the edge of the desert, was to betray their humanity. It was to break out of the confines of their cell and to expunge the regular alternations of vigil and prayer, eating and fasting. In moments when he was close to breakdown, the ascetic felt driven to wander as free and as mindless as a wild beast, gnawing at the scattered herbs, mercifully oblivious, at last, to the terrible ache of a belly tied to morsels of human bread, cruelly spaced out by the human rhythms of prayer and fasting. This was the dire state of *adiaphoria*. In it, the boundaries of man and desert, human and beast collapsed in chilling confusion. *Adiaphoria*, and not sexual temptations, flamboyant and deeply humiliating though these might sometimes be, was the condition that the Desert Fathers observed most anxiously, and described most graphically, because they feared it most deeply in themselves.[25]

Once they had faced out the terrible risks involved in remaining human in a nonhuman environment, the men of the desert were thought capable of recovering, in the hushed silence of that dead landscape, a touch of the unimaginable glory of Adam's first state. Hence the importance of fasting in the world of the Desert Fathers. It was widely believed, in Egypt as elsewhere, that the first sin of Adam and Eve had been not a sexual act, but rather one of ravenous greed. It was their lust for physical food that had led them to disobey God's command not to eat the fruit of the Tree of Knowledge. By so doing, they had destroyed the perfect physical equilibrium with which they had been first created. No longer content to contemplate the majesty of God largely (if not wholly) unconscious of the needs of their body, Adam and Eve had reached out to devour the forbidden fruit. In this view of the Fall, greed and, in a famine-ridden world, greed's blatant social overtones—avarice and dominance—quite overshadowed sexuality.

To fast for Lent was to undo a little of the fateful sin of Adam.[26] To fast heroically, by living in the desert, the land without food, was to

---

25. Palladius, *Laus. Hist.* 26 and 27; Evagrius, *Antirrhetikos* 1. 37, W. Frankenberg, ed. *Abhandlungen der königlichen Gesellschaft der Wissenschaften zu Göttingen, Philol.-Hist. Klasse,* pp. 478–479. Long periods of wandering were permitted, as long as the monk recognized his continued link to his cell: *Apophthegmata Patrum,* Bessarion 4: 141D.

26. For example, Basil of Caesarea, *de ieiunio, hom.* 1. 4: *Patrologia Graeca* 31: 168B and *hom. 7 in temp. famis* 31: 324C, and Romanos Melodes, *Hymn* 1. 3–22, in G. Grosdidier de Matons, ed., *Romanos le Mélode: Hymnes,* pp. 72–92.

relive Adam's first and most fatal temptation, and to overcome it, as Adam had not done.[27] Little wonder, then, that food frequently pushed sexuality to one side, as the major preoccupation of the monk. On the walls of a cell in Kellia, one monk had scrawled, as warning to himself, the fatal cry by which Esau had fallen from his birthright: "Jacob, my brother, [o, give me] lentils!"[28]

Perched on the edge of the desert along the valley of the Nile, within sight of the settled land, the monks of fourth-century Egypt stood as a perpetual challenge to the situation of hunger and of bitter dependence on the marketplace that characterized the society of a starving and laborious Near East. They, at least, had broken the dark cycle of hunger and avarice. In the legends that clustered around their persons at the end of the fourth century, we can glimpse the dreams of men who knew what it was to starve. The Christians of Egypt firmly believed that a few great monks had been able to make their way back to the imaginative antipodes of the sterile sands of the desert. When a party of pilgrims compiled the *Historia Monachorum*, the *Survey of the Monks of Egypt*, around 400, the heroes they visited were men believed to have touched, and to have released for others, the huge, frankly physical exuberance of Adam's Paradise. Angels once arrived at the cell of Apa Apollonius and his companions, to bring them giant apples, great clusters of grapes, exotic fruits, and loaves of warm white bread. It was a foretaste of the sensual delights of Paradise, granted to men who, by fasting, had chosen of their own free will to starve. This Paradise was a land without the burning heat of day or the icy cold of the desert nights. Its gentle slopes were covered with rustling fruit trees, through which wafted nourishing, perfumed breezes. It lay just beyond the horizon of the cruel desert.[29]

Visitors to Apa Copres noticed that, while he walked with them on the edge of the desert, farmers would come up from the valley below to scoop the sand from his footsteps. They would scatter it on their fields in order to produce a harvest richer than that of any other village in the middle Nile. The anecdote, taken from a notoriously poor re-

27. Flusin, *Miracle et histoire*, p. 104.   28. Kasser, *Kellia*, p. 22.

29. *Historia Monachorum* 7: *Patrologia Latina* 21: 416BC; *Apophthegmata Patrum*, Macarius 2: 260C–261A; *Bohairic Life of Pachomius* 114, Veilleux, *Pachomian Koinonia 1*, pp. 167–168. For the Syriac world, see Ephraem of Nisibis, *On Paradise* 9.13 and 10.2–13, in R. Lavenant, trans., *Éphrem de Nisibe: Hymnes sur le Paradis*, pp.126, 135–140.

gion, enables us to sense the urgency that had come to gather around the figures of those who bore in their bodies the primal themes of desert, settled land, and food.[30]

In the *Sayings of the Fathers*, the memories of the great monks of Nitria and Scetis collected in the mid-fifth century, in the *Lausiac History* of Palladius, and in the lives and rulings of Pachomius and his successors, we can sense the huge weight that the myth of Paradise regained placed on the frail bodies of the ascetics. It is precisely the bleak and insistent physicality of ascetic anecdotes that shocks the modern reader. They have led scholars to speak of "Contempt for the human condition and hatred of the body" as the principal motive that led the monks to undergo so much physical privation.[31] Far from confirming this view, the mood prevalent among the Desert Fathers implicitly contradicts it. The ascetics imposed severe restraints on their bodies because they were convinced that they could sweep the body into a desperate venture. For the average ascetics—ordinary, pious Christian men and women, squatting in cells within sight of the green fields of their villages,[32] or huddled together in the mudbuilt shelters of the Pachomian monasteries[33]—the imagined transfiguration of the few great ascetics, on earth, spoke to them of the eventual transformation of their own bodies on the day of the Resurrection.

They said of Apa Pambo, that just as Moses had taken on the likeness of the glory of Adam, when his face shone with the glory of the Lord, in the same way, the face of Apa Pambo shone like lightning, and he was like an Emperor, seated on a throne. The same effect was to be seen in Apa Silvanos and in Apa Sisoes.[34]

The ascetics thought of themselves as men and women who had gained a precious freedom to mourn for their sins and to suffer in this life so that they might regain a future glory for their bodies:

Let the soul then, brothers, teach wisdom to this thick body every day when we come to our bed at evening, and say to each member of the body, "O

30. *Hist. Mon.* 11: 431D, cf. 9: 426A.
31. E. R. Dodds, *Pagan and Christian in an Age of Anxiety*, p. 35.
32. E.g., *Apophthegmata Patrum*, Poimen 110: 349C; *Anon. Copt. Apophth.* 42, Chaine, ed., p. 92—Ama Sara never once saw the Nile flowing beneath her cell.
33. Rousseau, *Pachomius*, pp. 77–86.
34. *Apophthegmata Patrum*, Pambo 12: 372A; for Adam enthroned like an Emperor among the beasts of Paradise, see M. Y. and P. Canivet, "La mosaïque dans l'église syriaque de Ḥuârte."

feet, while you have the power to stand and to move before you are laid out and become motionless, stand eagerly for your Lord." To the hands, let it say, "The hour comes when you will be loosened and motionless, bound to each other [crosswise over the breast] . . . then before you fall into that hour do not cease stretching yourself out to the Lord." "O body . . . bear me as I eagerly confess God, before you are borne away by others. . . . For there will be a time when that most heavy sleep will surely overcome you. But if you listen to me, we shall together enjoy the blessed inheritance."[35]

There is no doubt as to the terrible privations that were involved even in the relatively stable life of the Pachomian monasteries. But we must remember that the body-image which the ascetics brought with them into the desert gave considerable cognitive and emotional support to their hope for change through self-mortification. It takes some effort of the modern imagination to recapture this aspect of the ascetic life. The ascetics of late antiquity tended to view the human body as an "autarkic" system. In ideal conditions, it was thought capable of running on its own "heat"; it would need only enough nourishment to keep that heat alive. In its "natural" state—a state with which the ascetics tended to identify the bodies of Adam and Eve—the body had acted like a finely tuned engine, capable of "idling" indefinitely. It was only the twisted will of fallen men that had crammed the body with unnecessary food, thereby generating in it the dire surplus of energy that showed itself in physical appetite, in anger, and in the sexual urge. In reducing the intake to which he had become accustomed, the ascetic slowly remade his body. He turned it into an exactly calibrated instrument. Its drastic physical changes, after years of ascetic discipline, registered with satisfying precision the essential, preliminary stages of the long return of the human person, body and soul together, to an original, natural and uncorrupted state.[36]

The Spirit calls them . . . [Anthony wrote to his disciples] . . . And He delivers to them works whereby they may constrain their soul and their body, that both may be purified and enter into their inheritance. . . . And it sep-

---

35. *Paralipomena* 9.20 in A. Veilleux, trans., *Pachomian Koinonia 2*, pp. 43–44.

36. Such autarky is assumed in Gregory of Nyssa, *On the Making of Man* 30. 11–23: *Patrologia Graeca* 44: 245D–252D. Valentinus, cited with approval by Clement of Alexandria, took it for granted that Christ did not defecate, his body being in a state of perfect equilibrium: Clement, *Stromata* 3.7.59. Excrement was always linked with luxury: it was the clear measure of overeating—e.g., John Chrysostom, *Hom. 13 in I Tim.* 5 4: *P.G.* 62: 570. See Brown, *Miracles of Feeding*, p. 19 for further evidence.

arates us from all the *fruits of the flesh* which have been mingled with all the members of the body since the first transgression.[37]

Contemporaries liked to think that they had sensed this state in Anthony, when he first emerged from his cell at the bottom of a ruined fort, after twenty years, in 305:

When they beheld him, they were amazed to see that his body had maintained its former condition, neither fat for lack of exercise, nor emaciated from fasting and combat with demons, but just as it was when they had known him previous to his withdrawal. The state of his soul was one of purity. . . . He maintained an utter equilibrium, as one guided by harmonious reason and steadfast in that which accords with man's true nature.[38]

This was a body that had already

received a portion of that *spiritual body* which it is to assume in the resurrection of the just.[39]

(II) "FOR YOU HAVE POSSESSED MY INMOST PARTS"

A deep serenity, therefore, was thought to come to rest on the bodies of the few great monks. This serenity, however, was only the physical byproduct of a spiritual state. It made magnificently palpable, for all to see, the ascetic's victory in a struggle that was less visible, more prolonged, and far more bitter than had been the effort to chasten the flesh. Only those who had won the long battle with their own "heart" could hope to be touched, as Pambo and Anthony had been, by the glory of Adam.

The ascetic had to learn, over the long years of life in the desert, to do nothing less than to untwist the very sinews of his private will. Fasting and heavy labor were important, in their own right, in the first years of the ascetic life, and especially for young monks in their full physical vigor. They were part of a "Cold Turkey Treatment," by which the ascetic leeched out of his body his former excessive dependence on food and sexual satisfaction. The young man's sexual drives were dramatically reduced, and his body was slowed down by the long fasts and sleepless nights of the desert. Loss of energy alone forced him to adopt the grave, ritualized movements that characterized the good monk. Fasting and vigils "clarified" the body:

---

37. Anthony, *Letter* 1, in D. J. Chitty, trans., *The Letters of Anthony the Great*, p. 2.
38. *Life of Anthony* 14: 865A; Gregg, p. 42.   39. Anthony, *Letter* 1, p. 5.

Increase for it, if you please, either the fast of the sabbaths, or the vigil of the nights, or the reading without interruption, and the body will not be taken ill, because it has got accustomed to them. The stomach has been reduced . . . the paths of the blood have become narrower and have only moderate claims. The kidneys have acquired their natural health and do not demand much warmth. The slime is driven out of all the bones, and on account of the smallness of the body they are not weakened or damaged by much vigil.[40]

Self-mortification, however, was only a preliminary. Once the florid symptoms of greed and sexual longing, associated with the ascetic's past habits, had subsided, he was brought face to face with the baffling closedness of his own heart. It was to the heart, and to the strange resilience of the private will, that the great tradition of spiritual guidance associated with the Desert Fathers directed its most searching attention. In Adam's first state, the "natural" desires of the heart had been directed toward God, with bounding love and open-hearted awe, in the huge delight of Paradise. It was by reason of Adam's willfulness that these desires had become twisted into a "counter-nature."[41] At the bottom of that counter-nature, active long after overt physical temptations had vanished as mere epiphenomena, there lay an unbroken love for a will of one's own, "deep down in the heart, like a snake hidden in the dung."[42] Only when that will lay buried in a heart that had become as dead to self as the sterile sand of the desert would the monk be at peace:[43] for he had learned, at long last, to take into his heart "the humility and the sweetness of the Son of God."[44] This sweetness could be gained and shown only in the hard school of contact with others—with one's spiritual guides, with one's cell-mates, with the neighboring villagers, and with the crowds of visitors that were never far away, in Egypt, from the imagined stillness of the desert.

The greatest sign of Anthony's recovery of the state of Adam was not his taut body. In his very last years, this state was revealed ever

---

40. Philoxenus of Mabbug, *Letter sent to a Friend* 18, in G. Olinder, trans., *Acta Universitatis Gotoburgensis*, p. 13*. This phenomenon has been observed in modern experiments: see A. Keys, J. Brožek and others, *The Biology of Human Starvation*, 2:839–853, 905–918. On monastic diet, see now M. Dembińska, "Diet. A Comparison of Food Consumption in some Eastern and Western Monasteries in the 4th–12th centuries."

41. Isaiah of Scetis, *Asceticon* 2.9.5, trans., *Abbé Isaie: Recueil ascétique*, p. 46.

42. John Climacus, *The Ladder of Divine Ascent* 15: *Patrologia Graeca* 88: 900A; C. Luibheid and N. Russell, trans., p. 183.

43. Ibid. 15: 881C; trans., p. 172.

44. *First Greek Life of Pachomius* 110, Veilleux, *Pachomian Koinonia* 1, p. 374.

more frequently in the quintessentially fourth-century gift of sociability. He came to radiate such magnetic charm, and openness to all, that any stranger who came upon him, surrounded by crowds of disciples, visiting monks and lay pilgrims, would know at once, in that dense press of black-garbed figures, which one was the great Anthony.[45] He was instantly recognizable as someone whose heart had achieved total transparency to others.

It was the human will, sensed by the monk as an impacted mass of willfullness lodged at the very bottom of his heart, and not the malleable "clay" of the body itself, that stood "like a brazen wall" between the monk and God.[46] For all but the greatest ascetics, direct experiences of the demonic were a distant prospect: normally, Apa Poimen insisted, "it is our own wills that play the demon to us."[47] "Throw your will behind you, be without care," said Apa Sisoes, "and you will find rest."[48] "Head bowed and a humble heart," Pachomius advised, "and gentleness in the hour of anger."[49] The heart was the accursed ground into which the fallen Adams of the desert found that they must dig "in the sweat of their brow."[50] The body, by contrast, was a mere "testing-bed." In the long and patient attrition of the desires of the flesh, the flaws that still lingered in the heart itself were revealed with stark exactitude.

The monks of Egypt brought about the reemergence, in a peculiarly radical form, of the early Christian preoccupation with "singleness of heart."[51] The quiet study-circles of an Origen or a Methodius had been groups of somewhat alienated soul-mates: they had been little concerned with the grinding clash of wills in a small community, such as had led simpler men to place so high a value on the virtue of "singleness of heart." Matters had always been different in the villages and small towns of Egypt. Texts such as *The Shepherd* of Hermas, which spoke so wistfully on just that theme, passed directly into Coptic. They circulated among a population which, for centuries, had admired gentleness and dignified reticence as the hallmark of the wise man.[52]

---

45. *Life of Anthony* 67: 940A. 46. *Apophthegmata Patrum* Poimen 54: 336A.
47. Ibid. Poimen 37: 337C. 48. Ibid. Sisoes 43: 405B.
49. *Instructions of Pachomius* 1.8, Veilleux, trans., *Pachomian Koinonia 3*, p. 14.
50. *Sentences des Pères*, 656, Regnault, trans., p. 160.
51. See esp. A. Guillaumont, "Monachisme et éthique judéo-chrétienne."
52. Rousseau, *Pachomius*, pp. 136–137. See Miriam Lichtheim, *Later Egyptian Wisdom Literature in the International Context*, and esp. p. 186 on the tone of the instructions contained in *Pap. Insinger*.

"Singleness of heart," the fear of the "divided heart," and a poignant wish for the simplicity of a little child in the midst of the cramped cunning of the settled world had given a quite distinctive flavor to the piety of Christian Egypt, in valley and desert alike. This was the Christianity that men like Anthony took with them out of the villages. The monk was the hero of the settled land, and not simply because he had risen above the iron laws of the belly. He bore the "heart of the righteous." He was a man who had gained a heart that was all of one piece, a heart as unriven by the knotted grain of private, unshared meanings and of private, covert intentions as was the solid, milk-white heart of the date-palm.[53]

Altogether, the most lasting impression of the monastic literature of fourth- and fifth-century Egypt, and of its later offshoots in Palestine and Sinai, was of a relentless ascesis of social relations. One saying of Anthony was held to have set the tone: "From your neighbor comes life and death."[54]

To the unchanging nexus of food and work that maintained the monk's humanity in the desert at all times, the Egyptian tradition added the nexus of acute dependence on others—of disciples on their masters, of cell-mates on each other. The company of one's fellows was the hardest trial of all to endure. As Apa Ammon remembered at Kellia:

I have accomplished all the mortifications of which my ear has heard, but among these, I have not found any so daunting as these two: to get up from table when still hungry, and to do our hearts violence so as not to say a disagreeable word to a brother.[55]

There was only one sure way to break the hard earth of the heart: "The Fathers say that to sit in one's cell is half, and to throw oneself before the Old Men is another half."[56]

The total dependence of small groups of disciples on a spiritual father, or on a group of spiritual fathers, was the *sine qua non* of survival and spiritual growth in the desert. It was through dependence on his

---

53. *Anonymous Apophthegmata* 362, in F. Nau, ed., *Revue de l'Orient chrétien* (1913) 18:138.

54. *Apophthegmata Patrum* Anthony 9: 77B.

55. *Ethiopian Collection* 14.17, *Sentences des Pères*, p. 317.

56. Dorotheos of Gaza, *Letter* 1.180, in L. Regnauult and J. de Préville, eds., *Dorothée de Gaza: Oeuvres spirituelles*, p. 488; see the translation of E. P. Wheeler, *Dorotheus of Gaza: Discourses and Sayings*.

spiritual father that the monk learned to understand his own heart, and to open that heart to others:

It is a universal and unambiguous symptom that a chain of thought is from the Devil, if we feel shame in bringing it out into the open before an Old Man.[57]

For nothing displeases the demon of fornication more than to reveal his works, and nothing gives him greater pleasure than to keep one's thoughts to oneself.[58]

The model of the person first made explicit by Origen lay at the back of this insistence on dependence on a spiritual guide. The "heart" was the center of the person:

The heart is the meeting point between body and soul, between the subconscious, the conscious and the supraconscious, between the human and the divine.[59]

Prolonged streams of thought, inspirations, and unshakable obsessions were invariably treated as symptomatic. The way they arose in the heart was thought to betray the guiding presence of the many impalpable beings who clustered along the fringes of the self. The "language of the Holy Spirit" might rise in the monk's heart, or his thought flow might slowly take on the quality of a demonic obsession.[60]

The good disciple sat in his cell, "twisting ropes while meditation floweth on as running water."[61] But the Devil, too, was a master-weaver: given the loose end of one sinful or unconsidered thought, he could plait a whole rope from it.[62] There was always a moment, then, when the thoughts of the monk could be sensed as no longer belonging wholly to the human mind, but to the demons or to the angels whose subtle presences were registered in the unaccustomed force of the flow, through the heart, of powerful trains of thought—the *logismoi*. Hence the crucial importance of the gift of discernment, of *diakrisis*, among

57. Cassian, *Institutiones* 4.9, in J. C. Guy, ed., *Jean Cassien: Les Institutions cénobitiques*, p. 132.

58. *Anonymous Apophthegmata* 164, Nau, ed., *Revue de l'Orient chrétien* (1908) 13:54.

59. Kallistos Ware, "Ways of Prayer and Contemplation," in B. McGinn, J. Meyendorff, and J. Leclercq, eds., *Christian Spirituality*, p. 401.

60. We must always remember that *logismoi* meant "streams of thought" or, even, "intentions": a clear distinction was always made between mere random thoughts and those that were persistent: *Barsanuphe et Jean de Gaza: Correspondance* 165, in L. Regnault, et al., trans., p. 141.

61. Cited in H. E. Winlock, *The Monastery of Epiphanius at Thebes, vol. 1*, p. 155, *n* 6.

62. *Sentences des Pères* 400, p. 50.

the Desert Fathers. This meant far more than self-knowledge and good sense, though it might, in fact, often include a large measure of both. It meant the rare spiritual gift of being able to see clearly what one could no longer call one's own in one's own stream of consciousness. It was the ability to heed a warning signal to depend on others.

As a result, the desert became the powerhouse of a new culture. For all his interest in such matters, Origen's spirituality had remained the spirituality of an urban study-group. The greatest powers of spiritual discernment were not directed to the heart: they were deployed in the long labor with which Origen and his disciples searched out the meaning of the sacred text. It was the precise meaning of Scripture, pondered by highly literate men and women, that caused the heart of the Christian "to burn." The discipline of meditation on the holy text often assumed philological resources that could be found only in upper-class circles, in close proximity to great cities. In the *Life of Anthony*, and in successive layers of monastic spiritual guidance, we can detect the emergence of an alternative. The monk's own heart was the new book. What required infinitely skilled exegesis and long spiritual experience were the "movements of the heart," and the strategies and snares that the Devil laid within it.[63]

Such movements were best conveyed orally to a spiritual father. It was a situation which tended to give priority to the languages closest to the heart, that is, the vernaculars of Egypt and the Near East—Coptic, Syriac, and demotic Greek.[64] The deepest relief of the soul came now, not from the written page, but from that tap of the Old Man's fingers on his disciple's chest, which assuaged the heart beneath.[65] The shift from a culture of the book to a *cultura Dei*,[66] based largely on the nonliterate, verbal interchange of a monastic "art of thought," was rightly hailed as the greatest and the most peculiar achievement of the Old Men of Egypt: it amounted to nothing less than the discovery of a new alphabet of the heart.[67]

The abiding presence of sexual desire, and of sexual feeling in the

---

63. Rufinus, *Historia Monachorum* 1: *Patrologia Latina* 21: 403B; and the classic speech of Anthony in the *Life of Anthony* 16–43: 868A–908A.

64. *Paralipomena* 27, Veilleux, *Pachomian Koinonia* 2, p. 51: Pachomius miraculously obtained the knowledge of Greek for this purpose.

65. *Sentences des Pères* 509–510, pp. 84–86.

66. The term is that used by the earliest Latin translation of the *Life of Anthony* to translate *askésis*: G. J. M. Bartelink, *Vita di Antonio*, prol. 2, p. 4.

67. *Apophthegmata Patrum* Arsenius 5: 89A.

mind of the monk, took on a new meaning. Sexuality became, as it were, a privileged ideogram. This did not mean that most ascetic spiritual guides treated sexual temptation as uniquely alarming. Far from it: sexual desire was frequently overshadowed, as a source of spiritual danger, by the dull aches of pride and resentment and by dread onslaughts of immoderate spiritual ambition. These could rock whole monasteries, destroying lives and littering the literature of the desert with chilling accounts of pathological cases of hatred,[68] hallucination,[69] and dire ego-inflation.[70] Regrettable though they were, sexual lapses were a fact of desert life. Monks were known to have become the fathers of sons: the hero of one such anecdote eventually brought his child back with him to the cell, resuming his handicraft just as he had left it before his escapade into the world.[71] Older men harassed the novices: "With wine and boys around, the monks have no need of the Devil to tempt them."[72] Bestiality with the monastery's donkeys could not be ruled out.[73]

What mattered, rather, was a sharpened awareness of the permanence of sexual fantasy. Because of this observed quality of permanence, sexual desire was now treated as effectively coextensive with human nature. Abiding awareness of the self as a sexual being, forever subject to sexual longings, and troubled—even in dreams—by sexual fantasies highlighted the areas of intractability in the human person. But this intractability was not simply physical. It pointed into the very depths of the soul. Sexual desire revealed the knot of unsurrendered privacy that lay at the very heart of fallen man. Thus, in the new language of the desert, sexuality became, as it were, an ideogram of the unopened heart. As a result, the abatement of sexual fantasy in the heart of the monk—an abatement that was held to be accompanied, quite concretely, with a cessation of the monk's night emissions—signaled, in the body, the ascetic's final victory over the closed heart. Only the hand of Christ Himself, reaching down from heaven—as in the marginal illuminations of Byzantine copies of *The Ladder of Divine*

---

68. See, for example, John Climacus, *Ladder* 8: 832A; trans., p. 148.

69. *Apophthegmata Patrum* Nicetas: 312B; Poimen 114: 352AB.

70. See the evidence collected in P. Canivet, "Erreurs de spiritualité et troubles psychiques," among these, *eparsis*, "spiritual elevation" notably preponderates. Palladius, *Hist. Laus.* 26 and 27 provides two florid examples.

71. *Anonymous Apophthegmata* 187, Nau, ed., *Revue de l'Orient chrétien* (1908) 13:273.

72. *Sentences des Pères* 545, p. 98.

73. John Climacus, *Ladder* 29: 1149A; trans., p. 283 and 4: 697A: trans., p. 102.

Ascent of John Climacus—could snatch the monk out of the tomb of his private will, by overcoming in him that most ineradicably private of his drives.[74] To receive from Christ the grace of a transparent chastity was to shatter the last weapons of the unsurrendered will: it was to complete the transformation of the heart.

Come now and look upon the works of the Lord, What awesome things He has done on the earth. It is He who makes war to cease in all the world; He breaks the bow, and shatters the spear, and burns the shields with fire.[75]

So intense a preoccupation with the monk's sexual thought-flow developed in ascetic circles because the aim of spiritual guidance had been the total expropriation of the inner world of the disciple. The inner world must be turned inside out. Nothing must linger in it that could not be placed unhesitatingly before others. In the words of Anthony:

I tell you, that every man who delights in his own will, and is subdued to his own thoughts, and takes up the things sown in his heart, and rejoices in them, and supposes in his heart that these are some great mystery, and justifies himself in what he does—the soul of such a man is a lair of evil spirits, counselling him to evil, and his body a store of evil mysteries in which it hides itself.[76]

The "thoughts" to which Anthony referred were not invariably sexual thoughts. But sexual thoughts had a pervasiveness and a resilience that soon led exponents of the desert tradition to place special emphasis upon them. They served as barium-traces, by which the Desert Fathers mapped out the deepest and most private recesses of the will.

Speaking to John Cassian at the end of the fourth century, Apa Chaeremon expatiated lovingly on the gift of God, bestowed on the few who enjoyed perfect "purity of heart." They had been freed from sexual fantasies in dreams associated with nocturnal emissions. For the continuance of sexual dreams and emissions served to warn the monk, in a mercifully concrete manner, of the presence within his heart of a more faceless, lingering desire—the wish to possess experiences of his own. The sexuality of the emission created a disjunction between his public, daylight self and a last oasis of incommunicable, privatized ex-

---

74. J. R. Martin, *The Illustrations of the Heavenly Ladder of John Climacus*, fig. 64.

75. John Cassian, *Collationes* 12.12, citing Psalm 45:9–10, in E. Pichery, ed., *Jean Cassien: Conférences*, Sources chrétiennes 54, p. 141.

76. Anthony, *Letter 6*, p. 19.

perience. When such dreams ceased, the last fissure between the private person and his fellows could be assumed to have closed: "And so he should be found in the night as he is in the day, in bed as when at prayer, alone as when surrounded by a crowd. *For you have possessed my inward parts.*"[77]

Quia tu possedisti renes meos: the "inmost parts" were the kidneys. These had been one of the traditional loci of sexual energy.[78] In monastic thought, they became the place where the shadows lingered longest in the private man. There is nothing strange, therefore, in the manner with which Apa Chaeremon opened his discourse on this delicate topic with a reference to the state of the first Christians of the Jerusalem community after the coming of the Holy Ghost: holding *all things in common* there was among them *one heart and one soul.*[79] The total expropriation associated with the life of the desert had begun, as in the case of Anthony, with the surrender of private wealth. It ended with the surrender of the last traces of sexual fantasy. This was a sure symptom, in Cassian's mind and in that of his Egyptian informants, that the dispersal of the last, most hidden treasures of the private will had taken place.

Cassian, as we shall see in a later chapter, was a theorist, writing to persuade Latin readers who did not necessarily share his views.[80] The most searching and humane material on monastic sexuality comes from a later age, and from a slightly different region—from the monasteries of Gaza and of Sinai in the sixth and early seventh centuries. Here we are no longer in a world of rugged pioneers. Rather, we see the sons of the local gentry, now turned monks, fighting the long battle for the will, with two centuries of ascetic experience behind them.[81]

Dorotheos of Gaza (who died around 560) is the most attractive figure among these.[82] The son of a notable from Antioch, an aura of past wealth and status continued to cling to him. It determined his role in the monastic settlement to which he came, in around 520—that of Apa

---

77. Cassian, *Collationes* 12.8 citing Psalm 138.13, Sources chrétiennes 54, p. 135.
78. E.g., Nemesius of Emesa, *On the Nature of Man* 28.45: *P.G.* 40: 716A.
79. Cassian, *Collationes* 12.2, Sources chrétiennes 54, pp. 123–124.
80. See below ch. 19, pp. 420–423.
81. See esp. Derwas Chitty, *The Desert a City*, pp. 132–181 and the excellent study of Palestinian monasticism by Flusin, *Miracle et Histoire*, pp. 12–32, 88–103.
82. See Chitty, *Desert a City*, pp. 136–140 and the introduction to Regnault and de Préville, *Dorothée de Gaza*, pp. 12–29.

Seridos, at Migdal Thavatha (now Khirbet Umm al-Tut), only a few miles south of Gaza.[83] He had arrived with a library of medical books. His brother, a good Byzantine, a "greater lover of monks," built the infirmary for the monastery; and Dorotheos found himself, predictably, placed in charge of the family foundation.[84]

For this delicate and marvelously vulnerable young man we possess evidence unique in late antiquity: the inner portrait of his life over two decades. This is revealed to us in a series of letters exchanged between himself and an ancient Egyptian recluse, the Great Old Man, Barsanuphius, from whose closed-in cell near the monastery there emanated over eight hundred letters of spiritual direction to Christians of every walk of life in the Gaza area, up to Barsanuphius' death in around 543.[85] As Lucien Regnault, the French translator of these remarkable documents, has said: "What the *Sayings of the Desert Fathers* let us glimpse only in the form of transitory flashes, is here played out before our very eyes like a film."[86]

Dorotheos appears in this film. His dependence on the Great Old Man was central to his early days in the new environment of the monastery. Dorotheos would kiss the closed door of the Old Man's cell as one would kiss the wood of the Cross.[87] A tap on the chest from the Old Man in a dream brought to an end a terrible period of depression.[88] Merely to write of his thoughts to Barsanuphius delivered him of their weight—and to such an extent that Dorotheos felt anxious that such apparent serenity should have come to him, at so young an age, with so little apparent effort![89] The young notable's son needed all the good nature that he could muster. Once, "whether to provoke me or out of simplicity," an elderly monk had stumbled across his cell in the middle of the night and urinated on the head of his bed, soaking Dorotheos through and through. At another time, a neighbor had shaken

83. Regnault and de Préville, *Dorothée de Gaza*, p. 14.

84. Dorotheos, *Life of Dositheos* 1, p. 122.

85. See Chitty, *Desert a City*, pp. 132–138 and his edition, *The Letters of Varsanuphius* in *Patrologia Orientalis* (1966) 31(3). This edition was sadly cut short by the death of Chitty: we are left with the Greek edition of S. Schoinos, *Biblios Barsanouphiou* and with the excellent French translation of L. Regnault and others, *Barsanuphe et Jean de Gaza: Correspondance.*

86. Regnault, *Barsanuphe*, p. 6.

87. Dorotheos, *Instructions* 4.56, p. 240; Wheeler, p. 117.

88. *Instructions* 5.67, p. 262; Wheeler, p. 128.

89. *Instructions* 1.25, p. 184; Wheeler, pp. 91–92.

his blanket in such a way that a swarm of bed bugs fell into Dorotheos' cell, a source of acute discomfort to him in the long summer heat.[90] Immensely aware of others, constantly tempted by "vain-glory" to pass on to his fellows the gems of spiritual advice given to himself alone by the Great Old Man,[91] prone to blushing with self-consciousness when he performed the obligatory prostration before certain colleagues,[92] and anxious lest he seem out of place by shutting his eyes in church in order to concentrate on the liturgy,[93] Dorotheos fell in love with a fellow-monk.

The first letter of the Great Old Man was harsh, "like wine on a new wound."[94] Dorotheos had found himself making pretexts to talk to the monk.[95] Now he was afraid that too brusque a cooling of relations would awaken his friend's suspicions.[96] Throughout, Barsanuphius is a stern but untroubled presence.

Often, my brother, in my youth, I was violently tempted by the demon of fornication, and I fought hard with toil against my thoughts. . . . And after I had done that for five years, God delivered me of it. . . . God, indeed, could release you speedily; but if that were to happen, you would not have gained the strength to stand up against other passions.[97]

Dorotheos stayed in the monastery. We see him settling down. He remained to the last the same man, clearly identifiable by being seen through the sharp eyes of the Great Old Man. When appointed to the infirmary, a position where his delightfully vulnerable personality would be at its most exposed and of most use to others, it is Barsanuphius who overrode his hesitations. Should he give his ample library to the monks?[98] Should he use the sophisticated medical recipes contained in these books, or should he, out of humility, be content to administer simple folk remedies?[99] Barsanuphius replied:

As we are not yet come to the perfection in which we are completely delivered from the captivity of the passions it is better to devote our time to medicine than to the passions.[100]

How could the busy supervisor retain the memory of God? The Great Old Man wrote back:

---

90. *Instructions* 4.57, p. 242; Wheeler, p. 118.   91. *Barsanuphe* 206, p. 207.
92. 302, p. 226.   93. 325, p. 236.   94. 256, p. 202.   95. 256, p. 201.
96. 258, p. 204.   97. 258, p. 205.   98. 326, p. 236.   99. 327, p. 237.
100. 327, p. 238.

Many hear all the time about a city and it so happens that they enter the city in question without knowing it. Brother, you are all day long in the memory of God and you do not know it. Indeed, to have a commandment and to devote yourself to keeping it, that is at one and the same time obedience and the memory of God.[101]

(III) "PURIFIED AND REFINED BY CLAY"

Almost three hundred years had passed from Anthony's first renunciation, around 270, to the death of Dorotheos of Gaza, around 560. This was a longer time than the period between the conversion of Saint Paul and the end of the reign of Constantine: it amounted to one half of the total lifespan of the Roman Empire in the eastern provinces. In this long period, ascetic reflection passed through many silent mutations, over an area that stretched from the coast of Provence in the West to the foothills of the Zagros mountains in the East. One feature, however, remained remarkably stable: a sense of the shared momentum of body and soul. This had first been made plain in Origen's grandiose system of transformation. It was later reasserted, frequently with significant modifications and with widely varying degrees of self-conscious dependence on Origen himself, by men as different from each other as were Anthony, Evagrius of Pontus, John Cassian, and Philoxenos of Mabbug.[102]

In the desert tradition, vigilant attention to the body enjoyed an almost oppressive prominence. Yet to describe ascetic thought as "dualist" and as motivated by hatred of the body, is to miss its most novel and its most poignant aspect.[103] Seldom, in ancient thought, had the body been seen as more deeply implicated in the transformation of the soul; and never was it made to bear so heavy a burden. For the Desert Fathers, the body was not an irrelevant part of the human person, that could, as it were, be "put in brackets."[104] It could not enjoy

---

101. 328, p. 238.

102. On this extremely intricate subject, I owe most to J. Gribomont, s.v. Monachisme, *Dictionnaire de la Spiritualité* pp. 1541–1544—on a "desert Origenism;" A. Guillaumont, *Les "Kephalaia Gnostica" d'Évagre le Pontique;* J. G. Bunge, "Origenismus-Gnostizismus: Zum geistesgeschichtlichen Standort des Evagrios Pontikos"; Flusin, *Miracle et Histoire*, pp. 76–86; Guy Lardreau, *Discours philosophique et discours spirituel. Autour de la philosophie spirituelle de Philoxène de Mabboug*, and K. Ware, "Ways of Prayer," pp. 397–400.

103. As by A. J. Festugière, *Antioche païenne et chrétienne*, p. 309: Toute la spiritualité de ce temps est foncièrement dualiste.

104. Lardreau, *Discours philosophique*, p. 39.

the distant tolerance that Plotinus and many pagan sages were prepared to accord it, as a transient and accidental adjunct to the self. It
was, rather, grippingly present to the monk: he was to speak of it as
"this body, that God has afforded me, as a field to cultivate, where I
might work and become rich."[105]

Theologians of ascetic background, throughout the fourth and fifth
centuries, would not have pursued with such ferocious intellectual energy the problems raised by the Incarnation of Christ, and the consequent joining of human and divine in one single human person, if
this joining had not been sensed by them as a haunting emblem of
the enigmatic joining of body and soul within themselves.[106]

Hence the double aspect of ascetic literature. Ascetic strategies of
exhortation continued to stress the sharp opposition between the pure
spirit and the sensual body. The Great Old Man did not mince his
words to young Dorotheos: "Torture your senses, for without torture
there is no martyrdom. . . . Trample on the passions by meditating
on this letter."[107]

But the cumulative experience of ascetic transformation quietly eroded
so stark an image of the self. Life in the desert revealed, if anything,
the inextricable interdependence of body and soul. When Dorotheos
himself came to write as an old man he noted that in some mysterious
way, it was possible to "humble" the body—by physical labor, fasting,
and vigils—so that one could actually bring humility to the soul. So
intimate a connection of body and soul both puzzled and reassured
him.[108] A monk's relations with his sexual fantasies brought his baffling relationship into exceptionally clear focus. What was most en-
duringly physical about him—his sexual needs and lingering sexual
imagination—seemed most intimately interwoven with the state of his
soul. The ebb and flow of sexual energy was consistently presented,
by Evagrius and John Cassian, as a symptom that reflected, in the
obscure but crucial frontier-zone between body and spirit, changes that
happened deep within the soul.[109] Speaking of the way a novice's
growing capacity for the love of God could even take sexual forms
"akin to the passion of fornication," Philoxenos of Mabbug exclaimed:

105. *Instructions of Horsiesius* 1.6, Veilleux, *Koinonia* 3, p. 138.
106. See most recently Lars Thunberg, "The Human Person as Image of God."
107. *Barsanuphe* 256, p. 202.
108. Dorotheos of Gaza, *Instructions* 2.39, pp. 204–206; Wheeler, pp. 101–102.
109. F. Refoulé, "Rêves et vie spirituelle d'après Évagre le Pontique."

"Oh how difficult this is to understand! Here the knowledge of the scholar is tried!"[110]

Phenomena such as this brought the Fathers of the Desert into a world where the "fixed components" of ancient thought no longer helped them.[111]

In the desert tradition, the body was allowed to become the discreet mentor of the proud soul. No longer was the ascetic formed, as had been the case in pagan circles, by the unceasing vigilance of his mind alone. The rhythms of the body and, with the body, his concrete social relations determined the life of the monk: his continued economic dependence on the settled world for food, the hard school of day-to-day collaboration with his fellow-ascetics in shared rhythms of labor, and mutual exhortation in the monasteries slowly changed his personality. The material conditions of the monk's life were held capable of altering the consciousness itself. Of all the lessons of the desert to a late antique thinker, what was most "truly astonishing" was "that the immortal spirit can be purified and refined by clay.[112]

The tradition of the Desert Fathers flowed into *The Ladder of Divine Ascent* of John Climacus—John "of *The Ladder*" (579–649), the undisputed masterpiece of Byzantine spiritual guidance.[113] Just because his body was so inextricably part of him, the monk was hailed by John as a charged anomaly: he "finds himself in an earthly and defiled body, but pushes himself into the rank and status of the incorporeal angels."[114] The huge labor of the monastic life happened because the body could never be abandoned: "Violence and unending pain are the lot of those who aim to ascend to Heaven with the body."[115]

"If people really understood it, no one would renounce the world."[116]

Sexuality was an abiding reminder of that pain: "For a man cannot conquer what he actually is. . . . Nature is on its side."[117] Only the hand of Christ could raise the monk above it.

---

110. Philoxenus of Mabbug, *Letter to a Friend* 13, p. 9*.

111. The term is that of A. D. Nock, *Sallustius: Concerning the Gods and the Universe*, p. xxxix.

112. John Climacus, *Ladder* 14: 868C; trans. p. 169.

113. See esp. K. Ware, Introduction to John Climacus, *The Ladder*, pp. 1–6 and 58–68. The classic treatment is that of W. Völker, *Scala Paradisi. Eine Studie zu Johannes Climacus und zugleich eine Vorstudie zu Symeon dem Neuen Theologen*, esp. pp. 108–122, on chastity; pp. 217–230, on discernment; and pp. 278–290, on spiritual perfection. Völker rightly emphasises the dependence of John on the traditions we have discussed so far.

114. John Climacus, *The Ladder* 1: 633B; trans., p. 74.   115. 1: 636B; p. 75.

116. 1: 641B; p. 79.   117. 15: 881A and 884AB; pp. 172, 174.

Yet John had inherited from the desert tradition the expectation that the power of Christ could embrace both body and soul. The body would share, in its own way, in the transfiguration of the human person that accompanied the final opening out of the clenched will. For John, as for Apa Chaeremon, a cessation of night fantasies could be expected, even demanded: "I do not think that anyone should be classed a saint until he has made his body holy, if indeed that is possible."[118]

What John seems to have envisaged in the perfected monk, touching on it hesitantly and in a language heavy with paradox, was an inversion of the normal properties of the fallen body. A redirection of its energies could take place. "I have watched impure souls mad for physical love but turning what they knew of such love into a reason for penance and transferring that same capacity for love to the Lord."[119]

This redirection took palpable physical form in the infinitely precious gift of tears. In the ancient medical tradition, excessive fluid humor had marked the temperament of the sensual man: the eyes of the lady-killer were damp and glistening with this superfluous humor; he was compassionate and given to tears.[120] Damp humors lurked in the lower parts, and were transformed, through the heat generated by excessive food, into sexual drives.[121] The fluidity of a temperament that blurred harsh boundaries ensured that the monks most prone to sensuality were often, so John had observed, more sensitive to others, and more gregarious, than were those harsh "dry" souls who were more naturally inclined to chastity.[122]

What John expected was that all this fluidity would be transformed. The damp humors would be released in an upsurge of spiritualized sensuality, associated with Christ's supreme gift of tears. The fine humor of the eyes would flow without inhibition.[123] The very blood of a broken heart would pour into the mouth.[124] The uncontrolled mourning of the perfect monk was a palpable physical state. Tears showed that men still stood before God, "on the dark side of the bay of his blessing."[125] But, in the tearful, the rigid heart had melted. By weep-

118. 15: 889C; p. 178.   119. 5: 77A; p. 129.
120. Pseudo-Aristotle, *Physiognomica* 29, in R. Förster, ed., *Physiognomici graeci*, 1:36.
121. It was a commonplace of the desert tradition that the Devil dried up the monk's tears of contrition and, by implication, diverted this humor to his lower parts: *Barsanuphe* 18, p. 25.
122. John Climacus, *The Ladder* 15: 889A; p. 177.   123. 7: 805c–808AC; p. 139.
124. 7: 816B; p. 144.   125. Gerard Manley Hopkins, *The Wreck of the Deutschland*, p. 16.

ing, they already stood close to the laughter of Paradise, "when pain, sorrow and lamentation will have taken flight."[126]

In a way that John was unwilling to analyze, a lover's ability to sense the deepest movements of the heart in the body of his beloved would change to a spiritual vision of others that was as exquisitely sharp.[127] The fierce boundlessness of sensuality, "a yearning for bodies, a shameful and terrible spirit that asserts itself at the very heart's core,"[128] would no longer reach out to break down the boundaries between one human being and another (and even, in the case of the errant keeper of the monastery's donkeys, between men and beasts).[129] It would be transmuted into an equally boundless transcendance of differences. Physical beauty would be sensed with unaccustomed intensity, but without temptation: John wrote: "There was a man who, having looked upon a body of great beauty, at once gave praise to its Creator, and after one look was stirred to love God and to weep copiously."

Maybe, he suggested, "the same guideline" applied to the sweet music of the Psalms. Former objects of sexual desire might be glimpsed, at last, in terms of the abstract beauty of their created form. Their beauty became translucent to the eye. It would shake the soul to its depths, but gently now, much as the impalpable sweetness of the liturgy now swayed the heart of the monk: "such a man," John declared, "has risen to immortality before the general resurrection."[130]

We can appreciate why sexuality had come to bear so unaccustomed a weight among the finest exponents of the desert tradition. It was not because men like Cassian, Dorotheos of Gaza, and John Climacus feared sexual temptation more than any other. It was rather that the body, in which sexuality lurked with such baffling tenacity, had come to be viewed in the searching light of a new, high hope: "What is this mystery in me? What is the purpose of this mixture of body and soul? How can I be my own friend and my own enemy?"[131] Yet everyone, John insists, "should struggle to raise his clay, so to speak, to a place on the throne of God."[132]

John's *Ladder of Divine Ascent* marks the end of late antiquity. Muslim armies had already entered Antioch, Jerusalem, and Alexandria by the time that John wrote those lines.[133] From then on, they would be read

126. John Climacus, *The Ladder* 7: 809C; p. 141.   127. 26: 1033D; p. 243.
128. 15: 884D; pp. 173–174.   129. 29: 1149A; p. 283.   130. 15: 892D–893A; p. 179.
131. 15: 904A; p. 186.   132. 26: 1064A; p. 248.
133. Chitty, *Desert a City*, pp. 168–175.

aloud in the refectory, every year at Lent, by the monks of the Orthodox churches.[134] A guide for souls, John had been content to sketch the mere outline of a trajectory, leaving the resolution of the paradoxes to which he alluded to the experience of his charges. John wrote with three centuries of spiritual wisdom behind him. The Christians of the fourth century, however, did not have the benefit of the long summer's afternoon of desert wisdom to guide them. In the fourth and early fifth centuries, other men, many of them less experienced, less endowed by temperament, and less free, by reason of their social position, to follow the slow patience of the desert art of souls, would turn their pens with new puzzlement to the facts of sex. Let us now turn away from the desert, to look more closely at the impact of the new ascetic ideals on the clergy, on lay persons, and on devout women in the cities and villages of the major Christian regions of the Mediterranean.

134. Ware, Introduction, *The Ladder*, p. 1.

TWELVE

"Make to Yourselves Separate Booths": Monks, Women and Marriage in Egypt

---

Some time in the 320s, a seventeen-year-old pagan boy in Alexandria decided to become baptized. For young Theodore, as for so many of his generation, committed Christianity meant continence: "If the Lord leads me on the way that I may become a Christian," he vowed "then I will also become a monk, and will keep my body without stain until the day when the Lord will come for me."[1] Immediately recruited into a local urban church, young Theodore's resolution was subjected to predictable strains: "He met with no woman at all. . . . When he read the lessons in church, he would strive not to let his eyes rove over the people."

Twelve years of such vigilance were enough. Theodore vanished up the Nile to the seclusion of a Pachomian monastery. The easygoing life of a well-fed and learned clergy were not for him: only a body rendered as dry as the desert sands could hope to keep its purity.[2]

---

1. *Bohairic Life of Pachomius* 89, in A. Veilleux, trans., *Pachomian Koinonia* 1:117.
2. Ibid., pp. 118, 120.

Theodore was not the only young clergyman of ascetic leanings to be driven into the desert through fear of his own susceptibility to women.[3] His anxieties were echoed in the desert itself. Fear of women fell like a bar of shadow across the paths that led back from the desert into the towns and villages.

The disciple of Apa Sisoes said to him, "Father, you have grown old. Let us move a little closer to the settled land." The Old Man said, "Where there is no woman, that is where we should go." The disciple said to him, "What other place is there that has no woman, if not the desert?" The Old Man said to him, "Take me to the desert."[4]

Such anecdotes reveal a side of the monastic movement very different from the gentle precision with which the few, great ascetic spiritual guides spoke about sexuality in themselves and in the small circle of their chosen disciples.

In the fourth and fifth centuries, the ascetic literature of Egypt became a repository of vivid anecdotes concerning sexual seduction and heroic sexual avoidance. In this new monastic folklore, the body leapt into sharp focus. Women were presented as a source of perpetual temptation to which the male body could be expected to respond instantly. For a nun simply to pat the foot of an elderly, sick bishop was considered enough provocation to cause both of them to fall instantly into fornication.[5]

The sheer physicality of such stories bruise the modern sensibility. A monk dipped his cloak into the putrefying flesh of a dead woman, so that the smell might banish thoughts about her;[6] a dutiful daughter repelled the advances of a young monk by warning him that he could not imagine the strange and terrible stench of a menstruating woman;[7] a novice carried his elderly mother across a stream, his hands prudently wrapped in his cloak: "for the flesh of all women is fire."[8] Their message to the laity was plain. The Emperor Zeno, so the Coptic legend said, was rightly puzzled when he learned that his daughter had slept in the same cell as a monk (the "monk," in fact, was a woman

3. See, for example, Palladius, Lausiac History 38.3–7, on Evagrius in Constantinople, and Ps.-Jerome, Letter 18.3: Patrologia Latina 30: 185C, on Praesidius, deacon of Piacenza.

4. Apophthegmata Patrum, Sisoes 3: Patrologia Graeca 65: 392D.

5. L. Regnault, trans., Les Sentences des Pères du Désert: Nouveau Recueil 32:22, also in F. Nau, "Histoires des solitaires d'Égypte," pp. 13:62–64.

6. Anonymous Apophthegmata 172, in Nau, ed., Revue de l'Orient chrétien (1908) 13:56.

7. Ibid. 52: (1907) 12:17.   8. Ibid. 159: (1908) 13:52.

in disguise): "I have heard that monks hate women and that they cannot bear even to speak with one."[9]

Many of the ugly stories that circulated in monastic circles in the fourth and fifth centuries would have struck contemporaries as banal. They were culled from the extensive rubbish heap of Near Eastern misogyny: the sayings and anecdotes concerning rabbis of this period were equally insistent on the need of the Sages and their young, married, disciples to avoid the touch, the sight, and the sound of women.[10] But the message of monastic anecdotes was no longer, simply, that men—even married men—were easily distracted from serious concerns by the wiles of women. Among the monks, male and female bodies came to be presented as equally charged with sexual feeling, because both were equally subject to an exacting obligation to preserve their virgin state. Emphasis on the infinite preciousness and fragility of a monk's virginity generated a totally new sense of peril. Monks were supposed to put an unbridgeable distance between themselves and the women of the settled land, and even between themselves and nuns. The virgin body of the monk was called upon to act as a landmark. Its untouched state spoke of a barrier between the Christian laity of the towns and villages—the *kosmikoi*, the men and women "of the world," who were most usually married persons—and the monks. It stood for a boundary that was as unmistakable as was the abrupt, ecological transition from the soft green fields of the valley to the shimmering dead sands of the desert. The words of prophet Nehemiah, *Make to yourselves separate booths*, was the motto of the age.[11]

Thus, the studied misogyny of much ascetic literature did not reflect merely a shrinking away from women as a source of sexual temptation. It was mobilized as part of a wider strategy. It served to contain and to define the place of the ascetic movement in late Roman society. Faced by the perpetual threat of an asceticism so radical that it blurred the distinction between city and desert, even between men and women, the leaders of the churches, in Egypt as elsewhere, fell back on ancient traditions of misogyny in order to heighten a sense of sexual peril. In

---

9. N. Giron, *Légendes coptes*, p. 59.

10. See *Babylonian Talmud: Berakhoth* 61a, in M. Simon, trans., *The Talmud*, p. 383 and *Babylonian Talmud: ʿAbodah Zarah* 20a, in A. Mishcon, trans., *The Talmud*, p. 105; but see *Babylonian Talmud: Soṭah* 21b, in A. Cohen, trans., *The Talmud*, p. 109. Only the "foolish pietist" would not rescue a woman from drowning for fear of looking at her!

11. *Nehemiah* 8:15 cited in *The Letter of Pseudo-Titus*, in E. Hennecke, ed., *New Testament Apocrypha*, 2:161.

so doing, they ensured that their heroes, the monks, remained in the prestige-filled, and relatively safe, zone of the desert. In fourth-century Egypt, fear of women acted as a centrifugal separator. It kept "world" and "desert" at a safe distance from each other.

Throughout the fourth century, Egypt was a region afflicted by troubling anomalies. It was more like Syria, as we know it to have been in the late third century, than the great Patriarchs of Alexandria and similar spokesmen of the official church would have cared to admit.[12] Gnostic groups still clung to the fringes of the local churches. One such contained eighty women members, who were said to be devoted to flamboyant inversions of conventional sexual morality, while remaining regular parishioners of their local church. The Manichaean Elect moved with ease up and down the Nile, following the normal contours of settled Christianity from town to town.[13] The Nile valley was filled with sturdy *apotaktikoi*, "renouncers," who would have resembled the "Holy Walkers" of Syria. Bands of rootless persons, given to chastity, to fasting, and to begging, filled the nooks and crannies of the towns.[14]

In the fourth century, it was far from certain that the desert would emerge as the unchallenged locus of Christian heroism. In Egypt, as previously in Syria, the growth of asceticism threatened to revive the radical expectations long associated with the Encratite movement. Hierakas was a younger contemporary of Saint Anthony.[15] A spiritual guide in a provincial town of the Nile Delta, Hierakas knew the Scriptures by heart. Like Origen, he enjoyed a reputation as an inspired exegete. A tireless writer and copyist, whose eyesight remained miraculously intact at the age of ninety, Hierakas wrote in Coptic as well

12. It is the particular merit of E.A. Judge, "The Earliest Use of the Word 'Monachos' for Monk," to have made this situation plain in all its complexity.

13. Epiphanius, *Panarion* 26. 3 and 17: *Patrologia Graeca* 41: 336D and 360A–361B. The evidence for Manichaean activity in Egypt has been assembled and analyzed, with rare good sense, by Philip Rousseau, *Pachomius. The Making of a Community in Fourth Century Egypt*, pp. 28–31; see now Gedaliahu G. Stroumsa, "The Manichaean Challenge to Egyptian Christianity," in Birger A. Pearson and James E. Goehring eds., *The Roots of Egyptian Christianity*, pp. 307–319, and, in general, Sam N. C. Lieu, *Manichaeism in the Later Roman Empire and Medieval China*.

14. Judge, "Monachos," pp. 78–85: Jerome, *Letter* 22.34: *Patrologia Latina* 22:419 is a classic denunciation of such figures; see J. Gribomont, s.v. Monachisme, *Dictionnaire de la Spiritualité* 68–69, pp. 1543: ils réfèrent non à une race depravée, mais aux héritiers directs des grands ancêtres, non modelés par les réformes.

15. Epiphanius, *Panarion* 67: *Patrologia Graeca* 42: 172C–184B.

as in Greek, and had even composed his own devotional psalms. He was the arbiter of ascetic opinion in his region. His views were clear. They were a radical extension of the "historical" presentation of virginity that we have seen in Origen and Methodius. The age of the Old Testament contained all the precepts necessary for decent, conventional living. The Gospel had added nothing to these. Christ had brought only one novelty to earth, and, with the novelty, the hope of salvation—chastity. Only the unmarried had a place in His Kingdom.[16]

What was disturbing about Hierakas was that the "true" Church he envisaged took the form of an old-fashioned federation of continent "cells" within the settled community. The desert was absent from his message. Men and women were to gather together into little confraternities, bound by personal vows of chastity. As in Encratite Syria, spiritual fathers of Hierakas' persuasion shocked their opponents by boasting of the close ties of service and spiritual companionship that linked them to their continent woman disciples. In Hierakas' opinion, continent persons were the only Christians in Egypt who would be saved: their presence in the towns and villages of the Nile Delta would have mocked the hopes of salvation of the average married householder. By advocating the formation of groups of continent men and women among the laity, Hierakas threatened to bring into the churches of the settled land the touch of a perilous freedom better left to occupants of the distant desert.[17]

Further up the Nile, the leaders of the Pachomian monasteries found themselves increasingly forced to face the problem of differentiating their own monks from the lay persons in the surrounding villages. The huge good nature of Pachomius had shown that it was possible to found a monastery that functioned as an alternative village in the midst of the settled world. His successors were a new kind of village headman. Born leaders, men of "gracious speech," they fitted only too well into the life of the valley.[18] For just that reason, the Pachomians had to struggle with particular self-consciousness, throughout the fourth and fifth centuries, to emphasize the boundaries that separated their all-too-notional "desert" from "the world." Hence the very explicit sense

---

16. Ibid. 67.1: 173AB.   17. Ibid. 67.8: 184AB.

18. On Petronios, see *Bohairic Life of Pachomius* 56 and *First Greek Life* 80, in A. Veilleux, trans., *Pachomian Koinonia* 1, pp. 77 and 352; on Theodore's "gracious speech:" *Bohairic Life* 32, p. 57.

of sexual danger that pervaded many of the rulings and exhortations of Pachomius' successors.

In the first place, the individual monks had to be separated from each other. Homosexual relationships were condemned in considerable detail. Disgust for such forms of sexuality was not the only cause of these rulings—the social texture of the community was at stake. Pathetically shorn of the normal affective bonds of the family, which counted for so much among Egyptian villagers,[19] the young monks had to learn to become "strangers" to one another.[20] The heavy injunctions of Horsiesius against pederasty betray more than the perils of unfulfilled sexual longings: they are a testimony to the poignant need of village boys to draw around themselves a little of the personal warmth associated with the crowded families from which they had come. They longed to re-create, within the monastery, a world of "easy laughing and playing with boys."[21] They would slip each other little presents, would wear their bandanas at a tilt, would call each other "father" and "son."[22] All this must end. The young monks had to learn to maintain a distance of one cubit between each other's bodies.[23]

By the end of the fourth century, the precautions that hemmed in Pachomian monks were complete. High walls marked off the monastery itself.[24] The monks were "bound around" with vows.[25] They appeared to the world dressed in a simple garment that had gained a

19. See the fourth-century letter from a man in a strange town: "You see in what a situation I find myself . . . for you know that I have no one with me, neither sister nor brother nor son, and nobody else, if not God alone." *PSI* 1161, *Papiri Greci e Latini*, 10:101–102.

20. Shenute of Atripe, *Letter 33*, in J. Leipoldt and W. E. Crum, eds., *Corpus Scriptorum Christianorum Orientalium 43: Scriptores Coptici* 3:100–101; H. Wiesman, trans. *C.S.C.O.*96: *Script. Copt.* 8:57.

21. Pachomius, *Precepts and Judgements* 7, in A. Veilleux, trans., *Pachomian Koinonia* 2:177.

22. Horsiesius, *Instructions* 7.5, 6 and 10: in *Pachomian Koinonia* 3:147, 149. Lesbian relations were punished (but by no means as severely as some other breaches of discipline) in the nunneries attached to the Pachomian confederacy: J. Leipoldt, *Schenute von Atripe*, p. 142.

23. Pachomius, *Precepts* 93–97, *Pachomian Koinonia* 2, p. 161.

24. H. Torp, "Les murs d'enceinte des monastères coptes primitifs," makes plain the symbolic function of the walls. The correspondence of Besa, Shenute's successor, reveals just how permeable such walls could be: *Fragment* 12.1.2 and 20.1.4, in K. H. Kühn, ed., *Letters and Sermons of Besa, Corpus Scriptorum Christianorum Orientalium* 157: *Scriptores Coptici* 21:28, and 53.

25. F. Ruppert, *Das Pachomianische Mönchtum und die Anfänge des klösterlichen Gehorsams*.

mystique of its own, as the *schema*, the distinctive dark robe of the monk. It was fastened with leather thongs, taken to symbolize the binding nature of monastic vows. Walking along the common paths and sailing up and down the Nile in their great boats, "harnessed up like donkeys"[26] in their monastic dress, members of the Pachomian community were called upon to make their own bodies act as landmarks of an unbreakable, but largely imperceptible, frontier: their continence spoke to the world at large of the integrity of their monastery—*a garden enclosed, a fountain sealed.*[27]

For many Pachomian monks, the lure of the world could take singularly chaste forms. It was the lure of an alternative form of Christian devotion that seemed more attractive, and more manageable, than were the unwieldy and economically vulnerable monastic federations of Pachomius.[28] Many a monk might dream of a return to the world for no worse reason than to convert his own family, by turning the ancestral house and property into a quiet domestic monastery—such as we know to have existed in Egypt as elsewhere.[29] Apa Zanos had thought of just that. He set out to return to his native Memphis:

And all of a sudden, looking behind me, I saw a nun. She was a very good-looking and beautiful woman, and she said to me, "Hello, Apa!" And I said to her, "Peace to you, Amma. Where are you going?" She answered, "I am a virgin from the monastery of the Tabennesiotes, and I am going to my family according to the flesh." And with these words the thought of fornication began to upset and disturb me. I was no longer able to stay the burning. I locked her in my embrace and, so it seemed, I tossed her down and stripped her naked; whereupon she gave me a slap, and I saw the whole place looking like fire. Then I arose, having ejaculated, but she had disappeared. . . . A fever and a shivering immediately seized me and I stayed lying there from the third to the ninth hour.[30]

Only cautionary tales of nightmarish sexual encounters were considered effective in blocking the way that led back, with such ease, from the desert into what were perfectly legitimate forms of Christian devotion in the settled land.

26. Shenute of Atripe, cited in H. E. Winlock, *The Monastery of Epiphanius at Thebes 1: The Archaeological Material*, p. 151.

27. *Testament of Horsiesius* 20, *Pachomian Koinonia 3*, p. 184.

28. On the terrible impact of famine on the Pachomian federation, see Theodore, *Instructions* 3.2 and 46, *Pachomian Koinonia 3*, pp. 93–94, 119 and B. Büchner, *Die Armut der Armen*, pp. 20–36.

29. R. Rémondon, "L'Église dans la société égyptienne à l'époque byzantine," p. 260.

30. *Draguet Fragment* 2.7: *Pachomian Koinonia 2*, p. 117.

Not surprisingly, a fog of sexual distrust gathered along the edge of the desert at exactly the same time as we find monks increasingly involved with the settled world, as arbiters, as privileged petitioners of the great, as the spiritual counselors of Christian lay persons, women included.[31] Defenders of the myth of the desert might write that letters from women asking for spiritual advice were arrows shot from a distance at the heart:[32] we know that, already by the middle of the fourth century, one monk, Paphnutius, could receive letters from a neighboring Christian lady, Valeria:

I trust by your prayers to obtain healing, for by ascetics and devotees revelations are manifested. For I am afflicted with a great disease in the shape of a grievous shortness of breath. . . . Even though in body I have not come to your feet, yet in spirit I come to your feet.[33]

The sense of sexual danger that lurked in the bodies of the monks weighed most heavily on novices. Converts to the desert life tended to be drawn from two distinct age-groups. By the end of the fourth century, some young monks might well have grown up in the desert, driven there with their parents by famine.[34] Others had been donated to the Old Men as human *ex voto* offerings by a pious laity—although, as the monks observed, the rich, who tended to give only used clothing to the orphans and widows and only their worst wine for banquets for the poor, also tended to give up only their least healthy and talented offspring to the desert, saving the better ones for marriage![35]

As much committed to virginity as were their sisters, the nuns, these young boys had to face the new challenge of having to pass through puberty in a monastic environment. Many leaders of the movement, however, were men who had lapsed into the life of the desert in middle age. Some were widowed, or had separated from their wives with their consent. Sexuality did not necessarily play a major role in their view of themselves: anger, pride, a lurking sensitivity to social status, and not fornication, were the temptations that afflicted them. They were persons with firm social roles; their sins were the hard sins of

---

31. Judge, "Monachos," p. 85.

32. *Karakaliou* 251, cited in *Abbé Isaïe, Recueil ascétique: Spiritualité orientale* 7:298.

33. H. I. Bell, *Jews and Christians in Egypt,* p. 109.

34. By famine, see, for example, *Apophthegmata Patrum* Cario 2: *Patrologia Graeca* 65: 249D–252A.

35. Evergetinos 4.2.1–9, *Sentences des Pères,* p. 192. For later examples of the donation of children: L.S.B. MacCoull, "Child Donations and Child Saints in Coptic Egypt."

the will. By contrast, the young monks were persons without clear social profiles: they were nothing but their vigorous young bodies. Their absorption into the life of the desert had to take the form of a pointedly sexual discipline.

By the end of the fifth century, ascetic literature had developed a code of deportment for novices that was quite as meticulous as had been the code once propounded to young Christians by Clement of Alexandria. The life of the cell had its own solemn reciprocities. The young monk must carry the bags of a visitor when he arrives,[36] must sit with him on the little bench outside the cell for an hour of reverent silence after the first greeting,[37] must always allow him to pass first through any door,[38] and must be sure to bring his own lunch when paying a visit to a monk known to be poor.[39] Such precepts show young men learning to live with a ceremonious dignity that had always been the pride of the ancient world. Other precepts, however, marked a new departure. While Clement's Christian young had chastened their bearing and their voices around a busy table where men and women had mixed unselfconsciously, in the desert the young were stripped down to their bodies. These were subjected to perpetual vigilance by reason of the sexuality that lurked within them:

For the snare of the Devil against mankind, and especially against the young, is the body.[40]

Accustom your eyes never to look at the body of any person, not even, if possible, at your own.[41]

Never say to anyone, "Take the vermin from my beard."[42]

Knees joined, robes drawn over the feet and belts well tied to stop wandering hands at night,[43] the young monks entered the world with lowered eyes,[44] careful never to eat with a woman.[45] They were stark reminders of a new code, whose weight no longer rested on the public gestures of the social person, and on public breaches of good taste that might come from violence of movement, loud voices, or inappropriate

---

36. Isaiah of Scetis, *Asceticon* 3.10.46, *Abbé Isaïe: Recueil ascétique*, p. 52.
37. *Sentences des Pères* 641, p. 154.   38. Isaiah of Scetis, *Asceticon* 4.11.12, p. 57.
39. Ibid. 4.11.18, p. 58.   40. *Sentences des Pères* 592/64, p. 129.
41. Ibid. 592/24, p. 122.   42. Ibid. 592/64, p. 130.
43. Isaiah, *Asceticon* 3.10.12 and 69, pp. 50 and 55.   44. Ibid. 7.13.18–19, p. 89.
45. L. Regnault, trans., *Barsanuphe et Jean de Gaza: Correspondance* 354, p. 254; *Apophthegmata Patrum* Daniel 2: 153B.

gestures. Two centuries after Clement's *Paidagôgos*, the codes of the desert placed their greatest weight on the untamed flesh itself.

The world of the novices was a narrow one. It lay at a distance from the life of the normal Christian congregation. It is exceedingly difficult to know how much and in what manner the sexual codes, elaborated to such a pitch of caution in the desert, trickled back into the churches. We must be very careful not to exaggerate their immediate effect on the sexual conduct of the average Christian. Studies of modern societies where the ascetic still enjoys great prestige have taught us to be prudent:

To say that something is the highest ideal, even if this is coupled with a high degree of cultural consensus, does not predict the place this ideal is made or allowed to occupy in social life.[46]

It is imprudent to attempt to deduce the state of mind of an early Byzantine layman simply from a cursory reading of the more melodramatic anecdotes purveyed by the Desert Fathers.

This is as true of Egypt as of any other region of the Christian world. The sexual codes that governed the relations of men and women in the Christian East undoubtedly hardened in the course of the fourth and fifth centuries. But the rise of Christian asceticism may have had less to do with this process than we might imagine. By the fourth century, for instance, the ancient Egyptian tradition of brother-sister marriages was finally abandoned. Such marriages, and those of close cousins, may well have maintained a certain ease of relations between girls and boys who grew up together in close proximity. Yet the prohibition of incest stemmed from the imposition of Roman law in Egypt, and had culminated in the edict of the pagan Emperor, Diocletian. The Christian clergy may have benefited from this change; but they did little to initiate it.[47]

In the same manner, the tendency to tie young men and women to early, arranged marriages, the growing emphasis on the binding na-

46. I. F. Silber, "Dissent through Holiness," p. 186.
47. See the thought-provoking study of Keith Hopkins, "Brother-Sister Marriage in Roman Egypt." In the late fifth century, a pagan philosopher married his first cousin, who resembled him so closely that no one could tell who was the father of whom: *Pap. Cairo* 3. 67295. 18–20, cited in J. Maspéro, "Horapollon et la fin du paganisme égyptien," pp. 166, 172. Christians had identical preferences: see the legend of Demetrius, bishop of Alexandria, in E. A. W. Budge, *Coptic Martyrdoms*, p. 398.

ture of the act of betrothal and the insistence that the bride be a virgin[48] were developments that coincided with the rise of Christianity, but were not exclusively caused by it. As the new leaders of local opinion in many villages, however, the Christian clergy came to play a part in securing the observance of these stricter codes. When the daughters of Sarapion brought shame on the village by rushing out of their seclusion with shouts of "We want men!" it was the priests of the church who were called upon to bring them to order.[49]

The monks and nuns of Egypt were as often as not the children of observant Christian families: they would have brought with them into the desert the current, harsh codes of sexual restraint and sexual segregration that their parents and neighbors had observed. They often represented what the average Christian "in the world" might have wished to have been, in his or her better moments. But whether Christian codes always rested as heavily on those who stayed in the world was quite a different matter. When Egyptians wanted a divorce, for instance, they did not allow Christian teaching to stand in their way. Though once persuaded by the priest to take back her ne'er-do-well husband, Aurelia Attiaena of Oxyrhynchus eventually had no hesitation about sending him a bill of repudiation, "according to Imperial law."[50]

If anything, a "zone of silence" was allowed to open up between the experience of sexuality in the settled world and the new awareness of sexuality pioneered by the monks. By the end of the fifth century, the tacit division between desert and settled land had become clear, and was accepted by both sides. A system of half-explicit checks and

48. Trouble ensued when the wife of the son of Apa Paham was revealed not to be a virgin: *KRU* 67.20–25, in W. C. Till, trans., "Erbrechtliche Untersuchungen," p. 171. See *Codex Theodosianus* 9.8.1 of 320 A.D. (in Italy)—girls entrusted to guardians must have their virginity examined for fear that they had been seduced by them; Ambrose, *Letter* 5.8: *Patrologia Latina* 16: 932AB gives cases of inspections. "Tokens of the virginity of the bride" were customarily brought by the servants from the bridal chamber: Budge, *Coptic Martyrdoms*, p. 398.

49. *Pap.Grenfell* 1.53 in L. Mitteis and U. Wilcken, *Grundzüge und Chrestomathie der Papyruskunde*, p. 157.

50. *Pap. Oxy.* 3581, *Oxyrhynchus Papyri*, 50:202–205; see A. H. M. Jones, *The Later Roman Empire*, 2:974–975 and S. Allam, "Le mariage dans l'Égypte ancienne," pp. 133–134. The denunciations of Shenute of Atripe seem to indicate that his hearers took such matters lightly: A. Shisha-Halevy, "Two New Shenoute-Texts from the British Library," pp. 176–182. See now the model treatment of Roger S. Bagnall, "Church, State and Divorce in Late Roman Egypt."

balances cushioned Christians "in the world" from the exceedingly exacting demands placed on the human body by the men of the desert.

This was not surprising, given the evolution of monasticism in the area. The ascetic movement had always been one of the greatest social diversity. At no time was it limited to the peasantry. Its main patrons and leaders usually came from the notables of the towns and villages.[51] Cells dating from the sixth century have been excavated in the desert outside Esna.[52] They must have taken at least ninety days of careful labor to construct.[53] They were no desert eyries. The arrangements for their ventilation, which led the cool breezes from the valley into the chapel, are the admiration of modern architects.[54] Though they were products of loving skill, they were carved into the rock like tombs; and like tombs they were pointedly empty of the clutter of furniture associated with the life of living persons.[55] Technically, their occupants were "dead" to the world.

In reality, such cells were often the carefully planned final resting places of middle-aged men of good family, who had found, in the *vida descansada* of the desert, a last avatar of the ancient notable's yearning for a dignified retirement. Such men had often been members of the clergy. Growing up as pious clients of the monks, they would have lived for decades in quiet symbiosis with the values of the desert to which they finally retired. Now bereavement, illness, or a brush with the local authorities had caused them to think that it was time, in Dante's gentle words, "to lower sail and gather in the ropes."[56] Such was the Archdeacon Joseph, writing the Apa Epiphanius at Thebes around 600:

For this cause, therefore, I have desired to withdraw myself . . . [and] to take thought for my sins. . . . broken, lying abed, being carried in and out. . . . a great grief is in my heart day and night. . . . And be so kind as to appoint

---

51. See esp. Annick Martin, "L'Église et la khôra égyptienne au ive siècle," pp. 14–17, E. Wipszicka, "Le degré d'alphabétisation en Égypte byzantine," pp. 284–285 and Rémondon, "L'Église dans la société," p. 259.

52. S. Sauneron and J. Jacquet, *Les ermitages chrétiens du désert d'Esna*, vols. 1: *Archéologie et inscriptions*, and 4: *Essai d'histoire*.

53. Sauneron, *Ermitages* 4:20.   54. Sauneron, *Ermitages* 1:47.

55. H. Torp, "Le monastère copte de Baouit," pp. 1–8, esp. p. 8, and Sauneron, *Ermitages* 1:vi.

56. Dante, *Inferno* 27.79–81:

Quando mi vidi giunto in quella parte
di mia etade, dove ciascun dovrebbe
calar le vele e raccoglier le sarte.

for me prayers and [a regime] convenient to sickness and old age, and even be it lying down, I will fulfill them.[57]

Measureless spiritual ambition was not likely to be the quality for which such men were noted. As a result, the desert tradition tended to fall in upon itself. The profound speculations on the role of sexuality in the human person, which we read of in the last chapter, took place among monks for monks. They were the product of a remarkable tradition of spiritual guidance whose main task had become to recruit candidates for true monastic perfection from among the thousands of distinctly average seekers after peace and quiet who made up the bulk of the monks of the fifth and sixth centuries. The habitual joining-points between the desert and the world tended to be manned by men who were close to the values and needs of married Christians. One such was Apa Paham, known to us from his will of around 600:

I had three children. I went and became a monk. I left them, still alive. All three continued living in the world. The eldest son, Papnute, married against my wishes. I was very sad about this. . . . I put the matter in the hands of God, the just Judge, and the prayers of my holy [spiritual] father. . . . My son [unhappily married by that time] often used to come and tell me his troubles.[58]

Monks such as Paham were the clients of spiritual fathers such as Barsanuphius. They received characteristically humane advice. Those who withdrew to the monastery when married must make careful provision for their wife and children: Barsanuphius and his colleague, John of Gaza, even suggested the best legal arrangement for such a separation.[59] They must allow their wives to visit them regularly once a week, to discuss family affairs.[60] Above all, they must be prepared to feel the pain of their wife's absence:

It is written on the subject of man and woman: *They shall be two in one flesh.* Consequently, just as if one cuts away a part of one's flesh, the rest of the body suffers for a time, until the wound is healed and the pain ceases; so it is necessary for you, in this present matter, to suffer for a time, your flesh having been mutilated by parting.[61]

57. W. E. Crum and H. G. Evelyn-White, *The Monastery of Epiphanius,* pp. 194–195.

58. Till, "Erbrechtliche Untersuchungen," p. 171, now trans. by Leslie S. B. Mac-Coull, "Coptic Documentary Papyri as a Historical Source for Egyptian Christianity," p. 49.

59. *Barsanuphe et Jean de Gaza* 571, p. 373.

60. Ibid. 595, p. 388.   61. Ibid. 129, p. 116.

We have come a long way from the shrill folklore of sexual avoidance with which the monks of the fourth century had first struggled to define their position over against the world. Barsanuphius' letters to lay persons and to recent converts to the ascetic life register a potentially revolutionary situation that had been brought to a halt by slow attrition over a period of two hundred years. His tone betrayed a serenity that came from a clear sense of hierarchy, in which the married life was allowed its due place.

In that hierarchy, it was agreed that virginity represented the pinnacle of Christian achievement: virginity, in monks as well as in nuns, was "the foundation of the Church."[62] This did not mean, however, that the life of the married laity was drained of all warmth and meaning. Writing against Hierakas, in the form of a treatise *On Virginity*, Athanasius (or, more probably, a later writer whose work survives under the name of the great Patriarch)[63] made that clear.[64] The presence of ascetics in the neighboring desert did not declare Christian marriage tainted or invalid. The monks were not to threaten to bring the "present age" to a dramatic end by urging the end of marriage and by canceling out the elemental division between men and women. In the view of Athanasius, the ascetic served as a signpost, as a living *demonstratio evangelica*, a proof of the truth of the Gospel for those who would follow its call to the utmost. The ascetic transformation of the few demonstrated the extent of the perfection made available, by the power of Christ, to human beings.[65]

The married Christians of the valley below had not answered Christ's call *If you would be perfect*, as Anthony had done; but they still belonged to the mercy of God. They lived the life of the righteous as this had been laid down in the Old Testament: if they did not do everything that the Gospels challenged them to do, at least they avoided everything that the book of Proverbs told them they should not do.[66] This

---

62. Epiphanius, *Expositio fidei catholicae* 23: *Patrologia Graeca* 42: 829A; cf. H. Chadwick, ed., *Sentences of Sextus* 86a, pp. 22–23.

63. T. Orlandi, "Giustificazioni dell'Encratismo nei testi monastici copti del iv–v secolo," in U. Bianchi, ed., *La Tradizione dell'Enkrateia*, pp. 344–345.

64. See the fine study of Y. M. Duval, "La problématique de la *Lettre aux vierges* d'Athanase," and L. Th. Lefort, "Saint Athanase: sur la virginité," Coptic text pages 97–98, translation, p. 247. This is now edited by Lefort, *S. Athanase, Lettres festales et pastorales en copte*.

65. J. R. Roldanus, *Le Christ et l'homme dans la théologie d'Athanase d'Alexandrie*, p. 338.

66. Lefort, *S. Athanase*, Coptic p. 135, trans. p. 259.

meant, in practice, that their lives could flow peaceably and with considerable decency along the riverbed of immemorial Near Eastern and Hellenistic traditions of courtesy, generosity, and marital restraint. At the same time, many pious practices linked the settled world to the life of the desert. During certain times of the year, every Christian household was encouraged to become a little monastery. At the high festivals of the church, rich householders were expected to experience a touch of the renunciation of all property practiced by their heroes in the desert, by giving away at least part of their goods in alms to the poor. In the season of Lent, the laity also would undergo, through fasting, a measure of the long hunger by which the monks unraveled in themselves the consequences of the sin of Adam. By periods of sexual abstinence, by vigils, by small repeated vows of renunciation, they breathed a little of the free air of the desert.[67] Their married duties as men and women "in the world" enjoyed the unchallengeable solidity of facts of nature. Marriage was

the more moderate form, suited to [normal] human life. . . .
It is a good thing if a young man becomes the head of a household and begets children.[68]

The assertion of a hierarchy, in which marriage had its due place, against more radical views, depended on one crucial assumption: the sexual life of the married couple was to be treated as unproblematic. The anxieties that hedged around the men of the desert in their relations with women, the sexual discipline imposed on the bodies of the young novices, and the deep preoccupations of the theorists of ascetic perfection with the permanence of sexual drives—these were concerns tacitly declared to be for monks only. Inevitably, some of these preoccupations entered into circulation among lay persons; but little effort was made by the monks to create, for married persons in the world, a code of sexual deportment such as had once been proposed, at such length, by Clement of Alexandria. For good or ill, Clement's embarrassed attempt to create a code of correct behavior for the marriage bed belonged to another age.

---

67. Epiphanius, *Expositio fidei catholicae* 23: *Patrologia Graeca* 42: 829A. The admission of such diversity is all the more remarkable in a man as certain of the primacy of monastic values as was Epiphanius.
68. Athanasius, *Letter to Amoun: Patrologia Graeca* 26: 1073 and Lefort, *S. Athanase*, Coptic p. 97, transl. p. 247.

The spiritual counsel offered by the Desert Fathers to married persons was limited to the most banal prohibitions. As long as it took place only within wedlock, and as long as the married couple observed traditional periods of abstinence, sexual intercourse posed no problems. The "chastity" of the lay couple consisted principally in their ability not to commit adultery. Intercourse was to be avoided on Saturday, on Sunday, on Wednesday, and on Friday, in the forty days of Lent and before the other feasts at which they might take the Eucharist.[69] Such prohibitions would test the will of any couple; but they hardly opened any new windows into the depths of their hearts. Married intercourse was a fact of nature: had Eve not been drawn from the side of Adam, and if both had not been granted the ability to procreate, the Word of God could not have been born of a woman and dwelt among men.[70]

The clergy in the towns and villages were not very different from the laity. The ascetic paradigm of total abstinence spread erratically among the village priests of Egypt. An Egyptian ascetic and hero of the Great Persecution, Paphnutius, a formidable figure, chaste from childhood up and blind in one eye from torture, was imagined to have intervened at the Council of Nicaea to make sure that total abstinence from married intercourse was not imposed on the clergy: "roaring at the top of his voice," he declared that "all men cannot bear the practice of rigid continence; neither perhaps would the chastity of the wife of each be preserved."[71] Bishops and members of the upper clergy were frequently recruited from the desert, but the village priests and minor clergy were usually married persons, who still slept with their wives. They were subjected to the same restraints as were the laity. We find the deacons of a village swearing, "to watch our beds on the days of the Eucharist, to master the Gospel according to Saint John, and to learn it by heart by the end of Pentecost."[72]

What the men of the desert offered the married householders was not advice as to how to conduct their sex life, but something more useful. The monks brought to men and women "in the world" the

69. W. E. Crum, ed. and trans., *The Answers of Apa [the Patriarch] Cyril*, Coptic p. 199, trans. p. 103.

70. Orlandi, "Giustificazioni dell'Encratismo," p. 349 and P. J. Sijpesteijn, "A Panegyric on John the Baptist," p. 235.

71. Socrates, *Ecclesiastical History* 1.11. On the legend, now see C. Cochini, *Origines apostoliques du célibat sacerdotal*, pp. 166–167.

72. W. E. Crum, *Coptic Ostraca*, no. 29, p. 9.

inestimable gift of mediation. The deep belief of all Byzantines in the intercessory powers of the monks betrays a tacit compact. It assumed that the monks, as "angelic men," still carried with them enough of the shared, common clay of human nature to enable them to stand before the throne of God as the representatives of common humanity and hence of its common, earthbound needs. The prayers of Pachomius for the farmers of the region were regarded as efficacious largely because he was known to have chosen the long hunger of the monastic life: as he said, at a time of famine, "Neither shall I eat while my fellow-members go hungry and find no bread."[73]

A myth of the desert built, from the ground up, around work and food, ensured that gossamer threads of supernatural power reached down from the desert to weave themselves around the fields,[74] and to embrace the sacred Nile.[75] By 400, the piety of the monks and nuns was believed, by Christians, to cause the yearly stirring of the great river.[76] The presence of the monks had brought blessing to precisely what they had renounced for themselves—the food-bearing fields of Egypt.

Seen from the desert, the "world" was no longer an engulfing "present age," whose imminent dissolution might be hastened through spectacular reversals of the facts of sex. By the fifth century, the "world" was a social fact, clearly defined, and rendered irremovable by the express blessing of God. Deep in the desert, monks would ask whether "The Water" still rose to give it life.[77] Even the most remote desert penitent could be asked to pray for the Church and the Empire of the Romans.[78] The anomalous body of the monk, standing in the desert between heaven and earth, had become a thread on which the society of East Rome was thought to hang. At Saqqara, a little to the south of Cairo, the monastery of Apa Jeremiah stands on the edge of a spur of sand so utterly dead that no flowers bloom there even after the January rains. Its back to a horizon ringed with the uncanny shapes of the pyramids, from Gizeh in the north to Dahshur in the south, the monastery looks down into a valley of exuberant, blue-green vegeta-

73. *Bohairic Life of Pachomius* 100: Veilleux, *Pachomian Koinonia 1*, p. 137.
74. Rufinus, *Historia Monachorum* Pref.; 2; 7; 9; and 11: *Patrologia Latina* 21:380; 405BC; 416C and 417A; 426A; 431D.
75. See F. Thélamon, *Païens et chrétiens au ivème siècle*, 159–279; 273–277; 375–417.
76. *Anonymous Apophthegmata* 177, Nau, ed., *Revue de l'Orient chrétien* 13 (1908): 269.
77. *Apophthegmata Patrum* Macarius 2: 260D.
78. *Vita Mariae Aegyptiacae* 24: *Patrologia Latina* 73: 687C.

tion. This was "the world" for Apa Jeremiah: "This is the spot on which our lord and father Apa Jeremiah bowed himself, until he removed the sins of the peoples of the whole world."[79]

Around Apa Jeremiah stood the mighty angels. They hovered above monastery and settled land alike, embracing their antithetical qualities in a vast prayer of intercession before the very face of God. The unwearied care of the Archangel Michael for all God's creatures, a care greater and more constant even than that of an "angelic" human being, stood as the silent ratification, in the back of the minds of all Egyptian Christians, of the humble, earthy values associated with life in the valley of the Nile. Through accepting the intercession of angels and archangels on behalf of all human beings, in all states of life, and for the state of the natural world on which the human race depended, God made plain His abiding sympathy for the joys and sufferings of the married Christian laity:

We find the intercession of Michael in the strenuous work of our hands. We find the intercession of the archangel in the quiet of the oxen and the growth of the lambs. . . . We find the intercession of Michael in the body of the vine and in the gladness [which is] in the wine. We find the intercession of Michael in the joy, and in the fatness and in the savour of the olives. We find the intercession of Michael in the slumber of man. . . . We find the intercession of Michael in the union of holy matrimony, wherein men beget their children for a blessing. . . . We find the intercession of Michael when he is gentle to those who are weary, and when he giveth them strength.[80]

79. J. E. Quibbell, *Excavations at Saqqara*, 4:55, inscription no. 188.
80. E. A. W. Budge, *Miscellaneous Coptic Texts in the Dialect of Upper Egypt*, pp. 757–758.

THIRTEEN

"Daughters of Jerusalem": The Ascetic Life of Women in The Fourth Century

The Son of God, our Lord and Saviour Jesus Christ, having become man for our sakes. . . . in addition to all His other benefits bestowed this also upon us, that we should possess upon earth, in the state of virginity, a picture of the holiness of the angels. Accordingly, such as have attained this virtue, the Catholic Church has been accustomed to call *the brides of Christ*. And the heathen who see them express their admiration of them as the temples of the Word. For indeed this holy and heavenly profession is nowhere established, but only among us Christians, and it is a very strong argument that with us is to be found the genuine and true religion.[1]

Thus the Patriarch Athanasius of Alexandria to the Emperor Constantius II, in 356. As all too often in the career of Athanasius this majestic claim was made against a background of unsavory local violence: dedicated virgins of the church of Alexandria had been subjected to ritual humiliation by his enemies. Any attack on the virgins of the church

---

1. Athanasius, *Apologia ad Constantium* 33.49: *Patrologia Graeca* 25: 640B; A. Atkinson, trans., *Saint Athanasius, Historical Tracts*, p. 185.

was an attack on the status of the formidable Patriarch himself. Athanasius was not alone in this. By the end of the fourth century, "benches in the apse raised on steps, thrones veiled with curtains, processions and the chanting crowds of virgins," were an integral part of a bishop's show of power.[2]

Attacking the Catholic clergy, a Manichaean polemist in North Africa pointed out that while they claimed that marriage was instituted by God, what they preached most fervently was virginity:

you always strive to outdo each other in persuading girls to adopt this vocation, to such an extent that in every church there is almost a greater number of virgins than of married women.[3]

It was no easy matter for a bishop to control and protect his symbolic retinue. Most virgins of the church were young girls of marriageable age. They had grown up in households where the control of parents over the marital prospects of young adolescents in general, and of girls in particular, had remained absolute. However much Christian authors wrote, in Platonic terms, of the innate love for virginity that stirred at the bottom of the heart of every Christian child,[4] such children were seldom free agents.[5] The family decided the fate of its girls. If a girl was to remain a consecrated virgin, she had to be hedged around with a heavy sacral language. The girl who found herself among the "brides of Christ" was spoken of by the clergy as a human *ex voto*. She was no longer a woman; she had become "a sacred vessel dedicated to the Lord."[6]

Teen-age "sacred vessels" could never feel secure. Ideally, girls did not commit themselves, by oath, to the virgin state until they were sixteen or seventeen. In many regions, the girl's resolution was not given final, public ratification, through the bestowing of a veil, until much later—frequently, not until the woman was safely past childbearing age, and was no longer a pawn in the game of family alli-

---

2. Augustine, *Letter* 23.3: *Patrologia Latina* 33:96.

3. Augustine, *Contra Faustum* 30.4: *P.L.* 42:492.

4. D. Amand and M.C. Moons, "Une curieuse homélie grecque sur la virginité," p. 35.

5. Evelyne Patlagean, *Pauvreté économique et pauvreté sociale à Byzance*, pp. 113–128, and "L'enfant et son avenir dans la famille byzantine."

6. Eusebius of Emesa, *Homily* 6.18, in E. M. Buytaert, ed., *Eusèbe d'Émèse: Discours conservés en latin*, 1:162.

ances.[7] But the decision was frequently made for girls by their parents at an early age, in order to relieve the family of dowry payments and similar expenses incurred by female children. Christian families regarded it as sinful to expose their children: they now found it convenient to dedicate their unwanted girl babies to the church.[8] As Basil of Caesarea wrote:

Parents, and brothers and other relatives bring forward many girls before the proper age, not because the girls have an inner urge towards continence, but in order that their relatives may gain some material advantage from so doing.[9]

Girls given to the church in this way were often withdrawn by their families, in an equally high-handed fashion, when a better use could be found for them. A newly discovered letter of Augustine shows him dealing with the case of a widow who had first dedicated her daughter's virginity to Christ when the child lay dangerously ill. Now that the mother had lost her son, and was faced with the prospect of having no grandchildren, she had decided to marry off her daughter and to offer to God, instead, a formal vow of her own to remain a widow.[10]

For this well-to-do lady, as for so many late Roman parents, women, like wealth, were there to circulate. The clergy's new language of *ex voto* dedication threatened in no uncertain manner to freeze the benign current of young girls that flowed from their parents' house so as to knit together the families of the locality. A gift to the church was "sacred," and, so, irrevocable. Dedicated virgins—precisely because they were known to have remained so vulnerable to the demands of their

7. The contrast between forty years in Spain and twenty years in Africa gives an idea of the variations from region to region, and of the very different social situations implied in the consecration of virgins: *Council of Saragossa* (380), canon 8 and *Council of Carthage* (397), canon 4.

8. See now John Boswell, "*Expositio* and *Oblatio*: The Abandonment of Children and the Ancient and Medieval Family," pp. 13–19 and Cynthia Patterson, " 'Not Worth the Rearing': The Causes of Infant Exposure in Ancient Greece." Baby boys, considered more useful, had frequently been given to friends to rear: L. and J. Robert, "Bulletin épigraphique," p. 500, inscription no. 468—a woman with seven sons gave three to friends. From giving children to friends to dedicating them to a local monastery is a very short step indeed.

9. Basil, *Letter* 119.18, in R. J. Deferrari, *Saint Basil: Letters*, 2:109; cf. Balsamon, *P.G.* 138:651 and *Novella* 6 of Majorian in 458.

10. Augustine, Epistola 3*.1.3, in J. Divjak, ed., *Sancti Augustini opera, epistulae ex duobus codicibus nuper in lucem prolatae*, p. 22. French trans. *Bibliothèque augustinienne. Oeuvres de Saint Augustin 46B: Lettres* 1* – 29*, pp. 98–100.

family—marked out, even more clearly than did the gold patens and chalices, the shimmering silks, and the translucent marbles of fourth-century Christian sanctuaries, the arrival of the church as a permanent institution in the Roman world.

Bodies withdrawn in perpetuity from the normal ebb and flow of marital strategies radiated the message that a church led by bishops of the caliber of Athanasius and his Western equivalents had every intention of holding on to the wealth and the human persons offered to it by a pious laity. No small part of the sudden chill of the short reign of a pagan Emperor, Julian the Apostate (361–363), had been that the wealth gathered in the great sanctuaries of the churches had been inventoried—as a sure prelude to confiscation—and that virgins of the church had been married off. His Christian successor made the return of Christianity public by threatening the death penalty for those who attempted to take such women as wives.[11] In the Imperial laws of the period, consecrated women were spoken of with elaborate respect: they were "most sacred persons."[12]

Throughout the fourth century, we are faced with a paradoxical situation. No *Life of Anthony* heralded a new departure in the piety of Christian women. The life of the "brides of Christ" always lay a little to one side of the great myth of the desert that had given new meaning to male asceticism in Egypt and elsewhere. The Christian household and the local church remained the *loci* of the female quest for holiness, as they had been, for men and women alike, in the earlier centuries of the church. Yet it is on the bedrock of this subdued, rather old-fashioned piety that a myth of the perpetual virgin state came to be elaborated. Sheltered nuns, the female "brides of Christ," and not the bearded heroes of the desert, have become the stereotypical representatives of the notion of "virginity" for Western readers.[13]

In the year 350, such an outcome was far from certain. In many world-renouncing religions, the growth of forms of heroic asceticism, asso-

---

11. Theodoret, *Ecclesiastical History* 3.8 and Sozomen, *Ecclesiastical History* 6.3. On the relation between the Church's encouragement of virginity and the redirection of inheritances, Jack Goody, *The development of the family and marriage in Europe*, pp. 42–64, 93–102, contains many interesting suggestions, but has been decisively criticized by Brent D. Shaw and P. Saller, "Close Kin Marriage in Roman Society?"

12. *Codex Theodosianus* 9.25.1 (354 A.D.).

13. Contrast the Armenian church, where the "virgins" who bring their lighted lamps to Christ are bearded monks, as on the tympanum of the portal at Hohannavank': Sirarpie Der Nersessian, *Armenian Art*, p. 174, fig. 133. I owe this information to the kindness of Professor Thomas Mathews.

ciated with extreme self-mortification, with physical danger, with mobility, and with the loss of a conventional social identity, tended to drain prestige away from pious women. Only men were considered able to practice such asceticism appropriately. In Buddhist Ceylon, for instance, after a short period, "Nuns left the stage of history as quietly as they had occupied it."[14]

Yet this did not happen in the Christianity of the fourth-century Roman world. Dedicated women came to be thought of as harboring a deposit of values that were prized, by their male spokesmen, as peculiarly precious to the Christian community. Women with ascetic vocations emerged in upper-class circles, where they had the wealth and prestige needed to make a permanent impact on the Christian church. The fate of the Buddhist nuns of Ceylon was certainly not that of the generation that produced women ascetics of the stature of Macrina, Melania the Elder, and Olympias of Constantinople. Before we turn to the few, well-known examples of devoted women from the governing classes of the Empire, it is important to attempt to grasp a little of the texture of the life and the horizons of the possible that existed for the average woman of ascetic leanings.

Female asceticism grew out of the Christian household. It was the individual householder who was thought to benefit most directly from the piety of his virgin daughter. He was encouraged to act as "a priest of the Highest God" in fostering the vocation and maintaining the seclusion of the family's dedicated women.[15] Such virgins had no life outside their parents' household. They were supposed to leave its inner rooms, if at all, only to participate in the ceremonials of the local church—a clearly designated group, their voices filling the church and the streets of their town with the sweet chanting of the Psalms.[16] Total seclusion was an ideal frequently propounded, and occasionally observed: one beautiful girl in Alexandria immured herself in a tomb.[17] But the very facelessness of pious women gave them supernatural powers in which the whole Christian community had an interest. In the words of an Egyptian writer:

---

14. R. A. L. H. Gunawardana, *Robe and Plough: Monasticism and Economic Interest in Early Medieval Sri Lanka*, p. 39.

15. Amand and Moons, "Une curieuse homélie grecque," p. 40.

16. Ibid., pp. 41–43 and *The Canons of Athanasius* 92 and 98, W. Riedel and W. E. Crum, ed. and trans. pp. 58, 64; for public psalm-singing, see Theodoret, *Eccles. Hist.* 3.14.

17. Palladius, *Lausiac History* 5.2.

In every house of Christians, it is needful that there be a virgin, for the salvation of the whole house is that one virgin. And when wrath cometh upon
the whole city, it shall not come upon the house wherein a virgin is. Where-
fore all inmates of great houses desire that this fair name may remain to them
in their house.[18]

In Upper Egypt, Piamun lived with her mother, "spinning flax and
only eating every other day at evening." Yet her prayers protected the
village from raids on its irrigation canals.[19] Figures such as Piamun
were normal throughout the eastern Mediterranean. Their continued
virginity was a matter of deep concern for their neighbors; for it brought
down the mercy of God on the locality. Pachomius was believed to be
able to detect whether a girl had lapsed simply by smelling her clothes.[20]

Similar arrangements prevailed in Asia Minor. Devoted women lived
in close dependence on their households, or on their own properties.
The ones that we know of were usually the sisters and daughters of
well-established clergymen or pious country gentry. The virgin, Rus-
siana, was a relative of Gregory Nazianzen. Gregory arranged in his
will for her to have an income and two servants, "so that she might
continue to live the life of a gentlewoman."[21]

Groups of consecrated, upper-class spinsters were a force to be reckoned with in many local churches in Cappadocia and elsewhere. By
the time of Basil of Caesarea, they had come to be called kanonikai:
they were thought of as committed to a "canon," to a regular rhythm
of daily observance that marked them off from other faithful women.[22]
Such were the daughters of Count Terentius, a pious Cappadocian
Christian and an exceedingly wily politician, "a man who walked
humbly and affected a somewhat sad expression, but . . . was a zealous abettor of dissensions."[23] Basil was careful to write to them in the
middle of a theological controversy. "Goodly scions of a goodly stock

18. Canons of Athanasius 98, pp. 62–63; cf. Eusebius of Emesa, Homily 7.24, p. 191.
19. Palladius, Historia Lausiaca 31.1.
20. Bohairic Life of Pachomius 43, A. Veilleux, trans., Pachomian Koinonia p. 67.
21. Gregory Nazianzen, Testament: P.G. 37: 392B.
22. In all this I am indebted to the differentiated study of Susannah K. Elm, "The
Organization and Institutions of Female Asceticism in Fourth Century Cappadocia and
Egypt" (Oxford: D. Phil in Litterae Humaniores, 1987); see now Ruth Albrecht, Das
Leben der heiligen Makrina auf dem Hintergrund der Thekla-Traditionen, pp. 119–238 and
Elizabeth Castelli, "Virginity and its Meaning for Women's Sexuality in Early Christianity."
23. Ammianus Marcellinus, Res Gestae 30.1.2.

. . . lilies among the thorns," their views on the Holy Ghost were worth canvassing.[24]

Even when no longer engulfed in the family, the organization of the ascetic life of any consecrated woman remained remarkably informal. Pious women did not share the urgent need of male ascetics to create for themselves a man-made "desert," by destroying all bonds of kin-ship and former friendship.[25] Virgins tended, rather, to coagulate into small groups in a more frankly organic manner. Intense friendships between female companions played an essential role.[26] We find com-panions renting rooms together in town,[27] or moving a soul-mate into their family home.[28] Well-to-do women, often rich widows or the un-married sister of members of the clergy or of ascetics, were crucial for the formation of larger groupings. Such women could gather around them groups of fifty, seventy, up to a hundred virgins.[29] But they did not do this as charismatic spiritual guides and still less as represen-tatives of the clergy. They were patronesses and heads of households in their own right. Many of the virgins under their protection had been their own friends, dependents, or poor relatives: Olympias was able to install 250 such dependents in the convent that flanked the Great Church at Constantinople.[30] Less organic groupings were less suc-cessful. In the large group settled on the estate of a pious ascetic, Elias, at Atripe in Egypt, "The women, gathered from every walk of life, quarrelled continuously with each other."[31]

24. Basil, *Letter* 105, ed. Deferrari, 2:199.

25. This aspect has been clearly seen both by Elizabeth A. Clark, "Authority and Humility: A Conflict of Values in Fourth Century Female Monasticism," now in *Ascetic Piety and Women's Faith: Essays in Late Ancient Christianity*, pp. 214–218, and, from a different perspective, by Caroline W. Bynum, "Women's Stories, Women's Symbols: A Critique of Victor Turner's Theory of Liminality," in R. L. Moore and F. E. Reynolds, eds., *Anthropology and the Study of Religion*, pp. 112–117.

26. See, for example, the cases in Socrates, *Eccles. Hist.* 9.2 and Theodoret, *Eccles. Hist.* 3.10.

27. R. Rémondon, "L'église dans la société égyptienne à l'époque byzantine," p. 260 and E. A. Judge, "The Earliest Use of 'Monachos,'" pp. 82–83.

28. Pseudo-Athanasius, *Sôtérios Logos peri parthenias* 9, in H. von der Goltz, ed., *Texte und Untersuchungen* 29.2, pp. 43–44.

29. Palladius, *Hist. Laus.* 1.4; 5.3; 67.1 and Theodoret, *Eccles. Hist.* 3.14.

30. *Life of Olympias* 6, in Elizabeth A. Clark, trans., *Jerome, Chrysostom, and Friends*, p. 132; see also Gregory of Nyssa, *Life of Macrina* 7.6; 11.9–13 and 26.31–34, in P. Mar-aval, ed., *Grégoire de Nysse: Vie de Sainte Macrine*, pp. 164, 176, and 232.

31. Palladius, *Hist. Laus.* 29.1; cf. Besa, *Letters and Sermons*, fgts. 13.1.5 and 20.1.4, K. H. Kühn, ed. and trans., *Corpus Scriptorum Christianorum Orientalium* 157: *Scriptores coptici* 21, pp. 36, 53.

These informal structures meant that ascetic women were free to seek protection and spiritual guidance from males of any kind—from relatives, from ascetic soul-mates, and from men of exceptional insight or learning. In communities where the public display of virginity spoke so clearly of the increased authority of the bishops and clergy, the world of female piety represented, in reality, a zone of exceptional fluidity and free choice. Reputations could be made and broken; deep spiritual friendships, based on elective affinities, were free to develop.

By ministering to the spiritual life of holy women in great cities, many cultivated clergymen were enabled to step to one side of the world of their own bishops. Origens of a new age, men like Arius, at Baucalis in Alexandria,[32] and Jerome, on the Aventine in Rome,[33] gained no small part of their public reputation by giving spiritual guidance to devoted women, most of whom would have been virgins or widows, living in their family houses. It was in such circles that the cultural and spiritual ideals of the *didaskaleion* of the Early Church survived into a harsher age.

An intense sense of spiritual companionship drew male and female ascetics together. Ascetic leaders, whose preaching regularly stirred wives to separate from their husbands, recognized that it was next to impossible to keep ascetic men and women apart once such friendships were formed.[34] We should not trivialize the tenacity of these bonds. Images of friendship and of passionate loyalty were essential to the inner life of ascetics of either sex. To have been in the presence of a pious male might place "an idol" in the heart of a woman, as she prayed to Christ. But such an "idol" was denounced as so dangerous precisely because images of intimacy and nurture were basic to the piety of men and women, who took joy from the glimpse of the "face of God" in holy persons.[35]

On a more mundane level, many virgins needed protection and lodging from Christians who sympathized with their courageous endeavor. To be a *philoparthenos*, a "lover of the virgins," was a form of charitable activity. Not all virgins enjoyed the protection of strong fam-

---

32. Epiphanius, *Panarion* 69.3: *Patrologia Graeca* 42: 208A; see esp. H. I. Marrou, "L'arianisme comme phénomène alexandrin," pp. 323–326.

33. Jerome, *Letter* 45.2: *P. L.* 22:481.   34. Sozomen, *Eccles. Hist.* 3.14.

35. Evagrius of Pontus, *Sententiae ad virginem* 6, in H. Gressmann, ed., *Texte und Untersuchungen* 39:146; see Peter Brown, "The Saint as Exemplar," pp. 6–8, 15–16, also in J. S. Hawley, ed., *Saints and Virtues*, pp. 6–10.

ilies: death, destitution, or a strong need for independence had thrown many of them on to the streets. To look after the needs of such persons, even to work to support them, was to do one's duty to the "deserving poor" *par excellence*.[36] Not surprisingly, a persistent campaign of preaching and canonical legislation came to be directed against monks and members of the clergy who sought female spiritual companions of this kind. Female spiritual friends and protegées were branded as *suneisaktai* in Greek or *subintroductae* in Latin, "call-in girls," and also *agapetae*, "love birds."[37] They stood for a disturbing category of persons: here were women who enjoyed a relationship of permanent companionship with a man who was neither father, brother, nor husband to them.[38]

Throughout the Roman world, the situation created by tenacious and vivid groupings of pious women provoked studiously fostered sexual alarm. In the literature of both the Greek and the Latin worlds, a steady flow of circumstantial evocations of the perils of sex were a byproduct of the rise of women's asceticism, and the consequent search, by men and women alike, for spiritual companions of the opposite sex. The most exhaustive of these cautionary works came from a bishop in Asia Minor, Basil, Bishop of Ancyra (modern Ankara), between approximately 336 and around 364. An older contemporary of Basil of Caesarea, and a former doctor, Basil wrote a treatise *On the Preservation of Virginity*.[39] In it, we see a man of recondite learning and singularly unruffled powers of observation conjuring up the facts of sex so as to keep the female ascetics of his region at a safe distance from male soulmates.

36. J. Lebon, "Athanase, Lettre à des vierges qui étaient allées prier à Jérusalem," Syriac text, pp. 185–186, trans. p. 201. The term is used of Elias, who was, appropriately enough, castrated by angels so as to equip him for his profession: Palladius, *Lausiac History* 29.1 and 2.

37. For the problem in general, see H. Achelis, *Virgines subintroductae* and Elizabeth E. Clark, "John Chrysostom and the *subintroductae*," now in *Ascetic Piety and Women's Faith*, with invaluable translations and commentaries in *Jerome, Chrysostom and Friends*. H. Baltensweiler, *Die Ehe im Neuen Testament*, pp. 176–184, writes with great good sense on this phenomenon in the earlier centuries. On the original meanings and implications of the name, see A. Guillaumont, "Le nom des 'Agapètes.'"

38. John Chrysostom, *Quod regulares feminae* 3: *Patrologia Graeca* 47: 519, Clark, trans., *Jerome, Chrysostom, and Friends*, p. 220. See also Rosemary Rader, *Breaking Boundaries: male/female friendship in early Christian communities*, pp. 62–71.

39. F. Cavallera, "La 'de virginitate' de Basile d'Ancyre," pp. 6–8. A French translation of fragments is available, made from an Old Slavonic version: A. Vaillant, *La "De Virginitate" de Saint Basile. Texte vieux slave.*

Parts of Basil of Ancyra's treatise were resolutely humane. He followed Plato and Jewish legend in speaking of Adam and Eve as a parted androgyne.[39] The male wished to cleave to the female with an inarticulate intensity that was as mysterious and as inevitable as the pull of a magnet.[40] Basil's appeal to the sense of a profound physical need for interdependence between men and women was unusual. It softened the harsh outlines of male domination. Basil was prepared to admit that men needed in women what they lacked in themselves; and he regarded this fact not as a sign of weakness in men, but as a gift bestowed on women by God.[41] Those indefinable qualities of sweetness, of damp eyes, soft flesh, and gliding movements that exercised an irresistible attraction on men's sexual nature turned what might otherwise have been an abrasive mastery of the strong over the weak into a more equally balanced relationship of care and mutual need.[42]

But Basil's deep sense of the "natural" interdependence of men and women served only to heighten his sense of the sexual dangers that surrounded the continent woman. Sexuality was not an aspect of the person that could be ignored by those who had given up marriage. An undiminished fountainhead of sensuality still continued to course through the whole person.[43] A touch, a glance, even a chaste kiss from a relative, could reverberate through the person as instantly, so Basil wrote, as the touch of a snake caused the whole body to shiver.[44]

In this life, there could be no such thing as sexual innocence, and hence no such thing as an innocent, asexual relationship between a man and a woman. The Bishop of Ancyra would have his readers believe that he had assured himself of this fact after long observation. Long before the onset of puberty, children could be seen to play at sex-games in the street.[45] Sexual stirrings occurred when young girls snuggled down together in bed.[46] Eunuchs, so he had heard from the confession of many women, were a constant danger: they were "quite exceptionally dissolute, there being no fear of pregnancy associated with their love-making."[47] Only by adopting strict codes of sexual avoidance and by taking on the firm contours of a man (in walk, in tone of voice, in a general "unnatural" masculine brusqueness)[48] could the virgin defend herself against the lure of false familiarity with fellow-militants of the opposite sex. Cordoned off in this way, the con-

---

40. Basil, de virginitate tuenda 3: Patrologia Graeca 30: 673D and 676B.   41. 3: 676C.
42. 3: 676CD and 18: 708A.   43. 4: 677B and 6: 681B.   44. 14: 700BC.
45. 65: 801BC.   46. 62: 797BC.   47. 61: 769BC.   48. 18: 708D.

tinent women would look only to their true spiritual friends, the bishop and his clergy. Basil's extraordinarily frank treatise was written, so he said, not to praise virginity in the abstract, as so many of his contemporaries were doing, but as a call to precise and anxious vigilance. By being fully aware of her sexuality and its continued dangers, the virgin would take greater care in fashioning herself as a living icon, whose severely drawn and luminous features, glimpsed in the local church, would instill awe into the Christian community.[49]

It is exceedingly difficult to see beyond this haze of anxiety into the true quality of female asceticism. We can assume a large overlap of ascetic practices between men and women. In whatever way they organized themselves, women had the hard labor of the heart in common with men. Male monks might suspect that Amma Sara must think that it was extraordinary that men should seek counsel from her, a woman. She could assure them that her *logismos,* her inner awareness of herself, was as attuned to the dangers of pride as that of any male: she had triumphed, as fully as had any man, in the long battle for the heart.[50] It was normal for young nuns to have close relations with older women, whom they saw as spiritual guides.[51] Deprived of the clear boundary of the desert, their energies less drained by hard physical labor and unable to expose themselves far from their place of residence for fear of sexual violence, virgins frequently defined themselves as separate from the world through an exceptionally rigid control of their diet. Woman ascetics were famous for their ability to endure preternaturally long fasts.[52] Nuns in a great monastery in Egypt were believed to have grown up not knowing what an apple looked like: the male equivalent of such stories would have been ignorance of the existence of women or of gold coins.[53]

49. 1: 669A–672A.

50. *Apophthegmata Patrum* Sara 4: *Patrologia Graeca* 65: 420D.

51. See for example the descriptions in *Vita Sanctae Eupraxiae* 2.15: *Acta Sanctorum. Mart.* II (Venice 1735), March 13th: 269C and *Vita Sanctae Febroniae* 4, 7 and 34: *Acta Sanctorum. Jun V* (Venice 1744), June 25th: 18F, 20E and 31C; Sebastian P. Brock and Susan Ashbrook Harvey, trans. *Holy Women of the Syrian Orient,* pp. 154, 156 and 172.

52. Paulos Eurgetinos 3.29.4 in *Sentences des Pères du Désert. Nouveau Recueil* 518, pp. 88–89. As single women, nuns were exposed to the danger of rape when far from their habitual surroundings: see the case of a nun raped when visiting a neighboring estate "for the sake of her wool-working," Augustine, *Letter* 15*.3.3, Divjak, ed. p. 85; trans. *Lettres* 1*–29*, p. 266. See esp. Caroline Walker Bynum, *Holy Feast and Holy Fast: The Religious Significance of Food to Medieval Women,* pp. 78–93.

53. *Vita Eupraxiae* 2.6: 267B.

Despite the widespread ideal of total seclusion, we should not exaggerate the unavailability to the outside world of these holy women. Monks continued to need to be told to avoid consulting female spiritual guides.[54] The growing segregation of the sexes in the churches often meant that holy women came to minister more frequently to the women of the Christian congregations.[55] When, in the fifth century, Matrona of Constantinople settled near Beirut in the course of her wanderings, the ladies of the town flocked to bring their daughters to her for instruction: "Let us go out," they said, "and look at the Christian."[56]

The legendary life of Saint Febronia, a martyred nun, was written in the early sixth century. It revealed very clearly what had long been considered normal in a great woman's monastery in northern Syria. Lay women would gather on Fridays at the oratory of the convent. They would hear long Scripture readings, accompanied by extensive exegesis and spiritual advice from a leading holy woman. Pious women, some of them widows subjected to constant pressure to remarry by their families or by high-ranking opportunists, visited Macrina, the elder sister of Basil of Caesarea, in her convent. They treated her as their spiritual guide and protector.[57] Thus, there is nothing strange, or necessarily sectarian, about a woman being addressed, in a mid-fourth century Egyptian papyrus, as "my lady, the teacher."[58]

We almost always see these women from the outside, and we have to live as best we can with that decisive limitation. Yet we can at least know, from such evidence, what gave dedicated women so much prestige in the local churches. They were, above all, women whose

54. *Barsanuphe et Jean de Gaza: Correspondance* 661, L. Regnault, trans., pp. 432–433.

55. In Gaul, widows of the church and nuns instructed women for baptism: *Statuta Ecclesiae Antiqua* 100, in C. Munier, ed., *Les Statuta Ecclesiae Antiqua*, pp. 99–100. The interventions of holy women in the affairs of great households could include issues as substantive as the humane treatment of slaves: John Chrysostom, *Homily 11 on 1 Thess.* 3: *Patrologia Graeca* 62: 464–465. It was a matter of constant concern to the clergy that virgins of the Church gave advice on marriage and intervened in matchmaking: Basil [of Ancyra], *de virg. tuenda* 21: 712C.

56. *Vita Sanctae Matronae* 22: *Acta Sanctorum. Nov. III*, 801B.

57. *Vita Febron.* 1.6 and 2.20; 19B and 25C; Brock and Harvey, trans., pp. 155, 163. See the warm appreciation of this source by Susan Ashbrook Harvey, "Women in Early Syrian Christianity," in A. Cameron and A. Kuhrt, eds., *Images of Women in Antiquity*, pp. 296–297; and Gregory of Nyssa, *Life of Macrina* 28:234, on Vetiana's dependence on Macrina.

58. *Pap. Graec. Strasburg.* 1900.12, in P. Nagel, "Lettre chrétienne sur papyrus," see also Albrecht, *Das Leben der heiligen Makrina*, pp. 221–225, 233–238.

lives had not been broken up by the discontinuities of marriage and childbearing.[59] To her male admirers, the consecrated virgin stood for continuity in its most pure state. Her sheltered, undisrupted life was prized by the members of a storm-tossed urban clergy. Here was a wellshaft of deep certainty for which they themselves thirsted. She was the one human being who could convincingly be spoken of as having remained as she had first been created.[60] Her physical integrity came to carry an exceptionally high charge of meaning. To late antique males, the female body was the most alien body of all. It was as antithetical to them as the desert was to the settled land. When consecrated by its virgin state, it could appear like an untouched desert in itself: it was the furthest reach of human flesh turned into something peculiarly precious by the coming of Christ upon it.[61]

A sense of the uncanny stability of the life of the virgin, and of the sacred nature of the integrity of her physical body, tended to link the virgins of the church, by association, to all that was most immovable and sacred in the midst of the cities. The monks were actively encouraged to leave the cities. They were expected to go away, to "make the desert a city." But it was the virgins who could call themselves "daughters of Jerusalem."[62] They stood for all that was most holy and enduring in the heart of the settled land. Very often, the local martyr's shrine was the place where virgins found shelter and a center for their daily devotions.[63]

Since the time of Constantine, the great urban and suburban shrines of the Mediterranean had tended to become privileged gathering places for Christian women of all kinds. It was only in their peaceful, sacred spaces that married women could find a momentary respite from their

---

59. See esp. Elena Giannarelli, *La tipologia femminile nella biografia e l'autobiografia cristiana del iv secolo*, pp. 29–47. On this, as on so much else, I am particularly indebted to the insights of Caroline Walker Bynum, most notably her *Holy Feast and Holy Fast* and her "Women's Stories, Women's Symbols." K. Hastrup, "The Semantics of Biology: Virginity," in S. Ardener, ed., *Defining Females: The Nature of Women in Society*, is an excellent survey of the wide range of meanings associated with the virgin state: we should never take those developed in the fourth-century Christian Roman Empire to be the only ones possible.

60. Eusebius of Emesa, *Homily* 6.18, p. 162; see Hastrup, "The Semantics of Biology," pp. 56–57.

61. Eusebius of Emesa, *Homily* 7.6, p. 179.

62. L. Th. Lefort, "Sur la virginité," Coptic text, p. 128; trans. p. 257.

63. Gregory Nazianzen, *Letter* 223: *P.G.* 37: 364C; Theodoret, *Historia Religiosa* 30.1 *P.G.* 82: 1492D.

families.[64] A young married woman, Matrona had been able to abandon her husband, and to arrange for the adoption of her daughter, by merging into the company of pious female "renouncers" who lodged unassumingly in the porticoes around the shrine of the Holy Apostles at Constantinople.[65] In the great sanctuary that had grown up in an idyllic grove outside the city of Seleucia, Saint Thecla received female renouncers, comforting them in their difficult resolve:

Dionysia, so they say, had begun to renounce her husband, children and house and, in a word, to abandon everything; and for that reason she went to the shrine. And the martyr passed the whole first night with her, holding her in her arms.[66]

All over the Mediterranean area, the controlled liminality of pilgrimage allowed women to experience, for long periods of time, the heartening freedom of the desert. Despite the frequently expressed disapproval of the clergy, little bands of women continued to live the life of Saint Thecla: they covered huge distances along the roads that led to the pilgrimage-shrines of the Christian East.[67] The anonymous Egyptian virgins of the church, who had returned to Alexandria from pilgrimage to the Holy Land in the early fourth century, already found there a pattern of piety, consisting of meditation in places touched by the presence of Christ interspersed with instruction at the feet of priests.[68] We recognize this pattern well from the lives of great Roman ladies, Melania the Elder, and, a decade later, Paula and Eustochium.

A piety of abiding closeness to the holy gave to women who could not vanish into the desert, or take to the open road, a means of inner withdrawal, linked to unmediated contact with invisible, enduring protectors. Macrina, for instance, always wore a ring containing what was supposedly a fragment of the Cross around her neck. It was a token of her indefinitely postponed betrothal. Her fiancé had died. His death had enabled her to resist further pressure to marry. She claimed that, having once been betrothed, she was, in effect, a widow, and should be allowed to remain faithful to her dead husband. But the ring and its relic were also the pledge of the enduring presence of Christ,

---

64. Peter Brown, *The Cult of the Saints*, p. 44.   65. *Vita Matronae* 30: 792A.

66. *Vie et Miracles de Sainte Thècle*, Miracle 46, in G. Dagron, ed. *Subsidia Hagiographica* 62:408.

67. Theodoret, *Historia Religiosa* 29.4: 1492B.

68. J. Lebon, "Athanase, Lettre à des vierges," Syriac text, pp. 170–171; trans., p. 189.

her true Bridegroom.[69] The invisible presences associated with relics of the saints stood between dedicated women and the profane world: the well-educated nuns whom Matrona drew to the convent that she finally established in the suburbs of Constantinople drove the memory of the classics from their minds as they kissed and embraced the relics of the saints.[70]

Unbroken loyalty is the most marked feature of descriptions of Saint Febronia in northern Syria, as it is of Saint Eupraxia in Egypt. The writers of these two lives describe the development of deep friendships between nuns and their older mentors.[71] The only miracle that immediately followed the brutal martyrdom of Febronia was a miracle of continuity. Febronia would always reappear in the convent church, to stand in her accustomed place among the sisters, from midnight to the third hour.[72]

Two great images of continuity emerged in the fourth century in connection with the piety of women. The first was the image of the childhood of Mary. It was derived from the earlier *Protoevangelium of James*.[73] This second-century narrative already presented Mary as a human creature totally enclosed in sacred space. It set the tone for all later descriptions of the consecrated woman: dedicated to the Temple at the age of three, Mary grew up in total isolation from the profane world. Later writers lingered insistently on this aspect of her life: it is the enclosed child, and not the grief-stricken mother of the Lord, that we meet most frequently in late antique literature.

She was pure in her body and her soul, she never put her face outside the door of the Temple, she never looked at a strange man, and she never moved herself to gaze upon the face of a young man. Her apparel was dainty. Her tunic came down to her seal; and her headcloth came down over her eyes. . . .

She never craved for a large quantity of food, neither did she walk about in the market-place of her city. . . .

There was no limit to her beauty, and the Temple was wont to be filled

---

69. Gregory of Nyssa, *Life of Macrina* 30.15–21, pp. 240–242 and note 2 at pp. 240–241.

70. *Vita Matronae* 47: 810C.

71. *Vita Euprax.* 3.15, 33 and 36–37: 296D, 273D and 274CD.

72. *Vita Febron.* 2.38: 32F; Brock and Harvey, trans., p. 174.

73. Translated in E. Hennecke and W. Schneemelcher, *New Testament Apocrypha* 1:370–388. The influence of this narrative is transparent in the fourth century Latin papyrus hymn on the Virgin: R. Roca-Puig, *Himne a la Verge Maria: "Psalmus responsorius."*

with angels because of her sweet odour, and they used to come to visit her for the sake of conversation.[74]

Whenever Mary appeared in public with her family, everyone was amazed at her poise. A young girl, she walked "as if she [already] had a master to keep a watch over her." She was, in fact, the most unusual of creatures: a young woman whose discipline sprang from deep within herself. She was controlled, not by any male guardian—a father or a husband—but only by the "holy thought" that rested in her.[75]

This concern for the continuous, unbroken loyalty of the virgin gave a quite distinctive flavor to the second image—that of the virgin as the "bride," espoused to Christ. It is noticeable that the language of the Song of Songs, which had been applied by Origen to the relation of Christ with the soul of every person, male or female, came, in the course of the fourth century, to settle heavily, almost exclusively, on the body of the virgin woman.[76]

As presented by Christian writers in the fourth century, the language of the Song of Songs spelled out the theme of unswerving loyalty and of abiding, intimate protection. Espousal to Christ rendered the virgin sacred and unavailable to any other marriage partner. No physical husband might be forced upon her by her family. This was why Basil of Caesarea decided that, while virgins of the church who had "fallen" (and this "fall" often consisted of nothing more lurid than marriage) had formerly been subjected to the penance only of fornicators, they should now undergo the heavier penance associated with adulterers:

since by God's grace, the church, as it advances, becomes stronger and the order of virgins is now increasing . . . it is far worse . . . that the bride should become an adulteress and, dishonouring her union with the bridegroom, give herself over to licentious pleasure.[77]

In this ruling, Basil spoke the harsh language of the irremovable *ex voto*. Yet this was not all that the image meant. It is exceedingly difficult to enter into the affective education of female children in late antiquity. One of its features may have been a careful socialization of

74. E. A. W. Budge, *Miscellaneous Coptic Texts in the Dialect of Upper Egypt*, pp. 655 and 641 (in that order, for the last part of the citation).

75. "Athanase, 'Sur la virginité.'" Coptic text, p. 93; trans., p. 246.

76. F. E. Consolino, *"Veni huc a Libano:* La sponsa del Cantico dei Cantici come modello per le vergini negli scritti esortatori di Ambrogio," pp. 399–415.

77. Basil, *Letter* 199.18, p. 107.

the young girl for loyalty to a future husband. Yet hers was to be a loyalty without freedom. Its affective element, love, had to be sternly inhibited. Augustine understood this only too well when he preached on the Song of Songs:

Nor is it said to her [the bride of the Song of Songs]: Do not love, as is sometimes said to any betrothed virgin not as yet married, and rightly said, do not love; when you have become a wife, then love. It is rightly said because it is a rash and irrational and an unchaste desire to love one she is not sure of marrying. For one man may be betrothed to her, and another man may marry her.[78]

Augustine's own betrothed wife, a Milanese girl in her early teens, had lost him as a future husband on his conversion to the life of continence. For all we know, she may have had to face the rest of her life as an unmarried woman.[79] One should not underestimate the freedom to love securely that came from an early promise of the self to Christ, made by girls who had already been subtly trained to considerably less dependable loyalties.

We know how decisive in the careers of males in the fourth century was the sense of the intimate presence of an invisible companion—of Chirst, of a guardian angel, or of a patron saint.[80] Without an equally strong language of loyalty, a young girl's autonomy could easily have been crushed. In the early fifth century, Eupraxia was already betrothed at the age of seven to a figure in the Imperial court when she was taken by her mother to visit a great convent near the family's estates in Egypt. The deaconess of the convent dandled the little girl on her knee, teasing her:

Eupraxia, my little lady, do you love our convent and all the sisters?" And she replied: "Indeed, my lady, I do." . . . "Between us and your betrothed, whom do you love best?" The girl replied: "I have neither known him nor he me: I have known you and I love you" . . . "But no one can remain here

78. Augustine, *Enarratio in Psalm 122.5: Patrologia Latina* 36:1633; in Mary T. Clark, trans., *Augustine of Hippo: Selected Writings* (New York: Paulist press 1984): 253.

79. Implied in *Confessions* 6.15.25 and 8.12.30; when two courtiers were converted to the ascetic life at Trier, their betrothed dedicated their virginity to Christ: *Confessions* 8.6.15.

80. Brown, *Cult of Saints*, p. 64; a girl had to claim that she had received "frightening visions" in order to persuade her parents to allow her to become a nun: Ps. Ambrose, *de lapsu virginis, Patrologia Latina* 16: 387B.

unless she has dedicated herself to Christ." To which the girl replied: "Where is Christ?" The deaconess gladly showed her an icon of the Lord, and Eupraxia, turning towards her, said to the deaconess: "Truly, I also dedicate myself to my Christ, and I will no longer go with my lady mother.[81]

Eupraxia would later wake up in the convent screaming, after she had dreamed that the Emperor had sent his officials to reclaim her for her betrothed at court.[82]

From the time of her betrothal onward, the virgin was thought to live in the company of Christ and His angels. She awaited His embrace with an intensity which those nourished on the works of Origen knew so well how to express. The full palette of physical delight had been used by the author of the Song of Songs; it would blaze forth in its most vibrant tints, as Christ touched the intact spirit at the end of time:

Their eyes will see the Lord, their ears will hear His words, their mouth will kiss their Bridegroom, and their nose will take in His sweet perfume. Virgins' hands will touch the Lord, and the purity of their flesh will give Him joy.[83]

In this life, the virgin's thought-world was presented as a tranquil conversation piece:

Your language with Him is your prayer, your fervour and your whole-hearted resolve; and His with you are the righteous thoughts that rise up in your heart, those thoughts by which He fans your fervour and increases within you your love of Him.[84]

It is a somewhat pastel image of the life of the dedicated girl, which was very far from the trials of sexual temptation, of envy and physical damage heroically endured that made up the life of Eupraxia in her convent. It would not have been so convincing to male writers if it had not been for one fact: the dedicated virgin was perceived as standing for an oasis of entirely sacralized culture in the midst of a church whose leaders were only too well aware of the tainted, profane roots of their own most brilliant achievements.

Given the low rate of literacy among women, and their exclusion

---

81. *Vita Euprax.* 2.8: 267D.　　82. Ibid., 3.18: 269E.

83. Evagrius, *Sententiae ad virginem* 55, Gressmann, p. 151; cf. Gregory of Nyssa, *In Cantica Canticorum Hom.* 1: P.G. 44: 776B.

84. "Athanase, 'Sur la virginité,'" Coptic, p. 116; trans. p. 253; cf. Palladius, *Hist. Laus.* 5.3.

from the public space in which males gained and demonstrated their mastery of the ancient classics, entry into a convent often meant entry into literacy across the sacred bridge of the Scriptures.[85] One of the most touching miracles of Saint Thecla was when a pious woman, who had been given a copy of the Gospels by her literate friend, suddenly found, to her surprise, that she could read it at sight.[86] Though beaten in public, Athanasius reported, one virgin of the church had continued to chant the Psalms from the book she held out in front of her.[87] The sacred page was the blazon of the devoted woman: "Let the rising sun see a book in your hands."[88]

In devout women, men met with a true cultural virginity: a culture of the sacred page, which had grown from childhood untainted by profane public space and by the pagan culture associated with public space. It was the women, protected by their loyalty to invisible protectors and nourished by their undisturbed absorption of a sacred culture, who brought into the urban churches a sense of permanence and of a purity as unalloyed as was the sand of the distant desert. In the virgins of the church, men with uneasy consciences, sensitive to their own continued dependence on a profane, pagan culture and to the ravages of power and competitiveness among themselves in the all-too-public forum of the fourth-century Church, could look wistfully at an innocence that they themselves had lost, "as if they looked on burning, phosphorescent gold."[89]

We need only turn to the *Life* of his elder sister Macrina, written by Basil's brother, Gregory of Nyssa, immediately after her death in 380, to appreciate what this could mean in practice. In this gem of late antique biography, Macrina represented for Gregory the quiet antipodes of the world of the city in which he and his great brother Basil had made their way at such great cost. That world was always far from her. She grew up with her widowed mother, Emmelia, helping her to keep together a large household, remaining as close to her "as if she were still in her mother's womb."[90] Her identity reached back to her

85. *Vita Euprax.* 2.8 and 3.37: 267E and 274D; *Vita Febron.* 4: 18F; Brock and Harvey, trans., p. 154.

86. *Vie et Miracles de Sainte Thècle* 45.8, p. 406.

87. Athanasius, *Encyclical Letter* 4: P.G. 25: 232B.   88. *Sôtérios logos* 12, p. 16.

89. John Chrysostom, *Quod regulares feminae* 4: Patrologia Graeca 47:527; Clark, p. 237.

90. Gregory of Nyssa, *Life of Macrina* 5.17 and 22, p. 156.

mother's vision of Saint Thecla in the midst of labor. Thecla's secret name rested on her: she would be what her mother had not been free to be.[91] She, and none of her brothers (who were sent out to wet-nurses) had sucked at her mother's milk.[92]

For her brothers, Macrina would always be the still eye of the storm. She was the "root that had blossomed"[93] from the very depths of the somber household of Old Christians. It was to the women of the household—and not to the men, tarnished as they were by the dark compromises of a century of public dominance—that Basil appealed as the guarantors of the purity of the creed of his region. These women were the "holy lineage" that linked Basil to the first days of Christianity in Pontus.[94]

Acting as "father, teacher, paedagogue, mother and counsellor in all good things" to the family's youngest brother, Peter, Macrina passed on to him a culture based exclusively on the Scriptures.[95] From her convent at Annesi, in the wooded hills of Pontus, some ten days journey from Caesarea,[96] Macrina presided over the disintegration of a civic dynasty. The death of the great Basil, a year before her own, came to her as a distant rumor.[97] When he came to her deathbed, nine years had passed since Gregory had last seen his sister; in that time, he had, among his many other misfortunes, been exiled for three years on a charge of embezzlement.[98]

He and his great brother had paid a heavy price for continued involvement in that last round of bitter civic politics that goes by the name of the Arian Controversy. In all that time, their sister's intact body, on a faraway estate, had mirrored the tenor of a life through which the storms of the city had not raged. Inviolate, profoundly unspecified, through having escaped the roles imposed on the normal woman by marriage and child-bearing, Macrina was the ancient "uncut meadow." Her body was a clear echo of the virgin earth of Paradise—untouched earth that bore within itself the promise of undreamed-of abundance,

91. 2.10, p. 144.   92. 3.2–3, p. 148.   93. 1.24, p. 140 and note 1, p. 141.
94. Basil, *Letter* 204; Deferrari, 3:168: this aspect of the family is well evoked by J. A. McNamara, "Cornelia's Daughters," p. 15.
95. Gregory of Nyssa, *Life of Macrina* 12.13–14, p. 182.
96. Maraval, *Grégoire de Nysse, Vie de sainte Macrine*, pp. 38–44.
97. Gregory of Nyssa, *Life of Macrina* 14.10, p. 188.
98. Ibid., 15.8, p. 192 and 21.9–17, p. 210.

which the ploughshare of the twisted will . . . has not broken; an earth virgin of thorns and thistles; where there runs clear flowing water past banks of deep repose.[99]

Macrina was only fifty-four when she died, in 380. But she belonged, in many ways, to an older generation. In the eyes of her brother, at least, the utter transparency of her existence summed up the deepest longings of a provincial gentry for solitude and sheltered piety. Macrina the woman could be what Gregory, the man, feared he might never be. But, now that Christianity was established in the highest classes of the Empire—among the great senatorial landowners of the West and in the families connected with the Imperial court at Constantinople—women with ascetic vocations found themselves making their way in an abrasive and fully public environment, very different from the dreamlike tranquility of the upland farms of Asia Minor. Like the crash of avalanches heard from the upper slopes of great mountains, women such as Melania the Elder and Olympias of Constantinople caused the clergy and ascetics of the late fourth century to look up with awe. They were startling phenomena. Their careers revealed possibilities and barriers greater than any encountered by humbler "daughters of Jerusalem."

To begin with, both Melania and Olympias were great heiresses. They were too valuable not to be married off as young girls. The granddaughter of a consul, Melania was given to a pagan family. By the age of twenty-two she was widowed. She had already lost two sons and suffered many miscarriages.[100] From then on, she created her own desert through self-imposed exile. She refused to sink back into the ranks of her powerful kin in Spain. She made for Rome, and appealed to the old-fashioned jurisdictional powers of the Urban Prefect—and not to her relatives—to have a guardian assigned to her sole surviving son: a young man who grew up to be an amiable and utterly conventional senator.[101]

99. Gregory of Nyssa, *On the Beatitudes* 7: *Patrologia Graeca* 44: 1212AB.

100. Paulinus of Nola, *Letter* 29.8. On Melania, see esp. A. H. M. Jones et al. *Prosopography of the Later Roman Empire* 1:502–593 and Nicole Moine, s.v. Mélanie l'Ancienne, *Dictionnaire de la Spiritualité* 66–67:955–960; in general, see Elizabeth A. Clark, "Ascetic Renunciation and Feminine Advancement: A Paradox of Late Ancient Christianity," now in *Ascetic Piety and Women's Faith.*

101. Paulinus of Nola, *Letters* 29.9 and 45.3.

By 374, she was in Alexandria, with all her portable wealth on board ship.[102] Making straight for Nitria, she placed at the feet of none other than Apa Pambo a great silver casket, like the great silver and gilt case, covered with scenes of a married woman adorning herself beneath the sensuous opulence of Venus at her toilet, that is known as the Esquiline Treasure in the British Museum.[103] It was filled with three hundred pounds of silverware. Pambo was impressively unimpressed.[104]

In fact, the arrival of so much ready wealth, distributed by a person of such unchallengeable social status, saved the overgrown and fragile monastic settlements outside Alexandria from ignominious collapse in the face of pressure from a hostile, Arian government. Melania supported the beleaguered settlement. When the leading holy men of Nitria were sent into exile in Palestine, in 377, Melania, a second Thecla, dressed herself as a servant to minister to them.[105] She confronted the governor: "I am So-and-So's daughter and So-and-So's wife. I am Christ's slave."[106] A woman whose Roman background conferred unanswerable authority, Melania could act in public as a "female man of God"[107] in a manner that the sheltered Macrina would have found impossible.

Settled in Jerusalem between 377 and 400, Melania ruled a monastery of fifty virgins, established on the slopes of the Mount of Olives. A schism involving four hundred monks gave way to her influence. All the time, regular installments of money forwarded to her by her son from her Western estates enabled her to pour oil on the notoriously troubled waters of ecclesiastical life in the Holy Land. Bishops, monks, and pilgrims from all over the Roman world were supported by her when in Palestine. Along with her favored male adviser, Rufinus of Aquileia, the lonely Roman enjoyed a privileged position in Jerusalem: for they "bestowed gifts and food on all the local clergy, and so finished their days without offending anyone."[108] By this means, Melania was able to live at the center of the Christian imagination of her age,

---

102. Palladius, *Lausiac History* 46.1.

103. Kathleen Shelton, *The Esquiline Treasure*, pp. 25–29 and *American Journal of Archaeology* (1985) 89:147–155.

104. Palladius, *Lausiac History* 10.2–4.   105. 46.3 and Paulinus, *Letter* 29.11.

106. 46.4.   107. 9.

108. 54.2 and 46.6: see E. D. Hunt, *Holy Land Pilgrimage in the Later Roman Empire*, esp. pp. 168–171.

in places that were thought still to bear the footprints of Christ, "without owning an inch of land" in her adopted country.[109]

Melania was free to choose two of the most talented intellectuals of the ascetic movement as her friends and advisers. Rufinus of Aquileia, the more tranquil and determined friend of Jerome's student days, joined Melania in Jerusalem in 381 until his return to Italy in 397.[110] In 387, it was her spiritual insight that diagnosed, as a mental breakdown brought about by an unfulfilled vocation, the lingering illness that had afflicted the brilliant Evagrius of Pontus, when he first fled from Constantinople to Jerusalem in order to disengage himself from a love affair.[111]

When controversy over the views associated with her protégés swept the Holy Land in the late 390s, Melania, now aged sixty, showed that she could resort, once again, to the hard expedient of exile. Though an old woman, she had never once stopped to bathe her feet in cold water as she and her little monastic group trudged, repeatedly, along the long coastal road from Jerusalem to Egypt, shunning the horses and sedan-chairs of the well-to-do. Melania had no fear of uprooting herself. In 399, she took ship straight to Italy.[112] Dressed in a black gown, riding a donkey, and given to reading late into the night, Melania duly impressed her fashionable relatives in Campania.[113] She had come to protect her own.

Though accused of heresy, Rufinus continued his careful labor of translation in her palace.[114] It was from one of her Sicilian villas, facing across the straits of Messina, that Rufinus and his fellow-ascetics watched the towns of mainland Italy going up in flames, as the Gothic army passed through them after the sack of Rome, in 410.[115] Now that the once-confident society of Rome had itself been reduced to a band of exiles, Melania, the woman for whom exile had long been the ascetic discipline *par excellence*, returned to the Holy Land, to die within a few months of her arrival. The very hatred with which Jerome (as we shall see) hounded her memory (expunging her name from the edition of his *Chronicle*, in which he had previously spoken of her as

---

109. Palladius, *Lausiac History* 54.8.   110. 46.5.   111. 38.9.
112. 55.2 and 54.3.   113. Paulinus, *Letter* 29. 12–13.
114. From the subscription of a manuscript of Rufinus' translation of the *Homilies* of Gregory Nazianzen, in A. Engelbrecht, *Corpus Scriptorum Ecclesiasticorum Latinorum* 46:233.
115. Rufinus, *Prologue to Origen: Homilies in Numbers*, in W. A. Baehrens, ed., *Corpus Christianorum* 20:285.

the "second Thecla,"[116] dismissing her theological views as those of "a silly old woman,"[117] and writing of Melania, "whose name [from *melané*: Greek for "black"] shows the darkness of her treacherous heart")[118] is some measure of the extent of her impact on contemporaries.

Such options were inconceivable for Olympias of Constantinople. The granddaughter of a major politician at the court of Constantine, Olympias was brought up by the sister of an episcopal colleague of Basil of Caesarea.[119] Through her, the somber world of the Cappadocians touched the court society of the capital. Designated to marry one of the many Spanish inlaws of the new Emperor, Theodosius I, Olympias duly received a poem on the occasion from Gregory Nazianzen: intercourse was granted by Christ as a boon, to give stability, through the begetting of children, to a human race caught in the millrace of death; but she should, at least, persuade her husband to observe abstinence on holy days, "for to such laws God's image must be bound."[120]

The husband died after twenty months, in 386. Olympias was a little over twenty. Her later admirers were convinced that she had remained a virgin.[121] She had no intention of remarrying, despite heavy pressure to accept another kinsman of the Emperor. In a world capital, whose recently arrived governing class were still out to make their fortune, wealth of the amount controlled by Olympias could never be a matter of indifference. In Rome, at a distance from the centers of power, no one had intervened to thwart Melania. Olympias's fortune was instantly put in trust until she reached the age of thirty. A zealous Prefect forbade her to receive bishops and clergymen in her palace.[122]

If she was to retain such wealth and remain unmarried, this could never be with the freedom enjoyed by Melania. So much wealth, dispensed by the pious resident of a world capital sought out by delegations of clerical fortune-seekers, threatened to place the clergy of the entire Greek world in Olympias' debt. Her admirers later took great pleasure in cataloguing the bishops who later opposed her protegé,

---

116. Rufinus, *Apologia* 2.26.   117. Jerome, *in Jerem.* 3.17 (70.4): *P.L.* 24: 786C.
118. Jerome, *Letter* 133.3: *P.L.* 22: 1151.
119. See *Prosopography of the Later Roman Empire*, 1:642–643.
120. Gregory Nazianzen, *Carmina* 2.2.6.86–94: *P.G.* 37: 1548A–1549A.
121. Palladius, *Lausiac History* 56.1 and *Life of Olympias* 2, Clark, trans. p. 128.
122. *Life of Olympias* 5, p. 130 and Palladius, *Dialogus de Vita Johannis Chrysostomi* 17 (61): *P.G.* 47:60.

John Chrysostom, recording how each of them had received favors from her. They pointed out that John's most bitter enemy, Theophilus, Patriarch of Alexandria, had once paid court to her, "kissing her hands and knees" in the hope of gifts, and had only received board and lodging.[123]

If Olympias were to handle so much wealth, its impact must be made to benefit the capital. Unlike Melania, she was not to be allowed to dispose of her wealth as she pleased. For Constantinople was a mushrooming city, filled with immigrants from Anatolia. Poverty was a dangerous feature of the city. When the Emperor and his courtiers attempted, spasmodically, to show that they were human, they usually did so through their womenfolk: it was the women who served as intermediaries of the governing class of the city by ministering to the urban poor. Thus, while Theodosius I wrapped himself in the full splendor of the Imperial office, it was his wife, Flacilla, who proved that even the Emperor and his family were human beings, subject to illness and death, by serving in the soup kitchens and visiting the hospitals of the poor.[124]

Flacilla died in 387. Next year, the Bishop's palace was burned down in an ugly riot, while Theodosius was away on campaign.[125] Someone had to act as protector of the poor. By the time Theodosius returned, in 391, the problem posed by Olympias had been resolved. The patriarch Nectarius—a former civil servant and a skilled diplomat—ordained her as a deaconess of the church of Constantinople. The young heiress was ordained thirty years earlier than the legal age of sixty.[126] For the formal office of deaconess obliged Olympias to use her wealth to support the Church of Constantinople. Her palace near the Great Church, only a few hundred yards from the murmurous Hippodrome, became a center for poor relief. An astonishing mansion, it already had its own tribunal for dispensing alms, its own extensive baths, and a bakery for de luxe bread.[127] A convent recruited from Olympias' own dependents formed a pious gatehouse to the gardens that abutted the Bishop's palace.[128] To these and other enterprises, Olympias contrib-

123. Ibid. 17 (61):61.

124. Theodoret, *Eccles. Hist.* 5.19; see K. Holum, *Theodosian Empresses*, pp. 22–30.

125. Socrates, *Ecclesiastical History* 5. 13.   126. *Codex Theodosianus* 16.2.27 and 28.

127. *Life of Olympias* 5:130–31; see esp. G. Dagron, *Naissance d'une capitale*, pp. 501–506.

128. *Life of Olympias* 6–7:131–132; see C. Mango, *The Brazen House*, pp. 55–56.

uted ten thousand pounds of gold, a hundred thousand pounds of silver, properties scattered all over western Asia Minor, and her family's share of the civic corn dole.[129] This one woman ensured that the bishops of the "Ruling City" would enjoy resources, both for the alleviation of the poor and for the fitting entertainment of the ambitious, equivalent to those lavished on the Holy Places of Jerusalem by a self-exiled Roman such as Melania.

In 397, Olympias was a woman still under forty. Her asceticism had rendered her "as frail as a spider's web," confined by modesty and ill health to the innermost rooms of her great convent.[130] She was known never to have taken a bath without draping her whole body in a capacious black robe.[131] She was an entirely appropriate recipient of Gregory of Nyssa's masterpiece, the *Commentary on the Song of Songs*.[132]

Olympias was in a strong position to welcome from Antioch the newly designated Bishop of Constantinople, the dazzling and intractable John Chrysostom—with what results we shall see. Having sketched out the sheer diversity of female ascetic experience and practice, from its humble bedrock in the pious household to its impact at the very top of Roman society, we must now step back a generation in time, to the late 360s and 370s, to deal with Macrina's energetic brother, Basil of Caesarea, with the more contemplative Gregory of Nyssa, and, a little later, with John Chrysostom of Antioch.

129. *Life of Olympias* 5, 7:130, 132.
130. John Chrysostom, *Letters to Olympias* 12. 1d, in A. M. Malingrey, ed., *Jean Chrysostome: Lettres à Olympias*, pp. 187–188.
131. Palladius, *Dialogus* 17 (61): P.G. 47:61.
132. Gregory of Nyssa, *In Cantica Canticorum*: P.G. 44: 756A: but note that the dedication to Olympias is missing in the Syriac version.

FOURTEEN

Marriage and Mortality:
Gregory of Nyssa

In Cappadocia and Pontus (that is, in eastern Anatolia and on the Black Sea coast of eastern Turkey) we find ourselves in a very different world from the Egypt of the Desert Fathers and from the court society of the new capital, in which Olympias was later constrained to live out her ascetic vocation. We are dealing with a provincial nobility, whose Christianity reached back, without a break, to the age of Origen. The great Basil, Gregory of Nyssa (his younger brother), and Gregory Nazianzen (Basil's friend) came from families of Old Believers. For generations, Christian families such as theirs had dominated the small cities of the region, as lawyers, *rhetors*, great landowners and, almost *ex officio*, as Christian bishops.[1] Theirs was a stern, ceremonious Christianity, firmly rooted in the continued life of great households. In these households, the women were crucial. They were the guarantors of physical and moral continuity. Gregory Nazianzen's mother, Nonna,

---

1. See esp. Raymond Van Dam, "Hagiography and History: the Life of Gregory Thaumaturgus," and T. A. Kopecek, "The Social Class of the Cappadocian Fathers."

had never once turned her back to the altar, had never spat on the pavement of the church, and had "never once grasped the hand or kissed the lips of any heathen woman."[2]

Gregory Nazianzen's sister, Gorgonia, would not allow male doctors to examine her body after she had suffered a serious accident in her coach.[3] Yet "performing those few services due to the world and to nature," she had duly produced two sons and three daughters, leaving behind "children and children's children."[4] Basil's own mother, Emmelia, had wished to remain a virgin, but was forced to marry when her father died. Thecla, the protectress of virgins, had been present in a vision at the birth of her first child, Macrina.[5] Nine other children followed in quick succession—four sons, four more daughters, and one baby who died in childhood.[6] Altogether, up to the middle of the fourth century, the Christian gentry of Cappadocia had shown an unbroken determination to face down "the common shame" of the grave[7] by the well-tried means of the marriage bed.

The new asceticism did not alarm well-to-do Christians of Cappadocia by taking the occasional girl out of her role as a bearer of children. Large families such as these could afford to shed daughters.[8] The ascetic calling did, however, threaten in no uncertain manner to sweep active males out of the city and out of the ranks of a Christian clergy that had become fully identified with the needs of the city.

To join the hermits in the forest-clad mountains of the Black Sea, or to vanish among the caves in the tufa-rock gulleys that lay at a temptingly short distance from the tranquil cities of Cappadocia, was worse than shocking; it caused the cold shadow of death to fall across the future of whole families. For young males, the potential fathers of noble families, to meditate sexual renunciation was to meditate social extinction. The family grave-houses along the roads leading from the city were already disturbing enough; the tumbled bones at the entrances

2. Gregory Nazianzen, *Oratio* 18.10: *Patrologia Graeca* 35: 99C, in C. G. Browne and J. E. Swallow, trans., *Library of the Nicene Fathers*, 7:257.

3. Ibid. 8.15: 808AD, trans. p. 242.   4. Ibid. 8.8.: 797B, trans. p. 240.

5. Gregory of Nyssa, *Life of Macrina* 2.10, in P. Maraval, ed., *Grégoire de Nysse: Vie de Sainte Macrine*, p. 144.

6. Ibid. 2.12-27, pp. 144–146.   7. Ibid. 35.5, p. 254.

8. Evelyne Patlagean, "Familles chrétiennes d'Asie mineure et histoire démographique du ive siècle," and Marcella Forlin Patrucco, "Aspetti di vita familiare nel iv secolo negli scritti dei padri cappadoci."

of the oldest of these acted as stark reminders of mortality.[9] But it would be yet more chilling if the line of tombs were to come to a halt. The last children of a noble line would join their parents (as Macrina did) in the great marble sarcophagi that now lined the martyrs' shrines.[10] A Christian family, and, with it, an ancient style of Christian leadership in the churches of Cappadocia, would come to an end.

In the late 350s and early 360s, Basil and his brothers seemed to have gone out of their way to confirm the worst fears of their compatriots. Naucratius, the second brother, left Caesarea (modern Kayseri) immediately after a brilliant first speech, in 352. By 357, he was dead, drowned in the river Iris, as it swept in a murderous whirlpool beneath the family's hunting-lodge at Annesi. He had been mending the nets with which he caught the fish he needed to feed a group of sick old men. Along with one servant, he had lived the life of a hermit, working with his own hands for the food with which he had fed himself and others.[11]

Basil returned from studying rhetoric at Athens in 356, at the age of twenty-six. It was soon obvious that, for Basil, Annesi was something more than a place of retirement, complete with a terrace shaded by the obligatory plane tree of the scholar gentleman, from which to view the wooded mountains veined with waterfalls and the river Iris as it meandered across the rich plain below.[12] The memory of Naucratius, the hermit, was the more powerful presence.

Basil's own spiritual guide at that time had been none other than the radical ascetic Eustathius, who became Bishop of Sebaste (modern Sivas) in 357.[13] In the years when Basil lived at Annesi (358–359 and 362–365), reading the Scriptures and excerpting the works of Origen with Gregory Nazianzen, his friend from his student days in Athens,

9. Gregory of Nyssa, *Encomium in sanctum Theodorum*: *P.G.* 46: 737C.

10. *Life of Macrina* 35.5, p. 254.

11. Ibid. 8.4-29, pp. 164–168. See esp. J. Gribomont, "Le panégyrique de la virginité, oeuvre de jeunesse de Grégoire de Nysse," p. 251, on the place of Naucratius' death.

12. Basil, *Letter* 14, in R. J. Deferrari, ed., *Saint Basil: The Letters*, 1:109–111: compare Gregory Nazianzen, *Letters* 5 and 6: *P.G.* 37: 29B and 32A, trans. 447; see esp. L. Robert, *Hellenica* (1948) 4:30, n 5.

13. Sozomen, *Ecclesiastical History* 3.14 and W. D. Hauschild, s.v. Eustathius, *Theologische Realenzyklopädie*, pp. 547–550. On the situation in Asia Minor in general, see esp. the judicious surveys of J. Gribomont, "Le monachisme en Asie Mineure au ive siècle," and "Le Monachisme au sein de l'Église en Syrie et en Cappadoce,"; see now R. Albrecht, *Das Leben der heiligen Makrina auf dem Hintergrund der Thekla-Traditionen*, pp. 174–189.

he also paid frequent visits to Eustathius's "brotherhoods," scattered through the region: "spending whole nights with them in prayer, speaking always . . . about God."[14]

Basil's interest in a man such as Eustathius was not reassuring. Eustathius was a widely respected spiritual guide and an ecclesiastical politician with loyal allies. His concern for the poor caused him to be remembered as the founder of monasticism in Constantinople, a city largely populated by destitute immigrants from Asia Minor.[15] In Cappadocia and Pontus, where Eustathius had been most active, ascetic lifestyles threatened to impinge directly on the urban churches. Ascetic preaching did not merely draw the few, talented leaders away from the city; it threatened to overturn the traditional structures of urban society. For, unlike Egypt, there was no desert into which radical activity might be deflected.[16] As early as the middle of the century, the bishops assembled at a council at Gangrae expressed alarm: they claimed that the disciples of Eustathius had endangered the institutions of slavery and of private wealth, and had denied the subjection of women. They were accused of expunging all social distinctions beneath a common dress, derived from the raw *pallium* of the philosopher: women and slaves would appear dressed alike, their social status and their sex obliterated by a common dress.[17] They also claimed that wealth was to be renounced *en bloc* and redistributed at once "among the saints."[18] Women gained their equality by shaving their heads. With the removal of the "natural veil" of long hair, so the bishops claimed, women were encouraged to throw off the sign "which God gave to every woman as a reminder of her subjection, thus annulling, as it were, the ordinance of subjection."[19]

As late as 390, Imperial laws threatened to depose any bishop who allowed such women into his church: for "under the inspiration of their ascetic persuasion [such women acted] against the laws human

14. Basil, *Letter* 223, in Deferrari ed., 3:305.

15. G. Dagron, "Les moines et la ville."

16. Sozomen, *Eccles. Hist.* 6.34. See esp. Évelyne Patlagean, "Sur la limitation de fécondité dans la haute époque byzantine," pp. 1365–1366, an essential study, now available in translation as "Birth Control in the Early Byzantine Empire," in R. Forster and O. Ranum, eds., *Biology of Man in History*.

17. *Council of Gangrae*, Letter and Canons 3, 10 and 13, in E. J. Jonkers, ed., *Acta conciliorum quae saeculo quarto habita sunt*, pp. 81, 83; E. J. Percival, trans., *The Seven Ecumenical Councils*, pp. 90, 93, 97.

18. Ibid. canon 7, Jonkers, p. 82; Percival, p. 95.

19. Ibid. canon 17, Jonkers, p. 84; Percival, p. 99.

and divine." A whole generation later, a Christian writer, worried by what struck him as the loosening of sexual discipline in Constantinople, cited the law with evident approval.[20]

In the early 360s, a decade after the council of Gangrae, the atmosphere of Cappadocia was marked by the tension that follows the first small, but unmistakable, tremor of an earthquake. The career of Aerius, a priest of Eustathius, showed very clearly what might still happen. Aerius broke with the Church over the administration of the dole for the poor in Sebaste. In his opinion, the Church should not accumulate wealth, even for the long-term care of the poor; all wealth must be given over directly to the needy. While Basil studied Origen and searched the Gospels in his quiet country retreat at Annesi, a mixed group of men and women set out, with Aerius at their head, to wander far from the cities in the cruel winter snow, along the hills that flanked the Halys River.[21]

Basil did what he could to reassure the Christian families of his city that to become a monk did not necessarily involve being swept over so terrible a cataract. He allowed himself to be ordained a priest in Caesarea in 364. He led the organization of poor relief during the famine of 368. In 370, he became Bishop of Caesarea. He died only nine years later, a comparatively young man of fifty, worn out by the strain of his double role as a leader of the monks and as a bishop ferociously loyal to his city and its province. In that short time, Basil had created a monasticism that was intended to exist alongside the churches of the cities. He wished to scatter the Christian landscape of Cappadocia and Pontus with carefully organized ascetic "brotherhoods."[22]

In this experiment, the notions of voluntary poverty and almsgiving predominated. Basil's "brotherhoods" were irrevocably committed to a new style of social relations by their vows of poverty. A life of shared poverty imposed its own intimate and unremitting discipline. Basil saw to it that no "brotherhood" could hope to survive without close economic collaboration between all its members.[23] This measure was, in itself, calculated to bring the "brotherhoods" to the poor and so back to the very gates of the city. Each "brotherhood" was to act as an ideal

---

20. *Theodosian Code* 16.2.27.1, cited by Sozomen, *Eccles. Hist.* 7.16.

21. Epiphanius, *Panarion* 75.1–3: P.G. 42: 504A–508C.

22. W. K. Lowther Clarke, *Saint Basil the Great. A Study in Monasticism,* remains the best English study. The *Greater* and *Lesser Rules* of Basil are available in English translation: M. M. Wagner, trans., *Basil of Caesarea, The Ascetical Works.*

23. Basil, *Regulae fusius tractatae* 7, 36 and 41: P.G. 36: 928C, 1009C and 1021A–1024D.

Christian household.[24] Each was an economic unit, whose surplus wealth would be given over to the poor. Many of the "brotherhoods," for whom Basil wrote his *Rules*, were converted country houses, like the one in which Macrina and Basil's youngest brother, Peter, were established—within easy distance of each other, in the plain at Annesi (they may even have continued to draw revenues from the estates on which they had been built).[25] But in these Christian households, made up of humble and hard-working celibates, surplus wealth was immediately handed over as alms to the poor; it was no longer soaked up by the ancient, tainted reflexes that led the average, married householder to spend large sums of money on ensuring the prestige and the continuity of his family.

The "brotherhoods" varied greatly in size and in organization. Some were little cottages at the edge of the villages, so small that the "brothers" could be warmed by a single fire.[26] They had little in common with the great monastic hospital and leper colony founded by Basil himself on the outskirts of Caesarea, a "city without the city," later called after him, the *Basileias*.[27] But each of Basil's "brotherhoods" found itself with substantial uncommitted surpluses that enabled it to meet the traditional duty of every Christian household—the care of the poor. In a province rocked by natural disasters, its farmers ruined by years of drought and by debts, and systematically expropriated by the great landowners in order to make room for the ranches that bred more profitable livestock (cattle, sheep and horses for the Imperial cavalry),[28] Basil's organization of poor relief through his private resources and, a little later, through the organization of monastic "brotherhoods," came to play an immediate, much-publicized role in the social life of Cappadocia.[29]

By such measures, Basil guaranteed that he and his followers would

24. E. L. Fellechner, *Askese und Caritas bei den drei Kappadokiern*, pp. 118 sees this clearly.

25. The family's wealth had increased enormously over the past generation, so that each of the nine children had as much as the parents once possessed: *Life of Macrina* 5.35–40, pp. 158–160 and 20.16–20, p. 206.

26. Basil, *Reg. fus.* 35.1-2: 1004A–1005B.

27. Gregory Nazianzen, *Oratio* 43.63: P.G. 36: 577C.

28. See esp. Basil, *Sermo in tempore famis*: P.G. 31:304–329. In 1873, a drought is reported to have killed 150,000 persons in Cappadocia: S. Kostof, *Caves of God. The Monastic Environment of Byzantine Cappadocia*, p. 3. See esp. Ramón Teja, *Organización economica y social de Capadocia en el siglo iv, según los padres capadocios*.

29. Greg. Nyss. *Contra Eunomium* 1.10: P.G. 45: 281C.

not vanish from the city. Instead, he brought a singularly consequential version of the ascetic life to the doors of an old-fashioned Christian gentry. He made clear that the baptized Christian was under an obligation to become, day by day, a little more like his own austere idea of a monk. The instinctive social reflexes of the well-to-do, to pile up wealth and to secure themselves against the future by producing the solid flesh of many sons and daughters, were, to him, quite simply, bad habits that a Christian must slowly learn to break. Basil wished to impose on the city of Caesarea as a whole an atmosphere of austerity and openness to the needs of the poor, similar to that which prevailed in his monastic "brotherhoods." For Basil, the issue was plain: if the Rich Young Man of the Gospel story had really done what he told Christ that he had done—followed all the commandments since his youth up—then he would not have been a *rich* young man by the time he met the Master![30]

Basil's stern message left many unpersuaded. It was therefore ostensibly to help his distinguished elder brother, at some time during Basil's episcopate (between 370 and 379), that Gregory of Nyssa, a man not many years younger than Basil, but of such an otherworldly disposition as to count as a child in comparison with the forceful Bishop of Caesarea,[31] committed himself to a formal panegyric in praise of virginity.[32] Gregory's *On Virginity* was a *virtuoso* composition that aimed to drench the reader in a fine golden rain of words. In it, he strove to persuade his readers, small-town intellectuals of rhetorical culture, that the sexual renunciation with which so many men and women in Cappadocia had begun their stormy ventures in the new ascetic life could be spoken of in public in elevating, old-fashioned terms. Like his brother,

---

30. Basil, *Hom. 7 in divitiis* 1: *P.G.* 31: 281A. See J. Gribomont, "Un aristocrate révolutionnaire, évêque et moine: S. Basile."

31. Basil, *Letters* 58 and 215, Deferrari 1:356 and 3:236, and A. D. Momigliano, "The Life of St. Macrina by Gregory of Nyssa," *The Craft of the Ancient Historian: Essays in Honor of C.G. Starr*, pp. 448–449; now with Raymond Van Dam, "Emperors, Bishops and Friends in late antique Cappadocia."

32. This is available with an exemplary introduction and commentary by M. Aubineau, *Grégoire de Nysse: Traité de la Virginité*; see also V. W. Callahan, trans., *Gregory of Nyssa: Ascetical Works*, pp. 3–75 (*On Virginity*), and 161–191 (*Life of Macrina*). With Gribomont, "Le panégyrique," p. 252 and G. May, "Die Chronologie des Lebens und der Werke des Gregors von Nyssa," in M. Harl, ed., *Écriture et culture philosophique dans la pensée de Grégoire de Nysse*, pp. 55–56, I see no reason why Gregory should not have written at any time after he became Basil's colleague. The genre itself must bear much of the blame for the "immaturity" that we tend to see in Gregory's *On Virginity*.

Gregory needed to reassure his peers. He wished to make plain that sexual renunciation did not necessarily lead to Spirit-filled extremes—such as a life of holy vagrancy and an indifference to sexual dangers—with which he himself may well have been acquainted, through his reading of spiritual works associated with the monks of northern Mesopotamia.[33]

Indeed, for all the studied banality of large parts of his *On Virginity*, Gregory was a man quite as unusual as his brother. In the 370s, it would have seemed to an outside observer that Gregory was the one male member of the family who had kept clear of the ascetic landslip that threatened to sweep his entire house into oblivion. A man in his early thirties, Gregory was the only brother who had married.[34] He loved to stay at his estate at Vanosa (modern Avanos). At Vanosa, the river Halys wound through a valley heavy with rich red soil, glowing in the evening light, "like a golden thread sewn through a robe of deep purple." A half-built martyr's shrine stood by the house. On an upper terrace, beneath a vine arbor, tame carp flashed and somersaulted in the fishpond.[35] Though only an hour's walk from the dramatic cliffs of Zilve and Çavuşin, later honeycombed with the caves of hermits, Gregory's Vanosa was no Annesi.

A loyal younger brother, Gregory left his estate in 371, to oblige Basil by becoming Bishop of the minor city of Nyssa. Yet, even at that time, he had learned to live with a great sadness. There is no evidence that his marriage to Theosebeia (who died in 385) produced an heir, or that Gregory had wished very strongly that it should do so. Upper-class bishops, in other regions, still felt that they owed male heirs to their family and to their city. Synesius of Cyrene wrote to the Patriarch of Alexandria, in 410, in order to make plain from the outset that he would consent to act as Bishop of Ptolemais only on condition that he would be allowed to continue to have intercourse with his wife: "I shall not be separated from her, nor shall I associate with her surreptitiously,

33. On the delicate, and as yet undecided, issue of Gregory's relations with "Messalian" spirituality, now see Reinhart Staats, "Basilius als lebende Mönchsregel in Gregors von Nyssa 'de Virginitate,'" pp. 51–54.

34. Aubineau, *Traité*, pp. 65–77.

35. Greg. Nyss. *Letter* 20: *P.G.* 46:1081A–1085A = *Letter* 15, in W. Moore and H. A. Wilson, trans., *Library of the Nicene Fathers*, 5:539-540. See Nicole Thierry, *Comptes-Rendus de l'Académie des Inscriptions et Belles Lettres* 1977, pp. 130–133, on the excavations at Avanos-Maçan-Çavuşin.

like an adulterer. . . . I desire and pray to have virtuous children."[36] Less diplomatic, the Bishop of Ephesus simply took his wife out of the convent to which she had retired in order to conclude his unfinished family business.[37]

Gregory showed no such dynastic leanings. He had come to share the family's drift toward a social void, but he did this very much on his own terms. A more profound, if less consequential, thinker than Basil, Gregory had made his own the boundless yearning of Origen.[38] For Gregory, the human soul lived forever in the grip of a "fine passion of insatiability." The familiar, solid ground of material existence led abruptly to the edge of a world unseen, a vast emptiness, toward which the soul's deepest love strained for fulfillment.[39] Why this "fine passion" seemed to be held in such a state of restless suspension, never free to find its true momentum in this life; by what means it could be set free; and what form the huge longing for fulfillment would take in the final reordering of all created things associated with the Resurrection: these were the preoccupations that underlay much of Gregory's thought. They formed the solemn *leitmotif* that ran beneath the virtuoso rhetorical passages of his *On Virginity*. They gave a quite distinctive tone to his views on sexuality, on marriage, and on the virgin life.

Gregory had come to the conclusion that the present constitution of the human person represented a nadir of uncertainty: "the life of man is at present subjected to abnormal conditions."[40] Men and women were poised between an original, lost prototype of human nature, created by God *in His own image*, and revealed to the visible world in the shimmering "angelic" majesty of Adam, and a fullness of humanity

36. Synesius, *Letter* 105: *P.G.* 66: 1485A, in A. Fitzgerald, trans., *The Letters of Synesius of Cyrene*, p. 199.

37. Palladius, *Dialogus de vita Johannis Chrysostomi* 13.48: *P.G.* 47.48.

38. As are all scholars, I am particularly indebted to the work of Jean Daniélou, most especially his *Platonisme et Théologie mystique* (Paris: Aubin 1944), and to W. Völker, *Gregor von Nyssa als Mystiker*. A masterly anthology of the writings of Gregory makes the themes studied here available in English: *From Glory to Glory*, ed. J. Daniélou, trans. H. Musurillo (New York: Charles Scribner's Sons, 1961). I have not been able to consult *The Biographical Works of Gregory of Nyssa: Proceedings of the Fifth International Congress on Gregory of Nyssa*, ed. A. Spira, Patristic Monograph Series 12 (Cambridge, Mass.: Philadelphia Patristic Foundation 1984).

39. *In illud "Tunc.": P.G.* 44: 1316D–1317A and *In Eccles. Serm.* 7:44: 729D–732A: *Glory to Glory*, pp. 127–128.

40. *Oratio Catechetica* 5:45: 24BC; in Moore and Wilson, trans., *Nicene Fathers* 5:479.

that would come about, through the restoration of Adam's first state, at the Resurrection.[41]

He had no doubt whatsoever that the present division of the sexes into male and female formed part of the present anomalous condition of human beings. This division made sexuality possible. Sexuality was designed for marriage and childbirth: it enabled mankind to continue its forlorn attempt to stem the tide of death by producing progeny. This had not been intended in God's first creation of the prototype of human nature. Adam's physical body had been unimaginably different from our own. It had been a faithful mirror of a soul which, itself, mirrored the utterly undivided, untouched simplicity of God.[42] *Katharotés*, "purity," was an essential concept for Gregory. With none of the antiseptic overtones that now afflict the word, *Katharotés* was a state of unshadowed clarity. It betrayed the perfect balance of potentially conflicting elements. It was like the diaphanous radiance of a still midday sky.[43] To return to such "purity" was the ultimate destiny of body and soul alike. For, "that which was made *in the image* was one thing, and that which is now plain to view in all its wretchedness is quite another."[44]

Sexuality existed in human nature as the result of a merciful afterthought. Like the *garments of skin*, with which God had gently clothed Adam and Eve, so that they might endure their long exile from Paradise,[45] sexuality had been added to the original serene undifferentia-

---

41. Gregory's thought on these issues was not always explicit or even consistent: scholars have varied accordingly. I have owed most to the following treatments: Monique Alexandre, "Protologie et eschatologie chez Grégoire de Nysse," in U. Bianchi, ed., *Arche e Telos. L'Antropologia di Origene e di Gregorio di Nissa*, E. Corsini, "Plérôme humaine et plérôme cosmique chez Grégoire de Nysse," in *Écriture et culture philosophique*, and G. B. Ladner, "The Philosophical Anthropology of Saint Gregory of Nyssa." These syntheses have not won universal acceptance: for helpful criticisms see esp. Paola Pisi, *Genesis e Phthora. Le motivazioni protologiche della verginità in Gregorio di Nissa e nella tradizione dell'enkrateia*, and H. J. Oesterle, "Probleme der Anthropologie bei Gregor von Nyssa." See now David L. Blank, "The Etymology of Salvation in Gregory of Nyssa's *De Virginitate*."

42. *De hominis opificio* 12.9: *P.G.* 44: 161C; 6: 137D.

43. *De virg.* 13.1, p. 26; *Katharon kai amiges kai ametochon*, cf. *Life of Macrina* 2.10, p. 144: Emmelia had hoped for the life of a virgin, described as *katharon . . . kai akélidôton diagôgén*. The sky blue of the priest's vestment: *Life of Moses* 2.191: *P.G.* 44: 388CD; cf. John Chrysostom, *de virginitate* 10.3: *P.G.* 47:540.

44. *De hom. op.* 16.7: 181A, trans. p. 404.

45. *Or. cat.* 8: 33CD. The *garments of skin* themselves were mortality, applied as a tourniquet to check the evil will of Adam; *De mortuis P.G.* 46: 524CD. But mortality itself was a sharing of the life of the animal kingdom, in which sexual intercourse had

tion of human nature, along with death, after Adam's fall. Far from being a punishment, sexuality was a privileged sign of God's abiding care. For God had foreseen that Adam would have need of it: in that sense, He had created human nature both *in his own Image,* and also as *male and female.*[46] But a capacity for sexual differentiation had been lodged in human nature only as a "safety device." In Adam's Paradise, the potential division between the sexes had been totally latent.

Plotinus had thought that a capacity for sense perception lay implicit even in disembodied souls; but that this capacity had remained unrealized in those mighty spirits who continued to soar forever above matter. It became active only in those weaker souls that had "fallen" into the physical world. In much the same way, for Gregory, the differentiation of the original human nature into two distinct sexes became active only when Adam's disobedient act of will brought upon him the loss of immortality.[47] It was the evil choice of his will that had been the cause of Adam's fall. Adam's fatal "slip" was his wish to possess and to control, rather than to contemplate, with laborless, buoyant joy, the visible world entrusted to his charge. He had wished to grasp for himself the material world whose stunning beauty God had laid out before his contemplative gaze, like the shimmering landscape of Vanosa viewed from a distant terrace.[48]

The wish to control and to possess such beauty had acted on Adam's soul like a drop of water poured into the oil of a lamp; it had caused the clear light of his love of God to gutter and grow dim. He no longer embraced the physical world with the serene and caring eyes of a mighty, angel-like being. By wishing to make such physical beauty his own, he found that the tragic transience inherent in the physical world seeped into his own nature.[49] He joined the beasts by becoming mortal.

Gregory was careful to make plain that Adam's "tilt" toward the animal world had nothing to do with a sexual act. The emergence of

---

been a necessary defense against extinction through death, to which animals, unlike Adam, had always been exposed: see J. Daniélou, *L'être et le temps chez Grégoire de Nysse,* pp. 154–164. For other, more radical, exegeses of the *garments of skin,* see now the perceptive study of P. F. Beatrice, "Le tuniche di pelle. Antiche letture di *Gen.* 3.21," pp. 455–458, on Gregory. We should remember that the taking off and the putting on of garments was a significant and readily intelligible part of the baptismal liturgy: Gregory's exegesis gained its cogency from this fact; see Daniélou, *Platonisme,* pp. 30–32.

46. *Genesis* 1:27.   47. Plotinus, *Ennead* 6.7.1–7; *de hom. op.* 17: 189C.
48. *De hom. op.* 1.5: 132AC.   49. *Or. cat.* 6: 29C.

a differentiated sexual nature in the first human beings was simply a secondary and necessary adjustment to the new conditions created by the fall; it had played no role whatsoever in causing the fall. Gregory, in fact, never spoke of it in any way as a punishment for the fall. Rather, God had allowed the subsequent division between the sexes, and the concomitant emergence of sexual drives in men and women, to unfold in the human person so that human nature should continue to enjoy, through physical reproduction, a continuity in time, tragically shattered though such continuity must be by the malevolent inroads of death.[50] It was, of course, a perilous solution: it was like trying to run an engine on an explosive *Ersatz* fuel. Human reproduction was inevitably associated with the moral dangers inherent in the present nature of sexual drives.

Gregory viewed such drives with ill-disguised discomfort. He even made clear that he himself would rather have remained continent than have faced the need for heightened moral vigilance involved, through marriage, in an active sexual relationship with his wife, Theosebeia.[51]

Specific sexual temptations remained peripheral for Gregory. Sexuality, for him, meant reproduction: and the continuity of the human race through reproduction was accepted by him as a sad, but faithful, echo of the abiding purposes of God. In a manner that Gregory wisely refused to itemize, the huge unfolding of the human capacities of Adam in Paradise would, in any case, have filled the visible world with Adam's "offspring," as surely as the invisible world was resonant with mighty throngs of angels.[52] The joyous abundance of God, His wish to draw from Adam, the single, perfect prototype, an exuberant multitude of like-minded beings—like a field grown from a single head of wheat to a full harvest rustling with a myriad golden ears[53]—continued to be mirrored, on earth, in the pathetic urge of human beings to *increase and multiply.* For this reason, Gregory always tended to present sexuality, along with other aspects of the instinctual life, not as a privileged anomaly, but as a token of the slow but sure cunning of God. Sexuality and marriage spoke of God's gentle persistence in carrying the human race to its appointed fullness, if, now, "by a long detour."[54]

What truly distressed Gregory was the way the entry of death into human nature had radically changed the human experience of time.

---

50. *De hom. op.* 22.4–5: 206B.   51. *De virg.* 8.1-9.2, pp. 358–364.
52. *De hom. op.* 17.2: 190A.   53. *De an. et res.* 4: 156C–157B; *de hom. op.* 16: 185C.
54. Ladner, "Philosophical Anthropology," p. 85.

If he had not been haunted by the wish to escape time, Gregory would not have advocated virginity, and, by implication, total male continence, with such conviction.[55] He might have been content with the somewhat disembodied reproductive duties that had been the norm in his family until his own generation. But only by the drastic step of abandoning marriage and childbirth was it possible to exorcise the anxiety created by a sense of the inexorable passing of time.

The creation had begun with a "pure" time. The soul of Adam might have stretched forever toward its goal, constantly changing, unfolding its capacities in measured sequence, according to the unimpeded growth of its love for God. This was a sense of time and of change so certain of its goal, so unwavering in its momentum, as to appear, by contrast to present time, as immobile as a rock.[56] The sense of time introduced by death was the opposite to such stability. It was time that could be likened to a treadmill,[57] to an unending filling up of one empty brick-mold after another,[58] to an attempt to struggle up a slope of sand.[59] The great festivals of the Church, the soft blaze of candelabra and the unbroken swell of male and female voices in responsorial Psalms, seemed to offer an experience on earth of "time out of time;" but even such solemn moments were no more than attempts to square the circle.[60] The present human experience of time was an experience of "tainted" time.[61] It was a factitious time, created within the self by unrelieved anxieties. It showed itself in the form of a perpetual, unquiet "extension" of the soul into an unknown and threatening future.[62]

For Gregory, the clock whose tick measured off most inexorably and most audibly the passing of tainted time was the clock of marriage. He saw human time as made up of so many consecutive attempts to block out the sight of the grave. Marriage, intercourse, and the raising of children were the most persistent, and the most highly valued, of such expedients.[63] It was precisely through the elemental power of the

---

55. The clearest statement is by Pisi, *Genesis e Phthora*, pp. 71–75.
56. *Life of Moses* 2.243: *P.G.* 44: 405B.   57. *In Flacillam P.G.* 46: 888D.
58. *Life of Moses* 2.60: 341D–344B.   59. Ibid. 2.244: 405C.
60. R. L. Wilken, "Liturgy, Bible and Theology in the Easter Sermons of Gregory of Nyssa."
61. The phrase is not Gregory's. It is used by a contemporary, maybe a compatriot; see F. Floeri and P. Nautin, eds. *Homélies Pascales 3*, pp. 100–102, 137.
62. See esp. *Hom. 15 in Cant. Cant. P.G.* 44: 1109AC.
63. *De virg.* 3.2, pp. 276–278; 14.1, p. 432.

hopes inspired by marriage—and through the tearing grief associated with the dashing of those hopes through the deaths of spouses and children—that it was possible to take the full measure of the burden of anxiety that rested upon men and women, caught as they were in "the blast of death's incessant motion."[64]

Hence the huge symbolic pressure that built up, in Gregory's mind, around the issue of marriage and virginity. What was at stake, for him, in the virgin life, was not the repression of the sexual drive. That was only a means to a greater end—the withering away in the human heart of a sense of time placed there by the fear of death. This fear could be dissolved most effectively by dispensing with the one social institution that had been brought into existence expressly by the fear of death. Marriage conferred the validation of organized society on that fear. Married intercourse had been the "last outward stopping place" of Adam and Eve in their sad exile from Paradise. It was by joining to have children that they had recognized, in themselves, the full extent of their terror of extinction.[65] To abandon marriage was to face down death. It was to deliver no further hostages to death in the form of children.[66] It was more than that: the abandonment of marriage implied that the soul had broken with the obsession with physical continuity that was the most distinctive trait of a humanity caught in "tainted" time. In the heart of the continent person, the heavy tick of the clock of fallen time had fallen silent.

At important moments of his career, Gregory used to visit Macrina and her companions, established in a farm house in the plain beneath the woods at Annesi. There he could observe for himself women no longer committed to the huge physical and emotional labor of maintaining the continuity of a Cappadocian noble household. The forms of time wished on them by society had stopped. They had not suffered the consecutive dislocations of marriage, childbirth, and bereavement. They were as close as any human beings could be to the original, openhearted straining of Adam toward God. In that sense, Macrina stood on the frontier of the invisible world.[67] Time, for her, had already ceased to consist of a succession of expedients to dull the blow of death: she could look directly into the immensity beyond the grave. It was she who consoled Gregory when Basil died, in 379, playing the role of the

---

64. George Herbert, *Church Monuments*, p. 60. 65. *De virg.* 13.1, p. 422.
66. Ibid. 3.6, p. 280. 67. *Life of Macrina* 11.33–45, pp. 178–180.

dying Socrates in Gregory's dialogue *On the Soul and the Resurrection.*[68] When her own death came to her in 380, in Gregory's presence, even her last movements revealed that her heart had placed no barrier against its approach. She did not even need to be laid out for burial: her body had settled itself, with perfect grace, into a position of deep repose.[69]

The virgin state, therefore, brought with it a touch of the "pure" time of Adam. In that unfissured time, the "fine passion of insatiability" was set free to gather an unwavering momentum. Gregory shared with Origen an acute sense of the soul's capacity for spiritual delight. But while, for Origen, spiritual delight had always remained a distant echo, muffled by the flesh, Gregory posited a more robust passion in the soul. He distrusted the material world largely because he had so acute a sense of the headlong capacity of the soul for love. Deprived of true objects of love, the soul could love material things with fierce tenacity. Like an "uncapped" fountain, it flooded exuberantly into the material world, turning the clear waters of its desire into a muddy morass. Led through the narrow pipe of continence, the soul's "fine passion" would rise again to heaven in a torrent, as unshakable as the steady surface of a cascade.[70] Freed from earthly cares, the soul might become again the virgin hunter, coursing after "divine, inviolate delights."[71]

Although Gregory was a married man, he plainly hoped for the same spiritual perfection as that achieved by his virgin sister. He made plain that, in his opinion, "virginity of body" was no more than a "method," "devised to further a disposition of the soul."[72] Without that disposition, continence in itself added nothing. Yet virginity could never be spoken about as if it were simply one method among many. Gregory was a Platonist of the school of Origen. To be effective, a method had also to be a mirror.[73] The virgin body was an exquisitely appropriate mirror, in which human beings could catch a glimpse of the immense purity of the *image of God.* The woman's untouched flesh was both a mirror of the purity of her soul and a physical image of the virgin earth of the garden of Eden. Byzantine nuns would continue to hope, as Macrina had hoped, that they might come to rest beside clear streams

68. M. Pellegrino, "Il platonismo di Gregorio di Nissa." Macrina is named throughout as "The Teacher."

69. *Life of Macrina* 25.24–28, p. 228.

70. *De virg.* 6.2, p. 344, cf. *Sermo 4 in Cant. Cant.*: 977C.   71. *De virg.* 5, p. 338.

72. Ibid. 5, p. 336.   73. Ibid. 2.2, p. 266; 12.1, p. 398.

in "the grassy garden of delight;" for their own, untouched bodies were already heavy with a sense of the unseen luxuriance of Paradise.[74]

When Gregory last dreamt of his sister, it was as if he held in his hands a precious relic, which flashed into his eyes, like a mirror catching the full light of the sun. This was an omen to him. He knew that he would carry Macrina to the grave. Her body was the untarnished mirror of a soul that had caught, at last, the blinding light of the *katharotés*, the radiant purity, of God.[75] The glow of her pale flesh against the coarse black robe in which she lay on her funeral bier confirmed Gregory's dream: Macrina's body had become a holy thing, on which the grace of God had come to rest.[76]

It is important to step back a little so as to view Gregory's thought as a whole, in order to appreciate its originality and distinctiveness. Gregory's writings show how, like a moving sand dune, the view of the human person held by Christians in Cappadocia had slowly shifted its position, to take on a different contour and orientation from that current in the pagan traditions on which he and his educated readers still depended. In most of what he wrote, Gregory moved in a "Platonic universe."[77] In the pages of the *On Virginity*, in particular, formulations from Plato and Plotinus dropped easily from his pen. They came naturally to him, like so many bars of ancient, reverential music. But they had changed their meaning.[78] For the soul to find itself in the body in its present, fallen state was a sad and perilous situation for Gregory; but it was no longer the principal cause of the present anomaly of the human condition. A man writing in an ancient, Platonic tradition, Gregory tended to assume that the mere fact of living in the physical world might tarnish the purity of the soul, as imperceptibly and as inexorably as the dire eye infections that were the scourge of Gregory's Near East clouded the bright vision of the eye:[79] human beings lived in the world of the senses as if in "a region heavy with infec-

74. C. A. Mango and I. Ševčenko, "Some recently acquired Byzantine inscriptions at the Istanbul Museum," p. 15, no. 18—a fourteenth-century inscription.

75. *Life of Macrina* 15.12–22, p. 192.   76. Ibid. 32.7–12, p. 246.

77. Aubineau, *Traité*, pp. 98–99, 213.

78. This is beautifully stated by P. Hadot, *Léçon inaugurale. Chaire d'histoire de la pensée hellénistique et romaine*, pp. 34–35, esp. p. 35: "La pensée évolue en reprenant des éléments préfabriqués et préexistants auxquels elle donne un sens nouveau."

79. *De mortuis*: 525D–528B.

tions."[80] A "negative attitude over against the material world . . . takes us into the deepest level of Gregory's piety."[81]

Yet we must be very careful to define precisely where the main burden of Gregory's distrust had come to lie. He was concerned less with the heaviness of the body than with the tight knot of anxieties that had gathered within the soul itself. These anxieties appeared to him to seek relief in continuities that stretched far beyond the body into society as a whole. Gregory's view of "fallen" time implied the notion of a fallen society. It was by the accumulation of wealth, by the retaining of power, above all, by marriage and the search for direct and palpable continuity in the form of sons and daughters, with all the social arrangements which dynastic continuity implied for members of the upper classes, that human beings sought to remedy the discontinuities inflicted on them by death. As a result, Gregory's thought tended to glance off the individual body into the extended body of a human society forever braced against death.[82]

The true "plunge" that accounted for the misery of the human condition was not that of the soul into the body; it was the plunge of the human person, body and soul together, into the present, fallen state of society. The urge to cheat death had made human beings collude with the needs of a society that lived by tainted time, a time measured by no other clock than that which registered, through marriage and childbirth, the passing of one generation after another into the grave. To adopt the virgin life was a decision with immediate social repercussions. It was a refusal of the body to serve society as "an instrument of succession unto death."[83]

In fourth-century Asia Minor, many persons quite as austere as Gregory in their philosophical outlook and in their personal discipline did not think in this way. Sosipatra, the daughter of a philosopher, was an exact pagan doublet of Macrina. As a child, she had grown up on a family farm in the Caryster valley behind Ephesus. There she had been consecrated to the service of the gods by mysterious strangers. And yet, when she met Eustathius, a philosopher-diplomat (a figure, indeed, with whom Basil may once have exchanged a polite note—so

---

80. *De virg.* 12.4, p. 420.
81. Völker, *Gregor von Nyssa*, p. 127, cf. Ladner, "Philosophical Anthropology," pp. 89, 91.
82. *De an. et res.*: 13A–16A.   83. *De virg.* 14.1, p. 432.

small was the world of the intellectuals of Asia Minor!)[84] she instantly agreed to marry him: "I shall bear you three children," she foretold, "but you will go hence before me. . . . Only five years longer will you devote your services to philosophy."[85]

Socially and morally, Sosipatra the pagan still lived in the same world of the married household as had the Christian women, Nonna, Gorgonia, and Emmelia. More than that: she still lived in the mighty cosmos of late pagan piety. She knew that she and Eustathius would be in their bodies only for a short time. She could speak with mystical fervor of the descent of the soul into its transient "garment of clay."[86] She had foretold not only the time of her husband's death, but the heroic resting place, "within the orbit of the moon," to which Eustathius' disembodied soul would soon return.[87]

The only time by which this philosophical couple lived was that measured by the vast, slow clock of an eternal universe. By contrast to the tranquil immensity of Sosipatra's spiritual world, Gregory's sense of time was hurried. It was a sense of time stretched out by human effort, through marriage and the creation of human society. Even among the continent, time was felt to race in the human heart as it strained toward the Resurrection. Such attitudes would have struck Sosipatra and Eustathius as quite unnecessarily frantic. The idea that the measureless lifespan of the cosmos could be spoken of as nothing more nor less than "that time which is necessarily coextensive with the development of humanity,"[88] would have been unthinkable to them. Living at ease in an unchanging world, Sosipatra would have seen little purpose in removing marriage from her life. Marriage was not a screen that had to be put aside, so as to bring about a mysterious foreshortening of time, as Macrina had done at Annesi. Gods and angels had hovered around Sosipatra from her childhood; but no Bridegroom awaited her, still less one whose coming might be hastened by a young

84. Basil, *Letter* 1, Deferrari 1:1. I see no reason why this note should not be to the philosopher Eustathius, rather than to Eustathius of Sebaste: see A. H. M. Jones, J. R. Martindale, and J. Morris, *Prosopography of the Later Roman Empire*, 1:310.

85. Eunapius, *Lives of the Sophists* 469, in W. C. Wright, ed., *Philostratus and Eunapius*, p. 409. There was nothing strange in possessing such knowledge: see Sencer Şahin, "Griechische Epigramme aus dem südlichen Propontisgebiet," in M. B. de Boer and T. A. Edridge, eds., *Hommages à M. J. Vermaseren*, 3:999–1000.

86. Ibid. 470, p. 414.

87. Ibid. 469, p. 408: see the ideas expressed on a contemporary pagan tomb: C. P. Jones, "A Family of Pisidian Antioch," pp. 264, 268.

88. *De hom. op.* 22.7: 205C, trans. *Nicene Fathers*, p. 412.

girl's brusque refusal to play her civic duty in the marriage bed. So-sipatra could bide her time. She could accept her role as a young woman, destined by nature to provide children for the ancient city, as serenely as she accepted her place as an embodied soul, woven, for a swift moment, into the material fabric of a timeless universe.

For Basil and for Gregory, neither the universe nor the city was se-cure. All creation was poised in tense expectation of the return of Christ, and, on earth, the little cities of Cappadocia were faced with momen-tous choices. Gregory wrote as he did to add an elevated, Platonic tone of voice to Basil's challenge to the ancient city. For all their differences of temperament and outlook, the two brothers were ringed by the same horizon. Both sensed acutely the power of the ancient, civic urge to pile up wealth, to gather kinsmen, and to beget descendants. The heavy blood of a Cappadocian gentleman still flowed in Gregory's veins. When he quoted Paul's Letter to the Romans on the law of sin in our mem-bers resisting the mind, and spoke of "the civil war that rages within each of us," he was not referring to his sexual urges: he was describing his sense of outrage when snubbed by a fellow-bishop: "What license does he have to insult us, if he is not superior in birth, nor distin-guished in rank, or more talented than I in rhetorical ability?"[89]

Basil and Gregory knew what it was to wrestle with such drives. It was to tame these, and only incidentally to tame the sexual urge, that Basil had written with passionate exactitude on the mode of life to be practiced in his "brotherhoods." Detailed rulings on the distribution of wealth, on the abandonment of marks of status, on uniform codes of dress fill the pages of Basil's ascetic writings.[90] Gregory, for his part, lingered by preference, not on sexual temptation, but on the tragic roots of pride, avarice, and family honor in the human condition since Adam's fall. Both believed that, through the new, reformed social life of a monastic "brotherhood," individuals set free from the demands of a family-based, conventional society could create a Christian society in miniature beside the city. The main effort of the "brotherhoods" would be less to tame sexuality in the few—desirable though that might seem to austere men such as themselves—than to create an example of the husbanding of resources in the light of the needs of the poor. They wished to open the hearts of a small-town gentry so that the

89. *Letter* 1: *P.G.* 46: 1005BC = *Letter* 13, trans. pp. 546–547.
90. Basil, *Asceticum parvum* 11: *Patrologia Latina* 121: 502–504—two full columns on dress as against half a column on sexual fantasies: 9: 501C.

river of Christian charity might flow again, from the doors of the rich into the hovels of the destitute.[91]

The stark economy of groups of men and women whose sexual renunciation had set them free from the urge to create, for themselves, a physical future, based upon physical progeny and the retention of family wealth, was meant to stand as a pointed rebuke to the habits of conspicuous expenditure that had made the ancient city what it was. Macrina's Annesi—a rural estate governed by the childless, whose entire surplus was turned over every year to the relief of the poor—was to eclipse classical Caesarea, whose walls and buildings, towering crags of brick and marble, spoke of wealth frozen by the pathetic wish to cheat the grave through civic fame and through civic family pride.[92] The towns of Cappadocia were small, and men of the status of Basil and Gregory of Nyssa could feel that they might, indeed, be able to make of them more truly Christian cities. Matters were less clear, however, in a sprawling and exuberantly profane metropolis such as Antioch. It was in Antioch that John Chrysostom, a man a decade younger than Gregory, began his career in 381, as a preacher of magnetic talent performing to entranced congregations beneath the spacious golden-domed octagon of the city's Great Church.

91. Gregory of Nyssa, *de pauperibus amandis: P.G.* 46: 464D; Basil, *Hom. 6 in div. P.G.* 31: 272B. It is an ancient, civic image: Artemidorus, *Oneirocritica* 2.27—it is good for a rich man to dream that a river runs from his house.

92. Basil, *Hom. 7 in div.* 4: 289C.

FIFTEEN

Sexuality and the City:
John Chrysostom

By the year 370, ascetics had come to settle all over the mountaintops of Syria. Small groups of monks were ensconced even in the caves of Mount Silpios, the mountain range that rose abruptly behind the most fashionable quarter of Antioch.[1] Every morning they would rise at cockcrow, gathering silently to pray, while, in the great city below,

the servants are asleep, the doors are shut, the muleteer rings his bells through empty streets . . . And we are snoring, or scratching our heads, or lying on our beds meditating on endless deceits.[2]

On the mountainside,

they gaze already upon the things of the Kingdom, holding converse with groves and mountains, springs and with great quietness and solitude . . . their souls free, refined and light, and far purer than the finest air. . . . Their

---

1. A. J. Festugière, *Antioche païenne et chrétienne*, pp. 245–289 and P. Canivet, *Le monachisme syrien selon Théodoret de Cyr*, pp. 114–132.

2. John Chrysostom, *Hom. 14 in I Tim.* 3: *Patrologia Graeca* 62: 575, in P. Schaff, trans. *Library of the Nicene and Post-Nicene Fathers*, 13: 455–456.

work is Adam's work in Paradise.[3] Take a long journey to visit them . . .
[John Chrysostom would tell his congregation] They have dropped anchor in
a safe port, drawing all men to their own calm.[4]

In the 370s, John, the son of a well-placed town clerk, felt the call
of these wild men of the mountains. Two years in a cave on Mount
Silpios proved enough for him. His gastric system permanently im-
paired by long fasts, half-dead with the winter cold, young John came
back into town. In Spring 381, he was ordained a deacon, and, in 386,
a priest. The city had claimed him for herself. For the next twelve
years, the Great Church of Antioch echoed with an oratory of quite
uncanny talent. John earned his later name, Chrysostom—John "Golden
Mouth"—on those occasions. As a deacon and young priest, John was
the link between the feelings of the Antiochene Christians and their
increasingly remote and preoccupied bishop. The Christian householders of Antioch were his audience. He identified with them with
the instinctive, almost mediumistic sensitivity of a great *rhetor*, conjuring up their own most unquestioned prejudices in support of his
message. "I know no other life but you and the care of souls."[5]

John Chrysostom was the most gifted Christian preacher of his age.
He was the last of the great urban *rhetors* of the ancient world. Yet his
sermons tolled the death knell of the ancient city. The poignant, tragically unrealized wish of his life was to be able to speak of Antioch as
a totally Christian city. The themes of marriage, of the household, and
of sexuality bulk so large in his sermons because it was through such
themes that John wished to express a new view of the civic community. The body and its vulnerability, and especially its universal vulnerability to sexual shame and to sexual temptation, became, for Chrysostom, the one sure compass that would enable the Christians of
Antioch to find their way in an urban landscape whose ancient, profane landmarks, so he dearly hoped, would soon disappear.

The practice of virginity, in John's opinion, posed a direct challenge
to the city. The church of Antioch already protected some three thousand virgins and widows.[6] The young priest, in his late twenties, took

3. *Hom. in Matt.* 68.3: *Patrologia Graeca* 57: 643, in G. Prevost, trans., *Library of the
Nicene and Post-Nicene Fathers*, 10:417–418.

4. *Hom.* 14 in I Tim. 3: 575, in Schaff, trans., p. 455.

5. *Hom.* 9 de statuis 1: *P.G.* 49: 103; see esp. Festugière, *Antioche*, pp. 181–220 and R.
L. Wilken, *John Chrysostom and the Jews. Rhetoric and Reality in the Late Fourth Century*,
pp. 5–10.

6. *Hom. in Matt.* 66.3: 630.

up their cause with gusto.[7] So many unused bodies showed that the passing of the ages had slowed the ancient, civic urge that had once led good citizens to provide for their city by marrying and begetting children. Marriage was a superfluity rendered necessary only by the fall of Adam: it had entered human existence "dragged on to the stage in death's somber train."[8]

Marriage and the pangs of labor, sensual pleasure and sexual joining, the gaining of wealth and the care of great estates, food and clothing, the labor of the farm and the sailing of the seas, arts and architecture, cities and households;[9]

all these would sink back into the vast stillness of the mountainside, as the earth fell silent before the coming of the Lord: "The things of the Resurrection stand at the door."[10]

Understatement was not a quality valued in a late antique rhetor, and John may have been a young man when he composed his treatise *On Virginity*. He was only too well aware that he addressed a captivated audience, that pressed into the Great Church so as to hear their brilliant priest speak, trooping out again immediately after the sermon, "as if I were a concert performance!"[11] Many of John's more flamboyant remarks on virginity were made under the discreet pressure of his situation as a rhetorical "star" in Antioch. He frequently spoke *pour épater les bourgeois*. The difference in tone between John's sermons and the treatise of Gregory of Nyssa is striking. With John, statements that had more usually circulated in the quiet study-circles of the converted, among the disciples of Methodius of Olympus and in the rural stillness of Annesi, now rang out defiantly beneath the dome of a great city church. The drift of John's preaching was plain. His aim was to rob the city of its most tenacious myth—the myth that its citizens had a duty to contribute to the continued glory of their native Antioch by marrying. Instead, he repeatedly told his Christian audiences that their bodies belonged to themselves, and no longer to the city.

Throughout his sermons, and not only in his star performance *On*

---

7. See the edition with commentary of H. Musurillo and B. Grillet, *Jean Chrysostome: La Virginité*, Sources chrétiennes 125; now trans. by Sally R. Shore, *John Chrysostom: On Virginity, Against Remarriage*. See also *De virg.* 14.3, p. 140.

8. 15.2. 19–23, p. 143.   9. 73.4. 63–67, p. 354.   10. 73.1.6, p. 350.

11. *De sacerdotio* 5.1: P.G. 48: 673.

Virginity, Chrysostom insisted that young men and women were no longer married so that their sexual energies might contribute to the city by producing children. They married, rather, so as to help each other to control their own bodies. An awareness of the sexual dangers that lurked in the young body, and not a sense of duty to the civic community, brought the Christian couple together. In his *On Virginity*, Chrysostom even went so far as to assert that the earth was already fully populated. The growth of civilization had brought the age of reproductive sex to an end. Indeed, in his effort to make his case, John even fell back on an ancient rhetorical argument in favor of homosexual love: pederasty, a rhetor had once insisted, represented the final refinement of love-making, in a society delivered, by its populousness, from the need for exclusively heterosexual relations![12]

In the Christian era, after Christ had preached virginity and the earth had been filled with human offspring, marriage was allowed to linger, on sufferance. Marriage served to place a limit on the sexual drives: it was there *by reason of fornications.*[13] Men did not marry women so as to check death by begetting children, as Gregory of Nyssa had insisted, with an ancient man's pathos, "but rather so as to bring down the high temperature" of their sexual needs.[14]

Women presumably did so for the same reason; but John, like many of his male Christian contemporaries, tended to present the sexual drives of women as weak compared with those of men.[15] For the young man, marriage was a "safe harbor." Like the late Roman harbors of the coasts of Syria and Cilicia, the walls of the married household acted as a simple breakwater: they created a tract of still water beyond which raged a deep salt ocean of potential debauch.[16] Seldom have the consequences latent in the original, lopsided character of Paul's presentation of marriage in the seventh chapter of his First Letter to the Corinthians been spelled out more clearly, and embraced with greater verve.

John's was a deliberately anxious vision. It stressed the power of sexuality in the young. "How shall we tie down this wild beast? What

---

12. *De virg.* 19.1, p. 156; Ps.-Lucian, *Amores* 35, in M. D. MacLeod, ed., *Lucian*, 8:208.

13. *De Virg.* 50.1.3–4, p. 284, citing I Cor. 7:2. *Dia de tas porneias*: "Nevertheless [to avoid] fornication, let every man have his own wife, and let every woman have her own husband." [Authorized Version].

14. Ibid. 19.1–2, p. 158.   15. *Hom. 10 in II Tim.* 3: P.G. 62: 659.

16. *De virg.* 9.6–10, p. 120.

shall we contrive? How shall we place a bridle on it? I know none, save only the restraint of hell-fire."[17]

He emphasized the dangers of sexual desire in the young largely in order to reinforce the structures of the Christian household against the perilous freedom of the great city. The father was to act as the undisputed head of the household. His anger was to be feared as if it were the wrath of God. He would help his sons and daughters to control their sexual urges by arranging early marriages for them.[18] Once married and established in their own household, the young husband and wife were to cling together, in order to protect each other, by means of the "suppressant drug" of sufficiently regular intercourse, from the dangerous tides of lust that lapped at their bedroom door—pretty girls in the servant's quarters and, beyond the walls of the Christian court-yard, the beguiling pleasures of the city. Because it led to the lasting joys of legitimate children, married intercourse was what young men needed: it kept them away from the transient pleasures of the brothel.[19]

John's was a bleak and deliberately atomistic vision that has elicited little sympathy from modern readers.[20] We must, however, realize that it was the shadow-side of Chrysostom's great hope—the creation of a new form of urban community through the reform of the Christian household.

Standing in the Great Church of Antioch, John saw himself, above all, as the "ambassador of another city . . . the ambassador of the poor."[21] It is a serious error of perspective to see him only as the preacher of sexual control. In one series of sermons on the Gospel of Saint Matthew, he touched on the issue of almsgiving on forty occasions, thirteen times on the state of the poor, thirty times on avarice, and twenty times on the abuse of wealth:[22]

17. *De inani gloria* 76, in A. M. Malingrey, ed., *Jean Chrysostome: Sur la vaine gloire et l'éducation des enfants*, p. 178; M. L. W. Laistner, trans., *Christianity and Pagan Culture in the later Roman Empire*, p. 117.

18. *De inani gloria* 44, 81; Malingrey, pp. 142, and 186–188; Laistner, pp. 106, 119–120.

19. *Hom. 12 in Coloss.* 5: P.G. 62: 388; *In illud "Propter fornicationes"*: P.G. 51: 210; *Hom. 12 in I Cor.* 5: P.G. 61: 102.

20. See esp. Elizabeth Clark, *Jerome, Chrysostom and Friends*, pp. 1–34. The bleak portrayal of Byzantine life in Cyril Mango, *Byzantium, The Empire of New Rome*, pp. 225–229 is drawn exclusively from the works of Chrysostom.

21. *De elemosyna* 1: P.G. 51: 261.

22. C. Baur, *John Chrysostom and his times*, 1:217; see esp. A. Natali, "Église et évergétisme à Antioche à la fin du iveme siècle d'après Jean Chrysostome."

How long will you not cease from continually introducing poor men and beggars into your sermons, prophesying disaster to us and our own future impoverishment, so as to make beggars of us all?[23]

Antioch was unlike Cappadocia. In Caesarea, Basil had faced the problems caused by terrible droughts that had thrown a starving peasantry into the little cities of the region. Antioch, by contrast, was a city of a quarter of a million inhabitants, surrounded by a rich agrarian hinterland. It did not need to fear famine.[24] Poverty was not the result of sudden catastrophes. Rather, what John saw all around him was a poverty built into the structures of urban life. Scenes of indigence that bruised the heart formed an unchanging backdrop to the life of the city:

wandering about like dogs in the alleys, [the poor] haunt the corners of the streets, they enter into the courtyards of great houses, they cry from their cellars, calling for charity.[25]

Beggars were forced to become buffoons in the hope of alms. They chewed on old shoes; they drove nails into their heads; they lay in frozen puddles; most terrible of all, they gave their children to be maimed in order to awaken compassion:[26] "and all this in Antioch, where men were first called Christians, Antioch wherein are bred the most civilized of mankind."[27]

A menacing human *débris* clustered around the porticoes of the Great Church. The members of John's congregation would have had to brush past the outstretched hands of the beggars on their way to pray in the basilica:

When you are weary of praying, and do not receive, consider how often you have heard a poor man calling, and have not listened to him. . . .[28]

---

23. *Hom. 30 in I Cor.*5: *P.G.* 61: 256, in T. W. Chambers, trans., *Library of the Nicene Fathers*, 12:180.

24. J. H. W. G. Liebeschuetz, *Antioch*, pp. 69–74.

25. *Hom. 11 in I Cor.* 10: 113, trans. p. 63, and *Hom. 13* 5: 113, trans. p. 76.

26. *Hom. 21 in I Cor.* 5: 177. This would remain true for the Islamic cities in the same area, see C. E. Bosworth, *The Medieval Islamic Underworld Vol. 1: The Banū Sūsān in Arabic Life and Lore*, 37–38, on the Mushaʿʿib, "the Improver," who made children better able to act as beggars by crippling them.

27. *Hom. 21 in I Cor.* 6: 178, p. 124.   28. *Hom. 11 in I Thess.* 30: 466, p. 373.

It is not for stretching out your hands [in the *orans* gesture of the Early Christian] that you will be heard. Stretch forth your hands, not to heaven but to the poor.[29]

In the course of his sixteen years at Antioch, the terrible weight of the poor came to press in on John. It left him in no doubt as to the fundamental duty of all Christians:

For the greatest of things is charity, an austere life-style and the giving of alms, which hits a higher peak of virtue than does virginity.[30] For without virginity, indeed, it is possible to see the Kingdom, but without almsgiving this cannot be.[31]

When John preached on the ideal relationship of husband and wife within the Christian household, we can always sense, behind the household, the somber presence of the poor and the challenge of Mount Silpios. John was unlike Basil of Caesarea in this respect. He did not expect the holy men of the mountains to come down, in great numbers, to minister to the needs of the city.[32] He feared, rather, that excessive admiration for the life of the monks might provide the Christian householders of the city with an alibi for abandoning their own quest for Christian perfection. It was only too easy for the average Antiochene to think that such things as Scripture-reading, chastity, and the support of the poor could be safely left to the monks, the professional Christians:

The Beatitudes of Christ were not addressed to solitaries only. . . . For if it be not possible, in the married state, to perform the duties of solitaries, then all things have perished, and Christian virtue is boxed in.[33] Why, it is just this that makes me sigh, that you think that monks are the only persons properly concerned with decency and chastity.[34] This notion has been the ruin of us all.[35]

If there were to be such things as "brotherhoods" in Antioch—austere cells of observant Christians committed to the care of the poor—they

---

29. *Hom.* 1 *in II Tim.* 606, p. 476.

30. *In Matt.* 46.4: 480–481, p. 291.   31. Ibid. 47.4: 486, p. 295.

32. This does not imply that John did not admire the monks or that he was unaware of their social activities: see esp. J. M. Leroux, "Saint Jean Chrysostome et le monachisme," in C. Kannengiesser, ed., *Jean Chrysostome et Augustin.*

33. *Hom.* 7 *in Hebr.* 7: P.G. 63: 67–68, in F. Gardner, trans., *Library of the Nicene and Post-Nicene Fathers* (Great Rapids, Mich.: Eerdmans 1978), 14:402.

34. *In Matt.* 7.8: 81, p. 49.   35. 2.10: 29–30, p. 13.

were to be none other than the existing Christian households. Each married couple, down to its solemn grace for meals, was to bring into the midst of the turbulent and hard-hearted city a touch of the Christian perfection practiced by the monks in the clean, city-less air of the mountaintops.[36]

In his sermons, John turned frequently to a topic long congenial to Greek males: *oikonomia*, advice on the creation of a model household. Much of his preaching on marriage and sexuality falls under that well-worn rubric.[37] Manipulating with ease a long tradition, that reached back through Plutarch to Xenophon, John made his position plain on issues that lay close to his heart. The successful running of a Christian household demanded the close collaboration of husband and wife. It assumed the dominance of the male within the family, of the husband over his wife, and of the father over his children.[38] By successfully absorbing the young wife into his household, the husband would cut her off from the alluring "vainglory" of civic life.[39] Gently, but firmly, she was to be molded, "like wax," by her husband.[40] She and her children were to be persuaded to adopt the same inward-looking austerity as himself. She would learn to cut back on her jewelry and dress; for she must not walk past the poor with the price of many dinners hanging from her ears.[41]

By appealing to the Greek and Jewish idyll of the biddable wife, "nailed" to the safe piety of domestic space, behind the walls of her husband's courtyard,[42] John hoped to integrate the young woman into a household whose meticulous discipline made of it a little monastery, ruled by the same precepts of the Gospel as those meditated by the monks on the distant mountainside. The money saved on public ex-

---

36. 55.5: 545.

37. This aspect of Greek attitudes to marriage has been most perceptively expounded by M. Foucault, *L'usage des plaisirs*, pp. 157–203, in R. Hurley, trans., *The Use of Pleasures*, pp. 143–184.

38. Carlo Scaglioni, "Ideale coniugale e familiare in Giovanni Crisostomo," in R. Cantalamessa, ed., *Etica sessuale e matrimonio nel cristianesimo delle origini*, is a responsible and clear survey; see now *St. John Chrysostom: On Marriage and Family Life*, C. P. Roth and D. Anderson, trans. for a convenient collection of texts.

39. *Hom. 20 in Ephes.* 8–9: P.G. 62: 146–148. The ability of the husband to absorb and make his own a wife who had grown up in a different household is a mystery as profound as baptism: A. Wenger, ed., *Jean Chrysostome: Huit Catéchèses baptismales inédites*, 1.11–12, p. 114.

40. *In Matt.* 30.5: 369.   41. *In Matt.* 89.4: 786.

42. *Hom. 61 in Joh.* 3: P.G. 59: 340.

travagance would be collected, every day, in a poorbox placed beside the marriage bed: it was a Jewish practice, which John reluctantly admired.[43] Households chastened by somber and protective fathers would make John's dream come true: poverty was unnecessary in Antioch, "with God's favor it would be possible for our city to nourish the poor of ten cities."[44]

John elevated the Christian household so as to eclipse the ancient city. He refused to see Antioch as a traditional civic community, bound together by a common civic patriotism, expressed by shared rhythms of collective festivity. He made no secret of the fact that he wished the theater, the hippodrome, even the busy agora, to fall silent forever.[45] The Antioch of his dearest hopes was to be no more than a conglomeration of believing households, joined by a common meeting-place within the spacious courtyards of the Great Church. He wished the doors of the Christian house to swing to, shutting out the murmur of a late classical metropolis. To him, the public life of Antioch was a "Devil's garbage tip," piled high outside the simple walls of Christian houses.[46] Only in individual Christian families would a touch of the holiness associated with the wild men of Mount Silpios survive in the midst of the suffocating profanity of the city.

The late antique city, however, was not to be wished away so easily. Its undiminished, deeply profane vigor mocked John's rhetoric. The forms of marriage ceremony celebrated in Antioch made brutally plain how far from fourth-century reality John's hopes had remained. When they joined their sons and daughters in marriage, the Christian families of the fourth century still breathed a heavy, civic air. A public procession led the unveiled bride through the city to her husband's house.[47] Songs and dances referred in no uncertain terms to love and to sexual exploits: for without a vigorous and, it was hoped, delightful sexual encounter in the marriage-bed, well-begotten sons would not be produced for the city.[48] Priests were rarely invited to these occasions; and those who came were advised to leave early.[49] For a moment, the raucous, whirling world of the theater burst through the walls of the Christian household.[50]

43. *Hom. 43 in I Cor.* 4: 383.   44. *In Matt.* 66.3: 630.

45. *Hom. 15 de statuis* 1: 153–354.   46. *Hom. 12 in I Cor.* 6–7: 105–106.

47. *Hom.* "Propter fornicationes." 2: 210–211.   48. Ibid. 2: 210.

49. *Hom. 48 in Gen.* 6: P.G. 54: 443; *Council of Laodicea*, canon 54, in E. J. Jonkers, ed., *Acta et Symbola Conciliorum quae saeculo quarto habita sunt*, p. 95.

50. "*Propter forn.*" 2: 211.

Nothing could have been more shocking to John. For him, marriage was a private affair, a part of an ascetic grooming, in which the marriage bed served only as a further means to bring the sexual urges of the young to a safe halt. By the ceremonial encouragement of passionate love, the traditional public wedding celebration heaped a very heavy load indeed of the "Devil's manure" around the tender roots of Christian matrimony.[51]

John's attacks on traditional weddings were only a symptom of his deep suspicion of the profane life of the city as a whole. The theater and the games in the circus and Hippodrome were a veritable obsession for him.[52] This was not simply because such games tended to be exuberantly immoral. With his unfailing *rhetor's* talent for finding an adversary, John sensed in the theater the perfect rival to the sense of community that he himself propounded so frequently in the Great Church.

In Antioch, the sense of the continued, joyous existence of a great civic community within a stable Empire had always been expressed through a carefully maintained mood of high good cheer, made available to the citizens of Antioch in their public baths, in their theater, and in their hippodrome. *Apolausis*—the shared enjoyment of the good things of life that only a great city ruled by generous families could savor—was more than self-indulgence: it was a precious collective ritual, a celebration of the will to survive.[53] Antioch was an unruly and divided city. In 387, it had exploded into a potentially catastrophic tax-revolt.[54] Christians, Jews, and pagans had come to eye each other anxiously across widening chasms.[55] The citizen body felt threatened by the press of the immigrant poor; and the families of local notables felt downgraded and pushed aside by powerful persons connected with the Imperial court.[56] In the Hippodrome, at least, Jews, pagans, and Christians could all sit down together, feeling through the long hot afternoons and in the joyous torchlit evenings the heavy swell of be-

51. *Hom. 12 in Coloss.* 4: 387.
52. Scaglioni, "Ideale coniugale," pp. 399–400.
53. Evelyne Patlagean, *Pauvreté économique et pauvreté sociale à Byzance*, pp. 182–183, on the importance of the urban quality of *apolausis*, dependent on the *megalopsychia* of the rich.
54. Studied by R. Browning, "The riot of A.D. 387 in Antioch."
55. Wilken, *John Chrysostom and the Jews*, pp. 29–33.
56. Libanius, *Orations* 2.26–29, 36; and 41.11.

longing to a common civic world.[57] *Apolausis* was the National Anthem of Antioch: not to join in it was to be a traitor to the ancient notion of the city as the most perfect of human communities.

John dearly wished for all that to wither away. What he offered in its stead was a fragile and novel theme. In his preaching on the public ceremonials of Antioch, his stress on the austere seclusion of the Christian household combined with a peculiarly sharp, ascetic sense of the privacy of the individual human body. By presenting the body, with great insistence, as a permanent abode of sexual desires and as universally vulnerable to personal sexual shame, John ensured that central features of the public life of Antioch stood condemned. Everyone knew that the Antiochenes were a notoriously easy-going people.[58] But what many observers mistook for unrepentant frivolity was, in fact, the expression of a civic code of propriety, based on an acute sense of what the bodies of particular persons could and could not do in particular social situations. The festive life of the city demanded moments of easy-going nudity in the great public baths and frank eroticism in its public spectacles.

In fourth-century Antioch, as in so many late classical cities, nudity had remained a fact of life. Nudity and sexual shame were questions of social status: the way people felt about being naked, or seeing others naked, depended to a large extent on their social situation. Thus, at the top of society, nudity in the public baths expressed the utter ease of the well-to-do, moving without a trace of sexual shame in front of their inferiors. An Antiochene lady would strip down in front of her mixed retinue. Her finely-nurtured, milk-white skin, across which lay strands of heavy jewelry, spoke, in itself, of a social gulf between herself and her male servants so huge that no sense of sexual shame could be expected to pass across it.[59]

57. *Huit catéchèses baptismales* 6.15, p. 22. It is noticeable how frequently Jews appear with specially marked seats in the hippodromes of the eastern empire: Alan Cameron, *Circus Factions*, p. 79. These seats expressed an immemorial civic right to participation in such ceremonies, as fellow citizens, despite the growing exclusion of Jews in other areas of the life of the Christian Empire.

58. Festugière, *Antioche*, pp. 63–89; see now Maud W. Gleason, "Festive Satire: Julian's *Misopogon* and the New Year at Antioch."

59. *Hom. 28 in Hebr.* 6:199 and *de inani gloria* 60, Malingrey, p. 158, Laistner, p. 11; compare Clement of Alexandria, *Paedagogus* 3.5: P.G. 18: 600: see E. Barbier, "La signification du cortège représenté sur le couvercle du coffret de 'Projecta,'" on late Roman bathing habits among the upper classes.

At the bottom of the social scale, the lower classes were not expected to be capable of protecting their womenfolk from exposure. The seclusion of one's womenfolk assumed power and wealth. The sexual vulnerability of poor girls was simply part of their general passivity to the powerful. Stage girls splashed naked in the newly constructed water-theaters of Antioch, their shining bodies re-creating the life-giving energy of the Nymphs and Nereids, whose presence in the streams on Mount Silpios brought to the heart of a sweltering Near Eastern city the supreme, sensuous delight of sparkling water. When they did so, to the evident enjoyment of members of John's congregation, a chasm was thought to separate their exposed bodies from the well-to-do Christian ladies and gentlemen who watched them.[60] For these young girls were *atimoi*, civic "non-persons;" they had no right to sexual shame.[61]

Only John was prepared to see in them a shared human body, subject to shared codes of modesty: "For say not this, that she that is stripped is a harlot; but that the nature is the same, and they are bodies alike, both that of the harlot and that of the free woman."[62]

By preaching incessantly on such themes, John wished to create in Antioch a new, more all-embracing sense of community, based on a sense of solidarity with a shared human nature. As a result, his exhortations came to place a quite unusual weight on the human body. For the body was the most vocal spokesman of all, in its manifest vulnerability, of the common descent of all human beings from Adam. John preached a brotherhood of bodies at risk. The two great themes of sexuality and poverty gravitated together, in the rhetoric of John and of many other Christians. Both spoke of a universal vulnerability of the body, to which all men and women were liable, independent of class and civic status. In his sermons, John made brilliantly explicit what was, in effect, a slow change in the climate of his age.

As Christianity gained more power in late Roman society, the sense that all human beings were equal, because leveled into a somber democracy of sexual shame, made itself felt throughout the Mediterranean. In Pontus, a high official, not necessarily a zealous Christian (he had served under the Emperor Julian the Apostate), was careful to point out, when he built a public bath for his locality, that it now

---

60. *In Matt.* 7.7: 79; see G. Traversari, "Tetimimo e Colimbétra. Ultime manifestazioni del teatro antico," pp. 18–19, 23–27.

61. *Hom. 12 in I Cor.* 1: 103.   62. *In Matt.* 6.8: 72.

boasted separate facilities for men and for women, "by reason of modesty."[63] In the Great Church of Antioch, a relatively new wooden partition separated the women's from the men's side, making plain the dangers of mixed company.[64]

The universal risk of sexual desire admitted no pockets of civic tolerance. On no occasion might the charged body be exposed to public view. Joined in a common sense of sexual shame, Christian men and women were urged, by John, to go one step further—to extend the heightened awareness of their own bodies so as to embrace with compassion the bodies of others. They must learn to see the faceless poor as sharing bodies like their own—bodies at risk, bodies gnawed by the bite of famine, disease, and destitution, and subtly ravaged by the common catastrophe of lust. Jerome, a Latin writer, but, like Chrysostom, a rhetor touched, from his youth onward, with nostalgia for the desert, expressed this new sensibility with peculiar sharpness:

He whom we look down upon, whom we cannot bear to see, the very sight of whom causes us to vomit, is the same as we are, formed with us from the self-same clay, compacted of the same elements. Whatever he suffers, we also can suffer. . . .
In silken robes or rags, the same lust holds sway. Desire neither fears the Emperor's purple nor keeps away from the beggar's filth.[65]

In 397, John was hurried across Asia Minor under armed guard, to become the patriarch of Constantinople, the Imperial capital. It was a disastrous choice. In Antioch, John's charisma had been that of a partisan; for the "Catholic" church in Antioch was only one religious group among others. John had striven to extend to his hearers an infectious sense of shared militancy; but he preached as a member of a church that still thought of itself as a minority religion, and so could afford the high-minded fervor of those who had not yet faced the responsibilities of power.[66]

Constantinople, by contrast, was a world capital, and, officially at least, a totally Christian city. Its patriarch had to be "representative;" he had to preside with benign good nature over the one city in the

63. *Studia Pontica* 3, J. G. C. Anderson, F. Cumont and H. Gregoire, eds., pp. 41–42.

64. *In Matt.* 73.3: 677.

65. Jerome, *Letters* 77.6 and 79.10: *Patrologia Latina* 22: 694 and 731.

66. Well seen by Wilken, *John Chrysostom and the Jews*, p. 13.

Roman world that could boast an impeccably Christian origin. In such a role, John was a resounding failure.[67] He instantly slipped into his role as a partisan. Instead of entertaining on a lavish scale, as a good bishop should, he dined alone, fed by the nuns of Olympias.[68] He persuaded Olympias to focus her use of wealth even more austerely than before on the needs of the poor, thus cutting back on those sections of the budget of the church that had provided pensions for retired gentlewomen and entertainment and funds for visiting ecclesiastical dignitaries.[69] He founded a leper colony on the edge of a fashionable suburb.[70] The local monks, bustling urban figures very different from the serene mountain dwellers to whom John was accustomed in Antioch, turned against him. They saw in the zealous Antiochene "a hard, passionate, morose and arrogant man."[71] When he denounced, in general terms, the abuses of the powerful, John's flashing eyes were thought to have come to rest too pointedly on particular dignitaries of the court.[72] By June 404, John was in exile; by September 407, he was dead, killed—perhaps intentionally—by cruel journeying from one place of detention to another in the mountainous fringes of eastern Anatolia.

In exile, John gained some of the chastened majesty of the last hours of Shakespeare's Richard II. His letters to Olympias show us a man and a woman joined under the huge sadness of the shipwreck of their dearest hopes for the Church.[73] The man who, in his younger days as a priest, had juggled unthinkingly with the soiled coin of classical misogyny in order to dissuade monks and clergymen from entering into spiritual companionships with ascetic women, now depended for the

67. The reasons for John's fall have been analyzed with particular skill by J. H. W. G. Liebeschuetz, "Friends and Enemies of John Chrysostom," in Ann Moffatt, ed., *Maistor: Classical, Byzantine and Renaissance Studies for Robert Browning.* See also K. Holum, *Theodosian Empresses,* pp. 70–78.

68. Palladius, *Dialogus de vita Johannis Chrysostomi* 45 and 61, P. R. Coleman-Norton ed., pp. 79, 107–108: *P.G.* 47: 41 and 61; see Liebeschuetz, "Friends and Enemies," pp. 102–106.

69. Palladius, *Dialogus* 5.20, Coleman-Norton, ed., p. 32: *P.G.* 47:20–21; Sozomen, *Ecclesiastical History* 8.9.

70. F. Van Ommeslaeghe, "Jean Chrysostome et Eudoxie," p. 151, citing the account of pseudo-Martyrius, whose value as a source he has reestablished.

71. Sozomen, *Eccles. Hist.* 8.9; see the important study of G. Dagron, "Les moines et la ville: le monachisme à Constantinople."

72. Van Ommeslaeghe, p. 150.

73. *Letters to Olympias* 3 1b, in A. M. Malingrey, ed., *Jean Chrysostome: Lettres à Olympias,* p. 97.

survival of what little remained of his ecclesiastical program on the "finesse" of a woman, "sitting in a small back room," in distant Constantinople.[74] "Was not the Crucified in exile from the first moment of his birth?"[75]

John died as the hero of a whole generation. He had summed up their hopes, and his reputation as a preacher of charismatic power was preserved untarnished through his early, tragic death. In the words of Isidore of Pelusium, like John, an urban priest, an admirer of the desert, and a fine connoisseur of Greek, here was a man whose sermons were such that "the divine Paul himself would not have spoken otherwise, if he had enjoyed John's gift for Attic eloquence."[76]

His failure was more than a personal tragedy; it marked the failure of one possible variant of East Roman Christianity. It was one of the truly significant shipwrecks of the fourth century. In 362, the ferocious loyalty of the Antiochenes to their own, studiously nonconfessional image of the city had made plain to the Emperor Julian that his hopes for a pagan revival were doomed. At the end of the fourth century, Antioch, and then Constantinople, broke the Christian revivalism of John Chrysostom quite as thoroughly. John's vision of the future of a Christian city was as stillborn as had been that planned for Antioch, as a pagan city, by the Apostate Emperor.

To hope that the eastern Mediterranean city would shed its profane traditions by becoming little more than an assemblage of pious Christian households involved a fatal underestimation of the power of the classical sense of the civic community. The East Roman cities retained their ancient festive rituals in order to do justice to a tenacious, pre-Christian civic pride. The governing classes of the cities—good, baptized Christians though they were—continued to make do with what they already had. A cheerful inconsequentiality reigned throughout the fifth and much of the sixth centuries. Public ceremonials remained indelibly profane, erotic, and cruel. Nereids continued to splash in many cities of the Christian East. On many occasions, the local Christian bishop found himself forming a common front with the civil governor to halt throngs of protesting monks who wished such shows to stop.[77]

74. *Letter* 12.1d, pp. 187–188.   75. *Letter* 7. 3c, p. 109.
76. Isidore of Pelusium, *Letters* 5.32: *P.G.* 78: 1347A.
77. Callinicus, *Vita Hypatii* 33; cf. *Barsanuphe et Jean de Gaza: Correspondance* 837, L. Regnault trans., p. 504.

It was largely in monastic circles, and not among the urban clergy, that John's anger against cruelty and oppression continued to burn most fiercely:

An important person took great pleasure in watching wild-beast shows, and hoped for one thing only, to see the fighters wounded by the animals. One day, he fell into danger and cried to God: "Lord, come to my help in this misfortune!" Then the Lord came to him, His body covered with wounds, and said: "This is how you wished to see me; how then have I the strength to help you?"[78]

The average well-to-do householder, of whom Chrysostom had demanded so much in his sermons, was less concerned about such matters. In the middle of the sixth century, Procopius of Caesarea wrote about the Empress Theodora. As a girl, she had performed in the circus of Constantinople. She had appeared dressed in nothing but a G-string; and geese had pecked seeds from between her thighs. A modern reader's sense of the erotic nature of Theodora's act should not dull for us the original, late antique brutality of the scene. Procopius wrote to prove that the Empress had once been a "non-person." What had happened to her body in public made plain that she was a girl of the lower classes: the good Christian senators of Constantinople could look on a body thus exposed with impunity.[79]

Antioch, in particular, held tenaciously to its traditions of profane good cheer. As late as the end of the sixth century, a bishop of Antioch returned from Constantinople with funds, obtained in his official capacity as bishop and spokesman of the city, to restore, yet once again, "the church of Satan"—none other than Chrysostom's dreaded Hippodrome![80]

John's ideal of the Christian household as a lay monastery, closed against the profane world, excluded too much of the life of the city outside its walls. It had little impact at the time. Only with the decline of the cities in the course of the sixth century and the subsequent arrival of the Muslim armies did John's ideal of the city come true: impoverishment and invasion, and not Christian preaching, silenced the

78. *Les Sentences des Pères du Désert. Nouveau recueil*, 442, L. Regnault trans., p. 64; cf. John Chrysostom, *Huit catéchèses baptismales* 1.43, p. 130.

79. Procopius, *Secret History* 9.20; see Averil Cameron, *Procopius*, pp. 81–82.

80. John of Ephesus, *Ecclesiastical History* 5.17, in E. W. Brooks, ed., *Corpus Scriptorum Christianorum Orientalium* 106, pp. 202–203. See also Severus of Antioch, *Homiliae cathedrales* 26, in M. Brière and F. Graffin, eds., *Patrologia Orientalis* 36:540–557, on chariot racing in the early sixth century.

ancient city. In the airless world of the towns of the early middle ages, both in Byzantium and in the Islamic Near East, the sense of privileged domestic space, with the moral values associated with this—a heightened sense of sexual shame, an attitude to marriage determined by sexual needs and by male sexual jealousy, and a further sharpening of the dominance of men over women—finally won out, as John had wished that it should, at the expense of the freer, more public codes associated with the classical city.[81]

A born orator, frequently at the mercy of his own uncanny talent, John had been content to perform set pieces, of little intrinsic originality, on the well-known themes of marriage, sexual desire, and the frailty of women. But these themes lay on the surface of his thought. His deepest concern and this most poignant legacy had been his insistence on solidarity with the shared bodies of the poor. At least his rhetoric of compassion survived. Themes taken directly from his sermons, or from sermons composed in his spirit, entered the great urban chants of the Byzantine church. The *kontakia* of Romanos Melodes, composed in the early sixth century, embraced the urban community in a spider-fine web of common feeling. They instilled, with heartfelt artistry, a sense of shared suffering, of shared fasting, of a shared duty to feed the city's poor.[82]

Chanted in the urban churches at great festivals, the solemn music of the *kontakia* maintained, for early Byzantines, a language of compassion that had first been carried by the voice of Chrysostom. Echoing a sermon of Chrysostom, Romanos insisted, in his great hymn *On the Ten Virgins*, that Christ regarded compassion for the poor, and not their virginity, as the rich oil with which the virgins must prime their lamps for His coming:

I renounce the fasts   of those who show no mercy.
I accept the prayers   of those who eat with kindness.
I hate all virgins   who shun human feeling.
I love the married   who love their fellow-creatures.
[and Romanos added, speaking of himself]

81. This point is made with particular force and perceptiveness by A. Kazhdan and A. Cutler, "Continuity and Discontinuity in Byzantine History," pp. 447–448 and 463–464, and by A. Kazhdan, with G. Constable, *People and Power in Byzantium*, pp. 29–34, 70–75. Hugh Kennedy, "From *Polis* to *Madina*: Urban Change in Late Antique and Early Islamic Syria," and "The Last Century of Byzantine Syria: A Reinterpretation," are crucial studies.

82. J. Grosdidier de Matons, *Romanos le Mélode*, pp. 22–23, 270–283.

I do not do what I now say, and what I urge the people.
For this reason, I fall down. Oh Savior, give me tears,
Contrition in my heart, and in all those who hear me.[83]

It is important to complete our survey of the Christian East by turning
now to the Syrian world that abutted John's Antioch, to see how other
Christians, formed by significantly different spiritual traditions, confronted the problems on which John had expended so much eloquence.

83. Romanos Melodes, *Hymn 31* 24.5–8 and 31.2–3, in J. Grosdidier de Matons, ed.,
Romanos le Mélode: Hymnes III, pp. 356, 364.

SIXTEEN

"These Are Our Angels": Syria

Antioch was a great Greek metropolis. It looked westward, into the
Mediterranean. Many of the ascetics who had come to settle in the
mountains around the city belonged to a profoundly different world.
They had been formed in the spiritual culture of eastern Syria. Some
had followed the call of the Spirit, in a life of holy vagrancy, that had
led them from their homelands near the Euphrates to the threshold of
the third largest city in the Roman Empire. They would even make an
occasional appearance at the gates of Antioch, impressing the inhabitants with pithy sayings in pidgin-Greek.[1] Most spoke only Syriac.[2] It
was enough to go out to "reap a blessing from their holy hands," and
to look with admiration at their gaunt bodies and stark living conditions.[3] John Chrysostom advised fathers worried by the sexual stir-

---

1. Theodoret, *Historia Religiosa* 8.2: *Patrologia Graeca* 82: 136B, now excellently translated by R. M. Price, *Theodoret of Cyrrhus: A History of the Monks of Syria*, p. 73.
2. E.g., Macedonius in Theodoret, *Hist. Relig.* 13.4 and 7: 1401CD and 1404D; Price,
p. 101–102 and 103.
3. Ibid. 8.15: 1377B; p. 79.

rings of their adolescent sons to take them on Sunday walks to visit a favorite holy man.[4] "These are our angels. . . ."[5]

Theodoret, later Bishop of Cyrrhus, was born in 393, four years before Chrysostom's fateful transfer to Constantinople.[6] He came from a family already "caught in the net" of intense dependence on a local hermit, Peter the Galatian (one of the rare Greek-speakers on the mountainside.)[7] The relationship had developed slowly. Theodoret's mother had first visited Peter when she was twenty-three, to seek a cure for an eye infection, on the advice of a high ranking lady whom he had cured of the same disease. It was by visits to Peter's cell (not, one suspects, by listening to the elegant misogyny of John's sermons against the vanity of women) that she began to change her dress style, abandoning "ear-rings, necklaces . . . and elaborate dress woven from silken thread."[8] Coming from a city where the segregation of the sexes was a matter of anxious concern for Christian moralists, she found that she could pour out her heart to this impassive figure, "seizing his feet, imploring loudly."[9] Her failure to conceive did not worry her at that time. A mature woman (she was thirty when Theodoret was born) she had wished to escape Hellfire by pursuing a devout life, not to be "brought to the very gates of death" by childbirth.[10] "But childlessness greatly distressed my father, who went round everywhere, begging the servants of God [the hermits] to ask for children."[11] After three years, one such hermit summoned her: "he would ask for a child and obtain one [but] it would be fitting to give the child back to God Who gave it."[12]

Only after reassurance that her child was a holy thing, blessed from the womb, was Theodoret's mother able to face pregnancy and a near-lethal childbirth. Theodoret was born already dedicated to God. Once a week, the little boy would walk out with his mother and climb the

4. John Chrysostom, de inani gloria 78, in A. M. Malingrey, Jean Chrysostome: Sur la vaine gloire et l'éducation des enfants, p. 180.

5. John Chrys. Hom. 55 in Matt. 6: P.G. 57: 548.

6. See esp. P. Canivet, Le monachisme syrien selon Théodoret de Cyr, pp. 7–63 and P. Canivet and A. Leroy-Molinghen, Théodoret de Cyr: Histoire des Moines de Syrie; Price, Theodoret of Cyrrhus, pp. ix–xxxvi is an outstanding introduction.

7. Theodoret, Hist. Relig. 9.7: 1384A: Price, p. 84.

8. 9.6: 1383B; p. 83.   9. 9.7: 1384A; p. 84.

10. 9.14: 1388A; p. 87; compare Ephraim the Syrian, Hymn 6. 29, in F. Graffin, trans., "Hymnes inédits de S. Éphrem sur la virginité," p. 233.

11. Theodoret. Hist. Relig. 13.16: 1408D–1409A; p. 106.   12. 13.16: 1409A; p. 106.

ladder that led to the upper story of a deserted tomb-house in which Peter lived with his companion, Daniel. He would listen as the holy men discussed his future. Old Daniel "often set me on his knees and fed me with grapes and bread."[13]

It is important to linger on these gentle anecdotes. They take us into the heart of the impact of the ascetic movement on the life of Christian families. For all the shrill public rhetoric deployed in favor of continence and virginity, ascetic values and ascetic vocations were nurtured in this intensely personal and informal manner. Theodoret grew up in the generation after the death of Chrysostom. He recalled his own childhood when he wrote his *Religious History* (or *History of the Lovers of God*) in around 440. All over the Mediterranean, similar patterns of behavior had been established. Young men now grew up with ascetic heroes to whom they might gravitate. In Arles, the father of Honoratus (a near contemporary of Theodoret) wanted to share in his son's youth by keeping him interested in the good life of a gentleman—hunting and play; but Honoratus had already begun to prefer the company of priests and holy monks.[14]

Above all, it was through the validation of conception and childbirth that the hand of the holy man reached into the Christian family. Theodoret's mother was only one of many women known to us who plainly felt that only a child marked out for a sacred life would redeem their own loss of virginity and exposure to the remorseless physical disruption of childbirth. Theodoret the boy, Macrina the girl: they bore the hopes for sanctity that their own mothers had been constrained to abandon on becoming married.[15] Men shared these preoccupations. Ajax of Gaza was widely admired because, although he had an exceptionally beautiful wife, he slept with her on only three occasions, producing three boys, two of whom became monks, leaving the third to carry on the family name![16]

It was not inevitable that such dedicated boys would find their way out onto the mountainsides or into the desert. Christian families admired "angelic" holy men; but the careers that they envisioned even

---

13. 9.4: 1381A; p. 83.

14. Hilarius of Arles, *Sermo de vita sancti Honorati* 6, in S. Cavallin, ed., *Vitae Sanctorum Honorati et Hilarii*, p. 53.

15. E.g., Martha, the mother of Symeon the Younger: P. van den Ven, *La vie ancienne de S. Syméon Stylite le Jeune* 2, 1:3–4.

16. Sozomen, *Ecclesiastical History* 7.28.

for those of their sons who had been consecrated to God were usually limited to their home town. Theodoret grew up in the shadow of the altar. He was to be a reader and a priest in the Church of Antioch. He received, in the city, a high Greek culture very different from that of his Syriac-speaking heroes.[17] But he was a clergyman already vowed to God and hence to continence. Maris of Omeros, a holy man whom Theodoret later came to know, had grown up in his village very much as Theodoret had grown up in Antioch:

He told me [that] his body had remained chaste as it had left his mother's womb, and this although he had taken part in many festivals of the martyrs when young and captivated the crowds [as a reader of the church] with the beauty of his voice.[18]

Large local churches depended on a steady supply of boys such as Theodoret, dedicated at birth, proud to have remained virgins, and enthusiastic admirers of the ascetic life.[19] These zealous young men, however, were frequently ruled by bishops and senior clergymen who belonged to a more old-fashioned world. They had married. Some had even sown their wild oats. John's suave predecessor at Constantinople, Nectarius, brought with him to the capital a doctor friend who had shared amorous escapades with him as a young man.[20] The Bishop of Ephesus had once been in the habit of dancing with chorus-girls on his shoulders at bachelor parties.[21] Not surprisingly, a certain coldness existed between two such very different groups of candidates for preferment in the church.

Debates on asceticism and on the value of married life would not have been so explosive, in the late fourth and early fifth centuries, if they had not coincided with tensions—almost with a war of the generations—within the clergy itself. The studied alienation of Jerome is so well known from his dazzling satires of clerical life that we often forget that Jerome's stormy career was part of a Mediterranean-wide pattern. The ascetic priest who rewrote the legend and recorded the miracles of Saint Thecla at Seleucia was a minor Greek Jerome: he had

---

17. Canivet, *Le monachisme syrien*, pp. 15–24.
18. Theodoret, *Hist. Relig.* 20.2: 1429BC; p. 131.
19. Gaudentius of Brescia, *Tractatus* 8: *Patrologia Latina* 20: 889A.
20. Sozomen, *Eccles. Hist.* 7.8, 10.
21. Palladius, *Dialogus de vita Johannis Chrysostomi* 15 (52): *P.G.* 47: 52.

no compunction about referring to his bishops as "that guttersnipe" and *"Schweinhund."*[22]

Literary jousts with conservative Christians, in the form of stirring panegyrics on virginity and vivid portrayals of the ills of marriage, enlivened the life of the more zealous members of the clergy. They now rest heavy on the shelves of modern libraries, contributing appreciably to the lurid reputation of this age among their modern readers. They did not, necessarily, affect the laity. The laity wanted holy persons and holy shrines. In Syria and in neighboring Cilicia (along the southeastern coast of Turkey), we can trace the way figures of uncanny, challenging strangeness were called upon to minister to the day-to-day needs of married persons. It was, indeed, precisely their strangeness that made them so available to their clients.

They were "angelic" persons. They were the products of a spiritual tradition whose roots lay in the Encratite movement of the second century A.D. They and those who consulted them believed that the Spirit of God could raise men and women above the normal constraints and perils of the human condition. Dedicated to a ferocious and fully visible asceticism and living a life shorn of all the normal attributes of human beings—perched in the open air on crags near their villages or, a little later, on the top of great columns—persons rendered so irrefragably sacred by the Holy Spirit could touch all that was most profane in the life of their admirers.[23] They could grapple with the polluted power and violence of the mighty in a manner that urban clergymen could never hope to do.[24] Though strictly segregated on most occasions from their women clients, they could receive, unmoved, the full charge of their love and need for solace. Childbirth, fertility, and marital wrongs were normal topics of consultation.

A woman of noble family, who shared the yoke of marriage with a debauched husband, came to the blessed man [Aphrahat] bewailing her misfortune. She told how her husband, in his attachment to a concubine, had been bewitched by some magical enchantment. . . . The woman told this standing in front of the outer door . . . for he . . . never admitted any woman inside. . . .

22. G. Dagron, *Vie et Miracles de Sainte Thècle* 12 and 46, Subsidia Hagiographica 62:318, 410—the Greek is "bear-hog."

23. Peter Brown, "The Rise and Function of the Holy Man in Late Antiquity," now in *Society and the Holy in Late Antiquity*, pp. 130–132.

24. E.g., the intervention of Macedonius after the Riot of the Statues in 387: Theodoret, *Hist. Relig.* 13.7: 1404CD; p. 103.

Taking pity on the woman who implored loudly, he quenched the power of magic by prayer, and blessing by divine invocation a flask of oil she had brought, told her to anoint herself with it. Following these instructions, the woman transferred to herself her husband's love, and induced him to prefer the lawful bed.[25]

Further to the West, along the coast of Cilicia at Seleucia (Silifke), we can see, at the great shrine of Saint Thecla outside the city (at Meryemlik), a figure still vibrant with radical associations, in the process of becoming encrusted with a coral reef of utterly mundane, down-to-earth preoccupations.[26] A legendary heroine, Thecla had come to mean many different things to different people. Her defense of her virginity made her a "monument of perpetual chastity" for sheltered nuns, a silent guardian figure with whom a Macrina could identify herself.[27] At the same time, the story of her daring journeys with Saint Paul provided a model for the self-exiled Melania, enabling her admirers to acclaim Melania as a "second Thecla."[28] Ascetic women would walk from Syria, fasting all the way, to visit her shrine.[29] Aristocratic women from the West, such as Egeria—restless souls disenchanted with the torpor of their local church—would come to Thecla's sanctuary and absorb the dramatic epic of her life. They would have found there many ascetic "renouncers," male and female, who had modeled themselves on Thecla as she was known through the many versions of her legend.[30]

Yet the Thecla of the day-to-day miracles eluded the precise and radical definition of her person contained in the *Life*. A hauntingly ambiguous figure, she would appear in visions, her human attributes swallowed up in an "angelic" shimmer, and dressed in a robe that was neither clearly male nor female.[31] Like the living holy man Aphrahat, Thecla would help wronged wives, counseling soap from her shrine as a love potion.[32] She showed far fewer qualms than did the prim

25. Theodoret, *Hist. Relig.* 8.13: 1376D–1377A; p. 78.

26. Dagron, *Vie et Miracles de Sainte Thècle*, pp. 55–139 is essential.

27. Isidore of Pelusium, *Letters* 1.87: *P.G.* 78: 214A; see now Ruth Albrecht, *Das Leben der heiligen Makrina auf dem Hintergrund der Thekla-Traditionen*, Forschungen zur Kirchen- und Dogmengeschichte 38, pp. 286–307.

28. Rufinus, *Apologia* 2.26.   29. Theodoret, *Hist. Relig.* 29.7: 1492C; p. 185.

30. Egeria, *Peregrinatio* 22.2–23.6, in P. Geyer, ed., *Itinera Hierosolymitana, Corpus Scriptorum Ecclesiasticorum Latinorum* 39, pp. 69–70. See the most interesting suggestion of Henry Chadwick, *Priscillian of Avila*, pp. 166–167.

31. *Vie et Miracles de Sainte Thècle* 14, Dagron, p. 328; see esp. pp. 97–99.

32. Ibid. 42, p. 401; cf. 20, p. 345.

ascetic priest who recorded her miracles, in engaging with the "vulgar, Jewish" hopes and fears associated with sterility, love-making, and pregnancy.[33] Outside the shrine, Thecla, the wild virgin girl bewitched by the message of Paul, could now be invoked, on her feast day, to give her blessing to an orderly hierarchy, in which every category of woman was expected to strive to maintain the purity appropriate to her state:

Let the widow maintain her affection for her dead husband as if he was to return to life. Let the wedded wife kill in herself all wish for pleasure with others. Let those who throb with fornication dampen their fire with the dew of matrimony.[34]

Far to the East of Antioch, in Edessa and Nisibis (Urfa and Nusaybin), the Syriac hymns of Ephraim the Syrian, who died in 373, served as the equivalent of the urban rhetoric of John Chrysostom. They filled the basilicas of the city with chants of extraordinary poetic power. The ancient Syrian institution of the Sons and Daughters of the Covenant placed groups of continent ascetics at the heart of the urban congregation: it was their pure voices—and not the Attic eloquence of a preacher such as John—that brought the ascetic message to the married householders.[35] Ephraim looked out of Edessa, his adopted city, at the men of the mountains with the same poignant admiration for distant heroes as did Chrysostom and Theodoret.[36] For all his wonder at their way of life, Ephraim's hymns gave a voice, also, to the hopes and tragedies of the married. Austerely ascetic,

He was a fine sight as he stood among the [virgin] sisters, singing a melody of praise.[37] Ephraim was the greatest poet of the patristic age and, perhaps, the only *theologian-poet* to rank beside Dante.[38]

Only a great poet could have done justice to the elemental paradox of late antique Christianity: an "angelic," ascetic way of life depended,

33. Ibid. 14, p. 326; see pp. 131:135.
34. M. Aubineau, "Le Panégyrique de Thècle attribué à Jean Chrysostome," pp. 352.
35. See esp. R. Murray, *Symbols of Church and Kingdom: A Study in Early Syrian Tradition*, pp. 29–32, and s.v. Ephraem Syrus, *Theologische Realenzyklopädie* (Berlin: de Gruyter 1982), 9:755–762; see now Sidney H. Griffith, "Ephraem, the Deacon of Edessa, and the Church of the Empire," in T. Halton and J. P. Williman, eds., *Diakonia: Studies in Honor of Robert T. Meyer.*
36. E. Beck, "Asketentum und Mönchtum bei Ephraem," pp. 356–361.
37. *Life of Ephraim* 31, cited in Murray, *Symbols of Church and Kingdom*, p. 30, n 1.
38. Murray, *Symbols of Church and Kingdom*, p. 131.

for its very existence, on the wild rootstock of intercourse and child-bearing. Marriage was the mother of virginity, as surely as the human flesh and blood of Mary gave human life to the infant Christ. The married had a share in the rewards of the "angelic" life, based on the ancient priority of the womb:

I will have my part in your high vision.
Because I carried you safe in my womb,
I will be shielded from the fires of Hell.
Because I brought you with pain into this world,
By your prayers, I shall pass the narrow gate into Eden.
Because I have not held you back from Paradise Regained on earth,
I will have my share in your reward—the Paradise above.[39]

Married persons would come to rest on the slopes of Paradise.

Ephraim was not one to ignore the carnage of the marriage bed. Its terrible cost demanded a reward:

There find their sweet repose
Wives with bodies broken,
Through pregnancy's dire curse,
Through birth's hard labors.
There do they see the babes,
That they buried with sighs,
Feed like the new born lambs,
Deep in the green of the Garden.[40]

By contrast to such verses, John's Attic idyll of the Christian household seems as frigid as the polished marble figures of husband and wife that had stood, in formal harmony, on the sarcophagi of well-to-do Greeks.

The juxtaposition of the profane world of the married and the "angelic" life of the ascetics was so close, in Syria, largely because the notional chasm that separated the average Christian from such "angels" was so profound. The Holy Spirit had descended on them, filling their bodies with otherworldly power. They lived a life "in imitation of the angels." In the Syrian tradition "imitation of the angels" admitted more vivid gestures than it did in the Greek world. The purity of the body was not, as it was for an Athanasius or a Gregory of Nyssa, a poignant, Platonic echo of an ever-distant spiritual reality. In Syrian

39. Ephraim, *Hymn* 9. 73–75, in Graffin, trans., *L'Orient syrien* (1961) 6:241.
40. Adapted from the beautiful translation of R. Lavenant, *Éphrem de Nisibe: Hymnes sur le Paradis* 8.8, p. 98.

thought, spiritual and physical lived side by side. Only a thin veil separated the world of the seen from the unseen realities that glowed beneath its surface. It was possible to use the body in a far more dramatic manner. The ascetic could assert, through singularly austere self-mortification, the visible, physical freedom of the body from the restraints of normal human living. By so doing, the ascetics were thought to have brought the vibrant energy of the angels through the half-translucent curtain that separated the unseen hosts of Heaven from the present world.[41] Robed in the Holy Spirit, human flesh could do on earth what the angels did in heaven.

An angel was a "wakeful" being.[42] It was a being set free by untiring awareness of the presence of God. By contrast, food and work defined the human condition. The ache of the belly and the back-breaking labor of the fields separated a care-worn humanity from the fiery, care-free spirits that hovered so close to earth:

The heavenly things were created together [with the earthly things], but the former are nourished by the rays of the Divine Presence, whilst the latter, if they do not labor they may not eat.[43]

To avoid labor and to make oneself free from the bondage of the fields, by begging if needs be, was to show that one had become identified with the "wakeful" beings who feasted on the love of God. It was to step out of the category of the human by making visible, among one's fellow-humans, the awesome freedom of the angels.

Hence the disturbing mobility associated with the monks of Syria and the comparative ease with which, unlike the monks of Egypt, they accepted food and protection from their lay clients. Unlike the monks of Egypt, they tended not to think of the desert as an absolute antithesis to the settled land, in whose bleak inhospitality the ascetic must strive to remain human, by maintaining human patterns of work and diet. In Egypt, Syrian versions of the "angelic life" were subjects of quiet ascetic humor. John the Dwarf had once announced to his cell mate that "I should like to be free from all care, like the angels, who do not work, but ceaselessly offer worship to God."

41. On this crucial difference, see Robert Murray, "The Theory of Symbolism in St. Ephrem's Theology," and Sabine MacCormack, "Christ and Empire, Time and Ceremonial in Sixth-Century Byzantium," p. 291. On these matters, I owe a particular debt to the advice and as yet unpublished papers of Professor Susan Ashbrook Harvey.

42. W. Cramer, Die Engelvorstellungen bei Ephräm dem Syrer, pp. 68, and 97–98.

43. Rabbi Abbahu cited in A. Levene, The Early Syrian Fathers on Genesis, p. 127.

A week in the Egyptian desert was enough for him. He was soon back, knocking on his companion's door. A crestfallen "angel," John was thought to have learned his lesson: "You are human, and you must work in order to eat."[44]

In Syria, a significantly different image of the desert lay in the back of men's minds. It reached back over a millennium to the story of Gilgamesh and Enkiddu. The desert was the land where men and beasts had once mingled in a state of pre-social liberty.[45] As a result, many ascetics were content to sink back into that state, by living with an angelic freedom that resembled that of beasts, wandering up the mountainsides to graze, with the sheep, on the natural grasses.[46]

Of all the restricting boundaries that defined settled society, that between the sexes was the most blatant. Hence, it also could be shown to vanish in a life lived in imitation of the angels. Syrian society was as deeply preoccupied with the segregation of women as was any other region of the Christian East.[47] But it was precisely by breaking this charged barrier that the freedom associated with the angelic life could be shown with most effect. In Syria and in regions touched by Syrian styles of asceticism, stories circulated about women who had stepped out of their sexual identity. They had reduced their bodies to an "angelic" indeterminacy by long fasting. They had cut off their hair. They had even adopted male clothes, so as to wander freely throughout the settled world.[48] It was possible for a woman to become a Stylite hermit, sitting on a column of her own outside Amaseia in Pontus.[49]

Delivered, in this drastic manner, from the accustomed marks of human bondage, the ascetic of either sex was a living sign of the power

44. *Apophthegmata Patrum*, John Colobos 2: *P.G.* 65: 204D–205A.

45. Elena Cassin, "Le semblable et le différent," in *Hommes et bêtes*, L. Poliakov, ed., pp. 117–120.

46. Sozomen, *Eccles. Hist.* 633.

47. It is, apparently, only in Syria that women were specifically ordained as deaconesses so that the male clergy should have no contact with women in the rituals associated with baptism: A. Martimort, *Les diaconesses*, pp. 31–71, 126–131. See esp. Susan Ashbrook Harvey, "Women in Early Syrian Christianity," in A. Cameron and A. Kuhrt, eds., *Images of Women in Antiquity*, pp. 295–298.

48. Evelyne Patlagean, "L'histoire de la femme déguisée en moine et l'évolution de la sainteté féminine à Byzance," pp. 605–607, 615–617. Sebastian P. Brock and Susan Ashbrook Harvey, *Holy Women of the Syrian Orient*, now provides a collection of texts with translation, commentary, and a masterly introduction.

49. *Studia Pontica* 3, J. G. C. Anderson, F. Cumont and H. Gregoire, eds., inscript. 134, p. 146.

of God placed among men. Crowds flocked out to catch a glimpse of Saint Symeon perched on his sixty-foot column on the mountain ridge of Telnesin. A figure standing with arms outstretched in prayer, the broken body of Symeon was a living image of the power of the Crucified.[50] He had been sent by God to men, "to arouse the world from the heaviness of its lethargy of sleep."[51]

Not surprisingly, living signs of so vivid a nature could be perceived as exotic and threatening to other Christians less attuned to their distinctive spiritual message. Speculations on the exact workings of the Holy Spirit in the heart and on the extent of the transformation of the normal person, brought about by the Spirit's descent upon the ascetic, disturbed bishops in neighboring regions. Syrian monks known as Messalians—the Men of Prayer, from the Syriac "to pray"—provoked genuine alarm in the late fourth and fifth centuries. In Asia Minor, the stricter colleagues of Basil and of Gregory of Nyssa and, in Antioch, Bishop Flavian, John Chrysostom's superior, were convinced that the little troops of "Messalian" monks, who passed occasionally through their cities, were the spearhead of a widespread subversive movement.[52] They claimed that the Messalian monks had taught men and women that perpetual prayer could bring down the Holy Spirit upon the believer in a measure that far exceeded that granted to the average Christian at baptism. A deep pessimism seemed to lie at the heart of such a view. The Messalians were accused of implying that the giving of the Holy Spirit in the rite of baptism was not enough to save men and women from themselves. The roots of evil reached too deep into the heart.[53]

50. H. J. W. Drijvers, "Spätantike Parallelen zur altchristlichen Heiligenverehrung unter besonderer Berücksichtigung des syrischen Styliten-Kultes," pp. 65–75.

51. *Life of Symeon Stylites*, p. 622; trans. F. Lent, *Journal of the American Oriental Society* (1915) 35:184.

52. J. Gribomont, "Le dossier des origines du messalianisme," in J. Fontaine and C. Kannengiesser, eds., *Epektasis, Mélanges offerts au cardinal J. Daniélou*, is a clear summary; see now R. Staats, "Messalianerforschung und Ostkirchenkunde," in W. Strothmann, ed., *Makarios-Symposium uber das Böse*. On the pseudo-Macarian *Spiritual Homilies* and *Letters*, now ascribed to Symeon of Mesopotamia, see H. Dörries, *Die Theologie des Makarios Symeon*; and V. Desprez, *Pseudo-Macaire: Oeuvres spirituelles* I, pp 32–47, 57–62.

53. Condemnation later cited by Timothy of Constantinople, *de receptione haereticorum: P.G.* 86: 48B; Theodoret, *Haer. fab. comp.* 4.11: *P.G.* 83: 429B. Baptism merely "shaved" sins, leaving their roots to grow again. See K. Ware, "The Sacrament of Baptism and the Ascetic Life in the Teaching of Mark the Monk."

Only a further measure of the Spirit, brought down by prayer and continence, could burn out the spirit of rebellion that lurked in the very core of the human person. Without full possession of the Spirit, the heart remained a depository of undiscovered drives, of which sexual desire was the most tenacious. It might erupt at any moment to humiliate the pious with bizarre misdeeds: a man once tortured for his faith, one writer pointed out, had then seduced the consecrated virgin who had brought him food in prison.[54] The monastic discipline on which Basil wrote and the pious works on which Chrysostom preached seemed threatened. It was said that the Messalians dismissed them both as equally irrelevant: compared with the flame of the love of God that burned like a high fever in the heart, such actions were external matters of no importance.[55]

The image of the Messalians put together by the Greek bishops of the late fourth and early fifth centuries spoke more of their own anxieties than about real men and women. The world East of Antioch was no spiritual "Wild West." The workings of the Spirit could take singularly humane forms. We see this best from an anonymous collection of sermons known as the Book of Degrees. Its author may have been a contemporary of John Chrysostom and Ephraim. He was a more marginal character than they were, but his perspective is revealing. The Book of Degrees took the form of addresses delivered to ascetics in search of the perfect life.[56] For all his insistence on the need to seek the gifts of the Spirit, the author looked out with singularly tranquil eyes on the married householders around him. What he demanded of them was, in fact, not so very different from what John had wished from the householders of Antioch. He was prepared to admit that they possessed the "first-fruits of the Spirit," conferred on them by baptism. They lived the life of the "righteous."[57] They opened their houses to the poor on cold winter nights; poorer households would even club together in groups of five to raise alms.[58] They prayed five times a day.[59] Solemn, decent persons, they addressed their Christian friends

54. Ps.-Macarius, Homilies 15.49 and 27.15: P.G. 34: 608B and 704D.

55. Ibid. 9.9: 537A; see the condemnation of such a view in Nilus of Ancyra, de voluntaria paupertate: P.G. 79: 907A.

56. M. Kmosko, ed., Patrologia Syriaca 3. See esp. A. Guillaumont, "Situation et Signification du Liber Graduum dans la spiritualité syriaque."

57. Liber Graduum 1.4: 18/19 (the paired columns refer to the Syriac and the parallel Latin translation).

58. 13.3 and 7.2: 311/312 and 147/148.   59. 7.19: 181/182.

and neighbors with a sweet sense of ceremony, never forgetting to use of each the correct form of address.[60]

Yet for all his gentle tolerance, the author of the *Book of Degrees* viewed the settled world of the "righteous" Christians as if from a mountain peak. He looked down from the great height of a heart fully opened to the Spirit. The "perfect," the "disciples of love," were unlike the "disciples of righteousness." For them there were no boundaries, no social statuses, no objects of avoidance. For them no thing was unclean.[61] They offered no judgment: when a monk from eastern Syria, settled in Egypt, saw a colleague making love to a boy, all that he said was "if God Who created them does not burn them up, who am I to blame them?"[62]

They exacted no penalties: they did not, for instance, kill off their local lunatics, as the Christian "righteous" tended to do.[63] They saw, with a clarity quite unusual in late Roman persons, that war was the product of human evil and that no war was ever wished on men by God. As a result, no war could claim the blessing of God—and this at a time when the East Roman government had begun to put the sign of the Cross on its coins, as a token of victory in its campaigns against Persia.[64] They could pass with the clear eyes of little children through the screens that hedged in the righteous. They could enter into distant cities.[65] The air of the city was not lethal to them. Filled with the Spirit, they felt as little shame at the robust profanity of urban life as a child wandering through a brothel.[66] They might even sit unmoved in the theater.[67]

In the sixth century, this tradition produced the "holy fools" of eastern Christian piety. Symeon of Emesa would enter the women's section of the public baths, stark naked, with his robe on his head as a turban; and he would dance the jig with the townsfolk in the local tavern.[68] At a time when the average Christians of Syria, zealous "dis-

---

60. 13.9: 311/312 and 16.2: 389/390.   61. 19.28: 501/502 and 4.5: 93/94.

62. 22.3: 630/640 and *Apophthegmata Patrum,* John the Persian 1: *P.G.* 65: 236C.

63. *Liber Graduum* 7.15: 173/174 and 22.3: 639/640.

64. 9.6: 215/216 and 22.7: 649/650; see K. Holum, "Pulcheria's Crusade A.D. 421–22 and the Ideology of Imperial Victory."

65. *Liber Graduum* 19.31: 505/506.   66. 15.4: 343/344.

67. Ps.-Macarius, *Homily* 15.8: 581A.

68. Leontius of Neapolis, *Life of Symeon the Holy Fool* 13–14, in A. J. Festugière and L. Ryden, eds., *Léonce de Néapolis: Vie de Syméon le Fou,* pp. 81–83, 135–136; see J. Grosdidier de Matons "Thèmes d'édification dans la 'Vie d'André Salos'."

ciples of faith," had provoked a wave of inter-village violence by destroying the temples of pagan villages, only the serene openness of these gentle wanderers, the "disciples of love," could hope to win over unbelievers.[69]

When you see a fool show no honor to himself, possess no house, no wife, no property, wear no clothes except his one tunic and own no food except what he can gain from day to day. When you see him speaking to all comers in his simple-minded way, feeling no anger when mocked . . . Then say: That is the life for me.[70]

The author of the *Book of Degrees* knew that he spoke for a minority in danger of emargination.[71] Yet the themes of his sermons touch on preoccupations that were common to all ascetic Christians in the Greek as well as in the Syriac-speaking worlds. Throughout this tradition, in its varying forms, human beings were thought capable of regaining a measure of Adam's angelic state in a long-lost Paradise. And Paradise regained involved no isolated achievement of an individual perfection. To regain Adam's state was to look with changed eyes at the present state of human society. Whether this took the form of Gregory of Nyssa's somber linking of marriage and death, of John's early idealization of the vast hush of the last days, in his *On Virginity*, or of the sense of human bondage challenged by those who lived a life "in imitation of the angels" on the hills of Syria, what these men felt they needed to explain was not so much the present weakness of the individual body; it was, rather, the tragic dislocation of present society as a whole, urged ever onward by fear of death and condemned to the long labor of the fields. Settled life, itself, stood under a question mark. Humanity had fallen from a state of angelic freedom into the inextricable compulsion of society.

According to the author of the *Book of Degrees*, Adam had fallen because he had looked around him in Paradise with a hot lust for the land. He had wished to possess its rich soil. He had wished, through property, to replace God as Creator. He had set about creating economic wealth by labor, and had wished to pile up the physical wealth of progeny by intercourse.[72] He had turned from the contemplation of

---

69. *Liber Graduum* 14.3: 329/330: see Libanius, *Oratio* 30.8–13, on violent mobs led by monks—plainly not the "disciples of love!"
70. *Liber Graduum* 16.7: 401/402.
71. 19.11 and 31: 471/472 and 507/508 and 30.4: 809/810.
72. 15.2 and 6: 339/340 and 347/348; cf. 21.2: 589/590.

God to build the society that we now know, a society ruled by the iron constraints of the "law of Adam."[73] When a holy man once allowed his eyes to wander from the holy page, to look at the farmers toiling in the rich valley of Tel ʿAde, he imposed a harsh penance on himself: for he had allowed himself to be tempted by Adam's fateful gaze.[74]

The righteous might live decently in this society by the simple code of fallen Adam—tilling their fields, doing good to their co-religionists, caring for the local Christian poor. God, who had shown mercy on Adam by allowing him to live by that law, would not deny the righteous their reward. But for those who had regained the first, Spirit-filled eyes of Adam, the present social world, the social structures of town, village, and family, must seem, forever, unaccountably strange. The power of the "present age," made manifest in the care-worn state of organized society, and, only tangentially, the present state of human sexuality, was what the most serious Christians of the East strove to explain.

Not all Christians were accustomed to thinking in such drastic terms. By the end of the fourth century, for the first time in the history of the Early Church, the distant, Latin-speaking provinces of the West —Africa, Italy, and Gaul—came into their own. It was the age of Ambrose, of Jerome and, a little later, of the great Augustine. Turning to the West, we will find a very different world. It was a world that originally knew little of the desert. In Milan, Rome, and Carthage, the relation of the Catholic church to the society around it was notably different from that which had prevailed in Egypt, Cappadocia, Antioch, and Syria. The structures of Western society forced very different social problems on the leaders of the Catholic church. A very different relationship between clergy and laity had emerged within the Church itself. In many influential centers of the Latin world, the ascetic movement rapidly took forms that gave less prominence to the slow wisdom of the Desert Fathers and that shunned the "angelic" freedom upheld by the monks of Syria. Even those Latins who were most attracted to continence and to the monastic life brought with them views on the relation between Church and society and on the limits of the human person that contrasted with those accepted by Egyptians, Greeks, and Syrians. Augustine wrote his very last words in Hippo, in 430, de-

73. 26.2: 759/760.   74. Theodoret, *Hist. Relig.* 4.6: 1344CD; p. 52.

fending an exegesis of the fall of Adam and Eve markedly different from any we have encountered so far, in the eastern regions of the Christian world. Two astonishingly creative generations in the Christianity of the Latin West ensured that the preoccupations of the Desert Fathers, of Gregory of Nyssa, of Chrysostom, and of Ephraim the Syrian always seem to speak to us from across a great gulf, while the attitudes to sexuality and society of Ambrose, Jerome, and, above all, of Augustine still appear, for good or ill, to run in the bloodstream of Western Europeans. It is, therefore, with these three Latin writers that we will end our book.

PART THREE

AMBROSE TO AUGUSTINE: THE MAKING OF THE LATIN TRADITION

SEVENTEEN

Aula Pudoris: Ambrose

In the late 340s, a little boy, the son of a Praetorian Prefect, was growing up in Rome with his widowed mother. Young Ambrose's elder sister, Marcellina, had already become a consecrated virgin. She lived at home with her mother, in the manner of so many "daughters of Jerusalem" all over the Mediterranean. But this home was a Roman palace, visited assiduously by the clergy:

He used to see bishops having their hands kissed by members of the family— his sister or mother—and would jokingly put out his hand to [Marcellina's lady-companion] and tell her that she ought to do the same to him; for . . . he was going to be a bishop.[1]

Thirty years later, Ambrose returned to the family palace. Now Bishop of Milan (since 374), he offered his hand once again to the lady-companion: "There now, I told you, you are kissing the hand of a bishop."[2]

This incident lays bare a peculiar feature of the upper-class Chris-

---

1. Paulinus, *Life of Ambrose* 4, in F. R. Hoare, trans, *The Western Fathers*, p. 151.
2. Ibid. 9, p. 155.

tianity of Italy. Italy was an intensely conservative, under-Christian-ized region. Active pagan worship had remained part of public life up to the last decades of the fourth century. A public career exposed the upper-class Christian to the smell of the sacrificial altar and, at Rome at least, to the stench of the blood of gladiatorial games. In pagan families, sons continued to follow the religion of their fathers in public, long after their mothers and wives had brought Christianity into the house.[3] As long as they wished to remain in public life, Christian no-blemen were unwilling to commit themselves prematurely or exclu-sively to the interests and the controls of the Church. They were con-tent to become catechumens, and to appear irregularly, if at all, in church.[4] Many preferred to postpone the final commitment of baptism for as long as possible. In the late 420s, Augustine still had to write to a Carthaginian nobleman, Firmus, urging him to accept baptism as a Christian. Firmus had already read more Christian literature than had his wife; but only his wife enjoyed the incommunicable hope of salvation conferred by baptism into the Catholic Church:

O Firmus, so unfirm in purpose. . . . O you men, who all fear the burdens imposed by baptism. You are easily beaten by your women. Chaste and de-voted to the faith, it is their presence in great numbers that causes the Church to grow.[5]

As a result of this imbalance, the upper-class families of Italy were taken by surprise by a new and assertive alliance between noble women and the Christian clergy. This alliance gave a quite distinctive flavor to the Christian literature of the Latin West in the age of Ambrose and Jerome. While it is possible to read all the works of Basil of Caesarea without being able to guess, for a moment, that he had a sister, much less that that sister was none other than the great Macrina, we know of some of Ambrose's most heroic confrontations with the Emperors in Milan only because he wrote about them in great detail to Marcel-lina, "my Lady, my sister, dearer to me than life and my very eyes."[6]

---

3. Peter Brown, "Aspects of the Christianization of the Roman Aristocracy," in *Religion and Society in the Age of Saint Augustine*, pp. 172–177.

4. E.g., *Council of Elvira*, canon 45.

5. Augustine, *Epistula* 2*. 4.1–7 and 7.4, in J. Divjak, ed., *Corpus Scriptorum Ecclesiasticorum Latinorum* 88, pp. 11–12, 14; *Lettres* 1*–29*, pp. 64–66, and 74.

6. Ambrose *Letter* 22: *Patrologia Latina* 16: 1062B = 77, in M. Zelzer, ed., *C.S.E.L.* 82: 126.

For it was through Marcellina that Ambrose chose to speak to Rome.

In Italy, the desert was all but unknown, and the Holy Places were a distant dream, available only to the enterprising or to the discontented few. Not many followed the heroic example of Melania.[7] The *cubiculum*, the inner bedroom of the well-to-do Christian house, rendered sacred by the presence of such consecrated women as Marcellina, her lady-companion, and her other protégées, was the one "desert" that Ambrose would have known, as he grew to manhood in the 350s and 360s.[8] Only in such secluded places could the Latin Christian hope to find deep holiness. The consecrated virgins brought into the Christian household and the Christian basilicas a breath of immortality: these grave women were like "gardens heavy with the scent of flowers, like shrines filled with solemn worship, like altars that touch their priests with holy awe."[9]

We should not underestimate the impact on Italian society of an ascetic movement whose principal exponents and patrons were noble women. Unlike the austere and populous families of Cappadocia, fourth-century Romans parted with their daughters with extreme reluctance. Among the senatorial families of Rome, the noble woman still carried with her the pride of the fertile womb. Anicia Faltonia Proba was acclaimed on her epitaph as "wife to a consul, the daughter of a consul, the mother of consuls."[10] Proba was a woman "by whose fertile births the power of Rome grows strong."[11]

The consecrated virgin, by contrast, denied that pride. When Simplicia, a Roman nun, died in middle age, all that needed to be said of her was that "she took no heed to produce children, treading beneath her feet the body's snares."[12]

Ambrose remembered one Roman girl who had rushed up to the altar and, in front of the bishop, wrapped the altar-cloth around her head as a veil, pleading for protection through consecration as a virgin of the church. In the stunned silence that followed, a relative shouted out:

---

7. See esp. E. D. Hunt, *Holy Land Pilgrimage in the Later Roman Empire,* pp 128–154.

8. *De institutione virginis* 1.7: *P.L.* 16: 307A: the bedroom stands for the inner life; Jerome, *Letter* 107.7: *P.L.* 22: 874; Pelagius, *ad Demetriadem* 22: *P.L.* 30: 37.

9. Ambrose, *de virginibus* 2.2.18, E. Cazzaniga, ed., p. 42; *P.L.* 16: 223A.

10. H. Dessau, *Inscriptiones latinae selectae,* 1269, 1: 283.

11. Claudian, *Panegyricus Probino et Olybrio consulibus dictus* 193–194.

12. *Année épigraphique* (1980) no. 138, p. 40.

Do you think that if your father was alive, he would have allowed you to remain unmarried? "Maybe he died," the girl snapped back, "so that no one should stand in my way."[13]

Conquer family-loyalty first, my girl: if you overcome the household, you overcome the world.[14]

Christian or pagan, these were chilling words indeed for any Roman to hear.

What made such incidents a matter of grave public concern was the fact that the majority of such young women were the daughters of widows.[15] They had acted as they did after their father had died, at a time when male control over the women of the family had been withdrawn. At such a moment in her life, a mature woman would have found herself with considerable wealth at her disposal, and was free to do with it as she pleased. Ascetic women were women of substantial private means. Manual labor, even of the most genteel kind, was unknown in the consecrated inner rooms of Italy.[16] The upper-class virgin was expected to be "powerful in revenue, a mother to the poor."[17]

The impact of upper-class ascetic women on the Latin church was far out of proportion to their numbers. This was a church that desperately needed lay patrons. Few provincial churches possessed extensive estates of their own: they depended on intermittent gifts of ready money and of valuables such as pious noblewomen could provide. Passing by Thagaste in Numidia as a refugee from Rome, the younger Melania, the great Melania's grand-daughter, endowed its church with

13. Ambrose, *de virginibus* 1.11.65–66, Cazzaniga, ed., pp. 33–34; *P.L.* 16: 218AC.

14. Ibid. 1.11.63, p. 32: 217B.

15. *De virg.* 1.10.58, p. 30: 216A. Widows, who should have been the ones to encourage their daughters, keep them away from his sermons. Juliana of Florence was the ideal widow: *Exhortatio virginitatis* 2.10–12 and 8.55; *P.L.* 16: 355A and 368A; see esp. F. E. Consolino, "Dagli 'exempla' ad un esempio di comportamento cristiano." Eusebius of Bologna was unusual in presenting his own daughter: *de institutione virginis* 1.1: 319A. She was called Ambrosia, and may well have been conceived or kept alive through the prayers of Ambrose, and had been dedicated for that reason.

16. See esp. Y. M. Duval, "L'originalité du *de virginibus* dans le mouvement ascétique occidental: Ambroise, Cyprien, Athanase," in Duval, ed., *Ambroise de Milan: xvième centénaire de son élection épiscopale*, pp. 56–58. Parents could threaten to withhold the girl's share in the inheritance: *de virg.* 1.11.62, p. 31: 217A.

17. Diehl, *Inscriptiones latinae christianae veteres*. 1700, 1:330—of Manlia Daedala, the sister of the Praetorian Prefect and Consul Manlius Theodorus and close client of Ambrose: see Peter Brown, *The Cult of the Saints*, p. 37 and P. Courcelle, "Quelques symboles funéraires du néo-platonisme latin."

revenues as well as offerings of gold and silver treasures, and valuable veils, so that this church, which formerly had been so very poor, now stirred up envy on the part of other bishops of the province.[18]

Without the wealth and the tenacity of Melania the Elder and Paula, the monastic and scholarly enterprises of Rufinus and Jerome in the Holy Land would have been inconceivable.[19] As distributors of wealth and patrons of individual writers, aristocratic Latin women acted as arbiters of intellectual life to a degree unparalleled in the Greek East.

Throughout the Empire, the governing classes were alarmed by this new development. The case of Olympias, at Constantinople, was not unique. Many aristocratic women threatened to dispose of their wealth in favor of the clergy and the monks.[20] In Roman society, the most significant transfers of wealth had always happened through legacies: by frequenting the palaces of devout women, priests joined in the time-honored Roman hunt for bequests from the childless.[21] In the Italy of Ambrose, treatises on virginity no longer circulated as exhortations to a sheltered piety. They were written so as to change upper-class opinion—to persuade emperors, prefects, and provincial governors to allow wealthy widows and virgins to remain dedicated to the Church, and to tolerate the redirection of parts of the wealth of great families, through such women, to pious causes.[22] No Latin writer saw the implications of this new situation more clearly than did Ambrose. The notion of virginity served him as a sounding board. By preaching on virginity, and especially by upholding the perpetual virginity of Mary, Ambrose made resonantly clear the position that he wished the Catholic Church to occupy in the Western territories of the Empire.

Although he came from a senatorial family, Ambrose was not simply a Roman grandee. He belonged to the more insecure and interesting

18. *Life of Saint Melania the Younger* 21, in D. Gorce, ed., *Vie de Sainte Mélanie;* Elizabeth A. Clark, *The Life of Melania the Younger,* p. 44—an invaluable translation and commentary.

19. Hunt, *Holy Land Pilgrimage,* pp. 138–141.

20. Jill Harries, "'Treasure in Heaven': Property and Inheritance among Senators of Late Rome," in Elizabeth M. Craik, ed., *Marriage and Property,* pp. 54–70.

21. Ramsay MacMullen, *Roman Social Relations,* pp. 101–102; Brent D. Shaw and Richard P. Saller, "Close-Kin Marriage in Roman Society?" pp. 438–439.

22. *Codex Theodosianus* 16.2. 20, 27, 28: a series of laws prohibiting legacies to the church by widows. Such restraints were a source of grievance to the clergy: Ambrose, *Letter* 18.14; *P.L.* 16: 1017C = 73, p. 42; Jerome, *Letter* 52.6: *P.L.* 22: 532. Ambrose said that he was careful to avoid such transfers: *de officiis* 3.9.58; *P.L.* 16: 171 A; *Letter* 82.7: 1333C = 24, p. 173.

class of young nobles who sought Imperial service because they needed power, and relished it. He came to Milan as Governor of Liguria shortly after 370, an experienced man in his mid-thirties.[23] When acclaimed bishop, in October 374, in the main basilica of the city, a huge building that held some three thousand persons,[24] his first reaction showed his personal eccentricity. He wished to withdraw into a life of philosophical retirement.[25] Caught between two conflicting claims for public service, in the Empire and, now, in the Church, his reflex was to blot out his public *persona*, much as Plotinus' Rogatianus had done, a century before. Memories of philosophical study groups, such as had once gathered around Plotinus in Rome, had been an element in Ambrose's culture during his early career as a senator.

His unusual philosophical background gave Ambrose a unique advantage: unlike most of his upper-class Latin contemporaries, he read Greek: Philo, Origen, even Plotinus (if only in "pre-digested" Christian extracts), and the sermons of his great Cappadocian contemporaries, were directly available to him in a library that few Westerners would have possessed.[26] Unlike Gregory of Nyssa, however, Ambrose did not use his wide reading to nourish a contemplative theology. The singularly austere spirituality he derived from his Greek reading provided him, instead, with the personal discipline he needed for a life of unflinching public action.

Ambrose was a man deeply preoccupied with the role of the Catholic Church in Roman society. He was dominated by a need to assert the position of the Church as an inviolably holy body, possessed of unchallengeable, because divine, authority. What angered him most was cowardice on the part of the clergy. He belonged to a younger generation of militant upholders of the Nicene Creed who were convinced that their bishops had allowed themselves to be browbeaten and seduced by the formidable anti-Nicene, "Arian" Establishment of Constantius II. Desire to curry favor with the powers that be, thereby

23. Ambrose was probably the protégé of Petronius Probus, a notoriously power-hungry nobleman: Paulinus, *Life of Ambrose* 8; see esp. John Matthews, *Western Aristocracies and Imperial Court*, pp. 37–38.

24. Richard Krautheimer, *Three Christian Capitals: Topography and Politics*, p. 76.

25. Paulinus, *Life of Ambrose* 7.

26. The uncovering of the sources that nourished the thought of Ambrose is one of the very finest achievements of post-war French patristic scholarship: see esp. Hervé Savon, *Saint Ambroise devant l'exégèse de Philon le Juif*; P. Courcelle, *Recherches sur les Confessions de Saint Augustin*, pp. 106–138 on Ambrose and Plotinus, and the exemplary study of Goulven Madec, *Saint Ambroise et la philosophie*, esp. pp. 61–71 on Plotinus.

surrendering Catholic truth to the dark powers of the "world," had brought a curse upon the Latin church.[27]

From 374 to his death in 397, Ambrose saw it as his duty, as Bishop of Milan, to make plain, on the very threshold of an Imperial court from which much of Western Europe was governed, the uncompromising antithesis between the true, Catholic Church and its manifold enemies, which had been an integral part of the rhetoric of Latin Christians since the days of Tertullian and Cyprian. He propounded a view of the world marked by sharp antitheses and by hard boundaries. In return for obedience to the commands of the Church, he proposed to the emperors the attractive mirage of a West Roman society held together by undivided loyalty to a single, mighty cause, that of Christ and His true, Catholic Church. It was a harsh, defensive view of the world; but it caught only too well the mood of Northern Italy in the 380s and 390s, after the collapse of the Danubian frontier and a series of civil wars had thrown the region into a state of perpetual mobilization.

We must always bear in mind this aspect of Ambrose, even when we study the most seemingly intimate and sheltered aspects of his thought. We are dealing with a man whose imaginative world was a tensile system. It was built up through a series of potent antitheses— Christian and pagan, Catholic and heretic, Bible truth and "worldly" guesswork, Church and *saeculum*, soul and body.[28] Any attempt to blur one antithesis, to breach one boundary, down to the most humble details of small-town life, such as easy tolerance for mixed marriages in the foothills of the Alps,[29] was calculated to set all the rest vibrating in his mind. To be a Catholic Christian was to keep these antitheses absolute: to admit "admixture" was to "pollute" one's own body and that of the Church. To surrender any boundary line was to court the ancient shame of the Roman male—it was to "become soft," to be "effeminated."[30]

What Ambrose wanted around him were men all of one piece. He simply refused to ordain as a member of his clergy a friend whose gestures seemed uncontrolled. Another's *incessus*, that telltale symptom of the measured stride of the public man in ancient Rome, "pained

---

27. Ambrose, *Expositio in Evangelium secundum Lucam* 5.71, in M. Adriaen, ed., *Corpus Christianorum*, 14:159; *P.L.* 15: 1740C.

28. Madec, *Ambroise et la philosophie*, p. 245.

29. *Letter* 19.2: 1024B.   30. E.g. *de officiis* 1.28.138: 68B.

my eyes." "Nor was I wrong." Both men, predictably, crumpled in the time of his nerve-wracking confrontation with the Imperial court over the Arian occupation of basilicas in Milan.[31]

No matter how deeply Ambrose read in Greek, he thought and felt in Latin. This was his moral "mother tongue." In effect, Ambrose reacted instinctively, for much of the time, like Cyprian:[32] he presented the Christian as tensed against the *saeculum*. The *saeculum*, for Ambrose, was a voracious sea, whipped by demonic gusts, across which there now drifted, in times of peace, the Siren songs of sensuality, of concern for worldly advantage, and of readiness to compromise with the great—beguiling, female figures who threatened always to "effeminate" the male resolve of the mind.[33]

Yet Ambrose was totally unlike Cyrpian in one crucial respect: he had been touched, in his own way, by the huge impatience of Origen.[34] A "skillfully maintained siege mentality"[35] always lay in the background of Ambrose's throught. But Ambrose's defensive posture toward the non-Catholic world was combined with a poignant longing for personal transformation. The heart of his preaching in Milan was the mysterious change promised to all Christians, through the "putting on" of Christ in the deep waters of the baptismal pool. It was on this transformation, prefigured in the state of Christ's own, pure body, that his thought lingered by preference.

The tension in Ambrose's thought—his deep suspicion of the *saeculum* contrasted with his high hopes of transformation for the baptized Christian—comes through most clearly in his view of the body. From Philo, Origen, and Plotinus, Ambrose had picked up a dualism of soul and body of exceptional sharpness.[36] He instinctively tended to identify Paul's somber and all-engulfing sense of the war between the spirit and the flesh with the more familiar, classical opposition of mind and body.[37] But Ambrose's dualism was not that of an ascetic

31. *De officiis* 1.18.72: 49A. 32. See above ch. 10, pp. 194–195.

33. *Expos. Luc.* 4.3, pp. 106–107: 1697A.

34. *Expositio Psalmi CXVIII.* 10.7–10 and 11.3–4 in M. Petschenig, ed., *C.S.E.L.* 62:207–210, 233–234; *P.L.* 15: 1401B–1403A, 1419C–3420D. See Savon, *Ambroise devant l'exégèse de Philon*, pp. 369, 376.

35. M. Meslin, *Les Ariens d'Occident*, p. 51.

36. See esp. W. Seibel, *Fleisch und Geist beim heiligen Ambrosius;* R. Holte, *Béatitude et Sagesse*, pp. 167–176 and E. Dassmann, *Die Frömmigkeit des Kirchenvaters Ambrosius von Mailand.*

37. Madec, *Ambroise et la philosophie*, p. 43 is the most nuanced statement of Ambrose's usage.

recluse; it was the dualism of a man of action. In stressing the superiority of the mind, he emphasized, in reality, the primacy of the will. The body was a mere "veil." Concern for material comfort and security must not be allowed to get in the way of the unflinching purpose of an active Catholic bishop, who must be prepared to stand in the way of an emperor's anger, to face, if not death, at least the near-lethal consequences of exile, and to go on dangerous diplomatic missions to distant courts.[38]

Ambrose's commitment to action led him to be peculiarly sensitive to the weakness of the "flesh." He viewed the body as a perilous mudslick, on which the firm tread of the soul's resolve might slip and tumble at any moment.[39] He had seen courtiers suffer the ultimate indignity of falling topsyturvy as they hustled along the smooth corridors of the Imperial palace. The word *lubricum*, "slippery," carried an exceptionally heavy charge of negative meaning for him: it signified moments of utter helplessness, of frustration, of fatal loss of inner balance and of surrender to the instincts brought about by the tragic frailty of the physical body.[40] When the mighty Paul had described the unrelenting war between the law in the members and the law in the mind, it seemed obvious to Ambrose that he was talking about the inadequacy of his own body: Paul was describing how he himself, and all Christians after him, "swerve, get stuck, are sucked into" the treacherous morass of the flesh.[41]

Yet Ambrose's sense of vertigo, of peril, of seasickness in the face of the heaving powers of the flesh[42] was only the shadow of a huge hope. A great baptismal pool flanked the main basilica of Milan. To enter into that seemingly anodine, clear water was to "put on Christ";[43] and, for Ambrose, to "put on Christ" meant, in a mysterious manner, to exchange the weakened flesh of human beings for flesh "re-

---

38. *Letter* 16.2: 1000B: describing Bishop Acholius of Thessalonica, a wiry old man of ascetic background, so active as a traveler that his junior colleagues found it hard to keep up with him!

39. *Hexaemeron* 3.1.4, in C. Schenkl, ed., *C.S.E.L.* 31, p. 61. 61; *P.L.* 14: 169AB.

40. Paulinus, *Life of Ambrose* 35: see esp. In Ps. 48. 9, in M. Petschenig, ed., *Expositio in XII Psalmos*, C.S.E.L. 34:366; *P.L.* 14: 1215B. This aspect of the fallen human condition was made dramatically visible by means of the baptismal liturgy: the feet of the baptized were washed separately, as sign of the innate weakness of the body—see esp. P. F. Beatrice, *La lavanda dei piedi*, pp. 103–127.

41. *In Ps. 118*. 20.46, p. 466: 1575C.

42. *In Ps. 118*. 5. 33, p. 100: 1329D–1330A.

43. *De mysteriis* 3.8 and 4.20; *P.L.* 16: 408B and 411B.

formed," flesh made perfect by having been taken up, in Christ, by God Himself. The flesh of Christ alone was a solid causeway that led from the quagmire of man's present state to heaven.[44] Christ's coming to humanity in human flesh had joined the huge antithesis of heaven and earth. "He lay in the crib, that you might stand at the altar; He came to earth, that you might come to the stars."[45]

Mighty images of ascent marked the crescendoes of Ambrose's preaching.[46] The same images suddenly leap out at us from the late-fourth-century sarcophagi in which his well-to-do listeners wished to rest. In the sarcophagi of Rome and Milan, great boundaries are crossed: Elijah's chariot breaks into the region of the stars, and the tiny figures of the dead bow before the four rivers of Paradise, which stood for the baptismal waters that had given them access to the feet of a towering Christ.[47]

Invisibly but certainly, so Ambrose believed, the baptized Christian would come to share in the tranquility that flowed from the spotless flesh of Christ. With Christ seated in the saddle of the inner person, it was possible, even in this life, to still the body's frisky steps.[48] "Your flesh was a pool of shade, which has cooled the high fevers of our desires, which has slaked the fires of our lusts."[49]

Ambrose presented conversion and baptism in terms of an intimate participation in the perfect flesh of Christ. There can be little doubt as to the immediate effect of such preaching: seen in the clear light that played around the untouched body of the Lord, every human body bore one ugly scar.[50] This scar was unmistakable—it was the scar of sexuality. Listening to Ambrose preaching, in the exciting years of 385 and 386, Verecundus, a well-placed Milanese teacher, decided that his bishop had implied that he could not yet become baptized, for he was a married man, "fettered" to an active sexual relation with his wife.[51] Another listener, a newly arrived African *rhetor*, Augustine, came to similar conclusions at that time. For an adult of serious religious in-

---

44. *In Ps. 39.* 2, C.S.E.L. 64, p. 215: 1109D.
45. *Expos. Luc.* 2.41, p. 49: 1649B.   46. *In Ps. 118,* 14.38, p. 323: 1479CD.
47. H. von Schoenebeck, *Der Mailänder Sarkophag und seine Nachfolge,* esp. figs. 4–6, pp. 28–29, and fig. 25, p. 66; A. Calderini et al., *La Basilica di San Lorenzo,* pp. 222–223; and C. Metzger, *Musée du Louvre: Sarcophages en pierre d'époques romaine et paléochrétienne,* pp. 312–313.
48. *Expos. Luc.* 9.9, p. 335: 1887B.   49. *In Ps. 118.* 19.5, p. 424: 1546D.
50. *Expos. Luc.* 5.24, p. 144: 1727D.   51. Augustine, *Confessions* 9.3.5.

tentions, to seek baptism at the hands of Ambrose meant exposing oneself to a glimpse of the "chaste majesty of continence."[52]

Ambrose had been driven to this daunting conclusion by the inner logic of his notion of salvation. The virgin birth of Christ was central to Ambrose's thought. The virgin birth offered the clue to understanding what it was that Christ had taken upon Himself that was common to all human beings, and what He had offered to human beings, in His own, human person, that they themselves had come to lack since the fall of Adam. The absence of sexual desire in the circumstances of Christ's own conception and in Christ's own human flesh was not, for Ambrose, simply a prodigy, incapable of imitation by others. Rather, Christ's sexless birth and unstirred body acted as a bridge between the present, fallen state of the human body and its future, glorious transformation at the Resurrection. Christ's flesh was a magnetically attractive token of human nature as it should be. A body "unscarred" by the double taint of a sexual origin and of sexual impulses stood for human flesh as it should be, flesh mysteriously "remade for the better," through baptism and continence, flesh that would eventually be restored to its full integrity at the Resurrection, "with all its flaws drained from it, [so that] all that would remain in human nature was the high happiness of life untouched by death."[53]

This way of thinking had been triggered in Ambrose's mind by powerful phrases of Origen.[54] Origen had wished to understand the pervasive sense of incongruity associated with the physical circumstances of conception and birth. Every human being had begun through a hot sexual act:

I too, indeed, am a mortal like all the rest . . . curdled in blood
by virile seed and the pleasure that is joined with sleep.[55]

Satirical poets positively enjoyed telling the high-minded that even they, for all their elevated pretensions, had originated in this indecorous

---

52. Ibid. 8.11.27.   53. *Expos. Luc.* 10. 125, pp. 380–381: 192B.

54. See esp. Madec, *Saint Ambroise et la philosophie,* p. 344 and Savon, *Saint Ambroise devant l'exégèse de Philon,* p. 378, on this trait in Ambrose.

55. *Wisdom of Solomon* 7.1–2. in David Winston, trans, *Anchor Bible,* p. 162, with commentary, pp. 163–166. The Latin *coagulatio* is notably less negative than *concretio,* which always has the overtones of a substance spoiled by admixture: e.g. *in Ps. 118.* 9.19, p. 201: 1397C.

manner.[56] With Origen, however, the widespread sense of the incongruity of human birth had hardened into the notion that conception and birth were inevitably associated with a series of "stains," of *contagia*. Jewish strictures on the "unclean" nature of the blood and debris of the womb, a sense of the "anti-spiritual" nature of the act of intercourse, and the fact of widespread infant baptism in the churches came together to form an ominous complex of *contagia*. They suggested to Origen that some deep, original "taint" must surely lie at the very beginning of human existence.

For Origen, however, this was a taint that could be transcended by the free will. The purificatory rites associated with the stain of birth served merely as signposts that pointed the Christian soul along the road of progressive purifications, by which the soul moved, in its long trajectory, toward ever greater freedom from stains of any kind. The sense of pollution conveyed by the stain of birth did not weigh very heavily upon Origen. Like a thumbprint on clear glass, it was visible only in the growing light of the glory that lay in store for the transformed body.[57] It did not speak of "original sin," as this was later understood in the Latin West: it was not the sign of an irrevocable fall of all mankind in Adam.

This was not so for Ambrose. The sheer sweep of Origen's cosmic view largely escaped him. The one transformation that riveted his attention was that brought about by conversion and baptism in the Catholic Church. He had no wish to consider the prospect of a long, slow purification of the soul, as it journeyed through a mighty universe. For him, human sexual feeling stood out in dark silhouette against the blaze of Christ's untouched body. Human bodies, "scarred" by sexuality, could be redeemed only by a body whose virgin birth had been exempt from sexual desire. It was a heady antithesis, with a long future ahead of it in the Latin Church. A generation later, those writings of Ambrose which stressed the contrast between the virgin birth of

---

56. Palladas in *Anthologia Palatina* 10.45, in W. R. Paton, ed., *The Greek Anthology*, 4:24.

57. Origen, *Comm. in ep. ad Romanos* 6.12; *Patrologia Graeca* 14: 1049C–1050A; cf. Ambrose, *de paen.* 1.3.13: 490C and *Apologia David* 1.11.56, in P. Hadot, ed., *Ambroise de Milan: Apologie de David*, pp. 150–152. See esp. P. F. Beatrice, *Tradux Peccati. Alle fonti della dottrina agostiniana del peccato originale*, pp. 174–185, 212–221; and now G. Sfameni Gasparro, "Le *sordes* (/*rhupos*), il rapporto genesis-phthorà dell'*Enkrateia* in Origene," in R. Hanson and F. Crouzel, eds., *Origeniana Tertia*, pp. 165–183.

Christ and the birth of ordinary human beings would provide Augustine with what he took to be irrefutable support of his own views on the intimate relation between the act of intercourse and the transmission of original sin: arguments on the virgin birth, taken from Ambrose, enabled Augustine to inject "a powerful and toxic theme into medieval theology."[58]

Ambrose would not have lingered on this theme unless it had struck some nerve of exquisite sensibility in the congregations he wished to move and in the governing circles whose opinions he wished to influence. His spirited championship of the perpetual virginity of Mary, in the last years of his life, reveal a slow hardening of attitudes among his Latin contemporaries. In the course of the fourth century, certain strings in the Christian sensibility had become more taut: Ambrose needed only to strike these, with his customary certainty of touch, for them to resound in such a manner as to lend a distinctive tone to contemporary discussions of issues that seem, at first sight, to have had little to do with the topic of virginity.[59]

What was at stake was the absolute nature of the boundaries that separated the Catholic Church from the world, as well as those which rendered individual virgins irrevocably "sacred" by reason of their vocation, and separate from their families. All forms of "admixture" and *concretio*—all confused jumbling of separate categories—were deeply repugnant to Ambrose. To avoid sexual intercourse was to avoid an act that involved "mixing," "relaxing," "becoming unstrung."[60] The cloying, labile mixture of male seed and female blood associated with the moment of conception struck him as a microcosm of the many smudged areas that weakened humankind: in its present fallen condition, the soul "stuck" to the body in an analogous glutinous and

58. Henry Chadwick, *Augustine*, p. 114. The principal passages are Augustine, *Contra ii epistulas Pelagianorum* 4.11.29: *P.L.* 44:626, citing Ambrose, *In Esaiam; Contra Julianum* 2.5.10: 680, citing *Expos. Luc.* 2.56; *C. Jul.* 2.5.14, 6.15, 7.19 and 8.24: 683, 684, 686 and 690, citing *de sacramento regenerationis vel de philosophia:* see Madec, *Ambroise et la philosophie,* pp. 256–260.

59. S. Alvarez Campos, *Corpus Marianum Patristicum,* vol. 3, provides a convenient collection of passages from Ambrose and contemporary Latin authors; C. W. Neumann, *The Virgin Mary in the Works of Saint Ambrose,* is a reliable summary of Ambrose's opinions and of those of his opponents.

60. *Hexaemeron* 5.21.67, p. 190: 248CD; compare *de virg.* 1.3.13, p. 8: 203A; *concretae confusionis labe; de paenitentia* 1.3.13: *P.L.* 16: 490C: *nec generationis aut conceptionis concretio fuscaverunt:* see Madec, *Ambrose et la philosophie,* pp. 295–299.

confused manner. The Christian always risked becoming "stuck" to the *saeculum;* for the soul's stern resolve had already become "effeminated" by having mixed indiscriminately with the body.[61] All such subversive joinings must be avoided. Ambrose's thought on virginity could be summed up in one word: *integritas.* This meant the precious ability to keep what was one's own untarnished by alien intrusion:

For in what does the chastity of a virgin consist, but in an integrity unexposed to taint from the outside?[62]

And, indeed, when a girl is deflowered by the customary process of marriage, she loses what is her own, when something else comes to mix with her.[63]

It was because she had avoided all admixture that Mary had been chosen by Christ as the source of His own flesh. In a phrase heavy with late Roman meaning, Mary was an *aula pudoris*, a royal hall of undamaged chastity.[64] Any inhabitant of Milan knew what that meant. The Imperial palace was a building rendered perpetually sacred by the presence of the Emperor. No private citizen, at any time, could dare to occupy its silent, golden halls. The body of Mary, and that of each of her followers as consecrated virgins, was such a hall.[65] An unbreakable "invisible frontier" lay between a virgin's body and the polluting "admixture" of the outside world.

Hence it was essential for Ambrose to assert, against other Christians, that Mary had remained a perpetual virgin. Her body not only had been intact at the time that she had conceived Christ through the Holy Spirit (that is, it had not suffered the intrusion and admixture of male seed)[66] but it also had been exempted, in a manner quite as marvelous, from the breaking of the closed boundary of the flesh associated with normal childbirth. Mary's womb stood for all that was unbroken and sacred in the world. It was the *"Gate of the Sanctuary, which looketh towards the East"* of Ezechiel's vision of the Temple:

61. *De Isaac vel anima* 1.2–2.5, in C. Schenkl, ed., *C.S.E.L.* 32:643–645: *P.L.* 14: 528B–530B; *in Ps. 118.* 4.6, p. 70: 1308C; *Expos. Luc.* 7.143, p. 264: 1826B.

62. *De virg.* 1.5.21, p. 10: 205C.   63. *Exhort. virg.* 6.35: 361C.

64. Neumann, *Virgin Mary,* p. 195: see also G. Sissa, "Une virginité sans hymen: le corps féminin en Grèce ancienne," pp. 1134–1136.

65. *Exhort. virg.* 4.27: 359A.

66. *Expos. Luc.* 2.56, p. 55: 1654C: *non enim virilis coitus vulvae virginalis secreta reseravit, sed immaculatum semen inviolabili utero spiritus sanctus infudit.* For a contemporary appreciation of the exact physiological implications of conception "in the womb" alone, without the intrusion of male seed, see Ps.- Jerome, *Letter 6: Ad amicum aegrotum* 6–7: *P.L.* 30: 82C–86B.

*The gate shall be shut, it shall not be opened, and no man shall enter in by it . . .
because the Lord, the God of Israel hath entered in by it, and therefore it shall be shut.*[67]

One could not have wished for a clearer statement of Ambrose's long concern to assert a view of the world in which the sacred was ringed by unbreakable frontiers. Throughout the 380s, Ambrose had threatened to bar the doors of his church, and of the sanctuary around the altar, to emperors polluted with the dark "admixture" of tolerance for pagans, heretics, and Jews.[68] (To be fair, he had also used the same sense of unbreakable boundaries to hold the Emperor Theodosius away from the altar until he had done due, public penance for a punitive massacre).[69]

In defending the perpetual virginity of Mary, in the years around 393, Ambrose knew that he was not only elevating the mother of the Lord: he found an apposite *Te Deum* with which to celebrate twenty years of tense concern for boundaries, for the dangers of admixture, and for the absolute and perpetual nature of the antithesis between the Catholic Church and the formless, disruptive confusion of the *saeculum*. In these years, it was always with the doors of the Church in mind that Ambrose ended his evocations of the perpetual virginity of Mary. The closed human person of Mary made concrete to his hearers the intangible screen that ringed the basilicas of the Catholic Church: "He of Whom it was said, in relation to the Church, *For he has strengthened the bars of thy gates,* how could He not have strengthened the bars of His own gate [the Virgin's womb]?"[70]

In the course of the 390s, events at Rome and on Ambrose's own doorstep, at Vercelli, made plain what issues were at stake in such a formulation of the status of Mary. Mary had come to be treated as the privileged exemplar of the virgin state. If she had merely conceived Christ while a virgin, and then had gone on, her miraculous role completed, to become an ordinary married woman, a *mulier*, the wife of Joseph and the mother of his children begotten by ordinary intercourse, her example would lose much of its power to protect young

---

67. *Ezechiel* 44:2 cited in *inst. virg.* 8.52: 234B.

68. *Letters* 17 and 18, on the pagan Altar of Victory; on the affair of the Arian basilicas, see esp. Krautheimer, *Three Christian Capitals*, pp. 69–92 and G. Gottlieb, "Der Mailänder Kirchenstreit von 385/6." P. Nautin, "Les premières relations d'Ambroise avec l'empéreur Gratien," in Y-M. Duval, ed., *Ambroise de Milan*, is essential on Ambrose's original position of weakness in Milan. On the incident of the burning of the synagogue at Callinicum, see *Letter* 40.

69. *Letter* 51; see Hadot, *Apologie de David*, pp. 22–43.   70. *Inst. virg.* 8.56: 335B.

virgin girls.[71] No Roman family, pagan or Christian, had any objection to the clergy when they encouraged their daughters to remain chaste and secluded, as Mary had been as a girl; but this was so that they should be given to their husbands as virgins. What was novel in Ambrose's unremitting exhortations to the virgin state was the cold shadow of perpetual withdrawal that fell across the family. To follow Mary, the *aula pudoris*, was to adopt a state of perpetual, irrevocable virginity. It meant to withdraw the womb in perpetuity from childbirth, and not merely to control one's teen-age desires before marriage. With the formal consecration of each virgin, a portion of the wealth of each family found itself frozen, with similar, sacralized perpetuity, in the treasuries of the Catholic Church: "A virgin is a royal palace hall, subject to no man, but to God alone."[72]

There was no denying the symbolic resonance of such notions in determining the public profile of the Catholic church in Italy and elsewhere. In Milan and Rome, as in the great churches of the East, the virgins of the church acted as nothing less than human boundary-stones. Their presence defined the Catholic basilica as a privileged, sacred space. The ceremony of the *velatio*, of the solemn veiling of consecrated virgins, was a fully public affair, celebrated at a few high festivals of the year. Though it was modeled on the veiling associated with a Roman marriage ceremony, echoes of the irrevocable and victorious transformation associated with baptism clustered around the woman's high moment of resolve.[73] In a crowded church, blazing with light and with the shimmer of white, triumphal robes, a burst of rhythmic shouting marked the moment when the consecrated woman took up her position behind a special pure white marble railing that marked her off from the rest of the basilica as clearly as did the chancel rail around the sanctuary. Noble men and women would push through the crowds to exchange with her the kiss of peace.[74]

The prominence accorded to consecrated women in the basilica raised

---

71. Gaudentius of Brescia, *Sermon* 9: *P.L.* 20: 899A and Zeno of Verona, *Tractatus* 1.5.3: *P.L.* 11: 303A report these views: see Duval, "L'originalité du *de virginibus*," pp. 61–64. Neumann, *Virgin Mary*, pp. 206–235 summarizes the views of Bonosus and the circumstances of their condemnation.

72. *Inst. virg.* 12.79: 339B.

73. See esp. R. D'Izarnay, "Mariage et consécration virginale au ivème siècle."

74. Ps.-Ambrose, *de lapsu virginis* 5.19 and 6.24: *P.L.* 16: 388A and 390A; for a later period, see E. de Benedictis, "The Senatorium and Matroneum in the Roman Church."

the explosive, because male, issue of the quality of the clergy of the Latin churches. In the 380s, it was an open question whether the *integritas* traditionally associated with consecrated virgin women would spill over into the ranks of the clergy as a whole, in the form of lifelong clerical celibacy. There had long existed a current of opinion that favored perpetual continence in the senior clergy as a visible symbol of the sacred nature of the Catholic priesthood. High theory had been one thing, however, and practice quite another. Ambrose realized that the best that most local churches could expect was that their bishops and priests should commit themselves to postmarital celibacy at the time of their ordination: all that could be demanded of the average clergyman was that he should "have had sons, and not continue to make sons."[75]

Only metropolitan churches, such as those of Rome and Milan, could attract large numbers of unmarried young men and encourage them to grow up from childhood as celibates, under the shadow of the altar (as did John Chrysostom and the young Theodoret in Antioch). The average provincial church, however, was chronically short of recruits to the clergy. It could not dispense with the services of married persons. On the contrary: good Romans tended to assume that the sons of clergymen would follow the profession of their fathers. In many regions, little clerical dynasties, where son followed father or nephew followed uncle, formed the backbone of the Church.

Whatever the practicability of the ideal of total clerical celibacy, appeals to it became surprisingly vocal at the end of the fourth century. This was because many Western Christian congregations found themselves caught in a dilemma.[76] In Spain, Gaul, and Italy, small and increasingly vocal groups of ascetics wanted a place in the clergy of the cities. The usual effect of pressure from these zealous and ostentatiously unmarried young men was to steel the determination of traditional Christians to choose their clergy from any group except the monks and the admirers of the monks. There were some bishops, Jerome complained, who would not ordain men priests until they saw

---

75. *De officiis* 1.50.258: 105A and *Letter* 63. 62: 1257A = *Extra. coll.* 14, C.S.E.L. 82, 2:267. See C. Cochini, *Origines apostoliques du célibat sacerdotal*, pp. 184–194.

76. See esp. C. Pietri, *Roma Christiana*, 1:684–721 and D. Callam, "Clerical Continence in the Fourth Century: Three Papal Decretals." Cochini, *Origines apostoliques du célibat*, pp. 277–278 offers a different view from that given here.

that their wives were well and truly pregnant![77] At the same time, however, the spread of Christianity in the upper classes brought into the churches potential leaders of beguiling power, effectiveness, and wealth.[78]

The potential new leaders posed a problem. They were not like the relatively humble, married clergy of an earlier age: they had fought wars; they had inflicted capital punishment; they had imposed judicial torture; their public duties in the cities had caused them to stain their eyes with the lust and cruelty of public games.[79] To old-fashioned Christians, they were as disturbing as were the new ascetics.

In parts of Spain, and later in Gaul, many bishops came to think that to forbid ordained clergymen to sleep with their wives would make the existing clergy an acceptable "middle party." Priests and bishops who were continent by that strict, if narrow, definition could stand between the shrill ascetics and the new men of power, grossly stained by the world.[80] This situation evoked a singularly self-confident letter from Pope Siricius to Himerius of Tarragona, in 384–385.

To Siricius, the issue seemed clear: service at the altar was only for those who were prepared henceforth to be perpetually free from at least one of the many stains of worldly life: the stain of intercourse. Those who stood before God to offer up the Eucharist must practice continence. Siricius cited Saint Paul's Letter to the Romans: "for those who are in the flesh cannot please God."[81] Siricius' ruling was one of the first, but by no means the last, occasion in the history of the Latin Church when Paul's mighty notion of the flesh, as all that was opposed to the Spirit of God, was whittled down to more manageable proportions, by being referred exclusively to sexual activity. Clergymen in the more insecure and warlike provinces of the Western Em-

77. Jerome, *Contra Vigilantium* 2: *P.L.* 23: 341. For opposition to monks in Gaul see esp. Clare Stancliffe, *St. Martin and His Hagiographer*, pp. 265–277 and J. M. Wallace-Hadrill, *The Frankish Church*, pp. 3–9; in Spain: Chadwick, *Priscillian of Avila*, pp. 8–36.

78. This is clearly seen by Ray Van Dam, *Leadership and Community in Late Roman Gaul*, pp. 69–78; see also Pedro de Palol Salellas, "La conversion de l'aristocratie de la Péninsule ibérique au ivème siècle," and Manuel C. Diaz y Diaz, "L'expansion du christianisme et les tensions épiscopales dans la péninsule ibérique," in *Miscellanea Historiae Ecclesiasticae* 6.

79. Siricius, *Letter* 10.5.13; *P.L.* 13: 1190.

80. The complexity of the situation is well seen by Callam, "Clerical Continence," pp. 25–26; see also Pietri, *Roma Christiana*, p. 894.

81. Siricius, *Letter* 1.7. 10: 1139A citing Romans 8.8–9.

pire could not be expected to have avoided violence and the dark taint of power in the course of their previous career: it was, indeed, their effectiveness as wielders of power that made them desirable as bishops. But, once ordained, they could at least be safely expected to abandon sex.

Siricius' views coincided with those of Ambrose in that both rested on the unquestioning acceptance of a notion of hierarchy. Both asserted the existence of distinct grades of perfection in the Christian life, and both believed that these distinctions could be measured in terms of the degree of a person's withdrawal from sexual activity. On this scale, the virgins came first, the widows second, and the married persons third. This was a universal scale, applicable to both sexes. The virgin state of the woman was hailed as a *norma integritatis:* it was both the pinnacle and the model of a state of sexual intactness that men, and especially members of the clergy, should strive to make their own.[82]

The long history of celibacy in the Catholic church makes it easy for us to forget the novelty of such a claim. Never before had Roman public men been expected to appropriate, in this way, virtues usually delegated to women. Watching Ambrose from a distance, in 385, the *rhetor* Augustine was puzzled by what he saw. Here was a man evidently honored by the powers that be; yet "his celibacy seemed the one difficult aspect of his life."[83]

So steep-pitched a notion of hierarchy was far from obvious to all Christians in Milan and Rome. The presence of a baptismal pool always spoke to Ambrose of an "ascent"; and Ambrose had little doubt that the peak of that ascent, in this life, was the virgin or the continent state. Jovinian, a serious minded ascetic in Rome, drew very different conclusions from the same pool of water: in his opinion, all Christians emerged from the baptismal waters equal. They had been equally rewarded with the gift of forgiveness and with the possession of the Holy Spirit. There was no further need for gradations of "grace and favor" within the Catholic congregation.[84] No groups of continent men and women needed to stand, in an ambiguous middle-ground, between a duly ordained clergy and the mass of the laity. For Jovinian,

---

82. Ambrose, *Letter* 63.66: 1259A, p. 270.   83. Augustine, *Confessions* 6.3.3.

84. Jerome, *Adversus Jovinianum* 1.3: *P.L.* 23: 214B; see Neumann, *Virgin Mary,* pp. 142–145 and David G. Hunter, "Resistance to the Virginal Ideal in Late-Fourth-Century Rome: The Case of Jovinian."

all baptized Christians were equally holy: they formed a single people of God, delivered, by baptism, from their sins. It was far from certain, therefore, that the further ceremonies of "consecration," associated with the solemn setting apart of virgin women, needed to be treated as valid and perpetual acts. They lacked the irrevocability of Christian baptism.

Jovinian had made this "horrifying" notion available, in writings, even to pagans.[85] This was a serious step to have taken. The early 390s was a time when paganism was once again "in the air" in Rome. A Prefect of the City, who might be a pagan or a Christian bitterly opposed to the ascetic movement, might at any time declare that the vocations of virgin girls were invalid, and that the dilapidation of family property, frequently associated with their renunciation of the world, must cease.[86]

Quite apart from the practical consequences of his preaching, Jovinian had touched a raw nerve in the clerical sensibility of his age. He was an old-fashioned Christian, in that, like Hermas, over two centuries previously, he believed that virginity was too potent and too serious an image of integrity to apply to particular human beings. The only "virgin" that mattered was the Christian congregation itself.[87] By such a notion, Jovinian denied the central tenet of the late Roman sense of hierarchy—that certain holy individuals could stand between heaven and earth, representing, on earth, the majesty of the invisible world. They, and not only the group as a whole, were holy.[88] As Siricius realized, Jovinian's views invalidated the role of the Catholic clergy in creating different statuses among the Christian people: for if priests could bestow their blessing on the veil of a married couple, why should they not also bestow the *honorificentia* of official consecration on the virgins of the Church?[89] For Ambrose, writing from a synod in Milan, Jovinian's delightfully old-fashioned denial of hierarchy was an *agrestis ululatus*, a "peasants' hue and cry."[90] It threatened to undo all that the

---

85. Siricius, *Letter* 7 = Ambrose, *Letter* 41a 4: 1171A; Extra coll. p. 299.

86. This was later the case with the trial that led to the confiscation of the properties of the young Pinianus and Melania the Younger: *Life of Melania* 19, Gorce, ed., p. 166, Clark, trans. p. 42.

87. Jerome, *Adv. Jovin.* 1.37: 263D–264A and 2.19: 314A.

88. Ambrose, *Letter* 42.3: 1173A = Extra coll. 15, p. 304.

89. Siricius = Ambrose, *Letter* 41a.5: 1171A = Extra coll. p. 300.

90. Ambrose, *Letter* 42.2: 1172B; p. 303.

revolution of late antiquity had achieved for the Christian church. Hierarchy, and not community, had become the order of the day.[91]

Unfortunately, the congregation of Vercelli, to whom two disciples of Jovinian came in 396, as lapsed monks from Ambrose's own monastery, were no peasants: they simply had a more secular, and commonsensical, notion of hierarchy. Rather than choosing to be ruled by a lifelong celibate drawn from the local monastery, the city decided, as many a city would do in later centuries, to select a powerful landowner as their next bishop.[92] The long letter that Ambrose wrote on this occasion makes plain the image of the Church to which he had devoted his life. It was a markedly ascetic image. The hardest battle of all that Adam's fallen progeny had to fight was an unremitting struggle of the mind against sensuality, against *voluptas*. To criticize monks, and to prefer nonascetic leaders, was to maintain that this struggle was unnecessary. It was to imply that *voluptas*, a capacity for sensual pleasure, had been a part of the human person intended by God at Creation. To say this was to deny the whole trajectory of man's painful return to Paradise through sexual abstinence and fasting: "how can sensuality recall us to Paradise, when it alone robbed us of its delights?"[93]

In this letter, *voluptas* was made to overlap almost entirely with sexual pleasure. Jovinian's disciples refused to admit a distinction between baptized Christians on the basis of their differing degrees of experience of the act of intercourse. They had claimed that virgins were equal to widows, even though widows had "once, and regrettably, undergone admixture with a man."[94]

Ambrose presented the people of Vercelli with a clear hierarchy: "Every day, in the readings of the Scriptures, and in the preaching of the bishops, the Church proclaims praise for marital morality, but the glory goes to virginal integrity."[95]

The integrity of the virgin state was the highest pinnacle of Christian virtue. Married sexuality lay in shadow of that one bright peak. The

91. Peter Brown, *The Making of Late Antiquity*, pp. 56, 97–101 and *The Cult of the Saints*, pp. 38–39, and 118–124; see now Victor Saxer, "Le culte chrétien au ive siècle," *Miscellanea Historiae Ecclesiasticae* 6.

92. Well explained by L. Ruggini, *Economia e società nell' "Italia annonaria"*, pp. 184–190.

93. Ambrose, *Letter* 63.13–14: 1244AB = Extra coll. 14, p. 242.

94. Ibid. 22: 1247B, p. 247–248.   95. Ibid. 10: 1243A, p. 240.

marriage bed was overgrown to an exceptional degree with the "tangled brushwood of human frailty."[96] Even within the respectable confines of legitimate wedlock, the Christian couple must be on their guard to maintain standards of conduct measured on a new, ascetic scale. The legal husband must not allow himself to be tempted, through love of sensuous delight, to play the adulterer to his own wife.[97]

This was a note never before sounded in public. Since the time of Clement of Alexandria, such a rigorous notion had circulated only in private works of philosophical grooming. To be "chaste" in marriage, the average Christian was expected to avoid adultery, to observe periods of abstinence before the great festivals of the Church, and to refrain from intercourse with women under certain conditions—when menstruating and even when pregnant and nursing. What Ambrose now demanded was that the couple should strive to minimize an ill-defined and ever-present possibility for "unchastity" connected with the pleasure that accompanied the act of intercourse itself. This ideal was held up to the Christians of Vercelli in order to persuade them to choose as their leaders and moral guides only men who had maximized their own control of the sexual urge—those who had lived lives of perpetual celibacy. In this long letter it is possible to glimpse, if only fleetingly, the future contours of the Catholicism of the Latin West.

In the writings of Ambrose's last years, no historian of the early middle ages can fail to catch that note of inward-looking intransigeance, that sharp fear of "admixture," and that exaltation of *integritas*, which enabled the Catholic clergy to provide the most formidable of all the "invisible frontiers" behind which the Roman populations of the post-Imperial West preserved their identity, long after the military frontiers of the Empire had been washed away by barbarian invasion and settlement. On a deep level, the preservation of the virgin bodies of Catholic women and the studied continence of Catholic clergymen echoed the cool, enclosed spaces of the Catholic basilicas. Along with the translucent marble surfaces and the shimmering golden vaults of Catholic shrines, the Catholic notion of virginity spoke of boundaries that no outsider, no heretical barbarian, would dare to breach.

Yet to emphasize this aspect of Ambrose's preaching alone is to anticipate the inflexible Catholicism of the fifth and sixth centuries. It is

96. Ambrose, *Letter* 2.8: 919B.
97. *Letter* 63. 32: 1249C, p. 252. The source is the *Sentences of "Sextus."* See Madec, *Ambroise et la philosophie,* pp. 316–317.

to miss what may have been the most significant aspect of his preaching on the virgin state, both for contemporaries and for all future ages. A connoisseur of Origen's allegorical style, Ambrose was a past master of the alchemy of imagery. His greatest gift as a preacher had been the instinctive artistry with which he conveyed the dynamism of change.[98] We must develop, for a moment, the ears of his late Roman audience in order to understand what else Ambrose had offered them, beneath his somewhat static notion of the virgin body as an *aula pudoris*.

Ambrose's language conveyed a sense of paradox that was essential to his view of the role of the Church in Roman society. His notion of virginity made concrete the integrity of the Catholic church in a hostile society while it endowed the Church with a sense of momentum over against the outside world. In his writings and sermons, the virgin's body was an object charged with powerful, conflicting associations. It was at one and the same time static and dynamic. Precisely because the normal, sexual associations of a woman's fecundity had been renounced in them, the bodies of virgins were calculated to conjure up, in the mind of believers, all that was most "untainted," and so most unambiguously exuberant, in the notions of fertility, of continuity, and of creativity.[99] The closed womb was not only a barred gate. Precisely because it was so closed, it could be most open: it was also a bubbling cauldron;[100] it was a source from which light streamed;[101] it was a cloud showering gentle rain.[102] By reason of the very closedness of her body, the mind, the heart, and the hands of the virgin woman had come to open wide—to the Scriptures, to Christ, and to the poor.[103]

What was truly significant in Ambrose's use of imagery was the way he took these paradoxical qualities in the individual virgin and applied them to the Catholic Church as a whole. Hence the Janus-like quality of his thought on the relation between Church and society. The Catholic congregations that he exhorted were still encouraged by him to think of themselves as on the defensive, and as hedged around with inflexible boundaries. Within the Catholic basilicas, however, the bap-

---

98. H. Savon, "Maniérisme et Allégorie dans l'oeuvre d'Ambroise de Milan," esp. pp. 218–220: a beautiful treatment.

99. See Brown, *The Cult of Saints*, pp. 74–85, for analogous psychological mechanisms mobilized in the cult of the relics of the martyrs.

100. *Inst. virg.* 12.79: 339B.   101. 9.56: 335B.   102. 13.81: 339C.

103. 9.58 and 62: 335C and 336A.

tismal pool and the cooled bodies of the continent spoke also of transformation.

For Ambrose, the exuberance connected with that transformation could spill over to embrace society as a whole. Like the virgin, the Catholic Church was an intact body endowed with a miraculous capacity for growth and nurture. The long-lost solidarity of all humanity would be regained through the Church.[104] Ambrose's imagery implied the possibility of a Catholic Roman world. The existing structures of Roman society might yet be bathed in the cool light of the Church, as it rose in the Empire, "like a moon waxing in its brightness."[105]

Alert listeners to Ambrose's sermons picked up this alluring message. A year after his baptism in Milan, Augustine could describe the Catholic church as "the true mother of all Christians," as if it might also be the mother of all humanity and the guarantor of all existing social bonds:

It is You who make wives subject to their husbands . . . by chaste and faithful obedience; you set husbands over their wives; you join sons to their parents by a freely granted slavery, and set parents above their sons in pious domination. . . . You link citizen to citizen, nation to nation, indeed, You bind all men together in the remembrance of their first parents. . . . You teach kings to rule for the benefit of their peoples; and You it is who warn the peoples to be subservient to their kings.[106]

In the next two generations, Augustine slowly laid bare the full implications of Ambrose's vision of a humanity transformed and disciplined, in all aspects of its social life, within the Catholic Church. It was a vision which, as Augustine's writings as a bishop in Africa soon made plain, caught the problems of human sexuality in a far finer and more exacting mesh of explanation than ever before.

The moral climate against which Augustine came to write first needs to be explained, in order to understand the choices that he faced in the 400s, and to enter into the frame of mind in which his first Latin readers absorbed his works on marriage, sexuality, and the fall of Adam, in the 410s and 420s. Let us, therefore, turn for a moment to Ambrose's dazzling near-contemporary, Jerome. In the vicissitudes of Jerome and his circle, we can measure some of the opportunities and the anxieties that the call of the desert had brought to the West in the late fourth

104. *De officiis* 1.33.170, 3.3.19: 78BC, 159B.
105. *Letter* 18.24, p. 47: 1020C.
106. Augustine, *de moribus ecclesiae catholicae* 1.30.63: P.L. 32: 1336.

and early fifth centuries. In Jerome's letters and commentaries, we can glimpse the devoted widows and virgins, whose symbolic role Ambrose had spoken of with such resonance, coming alive, as real women, actively engaged in the politics of erudition. In Jerome, we can follow the unresolved tensions of a man who had defined himself as the spiritual guide of upper-class women and as the arbiter of the ascetic taste of his age. More than any secular Latin author and second only to Augustine, Jerome made of this astonishing generation the last, and certainly the most stormy, of the "Three great epochs" of Latin literature.[107]

107. R. Syme, *Ammianus and the Historia Augusta,* p. 210.

EIGHTEEN

"Learn of Me a Holy Arrogance:"
Jerome

In August 385, a council of the Roman clergy summoned before them a Dalmatian priest of pronounced ascetic views, and told him to leave their city. Jerome had come to Rome in the autumn of 382, as the protégé of the former Pope, Damasus. A man entering his forties, if not older,[1] Jerome already had long experience in playing the role of the influential outsider. He had returned from the Greek world with a reputation for unusual erudition. He had learned Greek at Antioch. Between 375 and 377, he had spent two years of boredom and mounting irritation in a hermit's cell in the Syrian desert, at Chalcis.[2] Returning to Constantinople, he had sat at the feet of Gregory Nazian-

---

1. The reader should be aware that opinions on the date of Jerome's birth vary by as much as fifteen years, an important point to bear in mind when considering his mood and authority at different moments in his career. For the arguments for an early date, 330, and a survey of contrary views, see J. N. D. Kelly, *Jerome*, pp. 337–339. I remain inclined toward the later date, of 347, adopted by F. Cavallera, *Saint Jérôme: sa vie et son oeuvre*, 2:3–12.

2. Philip Rousseau, *Ascetics, Authority and the Church*, pp. 99–108, is a particularly sensitive study of this period of Jerome's life.

zen, and so he could refer to the friend of Basil of Caesarea as "my teacher"—no small credential for a wandering scholar of Latin origin.[3] In a very short time, Jerome set about using his erudition and his memories of the ascetic life to make the Roman clergy feel small. To make matters worse, he turned away from his male colleagues, with ill-disguised contempt, in order to lavish his erudition on the devoted women of the Roman Church. To Marcella, a widow of many decades' standing, and to Paula, a woman in her thirties, recently devastated by the loss of her husband, Jerome adopted the persona of Origen.

Though dedicated to Pope Damasus, Jerome's translation of Origen's *Homilies on the Song of Songs* was intended for his new circle of female spiritual charges. Origen's daunting erudition, and the warm gusts of his notion of "spiritual delight," would be brought to Rome, by Jerome, in order to minister to the spiritual needs of a circle of well-born women on the Aventine hill. Unfortunately for Jerome's future chances in Rome, these noble ladies were also treated to Jerome's most candid strictures on the worldliness and the Philistinism that he chose to see all around him. When he wrote to Paula's daughter, Eustochium, a consecrated virgin, on how best to shield her spiritual life from corruption, his descriptions of church society in Rome were so vivid that even pagans scrambled to make copies of the letter.[4] It was an album of caricatures in which too many clergymen and upper-class Christians recognized themselves. "Learn of me a holy arrogance; know that you are better than them all."[5]

When Damasus died in December 384, the "cauldron" of irritation boiled over.[6] Jerome had to go. But he ensured that all future ages would see the ugly incident through his eyes alone: "It often happened that I found myself surrounded by virgins, and to some of these I expounded the Divine Books as best I could."[7]

By next year, Jerome was settled in Bethlehem, "a somewhat more distinguished city."[8] Following the example set, a decade previously, by Melania the Elder, Paula sailed to the Holy Land with Eustochium.

3. Jerome, *de viris illustribus* 117: *Patrologia Latina* 23: 707C.

4. Rufinus, *Apologia contra Hieronymum* 2.5, in M. Simonetti, ed., *Corpus christianorum*, p. 86.

5. *Letter* 22.16: *P.L.* 22: 403.

6. Jerome, *Interpretatio libri Didymi de Spiritu Sancto: P.L.* 23: 102A.

7. *Letter* 45.2: 481.

8. Jerome, *In Ecclesiasten*, Praef. in M. Adriaen, ed., *Corpus Christianorum* 72:249—others read *angustiori*, "somewhat smaller;" the irony is equally clear.

Jerome joined them on the last lap of their pilgrimage. They settled within sight of the cave where Christ was born, in a silent, sun-soaked landscape, dotted with hill-villages. The songs of the peasants working in the valley below wafted echoes of the ancient Psalms of David into the cells of these erudite Latins. It was good to have come to the imagined center of the world:

We shall go into His tabernacle; we shall worship in the place where His feet have stood.[9]

Paula used her wealth to found a convent for fellow-exiles. Disaffected gentlewomen, their vocations thwarted in the West, gathered around her at Bethlehem. The lady-companions of these women were lodged in a separate building, lest the senatorial ladies still be tempted to treat them as their servants.[10] A short distance away, Jerome was established at the head of a small monastery. The considerable expenses involved in the setting up of his library, in the hiring of stenographers, and in retaining a Jew to give him lessons in Hebrew were paid for out of Paul's resources.

Jerome enjoyed a decade of deep happiness: he had begun, at last, to reap the reward of the truthful:

He shall fill thy mouth with laughing and thy lips with rejoicing.[11]

After many hastily abandoned sketches, he had hit upon the self-portrait that would become a classic. Jerome the sheltered scholar-monk of Bethlehem was the Jerome to whom the medieval West looked back with love and admiration: "the sound, the well-tongued sage, fair Jerome of Bethlehem, whom our sisters used to visit."[12]

Our familiarity with this aspect of the personality and career of Jerome should not lull us into overlooking the novelty and the potential dangers of his situation. In the 380s and early 390s, he made the persona of Origen his own in one crucial respect. He took for granted the profound identity of the minds of men and women. He saw no reason

---

9. *Letter* 46.11: 491 and 108.10: 885, citing Psalm 131.7. See esp. E. D. Hunt, *Holy Land Pilgrimage in the Late Roman Empire*, pp. 171–179 and C. Saulnier, "La vie monastique en Terre Sainte auprès des lieux de pélérinage," *Miscellanea Historiae Ecclesiasticae*, 6.

10. *Letter* 108.19: 896.

11. *In Eccles.* 3.13, p. 278, citing Job 8:21—I have used the fuller citation from the Authorized Version.

12. W. Stokes, ed., *The Martyrology of Oengus the Culdee*, p. 197.

why Origen's ideal of an unrelenting ascetic labor of the mind, associated with the Christian's daily meditation on the "delights of the Law," should not be extended in its full rigors to mature and well-educated women such as Marcella and Paula. Such women had both the spiritual and the cultural advantages that made such a style of life eminently practicable. They could read impressive quantities of Greek. Melania had read three million lines of Origen and two and half million lines of more recent authors, the Cappadocians included. She had mastered, that is, a body of Christian literature three hundred times larger than Homer's *Iliad*. "And she did not read them once only and in an offhand way, but she worked on them, dredging through each work seven or eight times." Melania could be trusted to know a heresy when she encountered one as well as did any other learned Christian.[13] Women copied and distributed commentaries and translations.[14] Paula eventually learned to read the Psalms in Hebrew without a trace of a foreign accent.[15]

In the upper classes, educated women were a common enough phenomenon. Aristocrats strove to raise their daughters in such a manner that, "Inspired by their sense of high birth, they rise above the ordinary behavior of mankind."[16] The imbalance between male and female commitment to the life of the Latin Church ensured that serious Christian women enjoyed advantages that few Western males possessed. Marcella's palace was a meeting place for clergymen from the East. Her Greek was probably as good as that of Ambrose, and her library as well stocked in up-to-date Greek books. This was a rarity in fourth-century Rome. For such a woman, the ideal "fecundity" associated with the virgin state was no highflown metaphor: it was a perfectly real matter, as demonstrable as that of any male spiritual leader, for whom images of asexual procreation, and of virginal fertility, through spiritual guidance and scholarship, had long carried a very heavy charge of meaning.[17] For such a woman, virginal fertility implied a high level of actual creativity, in the mind, by word of mouth, and through the

13. Palladius, *Lausiac History* 55.3, in R. T. Meyer, ed., *Palladius: The Lausiac History*, pp. 136–137; cf. Jerome, *Letter* 37.3–4: 463; 38.4: 464; 39.1: 466 and 65.2; 512. See the excellent survey of Franca Ela Consolino, "Modelli di comportamento e modi di santificazione per l'aristocrazia femminile d'Occidente."

14. *In Ephes.* 2, Praef.: 507BC; *Letter* 49.2: 512.   15. *Letter* 108.26: 902.

16. Pseudo-Jerome, *de virginitate* 12: *P.L.* 30: 178A; see Peter Brown, "Pelagius and His Supporters," in *Religion and Society in the Age of Saint Augustine*, pp. 186–189.

17. Jerome, *Letter* 52.4: 530, on himself.

pen. There was nothing strange about speaking of an educated Christian virgin as "generous in giving . . . outstanding in nobility, fertile in writing, worthy of the esteem of the whole world."[18] The culture that Jerome offered assumed that an upper-class woman, as much as any man, carried within her "a heart in which a library of books is stored."[19]

That Jerome did not encourage women to become theological authors in their own right meant no more than that he, like all other late antique males, wished to keep for himself the dubious privilege of being aggressive to other men. Given the contemporary preoccupation with the need to preserve an oasis of Christian culture untainted by male profane learning and by male competitive urges, well-educated "daughters of Jerusalem"—prodigious readers and memorizers of the holy texts and their learned commentaries—could maintain, quite as effectively as could any male monks, the quiet heartbeat of unsullied Christian truth. Face to face spiritual guidance by women with a formidable command of the Scriptures touched men as well as women. We have seen how, in Jerusalem, Melania the Elder induced the deeply disturbed Evagrius to live up to his ascetic vocation.[20] Two decades later, a young man wrote back to his home, to report that

In the land of Sicily I found a woman, most distinguished in the eyes of the world, but even more outstanding in the things of God. She showed me the way of truth in all things. . . . convincing me [on how best to live the Christian life] by reason and out of the Scriptures.[21]

Upper-class women were often the only persons from whom new books could be borrowed for transcription.[22] They intervened firmly, if only by word of mouth, as arbiters of right and wrong in theological controversies.[23] In Rome, Marcella and her equivalents helped Christians

---

18. *Laus Eunomiae: Patrologia Latina Supplementum* 3: 1430. I am uncertain whether this is the Eunomia, daughter of the *rhetor* Nazarius—see Jerome, *Chron.* ad ann. 340: 499, or the daughter of Turcius Apronianus and Avita, friends of Rufinus and of Paulinus of Nola: see J. R. Martindale, ed., *The Prosopography of the Later Roman Empire*, 2:421.

19. Bachiarius, *Letter 1: P.L.Suppl.* 1: 1036.

20. Palladius, *Lausiac History* 38.9; Meyer, trans., p. 113.

21. Pelagian letter, *Honorificentiae tuae* 5: *P.L. Suppl.* 1: 1692–1693.

22. Jerome, *in Ephes.* Praef. 469B and *The Life of Melania the Younger* 26, in D. Gorce, ed., *Vie de Sainte Mélanie*, p. 178; Elizabeth A. Clark, trans., *Life of Saint Melanie*, p. 46 and comment on p. 12.

23. *Letter* 127.7 and 9: 1091, 1092.

of both sexes to make sense of a world in which letters, manuscripts, and doctrinal statements flooded into Italy from the Greek East.

In the Holy Land, the somewhat marginal colonies of upper-class Latins and the crowded retinues of great ladies on pilgrimage offered opportunities for the flowering of spiritual companionship between male and female ascetics that were unique in the Mediterranean world. By a readily understandable paradox, those ascetics who profited most, both spiritually and (we must always remember) financially, from close contact with devout women deplored such companionships when practiced by anyone except themselves. Jerome attacked one distinguished lady for having "mixed insouciantly" with male clergymen when traveling in the Holy Land.[24] He poured scorn on a rival who had remained active in Rome, "running around the cells of virgins and pious widows and discoursing gravely on the Scriptures."[25]

In both attacks, we see Jerome himself as others saw him. The unknown author of the text that may later have served as the basis for Palladius' *Lausiac History*, the classic contemporary description of the monks of Egypt, faced the same dilemma as did Jerome. He wrote that monks should avoid ascetic women. Their silver hair and wrinkled faces might give rise to disturbing thoughts. Worse still, monks might be tempted to speak of such women with contempt, as ridiculous old creatures. Yet this author wrote for a woman and ascribed his own conversion to the ascetic life to a visit that he had made to Egypt in the company of that woman's "holy mother."[26] It is easy to be cynical about such gyrations. Yet they reflected genuine anger that an ancient, poignant hope might be betrayed by lack of circumspection: if men and women could not learn to see each other as sexless creatures, as *"neither male nor female,* [but] . . . *one in Christ Jesus,"* in the most sacred places of the Christian world, where would they ever be able to do so?

The constant literary preoccupation with female companionship showed that such practices were common among the privileged ex-

24. *Letter* 54.13: 556. At least Jerome cannot be said to be obsequious in his choice of targets—the lady may have been Poemenia, a relative of the Emperor! Paul Devos, "Silvie la sainte pélérine."

25. *Letter* 50.3: 514; see Y. M. Duval, "Pélage est-il le censeur inconnu de l'Adversus Jovinianum à Rome en 393; ou: du 'portrait-robot' de l'hérétique chez S. Jérôme," pp. 535–536.

26. R. Draguet, *Les formes syriaques de la matière de l'Histoire Lausiaque*, 1.19*–20*.

patriates of the Holy Land. Other regions were less tolerant. The case of Priscillian revealed the savagery of local reactions to pious women caught in positions of invidious eminence in the provincial societies of Spain and southern Gaul. In 380, little groups of men and women had begun to alarm Spanish bishops. On the eve of the great festivals, they would withdraw together from the city, to hold "retreats" in mountain villas, under the guidance of inspired, self-styled "teachers" of the Scriptures.[27] In 382, Priscillian settled outside Bordeaux, on the estate of Euchrotia, the widow of Delphidius, a local professor of impeccable conventionality.

By 386, everyone agreed that Delphidius had been lucky to have died when he did; the subsequent behavior of his womenfolk would have brought crushing shame upon him. Priscillian and Euchrotia were executed on a charge of sorcery and immorality. Euchrotia's daughter was rumored to have been seduced by her mother's spiritual guide. Another noble woman was stoned to death by a mob in the streets of Bordeaux.[28] It was a chilling reminder that, outside a few privileged milieux, intimacy with influential and militant Christian women might lead to violent death and, at the very least, to the lasting stigma of sexual innuendo. In the West, as a generation earlier in the East, the clergy came to learn that true Christian courage lay in cultivating a holy timidity with regard to women.[29] Spiritual friendships, such as might easily spring up between serious men and women faced by the moral torpor of their local churches, were condemned. They were branded as a form of "clandestine subversion."[30] They threatened to undermine the "wall of moral rigor, the overcoming of lower-class habits,"[31] that made the celibate clergy of the West, "a pure white Senate house . . . [in which] severity, to women holds undisputed sway."[32]

By the late 390s, the clouds that these fears had silently generated in Italy, Spain and Gaul came to darken Jerome's horizon. He found

27. Council of Saragossa, canons 1, 4 and 7, in J. Vives, ed., Concilios Visigóticos y Hispano-Romanos, pp. 17–18.

28. The best discussion of this aspect of Priscillian's career is in Ray van Dam, Leadership and Community in Late Antique Gaul, pp. 67–76.

29. Pseudo-Cyprian, de singularitate clericorum 2, in G. Hartel, ed., Corpus Scriptorum Ecclesiasticorum Latinorum, 3:176. It would be helpful to know more exactly the date and location of this tract. A. von Harnack, Texte und Untersuchungen, suggests a Donatist writing in Rome in the mid-fourth century; R. Gryson, Les origines du célibat ecclésiastique, p. 195 n 6—Toulouse or Bordeaux in the early fifth century.

30. De sing. cler. 6, p. 178.   31. 39, p. 214.   32. 45, p. 220.

himself in a peculiarly intimate dilemma. In the 380s, he had based his own, remarkably generous attitude to the cultural role of women on a model of the human person that was drawn from the exegetical works of Origen. This model had been based on an austerely spiritual view of human beings. Bodies endowed with the sexual characteristics of men and women were ephemeral things, into which the vibrant spirit had been placed for a short moment. It was possible for "spiritual" persons to live as if the restraints and perils of the body did not affect them. They could form companionships based on the meeting of like minds. A textual scholar first and foremost—and, therefore, not greatly given to reflection—Jerome accepted this model of the human person because he found it in the pages of Origen's commentaries and because it enabled him to live at ease with gifted and influential women such as Marcella at Rome and, then, with Paula at Bethlehem.

He was less prepared to allow others to draw such radical consequences from his own behavior. Once settled in Bethlehem, he maintained an avid readership for letters of advice as to how to conduct the ascetic life. In these letters, Jerome the heir of Origen clashed with Jerome the satirist, the passionate exponent of the weaknesses of the flesh. He rapidly established himself, in the Latin world, as a monastic Jean Jacques Rousseau: for all his notorious irritability, Jerome was a man whom a younger generation of militants loved to love. He passed on to his readers a vivid sense of the challenge and romance of the desert. But he also communicated to them an acute awareness of the sexual dangers of the body.

Jerome, in fact, knew little of the desert about which he wrote and next to nothing of the patient disciplines on which the Desert Fathers based their certainty that even the sexual urge might be transcended. It was his contemporaries who had explored the life of the Egyptian desert most thoroughly, bringing back news of its exciting possibilities to the monastic settlements of the Holy Land. When Jerome had lived in Constantinople, in 380, he could have met a young deacon in the entourage of Gregory Nazianzen, Evagrius of Pontus. Evagrius' career was destined to be quite as dramatic as his own. The brilliant young deacon fled from Constantinople to avoid becoming involved in a love affair with a well-placed, married lady. Melania helped him to recover from the experience in Jerusalem. By 382, he was settled in the sands of Nitria, moving deeper into the desert, a little later, to the harsh cells at Kellia. At Kellia, he suffered quite as terribly as Jerome had done at Chalcis.[33] His *Antirrhetikos*, on *How to Answer Back*, was a notebook of day-to-day temptations. It is an extraordinary portrait of the inner life of a late antique Christian. In it Evagrius recorded 487 separate *logismoi*, powerful or obsessive trains of thought, each accompanied with appropriate words of Scripture with which to banish or to welcome the experience. They included sexual fantasies of the most overt kind:

Against the demon of fornication taking on the likeness of a naked woman, with languishing walk, her whole body indicating sensual delight.[34]

Against thoughts of spending long periods of time with a married woman, with frequent visits at close quarters, as if she were deriving great spiritual benefit from us.[35]

Against the thought which takes the form of a beautiful woman engaging us in serious conversation, while we wish to do evil and shameful things with her.[36]

Against the demon who puts into my mind that I should marry a wife and become a father of sons, and not spend my time here starving and battling with foul thoughts.[37]

Yet Evagrius, for all his terrible precision, was a man in the tradition of Origen. This meant that the life of the desert, with its stretches of time quite as huge and frequently as bleak as the unending sands, stood for him as an intimation of the limitless patience of God. He had not intended the *Antirrhetikos* to be read as an anxious document. It was, rather, a route-map. It recorded, with merciful clarity, phases of temptation that the monk must pass through before a vast peace could settle in his soul.

From Kellia, Evagrius wrote to Melania at Jerusalem, addressing her, quite simply, as "my lord."[38] He composed highly condensed precepts for the monks and nuns connected with Melania on the Mount of Ol-

33. Palladius, *Lausiac History* 38.3:10; Meyer, pp. 111–113; see esp. A. Guillaumont, *Les "Kephalaia Gnostica" d'Évagre le Pontique*, pp. 47–61, F. X. Murphy, "Evagrius Ponticus and Origenism," R. Hanson and G. Crouzel, eds., *Origeniana Tertia*, and J. G. Bunge, "Origenismus-Gnostizismus. Zum geistesgeschichtlichen Standort des Evagrios Pontikos," pp. 36–44.

34. Evagrius, *Antirrhetikos* 2.32, in W. Frankenberg, ed., *Evagrius Ponticus*, pp. 488–489. Syriac translated back, inconveniently for us frail moderns, into Greek.

35. 2.35, pp. 488–480.   36. 2.36, pp. 490–491.   37. 2.49, pp. 490–491.

38. Evagrius, *Letter to Melania*, in Frankenberg, ed., p. 612.1; now trans. G. Bunge, *Evagrios Pontikos: Briefe aus der Wüste*, p. 303; see esp. pp. 193–200.

ives.[39] The state of *apatheia*, of transcendance of the "passions," which Evagrius and his supporters regarded as the culmination of the spiritual life, was not a state envisioned only for disembodied recluses. Rather, it was a grace conferred on spiritual guides of both sexes, giving them a vast openness to others. Their hard-won purity "shone in a gentle soul, like the daystar in a dawn sky."[40]

One such "passionless" person was Amma Talis, a mother superior of a great Egyptian convent:

Sixty nuns were with her. They loved her so much that no lock was ever placed on the courtyard gate of the monastery. . . . The old woman had such a high degree of serenity [wrote Palladius, a bishop greatly preoccupied with the dangers of female company] that she came in and sat down beside me, and placed her hands on my shoulder in a spontaneous gesture of companionship.[41]

It was a transcendance many would envy. Only three years before his own death, even the scrupulous Evagrius could sense, in the ebbing of his sexual fantasies, the onset of the crowning grace of purity of heart.[42]

Jerome the Latin, by contrast, was a man in a hurry, writing to a generation in a hurry. All that he had allowed his readers to know of his own experience in Chalcis had been deliberately calculated to heighten their anxiety:

O how often, when I was living in the desert, in that lonely waste, scorched by the burning sun, that affords to hermits their primitive dwelling place, how often did I fancy myself surrounded by the pleasures of Rome . . . though in my fear of Hell, I had condemned myself to this prison house, where my only companions were scorpions and wild beasts, I often found myself surrounded by bands of dancing girls. My face was pale with fasting; but though my limbs were cold as ice, my mind was burning with desire, and the fires of lust kept bubbling up before me while my flesh was as good as dead.[43]

---

39. Bunge, "Origenismus-Gnotizismus," pp. 35–39.

40. Evagrius, *Sententiae ad monachos*, translated by Rufinus, *Patrologia Graeca* 40: 1281C.

41. Palladius, *Lausiac History*, 59.1; Meyer, trans., p. 140.

42. *Lausiac History*, 38.13; Meyer, trans., p. 114.

43. Jerome, *Letter* 22.7: 398, expanded in *Vita Hilarionis* 7: *P.L.* 23: 32A. Evagrius, we should note, described exactly the same experience: *Practicus* 54, in A. Guillaumont, ed., *Traité Pratique ou le Moine*, pp. 624–625. For an excellent study of one such image of Jerome in the Renaissance, see Bernard Aikema, "Lorenzo Lotto and the 'Ospedale de San Zuane Polo,' in D. Rosand, ed., *Interpretazioni veneziane. Studi di storia dell'arte in onore di Michelangelo Muraro*, and, recently, Eugene F. Rice, *Saint Jerome in the Renaissance*.

This artistically brilliant *contraposto* of the sweltering body of the monk and the untamed sexual drives of his mind was a device so transparently simple as to become almost instantly canonical in the Latin world. Jerome applied it briskly to the problems of young girls in Rome. Eustochium must beware: "If those whose bodies are eroded can still be assailed by such thoughts, what must a girl endure, who is exposed to the thrills of easy living?" She must always remember that she carried her worst enemy "shut up inside herself"; her "hot little body" must be spared the devastating touch of wine, of heavy food, and, of course, the risks of close male company.[44]

The human body remained for Jerome a darkened forest, filled with the roaring of wild beasts, that could be controlled only by rigid codes of diet and by the strict avoidance of occasions for sexual attraction.[45] No amount of ascetic labor, no shared intellectual enthusiasms could overcome this fact. Writing letters of advice to distant ladies, Jerome placed the sayings of Jesus Christ on the same footing as the authors of Roman Comedy: both the Creator of human nature, and the Roman authors, sharp observers of humanity's coarser antics, agreed that men and women were irreducibly sexual beings, and a constant source of temptation to each other.[46]

Those who delighted in Jerome's letters were not unduly worried by such bleak observations: optimism was out of place in a Roman satirist. Yet Jerome's authority as a militant ascetic was supposed to rest on more solid foundations. He posed as an exegete, with opinions of his own, in a generation of Latins who had rediscovered Saint Paul.[47] For Jerome and his contemporaries, Paul was, in the words of Ambrose, "the teacher of the gentiles, the skillful driver of our moral life, the judge of our most intimate emotions."[48] What Paul had revealed about himself in his letters was held to be the surest guide of all to the strengths and limitations of the human person.

Faced by the letters of Paul, Jerome caricatured himself. In his exegesis of the Apostle, he contributed more heavily than did any other contemporary Latin writer to the definitive sexualization of Paul's notion of *the flesh*. An unrelieved sense of sexual danger, lodged deep

---

44. *Letter* 22.8: 399.
45. *Letters* 22.11: 400; 54.9: 554; 79.7: 729 and *in Titum* 1: *P.L.* 26: 601D.
46. *Letter* 54.9: 554.   47. Peter Brown, *Augustine of Hippo*, p. 151.
48. Ambrose, *de viduis* 13.79: *P.L.* 16: 272B.

within the physical person, swallowed up all other meanings of the flesh:

If after nakedness, after fasting, after prison, beatings and torments, Paul still used to cry: *Oh wretched man that I am, who will deliver me from this body of death,* do you think that you, my lady, can feel secure?[49]

What human being is not terrified by the Apostle's line of argument?[50]

In 393, Jerome intervened in Roman affairs, in order to chastise Jovinian for having placed married couples on the same level as consecrated virgins of the church. The pamphlet was a disaster. One of his own friends, Pammachius, simply withdrew it from circulation.[51] Roman Christians were shocked by Jerome's assertion that even first marriages were regrettable, if pardonable, capitulations to the flesh, and that second marriages were only one step away from the brothel.[52] He went on to suggest that priests were holy only in so far as they possessed the purity of virgins. The married clergy were mere raw recruits in the army of the church, brought in because of a temporary shortage of battle-hardened veterans of lifelong celibacy.[53] It was a memorable statement of the ascetic viewpoint at its most unpleasant and impracticable.

Jerome's *Against Jovinian* acted as an inspiration and as an irritant throughout the Latin world. Some militants were evidently delighted with it: they were prepared to agree that marriage was "suspiciously like an evil way of life."[54] Others were less impressed. An anonymous Roman priest, whom modern scholars call "Ambrosiaster" (the "would-be Ambrose"), went out of his way to show that it was quite possible to enjoy the dignity of a celibate priesthood without sharing Jerome's undisguised contempt for once-married clergymen. Like the High Priests of Israel, priests in the Catholic church abstained from their wives because they had to approach the altar; they abstained permanently, because the altar of the New Dispensation was holier than that of the

---

49. Jerome, *Letter* 22.5: 397.

50. Ibid. 79.5: 727, cf. *Adversus Jovinianum* 2.3–4: *P.L.* 23: 297D–302B.

51. *Letter* 49.2: 512.   52. *Adv. Jov.* 1.13, 15: 231C–232B, 234D.

53. Ibid. 1.34: 268D–269A.

54. *Epistula de castitate* 10.6: *Patrologia Latina: Supplementum* 1: 1483—written by a follower of Pelagius.

Old.[55] It was a view more acceptable to the *esprit de corps* of the clergy than was Jerome's invidious exaltation of a purity better left to nuns. In order to make his point, "Ambrosiaster" adopted a less alarmist, more old-fashioned, attitude to the power of the sexual drive. He presented sexuality as amenable to self-control. The postmarital celibacy of the clergy was a practicable course. The aging process, by which the body lost its youthful heat, could be counted on to support the will. It reduced the force of sexual desire to manageable proportions in middle-aged clergymen. Even among the young, the prolonged periods of sexual abstinence imposed on married couples by the ceremonial life of the Roman Church, with its feast-days, fasts, and vigils of preparation for the Eucharist, ensured that Christian couples had little enough time for sex. They did not need to fill their heads with misplaced anxiety about the subtle and perpetual ravages of sexual feeling that so evidently obsessed Jerome.[56]

Other writers felt that they needed to reassure married Christians. The later author of a treatise addressed to a certain Gregoria fell back on Chrysostom's sermons in order to prove that it was possible to be married and yet to lead a pious Christian life. The pious woman could turn a large Roman household into a holy place. But, in order to do this, she must accept the laws of the household. She had been given over entirely to her husband, "bought by the marriage contract and bound in as many knots as you have parts of the body."[57] Yet docility, combined with the frank use of "the embraces permitted to marital good cheer,"[58] would enable her to establish her own religious authority in the home.

On religious matters, her will would rule supreme, "as if to contradict it were sacrilege."[59] Instead of the virginity and self-exile proposed by Jerome, Gregoria was urged to become the benevolent head of a Roman *palazzo*, where the servants were well-behaved, well-dressed, and well-fed.[60] Of all the ways in which a Christian upper-class woman could show a "holy arrogance,"[61] the course propounded in this treatise was the most deliberately moderate. It was a firm, and rare, answer to the zeal of Jerome and his supporters.

---

55. Ambrosiaster, *in 1 Cor.7.9*, in H. J. Vogels, ed., *Corpus Scriptorum Ecclesiasticorum Latinorum* 82(2): p. 74. A. Stuiber, "Ambrosiaster," summarizes what has been suggested by modern scholars about this elusive figure.

56. Ambrosiaster, *in 1 Cor. 7.5*, p. 72.   57. *Liber ad Gregoriam* 7: P.L. Suppl. 3: 228.

58. 7: 230.   59. 7: 229.   60. 18–19: 243–247.   61. 24: 255.

Meanwhile, on his own doorstep, in Jerusalem, it seemed as if Jerome's orthodoxy itself might be impugned. He had only recently acclaimed Origen as "an immortal genius,"[62] and had made frequent use of his authority as an exegete to bait the Philistines of the Latin world, calling him "the man whom no one but an ignoramus could fail to admit to have been the greatest teacher of the church since the Apostles."[63] But, after 393, Origen came to be touched by the fatal stigma of heresy. The "face of the dragon" was unveiled.[64] On issues that touched on the nature of the human person, and most particularly on the extent to which the differences between the sexes could be regarded as transcendable, Origen was shown to have belonged to a very distant age. He stood before the men of the late fourth century with all the chilling majesty of a great, long-extinct creature. Jerome was forced to choose. He could no longer base his *persona* as a spiritual guide to noble ladies on so unpopular a figure. After 395, he came down firmly on the side of views that stressed the lasting differences between the sexes and the irremovable risk of sexual temptation between men and women.

By contrast, Jerome's boyhood friend, Rufinus, had been installed with Melania on the Mount of Olives since 378. He had eight years more experience of the venomous ecclesiastical politics of the Holy Places. Seen from Jerusalem, Jerome was a domineering and envious man: one holy man had declared that

The lady Paula, who looks after him, will die first and will be set free at last from his meanness. [For] because of him no holy person will live in those parts. His bad temper would drive out even his own brother.[65]

Jerome and his circle were isolated. Melania and Rufinus had retained their contacts with Italy. Unlike Jerome and Paula, they had not burned their boats in Rome. Rather than face a "witch-hunt," Melania and Rufinus were prepared to withdraw from Jerusalem. Rufinus returned to Rome in 397, quietly determined to take up where Jerome had left off in 385. He would make the works of Origen available to an Italian public. In the Preface that he wrote to the translation of Origen's great

62. Jerome, *de vir. ill.* 54: 665C.
63. *Liber de nominibus Hebraicis: P.L.* 23: 771A; see now P. Meyvaert, "Excerpts from an Unknown Treatise of Jerome to Gaudentius of Brescia," pp. 213–234—a most important discovery.
64. *Contra Johannem Hierosolymitanum* 1.25: *P.L.* 23: 375B.
65. Palladius, *Lausiac History* 36.6–7; Meyer, trans., pp. 104–105.

handbook, *On First Principles,* he referred explicitly to Jerome's translation of Origen's *Homilies on the Song of Songs* as the justification of his own enterprise. He went on to imply that, in turning away from such translations, Jerome had betrayed his early promise.[66]

Nothing could have caused Jerome more acute annoyance. If Origen's views were not condemned in the West, Rufinus would replace him on the spot as the mentor of the Latin world. If Origen were condemned, however, then Rufinus' appeal to his own example would ensure that Jerome would be condemned along with him. Once Jerome was thought heretical, his lifetime of scholarly labor would be wasted: he would no longer be appreciated in the Latin world, and his little community would no longer receive visits, and funds, from appreciative Latin pilgrims to the Holy Land.[67] Even for a man blessed with a more placid temperament than Jerome was, it was not a situation conducive to good nature.

It is, however, important to step back a little, in order to appreciate the long-term implications of Jerome's sudden disillusionment with his former hero, Origen, and his savage breach with his life-long friend, Rufinus. In the Origenist controversy of the late fourth century, we are dealing with the visceral reaction of a whole generation to views of the person that had come to seem deeply disturbing to them. In condemning Origen, Greek and Latin Christians, Jerome the most strident among them, turned away forever from the prospect of a limitless fluidity of the human person that they thought they perceived (not always correctly) to have lain at the very heart of Origen's thought. They did not wish their own bodies, and, with their bodies, the landmarks of their own society, to be rendered evanescent by the vertiginous immensity implied in Origen's notion of the slow transformation of all created spirits.

Jerome remained loyal to Origen as an exegete and textual scholar. What he may have realized only for the first time, after 393, was that the works of Origen harbored a view of the person deeply alien to his deepest prejudices and to those of his Latin readers. On such issues, Jerome reacted to Origen with all the sharpness of a man disowning a part of his own past.[68]

---

66. Rufinus, *Praefatio in Libros Origenis Peri Archon* 1, in Simonetti, ed., *Corpus Christianorum* p. 245.
67. Well seen by Kelly, *Jerome,* pp. 225–226.
68. Robert F. Evans, *Pelagius: Inquiries and Reappraisals,* pp. 11–17.

What was at stake, in the first place, was the immediacy of God's rewards for those who had undertaken the ascetic life. Epiphanius of Salamis, the Grand Old Man of Palestinian monasticism, had made this plain when he had preached in Jerusalem, in 393. He attacked Origen's notion of a purely spiritual Paradise. On that occasion, Jerome observed, the bright young men of the Bishop of Jerusalem's entourage had ostentatiously wrinkled their noses, coughed and tapped their foreheads.[69] The old man appeared, to them, to have advocated the most crassly materialist views on Paradise and on the resurrection of the body. But Jerusalem was filled with monks, who had streamed into the city for the festival.[70] For such monks, Paradise was not some supra-celestial, spiritual state, from which their souls had fallen on to the dull earth. Paradise was close to hand. It had always been on earth. The rivers Geon and Euphrates flowed from it: Epiphanius himself had drunk from their very waters.[71] Paradise was within their grasp. It could be regained, in their own desert, in their own time, by mighty monks. When Saint John had written, *we do not know what we shall be*, he did not intend to make the labors of the monks seem but one, rather insignificant, stage in a process of transformation so gigantic that the final features of the human person who emerged from it, at the resurrection of the dead, would be frighteningly unrecognizable. Rather, the glory of the Lord could flash out from their own humbled countenances, in their own times, and in its fullness, as it had once glowed from the faces of Moses and Saint Stephen.[72]

It was the same with the resurrection of the flesh. What was to rise again was the flesh that they could pinch between their fingers.[73] The flesh that hung loose about their bones from long fasting, that was cooked hard as a clay pot in the purifying heat of the desert: this was the same flesh that would finally put on its full glory. Their own peculiarly intimate, physical experience of the body's drastic changes, as it shriveled about them in the desert, would lead directly to the final transformation that lay in store for it at the end of time. The bodies

---

69. Jerome, *Contra Joh. Hieros.* 11: 362A.

70. P. Nautin, "Études de chronologie hiéronymienne (393–394) 2," p. 73. See now Elizabeth A. Clark, "The Place of Jerome's Commentary on Ephesians in the Origenist Controversy."

71. *Letter* 51.5: 522—taken from Epiphanius' letter to John of Jerusalem, translated and prudently circulated by Jerome: see Nautin, "Études de chronologie," pp. 84–85.

72. *Letter* 51.7: 526, cf. *Apophthegmata Patrum*, Pambo 12: *Patrologia Graeca* 65: 372A.

73. *Letter* 84.5: 747.

on which they had labored so hard would not simply evaporate into thin air, as Origen seemed to imply.[74]

Jerome had always lived close enough to the thought of Tertullian, whom he savored as a Latin stylist and frequently consulted as a theological dictionary, to tend to take for granted Tertullian's grippingly physical view of the body and its resurrection. He had no difficulty in mobilizing Tertullian's telling phrases in his defense of Epiphanius against the Bishop of Jerusalem.[75] But he was also aware of the changing temper of his times. He himself had contributed handsomely, in his letters, to the sharp tone of sexual anxiety that stressed the irreducible sexual differences between male and female bodies, and that lingered with studied alarm on the dangers that stemmed from these differences. He immediately drew attention to the further implications of Origen's notion of fluidity. He wrote to his friends in Rome that it was absurd to expect, as Origen and Rufinus seemed to imply, that women were creatures destined to be divested forever of the sexual characteristics that separated them from "us" males:

So now the little ladies hold up their breasts, they slap their bellies, groin and thighs, and stroke their hairless cheeks. "What use is it to us," they say "if it is this frail body that rises from the dead."[76]

In remarks such as this, Jerome canceled an unspoken charter. Previously, radical Christians had striven, in heroic defiance of the "commonsense" notions of their contemporaries, to find a place for intimacy with devout women as colleagues, disciples, and mentors. A constant preoccupation with the transcendance of sexual differences associated with the resurrection state of the body fed back into such groups. Views on the resurrection provided a mythic charter for their own attempts to justify close collaboration with women. By meeting women as equals in their study-groups, they anticipated a future age when the ache of sexual division would be abolished. Almost without knowing it, Jerome had betrayed his own past as the mentor of Marcella, Paula, and Eustochium. In rounding on what he took to be the views of Origen, he declared that an ancient Christian image of trans-

74. *Letter* 92.2: 763—letter of Theophilus of Alexandria, translated by Jerome.
75. See esp. Y. M. Duval, "Tertullien contre Origène sur la résurrection de la chair."
76. *Letter* 84.6: 748.

formation, by which male and female became one in Jesus Christ, was irrevocably inapplicable to his own times.[77]

It was important for Jerome's readers in the West that men should remain men, and women should remain women. Both Ambrose and Jerome had placed a heavy symbolic weight on the perpetual, closed state of the virgin body. Such a view implied that human beings were fixed within irrevocable boundaries. Virginity involved the heroic defense of the integrity of a specifically male or female body: *I am a wall, and my breasts are as a strong tower.*[78] Bodies defended with such care were not destined to melt away in some distant transformation. Far from being a superficial and transitory layer of the person, sexual differences, and the behavior appropriate to them, were validated for all eternity.[79]

To validate the body, in this manner, meant locking male and female bodies into their present, observed constraints. No imaginative alternative might relativize the cramping particularity of the body. No dream of a far-distant transformation could make the present body seem transparent to the spirit. Such a view could have cruel results. The drift in theological attitudes, though limited to sheltered circles of monks and scholars, coincided with a marked hardening of official attitudes. For the first time in history, in 390, the Roman people witnessed the public burning of male prostitutes, dragged from the homosexual brothels of Rome. The Emperor Theodosius' edict (preserved in full, significantly, by a writer anxious to prove the agreement of the Mosaic with the Roman laws) shows clearly, in the very incoherence of its moral indignation, the slow turning of the tide. For a male to play a female role, by allowing himself to become the passive partner in a sexual act, had long been repugnant. The Emperor declared that to do so "sapped the rude rural vigor of the Roman people." But it was now assumed to be equally shocking that a soul allotted in perpetuity to the "sacrosanct dwelling-place" of a recognizably male body should have tried to force that body into female poses.[80]

77. Jerome, *in Ephes.* 3.5.29: *P.L.* 26: 564D. explained away in *C. Rufinum* 1.28–29, *Corpus Christianorum* 79, pp. 27–29: *P.L.* 23: 419C–421A.

78. *Letter* 107.7: 874.

79. *C. Joh. Hieros.* 31: 383A; *Letter* 108.22–23: 899–901.

80. *Mosaicarum et Romanarum Legum Collatio* 5.3, in S. Riccobono, ed., *Fontes Iuris Romani Anteiustiniani*, 1.2: 481, cf. *Codex Theodosianus* 9.7.6, where only the penalty is given.

Behind these sharp anxieties, there lay a yet more serious issue, which Jerome exploited with a polemist's flair. Origen's view of the human person provided too unstable, too shifting a screen for believers to project upon it their deepest hopes for the world beyond the grave. Theodora, a Spanish widow, who had lived with her husband in continence in the last years of his life, was reassured, by Jerome, that the sexual differences whose perils Theodora and her husband had overcome, would remain in the next world. She would be rewarded, in heaven, by a bond to a recognizable man, in a love that was finally shorn of the taint of physical desire.[81]

It was a powerful message. In the late fourth century, Latin Christians (especially those of the class Jerome addressed) had peopled the other world with saints. They were prepared to draw in their own likeness the men and women whom God had taken into His glory. As saints, such men and women had plainly not lost their accustomed features by fading into a supra-mundane paradise, as Origen seemed to imply. They had remained patrons, friends, partners, and intercessors, physically recognizable and comfortingly accessible to their devotees through the same codes of social interchange with which the great and the merciful might be approached on earth.[82] Origen had overlooked that yearning for another world in which the most beloved features of the present life would be preserved: he "promises the unknown and the grandiose, in exchange for what is more modest but more sure."[83]

The heaven now imagined by Jerome and his Latin readers was no place of featureless, entirely spiritual perfection. It was a Roman society from which the corrosive flaws introduced by personal desire had been expunged. A heaven where the disorder of earthly life had ceased would cast a glow of glorious stability on social structures which seemed, for the first time, to be at risk.

The issues raised in the literary skirmishes that followed the breach between Jerome and Rufinus, in the years immediately after 397, were almost too large to be seen. The controversy itself was a studied anticlimax. As was so often the case in the politics of the Roman church, a "Center Party" emerged very rapidly.[84] The controversy was not al-

81. Jerome, *Letter* 75.2: 686.   82. Peter Brown, *The Cult of the Saints*, pp. 64–67.
83. Jerome, *Letter* 75.2: 687.
84. Very well studied by C. P. Hammond, "The Last Ten Years of Rufinus' Life," pp. 383–385.

lowed to spill over into the Church as a whole. Rufinus continued to enjoy protection and esteem until his death, in Sicily, in 411.

New faces had appeared in Italy since he had left Aquileia almost thirty years before. Paulinus, an Aquitainian relative of Melania the elder, had come to settle as a monk at Nola, in Campania, to the south of Rome, in 395. A man of huge wealth and genuine good nature, Paulinus, a poet and not a scholar, was delighted with Rufinus' quiet confidence: here was the only man "in these regions," he wrote to his friends, who could tell him all about the mystic meaning of the pelican![85]

Patronage, however, imposed its own, discreet restraints. Rufinus, infuriatingly placid and careful (a man "with the stride of a tortoise," Jerome wrote)[86] defused the charged issue of the role of women in a Christian culture. Collections of sermons, and not controversial writings, were what the wives of senators should now read: as in the human body, he wrote, there was room for the soft flesh as well as for hard bones.[87] Jerome, for all his fashionable misogyny and his sharp sense of sexual danger, would never for a moment have doubted that the minds of Paula or Marcella, and his other female allies and clients, did not have their full share of "male" bone and muscle.

Paula died on January 26, 404. Jerome now had only her prayers in Paradise, and no longer her own, frail physical presence, to help him through the last, empty years of his old age.[88] A letter that finally arrived in Bethlehem, by a suspiciously roundabout route, from an African bishop, Augustine of Hippo, confirmed his worst fears. Yet another self-satisfied mediocrity had arisen in the West to plague him. With courteous, yet ominous, tenacity, Augustine had taken Jerome to task for his translation and exegesis of the Scriptures. Jerome was in no mood to take on such an ignoramus:

For it does not become me, who have spent my life from youth until now sharing the arduous labors of pious brethren, in a monastery tucked away in the depths of the countryside, to presume to write anything against a bishop. . . . So huge a stretch of land and water lies between us, that the sound even of your voice, sir, can hardly reach me.[89]

85. Paulinus, *Letters* 28.5 and 40.6.

86. Jerome, *Contra Rufinum* 1.17, *Corpus Christianorum* 79, p. 16: *P.L.* 23: 411B.

87. Rufinus, *Praef. in Omelias Sancti Basilii*, Simonetti, p. 237: see esp. Consolino, "Modelli di comportamento e modi di santificazione per l'aristocrazia femminile," pp. 296–297.

88. Jerome, *Letter* 108.33: 906.   89. Ibid. 112.18: 928.

Fortunately, old age was not as terrible for Jerome as he had feared in 404. After 410, the sack of Rome and the devastation of the Western provinces brought a new flood of Latin refugees to the Holy Land. Jerome gained new friends and, equally invigorating, new enemies. But he was now an old man. Time had begun to stand still for him. He saw the world in terms of ancient enmities. Pelagius arrived in the Holy Land, after 413. He asserted that men had been endowed by God with free will, so that they should follow His law and live perfect Christian lives.

Jerome had seen it all before. Such talk was "a new heresy come out of the old."[90] It echoed the wild doctrine of Evagrius, that the ascetic might achieve a "passionless" state. It reminded Jerome of Melania, "the crazy old woman,"[91] whom thirty years previously he had described as "the second Thecla."[92] Writing against Pelagius in 415, Jerome went out of his way to destroy all hope of Christian perfection on earth. The facts of sex were against it. These now proved far more than the inadvisability of female companionship. To a new generation, which had begun to listen to Augustine, sexual desire revealed the inescapable solidarity of all mankind in Adam's sin. Only Pelagius, Jerome wrote, would dare to claim,

that I alone, and my groupies, are not held down in Adam's grip. Other poor fellows who have not heard my words may live shut up in cells and, without so much as seeing a woman, may remain still tormented by desire. As for me, though surrounded by droves of women, I feel not the slightest tingle of concupiscence. . . . I remain unmoved: by the power of my own free will, I bear wherever I go the conquering sign of Christ.[93]

Jerome had lived into an age very different from that in which he had begun his career. Both he and Rufinus had come to seem equally out of date. The emergence of Augustine, whom he had snubbed with such consummate skill in 404, proved the truth of the adage, that genius marks the end, and not the beginning, of an epoch. It is, then, to Augustine that we must turn, to bring to an end our account of the thought and practice of the Early Church.

90. *In Hieremiam* 1.17.3, in S. Reiter, ed., *Corpus Christianorum* 74:15.
91. Ibid. 3.70.4, p. 162.
92. Rufinus, *Apologia contra Hieronymum* 2.29, p. 105.
93. Jerome, *Dialogus adversus Pelagianos* 2.24: *P.L.* 23: 562BC.

NINETEEN

Augustine: Sexuality and Society

(I) *SERENITAS DILECTIONIS*

In the late August of 386, a thirty-two-year-old teacher of rhetoric, recently arrived in Milan from Africa, had begun to face the personal consequences of his wish to seek baptism at the hands of Ambrose. For Augustine, commitment to the Catholic Church had come to appear inexorably, over the previous months, to imply that he must also commit himself to a life of perpetual continence. In the garden in Milan, where Augustine struggled to reach a decision, the baleful shimmer of the "hope of this world" (that alluring and diffuse conglomerate of predominantly social expectations associated with success, with status, with comfort and security, against which so many young men and women touched by the ascetic movement had set their face in the course of the fourth century) had narrowed down to a choice of merciless precision; Augustine had to abandon an active sex life:

plucking at my garment, my flesh, these my past sweet joys softly murmured: "Are you dismissing us? . . . From this moment, will you never be allowed to do this, or to do that?" And, oh my God, what was it they suggested in those words, "this" and "that?"[1]

---

1. *Confessions* 8.11.26: *Patrologia Latina* 32: 761; cf. *Soliloquia* 1.10.17 and 1.14.25: 32: 878 and 882–883. The bibliography contains a comprehensive list of Augustine's writings

Of all the writers of the Early Church, Augustine is the only one whose past sexual activity is known to us. This is because he looked back on it with quite unusual attentiveness, ten years after his moment of decision, when he wrote his *Confessions,* around 397.

By 397, Milan was a long way away from him. Ambrose was dead; Rufinus had returned to Italy, to Jerome's vociferous annoyance; Augustine himself had changed deeply. The ascetic layman of 386 had become, since 395, a Catholic bishop in the North African seaport of Hippo Regius (modern Bône/Annaba in Algeria). It now seemed to Augustine that the outcome of the bitter struggle to live the continent life revealed, more clearly than did any other incident in his life, the hand of God as it reached down into his heart. For the decisive act of renunciation had set Augustine free to serve God, and, eventually, to become a bishop in the Catholic Church.[2]

Augustine's *Confessions* were written to address—and, in addressing, to help to form—a distinctive group. The book spoke most directly to "servants of God": to Catholics of ascetic experience similar to Augustine's own. Many had recently found themselves placed in positions of leadership in the Catholic churches in Africa and Italy.[3] Augustine brought the intimate force of his past sexual habits into painfully sharp focus in the *Confessions.* But he also addressed the hopes of a group for their Church and, by implication, for their society. In the *Confessions,* sexuality was presented as a facet of human social relations quite as frequently as it was analyzed as a problem for the human will. This book enables us to glimpse a little of the idiosyncrasy of Augustine's experiences of sex as a young man. At the same time, it communicated the views on the relationship between sexuality and society which Augustine had come to adopt in his middle age.

As he wrote the *Confessions,* Augustine wished to convey a sense of the sharp contrast between his sexual needs and his longing for clear, unproblematic relationships. He plainly regretted that both the strictly nonsexual ties of intellectual friendship and the sober concord of a legitimate Roman marriage had eluded him as a young man. The clear blue sky of unsullied love—the *serenitas dilectionis*—had been all around

---

cited in this chapter, along with translations of the most relevant of these to the themes treated in this book.

2. *Confessions* 9.1.1 and 10.30.41: 763 and 796.

3. Peter Brown, *Augustine of Hippo,* pp. 159–163.

him; but it had remained forever distant. Swirling mists of sexual desire had clouded his vision, as he attempted, in the serious manner of a sixteen-year-old, to tread the *luminosa limes*, the radiant knife edge, of intimacy.[4]

A sad sense of disjunction hovered over the only lasting sexual relationship in his life. It began in 372 when, at eighteen, newly arrived in Carthage, Augustine found a woman with whom he lived for thirteen years, until 385. A son, Adeodatus, was born in 373. In the same year, Augustine's reading of Cicero's *Hortensius* had provoked the first of his many "conversions" to a serious search for Wisdom. The relations he established with his concubine were all of a piece with his growing austerity. He remained faithful to her throughout their time together, which was considerably more than his own father, Patricius, had ever done for his mother, Monica.

Looking back at those years in Carthage, the forty-three-year-old bishop was inclined to judge them gently. His loyalty to his concubine had been a fragile spark of *fides* in the topsy-turvy world of a young professor on the make: it had contained that element of good faith and reliability which Romans valued highly in a regular marriage.[5] He had no doubt, however, that, in his early twenties, the sweetest joy of his life had been an ever-deepening friendship with a fellow-student and childhood acquaintance.[6] The "pleasures of the bed" with a woman were not necessarily the most important aspect of Augustine's life at that time.[7] For a young intellectual of the fourth century, male friendship opened the door to deeper satisfactions:

To talk and laugh. To do each other kindnesses. To read pleasant books together; to pass from lightest joking to talk of deepest things, and back again. To differ without rancor, as a man might differ with himself. . . . these, and such like things, proceeding from our hearts as we gave affection and received it back, and shown by face, by voice, by eyes, and by a thousand pleasing ways, kindled a flame which fused our very souls together, and, of many, made us one.[8]

Augustine had few options. Intense male friendships and the less public pleasures of life with a concubine were the best he could expect. He belonged to a small but influential class of young males whose sexual arrangements reflected only too faithfully the marginality of their social position. Marriage was out of the question for him. Those who

4. *Confessions* 2.2.2: 675.
5. 4.2.2: 693–694. 6. 4.4.7: 696. 7. 4.7.12: 698. 8. 4.8.13: 699.

wrote and preached for more settled persons—for landed aristocrats or for less ambitious townsfolk—might think that sexuality could be rendered magnificently unproblematic, by linking it to early marriage, and by limiting sexual experience to the solemn duties of reproduction performed in the marriage bed. Such high-minded mystifications did not apply to boys who intended to live by their wits.

Augustine's mother, Monica, was a convinced Christian. She had warned him "with huge anxiety" against fornication; but she showed no intention whatsoever of offering him the one remedy that Christian parents had been urged for centuries to provide for their adolescent sons—the comfort of a wife.[9] Augustine was the only member of his family to receive an intensive education. His huge talents could not be shackled by an early, arranged marriage that would have tied him forever to a wife chosen from among the same class as himself, the petty squirearchy of upland Thagaste. Instead of early marriage, he joined a circle of hard young careerists. His lifelong friend, Alypius, maintained as best he could a *de facto* continence. After one unhappy experience, he decided that sex was not for him. Committed to an active career in the late Roman administration, the public cruelty of the gladiatorial games fascinated and distressed him far more than did the prospect of a love affair.[10]

Unlike Alypius, Augustine plainly enjoyed sleeping with a woman. He opted for the next best thing to marriage—a strictly monogamous relationship with a concubine. Such a relation was common in intellectual circles. It was accepted as valid even by Christians. An "acceptable and often openly acknowledged sexual relationship, not covered by the law but with some rules of its own," concubinage was the very opposite of a dissolute arrangement.[11] It lacked the essential ingredient of a legally valid marriage—the declared intention to produce legitimate offspring. It was frankly sexual. Augustine chose his companion because he loved her; and he slept with her because he loved to do so, and not so as to produce grandchildren for his mother or citizens for his home town. Since they had only one child in thirteen years, it seems more than likely that Augustine and his concubine practiced birth-control of some kind.[12]

9. 2.3.8: 678.   10. 6.7.i2–8.13: 725.
11. Susan Treggiari, "*Concubinae*," p. 59; see also Aline Rousselle, *Porneia*, pp. 121–137.
12. *Confessions* 4.2.2: 693–694 and *de bono coniugali* 5.5: 40: 376–377.

To add to his idiosyncrasy, Augustine had been an *auditor*, a "hearer" or catechumen, of the church of Mani since 373. This meant, in effect, that he treated with studied reverence the Manichaean Elect, who represented the core of the Manichaean mission in Carthage as elsewhere.[13] He would bow before them to receive the blessing of their hands on his head.[14] He would bring them the special foods necessary for their ritual meals.[15] He would have fasted all Sunday, and would have gathered to hear solemn readings of the great cosmic myths that explained the destiny of his soul.[16]

Such visits to the Elect brought Augustine into close contact with little groups of men and women whose pale faces spoke of a quite unearthly continence. It is not easy to know exactly what Augustine's experiences on the fringe of the Manichaean movement meant to him. He never became a member of the charmed circle of the Elect.[17] One thing is certain: by gravitating to the edge of a radical, intermittently persecuted sect, Augustine sharpened the hiatus that existed in his mind between his own *ad hoc* sexual relationship and a marriage entered into, in the Roman manner, for the good of society. For Augustine the Manichaean *auditor*, sexuality and society were antithetical. Only in a "true church," composed of the continent Elect, would a true society be found, in the form of a light-filled harmony of souls set free from matter. Intercourse, and especially intercourse undertaken to produce children, collaborated with the headlong expansion of the Kingdom of Darkness at the expense of the spiritual purity associated with the Kingdom of Light.[18]

The Manichaeans maintained the sharp dichotomies that had first been proposed by the Encratites. For them, as for the Encratites, there could be no such thing as innocent sexuality—one whose use was validated by its social function within wedlock. All sexual activity, in whatever circumstances, aided the powers of the Kingdom of Dark-

---

13. See esp. F. Decret, *Aspects du manichéisme dans l'Afrique chrétienne* and Samuel N.C. Lieu, *Manichaeism in the Later Roman Empire and Medieval China*, pp. 117–153.

14. See esp. *Letter* 236.2: 33: 1033. 15. *Confessions* 4.1.1: 603.

16. *De utilitate credendi* 1.1.2: 42: 66–67 and *Contra Faustum* 15.4–6: 42: 307–309; see esp. Lieu, *Manichaeism*, pp. 134–136.

17. Decret, *Aspects du manichéisme*, pp. 27–38 and Lieu, *Manichaeism*, pp. 143–152 are the most reliable. See also the careful study of Erich Feldmann, *Der Einfluss des Hortensius und des Manichäismus auf das Denken des jungen Augustinus.*

18. *De moribus manichaeorum* (2).18.65–66: 32: 1372–1373 and John T. Noonan, *Contraception*, pp. 106–126.

ness. Marriage was no less regrettable than a more frankly sexual relationship with a concubine. Both held the *auditor* at a distance from the true Church of Mani, represented by the enclosed bodies of the Elect. The Elect did not belong to this world. They abstained as much as was humanly possible from those processes of eating, or producing and preparing food, and of begetting children that maintained conventional human society.[19] Their emaciated bodies spoke of spirits already liberated from the Kingdom of Darkness. Only the solemn intercessions of sexless, rootless, and studiously asocial creatures—such as were the Elect—would slowly deliver their *auditors* from the toils of that Kingdom.

Hence the surprising tolerance with which the austere Manichees could accept young men in such marginal positions as the one Augustine occupied in Carthage throughout the 370s. Viewed from the high pinnacle of their own total continence, Augustine's punctilious relationship with his concubine was neither better nor worse than marriage. It was the best he could do. Being still enslaved, through his career, to the tyranny of the world, Augustine, as a mere *auditor*, was no more expected to abandon sex than he could be expected to imitate the Elect in abstaining from meat or to abandon the pursuit of wealth. He was dependent for his salvation on their mysterious prayers. Standing with his fellow-*auditors* around the Elect, Augustine doubtless listened to their exalted hymns in praise of virginity; but he felt sure that such stirring sentiments did not yet apply to himself: "and I, an unfortunate young man . . . would pray: 'Lord, give me chastity and continence, *sed noli modo*, but not now.' "[20]

It was only when his career took him to the Imperial residence in Milan, in late 384, at the age of thirty, that Augustine found he had to make up his mind as to the social ties to which he might wish to be committed for the rest of his life. For a few months, he allowed himself to be lured by the prospect of unquestioning and advantageous integration into the social world around him. An alliance, through legitimate marriage, to a Milanese Catholic family close to Ambrose offered him an entry into the governing class of the Western Empire. A provincial governorship, secure wealth, and privileged leisure were the rewards he might expect.[21] Monica found him such a wife—a girl not yet old enough to marry, possibly, even, a twelve-year-old, some

19. *De mor. man.* (2).10.19–18.65: 1353–1373.   20. *Confessions* 8.7.17: 757.
21. Ibid. 6.11.19: 729 and *Soliloquia* 1.11.18: 897.

nineteen years younger than himself! She had hoped that her son might become a baptized Catholic as a result of the match.[22]

Augustine's concubine did what was expected of her on such occasions. She returned to Africa, bound by a vow to have no further sexual relationship. She could claim the protection of the Christian community, as a voluntary widow.[23] For all we know, she may have ended her life as a pillar of some local church. She had played her part with dignity according to the icy rules of a late Roman politic marriage. Her *fides* to Augustine had remained unbroken. It was Augustine who failed:

This problem often arises: If a man and a woman live together without being legitimately joined, not to have children, but because they could not observe continence; and if they have agreed between themselves to have relations with no one else, can this be called a marriage? Perhaps: but only if they had resolved to maintain until death the good faith which they had promised themselves. . . . . But if a man takes a woman only for a time, until he has found another who better suits his rank and fortune: and if he marries this woman, as being of the same class, this man would commit adultery in his heart, not towards the woman he wished to marry, but towards the woman with whom he had once lived.[24]

Bruised by her departure, Augustine fell back on a stopgap mistress. As a result, his own sexual needs were bleakly demystified. It seemed to him that any further relationship with a woman, lawful marriage included, could be based on nothing other than his own compulsive need for sex. A chain of habit, its links silently formed around his will in the course of thirteen years of unproblematic enjoyment of sexual companionship, now held him fast.[25] It conducted him, as with an armed escort, straight toward a wife;[26] and behind his arranged marriage, there lay the dark shadow of surrender to the "hopes of this world," implied in an alliance between a gifted *parvenu* and the Milanese families grouped round the Imperial court.

The winter of 385 and the spring of 386 marked the nadir of Au-

---

22. *Confessions* 6.13.23: 729–730.
23. Ibid, 6.15.25: 732. See the newly discovered letter of Augustine for an analogous case: *Letter* 20*. 1.3–4, in J. Divjak, ed., *Sancti Aurelii Augustini epistulae nuper in lucem prolatae*, pp. 94–95. trans. *Bibliothèque augustinienne. Oeuvres de Saint Augustin 46B: Lettres 1*–29*, p. 294.
24. *De bono coniugali* 5.5.: 376–377; cf. *Sermon* 392.2.2: 39: 1710.
25. *Confessions* 6.12.21–22: 730 and 8.5.10 and 12: 753 and 754.
26. Ibid. 6.15.25: 732 and *Soliloquia* 1.11.19: 880.

gustine's morale: "And now my first youth was dead."[27] We should not underestimate what it meant, in the ancient world, to pass from youth into one's prime. Late Roman society weighed relentlessly on young men in their twenties. Their energies were drained by an unremitting search for patrons, for allies, and for public acclaim. After thirty, many men came to discover in themselves reserves of feeling of disturbing force and texture. It was a dangerous hour. Augustine had begun to catch the drift of Ambrose's most excitedly otherworldly sermons. He gained access to some of the works of Plotinus and Porphyry in Latin translation. In a few months, in the summer of 386, the sudden touch of a strange new capacity for spiritual delight destroyed forever Augustine's hankering for a conventional future as a married man and a successful courtier.

We should not underestimate what that first experience of "sure, sweet delight"[28] meant to Augustine. It abruptly deflected his attitude to sexual joys. Through Ambrose and, possibly, through his Neo-Platonic readings, Augustine was brushed, for a crucial moment, by the "wild" Platonism that we have met with in the mystical thought of Origen. Direct experience of the sharp joys of the spirit made physical pleasure seem shadowy, even repugnant, to him. "Limbs asking to receive the body's embrace"[29] mirrored the enduring sweetness of the touch of God with disturbing congruence. Compared with the dawn light of the coming of Christ to embrace the soul, even the sober joys of a Catholic marriage now seemed to lie under a chill shadow of regret.[30] By abandoning sexual pleasure of any kind, Augustine hoped to uproot within himself the dark mirror-image of a fierce longing to hold God's Wisdom in "an utterly untroubled gaze, a most clean embrace; to see and to cling to Her naked, with no veil of bodily sensation in between."[31]

A deep sense of sadness lingered with Augustine for the rest of his life. Sexual love remained, for him, a leaden echo of true delight. He dearly wished that he had grown up chaste from his youth, his heart

---

27. *Confessions* 7.1.1: 733.   28. 8.5.10: 753.   29. 10.6.8: 782.

30. The crucial verses, Romans 13:13, that prompted Augustine's final decision for continence—*not in rioting and drunkenness, not in chambering and wantonness*—are interpreted in this manner by Origen: *Fragments on I Corinthians* xxxix, in C. Jenkins, ed., p. 510.

31. *Soliloquia* 1.13.22: 881.

kept open by the discipline of continence, to receive the embrace of Christ: *o tardum gaudium meum,* "O, my late joy!"[32]

The earthquake in Augustine's intimate life that took place in August 386 went hand in hand with the creation of a new set of social relations. The immediate effect of his conversion was to bring him back to his friends. In Milan he had never been alone. Alypius, Verecundus, Nebridius, even his busy patron, Romanianus, had wished for over a year to found some form of philosophical community around their brilliant friend. Like the upperclass students and patrons of Origen and Plotinus, these men were striking examples of the energy that late Roman gentlemen of leisure were prepared to deploy in the high art of intellectual friendship. Augustine's prospective marriage would have caused their ideal of a shared life to crumble.[33] In August 386, Augustine came to know, for the first time, of the ascetic movement. The story of the conversion of Saint Anthony and tales of the desert settlements in Egypt were crucial in bringing about his own decision.[34] A distant glimpse of the continent sociability of the desert resolved the dilemma that had weighed upon Augustine, Alypius, and their friends.

Augustine's conversion was a group experience. By choosing a life of continence, both Augustine and his closest friends hoped to recapture, through living together "in a holy plan of life," the joys of "a truly chaste because untarnished joining" of like souls.[35] The collective decision taken in August 386, in Milan, pointed directly toward the little monastery that Augustine would found five years later, on becoming a priest in Hippo, in a garden given to him by the bishop. This monastery, and the single-hearted interpersonal bonds fostered within it by continence and poverty, remained the calm eye of the storm for the remaining forty years of Augustine's life as a Catholic bishop. It provided the ideal against which he would henceforth judge the heartrending dissensions of the society around him.[36]

---

32. *Confessions* 2.2.2–3: 676.
33. 6.14.24: 731.
34. 8.6.15: 755.
35. 9.8.17: 771 and *Soliloquia* 1.13.23: 881.
36. Andre Mandouze, *Saint Augustin. L'aventure de la raison et de la grâce,* pp. 188–191, provides the most balanced survey of this aspect of Augustine's conversion. See now Henry Chadwick, "The Ascetic Ideal in the History of the Church," in W. J. Sheils, ed., *Monks, Hermits and the Ascetic Tradition,* pp. 8–23.

(II) *DISCORDIOSUM MALUM*

The agenda that Augustine brought with him from Ambrose's Milan changed subtly and irrevocably in his first decade as a bishop in the African church. By 400, Augustine was no longer the convert who had broken, so suddenly and with such evident relief, from his need for a physical relationship with a woman. The sharp tone with which he had spoken of material things, immediately after his conversion, had mellowed. He had quietly discarded views of the human person, of society and, consequently, of sexuality, that had been taken for granted in ascetic circles in Italy. He had become a very different man from Ambrose and Jerome.

As a Catholic bishop in Africa, Augustine found himself in a religious and moral landscape notably different from the Milan of Ambrose and from the Italian and Gallic circles addressed by Jerome. Late-fourth-century Africa lay a little to one side of the ascetic sensibility of the Mediterranean. Many of the features that rendered Italy and the Latin communities in the Holy Land so distinctive were lacking in this self-confident but rather old-fashioned province. Female asceticism was a deeply rooted institution in the African church; yet continent women of the caliber of Melania, Marcella, and Paula were notably absent.[37] The perils and excitements associated with what one might almost call a "High Church" asceticism had been studiously avoided by the African clergy: there was little nostalgia for the angelic life and no examples of spiritual companionship with gifted and influential ascetic women. Compared with Jerome, and even with Ambrose, Augustine moved in a monochrome, all-male world. He imposed strict codes of sexual avoidance on himself and his own clergy. He would never visit a woman unchaperoned, and did not allow even his own female relatives to enter the bishop's palace. He expelled a young clergyman who had been found speaking with a nun "at an inappropriate hour of the day."[38]

---

37. Augustine knew aristocratic pious ladies in Hippo and Carthage: *de civitate Dei* 5.6 and 22.8.3: 41: 146 and 763 and *Letter* 20*.17.2, Divjak, p. 103; trans. *Lettres 1*-29*, p. 318. His relations with the family of Melania the Younger were distinctly strained when they arrived in Africa: *Letter* 125. 2-5: 474-476.

38. Possidius, *Life of Augustine* 26.1-3: 32: 55; *Letter* 20*.5.1, Divjak, p. 96 *Lettres*, p. 298.

Paradoxically, Augustine, the most searching exponent of the frailty revealed by sexual desire, was utterly unlike Jerome. For all his strictness on himself and his clergy, he was no alarmist. Nor did the issue of celibacy preoccupy him greatly. The Catholic church in Africa was a beleaguered institution that had to make do with whatever clergy it could get. If a married man suddenly found himself ordained, then God would give him the grace needed to give up sleeping with his wife.[39] In a newly discovered letter, we find Augustine dealing with the case of a young clergyman who was accused of having once seduced a nun while staying at her parents' home in the countryside. He was surprisingly unruffled by the case. For a young girl to climb into one's bed, in order to complain about her parents' lack of understanding, was, Augustine wrote, "a trial that can befall any serious and saintly person." Nothing further need have happened. In any case, he added, the Catholic Church had few enough priests in country districts. He could not insist that they always travel in pairs in order to avoid such encounters.[40] One can imagine what Jerome would have made of the incident!

On a deep level, Augustine's priorities, and those of the Christian piety of Africa, remained different from those advocated by Italian admirers of virginity. For Augustine, martyrdom always represented the highest peak of human heroism. To have triumphed over the bitter fear of death was a far greater sign of God's grace than to have triumphed over the sexual urge. Many African martyrs were known to have been married women and mothers of children, as were Perpetua and St. Crispina of Theveste. At a time when Jerome could state that even the blood of martyrdom was barely able to wipe away "the dirt of marriage" from a Christian woman,[41] and when Italian writers found it difficult to imagine female martyrs other than as young virgins, intent, above all, on preserving their integrity,[42] Augustine wrote to African nuns, warning them never to look down on married women. The workings of God's grace were deeply hidden; the fashionable fascination with virginity paled before the ancient and terrible grace of martyrdom: "For a virgin of the church may not yet be able to be a

39. *De conjugiis adulterinis* 2.20.22: 40: 486.
40. *Letter* 13*.1.2 and 3.3., Divjak, pp. 81 and 82; he later had to admit that the young man was guilty: *Letter* 18*, Divjak, pp. 89–90; *Lettres*, pp. 256, 260, 280–284.
41. Jerome, *Adversus Jovinianum* 1.26: P. L. 33: 247A.
42. F. E. Consolino, "Modelli di santità femminile nelle più antiche passioni romane."

Thecla, while she [the married woman] may have been called by God to be a Saint Crispina."[43]

While the desert seemed distant in Africa, the texture of Roman society was an ever-present concern for Augustine and his Catholic colleagues. Society itself seemed under threat. In the years around 400, the Donatist schism occupied the forefront of Augustine's mind. All over Africa, two conflicting groups of male clergymen had faced each other, for almost a century, in the public squares of over four hundred small towns and villages. Each claimed to be the true leaders of the Christian community. In Hippo, Augustine found a situation where religious differences appeared to have undermined the basic unit of society, the family:

how great and miserable is the calamity by which the peace of Christian homes and families is broken. Husbands and wives, agreeing together at the family hearth, are divided at the altars of Christ. . . . Servants and masters divide their common Lord.[44]

A young man had threatened his mother:

I will pass over to the party of Donatus, and I will drink your blood.[45]

"Love for Christian peace" was the professed keynote of Augustine's activity as a Catholic bishop throughout his middle age. The broken unity of the Church in Africa obsessed him. So blatant a failure of Christians to agree prompted him to appreciate ever more deeply the cohesive strength of conventional Roman society. By 405, he accepted that the Roman state could bring to bear the force of its own laws so as to "reunite" Donatist congregations to the Catholic Church under threat of punishment. In so doing, he upheld the view that the structures of authority that gave cohesion to profane society might be called upon to support the Catholic church: Emperors should command their subjects, landowners their peasants (flogging them when necessary), heads of households, their wives and children, in order to bring them back into the unity of the Catholic church.[46]

It was a decision with profound consequences. A man whose own conversion had been prompted, in part, by the call of the desert, Au-

43. *De sancta virginitate* 44.45: 40: 422.
44. *Letter* 33.5: 131. 45. *Letter* 34.3: 132–133.
46. Brown, *Augustine*, pp. 212–243, esp. 235–240, sums up a complicated situation that has been abundantly studied.

gustine had come, within only ten years, to think about the Catholic Church from a viewing point deep within the structures of the settled world. Augustine left little room in his imaginative horizon for that wistful glimpse of a humanity laboring beneath the cares of society, seen, as it were, a little from the outside, from the free spaces of the desert or from the great height of an "angelic" life. If the Catholic church was to remain united, it could do so only by validating Roman society. The bonds that held subjects to emperors, slaves to masters, wives to husbands, and children to parents could not be ignored, still less could they be abruptly abandoned in order to recover an "angelic" mode of life. They must, rather, be made to serve the Catholic cause.

Augustine's handling of the story of the creation of Adam and Eve, and of their fall, made plain the extent to which he was prepared to shift the center of gravity of Christian thought on the human person. A man like Gregory of Nyssa would have found the Bishop of Hippo's *Literal Commentary on Genesis* (a long work, begun around 401, and not completed until 416) a highly idiosyncratic book.[47] So, even, would have Ambrose and Jerome. All three had shared an instinctive, largely unanalyzed, assumption about the origins of marriage and of sexuality. Marriage, intercourse and Paradise were as incompatible, in their minds, as were Paradise and death. Of that, at least, they felt they could be certain.[48]

This meant that sexuality, hence marriage and the creation of the family, could only have followed the Fall of Adam and Eve. They were the result of a sad decline, by which Adam and Eve had lapsed from an "angelic" state into physicality, and so into death. A question mark was allowed to hover over human society. Marriage, and the structures that sprang from it, could not be derived from the original nature of the human person. Ascetic exegesis of the Fall of Adam and Eve tended to preserve, at the back of the minds of its exponents, a lingering doubt: society, marriage, and, if not those, certainly sexual intercourse, were fundamentally alien to the original definition of humanity. They had come as an afterthought. They had imposed

47. Elizabeth A. Clark, "Heresy, Asceticism, Adam and Eve: Interpretations of Genesis 1–3 in the Later Latin Fathers," p. 370, makes a convincing case for the possibility that the books which dealt with the creation and fall of Adam and Eve were already drafted soon after 401.

48. Jerome, *Adversus Jovinianum* 1.29: 251C; for Ambrose, see G. Madec, *Saint Ambroise et la philosophie*, pp. 296–298.

limitations on the first angelic majesty of Adam and Eve. The seemingly unchallengeable order of society had not always been there: it was doomed to fade away. Already in this life, the radiance of the virgin state showed it to be as evanescent as a spider's web.[49] An angelic state of Paradise, which had once existed in the distant past, shimmered on the far horizon of late antique society as the "angelic life" of the desert. The state in which Adam and Eve would have continued, had they not fallen, was not like that of any contemporary married couple. In the words of Gregory of Nyssa, it had been "inconceivable by human conjecture, except that it had assuredly existed."[50]

In proposing a markedly different exegesis of the opening chapters of the book of Genesis from any that we have met so far, Augustine ensured that the golden mist that had hung over the slopes of Paradise would lift forever in the Latin West. From around 400 until the end of his life, Augustine invariably wrote of Adam and Eve as physical human beings, endowed with the same bodies and sexual characteristics as ourselves. God had created them for the joys of society. He had implanted in them both "the further attractive power of friendship."[51] They had been set in Paradise to found a *populus;* and to found a *populus* implied more than the disembodied meeting of like-minded souls. It involved physical intercourse, childbirth, and the rearing of children. Adam and Eve's original state even implied a measure of hierarchy: Augustine's exegesis validated the rule of men over women and the rule of the father over his children as part of God's original order.[52] Had they remained in Paradise, Adam and Eve would have begotten children and would have nurtured them with parental authority. Thus, central features of the social landscape of Paradise, marriage and the rule of the father over his children, would have been recognizable to a Roman of fourth-century Africa.[53] The angelic state of Adam and Eve had lain in the future. They had been placed in Paradise for a probationary period, so that they should learn to experience and to accept, with unswerving obedience and with openhearted gratitude, the full range of the joys of fully physical, fully so-

49. Gregory of Nyssa, *In Psalmos* 1.7: *P.G.* 44: 464A.
50. Gregory of Nyssa, *de hominis opificio* 17.2: *P.G.* 44: 189AB.
51. *De bono coniugali* 1.1 and 8.8: 373 and 379.
52. *De Genesi ad litteram* 9.5.9: 34: 396.
53. On the North African family, and particularly on the power of the father within it, see Brent D. Shaw, "The Family in Late Antiquity: the Experience of Augustine,"— a solid and persuasive study.

cial and, Augustine was quite prepared to conclude, of fully sexual beings.[54] Compared with the notions of many of his most vocal contemporaries, it was a singularly sociable and full-blooded vision.

The practical effects of this change of viewpoint were immediately apparent. In 401, a group of wandering monks appeared in Carthage. Like the Manichaean Elect of Augustine's youth, they brought with them a tempting breath of the East. Wild, long-haired men, dedicated to a life of perpetual prayer, they intended to live as freely as the birds in heaven, supported by the alms of the faithful. Local opinion was hotly divided for and against the awesome strangers.[55] To many, they had brought to Africa a touch of the untrammelled, pre-social majesty of Adam. To Augustine and his colleagues, their behavior showed that the nature of that majesty had been gravely misunderstood: they had no intention of allowing such persons to "pullulate in Africa, as they have done in other countries."[56]

In the same year, Augustine went out of his way to distance himself, also, from the high ascetic views of Jerome on marriage and virginity. These had left many Carthaginian Christians unsatisfied. It seemed to them as if the upholders of the ascetic sensibility could defend their views only by denigrating marriage.[57] The notion of a pre-sexual and pre-social majesty of Adam and Eve might speak with great force to the vocal few, of a hitherto undreamed-of freedom of the human person that might be reconquered by virginity. But many married couples were baffled by so ethereal a view of Paradise. When they had asked the priest to add his blessing to their marriage, he spoke over them the words that God had spoken to Adam and Eve before their Fall, at the first moment of their creation—*Increase and multiply*.

On Roman sarcophagi of that time, Adam and Eve were frequently shown with their right hands joined in the *dextrarum iunctio* that rendered visible the concord of a Roman marriage. Such scenes spoke for the views of a silent majority that believed as firmly as did their Jewish neighbors that God had created humanity for marriage and childbirth.[58] Good Catholic Christians needed to be reassured that the mar-

---

54. *De Genesi ad litteram* 9.6.10: 396 and *de bono coniugali* 2.2: 374.

55. *Retractationes* 2.21: 32: 638–639; *de opere monachorum* 17.20; 23.27–29 and 31.39: 40: 565, 569–570 and 578.

56. *De opere monachorum* 28.36: 576.   57. *Retractationes* 2.22: 639.

58. Pope Innocent, *Letter* 4.6.9: *P.L.* 20: 474–475; see esp. Charles Pietri, "Le mariage chrétien à Rome," in J. Delumeau, ed., *Histoire vécue du peuple chrétien*.

riages on which their whole society was based were not merely the result of a regrettable accident. In his *On the Good of Marriage* and *On Holy Virginity*, Augustine took up this challenge. He both defended marriage and found a place for virginity within the Church. He did this by making them both magnificently social. He presented marriage and continence as no more than two successive stages of human concord. The one form of friendship happened so as to produce children, and so it included physical intercourse; the other did not. Both pointed, however, if with different degrees of transparency, to the final unanimity of the redeemed in the Heavenly Jerusalem, the City of God.[59]

This view of marriage deliberately looked past the physicality of married intercourse. Sexual desire still disquieted Augustine. In mankind's present state, the sexual drive was a disruptive force. Augustine never found a way, any more than did any of his Christian contemporaries, of articulating the possibility that sexual pleasure might, in itself, enrich the relations between husband and wife.[60]

He presented sexual intercourse as secondary to friendship. In Paradise, Adam and Eve had been what he himself had once so dearly wished to be. Friendship, and not sexual desire, had set the pace of their relations. Their married intercourse, had it occurred, would have been a physical concretization of their pre-existing concord. Augustine was adamant that Eve had used no sexual attraction to lure Adam to eat the fatal fruit: he had eaten with her *amicali benevolentia*, "out of the good nature of a friend," so as to share her life at all times and in every way.[61] It was necessary that Adam should have had a woman for a friend—even though, Augustine admitted, in a manner that recalls his early student days, a woman's company was plainly less stimulating than a man's—so that, through intercourse, they should fill Paradise with children.[62] In Adam and Eve's first state, sexual desire was not absent, but it coincided perfectly with the conscious will: it would have introduced no disruptive element into the clear serenity

---

59. *De bono coniugali* 7.7: 378; Emile Schmitt, *Le mariage chrétien dans l'oeuvre de Saint Augustin*, pp. 260–295 is a warm statement of this aspect of Augustine's thought. Elizabeth Clark, " 'Adam's Only Companion': Augustine and the Early Christian Debate on Marriage" is an important recent contribution.

60. See esp. Eric Fuchs, *Sexual Desire and Love*, p. 117: "Augustine, although he was more sensitive than others to the social dimension of the couple, was unable to conceive of the possibility that sexuality could hold tenderness, friendship, spirituality, and this lack of insight was very influential on the later tradition."

61. *De Genesi ad litteram* 11.42.59: 454.   62. Ibid. 9.5.9: 396.

of their marriage. Marriage, therefore, was an expression of the primal and enduring nature of men and women as ineradicably social beings, created by God for concord.

In a fallen humanity, where so much of the original harmony of Paradise had been shattered, the bond of friendship between husband and wife still preceded, justified, and—so Augustine hoped—would long outlast the relatively short interlude of active sex. The *vena caritatis*, the clear, deep spring of charity, ran through the human race.[63] This stream had flowed through the lives of the ancient Patriarchs as they solemnly begot children for the future of Israel. Now the same stream ran in the lives of the Catholic married couple. Unlike Methodius of Olympus and John Chrysostom, Augustine did not think that the coming of Christ and the preaching of virginity had marked a turning point in human history. Marriage was not an out of date institution, a relic of the unregenerate physicality associated with the Old Testament, that lingered on sufferance in the new age of the Gospel. Far from it: the present concord of a husband and a wife pointed forward to the final unity of the City of God.[64]

Augustine, however, remained convinced that the stream of charity flowed more deeply and faster in those committed to a life of continence. In man's fallen state, sexual desire invariably created eddies in the will that stood in the way of true concord. Viewing the world from his continent household at Hippo, he chose his heroes and heroines with care. Many had been married and now lived together in a life of continence. He drew deep reassurance from the continent relationship of Paulinus of Nola with his wife Therasia. Here were a couple whom the renunciation of sexual relations had plainly set free to enjoy a single-minded intimacy, such as Romans had always relished in a well-established marriage.[65]

Ecdicia, by contrast, a local lady of high status, had considered that her marriage with her husband was at an end when she no longer slept with him. When once she had defied her husband's authority over her body, Ecdicia plainly felt that she could deny his authority over her in all other matters. He was "dead" to her. She put on a widow's dress and promptly took back control of her own property, which she then gave away to a pair of wandering monks.[66] Though

---

63. *De bono coniugali* 16.18: 385–386.   64. *Ibid.* 7.7: 378.
65. *Letter* 31.6: 424; cf. *Letter* 127.9: 487—to a similar Roman couple.
66. *Letter* 262.1,5 and 9: 1078–1080.

perfectly intelligible in an ancient, radical tradition of Christian renunciation, such as that represented in the *Acts of Judas Thomas*, Ecdicia's
gesture was intolerable in a region where the security of the Catholic
church depended on the authority of male heads of households. (Even
young girls were not encouraged, by the Catholic bishops, to commit
themselves to adolescent vows of virginity if marriage to the right suitor
might strengthen the Church in their city.)[67]

Ecdicia's action alarmed Augustine. It also bruised his deepest sensibilities. He wrote to remind her, as he frequently reminded his congregation, that concord and the solemn order of a household, and not
the sexual bond, were the abiding essence of a Christian marriage.[68]
Quite as much as the little group of monks and continent clergymen
gathered around him in the bishop's palace, the dignified concord of
married couples, from whom the mists of sexual desire would soon
blow away, summed up for Augustine the great hope that had begun
to fill his mind—the ideal of the total transparency of all human wills
within the City of God:

For a fulfillment of our unity lies in store for us at the end of our present
exile, in which the thoughts of each of us will no longer be hidden from each
other, nor will our intentions clash in any way.[69]

In such writings, Augustine removed the question mark that had
hung over human society. He did so by shifting the question mark
inwards. The catastrophe that needed to be explained was not the fact
of a human society, where men and women married, made love and
begot children. That would have happened had Adam and Eve not
fallen. What remained a dark enigma to him was the distortion of the
will of those who now made up society. The twisted human will, not
marriage, not even the sexual drive, was what was new in the human
condition after Adam's Fall. The fallen will subjected the original, God-
given bonds of human society—friendship, marriage, and paternal
command—to sickening shocks of willfulness, that caused these to sway,
to fissure, and to change their nature. It was the present twisted will
that had led to the development of slavery and to the sinister emergence of the state as a necessary agent of coercion. The social insti-

67. *Letter* 254: 1069–1070.
68. *Sermon* 51.17.27 and 20.30: 38: 348–349 and 350–351, on the chaste marriage of
Mary and Joseph; cf. *de sancta virginitate* 12.12: 401.
69. *De bono coniugali* 18.21: 388.

tutions within which an unfallen human race might have unfolded to form a mighty commonwealth, a *Res Publica* such as Cicero had sighed for, had become harsh prison walls that now merely confined the worse excesses of the egotism, violence, and self-destructiveness of a fallen humanity. Men and women had not fallen "into" society from an angelic state of Paradise; they had swept even society into their fall: "Man . . . has become antisocial by inner corrosion."[70]

So tragic a distortion of the will could no longer be ascribed to the mere fact of possessing a body. Augustine refused to believe that Adam and Eve had fallen from an angelic into a physical state. He did not see human beings as essentially spiritual creatures, to whom physical, sexual and social needs had once been irrelevant. Adam and Eve had originally enjoyed a harmonious unity of body and soul. Their bodies had followed the dictates of their wills with the same loving and familiar concord as they themselves had followed the will of God. The evident misery of the human race consisted in an awareness that such harmony no longer existed on any level.

For this reason, death always remained for Augustine the most bitter sign of human frailty. For death frustrated the soul's deepest wish, which was to live at peace with its beloved, the body. Death could never be welcomed as a freeing of the soul from a body to which it had been joined by accident. It was an unnatural occurrence. Its frightening wrench revealed the strength of the "binding force" associated with the "sweet marriage-bond of body and soul."[71] Even the most courageous and otherworldly Christians must wish that this disruption would not happen. Only the burning love of His commands, granted by Christ to the martyrs, could overcome so deep, and so natural, an affection.

I know you want to keep on living. You do not want to die. You want to pass from this life to another in such a way that you will not rise again, as a dead man, but fully alive and transformed. This is what you desire. This is the deepest human feeling: mysteriously, the soul itself wishes and instinctively desires it.[72]

70. Henry Chadwick, *Augustine*, p. 68. On this topic, R. A. Markus, *Saeculum: History and Society in the Theology of Saint Augustine*, esp. pp. 91–102, 202–206, remains outstandingly the best treatment. See also G. R. Evans, *Augustine on Evil*, p. 97: "a permanent twist arose in his [Adam's] will." Along with those studies, I have owed most to Albrecht Dihle, *The Theory of Will in Classical Antiquity*, pp. 125–132 and R. Lorenz, "Gnade und Erkenntnis bei Augustin."

71. *Letter* 140.6.16: 544.   72. *Sermon* 344.4: 39: 1514.

Such a way of seeing things placed a far greater weight than hitherto on sexuality. In the ascetic literature that we have met so far, the heats of young love and the cares of the married household, the itch of sexual temptation and the dull ache of the belly tended to mingle indiscriminately. They all formed part and parcel of the great aboriginal catastrophe of physical existence. If anything, physical greed—the most sinister inversion of all of Adam's primal hunger for the Wisdom of God, and the most blatant cause of human suffering in a famine-ridden society—stood out in slightly higher relief, above the generalized blur of sensuality and aching care associated with man's loss of the angelic state.[73] For a late antique ascetic, touched by the views of Origen, there was nothing at all strange in bursting into tears when sitting down to lunch: the very act of eating physical food, in the state of near-starvation induced by monastic fasting, reminded him of the rich feast of spiritual delight from which Adam had turned away in Paradise.[74] Sexuality, by contrast, lacked a distinctive flavor.

Augustine, however, could no longer regard sexual desire as no more than one irritant among so many others. It edged itself forward, in his thought, with ever-increasing circumstantiality. He came to scrutinize it, in the years in which he wrote the *Confessions* and the *Literal Commentary on Genesis*, as an exceptionally sharply delineated symptom of Adam's fall. That sexual desire existed in human beings, and that it might occasionally be connected with passions of distressing force, interested the middle-aged Augustine not in the slightest. His concern was more clearly focused and, for that reason, far more idiosyncratic. Writing the *Confessions*, he took the measure of the compulsive force of sexual habit. It was a cruel chain which only God could unloose. Far from vanishing, sexual fantasy, in the form of dreams accompanied by pleasurable nocturnal emissions, still lingered within him. Such sexual dreams may not have caused him great revulsion in 397; but they did point, in no uncertain fashion, to a disjunction between his conscious image of himself and a mysterious inability to follow his own will

Surely I have not ceased to be my own self . . . and yet there is still a great gap between myself and myself. . . .

73. E.g. Ambrose, *In Lucam* 7.142: *P.L.* 15: 1826A.
74. Palladius, *Lausiac History* 1.3.

Oh that my soul might follow my own self . . . that it might not be a rebel to itself.[75]

Such instances of the disjunction between conscious will and sexual feeling seemed to betray a dislocation of the human person quite as shocking as was the obscene anomaly of death. It had not been so in Paradise. For Adam and Eve, will and sexual delight had run together in perfect concord.

Only in the virgin birth of Christ had Mary recaptured Eve's first harmony. Overshadowed by the Holy Spirit, Mary had felt not the slightest eddy of uncontrolled feeling at the moment when she conceived Christ: the physical sensation associated with the sexual act had been fully consonant, in her case, with the untroubled movement of her will. The contrast with other Christian authors is striking. For Ambrose, the virginity of Mary had consisted principally in the fact that her body had not been entered by a male penis, and that her womb had received no alien seed: it was, for him, a potent image of a sacred boundary, unbreached by intrusion from the outside world. For Augustine, Mary's conception of Christ stood rather for an act of undivided obedience. It recaptured the ancient harmony of body and soul, in which the will was not the maimed thing that it so soon became.[76] A yearning for harmony and for untroubled obedience on every level, and not, as for Ambrose, the defense of a sacred inner space against a polluting world, was what now held the center of Augustine's thought. His ideal was a human soul, a human body and a human society unfissured by the dark twist of the fallen will.

By contrast to the present, the married intercourse of Adam and Eve, had this occurred before the Fall, would have been an object lesson in the balanced rapture with which all human beings might have used the physical joys showered upon them by their Creator. The sweet attractive power of physical beauty and the delicious onset and sharp climax of sexual delight, traditionally associated with the act of conception, may not have been absent in Paradise; but, in Paradise, such delight would have coincided entirely with the will. On the social plane, the personal, physical joy of each would have been swept up into an

75. *Confessions* 10.30.41–42: 796–797.
76. *Enarratio in Ps.* 67 21.37: 826; *Sermon* 287.4: 39:1302 and *de Trinitate* 13.18.23: 42: 1032; cf. *Contra Julianum* 4.13.62: 44: 768.

unswerving concord of wills. Adam and Eve would have served God by filling His Paradise with human beings capable, in all their actions, of a resonant unity of will and sensation, of individual and society.[77]

The human race still depended for its continuity on the sexual drive. But in mankind's fallen state, the precise quality of sexual intercourse could no longer be taken for granted. It was not what it had been to Gregory of Nyssa and John Chrysostom—a merciful, if clumsy, remedy against death. For Augustine, it was, in itself, a miniature shadow of death. Like death, the onset and culmination of sexual sensation mocked the will. Its random movements spoke of a primal dislocation. It betrayed a *discordiosum malum*,[78] an abiding principle of discord lodged in the human person since the Fall.

The rest of Augustine's life would be spent defending this view. After 413, controversy with Pelagius and Caelestius, and, after 418, a prodigious literary duel with their most gifted and tenacious supporter, Julian, Bishop of Eclanum, revealed to the Christian world at large the full implications of the views that Augustine had come to adopt in the decade after his return from Milan to the relative isolation of North Africa. It is as if, in the archipelago of the ancient Christian culture of the Mediterranean, an earthquake had forced another island to the surface. Many articulate Christians came to look with considerable disquiet at its unaccustomed and precipitous contours. The controversies of Augustine's old age take us into almost every region of the Greek and Latin worlds. They give us a unique opportunity to see Augustine's novel attitudes to sexuality and to the human person through the eyes of those who belonged to very different Christian traditions.

(III) *POENA RECIPROCA*

Julian, Bishop of Eclanum, in Southern Italy, was the last, and by far the most relentless, of Augustine's many critics. He had been forced to leave Italy, for his support of the views of Pelagius, around 419. He was about forty when he was exiled. He was Augustine's junior by almost a generation. Yet he had grown up in a more ancient world. He came from the aristocratic Italy that Jerome had abandoned so abruptly, and to which the more patient Rufinus had returned. His

---

77. *de civitate Dei* 14.10: 417.   78. *Contra Julianum* 4.8.49: 763.

polemics, written in vivid Latin, assumed an upper-class Italian audience whose experiences differed markedly from those of Augustine in Africa. In the debate on marriage and sexuality between Augustine and Julian, we can witness the confrontation of two worlds.[79]

Julian had thought nothing of becoming a married clergyman. He had married as a young man in minor orders, around 400–403. This was hardly surprising. He was the son of a bishop, and he married the daughter of a bishop. None other than Paulinus of Nola wrote an *Epithalamium* for the young couple. Paulinus presented Julian and his bride as standing before the Bishop of Beneventum (Julian's father-in-law) as Adam and Eve had once stood before God in Paradise, to receive the blessing *Increase and multiply*. For Paulinus, the young couple's options could be expressed in terms of an uncomplicated either-or. Either Julian and his wife would decide to live in virginal concord "bearing a body innocent of the flesh" (as Paulinus had eventually come to do with his own wife, and as some of Paulinus' friends had done)[80] or "should they be agreeable to each other in the body," then, "may chaste offspring come to form [yet once again, for the third generation!] a priestly race."[81]

Sexuality remained unproblematic among such persons. For a continent aristocrat like Paulinus, sexual needs had proved easy enough to forgo. They may never have bulked large in his life. As a young man of high family placed under an obligation to produce male heirs, he had duly begotten a son. When the child died, Paulinus and Therasia settled down into a life of post-marital continence. Julian had followed this course. By the time that he wrote against Augustine, he had long been continent. He had no son, as far as we know. His wife may have died, or she may have retired to a convent when he became a deacon, around 409. It was an altogether unremarkable evolution.

79. On Julian, see esp. the excellent preface of A. C. de Veer, *Premières polémiques contre Julien* pp. 9–25 and Y. M. Duval, "Julien d'Éclane et Rufin d'Aquilée." See also Peter Brown, "The Patrons of Pelagius: the Roman Aristocracy between East and West," now in *Religion and Society*, esp. pp. 214–215 and "Sexuality and Society in the Fifth Century A.D.: Augustine and Julian of Eclanum."

80. Paulinus of Nola, *Carmen* 25.233 in W. Hartel, ed., *Corpus Scriptorum Ecclesiasticorum Latinorum* 30:245. Turcius Apronianus and Avita were one such couple: A. H. M. Jones, J. R. Martindale and J. Morris, *The Prosopography of the Later Roman Empire*, 1:87–88. Friends of Paulinus, Avita received from Rufinus a translation of the *Sentences of Sextus*, a perfect "Rule" for a continent couple: for its influence on Pelagius, see R. F. Evans, *Pelagius: Inquiries and Reappraisals*, pp. 43–66.

81. Paulinus, *Carmen* 25.235–337, p. 245.

Unlike Augustine, no mighty earthquake on the ocean-bed of the self need have accompanied Julian's dignified resolve to abandon sex.

Compared with the truly sinister pressures placed on aristocrats by their social status, the sexual eddies of the body seemed a small matter. The habits against which young men and women had to pit themselves, in Rome and southern Itay, were those created by the possession of enormous wealth, by the crushing weight of social expectations, and by the avarice and cruelty associated with the exercise of power. It was a very different world from that of the marginal young careerists in which Augustine had grown up. In the narrow circle of the Christian aristocracy, the trials of outstanding men and women were known to everyone. Sexual temptation was the least important among them.

To take one example: the grand-daughter of Melania the Elder, Melania the Younger, and her husband, Pinianus, were known by all of the main protagonists in the controversy between Julian and Augustine.[82] Melania had been married, around 400 A.D., when she was fourteen and Pinianus seventeen. She had attempted to make plain, by refusing to wash, that she did not want her body to be used for marriage.[83] Her experience of the marriage-bed replicated that of her grandmother. Yet she had to agree to continue intercourse until Pinianus had a son.[84] The first child, a girl, was immediately dedicated to God.[85] The second child, a boy, died after an extremely difficult premature birth. Soon after, her daughter died.[86]

At the age of twenty, she finally persuaded Pinianus to live in continence. Sexual experiences were not what young persons, bruised by the tyranny of the marriage-bed, wished to linger on. What weighed most terribly on Melania was the huge wealth that had made her body the joining point of two relentless families. Long after their conversion to continence, their relatives were bitterly divided over the young couple's disposal of their wealth.[87] Looking back on that period of her life, she told her biographer of how the Devil once caused her palace to glow with fiery gold and evoked in her mind the rustling glades and the dazzling marble bathhouse of her favorite country villa.[88]

Pelagius moved in this distinctive world as a teacher of deep moral

82. Brown, "Patrons of Pelagius," pp. 212–213.

83. *Life of Melania* 2, in D. Gorce, ed., *Vie de Sainte Mélanie*, p. 132; Elizabeth A. Clark, trans. *The Life of Melania the Younger*, p. 28.

84. 3:132, Clark, p. 29.　　85. 6:136, Clark, p. 29.　　86. 56–6:136, Clark, pp. 29–30.

87. 19:162–166, Clark, pp. 41–43.　　88. 17–18:160–162, Clark, pp. 39–40.

fervor. He came from distant Britain to Rome, at some time in the 390s.[89] It was precisely for men and women whose ascetic militancy had been inspired by the examples of Melania and Pinianus that he wrote to uphold the freedom of the will. Spectacular renunciations, in the face of aristocratic opinion, showed what Christians were capable of doing, once they had seized upon the "sword of the free will."[90] Those who read Pelagius' commentaries on the letters of Saint Paul or the exhortations of his followers were challenged to remember the extent of their freedom. They could rid themselves of the heavy rust of corrupt social habits associated with the cruel and deeply profane society of the Roman governing classes.[91] For Pelagius, Adam's sin had brought about no irrevocable weakening of the will. No insuperable, inherited frailty stood between modern Christians and the capacity first bestowed on Adam and Eve to follow God's commands to the full.[92] Pelagius and his followers refused to believe that religious men and women were at the mercy of forces beyond the will's control.[93] Such a view struck Pelagius and his supporters as tantamount to condoning moral torpor. Once such views gained a hold on the Church, Julian asserted, all vices would be shrugged off as no more than the inevitable foibles of a human nature that had fallen beyond recall.[94] It was not by such dangerous ruminations on human frailty that the glory of God and of His saving commands would be made manifest in the under-Christianized provinces of the West.[95]

In the 400s, the ascetic sensibility of Italy ran in favor of Pelagius' views. Pelagius himself had been inspired by Rufinus' translations of the works of Origen.[96] Pelagian pamphleteers in favor of the ascetic life were among the few Roman Christians to welcome Jerome's *outré*

---

89. Peter Brown, "Pelagius and his Supporters: Aims and Environment," now in Brown, *Religion and Society*, pp. 183–207. See also Y. M. Duval, "Pélage est-il le censeur inconnu de l'Adversus Jovinianum?" F. G. Nuvolone and A. Solignac, s.v. Pélage et Pélagianisme, in *Dictionnaire de la Spiritualité*, provide a summary and a complete bibliography.

90. Pelagius, *Ad Demetriadem* 1: *Patrologia Latina* 30: 16B.

91. Brown, "Pelagius and His Supporters," pp. 195–197 and Evans, *Pelagius*, pp. 90–121.

92. *Epistula de castitate* 3.5: *Patrologia Latina Supplementum* 1: 1467–1468.

93. Pelagius, *Comm. in Rom.* 7:18–24: *P. L. Suppl.* 1: 1144.

94. *Opus Imperfectum* 2.8: 45: 1145.

95. Brown, "Pelagius and his Supporters," in *Religion and Society*. pp. 194 and 201–207 and Gisbert Greshake, *Gnade als konkrete Freiheit*, pp. 93–99 and 189–192.

96. Evans, *Pelagius*, p. 38.

statements in his *Against Jovinian*.[97] After Pelagius had been condemned by the Bishop of Rome in 417, Julian found it easy to appeal to Italian ascetic opinion. Their dearest hopes had been betrayed. Augustine preached despair:

despair at ever achieving chastity . . . presenting the power of indecent lust as so strong that neither reason could rule nor restrain it, nor the combined experience of the Apostles prove that it can ever be held at bay.[98]

Julian, however, was far more consequential than his mentor Pelagius had been. He realized that Augustine's notion of the abiding corruption of human nature since the Fall was intimately linked to his conviction that this corruption was made explicit by a permanent derangement of the sexual urge. It was not enough, therefore, to insist, as other Pelagians had done, that sexual needs could be renounced without insuperable difficulty. Julian had to go on to demonstrate that, in strict theory, sexual desire did not have to be renounced at all. It was in no way corrupted. It was both irrational and impious to suggest that the sexual urge, as now used in married intercourse, was in any way different from that which God had first placed in Adam and Eve. When the Christian couple stood before their priest, (as Julian and his bride had done, some twenty years before) they bore in their bodies a capacity for sexual desire and for sexual delight identical to that which God had blessed in Adam and Eve. Sexual desire might, at times, have to be controlled, but it could never be said to be "fallen." By such an argument, Julian brought about a dramatic shift of venue for the controversy. A storm whose first rumbles had taken the fashionable, ascetic form of treaties on virginity[99] now came to rage above the marriage-beds of the Christian laity.

Julian was careful to point out that he wrote to defend the sexual urge,

not as some oustandingly good thing, but as a drive in our bodies made by God—a drive which you claim has been placed deep within us by the Devil,

97. Evans, *Pelagius*, pp. 19–20; cf. R. Lorenz, "Die Anfänge des abendländischen Mönchtums im 4. Jahrhundert," pp. 36–38.

98. *Contra Julianum* 3.26.65: 735–736.

99. Thus, Demetrias, a young woman from the Anician family, received letters for Pelagius, Augustine, and Jerome on the occasion of her consecration as a virgin of the Church; each urged a distinctive theological viewpoint: Pelagius, *Ad Demetriadem*: P.L. 30: 15–45; Jerome, *Letter* 130: P.L. 22: 1107–1124; Augustine wrote to Demetrias' grandmother: *Letter* 130: 494–507.

making your whole doctrine stand or fall upon little more than the discreet behavior that surrounds the sexual act.[100]

In taking this stand, Julian knew that he could appeal to married Christians in an ancient language. Conventional medical opinion was on his side. It was known that physical pleasure was necessary for reproduction: it was the *confectrix commixtrixque seminum*, the force that brought male and female seeds harmoniously together.[101] A *calor genitalis*, a diffused heat, accompanied by pleasurable excitement, was necessary for reproduction. Without this, and the pleasurable sensations that accompanied it, conception simply would not happen. Marriage would have no point. Far from being the symptom of a sinister dislocation of the human person, sexual pleasure was the "chosen instrument of any self-respecting marriage . . . acceptable in and of itself, and blameworthy only in its excesses."[102]

Those who accepted marriage must accept the libido for what it was, an innocent and necessary instinctual drive. The more antisocial and immoral uses of the libido were banal and unrevealing byproducts: they were an "itch" that could be soothed, even in the headstrong young, by the salutary ointment of the Gospels.[103] To deny this was tantamount to deny that Christian marriage was a state blessed by God.

Julian combined this physiological attitude with a Pelagian's robust faith that sexuality was amenable to the will. The Christian couple were free to "trigger" the sexual mechanism, and to set it aside without great difficulty, despite its solemn onset and admittedly uncontrollable conclusion.[104] Sex was therefore what free choices made it. Good choices made it for marriage and children. The social function of Christian marriage explained and entirely justified the physical facts of sex.[105]

The foundation of Julian's attack on Augustine was solidly laid, from well-known materials. Writing for much of the time as an exile in the Greek world, and anxious to mobilize its leaders against the African Church, Julian appealed to a long tradition of Eastern Christian thought

100. *Opus Imperfectum* 3.142: 1303.
101. Ibid. 5.11: 1440.
102. *Contra Julianum* 4.2.7: 739.
103. *Opus Imperfectum* 2.10: 1145.
104. *Contra Julianum* 5.5.22: 797. Similar views were taken for granted by a Greek bishop: Nemesius of Emesa, *On the Nature of Man* 17.37 and 25.42: *Patrologia Graeca* 40: 677A and 700A.
105. *Opus Imperfectum* 1.79: 1102.

on marriage. Even the most austere Greek Christians had tended to agree that as long as men and women had to have children so as to overcome death, sexuality was indispensable for the majority of Christians. It had been given by God in His mercy to mankind. A preacher such as John Chrysostom might stress the dangers of sexual temptation, but in so doing he envisaged banal situations: he referred to young husbands who might be lured from their marriage-bed by slave girls, and tempted by the strident eroticism of the city. Sexual intercourse, in itself, between the married couple, posed no problems to him. In his more relaxed moods as a preacher, he could even describe the woman's conception of a child with evident warmth: "as if she were gold receiving the purest gold, the woman receives the man's seed with rich pleasure."[106]

The only Christians who seemed to think otherwise were those who had inherited the radical traditions of Encratite Syria—the Manichees and the Messalians. Unlike Augustine, Julian knew Greek well. He took up residence in Cilicia, close to Asia Minor and to Syria, where the Messalian movement had caused most disquiet. He knew that the radicalism associated with the Messalian monks was viewed with peculiar fear by the established bishops of the Greek world. The Messalians were said to have cut the link between sexuality and society. The sexual instinct, for them, was not a merciful adjunct, granted by God to a fallen Adam, so as to overcome death. It was a demonic intrusion, a terrible force that had come to possess men and women, and that lingered deep in the heart, like an evil spirit, even among baptized Christians. Messalians were said to have dismissed Christian baptism as a mere "shaving" of sins: the stubble of lust would soon grow again. Julian accused Augustine of saying the same.[107] He presented Augustine's notion of the *discordiosum malum* as if it implied the presence in the believer of an ineradicable force of evil that mocked the efforts of the will. The widespread fear of the Messalians, frequently identified with the Manichees, provided Julian with a perfectly

---

106. John Chrysostom, *Homily 12 on Colossians* 5: *Patrologia Graeca* 62: 388, in C. P. Roth and D. Anderson, trans. *St. John Chrysostom: On Marriage and Family Life* p. 76.

107. Julian, cited in Augustine, *Contra ii epistulas Pelagianorum* 1.13.26: 44: 562; Theodoret, *Haereticorum fabularum comp.* 4.11: *Patrologia Graeca* 83: 429B. See now O. Hesse, Dàs Bőse bei Markus Eremites," in W. Strothmann, ed., *Makarius-Symposium über das Bőse.*

apposite lay figure on which to drape the garments of the Augustinian notion of an abiding derangement of the sexual urge.[108]

Italian readers may not have known as much about the Messalians as Julian came to know, through his exile in the East. They did know that Augustine had once been a Manichee. Julian warned them that the leopard had not changed his spots. They should be careful: Augustine still believed, with his old masters, both that an element of permanent evil existed in human beings, and that this evil was itself responsible for the mindless continuation of a damned humanity, through the act of intercourse.[109]

It was with Manichaeism in mind that Julian made his first moves in the controversy. As early as 418, on the eve of his impending exile, he approached Count Valerius, an influential figure at the court at Ravenna. Valerius was a married man. He may have been a young man, still intent on founding a family. The illustrious Count must have no illusions. Julian warned him that Augustine taught that the capacity for physical pleasure, without which he and his wife could not conceive children, had been "the Devil's gift" to man.[110]

That was not what a distinguished and potentially influential Christian layman wished to hear about his own marriage. For the first, and last, time that we know of in the history of the Early Church, the clergy sought out the opinion of a married layman on the delicate issue of sex and marriage. It was a dangerous moment. Augustine knew that once the Greek churches were alarmed by Julian's claim that his views on marriage and concupiscence resembled those of the Manichees and the Messalians, and once powerful married courtiers were alienated in Italy, the chance of securing an Empire-wide condemnation of Pelagian ideas would be doomed. From 418 onward, therefore, Augustine wrote unceasingly against Julian, first to reassure Valerius with a work *On Marriage and Concupiscence* and, later, with extensive

108. The tradition with which Julian wished to identify Augustine has been well studied by P. F. Beatrice, *Tradux peccati. Alle fonti della dottrina agostiniana del peccato originale*, pp. 222–259; see now G. Sfameni Gasparro," Il tema della concupiscenza in Agostino e la tradizione dell'enkrateia."

109. Elizabeth M. Clark, "Vitiated Seed and Holy Vessels: Augustine's Manichaean Past," is the most serious recent study of the extremely delicate issue of "survivals" of Manichaean modes of thought in Augustine. I am, as yet, uncertain on this issue.

110. *Opus Imperfectum* 2.88: 1177: on Valerius, see Brown, "Sexuality and Society," p. 58—all suggestions, however, must remain tentative.

refutations addressed to learned Latin Christians. Seldom do we see so clearly the end of an epoch in the history of the Church.

We have already seen why Augustine had come to the view that the way sexual drives escaped the control of the will was a peculiarly resonant symptom of the frailty inherited by mankind from Adam's first act of disobedience. What he now came to insist upon, against the Pelagians, was that the hiatus between will and sexual feeling had been inflicted on Adam and on all his descendants as a *poena reciproca*, a punishment imposed to fit the crime.[111] Hence its immense symbolic power. Other signs of Adam's fall invariably struck Augustine, in his later years, as playing a far more powerful role in human affairs. The terrible cascade of helpless misery, of ignorance, arrogance, malice, and violence set up a deafening roar. Beside these devastating ills, sexual temptation was no more than an irritating trickle.[112] But sexuality and the grave stood one at each end of the life of every human being. Like two iron clamps, they delineated inexorably mankind's loss of the primal harmony of body and soul.

Hence the extreme circumstantiality of Augustine's later exegesis of the precise moment of the fall of Adam. Uncontrolled sexual feelings had immediately rendered palpable the *poena reciproca* that fell upon Adam and Eve as a result of their act of disobedience. They had eaten the forbidden fruit,

And the eyes of them both were opened, and they knew that they were naked.

In marked contrast to most Greek and Syrian writers Augustine identified this moment with an instant of clearly felt sexual shame.[113] He went on to insist that such shame was "more than just;" it was "utterly appropriate."[114] As soon as they had made their own wills independent of the will of God, parts of Adam and Eve became resistant to their own conscious will. Their bodies were touched with a disturbing new sense of the alien, in the form of sexual sensations that

111. *De civitate Dei* 14.17: 425.

112. Ibid. 22.22: 784–785. In a standard edition, out of sixteen lines devoted to deliberate human sins, only two refer to sexuality; cf. *Enarratio in Ps.* 41 14:474.

113. Genesis 3: 7; see *de Genesi ad litteram* 11.32.42: 447 and *de civitate Dei* 14.17–19: 425–427. For a very different exegesis of this moment, see M. Harl, "La prise de conscience de la 'nudité' d'Adam;" for Ephraim the Syrian, see Robert Murray, *Symbols of Church and Kingdom*, pp. 304–306 and J. Martikainen, "Das Böse in den Schriften des Syrers Ephraim, im Stufenbuch und im *Corpus Macarianum*," pp. 36–46.

114. *De Genesi ad litteram* 9.11.19: 400.

escaped their control.[115] The body could no longer be embraced entirely by the will. A tiny but ominous symptom—in Adam's case, the stirring of an erection over which he had no control—warned them both of the final slipping of the body as whole from the soul's familiar embrace at death.[116]

This was an austerely psychological doctrine. Augustine felt that he could brush aside Julian's defense of the *calor genitalis*. A learned man in the ancient tradition, and himself the father of a son, he did not attempt to challenge the medical fantasies of his age. He saw no reason why conception should not depend upon a moment of intense pleasure, and he was quite prepared to allow that such pleasure might have occurred in Paradise—no small imaginative feat for a late antique person of ascetic lifestyle. What concerned him was that, after the fall of Adam and Eve, this pleasure had gained a momentum of its own, and that it clashed with the intentions of the will. The sharp *summa voluptas* of orgasm notoriously escaped conscious control. This meant that a revelation of the limits of the conscious self that had first stunned Adam and Eve lingered on, as a sad reminder of the precise moment of the Fall, in the hot act by which each new human being was conceived.[117] In this psychological model, impotence was of equal interest to him. For in impotence, also, the will was mocked by the body quite as bluntly as in the incontrollable delight of orgasm: "lust itself does not serve lust . . . and is divided against itself."[118]

By directing attention to such a phenomenon, Augustine turned the flank of the ancient medical tradition. Impotence had either been treated as a physiological problem, amenable to exercise and diet, or it had been held to be the result of sorcery. A contemporary doctor, indeed, had been content to advise well-to-do clients afflicted with this disorder to eat many onions (rich in vital spirits), to take their siestas on soft beds . . . and to read Greek novels![119] Augustine, by contrast,

115. *De civitate Dei* 14.23.2: 431.
116. *De Genesi ad litteram* 9.9.17: 399 and *de civitate Dei* 14.25: 433.
117. *De civitate Dei* 14.20: 428 and *de nuptiis et concupiscentia* 1.7.7: 44: 417–418.
118. *De civitate Dei* 14.16: 424–425.
119. Theodorus Priscianus, *Euporiston* 2.11.34, V. Rose, ed. pp. 132–133; cf. Petronius, *Satyricon* 130.7 and 131.5–7; Marcellus of Bordeaux, another contemporary of Augustine, recommended apotropaic devices to ward off spells that caused impotence and spells to cause it in others: Marcellus, *de medicamentis* 33.49, 65, M. Niedermann, ed., 2:566, 570. Little changed in medical circles in the Middle Ages: D. Jacquart and C. Thomasset, *Sexualité et savoir médical au Moyen-Âge*, pp. 230–235.

presented impotence and frigidity, for the first time, as psychosomatic symptoms whose causes lay deep within the self. Sexuality was effectively taken from its physiological context and made to mirror an abiding, unhealed fissure in the soul.

The uncontrollable elements in sexual desire revealed the working in the human person of a *concupiscentia carnis*, of a permanent flaw in the soul that tilted it irrevocably towards *the flesh*. Unlike the hasty Jerome, and even unlike Ambrose, Augustine was exceptionally careful to point out, in frequent, patient expositions of the Letters of Paul, that *the flesh* was not simply the body: it was all that led the self to prefer its own will to that of God.[120]

The *concupiscentia carnis*, indeed, was such a peculiarly tragic affliction to Augustine precisely because it had so little to do with the body. It originated in a lasting distortion of the soul itself. With Adam's Fall, the soul lost the ability to summon up all of itself, in an undivided act of will, to love and praise God in all created things. Concupiscence was a dark drive to control, to appropriate, and to turn to one's private ends, all the good things that had been created by God to be accepted with gratitude and shared with others. It lay at the root of the inescapable misery that afflicted mankind.[121] Sexual desire was no more tainted with this tragic, faceless concupiscence than was any other form of human activity.[122] But the very incongruities associated with sexual feelings used the human body as a tiny mirror, in which men and women could catch a glimpse of themselves. They saw themselves, from this unexpected angle, as God had first seen the fallen Adam and Eve. They were beings estranged from Him and from each other as surely as their own sexual feelings were now estranged from their own conscious selves. At no other time in the history of the early Church had the opaque and somewhat banal facts of sex been held for so long in a single, searching light, as in Augustine's invocation of them to express the *poena reciproca* that lay so heavy on the human race.

The indirect and momentous result of Augustine's emphasis on the psychological momentum behind the sexual drive was to destroy the neat compartments with which Christians of an earlier age had tended

120. *De Genesi ad litteram* 10.12.10: 416 and *de civitate Dei* 14.3: 405–408.
121. *De Trinitate* 12.10.25: 1006 and *de civitate Dei* 14.28: 436.
122. *De Genesi ad litteram* 10.20.36: 424; see Margaret Miles, *Fullness of Life*, pp. 114–115: "His concern was not to locate an 'evil' of human life in any particular act, but to recognize and acknowledge its presence in all human actions. Julian denied its existence in married sex, so Augustine insisted on it even there."

to contain the anxieties raised by the sexual components of the human person. Sexuality could no longer be taken for granted as a problem that mainly concerned the young. Unlike Julian's *calor genitalis*, Augustine's *concupiscentia carnis* was not a physiological drive, safely confined to the body. It was not a physical reserve of heat that might be expected to burn off with the passing of age, permitting the old to sink back, without undue anxiety, into the postmarital celibacy that had been the normal form of male continence in earlier centuries.

As a result, the ascetic struggle seemed that much more uncertain. No one could gauge his own capacity to resist so subtle and continuous a source of temptation. For all his shrill sense of sexual danger, Jerome, for instance, had been a monk of the old school. The intense physicality of his descriptions of the ascetic life contained an unadmitted optimism. He was confident that the body was directly amenable to diet: long fasting, the studious avoidance of wine and of mixed company would cause the sexual drive to slacken.[123] Contemporary doctors had said as much.[124] Augustine could never allow himself to be so certain. As the manifestation of an impalpable concupiscence, sexuality was a disturbingly ageless adversary:

For when I had this work in hand, it was announced to us that an old man of eighty-three, who had lived with his wife in continence for twenty five years, had just now purchased a lyre girl for his pleasures.[125]

It was a disturbing doctrine, also, for the married laity. In the covering letter that Augustine sent to Count Valerius, along with his book *On Marriage and Concupiscence*, he praised Valerius for the "chastity" of his married life. Such chastity was more than the avoidance of blatant infidelities. It was closer to the sharply honed notion of marital restraint that Ambrose had propounded to the church at Vercelli in 396. It involved a personal struggle with desire that could be known only to the Count's most intimate spiritual advisers.[126] A sense of the lingering force of concupiscence, which had been more usually associated with the lonely struggles of the Desert Fathers, now tinged Augustine's view of the marital relations of every Catholic.

123. Jerome, *in Tit. 1: P.L.* 26: 602D and *Letters* 22.11, 54.9, 79.7: *P.L.* 22: 400–401, 554, 729–730.

124. Jerome, *Letter* 54.9 cites Galen: cf. Oribasius, *Medical Collection* 22.2.17 and *Libri Incerti* 2.10–17, in U. C. Bussmaker and C. Daremberg, eds., *Oeuvres d'Oribase*, 3:45, 84–85. Oribasius was doctor to Julian the Apostate.

125. *Contra Julianum* 3.20.22: 713.   126. *Letter* 200.3: 926.

For this reason, it is singularly appropriate that the most discreet and authoritative rebuttal of Augustine's views came from an authentic representative of the desert tradition. John Cassian had been a disciple of Evagrius in Egypt and, later, of John Chrysostom in Constantinople. He was a member of the monastic diaspora that had been scattered from Egypt and Constantinople as a result of the Origenist controversy. Settled in Lérins, a deserted island opposite Cannes, within sight of the sun-scarred slopes of the Alpes Maritimes, Cassian wrote his *Collationes*, his *Conferences*, and his *Institutes of the Monastic Life*, in the period from about 420 to 426. Cast in the form of extensive interviews with the Old Men of Egypt, he wished to bring the still voice of the desert into a Western Mediterranean lashed by the storms of the Pelagian controversy.[127] In his *Thirteenth Conference*, he had attempted, with the utmost tact, to modify what he thought was a dangerous denial of the freedom of the will implied in Augustine's notion of grace and predestination. The indirect criticism was immediately recognized for what it was by Augustine's supporters in southern Gaul.[128]

Cassian's rebuttal of Augustine's notion of concupiscence, in his other *Conferences*, was indirect but equally firm. The war with sexual temptation, the Old Men agreed, was indeed a conflict "woven into the very fibers of our being."[129]

When a thing exists in all persons without exception [Apa Paphnutius assured him] we can only think that it must belong to the very substance of human nature, since the fall, as if it were "natural" to man.[130]

But the conclusions that the Old Man drew from this observation were not those that readers of Augustine had come to expect: for

when a thing is found to be congenital . . . how can we fail to believe that it was implanted by the will of the Lord, not to injure us, but to help us.[131]

127. *Collationes*, in E. Pichery, ed., *Jean Cassien: Les Conférences: De Institutis coenobiorum*, in J. C. Guy, ed. *Jean Cassien: Institutions cénobitiques*. Edgar C. S. Gibson, in *The Library of the Nicene and Post-Nicene Fathers*, vol. 11 provides a reliable English translation. See esp. Peter Munz, "John Cassian"; Philip Rousseau, *Ascetics, Authority and the Church*, pp. 169–234; and M. Foucault, "Le combat de la chasteté," a brilliant essay, now available in P. Ariès and A. Béjin, eds., *Western Sexuality: Practice and Precept in Past and Present Times*.

128. Owen Chadwick, *John Cassian*, pp. 120–135 and Rousseau, *Ascetics, Authority and the Church*, pp. 231–234.

129. Cassian, *Collationes* 4.7, p. 172.   130. Ibid. p. 172.   131. Ibid. p. 172.

Through his continued exposure to temptation, the monk was held in the merciful tardiness of the flesh. Only the icy demons were exempt from the battle with concupiscence. For they were beyond God's mercy. Unlike the monk, they did not suffer from occasional wet dreams:

And from this fact we can clearly gather that the struggle of the flesh and the spirit against each other is not merely harmless, but is, in fact, extremely useful to us. . . . *These are the nations that the Lord has left in the land, that He might instruct Israel through them.*[132]

The lingering presence of the sexual drive did more than save the monk from pride, by imposing on him the intermittent shame of nocturnal emissions. Sexual fantasies were like signals on a screen. They registered processes that lay out of sight, in the depths of the self. They informed the monk of the movement of forces in himself that lay beyond his immediate consciousness. Only when the more faceless drives of egotism and rage were stilled would the monk come to sense a delicious freedom from sexual fantasy, associated with the state of total *purity of heart.*[133] Until that time, sexual temptations continued to warn him that these drives still lingered, unconsciously, within his soul.

Cassian deliberately chose the medical terminology of his age in order to express his sense of psychic powers that burned like subcutaneous fevers within the unconscious self. Sullen resentments, unacknowledged egotism, and a diffuse anger lay congealed, in the soul, like undispersed residues of noxious humors. Only by remaining alert to his own sexual temptation could the monk measure the continued, debilitating presence within him of more tenacious spiritual ailments. He must approach his sexual fantasies much as a doctor felt the pulse to learn about his patient's true condition.[134]

Such medical terminology bears so striking a resemblance to the clinical language of "depth psychology" that a modern reader is easily misled. Cassian, however, was a loyal follower of the Desert Fathers on this issue. Sexuality, for him, was not what it has become in the lay imagination of a post-Freudian age. It was not the basic instinctual drive, of which all others were secondary refractions. It was the other way around. The colder drives that lured the human person into col-

132. Ibid. 4.14, p. 179; Judges 6:1–2 cited in *Collationes* 4.6, 7.2, pp. 171, 245.
133. Ibid. 7.2, p. 245 and 12.16, p. 145.
134. Ibid. 3.7, p. 147; *Institutes* 6.11, p. 274.

lusion with the demonic world were more basic to the monk's concern. They lay deeper in his identity than did sexual desire. Sexuality was a mere epiphenomenon. Sexual dreams and sexual temptations betrayed the tread of far heavier beasts within the soul—anger, greed, avarice, and vainglory.[135]

Augustine, by contrast, had placed sexuality irremovably at the center of the human person. He had done this because, by the time that Cassian wrote, sexuality was held inflexibly in the grip of his notion of a human race condemned, by the justice of God, to endure, in their bodies and their minds, the permanent presence of a *poena reciproca*—an exquisitely apposite and permanent symptom of Adam's fall.

It was not that Augustine's sense of the strength and the disruptive power of sexual temptation was any stronger than that of the Desert Fathers. For both it was a fearsome and debilitating trial. Both feared the lingering power of sexual fantasy. Thoughts of sexual matters weakened the Christian's capacity for true delight; sexual fantasies and sexual dreams silently eroded "the spiritual joys of the saints."[136] But, in Augustine's mind, sexuality served only one, strictly delimited purpose: it spoke, with terrible precision, of one single, decisive event within the soul. It echoed in the body the unalterable consequence of mankind's first sin. It was down that single, narrow, and profound shaft that Augustine now looked, to the very origins of human frailty. Nocturnal emissions could not tell him anything about the silent shift of forces within the soul of a particular individual: they spoke to all men, and of one thing alone—of a fatal deposit of concupiscence left there by Adam's fall.[137] It was a drastically limited vision of a complex phenomenon.

Cassian wrote as he did because he had been a distant heir of the thought of Origen. He was convinced that the very depths of the person could shift. Not fully available to his consciousness, the forces within him nevertheless lay within the power of the free will to master, in vigilant collaboration with the grace of God. The inner world of the monk could be transformed, slowly but surely, in the same way as the huge universe of Origen would sink back, after the disciplined use of freedom by innumerable beings over endless ages, into the primal fire of Christ's embrace. A *fullness of peace* would flood into the

135. Cassian, *Collationes* 1.22, p. 106.
136. E.g. *Contra Julianum* 4.2.10–11, 13.69–70: 741, 772–773.
137. *Confessions* 10.30.42: 797 and *de Genesi ad litteram* 12.15.31: 466.

heart of the monk. The dark recesses of the self would come, at last, into the light:

and I will give thee the treasures of darkness, and riches hidden in secret places.[138]

Meanwhile, the monk was encouraged to scan his dreams for welcome signals of the approach of peace of heart. Businesslike as ever, Apa Moses declared that three emissions a year, without sexual fantasies, would be what the good monk might expect; and Moses had once been a brigand chief, of legendary physique and gusto, who had passed through many years of particularly cruel sexual temptation.[139] Augustine, by contrast, never thought that such deliverance would occur in this life. It is seldom that two Latin writers, each as gifted in their differing ways with such powers of introspection and each capable of such magnetic literary expression as Augustine and John Cassian, have reached such diametrically opposite conclusions as to what precisely they had seen in their own hearts.

(IV) PAX PLENA

Stung by Julian's invective, Augustine may not even have been aware of Cassian's quiet, but pertinent, dissagreement.[140] We now know from a recently discovered letter that, in the years when Cassian wrote, Augustine had approached none other than Atticus, the canny successor of John Chrysostom as Bishop of Constantinople.[141] It is the letter of an old, frail man. Augustine was nearing seventy. He opined that Atticus had not written to him in the first place because it was believed in Constantinople that Augustine was already dead. This was hardly surprising, Augustine observed, with his unfailing literary *aplomb:* "for what is so easy to believe than that a man, born to die, should, in fact, be dead?"[142]

The letter is remarkable for its careful choice of words and for the concision with which Augustine spelled out his final position. Atticus

---

138. Isaiah 45: 2–3 cited in Cassian, *Institutes* 5.2, pp. 190–192.

139. Ibid. 2.23, p. 134; Palladius, *Historia Lausiaca* 19.5–11.

140. U. Duchrow, "Zum Prolog von Augustins *de doctrina christiana*," suggests that Augustine knew something of the writings of Cassian.

141. Letter 6*, pp. 32–38; *Lettres,* pp. 126–145: see esp. M. F. Berrouard, "Les lettres 6* et 19* de Saint Augustin," Brown, "Sexuality and Society," pp. 50–51 and G. R. Bonner, "Some Remarks on Letters 4* and 6*."

142. *Letter* 6*.1.3, p. 32; *Lettres,* p. 126.

was left in no doubt as to the view to which Augustine and his Latin colleagues wished to commit the Christian church: the letter summed up over thirty years of Augustine's thought on sexuality, marriage, and society.

The Pelagians, he wrote, had been wrong to spread the libelous rumor that, by drawing attention to the present state of sexuality as an enduring symptom of the Fall, Augustine had in any way condemned the "urge to marry," the *concupiscentia nuptiarum:*[143]

What Catholic could say that the urge to marry was an urge implanted by the Devil, when, by means of it, the human race would surely have been propagated, even if it had never sinned. . . . What Catholic, faced by God's creation, in souls and in our human flesh, does not acclaim His works, and summon up from deep within a hymn to the Creator, Who, not only at that time, before man's first sin, but even now, makes all things truly good?[144]

But this urge must be distinguished from the *concupiscentia carnis:*

An urge which burns quite indiscriminately for objects allowed and disallowed; and which is bridled by the urge for marriage, that must depend upon it, but that restrains it from what is not allowed. . . . Against this drive, which is in tension with the *law of the mind,* all chastity must fight: that of the married couple, so that the urge of the flesh may be rightly used, and that of continent men and virgins, so that, even better and with a struggle of greater glory, it should not be used at all. This urge, had it existed in Paradise . . . would, in a wondrous pitch of peace, have never run beyond the bidding of the will. . . . It would never have forced itself upon the mind with thoughts of inappropriate and impermissible delights. It would not have had to be held upon the leash by married moderation, or fought to a draw by ascetic labor. Rather, when once called for, it would have followed the will of the person with all the ease of a single-hearted act of obedience.[145]

Along with this late letter, the sermons that Augustine preached in the last decades of his life set his final views on sexuality in their true perspective. Preaching to married persons, he was content with the most banal exhortations to restraint: it was difficult enough for him to persuade husbands to be faithful to their wives, and married couples to attempt to abstain during the season of Lent, without laboring the more erudite ravages of concupiscence.[146] When a bishop preached,

---

143. 3.3, 5.1, pp. 33, 34; *Lettres,* p. 128, 130.   144. 3.3–5. p. 33; *Lettres,* pp. 128–130.
145. 5 and 8, pp. 34 and 38; *Lettres,* pp. 130–132 and 143.
146. *Sermons* 205.2: 1040; 224.3.3: 1094–1095; 392.2: 1710.

he was expected to preach, rather, against *scelera*, against violence, fraud, and oppression, not on sexual sins.[147]

Augustine's Africa had been spared barbarian invasions. But African society creaked with ancient ills. The powerful victimized the poor. Armed gangs of slave traders wandered with impunity through a defenseless countryside. Members of Augustine's own clergy set themselves up as petty tyrants in the villages.[148] The secular society whose right to exist Augustine had validated, by abandoning the ascetic myth of a pre-social Paradise, and whose coercive powers he had come to accept, by justifying the official suppression of his religious rivals, now wore a cruel face.[149]

The Catholic church would never be able to embrace it, as its "true mother," as he had once been tempted to hope, now forty years ago, in Milan and in his first years in Africa. All that he and his Catholic colleagues could now do was stand aside "and groan in vain for the wretched" as the powerful ground down the poor.[150] Augustine's somber sense of the Christian life as one of unresolved moral conflict was widened, tragically, in his later preaching: the Church itself, the great invisible body of Christ, and not only the individual believer, ached with the strains of living in this world; its final peace was forever withheld.[151]

Throughout these years of bitter frustration, Augustine never abandoned the hope against which he judged, ever more sadly, the present misery of the human race. It was still a hope for unity. A shattered harmony would be regained at the end of time. In his sermons we can sense the momentum of an unwearied heart. The fatal flaw of concupiscence would not have seemed so tragic to Augustine, if he had not become ever more deeply convinced that human beings had been created to embrace the material world. The body was a problem to him precisely because it was to be loved and cherished:

147. *Sermon* 137.11.13: 761.   148. Notably *Letters* 10*, 20*, 22*, 23*.

149. See esp. C. Lepelley, "La crise de l'Afrique romaine au début du vème siècle," and M. F. Berrouard, "Un tournant dans la vie de l'Eglise d'Afrique: les deux missions d'Alypius." Suzanne Poque, *Le langage symbolique dans la prédication d'Augustin d'Hippone*, pp. 57–60, is revealing on the reflection of this situation in Augustine's choice of imagery.

150. *Letter* 22*.2.5, p. 114; *Lettres*, p. 348.

151. *Enarratio* 2 *in Ps.* 29 5–7; 1 *in Ps.* 70 6–10 and *in Ps.* 83 3–10: 219–221, 879–881 and 1057–1065.

Let me put it to you yet more intimately. Your flesh is like your wife. . . . Love it, rebuke it; let it be formed into one bond of body and soul, one bond of married concord. . . . Learn now to master what you will receive as a united whole. Let it now go short, so that it will then enjoy abundance.[152]

In man's fallen state, the body must still be disciplined. It remained, for Augustine, a source of unrelieved disquiet. In order to convince the learned readers of his *City of God* and of his tracts against Julian, Augustine appealed to the authority of the ancients. He opened the sluice-gates of Latin Christian literature, quite as drastically as had Jerome, to let in the hard male puritanism that Romans relished in their ancestors and in their favorite authors. An ancient Roman's harsh distrust of sensual delight and a fear that the body's pleasures might weaken the resolve of the public man added a peculiarly rigid note to Augustine's evocation of human beings forever exposed to a merciless concupiscence. He created a darkened humanism that linked the pre-Christian past to the Christian present in a common distrust of sexual pleasure.[153] It was a heavy legacy to bequeath to later ages.

Augustine's sermons, by contrast, were notably free of this icy tone. In them he spoke of married love with a deep sense of sadness. Preaching in Carthage, at a time when a great civic celebration was taking place in the amphitheater, the nominal triumph of the Catholic Church in African society meant little to him.[154] He needed to speak, rather, of a deeper peace than Carthage could provide. Married couples now had to exercise constant vigilance in their sexual relations. He accepted the fact that they often experienced considerable difficulty in abstaining from intercourse at times of fast and vigil. Augustine reminded them that they should learn to yearn for a final resolution of the discord that made their present sexual abstinence so necessary:

God has not taken this punishment from us, in order that each of us might still remember to what place we have been called, and by Whom; so that each one of us might seek out that embrace, in which no instability is found.[155]

To beget children with a certain, medically approved zest, as a duty to the earthly city, was no longer enough. The Christian married couple must "descend with a certain sadness" to that particular task: for

---

152. *Enarratio in Ps. 140* 16: 1825–1826.
153. *Contra Julianum* 4.14.72 and 5.10.42: 774 and 808, citing Cicero's *Hortensius;* and *Contra Julianum* 5.5.9: 806–807, on the austerity of Cato.
154. See C. Lepelley, *Les cités de l'Afrique romaine au Bas-Empire,* 1:376–385.
155. *Sermon* 51.3.4: 335–336.

in the act of married intercourse itself, their very bodies spoke to them of Adam's fall.[156] In Augustine's piercing vision, the Roman city and the walls of the married household within it—those solid, magnificently self-reliant creations of an ancient Mediterranean way of life—were now washed by a dark current of sexual shame. Adam's shame knew no frontiers. All men and women must feel it. All ancient boundaries crumbled beneath the weight of the sadness that he had brought upon mankind. City and countryside, Roman and barbarian cultures, carefully groomed members of the upper classes and ordinary Christians, ascetics in the shimmering desert and married couples in the cities—all had been touched by the same bitter flood of a discordant sexuality. All mankind belonged to one single city of the doomed—they were all by birth citizens of Babylon. Only by baptism and by incorporation into the Catholic Church, a church whose basilicas were now plainly visible in every city of the Roman world, and whose hierarchy embraced and disciplined all forms of Christian life, would human beings be enabled to join the one city of which *Glorious things* might be spoken: the Heavenly Jerusalem, the City of God. Only in a city at the end of time, and in no city of the Western Empire in its last century, would the ache of discord, so faithfully mirrored in the flesh by sexuality, give way to a *pax plena*, to a fullness of peace:

When will full peace come to even one single person? The time when full peace comes to each is the time when peace in its fullness will have come in all the citizens of our Jerusalem.[157]

156. *Sermon* 51.15.25: 348.   157. *Enarratio in Ps. 147* 20: 1930.

Body and Society: The Early Middle Ages

By the middle of the fifth century A.D., the Christian church stood out in the Roman world as an institution that gave pride of place to the continent. When, around 430 A.D., Saint Patrick wrote to defend his eccentric mission to a barbarous land beyond the Roman frontiers, he reported that "In Ireland, which never had any knowledge of God . . . the sons and daughters of the chieftains are now seen to be monks and virgins of Christ."[1]

Later in the century, a local synod made plain that the coming of Christianity to Ireland had meant the arrival of codes of "Roman," that is, of Mediterranean, Christian, decorum among a people not hitherto noted for sexual restraint. The bishops condemned

Any cleric . . . who is seen without a [long] tunic, and does not cover the shameful parts beneath his belly, whose hair is not cut in the Roman fashion, and whose wife goes about with her hair unveiled.[2]

1. Patrick, *Confessio* 41, in A. B. E. Hood, ed., *St. Patrick*, pp. 31, 50.
2. *Synodus I Sancti Patricii* 6, in L. Bieler, ed., *The Irish Penitentials* pp. 54–55. I have followed the advice of my friend Dr. Francis J. Byrne in accepting a fifth-century date for this council.

At the other end of the Christian world, a Zoroastrian Persian governor berated the Christians of Armenia:

Do not believe your spiritual guides. . . . What they teach in words they belie by their actions. They say that it is no sin to eat meat, but they refuse to touch it; that it is permissible to take a wife, yet they do not so much as wish to look at a woman; that whosoever piles up treasure sins; and they exalt poverty as the highest virtue. . . . They love misfortune and despise prosperity. . . . If you listen to them, you will never go near your wives again, and the end of the world will soon be upon you.[3]

Within the territories of the Empire, members of a clearly recognizable elite now walked the streets of every city. Their very visibility drew upon them the usual consequences of unpopularity and satire. Bishops preached against those who treated it as a bad omen for the day, if the first person they saw on entering the street was a priest, a monk, or a virgin of the Church.[4] In 546, the Emperor Justinian forbade actors to dress up in the "holy robes" of monks and nuns, so as to portray them in comic skits in the theater.[5] In the course of three centuries, since the age of Galen and Justin Martyr, we have come appreciably closer to a world that resembles our current notion of the Catholic Middle Ages—a world of celibate priests, monks, and nuns.

We should, however, remember that we have followed the destinies of a small and vociferous minority, in an ancient society that changed very slowly. Even the minority was divided in its opinions. The Early Church was so creative largely because its most vocal members so frequently disagreed with each other. As in the history of all great revolutions brought about by the militant few, room must also be found in any history of sexual renunciation in the Early Church for tragedy, for disillusionment, and for sheer boredom on the part of the unheroic majority of believers. The reaction to Jerome's *Against Jovinian*, to mention only one example, shows Christian congregations baffled and angered by the fashionable radical stances of one of their more articulate leaders. There were also moments of bitterness, as former members of the ascetic movement turned against their own past. In Vercelli, lapsed monks from his own monastery had led the campaign to defy

3. Elishe Vartapet, *History of Vartan* 2, from V. Langlois, *Collection des historiens anciens et modernes de l'Arménie*, 2:191.

4. *Sermo de sacrilegio* 11: *Patrologia Latina: Supplementum* 4:971.

5. Justinian, *Novella* 123.44.

Ambrose, when he had wished to have a monk as bishop for the city. We meet Tiberianus, a bishop in southern Spain, in a short, cold notice by Jerome. For a time, Tiberianus was caught up in the Priscillianist movement. He even suffered exile. Then he lost faith in his radical friends: continence was no longer the watchword of his life; *"as a dog returns to his vomit,* he married off his daughter, who had been a virgin dedicated to Christ."[6]

We know less of the regrets and the human casualties among the few than we do about the cheerful impermeability of the many. The "pale Galilaean" may have conquered the Empire; but Mediterranean Romans did not "grow grey" to any appreciable extent. When Jerome was serving as secretary to Pope Damasus in Rome, in 384, he witnessed a strange funeral. A husband, the veteran of twenty wives, buried a wife who had, in her time, got through twenty-two husbands. The husband led the procession around her bier, "crowned and carrying a palm of victory, with all the people of the City in attendance, to the chant of 'Lay 'em out in hundreds.' "[7]

A century later, in 495, the festivities of the Lupercalia—an archaic, pagan rite associated with fertility and with the good behavior of the City's women—were now enlivened by ditties on the adulteries of the Roman clergy.[8] A little later, many Romans were convinced that the Pope kept a mistress, known in the City as *Conditaria,* "Sugar and Spice."[9]

In the eastern Empire, divorce by consent, in the Roman manner, remained the norm, despite persistent clerical pressure. In the marriage legislation of the Christian Emperors, indeed, considerations of wealth and status spoke louder than did the rulings of the Gospels.[10] The career of Theodora shows a woman caught up in the life of a fully Christian governing class, whose sense of erotic privilege and social prejudices had changed little since the days of Augustus.[11] Courtesan,

6. Jerome, *de viris illustribus* 123: *P.L.* 23: 711.

7. Jerome, *Letter* 123.10: *P.L.* 22: 1052–1053.

8. Gelasius, *Ad Andromachum* 2, in G. Pomarès, ed., *Gélase 1er: Lettre contre les Lupercales* p. 162.

9. See Henry Chadwick, *Boethius,* p. 32.

10. A. H. M. Jones, *The Later Roman Empire,* 2:974–975. Now add Roger Bagnall, "Church, State and Divorce in Late Roman Egypt," pp. 50–54.

11. See esp. David Daube, "The Marriage of Justinian and Theodora," and Averil Cameron, *Procopius,* pp. 67–83; see also R. S. McCail, "The Erotic and Ascetic Poetry of Agathias Scholasticus," and the important survey of H. G. Beck, *Byzantinisches Er-*

concubine and, finally, the Imperial wife of Justinian, Theodora also acted as the devout and powerful protector of the monks of Syria, by whom she was remembered, frankly enough, as "Theodora, she of the brothel."[12]

In 630, three hundred prostitutes demonstrated against the Byzantine governor of Syracuse as he relaxed in the public baths. We know of the incident only because the Pope, Honorius, was shocked to hear that the governor had pacified the protestors by appointing the Catholic Bishop of Syracuse as Imperial Inspector of Brothels.[13] Good citizens of the Roman Empire in its last days, governor and bishop took for granted that their first duty was to preserve law and order in the city. In Syracuse, as elsewhere, the codes of behavior associated with the Catholic church still had to co-exist with a texture of urban life that had come of age long before the rise of Christianity.

Further to the northwest, in Gaul, the cities were less colorful; but the ancient codes of the Roman aristocracy still governed the lives of the Catholic episcopate. Representatives of great families, allied to others by marriage, these men brought their rhetorical skills into the pulpit, their experience of Roman administration to the bishop's court, and their wives, as "sisters in Christ," into the bishop's palace.[14] The strict continence of the Catholic clergy in much of the Latin West still rested on the time-honored institution of postmarital celibacy. The arrangement had its strains. Around 570, Bishop Felix of Nantes, "when talking about such matters," confided to his friend, Gregory of Tours, how he had first begun to sleep apart from his wife when elected bishop. Far from taking such behavior for granted in a Catholic bishop, Felix's wife immediately suspected that he had found another woman. Bursting into his room, she saw the Bishop, stretched out for his siesta, fast asleep, with a "lamb of unparalleled radiance" curled up on his chest: for *lo, I am with you always, to the close of the age.*[15] Only in the late sixth

---

otikon. Orthodoxie-Literatur-Gesellschaft, Sitzungsberichte der bayerischen Akademie der Wissenschaften. Philos.-Hist. Klasse 1984, esp. pp. 69–75.

12. John of Ephesus, *Lives of the Eastern Saints* 12: *Patrologia Orientalis* 17:189.

13. Honorius, *Letter* 14: *P.L.* 80:841.

14. Constantius, *Life of Germanus of Auxerre* 1. 1–2, in R. Borius, ed., *Constance de Lyon: Vie de Saint Germain d'Auxerre,* pp. 122–124; see C. Cochini, *Origines apostoliques du célibat sacerdotal,* pp. 125–143, 288–379.

15. Gregory of Tours, *Liber de gloria confessorum* 75, in B. Krusch, ed., *Monumenta Germaniae Historica: Scriptores Rerum Merovingicarum* 1.2 p. 343.

century, when their wives finally disappeared from the households of the clergy and the majority of the bishops came to their cities from the monastery, would an ancient style of Christian leadership vanish from the West, and the clerical celibacy associated with the Middle Ages proper be said to have begun.[16]

Yet, by the time that Augustine laid down his pen, in 430, the leaders of the Christian Church already carried in the back of their minds a deposit of assumptions that marked them off irrevocably from the elites of the age of Plutarch, Galen, and Marcus Aurelius. Subjected to repeated, violent shocks, the ancient notion of the human person had fractured in many places.

Christian notions of sexuality had tended to prise the human person loose from the physical world. The *calor genitalis*, the fiery spirit unleashed in the sexual act, was no longer treated with an ancient reverence. Sexuality was not seen as a cosmic energy that linked human beings both to the fertile herds and to the blazing stars. Nothing is more marked than the severity with which the bishops of the Latin West now censured those occasions on which the animal and the human might be seen to join. In the early sixth century, Caesarius of Arles was genuinely appalled that human beings should dance through the streets of his city, bearing the great horns of the stag and uttering the calls of wild beasts.[17] The pagans of the first century A.D. had not been greatly disturbed by the presence of an animal nature in the act of love: the gods themselves had joined the human and the wild in their *amours*. What had worried ancient Romans was that a free man might upset the stern civic hierarchy that separated him from a woman by indulging in oral sex with her, or by offering himself, like a woman, to be penetrated by his lover. In Dark Age Ireland and Frankish Gaul, by contrast, it was also the animal world that had to be kept away from the marriage-bed: intercourse "from behind, in the manner of dogs" was one form of sinful act, among many others, for which married persons must do penance.[18]

Detached from nature, preoccupation with the human body was eclipsed by concern for the frail workings of the human will. Augus-

16. Suzanne F. Wemple, *Women in Frankish Society*, pp. 134–135.

17. R. Arbesmann, "The 'Cervuli' and 'Anniculae' in Caesarius of Arles," and A. J. Gurevič, *Contadini e santi*, pp. 101–113, 154. See also L. Schneider, *Die Domäne als Weltbild. Wirkungsstrukturen der spätantiken Bildersprache*, pp. 134–141, on the changing representation of nature and mythology in late antique mosaics.

18. Pierre J. Payer, *Sex and the Penitentials*, pp. 29–30.

tine's somber doctrine of concupiscence brought to the fore "the indistinct but persistent voluntarism" that had permeated the Biblical tradition, and that had found expression in the Early Christian longing for singleness of heart.[19]

Christianity brought from its Jewish background the distinctive flavor of a view of the human person that tended to peer past the body, that restless reminder of man's enduring kinship with the beasts, into the heart. Sexual motivations and the abiding, protean force of sexual fantasy attracted the attention of Christian ascetic thinkers: their very privacy and persistence spoke more resonantly than did other forms of human cunning and malevolence, of the black shadow of self-will that lay at the very back of the heart. The transparency that John Cassian associated with the gift of "purity of heart" was shown in the body by the ebbing of the sexual drive. But the gift was won only through a struggle with the heart itself, in the slow and intricate untwisting of the private will. If Augustine disagreed with Cassian, it was not because he believed that the body's instincts were any stronger or more corrupt: rather he held that the most humble details of the body's experience of sexuality—erection, impotence, orgasm, and instinctive shame—mirrored a failure of the will more drastic and irrevocable than Cassian had been prepared to admit.

Prohibitions that were directly linked to the physical state of the body weakened, if only a little, in the West, as a result of this preoccupation with the fallen will. The more pensive readers of Augustine made this change most plain. When he wrote in 601, to answer questions raised by the first monks from Rome to settle among the heathen at Canterbury, Pope Gregory I showed surprisingly little sympathy for their concern with ritual prohibitions that had to do with blood and semen. Taboos taken from the book of Leviticus had been maintained by most Christians of the eastern Mediterranean. A third-century Bishop of Alexandria, a pupil of Origen, had written that it was unnecessary to tell menstruating women to keep away from the Eucharist: good Christian women did not need to be reminded of so obvious a prohibition.[20] Temporary denial of access to the altar, due to menstruation

---

19. Albrecht Dihle, *The Theory of Will in Classical Antiquity*, p. 127.

20. Dionysius of Alexandria, *Canonical Letter* 2: *Patrologia Graeca* 10: 1281A. Gregory's intervention did not prevent this prohibition from also becoming normal in the early medieval West: see Charles T. Wood, "The Doctor's Dilemma: Sin, Salvation and the Menstrual Cycle in Medieval Thought."

and childbirth among women and to ejaculation among men, had underscored the position of human beings as creatures perched between nature and the city. They had protected human sacred space from the formless, purely biological, products of the body that periodically reminded the faithful of their indissoluble connection with the natural world.

A follower of Augustine in his magnificent obsession with the will, Gregory turned his back on that tradition. Neither the woman's blood nor the man's semen counted for anything. The "primitive nation of the English" must be told that what kept human beings away from the sacred had nothing to do with their physical bodies. It was the subtle, impalpable flaw within the human will that stood between them and God. The dislocation of the will caused telltale eddies of "illicit delight" to form in the wake of every act of married intercourse. Such delight was no longer seen as an eminently physical experience, caused by the exuberant rush of vital spirit through the veins; it lingered, rather, as a sharp, sweet flicker in the heart. Pious Romans, Gregory added, usually kept away from church until such feelings had subsided in their minds. They did not do so because their bodies had emitted seed.[21] Will and memory, topics of absorbing interest to thinkers of an introspective turn of mind, and not the body, were at stake: "Such matters must be weighed with the utmost subtlety."[22] "For, behold, this is what it is to be human . . . a creature with a will, at once bound and free."[23]

The human body was no longer set in place, as a link in the great chain of being. It was not encouraged to share with the animal world pleasures that might be indulged frankly (if within reason) before disease and the dread approach of age snatched them away. In the Catholic thought of the early Middle Ages, human flesh emerged as a quivering thing. Its vulnerability to temptation, to death, even to delight, was a painfully apposite concretization of the limping will of Adam.[24]

Other Christian regions did not share so stark a notion of the errant will as that spelled out by Gregory the Great. From the time of Am-

21. Gregory, *Letters* 11.64, question 10: *P.L.* 77: 1196C; also cited in Bede, *A History of the English Church and People* 1.27, pp. 80–81; see now Paul Meyvaert, "Le *Libellus Responsionum* à Augustin de Cantorbéry."
22. Ibid. question 11: 1198C.   23. Ibid. 1200A.
24. *Moralia* 8.6.8: *P.L.* 75: 805CD; see now Carole Straw's forthcoming *Perfection in Imperfection: Body, Soul and Spiritual Progress in Gregory the Great.*

brose and Jerome, indeed, leaders of Latin Christianity had been un-
usually swift as they moved toward accepting the existing structures
of society as good in themselves, while casting the blame for human
evil squarely on the mysterious perversity of the will. The Catholic
bishops of the West faced an uncertain future. They maintained a truly
Roman sense of the need to discipline the libido, to hold in check the
stirrings of a measureless self-will in themselves and in others, if their
threatened society was not to disintegrate. They lived in a world for
which Augustine had already drawn a clear map in his writings of the
early 400s: the familiar social landmarks were maintained; but against
each one of these the fallen human will beat mercilessly, and nowhere
more insistently (so many thought) than in the bedroom.

In the eastern Mediterranean, by contrast, we meet, from the first
beginnings of the Church, relatively humble men and women locked
into the inexorable logic of the settled world: "Every day a voice calls
from Heaven, declaring: 'The daughter of so-and-so will marry so-and-
so; and the field of so-and-so will pass on to so-and-so.' "[25]

Generation after generation of militants had used the elemental gesture of sexual renunciation to break free from that iron chain. When,
for instance, the "kingdom" failed to arrive, around 200 A.D., a group
of Christians in Pontus returned, dispirited, to normal life. The dashing of their hopes was summed up in a simple phrase: "the young
girls got married; the men went back to the fields."[26]

By the mid-fifth century, however, throughout the Christian East,
the settled land was flanked by men and women who owned no land
and had taken no spouses. In great, walled-in monasteries and convents, in clusters of cells built into the sandy plateau of Egypt like
ancient grave-houses, on the tops of mountains, perched on columns,
walled up in the nooks and crannies of the cities, sheltered in the depths
of the women's quarters, or huddled in grottoes carved into the cliffs
and in the fairy-tale rock formations of great ravines, monks and nuns
made plain that, for some Christians at least, the kingdom had come:
they had made for themselves a world without marriage and without
private fields. Riding from Jerusalem to Jericho, in the reign of the
Emperor Justinian, two young Syrian boys of good family caught sight
of the monasteries perched on the cliffs above the river Jordan: " 'Who

25. *Babylonian Talmud: Mo°ed Ḳaṭan* 18b. in H. M. Lazarus, trans., *The Talmud*, p. 118.
26. Hippolytus, *Commentary on Daniel* 4.18 p. 234.

are these men who live in the houses over there?' one asked his friend. 'Why, don't you know? They are the angels of God.' "[27]

We should have no illusions about such "angels of God." Many monasteries had become ferociously organized landowning concerns, with properties spread over the best agricultural land in Egypt and Syria.[28] Hermits lived close to the settled land. Far from being creatures from another world, no chasm separated them from the values of the average Christian. Some "angels" were no more than amiable seekers after a quiet old age, such as were many of the monks who signed a petition in Constantinople, in 451, on the eve of the Council of Chalcedon. Vetting the signatures, the bishops overturned a stone from which many a peculiar creature crawled into sight: there was "Euthychius, who lives in the martyr's shrine of Celerina, for he has no monastery . . . Nemesinus, of whom we know nothing . . . Leontius, former keeper of performing bears."[29]

Even the numbers of these black-robed figures may not have been as overwhelming as we have been inclined to think. Sixth-century Aphrodito, with 79 priests, 18 deacons, 33 monks and nuns, and one Stylite hermit, in a population of fewer than 2000 identifiable taxpayers, shows an early Byzantine society with an appreciable ecclesiastical and ascetic presence. Yet the town may have sheltered no more unmarried males than did an Egyptian village of the second century, where about ten percent of the men had no wives.[30] What matters is that unmarried men and women were now effectively dragooned into a distinct and privileged class: as monks and nuns, they might produce no children for their city; but, at least, they would not compete for private land.[31] They were made to bear in their unpretentious persons the great, late antique myth of the desert.

This myth had wrenched the body free from ancient solidarities. The

27. Leontius of Neapolis, *Life of Symeon the Holy Fool* 1, in A. J. Festugière and L. Ryden, eds., *Léonce de Néapolis: Vie de Syméon le Fou*, pp. 58, 109.

28. Evelyne Patlagean, *Pauvreté économique et pauvreté sociale à Byzance*, pp. 318–333 and E. Wipszycka, "Les terres de la congrégation pachômienne." Not all monasteries were as fortunate: F. Villeneuve, "L'économie rurale et la vie des campagnes," pp. 118–121.

29. *Acts of the Council of Chalcedon* 4.64, in A. J. Festugière, trans., *Actes du Concile de Chalcédoine: Sessions iii–vi*, p. 50.

30. L. S. B. MacCoull, "Notes on the Social Structure of late antique Aphrodito;" cf. Keith Hopkins, "Brother-Sister Marriage in Roman Egypt," p. 333, as interpreted by B. W. Frier's forthcoming "The Demography of the Early Roman Empire."

31. Patlagean, *Pauvreté*, pp. 338–340.

perfected ascetic of the East Roman imagination was thought to have recovered the glory of Adam against a landscape where the benevolent chain of life had snapped. He had moved from fertile fields, protected by so many ancient gods, into dead wastes, touched by the deathly chill of the demonic hosts. Yet he brought back from a land hateful to gods and men a body suffused with sweet perfume.[32] The prayers offered by the monks and consecrated virgins bound heaven to earth in an impalpable chain of intercession. Human prayer to the one God, offered up by the continent, replaced the natural, cosmic hierarchy that had been thought to link the exuberant earth, through ethereal ministering spirits, to the gods who dwelt among the stars. Egyptian Christians now believed that the shriveled, sterile bodies of monks and virgins caused the valley to turn green every year.[33] When Symeon Stylites fasted throughout Lent, the pot of lentils that had been given him as his only food for forty days was found still unopened:

they found it full, just as they had left it, and they wondered and were astonished. Then the elders and the deacons arose, and gave a part from it to all the people, from three o'clock until nine, and it was not exhausted. Then there went up also widows of the city, and received their skirts full and went down, and it remained just as it was.[34]

In even the most stable regions of the Mediterranean, the city itself had come to lose its ancient shape. The classical notion of the civic community had weakened its hold on the Christian inhabitants of the towns, both in reality and in the imagination. Christian attitudes to sexuality delivered the death-blow to the ancient notion of the city as the arbiter of the body. Christian preachers endowed the body with intrinsic, inalienable qualities. It was no longer a neutral, indeterminate outcrop of the natural world, whose use and very right to exist was subject to predominantly civic considerations of status and utility. God had created the human body and Adam had brought upon it the double shame of death and lust. The new sensibility to nudity showed this slow change in the collective imagination of the late antique world. Late Roman codes of upper-class dress made the social status of their wearers, if anything, more blatant than ever before; but they did so

32. *Vita Mariae Meretricis* 7: *P.L.* 73: 655D.
33. Serapion of Thmuis, *Letter to the Monks* 3: *P.G.* 40: 929A.
34. *Life of Symeon Stylites*, in F. Lent, trans., *Journal of the American Oriental Society* (1915) 35:132.

by carefully sheathing the body itself. No longer were the body's taut musculature and its refined poise, signs of the athlete and the potential warrior, put on display, as marks of upper-class status. Emperors no longer showed their unchallenged power by posing in the nude, thereby recapturing the heroic ease and readiness associated with the deathless gods.[35] What now lay behind the rustling, gold-embroidered silks and the splendor of the Imperial robes was mortal clay, fragile stuff, gnawed by the same stirrings of desire and subject to the same sexual shame as was the flesh that shivered beneath a beggar's rags.[36]

Christians were as appalled as Jews had been by the indeterminacy of the body. The body of young males might no longer enjoy the time of the *ludus*, that period of frankly bisexual free play, before the city set the young man firmly in place as a married statesman. Spiritual guides now asked a young man whether he had lost his virginity—a question which would have concerned only his sister three centuries earlier.[37] Men were now expected to derive from the body itself the laws that limited their love-making. The body was a "sacrosanct temple," intended by God to be joined, if at all, only to members of the opposite sex, and then, ideally, only so as to produce children. Indeterminacy of any kind was disturbing to late antique persons. In the fourth century, the soft, tumbling locks and the haunting, godlike ambivalence of a head of Antinous, the Emperor Hadrian's true love, was recarved so that his smooth cheeks and heavy hair now represented an Imperial lady![38]

Nor did the products of sexual intercourse lie any longer in a neutral zone, waiting for the family to decide whether they were relevant or not to human society: contraception, abortion, and the placing out of children were equally condemned. By the sixth century, the ancient right of the Roman father to decide whether or not he would accept a newborn child was spoken of as a custom that belonged to a distant, pagan age.[39] As Tertullian put it, with lapidary brevity: "What will be human *is* human."[40] It was not for the couple to decide whether they

---

35. See esp. H. I. Marrou, *Décadence romaine ou antiquité tardive?* pp. 15–20.

36. Jerome, *Letter* 77.6: *P.L.* 22: 694.

37. *The Penitential of John the Faster: P.G.* 88: 1893AB.

38. H. Blanck, *Wiederverwendung alter Statuen als Ehrendenkmäler bei Griechen und Römern*, 45 and plates 14–15. I owe this reference to the kindness of Professor Patricia Erhart.

39. *Codex Justinianus* 8.46.10.   40. Tertullian, *Apologeticum* 9.8.

would create a child, by resorting to contraception and abortion, or whether they would rear it once born.[41]

The silent withdrawal of the city affected some of the most intimate aspects of married life. Emphasis on the role of God in forming the child from its first moment in the womb, and a heightened sense that the sexual act itself escaped rational control, may well have tended to brush aside the learned fantasy of eugenic sex.[42] No longer was civic decorum, even a certain measure of courtesy and considerateness, shown by one partner to another in the act of intercourse, thought to have any appreciable effect on the temperament of the ensuing child. This aspect of procreation was removed from the realm of human choice. The new codes of eugenic sex stressed only the wrath of God. Those who had intercourse, "like peasants," by sleeping together on Sundays and on other days of abstinence, would beget lepers and epileptics.[43]

Behind this unpleasant rhetoric of the body, we can sense a Mediterranean-wide phenomenon. In Byzantium and in the West, the family tended to turn inward. Its simpler structures proved more resilient, in a less certain age, than did the more complex, more abstract solidarity offered by the ancient city.[44] The preaching of John Chrysostom had merely brought out into the open the centuries-old reflex of the Christian family to huddle, distrustfully, behind its high walls. The evolution of the early Byzantine city was on John's side. Piled into rabbit-warrens of one-family rooms around busy courtyards, the average city-dweller of the eastern Mediterranean of the fifth and sixth centuries lived in simple, private housing, which encroached relentlessly on the tidy, open spaces once associated with the ancient city. In cities that had already taken on the features of an Islamic town, with cluttered lanes, closed-in quarters, and narrow streets lined with busy shops, the Christian basilica, with its spreading courtyard and magnificent episcopal palace, provided the populace with all the sense

41. John T. Noonan, *Contraception*, pp. 47–146 remains a masterly and humane study of this development.

42. *Babylonian Talmud: Nedarim*, 20a, in I. Epstein, trans., pp. 57–58 *The Talmud*, seems to indicate this change.

43. Caesarius of Arles, *Sermon* 44.7, in G. Morin, ed., *Corpus Christianorum* 103:199.

44. See esp. A. Kazhdan with G. Constable, *People and Power in Byzantium* pp. 32–34 and Brent D. Shaw, "Latin Funerary Epigraphy and Family Life in the Later Roman Empire."

of shared public space deemed suitable to the subjects of an orthodox Empire.[45]

The city fell silent, even among the dead. After 500 A.D., all but a few monuments of old-fashioned grandees and of bishops of the Church were content to give more than the most laconic messages: the great marble sarcophagi and verse inscriptions belonged to an earlier, more demonstrative age. In the telling words of a recent study, "No longer do the secular lines of kinship and family converge on the grave-stones."[46]

The dead person became an isolate. The next of kin alone spoke, and with growing reticence, of its grief for the dead—for spouses and for children. God had called their souls to Himself; a few, interchange-able emblems of hope and salvation told the living of His mercy to the dead. No longer did the monuments of the dead use the tomb to speak volubly to the city about the things of the city, by praising ancestral virtues and public decorum, and by lingering lovingly on high mo-ments of civic eminence. We do not meet the Christians of the age of Augustine going about their business "in life's sweet air." The society of the high Empire seems so immediately accessible to us largely be-cause of the vivid scenes of their daily life that the dead wished to have carved on their tombs. After the fourth century, all this vanishes. No longer do Roman soldiers stolidly clutch the standards or ride down conquered barbarians. No longer does a lady toy with her jewelry as she reaches down a hand to pat a small dog. No longer do we see small boys, each dressed in a carefully folded toga, clutching their scroll with hand outstretched, solemnly orating, as they had once done, be-fore the black envy of death snatched so much promise from the city.

Looking out from behind the walls of the Christian household, we see only the poor. Human bodies at their nadir, the poor were mo-bilized by the bishops and clergy in every city. They spoke for all hu-manity, the humbled offspring of Adam, leveled before God by the common misery of distance from Him, associated with the common shame of sexual desire and destined to answer the common call of the

45. See the survey of Dieter Claude, *Die byzantinische Stadt im 6. Jahrhundert*, Byzan-tinisches Archiv 13, pp. 89–97, 101–106, and the more up-to-date study of Hugh Ken-nedy, "From *Polis* to *Madina*: Urban Change in Late Antique and Early Islamic Syria," pp. 12–15. The change is most apparent in Justiniana Prima, a new foundation by Jus-tinian in the Balkans: see Dj. Mano-Zisi, s.v. Justiniana Prima (Caričin Grad), *Reallex-ikon zur byzantinischen Kunst*, cols. 702–710, and the plan at col. 694.

46. Shaw, "Latin Funerary Epigraphy," p. 482.

grave. On Maunday Thursday, and on other feast days, the poor marched to the public baths, a new class of citizens, called to enjoy a new form of public benevolence. There they received a ritual wash and massage.[47] As they went, they chanted the psalms of a high God, who was now thought to come closest to mankind when the body was at its weakest, and, hence, of least obvious use to the classical city:

Who is like the Lord our God, Who sits enthroned on high,
but stoops to behold the heaven and the earth?
He takes up the weak out of the dust
and lifts up the poor from the ashes.[48]

By a paradox which remains to be explained, the physical body became an object of "obsessive compassion," in the afflicted poor,[49] at exactly the same time as it was made to bear increasingly cruel punishments. The use of mutilation, as permitted in early Byzantine penal codes, treated the human body as a "blazon," on which society might leave permanent marks of punishment.[50]

When in the course of the late fifth and the sixth centuries profound changes sapped the political and economic structure of the cities of the Mediterranean, the Christian notions we have just described came to the fore. They ratified a very different sense of the community and of the human person within it from that current in the age of Marcus Aurelius. They made plain what Jacques le Goff has described, in a memorable phrase, as *la déroute du corporel*, the definitive "rout of the body," that marked the end of the ancient world and the beginning of the middle ages.[51]

It is important to see what else so profound a change could mean. Writing to a friend stricken with arthritis in the late fifth century, a Latin Christian consoled him by extolling the power of God. God would "make our nature translucent." At the resurrection, human flesh would "turn molten to regain its lost solidity," as base metal flowered into

---

47. H. I. Marrou, "L'origine orientale des diaconies romaines," now in *Patristique et Humanisme*, pp. 97–100.

48. Psalm 113:5–7.

49. Patlagean, *Pauvreté*, p. 430; cf. S. Averincev, "Notion de l'homme et tradition littéraire à Byzance," p. 25.

50. S. Averincev, *Poetika rannevizantijskoj literaturi*, pp. 60–76 and E. Patalagean, "Byzance et le blason penal du corps," p. 421.

51. Jacques Le Goff, *L'imaginaire mediéval*, p. 123.

gold in the alchemist's crucible. "No Christian mind can ever weary of thinking of such things."[52] The human body was poised on the threshold of a mighty change. In Christian circles, concern with sexual renunciation had never been limited solely to an anxious striving to maximize control over the body. It had been connected with a heroic and sustained attempt, on the part of thinkers of widely different background and temper of mind, to map out the horizons of human freedom. The light of a great hope of future transformation glowed behind even the most austere statements of the ascetic position. To many, continence had declared the end of the tyranny of the "present age." In the words of John Chrysostom, virginity made plain that "the things of the resurrection stand at the door."[53]

To the Desert Fathers, the gift of true chastity of heart revealed, in the very slowness with which it came, the immensity of the *abundance of peace* that might yet descend upon the human body. From the age of Valentinus and Origen to that of Jerome and Evagrius, the delicious suspicion that even the rigid boundaries between the sexes might trickle away in the liquid gold of a "spiritual" body, caused disturbing gusts of freedom to blow, intermittently, among the intelligentsia of the church. For Augustine, the bondage of the will to sexual desire spoke of the postponement of that great hope to the end of time: though tragically deferred, the yearning for transfiguration still remained.

The pain of Christian asceticism consisted in the fact that the present human person was an unfinished block, destined to be cut into the form of an awesome model. The body required the deep chisel-bites of permanent renunciation, if the Christian was to take on the lineaments of the risen Christ. Around the year 400, late Roman Christian mosaics made plain what that might mean. In these, Christ and his saints are shown carrying bodies of exquisite classical grace and proportion. But they are bodies lighter than air. The dull weight of death has been lifted from them, and, with that, their physicality. They stand on the green grass of Paradise, now effortlessly alive, like the shadowless figures of dead friends, glimpsed in a deep, clear dream.[54]

The ascetics, of course, were a tiny if magnetic minority among Christians of the fifth and sixth centuries. In the public world of the

---

52. Ps.-Jerome, *Ad amicum aegrotum* 4 and 8: *P.L.* 30: 80B and 89C; see now H. Savon, "Une consolation imitée de Sénèque et de saint Cyprien."

53. John Chrysostom, *On Virginity*, 73.1.6: *Sources chrétiennes* 125, p. 350.

54. Gregory Nazianzen, *Oration* 7.21: *P.G.* 35: 784B.

cities, the pointed absence of sexuality in the elites of the church and in its imagined heroes and heroines played a crucial role in the collective imagination of what had become a predominantly Christian society. It forced to the fore a whole range of images of authority and solidarity, among both Latin and East Roman Christians.

In the Latin West particularly, laymen eyed their new leaders anxiously. They instantly denounced priests who continued to beget children with their wives once ordained to serve at the altar.[55] The clergy were not allowed to maintain for themselves the ancient means by which secular elites took care for the continuity of their cities. The holiness of the altar stood between them and their wives, prohibiting the biological act by which they would normally, as civic leaders, have provided for their own future. And rightly so: bishops were ever more frankly recruited from the upper classes. There was no guarantee that, if bishops were once allowed to perpetuate themselves in the ancient manner, they might not also come to use the increasing communal power and wealth of the Church in the ancient manner, by treating it as their private property.

The church was based, ideally, on the ethereal, nonphysical continuities of teaching and baptism administered by the clergy. Birth alone did not guarantee salvation. By insisting that its leaders no longer beget children, the Catholic Church in the West made plain that it enjoyed a supernatural guarantee of continuity that no ancient city could claim. If they were to be respected as the leaders of a "holy" institution, bishops and priests had to remain anomalous creatures. The celibacy of the clergy ensured that the Church's connection with normal sources of power was carefully masked out in perceptions of their role in society. They were to live with their wives, "as if they were no wives." They administered the palpable wealth of their churches as if they were men without possessions.[56]

In entering the light-filled basilicas of the Catholic church, the townspeople wished to feel that here, at last, they trod on holy ground. Despite the undeniable message of vast private wealth and family power congealed in the splendor of such buildings—with their marble columns, their mosaics, and their shimmering furnishings—each Catholic basilica was a "City of God," sharply distinguished from the an-

55. Pope Innocent, *Letter* 38: *P.L.* 20: 605B.
56. Ps.-Jerome, *de septem ordinibus ecclesiae*: *P.L.* 30: 160B.

cient city. The double knot of physical procreation and of privately owned wealth had been cut away from its white-robed clergy.

Within a church endowed with a strong aura of the sacred in that trenchant manner, the sudden rise of the cult of the Virgin Mary and of other virgin saints spoke of a poignant need for untainted solidarity with perfect human beings. Late antique Christians placed a heavy stress on the fact that the flesh of Christ and that of his virgin mother were utterly continuous with human flesh. Theirs had been human flesh "reformed" in the strict sense: the flaws that rendered the body so burdensome, and so difficult to control in ordinary men and women, before it melted into the glory of the Resurrection, were already absent in the flesh of Christ and in the circumstances of his birth from Mary. As Rufinus pointed out: Christ's birth from Mary had been no prodigious anomaly, as when Athena had burst violently from the head of Zeus. In the conception, the birth, and the nurturing of Christ, every human physiological process had been respected, except for the hot act of male procreation and the wrenching-open of the womb at childbirth.[57] To a late antique sensibility, the miraculous quality of the virgin birth shimmered all the more hypnotically because the two violent and indispensable links of a normal human process had been excised. The *pudor aureus* of Mary spoke of the resilience of a human body from which the disorder introduced into it by Adam's fall had been expunged.[58] Virgins of the church bore bodies analogous to that of Mary: unshaken by intercourse and childbirth, here was a body "that has the marks of sex without its dire constraint."[59]

Mary's female body had been yet more wonderful. She had conceived and given birth to a child; she had offered her breast as a nursing mother; and yet she had suffered no dislocation: soft as a fleece to receive the Word of God into herself, she had remained solid and unfissured as unalloyed gold.[60] The suppression of the associations of normal sexual intercourse and of the violence of normal childbirth caused a shaft of golden light to fall on the other, intensely physical relationships associated with the Virgin birth and shared with Mary by all human beings—nurture, intimacy, the continuity of one's own flesh and blood.

57. Rufinus, *Expositio Symboli* 9, *Corpus Christianorum 20*, pp. 146–147.
58. Ps.-Jerome, *Ad amicum aegrotum* 6: 83B.
59. Leander of Seville, *de institutione virginum: P.L.* 72: 880A.
60. Maximus of Turin, *Sermon* 97.3, *Corpus Christianorum 23*, pp. 387–388.

The shrines of the martyrs were visited with increasing fervor in the fifth and sixth centuries, as places where new life and healing bubbled up for the faithful from the cold graves of the dead. For the martyrs' shrines contained the bones of men and women on whom the Holy Spirit had come to rest.[61] The presence of the Spirit removed from the remains of these dead human beings the grim associations of normal death.[62] The bodies of the Virgin and of virgin men and women carried a similar charge. "Bathed in viriginity's clear light, radiant limbs,"[63] because suffused by the Holy Spirit, these were bodies identical with those of the average Christian in all but the physical act that continued the human race by physical means. They mediated between the congregations of the shrunken Roman towns of the West and a Christ who had borne a body of the same flesh as themselves. By the tenth century, upland Clermont had 112 altars with relics and 54 churches, while it sheltered 48 known tombs of the saints, every one of which was believed to house a continent person. Beside the river Rhône, Vienne could rest secure, reassured by the presence of some 1500 monks and nuns, settled in 12 convents, and by the graves of the virgin dead, placed in the great basilicas that "formed a garrison of sacred buildings" around the city.[64]

Overarching the Christian urban community, the cult of the Virgin offered the luminous inversion of the dark myth of shared, fallen flesh. Standing in church, a Byzantine such as Romanos Melodes knew that his own flesh was "flesh out of joint with nature." It was as weak, as slippery, as uncontrolled as were the bizarre thoughts that flitted through his wandering mind. Gazing at the still body of Christ, he saw all that he lacked. And yet he looked on the flesh of a kinsman, taken from the tranquil human substance of the Virgin's womb.[65] In

---

61. A. Tanghe, "Memra de Philoxène de Mabboug sur l'Inhabitation du Saint Esprit," p. 53, trans. p. 68. I owe this reference to the kindness of Dr. Sebastian Brock.

62. Peter Brown, *The Cult of the Saints*, pp. 74–85.

63. E. Diehl, *Inscriptiones latinae christianae veteres* 1714.1, 1:333.

64. I. N. Wood, "A Prelude to Columbanus: The Monastic Achievement in the Burgundian Territories," in H. B. Clarke and M. Brennan, eds., *Columbanus and Merovingian Monasticism*, p. 9.

65. Romanos Melodes, *Hymns* 20.8.6 and 22.14.5, in J. Grosdidier de Matons, ed., *Romanos le Mélode: Hymnes*, Sources chrétiennes 110 and 114, pp. 357 and 78, respectively. On the elaboration of the cult of the Virgin, see esp. Averil Cameron, "The Theotokos in Sixth-Century Constantinople: A City Finds its Symbol," pp. 7. Michael P. Carroll, *The Cult of the Virgin Mary* has the merit of suggesting an approach related to family structures, although I am utterly unconvinced by his historical argument.

sixth-century icons of the Virgin, Christ is often held on her lap, as if indissolubly tied to humankind by the bond of her womb.[66] It was a link to the flesh rescued from all ambivalence. In such an image, the physical bonds created between human beings by their bodies could be sensed at their most sweet, at their most harmonious, and at their most cohesive because effectively disconnected, in the believer's mind, from the black shadow of the sexual act that lay at the root of normal, physical society. Such a validation of the ideal links between mother and child spoke with peculiar force to a society that thought of itself no longer as an assembly of citizens, but rather as an agglomeration of pious households, made up of Christian fathers, mothers, and children. In the hymns and sermons of the age, the great hope of the accessibility of fallen man to God, of the weak to the powerful, and of each member of the Christian community to each other, as bearers of the common flesh of Adam and Eve, was condensed in the ideal of the shared flesh of Christ and Mary:

Thou, Mary, didst bend thy neck and let thy hair fall over Him. . . . He stretched out His hand, He took thy breast, and He drew with His mouth the milk that is sweeter than pure manna. . . . And He, into whose face the angels dared not gaze. . . . the holy virgin made bold to approach, intimately and without fear, calling Him, "My son," and He called her also, "My Mother."[67]

With such scenes of haunting tenderness, we have entered the dreams of a very different age from the one in which we began our story, more than three hundred years before, in Palestine, in Rome, and in the Greek cities of Asia Minor.

To modern persons, whatever their religious beliefs, the Early Christian themes of sexual renunciation, of continence, celibacy, and the virgin life have come to carry with them icy overtones. The very fact that modern Europe and America grew out of the Christian world that replaced the Roman Empire in the Middle Ages has ensured that, even today, these notions still crowd in upon us, as pale, forbidding pres-

66. See the Mount Sinai icon, discussed by E. Kitzinger, *Byzantine Art in the Making*, pp. 117–118 and fig. 210, and the Coptic textile of the Virgin in the Cleveland Museum of Art: Dorothy G. Shepherd, "An Icon of the Virgin: A Sixth Century Tapestry Panel from Egypt."

67. E. A. W. Budge, *Miscellaneous Coptic Texts in the Dialect of Upper Egypt*, pp. 701, 717.

ences. Historians must bring to them their due measure of warm, red blood. By studying their precise social and religious context, the scholar can give back to these ideas a little of the human weight that they once carried in their own time. When such an offering is made, the chill shades may speak to us again, and perhaps more gently than we had thought they might, in the strange tongue of a long-lost Christianity. Whether they will say anything of help or comfort for our own times the readers of this book must decide for themselves.

Bibliography

Abbreviations

CSCO   *Corpus Scriptorum Christianorum Orientalium*, Louvain: 1903–
CSEL   *Corpus Scriptorum Ecclesiasticorum Latinorum*, Vienna: 1866–
PG   *Patrologia Graeca*, (Migne)
PL   *Patrologia Latina*, (Migne)
PL Supp. *Patrologia Latina, Supplementum*

Primary Sources

Acta Iohannis. Eds. E. Junod and J.-D. Kaestli. *Corpus Christianorum, scriptorum apocryphorum* 1. Turnhout: Brepols, 1983. English translation: *New Testament Apocrypha*, vol. 2, q.v.

Acta Philippi. In M. Bonnet, ed. *Acta Apostolorum Apocrypha*, vol. 3. Leipzig: H. Mendelssohn, 1903. English trans. A. Walker. *The Ante-Nicene Fathers*, vol. 8. Grand Rapids, Michigan: Eerdmans, 1951.

Acta Saturnini. PL 8.690–703.

Acts of [Judas] Thomas. Trans. with commentary, A. F. J. Klijn. Supplements to Novum Testamentum 5. Leiden: Brill, 1962.

Acts of Paul and Thecla. New Testament Apocrypha, vol. 2, q.v.

Acts of the Christian Martyrs. Ed. and trans. H. Musurillo. Oxford: Clarendon Press, 1972.

Adam, A., ed. *Texte zum Manichäismus*. Berlin: de Gruyter, 1954.

Allberry, C. R. C., ed. *A Manichaean Psalmbook. Pt. II. Manichaean Manuscripts in the Chester Beatty Collection.* Stuttgart: Kohlhammer, 1938.

Alvarez Campos, S., ed. *Corpus Marianum Patristicum.* Vol. 3: *Scriptores Latini.* Burgos: Ediciones Aldecoa, 1974.

Ambrose. *Apologia prophetae David.* Ed. P. Hadot. *Ambroise de Milan: Apologie de David.* Sources chrétiennes 239. Paris: Éditions du Cerf, 1977.

—— *De Isaac et anima.* PL 14.527–559. Ed. C. Schenkl. *CSEL* 32. Vienna: Tempsky, 1897.

—— *De institutione virginis.* PL 16.319–347.

—— *De mysteriis.* PL 16.409–426.

—— *De officiis.* PL 16.25–194.

—— *De poenitentia.* PL 16.486–545. Ed. R. Gryson. *Ambroise de Milan: La Pénitence.* Sources chrétiennes 179. Paris: Éditions du Cerf, 1971.

—— *De viduis.* PL 16.247–275.

—— *De virginibus.* PL 16.197–243. Ed. E. Cazzaniga. Turin: G. B. Paravia, 1984.

—— *Exhortatio virginitatis.* PL 16.347–379.

—— *Expositio in Evangelium Secundum Lucam.* PL 15.1603–1945. Ed. M. Adriaen. *Corpus Christianorum, series latina* 14. Turnhout: Brepols, 1957.

—— *Hexaemeron.* PL 14.131–288. Ed. II Schenkl. *CSEL* 32. Vienna: Tempsky, 1897.

—— *In Psalmum 39 enarratio.* PL 14.1057–1068. In M. Petschenig, ed. *Expositio in XII Psalmos.* CSEL 34. Vienna: Tempsky, 1919.

—— *In Psalmum 48 enarratio.* PL 14.1211–1224. Petschenig, ed. *Expositio in XII Psalmos.* CSEL 34.

—— *In Psalmum 118 expositio.* PL 15.1257–1603. In M. Petschenig, ed. *CSEL* 62. Vienna: F. Tempsky, 1913.

—— *Letters.* PL 16.913–1342. In M. Zelzer, ed. *CSEL* 82. Vienna: Tempsky, 1982.

Ps.-Ambrose. *De lapsu virginis.* PL 16.383–399.

Ambrosiaster. *In 1 Cor.* In H. J. Vogels, ed. *CSEL* 82:2. Vienna: F. Tempsky, 1968.

Anthony. *The Letters of St. Anthony the Great.* Trans. D. J. Chitty. Oxford: SLG Press, 1977.

Aphrahat. *Demonstrations 18.* In J. Neusner, trans. *Aphrahat and Judaism: the Christian-Jewish Argument in fourth-century Iran.* Studia Post Biblica 19. Leiden: Brill, 1971.

—— *Demonstrations.* Ed. J. Parisot. *Patrologia Syriaca,* vol. 1. Paris: Firmin Didot, 1894.

L'Apocalypse de Baruch. Ed. and trans. P. Bogaert. Sources chrétiennes 144. Paris: Éditions du Cerf, 1969.

Apocrypha and Pseudepigrapha of the Old Testament. Vol. 2: *Pseudepigrapha.* Ed. and trans. R. H. Charles. Oxford: Clarendon Press, 1913.

Apophthegmata Patrum. PG 65.72–440.

—— *Anonymous Apophthegmata: MS Coislin 126.* Ed. F. Nau. "Histoire des solitaires égyptiens (MS Coislin 126, fol. 158f.)" *Revue de l'Orient chrétien* (1908) 13:47–57, 266–83; (1913) 18:137–40.

—— *Anonymous Coptic Apophthegmata*. Ed. M. Chaine. *Institut français d'archéologie orientale: Bibliothèque des études coptes* (1960) 6:85–127.

—— *The Sayings of the Desert Fathers*. Trans. Benedicta Ward. Cistercian Studies 59. Kalamazoo, Michigan: Cistercian Publications, 1975.

—— *Sentences des Pères du Désert: Nouveau Recueil*. Trans. L. Regnault. Sablé-sur-Sarthe: Abbaye de Solesmes, 1970.

Aretaeus. *The Extant Works of Aretaeus the Cappadocian*. Trans. F. Adams. London: The Sydenham Society, 1856.

Aristaenetus. *Aristénète: Lettres d'Amour*. Trans. J. Bernous. Paris: Belles Lettres, 1938.

Ps.-Aristotle. *Physiognomica*. In R. Förster, ed. *Physiognomici graeci*, vol. 1. Leipzig: Teubner, 1893.

Artemidorus. *Oneirocritica*. Ed. R. A. Pack. Leipzig: Teubner, 1963. Trans. R. White. *The Interpretation of Dreams*. Noyes Classical Studies. Ridge Hill, New Jersey: Noyes Press, 1975.

Athanasius. *Apologia ad Constantium*. PG 25.593–642. In A. Atkinson, trans. *Saint Athanasius, Historical Tracts*. Library of Fathers of the Holy Catholic Church 13. Oxford: J. H. Parker, 1873.

—— *Encyclical Letter*. PG 25.219–240.

—— *The Festal Epistles of Saint Athanasius*. In W. H. Burgess, trans. *Saint Athanasius, Historical Tracts*. Library of Fathers of the Holy Catholic Church 38. Oxford: J. H. Parker, 1873.

—— *Letter to Amoun*. PG 26.1169–1179.

—— *Lettre à des vierges qui étaient allées prier à Jérusalem*. Trans. J. Lebon. "Athanasiana Syriaca. Une lettre attribuée à saint Athanase d'Alexandrie." *Le Muséon* (1928) 41:169–215.

—— *S. Athanase: lettres festales et pastorales en copte*. Ed. L.-Th. Lefort. CSCO 150, 151, Scriptores Coptici 19, 20. Louvain: L. Durbecq, 1955.

—— *The Life of Anthony*. PG 26.835–976. Earliest Latin translation: G. J. M. Bartelink, ed. *Vita di Antonio*. Vite dei Santi 1. Fondazione Lorenzo Valla: Mondadori, 1974. Syriac *Life*: R. Draguet, ed. *La vie primitive de Saint Antoine*. CSCO 417, Scriptores Syri 184. Louvain: CSCO, 1980. English translation: in Robert Gregg, trans. *Athanasius: The Life of Anthony and the Letter to Marcellinus*. New York: Paulist Press, 1980.

"Saint Athanase: Sur la Virginité." L.-Th. Lefort, trans. *Le Muséon* (1929) 42:197–274.

Ps.-Athanasius. *Sôtérios Logos peri parthenias*. Ed. H. von der Goltz. *Texte und Untersuchungen* 29.2. Leipzig: J. C. Hinrichs, 1906.

—— *Vita Sanctae Syncleticae*. PG 28.1485–1558.

—— *The Canons of Athanasius, Patriarch of Alexandria*. W. Reidel and W. E. Crum, eds. and trans. Text and Translation Society 9. London: William and Norgate, 1904. Reprint. Amsterdam: Philo Press, 1973.

Athenagoras. *A Plea for the Christians*. In B. P. Pratten, ed. *The Ante-Nicene Fathers*, vol. 2. Grand Rapids, Michigan: Eerdmans, 1977.

Augustine. *Confessions*. PL 32.659–868.

—— *Contra ii epistolas Pelagianorum*. PL 44.599–640. English translation: *Against the two letters of the Pelagians*. In P. Holmes and R. E. Wallis, eds. *Library of the Nicene and Post-Nicene Fathers*, vol. 5. New York: Christian Library Company, 1887.

—— *Contra Faustum*. PL 42.207–518.

—— *Contra Julianum*. PL 44.641–880. English translation: W. A. Schuhmacher, trans. *Against Julian*. Fathers of the Church 35. New York: Fathers of the Church, Inc., 1957.

—— *Contra Secundum Juliani Responsionem imperfectum opus*. PL 45.1049–1608.

—— *De bono coniugali*. PL 40.373–396. English translation: *On the Good of Marriage and On Holy Virginity*. In R. J. Deferrari, ed. *Treatises on Marriage and Other Subjects*. Fathers of the Church 29. New York: Fathers of the Church, Inc., 1955.

—— *De civitate dei*. PL 41.13–804.

—— *De conjugiis adulterinis*. PL 40.415–475.

—— *De Genesi ad litteram*. PL 34.245–486. English translation: *The Literal Meaning of Genesis*. In J. H. Taylor, ed. *Ancient Christian Writers* 41–42. New York: Newman Press, 1982.

—— *De haeresibus*. PL 42.21–50.

—— *De moribus ecclesiae catholicae et de moribus manichaeorum*. PL 32.1300–1377.

—— *De nuptiis et concupiscentia*. PL 44.415–475. English translation: *On Marriage and Concupiscence*. In Holmes and Wallis, eds. *Library of the Nicene and Post-Nicene Fathers*, vol. 5.

—— *De opere monachorum*. PL 40.547–582.

—— *De sancta virginitate*. PL 40.395–428.

—— *De Trinitate*. PL 42.819–1098.

—— *De utilitate credendi*. PL 42.63–93.

—— *Enarrationes in Psalmos*. PL 36.67–1028.

Enarratio in Psalmum 122. English translation: in Mary T. Clark, trans. *Augustine of Hippo: Selected Writings*. New York: Paulist Press, 1984.

—— *Letters*. PL 33.

—— *Retractationes*. PL 32.583–659.

—— *Sancti Augustini opera, epistulae ex duobus codicibus nuper in lucem prolatae*. Ed. J. Divjak. CSEL 88. Vienna: Hölder, Pichler and Tempsky, 1981. French translation: in *Bibliothèque augustinienne: Oeuvres de Saint Augustin 46 B: Lettres 1*–29**. Paris: Études augustiniennes, 1987—newly discovered letters.

—— *Sermones*. PL 38, 39.

—— *Soliloquia*. PL 32.869–905.

Babylonian Talmud. I. Epstein, general editor. 35 vols. London: Soncino Press, 1935–62.

—— *ʿAbodah Zarah*. Trans. A. Mishcon. 1935.

—— *Baba Bathra*. Trans. M. Simon. 1935.

—— *Berakhoth*. Trans. M. Simon. 1948.

—— *ʿErubin*. Trans. I Epstein. 1938.

—— *Ḥullin*. Trans. E. Cashdan. 1936.

—— *Moʿed Ḳaṭan*. Trans. H. M. Lazarus. 1938.

—— *Nedarim*. Trans. I. Epstein. 1936.

—— *Niddah*. Trans. I. Epstein. 1948.

—— *Pesaḥim*. Trans. I. Epstein. 1938.

—— *Sanhedrin*. Trans. I. Epstein. 1935.

—— *Shabbat*. Trans. I. Epstein. 1938.

—— *Soṭah*. Trans. A. Cohen. 1936.

—— *Sukka*. Trans. W. Slotki. 1938.

—— *Yebamoth*. Trans. W. Slotki. 1936.

—— *Yoma*. Trans. I. Epstein. 1938.

Bachiarius. Letter. *PL Supp.* 1:1035–1044.

Barsanuphius. *Biblios Barsanouphiou*. Greek text edited by S. Schoinos. Volos: 1960.

—— Letters. Ed. D. J. Chitty. *Barsanuphius and John, questions and answers. Patrologia Orientalis* 31. Paris: Firmin Didot, 1966.

—— *Barsanuphe et Jean de Gaza: Correspondance*. Trans. L. Regnault et al. Sablé-sur-Sarthe: Abbaye de Solesmes, 1972.

Basil of Ancyra. *La "De virginitate" de Saint Basile: texte vieux-slave*. Ed. and trans. A. Vaillant. Paris: Institut des études slaves, 1943.

—— *De virginitate tuenda [Liber de vera virginitate.]* PG 30.669–810.

Basil of Caesarea. *Homilia 7 in divites*. PG 31.227–304.

—— *St. Basil: Letters*, 4 vols. Trans. R. J. Deferrari. Loeb Classical Library. Cambridge: Harvard University Press, 1961–62.

—— *Praevia instituta ascetica [Asceticum Parvum.]* PG 31.619–626.

—— *Regulae fusius tractatae*. PG 31.889–1052. English translation: in M. M. Wagner, trans. *St. Basil. The Ascetical Works*. Fathers of the Church. New York: Fathers of the Church, Inc., 1950.

—— *Sermo in tempore famis*. PG 31.303–328.

Bede. *A History of the English Church and People*. Trans. Leo Shirley-Price. Harmondsworth: Penguin, 1955.

Besa. *Letters and Sermons of Besa*. Ed. K. H. Kühn. *CSCO* 157, *Scriptores Coptici* 21. Louvain: L. Durbecq, 1956.

Bohairic Life of Saint Pachomius. In A. Veilleux, trans. q.v. *Pachomian Koinonia*. Vol. 1: *The Life of Saint Pachomius and his Disciples*.

Book of Degrees, The. See *Liber Graduum*.

Budge, E. A. W., ed. *Miscellaneous Coptic Texts in the Dialect of Upper Egypt*. London: British Museum, 1915.

—— *Coptic Martyrdoms in the Dialect of Upper Egypt*. London: British Museum 1914.

Caesarius of Arles. *Sermones*, vol. 1. Ed. G. Morin. *Corpus Christianorum, series latina*, 103. Turnhout: Brepols, 1953.

Cassian, John. *Collationes*. Ed. E. Pichery. *Jean Cassien: Les Conférences*. Sources chrétiennes 42, 54, 64. Paris: Éditions du Cerf, 1953, 1958, 1959.

—— *De Institutis coenobiorum*. Ed. J. C. Guy. *Jean Cassien: Les Institutions cénobitiques*. Sources chrétiennes 109. Paris: Éditions du Cerf, 1965. English translation: in Edgar C. S. Gibson, ed. *Library of the Nicene and Post-Nicene Fathers*, vol. 11. New York: Christian Literature Company, 1894.

Ps.-Clement. *Epistolae ii ad virgines*. PG 1.350–452. English translation: in M.

P. Pratten, ed. *The Ante-Nicene Fathers*, vol. 8. Grand Rapids, Michigan: Eerdmans, 1951; and trans. H. Duensing. "Die dem Klemens von Rom zugeschriebenen Briefe über die Jungfräulichkeit." *Zeitschrift für Kirchengeschichte* (1950) 63:166–188.

—— *Homiliae. PG* 2.57–468.

Clement of Alexandria. *Opera*. Ed. O. Stählin. Die griechischen christlichen Schriftsteller der ersten drei Jahrhunderte, 12, 15, 17, 39. Leipzig: J. C. Hinrichs, 1905–1909. English translation: in A. C. Coxe, ed. *The Ante-Nicene Fathers*, vol. 2. Grand Rapids, Michigan: Eerdmans, 1977.

—— *Excerpta ex Theodoto*. In F. Sagnard, ed. and trans. *Clément d'Alexandrie: Extraits de Théodote*. Sources chrétiennes 23. Paris: Éditions du Cerf, 1948.

—— *Paedagogus. Clément d'Alexandrie: Le Pédagogue*. Ed. M. Harl with an introduction by H. I. Marrou. Sources chrétiennes 70, 108, 158. Paris: Éditions du Cerf, 1960, 1965, 1970.

—— *Stromata* III and VII. In H. Chadwick, trans. *Alexandrian Christianity*. Philadelphia: Westminster Press, 1954.

Constantius. *Life of Germanus of Auxerre*. Ed. R. Borius. *Constance de Lyon: Vie de Saint Germain d'Auxerre*. Sources chrétiennes 112. Paris: Éditions du Cerf, 1965.

Cornutus. *Theologiae Graecae Compendium*. Ed. C. Lang. Leipzig: Teubner, 1881.

Cyprian of Carthage. Letters and Writings. Ed. G. Hartel. *CSEL* 3. Vienna: G. Gerold, 1868.

—— *The Letters of Saint Cyprian of Carthage*. Trans. and commentary, G. W. Clarke. Ancient Christian Writers 43, 44. New York: Newman Press, 1983, 1984.

—— Letters. English translation: in E. Wallis, ed. *The Ante-Nicene Fathers*, vol. 5. Grand Rapids, Michigan: Eerdmans, 1981.

Ps.-Cyprian. *De singularitate clericorum*. Ed. G. Hartel. *CSEL* 3:3. Vienna: G. Gerold, 1871.

Cyril the Patriarch. *The Answers of Apa [the Patriarch] Cyril*. In W. E. Crum, ed. *Der Papyruskodex der Philippsbibliothek*. Strasbourg: Faculté des Lettres, 1915.

Dead Sea Scrolls in English, The. Trans. G. Vermes. Harmondsworth: Penguin, 1968.

Dessau, H, ed. *Inscriptiones latinae selectae*, vol. 1. Berlin: Weidmann, 1892.

Didascalia et Constitutiones Apostolorum. Ed. F. X. Funk. Paderborn: F. Schoeningh, 1905. English trans. R. H. Connolly. *Didascalia Apostolorum*. Oxford: Clarendon Press, 1929.

Diehl, E., ed. *Inscriptiones latinae christianae veteres*, 3 vols. Zürich: Weidmann, 1970.

Dionysius of Alexandria. *Canonical Letter. PG* 10.1271–1290.

Dittenberger, W., ed. *Sylloge Inscriptionum Graecarum*, vol. 3. Hildesheim: G. Olms, 1960.

Dorotheus of Gaza. *Discourses*. In L. Regnault and J. de Préville, eds. *Dorothée de Gaza: Oeuvres spirituelles*. Sources chrétiennes 92. Paris: Éditions du Cerf,

1963. English translation: E. P. Wheeler, *Dorotheus of Gaza: Discourses and Sayings*. Cistercian Studies. Kalamazoo, Michigan: Cistercian Publications, 1977.

Egeria. *Peregrinatio*. In P. Geyer, ed. *Itineraria Hierosolymitana*. CSEL 39. Vienna: Tempsky, 1898.

Elishe Vartapet. *History of Vartan*. In V. Langlois, ed. *Collection des historiens anciens et modernes de l'Arménie*, vol. 2. Paris: Firmin Didot, 1869.

Ephraim the Syrian. *De Paradiso*. Trans. R. Lavenant. *Éphrem de Nisibe: Hymnes sur le Paradis*. Sources chrétiennes 137. Paris: Éditions du Cerf, 1968.

—— "Hymnes inédits de S. Éphrem sur la virginité." Trans. F. Graffin. *L'Orient Syrien* (1961) 6:213–242.

—— *Hymns on the Resurrection*. English translation: S. P. Brock, *The Harp of the Spirit*. Studies Supplementary to *Sobornost* 4. London: Fellowship of St. Alban, 1983.

Epictetus. *Enchiridion*. In W. A. Oldfather, ed. and trans. *Epictetus*. Loeb Classical Library. Cambridge: Harvard University Press, 1965.

Epiphanius. *Expositio fidei catholicae*. PG 42.773–832.

—— *Panarion*. PG 41.155–1200.

Eunapius. *Lives of the Sophists*. In W. C. Wright, ed. *Philostratus and Eunapius*. Loeb Classical Library. Cambridge: Harvard University Press, 1952.

Eusebius of Caesarea. *Demonstratio Evangelica*. Trans. W. S. Ferrar. *Eusebius: The Proof of the Gospel*, vol. 1. London: SPCK, 1920.

—— *Ecclesiastical History*. Trans. H. J. Lawlor and J. E. L. Oulton. *Eusebius: The Ecclesiastical History and the Martyrs of Palestine*. London: SPCK, 1927. Also trans. A. C. McGiffert. *Library of Nicene and Post-Nicene Fathers*, vol. 1. Grand Rapids, Michigan: Eerdmans, 1979.

—— *Life of Constantine*. English translation: in E. C. Richardson, ed. *Library of Nicene and Post-Nicene Fathers*, vol. 1. Grand Rapids, Michigan: Eerdmans, 1979.

—— *The Martyrs of Palestine*. In Lawlor and Oulton, trans. *Eusebius: The Ecclesiastical History and the Martyrs of Palestine*.

Eusebius of Emesa. Sermons. In E. M. Buytaert, ed. *Eusèbe d'Émèse: Discours conservés en latin*. Spicilegium Sacrum Lovaniense 26. Louvain: Spicilegium Sacrum, 1953.

Evagrius of Pontus. *Antirrhetikos*. In W. W. Frankenberg, ed. *Evagrius Ponticus*. Abhandlungen der königlichen Gesellschaft der Wissenschaften zu Göttingen, Philol.-Hist. Klasse, N. F. 13.2. Berlin: Weidmann, 1912.

—— *Letter to Melania*. In Frankenberg, ed. *Evagrius Ponticus*. German translation: G. Bunge, trans. *Evagrios Pontikos: Briefe aus der Wüste*. Trier: Paulinus Verlag, 1986.

—— *Praktikos*. In A. and C. Guillaumont, eds. *Évagre le Pontique: Traité Pratique ou le moine*. Sources chrétiennes 171. Paris: Éditions du Cerf, 1971. English translation: J. E. Bamberger, trans. *Evagrius Ponticus: The Praktikos and Chapters on Prayer*. Cistercian Studies 4. Kalamazoo, Michigan: Cistercian Publications, 1978.

—— *Sententiae ad monachos*. PG 40.1277–1282.

—— *Sententiae ad virginem*. Ed. H. Gressmann. *Texte und Untersuchungen* 39. Leipzig: J. C. Hinrichs, 1913.

Festugière, A. J., trans. *Actes du Concile de Chalcédoine: Sessions iii–vi.* Cahiers d'orientalisme 4. Geneva: P. Cramer, 1983.

Galen. *Galeni Opera Omnia.* Ed. C. G. Kühn. Leipzig: K. Knobloch, 1823.
—— *De cognoscendis animi morbis.* Ed. Kühn, *Opera,* vol. 5. English translation: P. W. Harkins, trans. *On the Passions and Errors of the Soul.* Columbus: Ohio State University Press, 1963.
—— *De locis affectis.* In Kühn, ed., *Galeni Opera,* vol. 8.
—— *De semine.* In Kühn, ed., *Galeni Opera,* vol. 4.
—— *De usu partium.* In Kühn, ed., *Galeni Opera,* vol. 4. English translation: M. T. May, trans. *Galen: On the Usefulness of the Parts of the Body.* Ithaca: Cornell University Press, 1968.
Gaudentius of Brescia. *Tractatus vel Sermones.* PL 20.843–1004.
Gelasius. *Ad Andromachum.* Ed. G. Pomarès. *Gélase 1er: Lettre contre les Lupercales.* Sources chrétiennes 65. Paris: Éditions du Cerf, 1959.
Gregory the Great. *Moralia.* PL 75.509–1162.
—— *Letters.* PL 77.431–1328.
Gregory Nazianzen. *Carmina.* PG 37.397–1600.
—— *Letters.* PG 37.21–389.
—— *Orationes.* PG 35.395–1252. Trans. C. G. Browne and J. E. Swallow. *Library of the Nicene Fathers,* vol. 7. Grand Rapids, Michigan: Eerdmans, 1974.
—— *Testamentum.* PG 37.389–396.
Gregory of Nyssa. *Contra Eunomium.* PG 45.243–1122.
—— *De hominis opificio.* PG 44.123–256. English translation: in W. Moore and H. A. Wilson, eds. *Library of the Nicene Fathers,* vol. 5. Grand Rapids, Michigan: Eerdmans, 1976.
—— *De mortuis.* PG 46.497–538.
—— *De pauperibus amandis.* PG 46.453–490.
—— *Encomium in Sanctum Theodorum* PG 46.735–748.
—— *From Glory to Glory.* J. Daniélou, ed., H. Musurillo, trans. New York: Scribner, 1961.
—— *In Cantica Canticorum.* PG 44.755–1120.
—— *In Flacillam* PG 46.877–892.
—— *In Psalmos.* PG 44.431–608.
—— *Letters.* PG 46.999–1108.
—— *Life of Macrina.* Ed. P. Maraval. *Grégoire de Nysse: La Vie de Sainte Macrine.* Sources chrétiennes 178. Paris: Éditions du Cerf, 1971.
—— *On the Beatitudes.* PG 44.1193–1302.
—— *On Virginity.* Ed. M. Aubineau. *Grégoire de Nysse: Traité de la Virginité.* Sources chrétiennes 119. Paris: Éditions du Cerf, 1961. English translation: in V. W. Callahan, trans. *Gregory of Nyssa: Ascetical Works.* Fathers of the Church 58. New York: Fathers of the Church, 1967; also Moore and Wilson, trans. *Library of the Nicene Fathers.*

—— *Oratio catechetica*. In Moore and Wilson, trans. *Library of the Nicene Fathers*.

Gregory of Tours. *Liber de gloria Confessorum*. Ed. B. Krusch. *Monumenta Germaniae Historica. Scriptores Rerum Merovingicarum*, vol. 1, pt. 2. Hannover: Hahn, 1885.

Hegemonius. *Acta Archelai*. Ed. C. H. Beeson. Die griechischen christlichen Schriftsteller der ersten drei Jahrhunderte 16. Leipzig: J. C. Hinrichs, 1906.

Hermas. *Hermas: Le Pasteur*. Ed. R. Joly. Sources chrétiennes 53. Paris: Éditions du Cerf, 1968.

Hilarius of Arles. *Sermo de vita sancti Honorati*. Ed. S. Cavallin. *Vitae Sanctorum Honorati et Hilarii*. Lund: Gleerup, 1952.

Hippolytus. *Apostolic Traditions*. Ed. and trans. G. Dix. *Apostoliké Paradosis: The Treatise of the Apostolic Tradition of S. Hippolytus of Rome*. 2nd ed. H. Chadwick, ed. London: SPCK, 1968.

—— *Commentary on Daniel*. Ed. N. Bonwetsch and H. Achelis. Die griechischen christlichen Schriftsteller der ersten drei Jahrhunderte 1. Leipzig: J. C. Hinrichs, 1897.

—— *Refutation of All Heresies*. English translation: in J. H. MacMahon, ed. *The Ante-Nicene Fathers*, vol. 5. Grand Rapids, Michigan: Eerdmans, 1981.

Homélies Pascales. Vol. 3: *Une Homélie Anatolienne sur la Date de Pâques en l'An 387*. Ed. F. Floëri and P. Nautin. Sources chrétiennes 48. Paris: Éditions du Cerf, 1957.

Honorius I. Letters. PL 80.469–484.

Horsiesius. *Instructions*. In A. Veilleux, trans. q.v. *Pachomian Koinonia*. Vol. 2: *Pachomian Chronicles and Rules*.

Huelsen, C., ed. *Corpus Inscriptionum Latinarum*. Berlin: Reimer, 1902.

Hunt, A. S., and C. C. Edgar, eds. and trans. *Select Papyri*, vol. 2. Loeb Classical Library. Cambridge: Harvard University Press, 1965.

Ibn al-Nadim. *The Fihrist of al-Nadim*, 2 vols. Trans. B. Dodge. New York: Columbia University Press, 1970.

Innocent I. Letters. PL 20.463–640.

Irenaeus. *Against the Heresies*. English translation: in A. Roberts and W. H. Rambaut, eds. *The Ante-Nicene Library: The Writings of Irenaeus*, vol. 2. Edinburgh: T. & T. Clark, 1869.

Irish Penitentials, The. Ed. Ludwig Bieler with an introduction by D. A. Binchy. Scriptores Latini Hiberniae 5. Dublin: Institute of Advanced Studies, 1975.

Isaiah of Scetis. *Asceticon*. French translation: the monks of Solesmes. *Abbé Isaie: Recueil ascétique*. Spiritualité orientale 7. Soicy-sur-Seine: Abbaye de la Bellefontaine, 1970.

Isidore of Pelusium. Letters. PG 78.177–1646.

Jerome. *Adversus Jovinianum*. PL 23.221–352.

—— *Contra Johannem Hierosolymitanum*. PL 23.371–412.

—— *Contra Rufinum*. PL 23.415–514. Ed. P. Lardet. *Corpus Christianorum, series latina* 79. Turnhout: Brepols, 1982.

—— *Contra Vigilantium*. PL 23.353–368.

—— *Dialogus adversus Pelagianos.* PL 23.517–626.

—— *De viris illustribus.* PL 23.631–764.

—— *In Ecclesiasten.* Ed. M. Adriaen. *Corpus Christianorum, series latina* 72. Turnhout: Brepols, 1959.

—— *In Ephesios.* PL 26.467–588.

—— *In Hieremiam.* PL 24.705–936. Ed. S. Reiter. *Corpus Christianorum, series latina* 74. Turnhout: Brepols, 1960.

—— *Interpretatio libri Didymi de Spiritu Sancto.* PL 23.109–162.

—— *In Titum.* PL 26.589–636.

—— *Letters.* PL 22.325–1197.

—— *Liber de nominibus Hebraicis.* PL 23.815–903.

—— *Life of Malchus.* PL 23.55–62.

—— *Vita S. Hilarionis.* PL 23.29–54.

Ps.-Jerome. *Ad amicum aegrotum.* PL 30.63–108.

—— *De septem ordinibus ecclesiae.* PL 30.157–168.

—— *De virginitate.* PL 30.163–175.

John Chrysostom. *Jean Chrysostome: À une jeune veuve sur le mariage unique.* Eds. B. Grillet and G. H. Ettlinger. Sources chrétiennes 138. Paris: Éditions du Cerf, 1938.

—— *De eleemosyna.* PG 51.261–272.

—— *De inani gloria.* In A. M. Malingrey, ed. *Jean Chrysostome: Sur la vaine gloire et l'éducation des enfants.* Sources chrétiennes 188. Paris: Éditions du Cerf, 1972. English translation: in M. L. W. Laistner, trans. *Christianity and Pagan Culture in the Later Roman Empire.* Ithaca: Cornell University Press, 1951.

—— *De sacerdotio.* PG 48.623–692.

—— *De virginitate.* PG 48.533–596. Ed. H. Musurillo and B. Grillet. *Jean Chrysostome: La Virginité.* Sources chrétiennes 125. Paris: Éditions du Cerf, 1966. English translation: Sally R. Shore, *John Chrysostom: On Virginity, Against Remarriage.* New York: Edwin Mellen Press, 1983.

—— *Homiliae de Statuis.* PG 49.15–222.

—— *Homiliae in Epist. ad Colossios.* PG 62.299–392.

—— *Homiliae in Epist. I ad Corinthios.* PG 61.11–382. English translation: in T. W. Chambers, ed. *A Select Library of the Nicene Fathers*, vol. 12. Grand Rapids, Michigan: Eerdmans, 1979.

—— *Homiliae in Epist. ad Ephesios.* PG 62.4–176.

Homiliae in Epist. ad Hebraeos. PG 63.9–236. English translation: in F. Gardner, ed. *Library of Nicene and Post-Nicene Fathers*, vol. 14. Grand Rapids, Michigan: Eerdmans, 1978.

—— *Homiliae in Epist. I ad Timotheum.* PG 62.501–600. English translation: in P. Schaff, ed. *Library of Nicene and Post-Nicene Fathers*, vol. 13. Grand Rapids, Michigan: Eerdmans, 1979.

—— *Homiliae in Epist. II ad Timotheum.* PG 62.599–662.

—— *Homiliae in Genesim.* PG 54.385–580.

—— *Homiliae in Johannem.* PG 50.23–482.

—— *Homiliae in Matthaeum.* PG 57.13–472. Trans. G. Prevost. *Library of Nicene and Post-Nicene Fathers*, vol. 10. Grand Rapids, Michigan: Eerdmans, 1978.

—— *In illud propter fornicationes. PG* 51.207–218.

—— *Jean Chrysostome: Huit Catéchèses baptismales inédites.* Ed. A. Wenger. Sources chrétiennes 50. Paris: Éditions du Cerf, 1957.

—— *Jean Chrysostome: Lettres à Olympias.* Ed. A. M. Malingrey. Sources chrétiennes 13. Paris: Éditions du Cerf, 1947.

—— *Quod regulares feminae. PG* 47.513–532. English translation: Elizabeth A. Clark, *Jerome, Chrysostom and Friends. Essays and Translations.* New York and Toronto: Edwin Mellen Press, 1979.

—— *St. John Chysostom: On Marriage and Family Life.* Trans. C. P. Roth and D. Anderson. Crestwood, New York: St. Vladimir's Seminary Press, 1986.

John Climacus. *The Ladder of Divine Ascent. PG* 88.623–1164. English translation: C. Luibheid and N. Russell, New York: Paulist Press, 1982.

John of Ephesus. *Ecclesiastical History.* Ed. E. W. Brooks. *CSCO* 106: *Scriptores Syri* 55. Louvain: L. Durbecq, 1936.

—— *Lives of the Eastern Saints. Patrologia Orientalis* 17. Paris: Firmin Didot, 1923.

John the Faster. *Penitential. PG* 88.1889–1918.

Jonkers, E. F., ed. *Acta et symbola conciliorum quae saeculo quarto habita sunt.* Textus Minores 19. Leiden: Brill, 1974.

Lactantius. *Divine Institutions. PL* 7.111–822.

Leander of Seville. *Regula. Liber de institutione virginum et contemptu mundi. PL* 72.873–894.

Leontius of Neapolis. *Life of Symeon the Holy Fool.* Ed. A. J. Festugière and L. Ryden. *Léonce de Néapolis: Vie de Syméon le Fou.* Paris: Geuthner, 1974.

Liber ad Gregoriam. PL Supp. 3.221–256.

Liber Graduum. Ed. M. Kmosko. *Patrologia Syriaca* 3. Paris: Firmin Didot, 1926.

Life of Melania the Younger. Ed. D. Gorce. *Vie de Sainte Mélanie.* Sources chrétiennes 90. Paris: Éditions du Cerf, 1962. English translation: Elizabeth A. Clark, New York: Edwin Mellen Press, 1984.

Life of Olympias. Trans. in Elizabeth A. Clark, *Jerome, Chrysostom and Friends. Essays and Translations.* New York and Toronto: Edwin Mellen Press, 1979.

Life of Symeon Stylites. F. Lent, trans. *Journal of the American Oriental Society* (1915) 35:103–198.

Ps.-Lucian. *Amores.* In M. D. MacLeod, ed. *Lucian*, vol. 8. Loeb Classical Library. Cambridge: Harvard University Press, 1967.

Ps.-Macarius. *Homiliae. PG* 34.449–822. In V. Desprez, ed. *Ps.-Macaire: Oeuvres Spirituelles,* vol. 1. Sources chrétiennes 275. Paris: Éditions du Cerf, 1980.

Mani. *Life of Mani.* A. Henrichs and L. Koenen, eds. and trans. "Ein griechischer Mani Codex (P. Colon. inv. no. 4780)." *Zeitschrift für Papyrologie und Epigraphik* (1970) 5:27–216, and in successive volumes: *Zeitschrift für Papyrologie und Epigraphik* (1975) 19:1–85; (1978) 32:87–199; (1981) 44:201–318; (1982) 48:319–377.

—— *The Cologne Mani Codex: "Concerning the Origin of his Body."* Ed. and trans. R. Cameron and A. J. Dewey. Missoula, Montana: Scholars Press, 1979.

Manichaean latin document. *PL Supp.* 2.1378–1388.

Mark the Deacon. *Marc le Diacre: Vie de Porphyre.* Ed. H. Grégoire and A. Kugener. Collection Budé. Paris: Belles Lettres, 1930.

Marcellus of Bordeaux. *De medicamentis.* Ed. M. Niedermann. Berlin: Akademie-Verlag, 1968.

Martyrdom of St. Theodotus of Ancyra. Ed. Pio Franchi de' Cavalieri. *Studi e Testi* (1901) 6:69–73.

The Martyrology of Oengus the Culdee. Ed. W. Stokes. Dublin: Institute for Advanced Studies, 1984.

Maximus of Turin. *Sermones.* Ed. A. Mutzenbecher. *Corpus Christianorum, series latina* 23. Turnhout: Brepols, 1962.

Melito. *Melito of Sardis: On Pascha and Fragments.* Ed. and trans. S. G. Hall. Oxford: Clarendon Press, 1979.

Menander. *Epideictica.* Ed. and trans. D. A. Russell and N. G. Wilson. Oxford: Clarendon Press, 1981.

Methodius. *On the Resurrection.* PG 18.235–330. English translation: in W. R. Clark, ed. *The Ante-Nicene Fathers.* New York: Charles Scribner's Sons, 1899.

—— *Symposium.* Ed. H. Musurillo, trans. V. H. Debidor. *Méthode d'Olympe: Le Banquet.* Sources chrétiennes 95. Paris: Éditions du Cerf, 1963.

Midrash Rabba: Ecclesiastes. Trans. A. Cohen. London: Soncino Press, 1939.

—— *Genesis.* Trans. H. Freedman and M. Simon. London: Soncino Press, 1939.

—— *Numbers.* Trans. J. Slotki. London: Soncino Press, 1939.

—— *Song of Songs.* Trans. M. Simon. London: Soncino Press, 1939.

Minucius Felix. *Octavius.* In G. H. Randall, ed. and trans. *Tertullian and Minucius Felix.* Loeb Classical Library. Cambridge: Harvard University Press, 1953.

Mitteis, L., and U. Wilcken, eds. *Grundzüge und Chrestomathie der Papyruskunde.* Leipzig: Teubner, 1912.

Mosaicarum et Romanarum Legum Collatio. In S. Riccobono, ed. *Fontes Iuris Romani Anteiustiniani,* vol. 1. Florence: G. Barbera, 1968.

Munier, C., ed. *Les Statuta Ecclesiae Antiquae.* Paris: Presses universitaires de France, 1960.

Musonius Rufus. Fragments. In Cora B. Lutz, ed. "Musonius Rufus. The Roman Socrates." *Yale Classical Studies* (1947) 10:3–147.

Nag Hammadi Library in English, The. Ed. James M. Robinson. Translated by the members of the Coptic Gnostic Library project of the Institute for Antiquity and Christianity. Leiden: Brill, 1977. New York: Harper and Row, 1977.

Nazarius. *Panegyric.* PL 8.581–640.

Nemesius of Emesa. *On the Nature of Man.* PG 40.503–818.

New Testament Apocrypha. E. Hennecke and W. Schneemelcher, eds., R. McL. Wilson, trans. Philadelphia: Westminster Press, 1965.

Nilus of Ancyra. *De voluntaria paupertate.* PG 79.967–1060.

Odes of Solomon, The. Ed. J. H. Charlesworth. Missoula, Montana: Scholars Press, 1977.

Oribasius. *Oeuvres d'Oribase,* vol. 3. Ed. U. C. Bussmaker and C. Daremberg. Paris: Imprimerie Impériale, 1858.

Origen. *Origène: Commentaire sur Saint Jean.* Ed. Cécile Blanc. Sources chrétiennes 157. Paris: Éditions du Cerf, 1970.

—— *Contra Celsum.* Trans. H. E. Chadwick. Cambridge: Cambridge University Press, 1965.

—— *De Principiis.* In H. Crouzel and M. Simonetti, eds. *Origène: Traité; des Principes.* Sources chrétiennes 252, 253, 268, 269, 312. Paris: Éditions du Cerf, 1978–1984. English translation: G. W. Butterworth, trans. *Origen: On First Principles.* New York: Harper and Row, 1966.

—— *Dialogue with Heraclides.* Trans. H. E. Chadwick. *Alexandrian Christianity.* Philadelphia: Westminster Press, 1954.

—— "Fragments on I Cor." Ed. C. Jenkins. *Journal of Theological Studies* (1907/08) 9:500–514.

—— "Fragments on Ephesians, no. 29." Ed. J. A. Gregg. *Journal of Theological Studies* (1901/02) 3:565–567.

—— *Origène: Homélies sur le Cantique des Cantiques.* Ed. O. Rousseau. Sources chrétiennes 37. Paris: Éditions du Cerf, 1954.

—— *Origenes Werke.* Ed. W. A. Baehrens. Die griechischen christlichen Schriftsteller der ersten drei Jahrhunderte. Leipzig: J. C. Hinrichs, 1899–1955.

Oxyrhynchus Papyri, vol. 50. London: Egyptian Exploration Society for the British Academy, 1983.

Pachomius. *Precepts and Judgements.* In A. Veilleux, trans., q.v. *Pachomian Koinonia.* Vol. 2: *Pachomian Chronicles and Rules.*

Palestinian Talmud: Soṭah. Trans. M. Schwab. *Le Talmud de Jérusalem,* vol. 4. Paris: Maisonneuve and Larra, 1972.

Palladas. *Anthologia Palatina.* In W. R. Paton, ed. *The Greek Anthology,* vol. 4. Loeb Classical Library. Cambridge: Harvard University Press, 1971.

Palladius. *Dialogus de vita Johannis Chrysostomi.* PG 47.3–82. Ed. C. R. Coleman-Norton. Cambridge: Cambridge University Press, 1928.

—— *Palladius: The Lausiac History.* Trans. R. T. Meyer. Ancient Christian Writers 34. New York: Newman Press, 1964.

—— *Lausiac History.* In R. Draguet, ed. *Les formes syriaques de la matière de l'Histoire Lausiaque,* vol. 1. CSCO 390: *Scriptores Syri* 170. Louvain: CSCO, 1978.

Pamphilus. *Apologia pro Origene.* PG 17.541–616.

Papiri Greci e Latini, vol. 10. Pubblicazioni della società per la ricerca dei papiri. Florence: E. Ariani, 1932.

Patrick. *Confessio.* In A. B. E. Hood, ed. *St. Patrick.* London and Chichester: Phillimore, 1978.

Paulinus of Milan. *The Life of Ambrose.* In F. R. Hoare, trans. *The Western Fathers.* New York: Harper Torchbooks, 1954.

Paulinus of Nola. *Carmina.* Ed. W. Hartel. CSEL 30. Vienna: Tempsky, 1904.

Pelagian Letters [Scripta Pelagiana]. "Honorificentiae tuae." PL Supp. 1. 1687–1694.

—— *Epistula de castitate.* PL Supp. 1.1464–1505.

Pelagius. *Ad Demetriadem. PL* 30.16–487.

—— *Expositio in epistolam ad Romanos. PL Supp.* 1.1112–1181.

Percival, E. J., ed. *The Seven Ecumenical Councils.* In *Library of Nicene and Post-Nicene Fathers,* vol. 14. Grand Rapids, Michigan: Eerdmans, 1977.

Peter of Alexandria. *Canonical Epistle. PG* 18.467–508.

Philo. *De vita contemplativa.* Ed. R. Arnaldez with an introduction by F. Daumas. *Philo: "De Vita Contemplativa": Oeuvres de Philon d'Alexandrie.* Paris: Éditions du Cerf, 1963. English translation: in F. H. Colson, *Philo,* vol. 9. Loeb Classical Library. Cambridge: Harvard University Press, 1967.

—— *Hypothetica.* In Eusebius, *Praeparatio Evangelica. PG* 21.

—— *Life of Moses.* In Colson, ed. *Philo,* vol. 6. Loeb Classical Library. Cambridge: Harvard University Press, 1950.

Philoxenus of Mabbug. "Memra de Philoxène de Mabboug sur l'Inhabitation du Saint-Esprit." Trans. A. Tanghe. *Le Muséon* (1960) 73:39–71.

—— *Letter sent to a Friend.* Trans. G. Olinder. *Acta Universitatis Gotoburgensis* (1950) 56.

Pliny. *Pliny: Natural History.* Ed. H. Rackham. Loeb Classical Library. Cambridge: Harvard University Press, 1969.

Plotinus. *Enneads.* Trans. S. MacKenna. London: Faber, 1956.

Plutarch. *Comparison of Lycurgus and Numa.* In B. Perrin, ed. *Plutarch's Lives,* Loeb Classical Library. Cambridge: Harvard University Press, 1948.

—— *De Iside.* In F. C. Babbitt, ed. *Plutarch's Moralia.* vol. 5. Loeb Classical Library. Cambridge: Harvard University Press, 1969.

—— *De sanitate tuenda.* In F. C. Babbitt, ed. *Plutarch's Moralia.* Loeb Classical Library. Cambridge: Harvard University Press, 1971.

—— *Praecepta conjugalia.* In Babbitt, ed. *Plutarch's Moralia,* vol. 2.

Polemo. *Physiognomica.* Ed. R. Förster, ed. *Physiognomici graeci,* vol. 1. Leipzig: Teubner, 1891.

Polotsky, H. J., ed. *Manichäische Handschriften der staatlichen Museen Berlins.* Vol. 1: *Kephalaia.* Stuttgart: Kohlhamer, 1940.

Porphyry. *Contra Christianos.* Ed. A. von Harnack. "Porphyrius. 'Gegen die Christen'." *Abhandlungen der königlichen preussischen Akademie der Wissenschaften 1916,* pp. 1–115. Berlin: Akademie der Wissenschaften, 1916.

—— *Porphyre: De l'Abstinence.* Ed. J. Bouffartigue and M. Patillon. Collection Budé. Paris: Les Belles Lettres, 1977. English translation: Thomas Taylor, *On Abstinence from Animal Foods.* London: Centaur Press, 1965.

—— *Porphyry: On the Cave of the Nymphs.* Ed. and trans. Arethusa Monographs. Buffalo: Department of Classics, SUNY Buffalo, 1960. English translation: Robert Lamberton, Barrington, New York: Station Hill Press, 1983.

—— *On Philosophy from Oracles.* In Eusebius. *Praeparatio Evangelica. PG* 21.

—— *Life of Plotinus.* Trans. S. MacKenna, *Plotinus: Enneads.* London: Faber, 1956.

Possidius. *Life of Augustine. PL* 32.33–66.

Quintilian. *Institutio Oratoria.* In H. E. Butler, ed. *Quintilian,* 4 vols. Loeb Classical Library. Cambridge: Harvard University Press, 1969–1979.

Roca-Puig, R., ed. *Himne a la Verge Maria: "Psalmus responsorius," papir llatí del segle iv.* Barcelona: Asociación Bibliófilos, 1965.

Romanos Melodes. *Romanos le Mélode: Hymnes III.* Ed. J. Grosdidier de Matons. Sources chrétiennes 114. Paris: Éditions du Cerf, 1965.

Rufinus. *Apologia contra Hieronymum.* In M. Simonetti, ed. *Tyrannii Rufini Opera. Corpus Christianorum, series latina* 20. Turnhout: Brepols, 1961.

—— *Expositio Symboli.* In Simonetti, ed. *Opera.*

—— *Historia Monachorum.* PL 21.387–462.

—— *Praefatio in Omelias Sancti Basilii.* In Simonetti, ed. *Opera.*

—— *Praefationes in Libros Origenis Periarchon.* In Simonetti, ed. *Opera.*

—— *Prologus in Omelias Origenis super Numeros.* In Simonetti, ed. *Opera.*

Sallust. *Sallustius: Concerning the Gods and the Universe.* Ed. A. D. Nock. Cambridge: Cambridge University Press, 1926.

Schermann, T., ed. *Die allgemeine Kirchenordnung frühchristlicher Liturgien.* Paderborn: F. Schoeningh, 1914.

Serapion of Thmuis. *Letter to the Monks.* PG 40.924–942.

Sermo de sacrilegio. PL Supp. 4:969–973.

Severus of Antioch. *Homiliae cathedrales.* Ed. M. Brière and F. Graffin. *Patrologia Orientalis* 36. Turnhout: Brepols, 1974.

Sextus. *The Sentences of Sextus: A Contribution to the History of Christian Ethics.* Texts and Studies, n.s. 5. Cambridge: Cambridge University Press, 1959.

Shenute of Atripe. Letters. Ed. J. Leipoldt and W. E. Crum. *CSCO*, 43, *Scriptores Coptici* 3. Leipzig: O. Harrassowitz, 1898. Trans. H. Wiesmann. *CSCO* 96: *Scriptores Coptici* 8. Louvain: L. Durbecq, 1953.

Siricius, Pope. Letters. PL 13.1131–1196.

Socrates. *Ecclesiastical History.* English translation: in A. C. Zenos, ed. *Library of Nicene and Post-Nicene Fathers,* ser. 2, vol. 2. Grand Rapids, Michigan: Eerdmans, 1979.

Soranus. *Gynaecia.* Ed. J. Ilberg. Leipzig: Teubner, 1927. English translation: O. Temkin, *Soranus' Gynaecology.* Baltimore: Johns Hopkins University Press, 1956.

Suidas. *Lexicon,* vol. 3. Ed. A. Adler. Leipzig: Teubner, 1933.

Synesius of Cyrene. Letters. PG 66.1321–1560. English translation: A. Fitzgerald, *The Letters of Synesius of Cyrene.* Oxford: Oxford University Press, 1926.

Tatian. *Oration* to the Greeks. English translation: in J. E. Ryland, ed. *The Ante-Nicene Fathers,* vol. 2. Grand Rapids, Michigan: Eerdmans, 1977.

Tertullian. *Ad Martyras.* Ed. E. Dekkers. In *Tertulliani Opera. Corpus Christianorum, series latina* 1. Turnhout: Brepols, 1954.

—— *Ad uxorem.* Ed. E. Kroymann. *Corpus Christianorum* 1.

—— *Adversus Marcionem.* Ed. E. Kroymann, *Corpus Christianorum* 1.

—— *Adversus Valentinianos.* Ed. E. Kroymann. *Tertulliani Opera. Corpus Christianorum, Series latina* 2. Turnhout: Brepols, 1954.

—— *De Anima.* Ed. J. H. Waszink. *Corpus Christianorum* 2.

—— *Apologeticum*. Ed. Dekkers, *Corpus Christianorum* 1.
—— *De cultu feminarum*. Ed. Kroymann, *Corpus Christianorum* 1.
—— *De exhortatione castitatis*. Ed. Kroymann. *Corpus Christianorum* 2.
—— *De ieiunio*. Ed. A. Reifferscheid and G. Wissowa. *Corpus Christianorum* 2.
—— *De monogamia*. Ed. Dekkers. *Corpus Christianorum* 2.
—— *De oratione*. Ed. G. F. Diercks. *Corpus Christianorum* 1.
—— *De virginibus velandis*. Ed. Dekkers. *Corpus Christianorum* 2.
Theodoret of Cyrrhus. *Dialogus*. PG 83.31–318.
—— *Epistolae*. PG 83.1171–1494.
—— *Haereticarum fabularum compendium*. PG 83.335–356.
—— *Historia Religiosa*. PG 82.881–1280. Ed. P. Canivet and A. Leroy-Molinghen. *Théodoret de Cyr: Histoire des Moines de Syrie*. Sources chrétiennes 234, 257. Paris: Éditions du Cerf, 1977, 1979. English translation: R. M. Price, *Theodoret of Cyrrhus: A History of the Monks of Syria*. Cistercian Studies 88. Kalamazoo, Michigan: Cistercian Publications, 1985.
Theodorus Priscianus. *Euporistôn libri*. Ed. V. Rose. Leipzig: Teubner, 1894.
Till, W. C., "Erbrechtliche Untersuchungen auf Grund der koptischen Urkunden." *Österreichische Akademie der Wissenschaften: Philol.-Hist. Klasse* 229. Vienna: R. M. Röhrer, 1954.
Timothy of Constantinople. *De Receptione Haereticorum*. PG 86.11–68.

Veilleux, A., trans. *Pachomian Koinonia. The Lives, Rules, and Other Writings of Saint Pachomius and his Disciples*. Vol. 1: *The Life of Saint Pachomius and his Disciples*. Vol. 2: *Pachomian Chronicles and Rules*. Vol. 3: *Instructions, Letters, and Other Writings of Saint Pachomius and his Disciples*. Cistercian Studies 45–47. Kalamazoo, Michigan: Cistercian Publications, 1980–1982.
Vie Ancienne de S. Syméon Stylite le Jeune. 2 vols. Ed. P. Van der Ven. Subsidia Hagiographica 32. Brussels: Société des Bollandistes, 1962.
Vita Mariae Aegyptiacae. PL 73.671–690.
Vita Mariae Meretricis. PL 73.651–660.
Vives, J. ed. *Concilios Visigóticos y Hispano-Romanos*. Madrid: Consejo Superior de Investigaciones científicas, 1963.
Vita Sanctae Eupraxiae. Acta Sanctorum. Mart. ii. March 13. Venice: 1735.
Vita Sanctae Febroniae. Acta Sanctorum. Jun. v. June 25. Venice: 1744.
Vita Sanctae Matronae. Acta Sanctorum. Nov. iii. Brussels: Société des Bollandistes, 1910.
Vita Theclae. In G. Dagron, ed. *Vie et Miracles de Sainte Thècle*. Subsidia Hagiographica 62. Brussels: Société des Bollandistes, 1978.

Secondary Sources

Abramowski, L. "Sprache und Abfassungszeit der Oden Salomos." *Oriens Christianus* (1984) 68:80–90.
Achelis, H. *Virgines subintroductae*. Leipzig: J. C. Hinrichs, 1902.
Adam A. "Erwägungen zur Herkunft der Didache." *Zeitschrift für Kirchengeschichte* (1957) 68:1–47.
Aikema, Bernard. "Lorenzo Lotto and the 'Ospedale de San Zuane Polo.'"

In D. Rosand, ed. *Interpretazioni veneziane: Studi di storia dell'arte in onore di Michelangelo Muraro*, pp. 343–350. Venice: Arsenale, 1984.

Aland, Barbara. "Marcion. Versuch einer neuen Interpretation." *Zeitschrift für Theologie und Kirche* (1973) 70:420–447.

Albrecht, Ruth. *Das Leben der heiligen Makrina auf dem Hintergrund der Thekla-Traditionen*. Forschungen zur Kirchen- und Dogmengeschichte 38. Göttingen: Vandenhoeck and Ruprecht, 1986.

Alexandre, Monique. "Protologie et eschatologie chez Grégoire de Nysse." In Ugo Bianchi, ed. q.v. *Arche e Telos. L'Antropologia di Origene e di Gregorio di Nissa*, pp. 122–159. Studia Patristica Mediolanensia 12. Milan: Vita e Pensiero, 1981.

Allam, S. "Le mariage dans l'Égypte ancienne." *Journal of Egyptian Archaeology* (1981) 67:116–35.

Amand, D., and M. C. Moons. "Une curieuse homélie grecque sur la virginité, adressée aux pères de famille." *Revue bénédictine* (1953) 63:18–69, 211–238.

Amat, Jacqueline. *Songes et Visions. L'au-delà dans la littérature latine tardive*. Paris: Études augustiniennes, 1985.

Anderson, Graham. *Ancient Fiction: The Novel in the Graeco-Roman World*. Totowa, New Jersey: Barnes and Noble, 1984.

Anderson, J. G. C., F. Cumont and H. Grégoire, eds. *Studia Pontica*. Brussels: H. Lamartin 1910.

Appelbaum, S. "Economic Life in Palestine." In S. Saffrai and M. Stern, eds. *The Jewish People in the First Century*, pp. 631–700. Assen: Van Gorcum, 1974.

Arbesmann, R. "Fasting and Prophecy in Pagan and Christian Antiquity." *Traditio* (1949–51) 7:1–71.

—— "The 'cervuli' and 'anniculae' in Caesarius of Arles." *Traditio* (1979) 35:89–119.

Archer, L. J. "The Role of Jewish Women in Graeco-Roman Palestine." In Averil Cameron and Amélie Kuhrt, eds. q.v. *Images of Women in Late Antiquity*, pp. 273–287.

Ariès, Philippe, and André Béjin, eds. *Western Sexuality: Practice and Precept in Past and Present Times*. Translated by Anthony Forster. Oxford: Basil Blackwell, 1985.

Armstrong, A. H. *The Cambridge History of Later Greek and Early Medieval Philosophy*. Cambridge: Cambridge University Press, 1967.

—— "Gnosis and Greek Philosophy." In B. Aland, ed. *Gnosis: Festschrift für Hans Jonas*, pp. 87–124. Göttingen: Vandenhoeck and Ruprecht, 1978.

—— "Neoplatonic Valuations of Nature, Body and Intellect." *Augustinian Studies* (1972) 3:35–59.

—— *Saint Augustine and Christian Platonism*. Saint Augustine Lecture for 1966. Villanova, Pennsylvania: Villanova University Press, 1967.

Aubineau, M. "Le Panégyrique de Thècle attribué à Jean Chrysostome (BHG 1720): La fin retrouvée d'un texte mutilé." *Analecta Bollandiana* (1975) 93:349–362.

Aune, D. E. *The Cultic Setting of Realized Eschatology in Early Christianity*. Supplements to Novum Testamentum 28. Leiden: Brill, 1977.

Averincev, S. "L'or dans le système des symboles de la culture protobyzantine." *Studi medievali* (1979), ser. 3, 20:47–67.

—— "Notion de l'homme et tradition littéraire à Byzance." *Studi medievali* (1977) ser. 3, 18:1–38.

—— *Poetika rannevizantijskoj literaturi*. Moscow: Akademiya Nauk, 1977.

Bagnall, Roger S. "Church, State and Divorce in Late Roman Egypt." In *Florilegium Columbianum: Essays in Honor of Paul Oskar Kristeller*, pp. 41–61. New York: Italica Press, 1987.

Bakhtin, M. *The Dialogic Imagination: Four Essays*. Edited by Michael Holquist. Translated by Caryl Emerson and Michael Holquist. Austin: University of Texas Press, 1981.

Baltensweiler, H. *Die Ehe im Neuen Testament*. Zürich: Zwingli Verlag, 1967.

Barbier, E. "La signification du cortège représenté sur le couvercle du coffret de 'Projecta'." *Cahiers Archéologiques* (1962) 12:15–33.

Barnes, T. D. "Angel of Light or Mystic Initiate? The Problem of the *Life* of Anthony." *Journal of Theological Studies* (1986) n.s. 37:353–68.

—— *Constantine and Eusebius*. Cambridge: Harvard University Press, 1981.

—— "Methodius, Maximus and Valentinus." *Journal of Theological Studies* (1979) n.s. 30:47–55.

—— "Porphyry *Against the Christians:* Date and the Attribution of Fragments." *Journal of Theological Studies* (1973) n.s. 24:424–442.

—— *Tertullian*. Oxford: Clarendon Press, 1971.

Baumgarten, J. M. "4Q502, Marriage or Golden Age Ritual?" *Journal of Jewish Studies* (1983) 34:125–135.

Baur, C. *John Chrysostom and His Times*. 2 vols. Translated by M. Gonzaga. Westminster, Maryland: Newman Press, 1959.

Batey, R. A. *New Testament Nuptial Imagery*. Leiden: Brill, 1971.

Baynes, N. H. "The Thought World of East Rome." In *Byzantine Studies and Other Essays*, pp. 24–46. London: Athlone Press, 1960.

Beard, Mary. "The Sexual Status of Vestal Virgins." *Journal of Roman Studies* (1980) 70:12–27.

Beatrice, P. F. "Continenza e matrimonio nel Christianesimo primitivo." In R. Cantalamassa, ed. q.v. *Etica sessuale e matrimonio nel cristianesimo delle origini*, 3–68.

—— *La Lavanda dei piedi*. Rome: Edizioni liturgiche, 1983.

—— *Tradux Peccati. Alle fonti della dottrina agostiniana del peccato originale*. Studia Patristica Mediolanensia 8. Milan: Vita e Pensiero, 1978.

—— "Le tuniche di pelle. Antiche letture di *Gen.* 3.21." In Ugo Bianchi, ed. q.v. *La Tradizione dell'Enkrateia*, pp. 433–484.

Beauchamp, Paul. *Création et Séparation*. Paris: Desclée de Brouwer, 1969.

Beck, E. "Asketentum und Mönchtum bei Ephraem." In *Il Monachesimo Orientale*, pp. 343–362. Orientalia Christiana Analecta 153. Rome: Vatican, 1958.

Beck, H. G. *Byzantinisches Erotikon. Orthodoxie, Literatur, Gesellschaft*. Sitzungsberichte der bayerischen Akademie der Wissenschaften. Philos.-Hist. Klasse 1984, no. 5. Munich: Verlag der Bayerischen Akademie der Wissenschaften: Kommission C. H. Beck, 1984.

Bell, H. I. *Jews and Christians in Egypt*. London: British Museum, 1924.

Berrouard, M.-F. "Les Lettres 6* et 19* de saint Augustin." *Revue des études augustiniennes* (1981) 27:264–277.

—— "Un tournant dans la vie de l'Église d'Afrique: les deux missions d'Alypius en Italie à la lumière des *Lettres* 10*, 15*, 16*, 22*, et 23*A de saint Augustin." *Revue des études augustiniennes* (1985) 31:46–70.

Betz, H. D. *Galatians*. Philadelphia: Fortress Press, 1979.

Bianchi, U., ed. *La Tradizione dell'Enkrateia*. Rome: Ateneo, 1985.

Black, Matthew. *The Scrolls and Christian Origins*. New York: Scribner's Sons, 1961.

—— "The Tradition of Hasidaean-Essene Asceticism: Its Origins and Influence." In *Aspects du Judéo-christianisme*, pp. 19–33. Colloque de Strasbourg, 1964. Paris: Presses Universitaires de France, 1965.

Blanck, H. *Wiederverwendung alter Statuen als Ehrendenkmäler bei Griechen und Römern*. Rome: Bretschneider, 1969.

Blank, David L. "The Etymology of Salvation in Gregory of Nyssa's *De Virginitate*." *Journal of Theological Studies* (1986) n.s. 37:79–90.

Blond, G. "L' 'hérésie' encratite vers la fin du quatrième siècle." *Recherches de science religieuse* (1944) 32:157–210.

Bonner, G. "Some Remarks on Letters 4* and 6*." In *Les Lettres de Saint Augustin découvertes par Johannes Divjak: communications presentées au Colloque des 20 et 21 Septembre, 1982*, pp. 155–164. Paris: Études augustiniennes, 1983.

Bornkamm, G. *Paul*. New York: Harper and Row, 1971.

Boswell, John. "*Expositio* and *Oblatio:* The Abandonment of Children and the Ancient and Medieval Family." *American Historical Review* (1984) 89:10–33.

Bosworth, C. E. *The Medieval Islamic Underworld*. Vol. 1, *The Banū Sāsān in Arabic Life and Lore*. Leiden: Brill, 1976.

Bourdieu, Pierre. *Outline of a Theory of Practice*. Translated by Richard Nice. Cambridge: Cambridge University Press, 1977.

Bowersock, G. W. *Roman Arabia*. Cambridge: Harvard University Press, 1983.

Brennan, Brian. "Athanasius' *Vita Antonii*: A Sociological Interpretation." *Vigiliae Christianae* (1985) 39-:209–227.

Brilliant, Richard. "Una statua ritratto femminile dal territorio di Tarquinia." *Bolletino d'Arte* (1984) 26:1–12.

Brisson, Luc, ed. *Porphyre. La Vie de Plotin I: Travaux Préliminaires*. Paris: J. Vrin, 1982.

Brock, Sebastian P. "Clothing Metaphors as a Means of Theological Expression in Syriac Tradition." In M. Schmidt and C. F. Geyer, eds. *Typus, Symbol, Allegorie bei den östlichen Vätern und ihren Parallelen im Mittelalter*, pp. 11–40. Regensburg: Pustet, 1981.

—— "Early Syrian Asceticism." *Numen* (1973) 20:1–19.

—— "Jewish Traditions in Syriac Sources." *Journal of Jewish Studies* (1979) 30:212–232.

Brock, Sebastian P., and Susan Ashbrook Harvey, eds. *Holy Women of the Syrian Orient*. Berkeley and Los Angeles: University of California Press, 1987.

Brooten, B. J. *Women Leaders in the Ancient Synagogue*. Chico, California: Scholars Press, 1982.

Brown, P. R. L. "Antiquité tardive." In Paul Veyne, ed. q.v. *Histoire de la Vie Privée*. Vol. 1, *De l'Empire romain à l'an mil*, pp. 226–299; English translation in A. Goldhammer, trans. *History of Private Life*. Vol. 1, *From Pagan Rome to Byzantium*, pp. 239–311.

—— *Augustine of Hippo*. Berkeley and Los Angeles: University of California Press, 1967.

—— *The Cult of the Saints*. Chicago: University of Chicago Press, 1981.

—— "The Diffusion of Manichaeism in the Roman Empire." *Journal of Roman Studies* (1969) 59:92–103. Now in *Religion and Society in the Age of Saint Augustine*, q.v., pp. 94–118.

—— *The Making of Late Antiquity*. Cambridge: Harvard University Press, 1978.

—— "The Notion of Virginity in the Early Church." In Bernard McGinn, John Meyendorff, and Jean Leclercq, eds. *World Spirituality*. Vol. 16, *Christian Spirituality: Origins to the Twelfth Century*, pp. 427–443. New York, Crossroad, 1985.

—— "Pelagius and His Supporters: Aims and Environment." *Journal of Theological Studies* (1968) n.s. 19:93–114. Now in *Religion and Society in the Age of Saint Augustine*, q.v., pp. 183–207.

—— "The Problem of Miraculous Feeding in the Graeco-Roman World." *Center for Hermeneutical Studies: colloquy 42*, pp. 19–24. Berkeley, California: Graduate Theological Union, 1982.

—— *Religion and Society in the Age of Saint Augustine*. London: Faber, 1977.

—— "The Saint as Exemplar." *Representations* (1983) 1:1–25. Also in J. S. Hawley, ed. *Saints and Virtues*, pp. 3–14. Berkeley and Los Angeles: University of California Press, 1987.

—— "Sexuality and Society in the Fifth Century A.D.: Augustine and Julian of Eclanum." In E. Gabba, ed. *Tria Corda. Scritti in onore di Arnaldo Momigliano*, pp. 49–70. Biblioteca di Athenaeum 1. Como: New Press, 1983.

Browning, R. "The Riot of A.D. 387 in Antioch." *Journal of Roman Studies* (1952) 42:13–20.

Brunt, P. A. *Italian Manpower, 255 B.C.–A.D. 14*. Oxford: Clarendon Press, 1971.

Büchner, B. *Die Armut der Armen*. Munich: Kosel, 1980.

Buckler, W. H., W. M. Calder, and C. W. M. Cox. "Asia Minor, 1924. IV.— A Monument from the Upper Tembris Valley." *Journal of Roman Studies* (1927) 17:49–58.

Bunge, J. G. "Origenismus-Gnostizismus: Zum geistesgeschichtlichen Standort des Evagrios Pontikos." *Vigiliae Christianae* (1986) 40:24–54.

Burkitt, F. *Early Christianity Outside the Roman Empire*. Cambridge: Cambridge University Press, 1899.

Burn, A. R. "Hic Breve Vivitur." *Past and Present* (1953) 4:1–31.

Bynum, Caroline Walker. *Holy Feast and Holy Fast: The Religious Significance of Food to Medieval Women*. Berkeley and Los Angeles: University of California Press, 1987.

—— "Women's Stories, Women's Symbols: A Critique of Victor Turner's Theory of Liminality." In R. L. Moore and F. E. Reynolds, eds. *Anthropology and the Study of Religion*, pp. 105–125. Chicago: Center for the Scientific Study of Religion, 1984.

Cacitti, Remo. "L'etica sessuale nella canonistica del iiio secolo." In R. Cantalamassa, ed. q.v. *Etica sessuale e matrimonio nel cristianesimo delle origini,* pp. 69–157.

Caird, G. B. *A Commentary on the Revelation of Saint John the Divine.* New York: Harper and Row, 1966.

Calder, W. M. "The Epigraphy of the Anatolian Heresies." In W. H. Buckler and W. M. Calder, eds. *Anatolian Studies Presented to Sir William Mitchell Ramsay,* pp. 59–91. Manchester: Manchester University Press, 1923.

Calderini, A., et al. *La Basilica di San Lorenzo.* Milan: Fondazione Treccani, 1951.

Callam, D. "Clerical Continence in the Fourth Century: Three Papal Decretals." *Theological Studies* (1980) 41:3–50.

Cameron, Alan. *Circus Factions.* Oxford: Oxford University Press, 1976.

Cameron, Averil. *Procopius and the Sixth Century.* Berkeley and Los Angeles: University of California Press, 1985.

—— "The Theotokos in Sixth-Century Constantinople: A City Finds Its Symbol." *Journal of Theological Studies* (1978) n.s., 29:79–108.

Cameron, Averil, and Amélie Kuhrt, eds. *Images of Women in Late Antiquity.* Detroit: Wayne State University Press, 1983.

Canivet, M. Y., and P. Canivet. "La mosaïque dans l'église syriaque de Ḥuârte." *Cahiers archéologiques* (1975) 24:49–60.

Canivet, P. "Erreurs de spiritualité et troubles psychiques." *Recherches de science religieuse* (1962) 50:161–205.

—— *Le monachisme syrien selon Théodoret de Cyr.* Théologie historique 42. Paris: Beauchesne, 1977.

Cantalamassa, R., ed. *Etica sessuale e matrimonio nel cristianesimo delle origini.* Studia Patristica Mediolanensia 5. Milan: Vita e Pensiero, 1976.

Carrithers, Michael. *The Forest Monks of Sri Lanka.* Delhi: Oxford University Press, 1983.

Carroll, Michael. *The Cult of the Virgin Mary.* Princeton: Princeton University Press, 1986.

Cassin, Elena. "Le Proche-Orient ancien: Virginité et stratégie de sexe." In *Le Mythe de la virginité perdue à travers les siècles et les continents,* pp. 241–258. Paris: Éditions Ramsay, 1981.

—— "Le Semblable et le différent." In L. Poliakov, ed. *Hommes et bêtes,* 115–127. Paris: Mouton, 1975.

Castelli, Elizabeth. "Virginity and Its Meaning for Women's Sexuality in Early Christianity." *Journal of Feminist Studies in Religion* (1986) 2:61–88.

Cavallera, F. "La *de virginitate* de Basile d'Ancyre." *Revue d'histoire ecclésiastique* (1905) 6:5–14.

—— *Saint Jérôme: sa vie et son oeuvre.* Spicilegium Sacrum Lovaniense, fasc. 1–2. Louvain: Spicilegium Sacrum, 1922.

Chadwick, H. E. "All Things to All Men." *New Testament Studies* (1955) 1:261–275.

—— "The Ascetic Ideal in the History of the Church." In W. J. Sheils, ed. *Monks, Hermits, and the Ascetic Tradition,* pp. 1–24. Oxford: Basil Blackwell, 1985.

—— *Augustine*. Past Masters. Oxford: Oxford University Press, 1986.

—— *Boethius, the consolations of music, logic, theology and philosophy*. Oxford: Clarendon Press, 1981.

—— *Early Christian Thought and the Classical Tradition*. New York: Oxford University Press, 1966.

—— *Reallexikon für Antike und Christentum*, 5: coll. 343–365, s.v. "Enkrateia." Stuttgart: A. Hiersemann, 1960.

—— "Origen, Celsus, and the Resurrection of the Body." *Harvard Theological Review* (1948) 41:83–102.

—— *Priscillian of Avila*. Oxford: Clarendon Press, 1976.

Chadwick, O. *John Cassian*. Cambridge: Cambridge University Press, 1963.

Chitty, Derwas. *The Desert a City*. Oxford: Basil Blackwell, 1966.

Chodorow, Nancy. "Family Structure and Female Personality." In M. Z. Rosaldo and L. Lamphere, eds. q.v. *Women, Culture and Society*, pp. 43–66.

Clark, Elizabeth A. " 'Adam's Only Companion': Augustine and the Early Christian Debate on Marriage." *Recherches augustiniennes* (1986) 21:139–162.

—— *Ascetic Piety and Women's Faith: Essays on Late Ancient Christianity*. New York and Toronto: Edwin Mellen Press, 1986.

—— "Ascetic Renunciation and Feminine Advancement: A Paradox of Late Ancient Christianity." *Anglican Theological Review* (1981) 6:240–257. Now in *Ascetic Piety and Women's Faith*, q.v., pp. 175–208.

—— "Authority and Humility: A Conflict of Values in Fourth-Century Female Monasticism." *Byzantinische Forschungen* (1985) 9:17–33. Now in *Ascetic Piety and Women's Faith*, q.v. pp. 209–228.

—— *Jerome, Chrysostom and Friends*. Lewiston, New York: Edwin Mellen Press, 1979.

—— "John Chrysostom and the *Subintroductae*." *Church History* (1977) 46:171–185. Now in *Ascetic Piety and Women's Faith*, q.v., pp. 265–290.

—— "The Place of Jerome's Commentary on Ephesians in the Origenist Controversy: the Apokatastasis and Ascetic Ideals." *Vigiliae Christianae* (1987) 41:154–171.

—— "Vitiated Seeds and Holy Vessels: Augustine's Manichaean Past." In *Ascetic Piety and Women's Faith*, q.v., pp. 291–349.

Clarke, W. K. Lowther. *Saint Basil the Great: A Study in Monasticism*. Cambridge: Cambridge University Press, 1916.

Claude, Dieter. *Die byzantinische Stadt im 6. Jahrhundert*. Byzantinisches Archiv 13. Munich: C. H. Beck, 1969.

Cochini, C. *Origines apostoliques du célibat sacerdotal*. Paris: Lethielleux, 1981.

Consolino, Franca Ela. "Dagli 'exempla' ad un esempio di comportamento cristiano." *Rivista storica italiana* (1982) 94:455–477.

—— "Modelli di comportamento e modi di santificazione per l'aristocrazia femminile d'Occidente." In A. Giardina, ed. *Società romana e impero tardoantico*. Vol. 1, *Istituzioni, ceti, economia*, pp. 273–306. Bari: Laterza, 1986.

—— "Modelli di santità femminile nelle più antiche Passioni romane." *Augustinianum* (1984) 24:83–113.

—— "*Veni huc a Libano*: La *Sponsa* del Cantico dei Cantici come modello per le vergini negli scritti esortatori di Ambrogio." *Athenaeum* (1984) n.s. 62:399–415.

Corsini, E. "Plérôme humaine et plérôme cosmique chez Grégoire de Nysse." In M. Harl, ed. q.v. *Écriture et culture philosophique dans la pensée de Grégoire de Nysse*, pp. 111–126.

Countryman, L. W. *The Rich Christian in the Church of the Early Empire: Contradictions and Accommodations*. Lewiston, New York: Edwin Mellen Press, 1980.

Courcelle, P. *Recherches sur les Confessions de Saint Augustin*. Paris: de Boccard, 1950.

—— "Quelques symboles funéraires du néo-platonisme latin." *Revue des études anciennes* (1944) 46:65–93.

Cox, Patricia. *Biography in Late Antiquity: A Quest for the Holy Man*. Berkeley and Los Angeles: University of California Press, 1983.

—— "Origen and the Bestial Soul." *Vigiliae Christianae* (1982) 36:115–140.

—— " 'Pleasure of the Text, Text of Pleasure': Origen's *Commentary on the Song of Songs*." *Journal of the American Academy of Religion* (1986) 54:241–251.

Cramer, W. *Die Engelvorstellungen bei Ephräm dem Syrer*. Orientalia Christiana Analecta 173. Rome: Vatican, 1965.

—— *Der Geist Gottes und des Menschen in frühsyrischer Theologie*. Münster Beiträge zur Theologie 46. Münster-in-Westfalen: Aschendorff, 1979.

Croke, Brian. "The Era of Porphyry's Anti-Christian Polemic." *Journal of Religious History* (1984) 13:1–14.

Crouzel, F. *Origène et la "connaissance mystique."* Paris: Desclée de Brouwer, 1961.

—— *Virginité et mariage chez Origène*. Paris: Desclée de Brouwer, 1963.

Crum, W. E. *A Coptic Dictionary*. Oxford: Clarendon Press, 1939.

—— *Coptic Ostraca*. London: Egypt Exploration Fund, 1902.

Crum, W. E., and H. G. Evelyn-White. *The Monastery of Epiphanius of Thebes, Pt. 2: Coptic Ostraca and Papyri*. New York: Metropolitan Museum of Art, 1926.

Dagron, Gilbert. "Les moines et la ville: le monachisme à Constantinople." *Travaux et Mémoires* (1970) 4:229–276.

—— *Naissance d'une capitale*. Paris: Presses Universitaires de France, 1974.

Daniélou, Jean. *Platonisme et Théologie mystique*. Paris: Aubin, 1944.

—— *L'être et le temps chez Grégoire de Nysse*. Leiden: Brill, 1970.

Dassmann, E. *Die Frömmigkeit des Kirchenvaters Ambrosius von Mailand*. Münster-in-Westfalen: Aschendorff, 1965.

Daube, David. "The Marriage of Justinian and Theodora. Legal and Theological Reflections." *Catholic University of America Law Review* (1967) 16:380–399.

De Benedictis, E. "The Senatorium and Matroneum in the Roman Church." *Rivista di archeologia cristiana* (1981) 57:69–85.

Decret, F. *L'Afrique manichéenne*, 2 vols. Paris: Études augustiniennes, 1978.

—— *Aspects du manichéisme dans l'Afrique chrétienne*. Paris: Études augustiniennes, 1970.

De Jonge, M. "The Pre-Mosaic Servants of God in the Testaments of the Twelve Patriarchs and in the Writings of Justin and Irenaeus." *Vigiliae Christianae* (1985) 39:157–170.

Deléani, S. "*Christum sequi.*" *Étude d'un thème dans l'oeuvre de saint Cyprien.* Paris: Études augustiniennes, 1979.

Démarolle, J. M. "Les femmes chrétiennes vues par Porphyre." *Jahrbuch für Antike und Christentum* (1970) 13:42–47.

Dembińska, M. "Diet. A Comparison of Food Consumption in Some Eastern and Western Monasteries in the 4th–12th centuries." *Byzantion* (1985) 55:431–462.

Dening, Greg. *Islands and Beaches.* Melbourne: Melbourne University Press, 1980.

Der Nersessian, Sirarpie. *Armenian Art.* London: Thames and Hudson, 1978.

De Ste. Croix, G. E. M. *The Class Struggle in the Ancient Greek World.* London: Duckworth, 1981.

De Veer, A. C. *Premières polémiques contre Julien.* Bibliothèque augustinienne 23. Paris: Desclée de Brouwer, 1974.

Devos, Paul. "Silvie la sainte pèlerine." *Analecta Bollandiana* (1973) 91:105–120.

Diaz y Diaz, Manuel C. "L'expansion du christianisme et les tensions épiscopales dans la péninsule ibérique." *Miscellanea Historiae Ecclesiasticae*, no. 6, pp. 84–94. Bibliothèque de la Revue d'Histoire Ecclésiastique, fasc. 67. Brussels: Nauwelaerts, 1983.

Di Benedetto, F. "Un nuovo frammento delle Ipotiposi di Clemente Alessandrino." *Sileno* (1983) 9:75–82.

Dihle, Albrecht. *The Theory of Will in Classical Antiquity.* Berkeley and Los Angeles: University of California Press, 1982.

Dillon, John. "The Academy in the Middle Platonic Period." *Dionysus* (1979) 3:63–77.

—— "Aesthésis Noété: a doctrine of spiritual senses in Origen and Plotinus." In A. Caquot, M. Hadas-Lebel and J. Riaud. *Judaica et Hellenica: Hommage à V. Nikiprowetzky*, pp. 443–455. Louvain and Paris: Peters, 1986.

Dionisotti, A. C. "From Ausonius' Schooldays? A Schoolbook and Its Relatives." *Journal of Roman Studies* (1982) 72:83–125.

D'Izarnay, R. "Mariage et consécration virginale au ivème siècle." *Vie Spirituelle: Supplément* (1953) 24:92–107.

Dodds, E. R. *Pagan and Christian in an Age of Anxiety.* Cambridge: Cambridge University Press, 1965.

Dörries, H. *Die Theologie des Makarios/Symeon.* Abhandlungen der Akademie der Wissenschaft in Göttingen, Philol.-Hist. Klasse, 3. Folge, Nr. 103. Göttingen: Vandenhoeck and Ruprecht, 1978.

Douglas, Mary. *Purity and Danger.* London: Ark Paperbacks, 1985.

Drijvers, Han J. W. "Conflict and Alliance in Manichaeism." In H. G. Kippenberg, ed. *Struggles of Gods*, pp. 99–124. Religion and Reason 31. Berlin, New York and Amsterdam: Mouton, 1984.

—— *East of Antioch.* London: Variorum Reprints, 1984.

—— "Hellenistic and Oriental Origins." In S. Hackel, ed. *The Byzantine Saint,* pp. 25–33. Studies Supplementary to Sobornost 5. London: Fellowship of St. Alban, 1981.

—— "Jews and Christians at Edessa." *Journal of Jewish Studies* (1985) 36:88–102.

—— "Die Legende des heiligen Alexius und der Typus des Gottesmannes im syrischen Christentum." In M. Schmidt and C. F. Geyer, eds. *Typus, Symbol, Allegorie bei den östlichen Vätern und ihren Parallelen im Mittelalter*, pp. 187–217. Regensburg: Pustet, 1981.

—— "Marcionism in Syria: Principles, Problems and Polemics." *The Second Century* (1987).

—— "Odes of Solomon and Psalms of Mani: Christians and Manichaeans in Third-Century Syria." In R. van den Broek and M. J. Vermaseren, eds. *Studies in Gnosticism and Hellenistic Religions Presented to Gilles Quispel*, pp. 117–130. Leiden: Brill, 1981.

—— "Spätantike Parallelen zur altchristlichen Heiligenverehrung unter besonderer Berücksichtigung des syrischen Styliten-Kultes." In F. von Lilienfeld, ed. *Aspekte frühchristlicher Heiligenverehrung*, pp. 54–76. Oikonomia 6. Erlangen: Copy Center, 1977.

—— In M. Eliade, ed. *The Encyclopedia of Religion*, 15:279–281, s.v. "Virginity." New York: Macmillan, 1987.

Dronke, Peter. *Women Writers of the Middle Ages*. Cambridge: Cambridge University Press, 1984.

Duchrow, Ulrich. "Zum Prolog von Augustins *De Doctrina Christiana*." *Vigiliae Christianae* (1963) 17:165–172.

Duckworth, Colin, and Eric F. Osborn. "Clement of Alexandria's *Hypotyposeis*: A French Eighteenth-Century Sighting." *Journal of Theological Studies* (1985) n.s. 36:67–83.

Dumont, L. "World Renunciation in Indian Religions." *Religion, Politics and History in India*, pp. 33–60. Paris, The Hague: Mouton, 1970.

Duncan-Jones, R. *The Economy of the Roman Empire*. Cambridge: Cambridge University Press, 1974.

Duval, Y.-M. "Julian d'Éclane et Rufin d'Aquilée." *Revue des études augustiniennes* (1978) 24:243–271.

—— "L'originalité de *de virginibus* dans le mouvement ascétique occidental: Ambroise, Cyprien, Athanase." In Duval, ed. *Ambroise de Milan: xvième centénaire de son élection épiscopale*, pp. 9–66. Paris: Études augustiniennes, 1974.

—— "Pélage est-il le censeur inconnu de l' *Adversus Iovinianum* à Rome en 393; ou: du "portrait-robot" de l'hérétique chez saint Jérôme." *Revue d'histoire ecclésiastique* (1980) 75:525–557.

—— "La Problématique de la *Lettre aux vierges* d'Athanase." *Le Muséon* (1975) 88:405–433.

—— "Tertullien contre Origène sur la résurrection de la chair: dans le *Contra Johannem Hierosolymitanum*, 23–36 de saint Jérôme." *Revue des études augustiniennes* (1971) 17:227–278.

Elm, Susannah K. "The Organization and Institutions of Female Asceticism in Fourth-Century Cappadocia and Egypt." D. Phil., Oxford, 1987.

Elze, M. *Tatian and seine Theologie*. Forschungen zur Kirchen- und Dogmengeschichte 9. Göttingen: Vandenhoeck and Ruprecht, 1960.

Evans, G. R. *Augustine on Evil*. Cambridge: Cambridge University Press, 1982.

Evans, Robert F. *Pelagius: Inquiries and Reappraisals*. London: Adam and Charles Black, 1968.

Evelyn-White, H. G. *The Monasteries of the Wadî'n Natrûn Pt. 2: The History of the Monasteries of Nitria and Scetis*. New York: Metropolitan Museum of Art, 1932.

Eyben, E. "Family Planning in Graeco-Roman Antiquity." *Ancient Society* (1980/81) 11/12:5–82.

Faivre, A. *Naissance d'une hiérarchie*. Théologie historique 40. Paris: Beauchesne, 1977.

Fantham, E. "Sex, Status and Survival in Hellenistic Athens: A Study of Women in New Comedy." *Phoenix* (1975) 29:44–74.

Feeley-Harnick, G. "Is Historical Anthropology Possible? The Case of the Runaway Slave." In G. Tucker and D. Knight, eds. *Humanizing America's Iconic Book*, pp. 95–126. Chico, California: Scholars Press, 1982.

Fehrle, E. *Die kultische Keuschheit im Altertum*. Religionsgeschichtliche Versuche und Vorarbeiten 6. Giessen: A. Töpelmann, 1910.

Feldmann, Erich. *Der Einfluss des Hortensius und des Manichäismus auf das Denken des jungen Augustinus von 373*. Inaugural Dissertation, Wilhelms-Universität, Münster-in-Westfalen, 1975.

Fellechner, E. L. *Askese und Caritas bei den drei Kappadokiern*. Inaugural Dissertation, Heidelberg, 1979.

Festugière, A. J. *Antioch païenne et chrétienne*. Bibliothèque des écoles françaises d'Athènes et de Rome 194. Paris: de Boccard, 1959.

—— *La Révélation d'Hermès Trismégiste*. 4 vols. Paris: J. Gabalda, 1944–1954.

Fiey, J. M. "Les Marcionites dans les textes historiques de l'Église de Perse." *Le Muséon* (1970) 83:183–88.

Flecker, G. *Amphilochiana*. Leipzig: J. A. Barth, 1906.

Flusin, R. *Miracle et Histoire dans l'oeuvre de Cyrille de Scythopolis*. Paris: Etudes augustiniennes, 1983.

Foucault, Michel. "Le Combat de la chasteté." *Communications* (1982) 35:15–25. Now in P. Ariès and A. Béjin, eds. q.v. *Western Sexuality: Practice and Precept in Past and Present Times*, pp. 14–25.

—— *Le Souci de Soi*. Paris: Gallimard, 1984. English translation: R. Hurley, trans. *The Care of the Self*. New York: Pantheon, 1985.

—— *L'usage des plaisirs*. Paris: Gallimard, 1984. English translation: R. Hurley, trans. *The Use of Pleasures*. New York: Pantheon Books, 1985.

Fowden, Garth. *The Egyptian Hermes: a historical approach to the late pagan mind*. Cambridge: Cambridge University Press, 1986.

—— "The Pagan Holy Man in Late Antique Society." *Journal of Hellenic Studies* (1982) 102:33–59.

—— "The Platonist Philosopher and his Circle in Late Antiquity." *Philosophia* (Athens/1977) 7:359–383.

Fraade, Steven D. "Ascetical Aspects of Ancient Judaism." In A. Green, ed.

World Spirituality. Vol. 13, *Jewish Spirituality: From the Bible to the Middle Ages*, pp. 253–288. New York: Crossroad, 1986.

Fredriksen, Paula. "Paul and Augustine: conversion narratives, orthodox traditions, and the retrospective self." *Journal of Theological Studies* (1986) n.s. 37:3–34.

Frier, Bruce W. "The Demography of the Early Roman Empire." In *The Cambridge Ancient History*. Cambridge: Cambridge University Press, forthcoming.

—— "Roman Life Expectancy: Ulpian's Evidence." *Harvard Studies in Classical Philology* (1982) 86:213–251.

Frischer, B. *The Sculpted Word: Epicureanism and Philosophical Recruitment in Ancient Greece*. Berkeley and Los Angeles: University of California Press, 1982.

Frye, Northrop. *The Secular Scripture: A Study of the Structure of Romance*. Cambridge: Harvard University Press, 1976.

Fuchs, Eric. *Sexual Desire and Love*. New York: Seabury Press, 1983.

Gager, J. M. *The Origins of Anti-Semitism*. Oxford: Oxford University Press, 1983.

Garnsey, Peter. *Social Status and Legal Privilege in the Roman Empire*. Oxford: Oxford University Press, 1971.

—— and Richard Saller. *The Roman Empire: Economy, Society and Culture*. London: Duckworth, 1987.

Giannarelli, Elena. *La tipologia femminile nella biografia e l'autobiografia cristiana del ivo secolo*. Istituto storico italiano per il Medio Evo: Studi storici 127. Rome: Sede dell'Istituto, 1980.

Giron, N. *Légendes coptes*. Paris: P. Geuthner, 1907.

Gleason, Maud W. "Festive Satire: Julian's *Misopogon* and the New Year at Antioch." *Journal of Roman Studies* (1986) 76:106–119.

Goehring, James E. *The "Letter of Ammon" and Pachomian Monasticism*. Patristische Texte und Studien 27. Berlin, New York: de Gruyter, 1986.

—— "New Frontiers in Pachomian Studies." In Birger A. Pearson and James E. Goehring, eds. q.v. *The Roots of Egyptian Christianity*, pp. 236–257.

Golb, Norman. "Les manuscrits de la Mer Morte." *Annales É.S.C.* (1985) 40:1133–1149.

—— "The Problem of the Origin and Identification of the Dead Sea Scrolls." *Proceedings of the American Philosophical Society* (1980) 124:1–24.

Goodman, Martin. *State and Society in Roman Galilee, A.D. 132–212*. Totowa, New Jersey: Rowman and Allanheld, 1983.

Goody, Jack. *The Development of the Family and Marriage in Europe*. Cambridge: Cambridge University Press, 1983.

Gottlieb, G. "Der Mailänder Kirchenstreit von 385/6." *Museum Helveticum* (1985) 43:37–55.

Goulet-Cazé, M. O. "L'arrière-plan scolaire de la *Vie de Plotin*." In L. Brisson, ed. q.v. *Porphyre. La Vie de Plotin I: Travaux Préliminaires*, pp. 231–276.

Green, Henry A. "Ritual in Valentinian Gnosticism: A Sociological Interpretation." *Journal of Religious History* (1982) 12:109–124.

Greshake, Gisbert. *Gnade als konkrete Freiheit*. Mainz: Grünewald, 1972.

Gribomont, J. "Un aristocrate révolutionnaire, évêque et moine: S. Basile." *Augustinianum* (1977) 17:179–191.

—— "Le dossier des origines du messalianisme." In J. Fontaine and C. Kannengiesser, eds. *Epektasis, Mélanges offerts au cardinal J. Daniélou*, pp. 611–625. Paris: Beauchesne, 1972.

—— *Dictionnaire de la Spiritualité*, fasc. 68–69, coll. 1536–1547, s.v. "Monachisme." Paris: Beauchesne, 1979.

—— "Le monachisme au sein de l'Église en Syrie et en Cappadoce." *Studia Monastica* (1965) 7:7–24.

—— "Le Monachisme au ive s. en Asie Mineure. De Gangres au Messalianisme." *Studia Patristica* 2, pp. 400–415. Texte und Untersuchungen 64. Berlin: Akademie-Verlag, 1957.

—— "Le panégyrique de la virginité, oeuvre de jeunesse de Grégoire de Nysse." *Revue d'ascétique et mystique* (1967) 42:249–260.

Griffin, Jasper. "Augustan Poetry and the Life of Luxury." *Journal of Roman Studies* (1976) 66:87–105.

Griffin, Miriam. *Seneca: A Philosopher in Politics*. Oxford: Oxford University Press, 1976.

Griffith, Sidney H. "Ephraem, the Deacon of Edessa, and the Church of the Empire." In T. Halton and J. P. Williman, eds. *Diakonia: Studies in Honor of Robert T. Meyer*, pp. 22–52. Washington D.C.: Catholic University of America Press, 1986.

Grodzynski, Denise. "Ravies et coupables: un essai d'interprétation de la loi ix.24.1 du Codex Théodosien." *Mélanges de l'école française de Rome: Antiquité* (1984) 96:697–726.

Grosdidier de Matons, J. *Romanos le Mélode*. Paris: Beauchesne, 1977.

—— "Thèmes d'édification dans la "Vie d'André Salos." *Travaux et Mémoires* (1970) 4:277–328.

Gryson, R. *The Ministry of Women in the Early Church*. Collegeville, Minnesota: Liturgical Press, 1976.

—— *Les origines du célibat ecclésiastique*. Gembloux: J. Duculot, 1970.

Guillaumont, A. "Christianisme et Gnoses dans l'Orient préislamique." *Annuaire du Collège de France 1981–82*, pp. 425–433.

—— "La conception du désert chez les moines d'Égypte." *Revue de l'Histoire des Religions* (1975) 188:3–21.

—— *Les "Kephalaia Gnostica" d'Évagre le Pontique*. Patristica Sorbonensia 5. Paris: Le Seuil, 1962.

—— "Monachisme et éthique judéo-chrétienne." *Judéo-christianisme: volume offert au cardinal Daniélou. Recherches de science religieuse* (1972) 60:199–218.

—— "Le nom des 'Agapètes'." *Vigiliae Christianae* (1969) 23:30–37.

—— "Situation et Signification du *Liber Graduum* dans la spiritualité syriaque." *Symposium Syriacum 1972*, pp. 311–325. Orientalia Christiana Analecta 107. Rome: Vatican, 1974.

Gunawardana, R. A. L. H. *Robe and Plough: Monasticism and Economic Interest in Early Medieval Sri Lanka*. Tucson: University of Arizona Press, 1979.

Gunday, R. H. *Sôma in Biblical Theology: with Emphasis on Pauline Anthropology*. Cambridge: Cambridge University Press, 1976.

Gurevič, A. J. *Contadini e santi.* Turin: Einaudi, 1986.

Hadot, I. "The Spiritual Guide." In A. H. Armstrong, ed. *World Spirituality.* Vol. 15, *Classical Mediterranean Spirituality: Egyptian, Greek, Roman,* pp. 436–459. New York: Crossroad, 1986.

Hadot, Jean. *Penchant Mauvais et Volonté Libre dans la Sagesse de Ben Sira (Ecclésiastique).* Brussels: Presses Universitaires, 1972.

Hadot, Pierre. *Exercices spirituels et philosophie antique.* Paris: Études augustiniennes, 1981.

—— *Léçon inaugurale. Chaire d'histoire de la pensée hellénistique et romaine.* Paris: Collège de France, 1983.

—— *Plotin.* 2nd ed. Paris: Études augustiniennes, 1973.

Hammond, C. P. "The Last Ten Years of Rufinus' Life and the Date of His Move South from Aquileia." *Journal of Theological Studies* (1977) n.s. 28:372–429.

Harl, Marguerite. "Adam et les deux arbres du Paradis." *Recherches de science religieuse* (1962) 50:321–388.

—— ed. *Écriture et culture philosophique dans la pensée de Grégoire de Nysse.* Leiden: Brill, 1971.

—— "Le langage de l'expérience religieuse chez les pères grecs." *Rivista di storia e letteratura religiosa* (1972) 12:5–34.

—— *Origène et la fonction révélatrice du Verbe incarné.* Paris: Le Seuil, 1958.

—— "La prise de conscience de la 'nudité' d'Adam. Une interprétation de Genèse 3, 7 chez les Pères Grecs." *Studia Patristica* 7, pp. 486–495. Texte und Untersuchungen 92. Berlin: Akademie-Verlag, 1966.

—— "Recherches sur l'origénisme d'Origène: la 'satiété' (kóros) de la contemplation comme motif de la chute des âmes." *Studia Patristica* 8, pp. 373–405. *Texte und Untersuchungen* 93. Berlin: Akademie-Verlag, 1966.

Harnack, A. von. *Marcion: das Evangelium vom fremden Gott.* Leipzig: J. C. Hinrichs, 1921.

—— *Mission und Ausbreitung des Christentums.* Leipzig: J. C. Hinrichs, 1906.

—— "Der pseudocyprianische Traktat 'de singularitate clericorum'." *Texte und Untersuchungen.* N.F. 9:3. Leipzig: J. C. Hinrichs, 1903.

Harrauer, H., and P. J. Sijpesteijn, "Eine neues Dokument zu Roms Indienhandel." *Anzeiger der österreichischen Akademie der Wissenschaften* (1986) 112, no. 7.

Harries, Jill. " 'Treasures in Heaven': Property and Inheritance among Senators of Late Rome." In Elizabeth M. Craik, ed. *Marriage and Property,* pp. 54–70. Aberdeen: Aberdeen University Press, 1984.

Harris, W. V. "The Roman Father's Power of Life and Death." In R. S. Bagnall and W. V. Harris, eds. *Studies in Roman Law in Memory of A. Arthur Schiller,* pp. 81–95. Leiden: Brill, 1986.

Harvey, Susan Ashbrook. "Women in Early Syrian Christianity." In Averil Cameron and Amélie Kuhrt, eds. q.v. *Images of Women in Antiquity,* pp. 288–298.

Haspels, C. H. Emilie. *The Highlands of Phrygia: Sites and Monuments,* vol. 1. Princeton: Princeton University Press, 1972.

Hastrup, K. "The Semantics of Biology: Virginity." In S. Ardener, ed. *Defining Females: The Nature of Women in Society*, pp. 49–65. New York: John Wiley, 1978.

Hauschild, W.-D. *Theologische Realenzyklopädie*, 10, pp. 547–550, s.v. "Eustathius von Sebaste." Berlin: de Gruyter, 1982.

—— *Gottes Geist und der Mensch*. Munich: Chr. Kaiser, 1972.

Helcke, W., and W. Westerdorf, eds. *Lexikon der Ägyptologie*, 4, pp. 292–294, s.v. "Nacktheit." Wiesbaden: Harrassowitz, 1982.

Helderman, Jan. *Die Anapausis im "Evangelium Veritatis."* Nag Hammadi Studies 18. Leiden: Brill, 1984.

Herbert, George. *Church Monuments*. Edited by R. A. Willmott. London: Routledge, 1854.

Héring, J. *The First Epistle of Saint Paul to the Corinthians*. London: Epworth Press, 1962.

Hesse, O. "Das Böse bei Markus Eremites." In W. Strothmann, ed. *Makarios-Symposium über das Böse*, pp. 109–122. Göttinger Orientforschungen 1, no. 24. Wiesbaden: Harrassowitz, 1983.

Holum, K. "Pulcheria's Crusade A.D. 421–22 and the Ideology of Imperial Victory." *Greek, Roman and Byzantine Studies* (1977) 18:153–172.

—— *Theodosian Empresses: Women and Imperial Dominion in Late Antiquity*. Berkeley and Los Angeles: University of California Press, 1982.

Holte, R. *Béatitude et Sagesse*. Paris: Études augustiniennes, 1962.

Hopkins, Keith. "The Age of Roman Girls at Marriage." *Population Studies* (1965) 18:309–327.

—— "Brother-Sister Marriage in Roman Egypt." *Comparative Studies in Society and History* (1980) 22:303–354.

—— "Contraception in the Roman Empire." *Comparative Studies in Society and History* (1965) 8:124–151.

—— "Murderous Games." In *Death and Renewal*, 1–30. Cambridge: Cambridge University Press, 1983.

—— "On the Probable Age Structure of the Roman Population." *Population Studies* (1966) 20:245–264.

Humphreys, Sarah C. *The Family, Women, and Death: comparative studies*. London: Routledge and Kegan Paul, 1983.

Hunt, E. D. *Holy Land Pilgrimage in the Later Roman Empire*. Oxford: Clarendon Press, 1982.

Hunter, David G. "Resistance to the Virginal Ideal in Late-Fourth-Century Rome: The Case of Jovinian." *Theological Studies* (1987) 48:45–64.

Isaacs, Marie E. *The Concept of Spirit. A Study of Pneuma in Hellenistic Judaism and its Bearing on the New Testament*. London: Heythrop Monographs, 1976.

Jacquart, Danielle, and Claude Thomasset. *Sexualité et savoir médical au Moyen-Âge*. Paris: Presses Universitaires de France, 1985.

Janowski, Bernd, and Hermann Lichtenberger. "Enderwartung und Reinheitsidee zur eschatologischen Deutung von Reinheit und Sühne in der Qumrangemeinde." *Journal of Jewish Studies* (1983) 34:31–62.

Jones, A. H. M. *The Later Roman Empire,* 3 vols. Oxford: Basil Blackwell, 1964.
Jones, A. H. M., J. R. Martindale, and J. Morris. *Prosopography of the Later Roman Empire,* vol. 1. Cambridge: Cambridge University Press, 1971.
Jones, C. P. "A Family of Pisidian Antioch." *Phoenix* (1982) 36:264–271.
—— *Plutarch and Rome.* Oxford: Clarendon Press, 1971.
Judge, E. A. "The Earliest Use of the Word 'Monachos' for Monk (P. Coll. Youtie 77) and the Origins of Monasticism." *Jahrbuch für Antike und Christentum* (1977) 20:72–89.
Junod, E., and J.-D. Kaestli. *L'Histoire des Actes Apocryphes des Apôtres du iiie au ixe siècle: le cas des Actes de Jean.* Cahiers de la Revue de Théologie et Philosophie 7. Geneva: Cahiers de la revue de théologie et de philosophie, 1982.

Kasser, R. *Kellia: Recherches suisses d'archéologie copte Pt. 1: Kellia 1965.* Geneva: Georg, 1967.
Kazhdan, A. P., and Giles Constable, eds. *People and Power in Byzantium: an Introduction to Modern Byzantine Studies.* Washington, D.C.: Dumbarton Oaks, Center for Byzantine Studies, 1982.
Kazhdan, A. P., and A. Cutler. "Continuity and Discontinuity in Byzantine History." *Byzantion* (1982) 52:429–478.
Kee, H.C. "The Ethical Dimensions of the Testaments of the XII Patriarchs as a Clue to Provenance." *New Testament Studies* (1978) 24:259–270.
Kelly, J. N. D. *Jerome.* London: Duckworth, 1975.
Kennedy, Hugh. "From *Polis* to *Madina*: Urban Change in Late Antique and Early Islamic Syria." *Past and Present* (1985) 106:3–27.
—— "The Last Century of Byzantine Syria: A Reinterpretation." *Byzantinische Forschungen* (1985) 19:141–184.
Keys, A., J. Brožek, et al. *The Biology of Human Starvation.* Minneapolis: University of Minnesota Press, 1950.
Kirk, K. E. *The Vision of God.* London: Longmans, 1932.
Kitzinger, E. *Byzantine Art in the Making.* Cambridge: Harvard University Press, 1977.
Klijn, A. F. J. "The 'Single One' in the Gospel of Thomas." *Journal of Biblical Literature* (1962) 81:271–278.
Koch, Hal. *Pronoia und Paideusis. Studien über Origenes und sein Verhältnis zum Platonismus.* Berlin: de Gruyter, 1932.
Kopecek, T. A. "The Social Class of the Cappadocian Fathers." *Church History* (1973) 42:453–466.
Koschorke, Klaus. *Die Polemik der Gnostiker gegen das kirchliche Christentum.* Nag Hammadi Studies 12. Leiden: Brill, 1978.
Kostof, S. *Caves of God. The Monastic Environment of Byzantine Cappadocia.* Cambridge: Massachusetts Institute of Technology Press, 1972.
Kötting, B. "Univira in Inschriften." In W. van den Boer, et al., ed. *Romanitas et Christianitas. Studien I. H. Waszink oblata,* pp. 195–206. Amsterdam: North Holland, 1973.
Kraeling, C. H. *Gerasa: City of the Decapolis.* New Haven, Connecticut: American Schools of Oriental Research, 1938.

Krautheimer, Richard. *Three Christian Capitals: Topography and Politics.* Berkeley and Los Angeles: University of California Press, 1983.

Kretschmar, G. "Ein Beitrag zur Frage nach dem Ursprung frühchristlicher Askese." *Zeitschrift für Theologie und Kirche* (1961) 64:27–67.

Kümmel, W. G. *Römer 7 und das Bild des Menschen im Neuen Testament.* Munich: Kaiser, 1974.

Ladner, G. B. "The Philosophical Anthropology of Saint Gregory of Nyssa." *Dumbarton Oaks Papers* (1958) 12:61–94.

Laeuchli, S. *Power and Sexuality: The Emergence of Canon Law at the Synod of Elvira.* Philadelphia: Temple University Press, 1972.

Laistner, M. L. W. *Christianity and Pagan Culture in the Later Roman Empire.* Ithaca, New York: Cornell University Press, 1951.

Lane Fox, Robin. *Pagans and Christians.* New York: Knopf, 1987.

Laqueur, Thomas. "Orgasm, Generation, and the Politics of Reproductive Biology." *Representations* (1986) 14:1–41.

Lardreau, Guy. *Discours philosophique et discours spirituel. Autour de la philosophie spirituelle de Philoxène de Mabboug.* Paris: Le Seuil, 1985.

Layton, B., ed. *The Rediscovery of Gnosticism.* Vol. 1, *The School of Valentinus.* Leiden: Brill, 1980.

Le Boulluec, Alain. *La notion d'hérésie dans la littérature grecque, iie-iiie siècles.* 2 vols. Paris: Études augustiniennes, 1985.

LeGoff, Jacques. *L'imaginaire mediéval.* Paris: Gallimard, 1985.

Leipoldt, J. *Schenute von Atripe.* Texte und Untersuchungen 25. Leipzig: J. C. Hinrichs, 1904.

Lepelley, Claude. *Les cités de l'Afrique romaine au Bas-Empire.* Vol. 1, *La permanence d'une civilisation municipale.* Paris: Études augustiniennes, 1979.

—— "La crise de l'Afrique romaine au début du vème siècle." *Académie des Inscriptions et Belles Lettres, Comptes rendus 1981,* pp. 445–463.

Leroux, J. M. "Saint Jean Chrysostome et le monachisme." in C. Kannengiesser, ed. *Jean Chrysostome et Augustin,* pp. 125–144. Théologie historique 35. Paris: Beauchesne, 1975.

Levene, A. *The Early Syrian Fathers on Genesis.* London: Taylor's Foreign Press, 1951.

Lévi-Strauss, Claude. *Structural Anthropology.* Translated by C. Jacobson and B. Grundfest Schoepf. Harmondsworth: Peregrine, 1977.

Lichtheim, Miriam. *Late Egyptian Wisdom Literature in the International Context.* Göttingen: Vandenhoeck and Ruprecht, 1983.

Liebeschuetz, J. H. W. G. *Antioch.* Oxford: Oxford University Press, 1972.

—— "Friends and Enemies of John Chrysostom." In Ann Moffat, ed. *Maistor: Classical, Byzantine and Renaissance Studies for Robert Browning,* pp. 85–111. Byzantina Australiensia 5. Canberra: Australian Association for Byzantine Studies, 1984.

Lieu, S. N. C. *Manichaeism in the Later Roman Empire and Medieval China.* Manchester: Manchester University Press, 1985.

Lilla, Salvatore R. C. *Clement of Alexandria: A Study in Christian Platonism and Gnosticism.* Oxford: Oxford University Press, 1971.

Lochner, C. *Die Ehre einer Frau in Israel*. Göttingen: Vandenhoeck and Ruprecht, 1986.

Long, A. A. *Hellenistic Philosophy*. London: Duckworth, 1974.

Lorenz, R. "Die Anfänge des abendländischen Mönchtums im 4. Jahrhundert." *Zeitschrift für Kirchengeschichte* (1966) 77:1–61.

—— "Gnade und Erkenntnis bei Augustin." *Zeitschrift für Kirchengeschichte* (1964) 75:21–78.

Lyne, R. O. A. M. *The Latin Love Poets*. Oxford: Clarendon Press, 1980.

McCail, R. S. "The erotic and ascetic poetry of Agathias Scholasticus." *Byzantion* (1971) 41:205–267.

MacCormack, Sabine G. *Art and Ceremony in Late Antiquity*. Berkeley and Los Angeles: University of California Press, 1981.

—— "Christ and Empire, Time and Ceremonial in Sixth-Century Byzantium." *Byzantion* (1982) 52:287–309.

—— "Roma, Constantinopolis, the Emperor and his Genius." *Classical Quarterly* (1975) n.s. 25:131–150.

MacCoull, Leslie S. B. "Child Donations and Child Saints in Coptic Egypt." *Eastern European Quarterly* (1980) 13:409–415.

—— "Coptic Documentary Papyri as a Historical Source for Egyptian Christianity." In Birger A. Pearson and James E. Goehring, eds. q.v. *The Roots of Egyptian Christianity*, pp. 42–50.

—— "Notes on the Social Structure of late antique Aphrodito." *Bulletin de la societé d'archéologie copte* (1984) 26:65–77.

Maclean, Ian. *The Renaissance Notion of Woman*. Cambridge: Cambridge University Press, 1980.

MacMullen, Ramsay. *Christianizing the Roman Empire (A.D. 100–400)*. New Haven, Connecticut: Yale University Press, 1984.

—— "Roman Attitudes to Greek Love." *Historia* (1982) 31:484–502.

—— *Roman Social Relations*. New Haven, Connecticut: Yale University Press, 1974.

—— "Woman in Public in the Roman Empire." *Historia* (1980) 29:208–18.

McNamara, Jo Ann. "Cornelia's Daughters: Paula and Eustochium." *Women's Studies* (1984) 11:9–27.

—— *A New Song: Celibate Women in the First Three Christian Centuries*. Binghamton, New York: Harrington Park Press, 1985.

Madec, Goulven. *Saint Ambroise et la philosophie*. Paris: Études augustiniennes, 1974.

Mahé, J. P. "Le sens des symboles sexuels dans quelques textes hermétiques et gnostiques." In J. E. Ménard, ed. *Les Textes de Nag Hammadi*, pp. 123–145. Nag Hammadi Studies 7. Leiden: Brill, 1975.

Mandouze, André. *Saint Augustin. L'aventure de la raison et de la grâce*. Paris: Études augustiniennes, 1968.

Mango, C. A. *The Brazen House*. Copenhagen: E. Munksgaard, 1959.

—— *Byzantium, the Empire of New Rome*. London: Weidenfeld and Nicolson, 1980.

Mango, C. A., and I. Ševčenko. "Some recently acquired Byzantine inscriptions at the Istanbul Museum." *Dumbarton Oaks Papers* (1978) 32:1–27.

Mano-Zisi, Dj. *Reallexikon zur byzantinischen Kunst*, 3, coll. 687–717, s.v. "Justiniana prima" [Caričin Grad]. Stuttgart: A. Hiersemann, 1976.

Markus, R. A. *Augustine: A Collection of Critical Essays*. New York: Doubleday Anchor, 1972.

—— *Saeculum: History and Society in the Theology of Saint Augustine.* Cambridge: Cambridge University Press, 1970.

Marrou, H. I. "L'origine orientale des diaconies romaines." *Mélanges d'archéologie et d'histoire* (1940) 47:95–142. In *Patristique et Humanisme*, pp. 81–118. Patristica Sorbonensia 9. Paris: Le Seuil, 1976.

—— *Décadence romaine ou antiquité tardive?* Paris: Le Seuil, 1977.

—— "L'arianisme comme phénomène alexandrin." In *Patristique et Humanisme*, pp. 321–330. Patristica Sorbonensia 9. Paris: Le Seuil, 1976. (First published in *Académie des Inscriptions et Belles Lettres, Comptes rendus 1973*, pp. 533–542.)

Martikainen, J. "Das Böse in den Schriften des Syrers Ephraim, im Stufenbuch und im *Corpus Macarianum*." In W. Strothmann, ed. *Makarios-Symposium über das Böse*, pp. 36–46. Göttinger Orientforschungen 1, no. 24. Wiesbaden: Harrassowitz, 1983.

Martimort, A. G. *Les Diaconesses: essai historique.* Rome: Edizioni liturgiche, 1982.

Martin, Annick. "Aux origines de l'église copte." *Revue des études anciennes* (1981) 83:35–56.

—— "L'église et la khôra égyptienne au ive siècle." *Revue des études augustiniennes* (1979) 26:3–26.

Martin, J. R. *The Illustrations of the Heavenly Ladder of John Climacus.* Princeton: Princeton University Press, 1954.

Martindale, J. R., ed. *The Prosopography of the Later Roman Empire*, vol. 2. Cambridge: Cambridge University Press, 1980.

Marx, A. "Les racines du célibat essénien." *Revue de Qumran* (1970) 7:323–342.

Maspéro, J. "Horapollon et la fin du paganisme égyptien." *Bulletin de l'Institut français d'archéologie orientale du Caire* (1914) 11:163–195.

Matthews, John. *Western Aristocracies and Imperial Court.* Oxford: Clarendon Press, 1975.

May, G. "Die Chronologie des Lebens und der Werke des Gregors von Nyssa." In M. Harl, ed. q.v. *Écriture et culture philosophique dans la pensée de Grégoire de Nysse*, pp. 51–66.

Meeks, Wayne A. *The First Urban Christians: The Social World of the Apostle Paul.* New Haven, Connecticut: Yale University Press, 1983.

—— "The Image of the Androgyne: some uses of a symbol in earliest Christianity." *History of Religions* (1974) 13:165–208.

Méhat, André. *Étude sur les 'Stromates' de Clément d'Alexandrie.* Patristica Sorbonensia 7. Paris: Le Seuil, 1966.

Ménard, J. E. *L'Évangile selon Philippe.* Strasbourg: Université de Strasbourg, Faculté de Théologie Catholique, 1969.

Mertens, C. "Les premiers martyrs et leur rêves." *Revue d'histoire ecclésiastique* (1986) 81:5–46.

Meslin, M. *Les Ariens d'Occident*. Patristica Sorbonensia 8. Paris: Le Seuil, 1967.

Metzger, C. *Musée du Louvre: Sarcophages en pierre d'époques romaine et paléochrétienne*. Paris: Réunion des musées nationaux, 1985.

Meyer, M. W. "Making Mary Male: The Categories 'Male' and 'Female' in the Gospel of Thomas." *New Testament Studies* (1985) 31:554–570.

Meyvaert, P. "Excerpts from an Unknown Treatise of Jerome to Gaudentius of Brescia." *Revue bénédictine* (1986) 96:203–218.

—— "Le *Libellus Responsionum* à Augustin de Cantorbéry: une oeuvre authentique de Saint Grégoire le Grand." In *Grégoire le Grand: Colloques internationaux du Centre National de Recherche Scientifique*, pp. 543–549. Paris: Éditions du C.N.R.S., 1986.

Miles, Margaret R. *Fullness of Life*. Philadelphia: Westminster Press, 1981.

Milovanović, C. "Apokrypha Dela Pavlova i njihov odnos prema antičkom grčkom romanu i kanonskim Delima Apostolskim." *Zbornik Radova Vizantinološkog Instituta* (1976) 17:295–407.

Mitchell, Stephen. "The Life of Saint Theodotus of Ancyra." *Anatolian Studies* (1982) 32:93–113.

Moine, Nicole. *Dictionnaire de la Spiritualité*, fasc. 66–67, coll. 955–960, s.v. "Mélanie l'Ancienne." Paris: Beauchesne, 1978.

Momigliano, Arnaldo D. "Ciò che Flavio Giuseppe non vide." *Rivista storica italiana* (1979) 91:564–574.

—— "The Life of Saint Macrina by Gregory of Nyssa." in J. W. Eade and J. Ober, eds. *The Craft of the Ancient Historian: Essays in Honor of C. G. Starr*, pp. 443–458. Ann Arbor: University of Michigan Press, 1975. (Now in *On Pagans, Jews, and Christians*, pp. 206–221. Middletown, Connecticut: Wesleyan University Press, 1987.)

Morony, Michael G. *Iraq After the Muslim Conquest*. Princeton: Princeton University Press, 1984.

Munro, W. *Authority in Paul and Peter*. Cambridge: Cambridge University Press, 1982.

Munz, Peter. "John Cassian." *Journal of Ecclesiastical History* (1960) 11:1–22.

Murphy, F. X. "Evagrius Ponticus and Origenism." In R. Hanson and F. Crouzel, eds. *Origeniana Tertia*, pp. 253–269. Rome: Ateneo, 1985.

Murray, Robert. *Theologische Realenzyklopädie*, 9, pp. 755–762. s.v. "Ephraem Syrus." Berlin: de Gruyter, 1982.

—— "The Exhortation to Candidates for Ascetical Vows at Baptism in the Ancient Syrian Church." *New Testament Studies* (1974–75) 21:59–80.

—— *Symbols of Church and Kingdom: A Study in Early Syriac Tradition*. Cambridge: Cambridge University Press, 1975.

—— "The Theory of Symbolism in St. Ephrem's Theology." *Parole de l'Orient* (1975/76) 6–7:1–20.

Musurillo, H. "The Problem of Ascetical Fasting in the Greek Patristic Writers." *Traditio* (1956) 12:1–64.

Nagel, P. "Lettre chrétienne sur papyrus." *Zeitschrift für Papyrologie und Epigraphik* (1975) 18:317–323.

Natali, A. "Église et évergétisme à Antioche à la fin du ivème siècle d'aprés

Jean Chrysostome." In E. Livingstone, ed. *Studia Patristica* 17, vol. 3, pp. 1176–1184. Oxford: Pergamon Press, 1982.

Nauerth, C., and R. Warns. *Thekla: ihre Bilder in der frühchristlichen Kunst.* Wiesbaden: Harrassowitz, 1981.

Nautin, P. "Études de chronologie hiéronymienne (393–397) 2." *Revue des études augustiniennes* (1973) 19:69–86.

—— *Lettres et écrivains chrétiens des iie et iiie siècles.* Paris: Le Cerf, 1961.

—— *Origène: sa vie et son oeuvre.* Paris: Beauchesne, 1977.

—— "Les premières relations d'Ambroise avec l'empereur Gratien." In Y. M. Duval, ed. q.v. *Ambroise de Milan*, pp. 229–244.

Nedungatt, G. "The Covenanters in the Early Syriac-Speaking Church." *Orientalia Christiana Periodica* (1973) 39:191–215.

Neumann, C. W. *The Virgin Mary in the Works of Saint Ambrose.* Paradosis 17. Fribourg-en-Suisse: University Press, 1962.

Neusner, J. *A History of the Mishnaic Law of Women.* Vol. 5, *The Mishnaic System of Women.* Leiden: Brill, 1980.

—— *Judaism, the Evidence of the Mishnah.* Chicago: University of Chicago Press, 1981.

Niederwimmer, Kurt. *Askese und Mysterium: Über Ehe, Ehescheidung und Eheverzicht in den Anfängen des christlichen Glaubens.* Göttingen: Vandenhoeck and Ruprecht, 1975.

Nietzsche, F. *Die fröhliche Wissenschaft.* Stuttgart: Kröner Taschenbuch, 1956.

Nock, A. D. "A Vision of Mandulis Aion." *Essays on Religion and the Ancient World*, 1:362–374. Oxford: Clarendon Press, 1982.

Noonan, J. T. *Contraception.* Cambridge: Harvard University Press, 1965.

Nuvolone, F. G., and A. Solignac. *Dictionnaire de la Spiritualité*, fasc. 83–85, coll. 2889–2942, s.v. "Pélage et Pélagianisme." Paris: Beauchesne, 1986.

Oesterle, H. J. "Probleme der Anthropologie bei Gregor von Nyssa." *Hermes* (1985) 113:101–114.

Oppenheimer, Aharon. *The ᶜAm ha-Aretz: A Study in the Social History of the Jewish People in the Hellenistic-Roman Period.* Leiden: Brill, 1977.

Orbe, A. "El pecado de Eva, signo de división." *Orientalia Christiana Periodica* (1963) 29:305–330.

—— "El pecado original y el matrimonio en la teologia del s. II." *Gregorianum* (1964) 45:449–500.

Orlandi, T. "Giustificazioni dell'Encratismo nei testi monastici copti del iv-v secolo." In Ugo Bianchi, ed. q.v. *La Tradizione dell'Enkrateia*, pp. 341–363.

Padel, R. "Women: Model for Possession by Greek Daemons." In Averil Cameron and Amélie Kuhrt, eds. q.v. *Images of Women in Late Antiquity*, pp. 3–19.

Pagels, Elaine. "Gnostic and Orthodox Views of Christ's Passion: Paradigms of the Christian Response to Persecution?" In B. Layton, ed. q.v. *The Rediscovery of Gnosticism 1: The School of Valentinus*, pp. 262–288.

—— *The Gnostic Gospels.* New York: Random House, 1979.

—— *The Gnostic Paul.* Philadelphia: Fortress Press, 1979.

—— *The Johannine Gospel in Gnostic Exegesis.* Society of Biblical Literature Monograph Series 17. Nashville and New York: Abingdon Press, 1973.

Palol Salellas, Pedro de. "La conversion de l'aristocratie de la Péninsule ibérique au ivème siècle." *Miscellanea Historiae Ecclesiasticae*, no. 6, pp. 47–69. Bibliothèque de la Revue d'Histoire Ecclésiastique, fasc. 67, Brussels: Nauwelaerts, 1983.

Patlagean, Evelyne. "Byzance et le blason pénal du corps." In *Du Châtiment dans la Cité*, pp. 405–427. Collection de l'École française de Rome 79. Rome: Palais Farnèse, 1984.

—— "L'enfant et son avenir dans la famille byzantine." *Enfant et Sociétés: Annales de démographie historique* (1973), pp. 85–93.

—— "Familles chrétiennes d'Asie mineure et histoire démographique du ive siècle." *Antiquitas* (1978) Reihe 1, no. 29:169–186.

—— "L'histoire de la femme déguisée en moine et l'évolution de la sainteté féminine à Byzance." *Studi medievali* (1976) ser. 3, 17:597–623.

—— *Pauvreté économique et pauvreté sociale à Byzance.* Paris and The Hague: Mouton, 1977.

—— "Sur la limitation de la fécondité dans la haute époque byzantine." *Annales É.S.C.* (1969) 24:1353–1369. English translation: R. Forster and O. Ranum, eds., and E. Forster and P. M. Ranum, trans. "Birth Control in the Early Byzantine Empire." *Biology of Man in History*, pp. 1–22. Baltimore: Johns Hopkins University Press, 1975.

Patrucco, Marcella Forlin. "Aspetti di vita familiare nel iv secolo negli scritti dei padri cappadoci." In R. Cantalamassa, ed. q.v. *Etica sessuale e matrimonio nel cristianesimo delle origini*, pp. 158–179.

Patterson, Cynthia. " 'Not Worth the Rearing': The Causes of Infant Exposure in Ancient Greece." *Transactions of the American Philological Association* (1985) 114:103–24.

Payer, Pierre J. *Sex and the Penitentials.* Toronto: University of Toronto Press, 1984.

Pearson, Birger A., and James E. Goehring, eds. *The Roots of Egyptian Christianity.* Philadelphia: Fortress Press, 1986.

Pellegrino, M. "Il platonismo di Gregorio di Nissa." *Rivista di filologia neoscolastica* (1938) 30:437–474.

Perkins, Judith. "The Apocryphal Acts and the Early Christian Martyrdom." *Arethusa* (1985) 18:211–230.

Peterson, E. "Einige Beobachtungen zu den Anfängen der christlichen Askese." In *Frühkirche, Judentum und Gnosis*, pp. 209–220. Rome: Herder, 1959. (First published in *Euntes docere* [1948] 1:295–302.)

Petrément, S. *Le Dualisme chez Platon, les Gnostiques et les Manichéens.* Paris: Presses Universitaires de France, 1947.

Pietri, Charles. "Le mariage chrétien à Rome." In J. Delumeau, ed. *Histoire vécue du peuple chrétien*, pp. 105–131. Paris: Privat, 1979.

—— *Roma Christiana.* 2 vols. Bibliothèque des écoles françaises d'Athènes et de Rome 224. Rome: Palais Farnèse, 1976.

Pisi, Paola. *Genesis e Phthora. Le motivazioni protologiche della verginità in Gregorio di Nissa e nella tradizione dell'enkrateia.* Rome: Ateneo, 1981.

Poque, Suzanne. *Le langage symbolique dans la prédication de saint Augustin.* 2 vols. Paris: Études augustiniennes, 1984.

Poupon, G. "L'accusation de magie dans les Actes Apocryphes." In F. Bovon, et al., eds. *Les Actes apocryphes des Apôtres*, pp. 71–93. Geneva: Labor et Fides, 1981.

Price, S. R. F. *Rituals and Power: The Roman imperial cult in Asia Minor.* Cambridge: Cambridge University Press, 1984.

Quibbell, J. E. *Excavations at Saqqara*, vol. 4. Cairo: 1908.

Rader, Rosemary. *Breaking Boundaries: Male/Female Friendship in Early Christian Communities.* New York: Paulist Press, 1983.

Rambeaux, C. *Tertullian face aux morales des trois premiers siècles.* Paris: Belles Lettres, 1979.

Rawson, B. "The Roman Family." In Rawson, ed. *The Family in Ancient Rome: New Perspectives*, pp. 1–57. Ithaca, New York: Cornell University Press, 1986.

Refoulé, F. "Rêves et vie spirituelle d'après Évagre le Pontique." *La vie spirituelle: Supplément* (1961) 14:470–571.

Reiling, J. *Hermas and Christian Prophecy: A Study in the Eleventh Mandate.* Supplements to Novum Testamentum 37. Leiden: Brill, 1973.

Rémondon, R. "L 'Église dans la société égyptienne à l'époque byzantine." *Chronique d'Égypte* (1972) 47:254–277.

Rice, Eugene F. *Saint Jerome in the Renaissance.* Baltimore: Johns Hopkins University Press, 1985.

Richardson, T. Wade. "Homosexuality in the *Satyricon*." *Classica et Medievalia* (1984) 35:105–127.

Ricoeur, Paul. *The Symbolism of Evil.* Translated by E. Buchanan. Boston: Beacon Press, 1969.

Roberge, M. "Anthropogonie et anthropologie dans la *Paraphrase de Sem* (NH VII, 1)." *Le Muséon* (1986) 99:229–248.

Robert, Jeanne, and Louis Robert. "Bulletin épigraphique." *Revue des études grecques* (1984) 97:419–522.

—— *La Carie.* Paris: A. Maisonneuve, 1954.

Robert, Louis. "D'Aphrodisias à la Lycaonie." *Hellenica* 13. Paris: Maisonneuve, 1965.

—— *Les Gladiateurs dans l'Orient grec.* Paris: Champion, 1940.

—— *Nouvelles inscriptions de Sardes.* Paris: A. Maisonneuve, 1964.

—— "Une vision de Perpétue." *Académie des Inscriptions et Belles Lettres, Comptes rendus 1982*, pp. 229–276.

Roberts, Colin H. *Manuscript and Belief in Early Christian Egypt.* Schweich Lectures 1977. London: Oxford University Press, 1977.

Robinson, J. M., and H. Koester. *Trajectories through Early Christianity.* Philadelphia: Fortress Press, 1971.

Rodenwaldt, G. "Über den Stilwandel in der antoninischen Kunst." *Abhandlungen der Berliner Akademie der Wissenschaften* (1935) 30, no. 3.

Roldanus, J. R. *Le Christ et l'homme dans la théologie d'Athanase d'Alexandrie.* Studies in the History of Christian Thought 4. Leiden: Brill, 1977.

Rordorf, Willy. "Marriage in the New Testament and in the Early Church." *Journal of Ecclesiastical History* (1969) 20:193–210.

Rosaldo, M. Z. "Women, Culture and Society: A Theoretical Overview." In M. Z. Rosaldo and L. Lamphere, eds. *Women, Culture and Society*, pp. 17–42. Stanford: Stanford University Press, 1974.

Rousseau, Philip. *Ascetics, Authority, and the Church in the Age of Jerome and Cassian*. Oxford: Oxford University Press, 1978.

—— *Pachomius: The Making of a Community in Fourth-Century Egypt*. Berkeley and Los Angeles: University of California Press, 1985.

Rousselle, Aline. "Gestes et signes de la famille dans l'Empire romain." In André Burguière, et al., eds. *Histoire de la famille*, vol. 1, pp. 231–269. Paris: Armand Colin, 1986.

—— "Parole et Inspiration: le travail de la voix dans le monde romain." *History and Philosophy of the Life Sciences* (1983) 5:129–157.

—— *Porneia: de la maîtrise du corps à la privation sensorielle*. Paris: Presses Universitaires de France, 1983.

Ruggini, L. *Economia e società nell'"Italia annonaria."* Milan: Giuffré, 1961.

Ruppert, F. *Das pachomianische Mönchtum und die Anfänge des klösterlichen Gehorsams*. Münster Schwarzacherstudien 20. 1971.

Sagnard, F. M. M. *La Gnose valentinienne et le témoignage de Saint Irénée*. Études de philosophie médiévale 26. Paris: J. Vrin, 1947.

Şahin, Sencer. "Griechische Epigramme aus dem südlichen Propontisgebiet." In M. B. de Boer and T. A. Eldridge, eds. *Hommages à M. J. Vermaseren*, vol. 3, pp. 997–1002. Leiden: Brill, 1978.

Salisbury, Joyce E. " 'The Bond of a Common Mind': A Study of Collective Salvation from Cyprian to Augustine." *Journal of Religious History* (1985) 13:235–247.

Saller, Richard P., and Peter Garnsey. *The Roman Empire: Economy, Society and Culture*. London: Duckworth, 1987.

—— and Brent D. Shaw. "Tombstones and Roman Family Relations in the Principate." *Journal of Roman Studies* (1984) 74:124–156.

Samuel, Alan E. "How many Gnostics?" *Bulletin of the American Society of Papyrologists* (1985) 22:297–322.

Sanders, E. P. *Jesus and Judaism*. Philadelphia: Fortress Press, 1985.

—— *Paul, the Law and the Jewish People*. Philadelphia: Fortress Press, 1983.

Saulnier, C. "La vie monastique en Terre Sainte auprès des lieux de pèlerinages." *Miscellanea Historiae Ecclesiasticae* 6, pp. 223–248. Bibliothèque de la Revue d'Histoire Ecclésiastique, fasc. 67. Brussels: Nauwelaerts, 1983.

Sauneron, S., and J. Jacquet. *Les ermitages chrétiens du désert d'Esna*. Vol. 1, *Archéologie et inscriptions*. Vol. 4, *Essai d'histoire*. Cairo: Institut français d'archéologie orientale du Caire, 1972.

Savon, H. "Maniérisme et Allégorie dans l'oeuvre d'Ambroise de Milan." *Revue des études latines* (1977) 55:203–221.

—— *Saint Ambroise devant l'exégèse de Philon le Juif*. 2 vols. Paris: Études augustiniennes, 1977.

—— "Une consolation imitée de Sénèque et de saint Cyprien." *Recherches augustiniennes* (1979) 14:153–190.

Saxer, Victor. "Le culte chrétien au ive siècle." *Miscellanea Historiae Ecclesiasticae*, no. 6, pp. 202–215. Bibliothèque de la Revue d'Histoire Ecclésiastique, fasc. 67. Brussels: Nauwelaerts, 1983.

—— "Le 'juste crucifié' de Platon à Théodoret." *Rivista di storia e letteratura religiosa* (1983) 19:189–215.

Scagloni, Carlo. "Ideale coniugale e familiare in Giovanni Crisostomo." In R. Cantalamassa, ed. q.v. *Etica sessuale e matrimonio nel cristianesimo delle origini*, pp. 273–422.

Schmitt, Émile. *Le mariage chrétien dans l'oeuvre de Saint Augustin.* Paris: Études augustiniennes, 1983.

Schneider, L. *Die Domäne als Weltbild. Wirkungsstrukturen der spätantiken Bildersprache.* Wiesbaden: Steiner, 1983.

Schoenebeck, H. von. *Der Mailänder Sarkophag und seine Nachfolge.* Rome: Pontificio Istituto di archeologia cristiana, 1935.

Schöllgen, G. *Ecclesia sordida? Zur Frage der sozialen Schichtung frühchristlicher Gemeinden am Beispiel Karthagos zur Zeit Tertullians.* Jahrbuch für Antike und Christentum: Ergänzungsband 12. Münster-in-Westfalen: Aschendorff, 1984.

Schrijvers, P. H. *Eine medizinische Erklärung der männlichen Homosexualität aus der Antike.* Amsterdam: Grüner Verlag, 1985.

Schürer, E. *The History of the Jewish People in the Age of Jesus Christ*, vol. 2. Revised and edited by G. Vermes, F. Millar, and M. Black. Edinburgh: T. and T. Clark, 1979.

Segal, Alan F. *Rebecca's Children: Judaism and Christianity in the Roman World.* Cambridge: Harvard University Press, 1986.

Seibel, W. *Fleisch und Geist beim heiligen Ambrosius.* Münchener Theologische Studien 14. Munich: K. Zink, 1958.

Seitz, O. J. "Antecedents and Significance of the Term δίψυχος." *Journal of Biblical Literature* (1947) 66:211–219.

Sfameni Gasparro, G. "Le motivazioni protologiche dell'*Enkrateia* nel cristianesimo dei primi secoli e nello Gnosticismo." In Ugo Bianchi, ed. q.v. *La Tradizione dell'Enkrateia*, pp. 149–261.

—— *Origene: studi di antropologia e di storia della tradizione.* Rome: Ateneo, 1984.

—— "Le *sordes* (/*rhupos*), il rapporto genesis-phthorà dell' *Enkrateia* in Origene." In R. Hanson and F. Crouzel, eds. q.v. *Origeniana Tertia*, pp. 165–183.

—— "Il tema della concupiscentia in Agostino e la tradizione dell'enkrateia." *Augustinianum* (1985) 15:155–183.

Shaw, Brent D. "The Age of Roman Girls at Marriage: Some Reconsiderations." *Journal of Roman Studies* (1987) 77:30–46.

—— "The Divine Economy: Stoicism as Ideology." *Latomus* (1985) 64:16–54.

—— "The Family in Late Antiquity: the Experience of Augustine." *Past and Present* (1987) 115:3–51.

—— "Latin Funerary Epigraphy and Family Life in the Later Roman Empire." *Historia* (1984) 33:457–495.

Shaw, Brent D. and Richard P. Saller. "Close Kin Marriage in Roman Society?" *Man* (1984) n.s. 19:431–444.

Shelton, Kathleen. *The Esquiline Treasure.* London: British Museum Publications, 1981.

—— "The Esquiline Treasure." *American Journal of Archaeology* (1985) 89:147–155.

Shepherd, Dorothy G. "An Icon of the Virgin: A Sixth-Century Tapestry Panel from Egypt." *Bulletin of the Cleveland Museum of Art* (1969) 59:90–120.

Shisha-Halevy, A. "Two New Schenoute-Texts from the British Library." *Orientalia* (1975) n.s. 44:149–185.

Sijpesteijn, P. J. "A Panegyric on John the Baptist." *Le Muséon* (1983) 96:231–238.

Silber, Ilana Friedrich. "Dissent Through Holiness: The Case of the Radical Renouncer in Theravada Buddhist Countries." *Numen* (1981) 28:164–193.

Sissa, Giulia. *Le corps virginal.* Paris: J. Vrin, 1987.

—— "Une virginité sans hymen: le corps féminin en Grèce ancienne." *Annales É.S.C.* (1984) 39:1119–1139.

Smith, A. *Porphyry's Place in the Neoplatonic Tradition.* The Hague: M. Nijhoff, 1974.

Smith, J. Z. *Map Is Not Territory.* Leiden: Brill, 1978.

Söder, R. *Die apokryphen Apostelakten und die romanhafte Literatur der Antike.* Stuttgart: Kohlhammer, 1932.

Sokolowski, F. *Les lois sacrées des cités grecques: Supplément.* Paris: de Boccard, 1962.

Speyer, W. "Zu den Vorwürfen der Heiden gegen die Christen." *Jahrbuch für Antike und Christentum* (1963) 6:129–135.

Staats, Reinhart. "Basilius als lebende Mönchsregel in Gregors von Nyssa *de virginitate.*" *Vigiliae Christianae* (1985) 39:228–255.

—— "Messalianerforschung und Ostkirchenkunde." In W. Strothmann, ed. *Makarios-Symposium über das Böse,* pp. 47–71. Göttinger Orientforschungen 1, no. 24. Wiesbaden: Harrassowitz, 1983.

Stancliffe, Clare. *St. Martin and His Hagiographer.* Oxford: Oxford University Press, 1983.

Steigman, E. "Rabbinic Anthropology." In W. Haase, ed. *Aufstieg und Niedergang der römischen Welt,* Reihe 2. Vol. 19:2, pp. 487–579. Berlin: de Gruyter, 1979.

Strack, H. and P. Billerbeck. *Kommentar zum Neuen Testament aus Talmud und Midrasch.* 4 vols. Munich: C. H. Beck, 1928.

Straw, Carole. *Perfection in Imperfection: Body, Soul, and Spiritual Progress in Gregory the Great.* Berkeley and Los Angeles: University of California Press, forthcoming.

Strobel, A. *Das Heilige Land der Montanisten.* Religionsgeschichtliche Versuche und Vorarbeiten 37. Berlin: de Gruyter, 1980.

Stroumsa, Gedaliahu A. G. *Another Seed: Studies in Gnostic Mythology.* Nag Hammadi Studies 24. Leiden: Brill, 1984.

—— "The Manichean Challenge to Egyptian Christianity." In Birger A. Pearson and James E. Goehring, eds. q.v. *The Roots of Egyptian Christianity*, pp. 307–319.

Stücklin, Christoph. *Tertullian: de virginibus velandis*. Europäische Hochschulschriften, ser.24.6. Bern and Frankfurt-am-Main: H. and P. Lang, 1974.

Stuiber, A. "Ambrosiaster." *Jahrbuch für Antike und Christentum* (1970) 13:119–123.

Syme, R. *Ammianus and the "Historia Augusta."* Oxford: Clarendon Press, 1968.

Tardieu, M. *Trois Mythes Gnostiques*. Paris: Études augustiniennes, 1974.

Teja, Ramón. *Organización economica y social de Capadocia en el siglo iv, según los padres capadocios*. Acta Salamanticensia: Filosofia y Letras 78. Salamanca: Universidad de Salamanca, 1974.

Tetz, Martin. "Athanasius und die Vita Antonii. Literarische und theologische Relationen." *Zeitschrift für neutestamentliche Wissenschaft* (1982) 73:1–30.

Theissen, Gerd. *Psychologische Aspekte paulinischer Theologie*. Göttingen: Vandenhoeck and Ruprecht, 1983.

—— *The Social Setting of Pauline Christianity: Essays on Corinth*. Edited and translated with an introduction by J. H. Schütz. Philadelphia: Fortress Press, 1982.

—— *Sociology of Early Palestinian Christianity*. Translated by John Bowden. Philadelphia: Fortress Press, 1978.

Thélamon, F. *Païens et chrétiens au ivème siècle*. Paris: Études augustiniennes, 1981.

Thierry, Nicole. "Un problème de continuité ou de rupture. La Cappadoce entre Rome, Byzance et les Arabes." *Académie des Inscriptions et Belles Lettres, Comptes rendus 1977*, pp. 98–146.

Thunberg, Lars. "The Human Person as the Image of God 1: Eastern Christianity." In B. McGinn, J. Meyendorff, and J. Leclercq, eds. *World Spirituality*. Vol. 16, *Christian Spirituality: Origins to the Twelfth Century*, pp. 291–312. New York: Crossroad, 1985.

Tissot, Y. "Encratisme et Actes Apocryphes." In F. Bovon, et al., eds. *Les Actes Apocryphes des Apôtres*, pp. 109–119. Geneva: Labor et Fides, 1981.

Tollinton, R. B. *Clement of Alexandria*. London: Williams and Norgate, 1914.

Torp, H. "Le monastère copte de Baouit. Quelques notes d'introduction." *Miscellanea Coptica, Acta Instituti Norvegiae Romani* (1981) 9:1–8.

—— "Les murs d'enceinte des monastères coptes primitifs." *Mèlanges d'archéologie et d'histoire* (1964) 76:173–200.

Traversari, G. "Tetimimo e Colimbétra. Ultime manifestazioni del teatro antico." *Dioniso* (1950) 13:18–35.

Tregenza, L. A. *The Red Sea Mountains of Egypt*. Oxford: Oxford University Press, 1955.

Treggiari, Susan. "Concubinae." *Papers of the British School at Rome* (1981) 49:59–81.

Trigg, J. W. *Origen: the Bible and Philosophy in the Third Century Church*. Atlanta: John Knox Press, 1983.

Urbach, E. E. *The Sages: Their Concepts and Beliefs.* Jerusalem: Magnes Press, 1975.

Van Bremen, Riet. "Women and Wealth." In Averil Cameron and Amélie Kuhrt, eds. q.v. *Images of Women in Antiquity,* pp. 223–242. Detroit: Wayne State University Press, 1983.

Van Dam, Raymond. "Emperors, Bishops and Friends in Late Antique Cappadocia." *Journal of Theological Studies* (1986) n.s. 37:53–76.

—— "Hagiography and History: The Life of Gregory Thaumaturgus." *Classical Antiquity* (1982) 1:272–308.

—— *Leadership and Community in Late Antique Gaul.* Berkeley and Los Angeles: University of California Press, 1985.

Van Eijk, Ton H. J. "Marriage and Virginity, Death and Immortality." In J. Fontaine and C. Kannengiesser, ed. *Epektasis: Mélanges offerts au cardinal J. Daniélou,* pp. 209–235. Paris: Beauchesne, 1972.

Van Ommeslaeghe, F. "Jean Chrysostome et Eudoxie." *Analecta Bollandiana* (1979) 97:131–159.

Vatin, C. *Recherches sur le mariage et la condition de la femme mariée à l'époque hellénistique.* Paris: de Boccard, 1970.

Vermes, Geza. "Leviticus 18:21 in Ancient Jewish Bible Exegesis." In J. J. Petruchowski and E. Fleischer, eds. *Studies in Aggadah, Targum, and Jewish Liturgy in Memory of Joseph Heinemann,* pp. 108–124. Jerusalem: Magnes Press, 1983.

—— *Jesus the Jew.* Philadelphia: Fortress Press, 1981.

—— "Methodology in the Study of Jewish Literature in the Graeco-Roman Period." *Journal of Jewish Studies* (1985) 36:145–158.

Veyne, P. *L'Élégie érotique romaine.* Paris: Editions du Seuil, 1983.

—— "L'Empire romain." In Veyne, ed. *Histoire de la Vie Privée.* Vol. 1, *De l'Empire romain à l'an mil.* pp. 19–224. Paris: Le Seuil, 1985. English translation: A. Goldhammer, trans. *A History of Private Life.* Vol. 1, *From Pagan Rome to Byzantium,* pp. 16–233. Cambridge: Harvard University Press, 1987.

—— "La famille et l'amour sous le Haut-empire romain." *Annales É.S.C.* (1978) 33:35–63.

—— "L'homosexualité à Rome." *Communications* (1982) 35:25–33. Translated in P. Ariès and A. Béjin, eds. q.v. *Western Sexuality: Practice and Precept in Past Times,* pp. 26–35.

—— "Rome devant la prétendue fuite de l'or." *Annales É.S.C.* (1979) 34:211–244.

Villeneuve, F. "L'économie rurale et la vie des campagnes." in J.-M. Dentzer, ed. *Hauran 1,* pp. 63–129. Paris: P. Geuthner, 1985.

Ville, Georges. "Religion et politique: comment ont pris fin les combats de gladiateurs." *Annales É.S.C.* (1979) 34:651–671.

Völker, W. *Gregor von Nyssa als Mystiker.* Wiesbaden: Franz Steiner, 1955.

—— "Scala Paradisi." *Eine Studie zu Johannes Climacus und zugleich eine Vorstudie zu Symeon dem Neuen Theologen.* Wiesbaden: F. Steiner, 1968.

—— *Das Vollkommenheitsideal des Origenes.* Tübingen: J. C. B. Mohr, 1931.

—— Der wahre Gnostiker nach Clemens Alexandrinus. Texte und Untersuchungen 57. Berlin: Akademie Verlag, 1952.

Vööbus, A. Celibacy, a Requirement for Admission to Baptism in the Early Syrian Church. Papers of the Estonian Theological Society in Exile 1. Stockholm: 1951.

—— A History of Asceticism in the Syrian Orient. CSCO 184, Subsidia 14. Louvain: CSCO, 1958.

Walzer, Richard. Galen on Jews and Christians. Oxford: Oxford University Press, 1947.

Ware, Kallistos. "The Sacrament of Baptism and the Ascetic Life in the Teaching of Mark the Monk." Studia Patristica 10, pp. 441–451. Texte und Untersuchungen 107. Berlin: Akademie-Verlag, 1970.

—— "Ways of Prayer and Contemplation 1: Eastern." In B. McGinn, J. Meyendorff, and J. Leclercq, eds. World Spirituality. Vol. 16, Christian Spirituality: Origins to the Twelfth Century, pp. 395–414. New York: Crossroad, 1985.

Wallace-Hadrill, J. M. The Frankish Church. Oxford: Clarendon Press, 1983.

Wemple, Suzanne F. Women in Frankish Society. Philadelphia: University of Pennsylvania Press, 1981.

Wenham, G. J. "Beṯûlāh: 'A Girl of Marriageable Age'." Vetus Testamentum (1972) 22:326–348.

Wilken, R. L. John Chrysostom and the Jews. Rhetoric and Reality in the Late Fourth Century. Berkeley and Los Angeles: University of California Press, 1983.

—— "Liturgy, Bible and Theology in the Easter Sermons of Gregory of Nyssa." In M. Harl, ed. q.v. Écriture et culture philosophique dans la pensée de Grégoire de Nysse, pp. 127–143.

Williams, Michael Allan. The Immovable Race. A Gnostic Designation and the Theory of Stability in Late Antiquity. Nag Hammadi Studies 29. Leiden: Brill, 1985.

—— "Uses of Gender Imagery in Ancient Gnostic Texts." In C. W. Bynum, S. Harrell, and P. Richman, eds. Gender and Religion: On the Complexity of Symbols, pp. 196–227. Boston: Beacon Press, 1986.

Wilson, Robert. McL. "Alimentary and sexual encratism in the Nag Hammadi Texts." In Ugo Bianchi, ed. q.v. La Tradizione dell'Enkrateia, pp. 317–339.

Winlock, H. B. The Monastery of Epiphanius at Thebes 1: The Archaeological Material. New York: Metropolitan Museum of Art, 1926.

Wipszycka, E. "Le degré d'alphabétisation en Égypte byzantine." Revue des études augustiniennes (1984) 30:279–96.

—— "Les terres de la congrégation pachômienne." In J. Bingen, ed. Le monde grec. Hommages à Claire Préaux, pp. 625–636. Brussels: Université de Bruxelles, 1975.

Wood, Charles T. "The Doctor's Dilemma: sin, salvation and the menstrual cycle in medieval thought." Speculum (1981) 56:710–727.

Wood, I. N. "A Prelude to Columbanus: the Monastic Achievement in the Burgundian Territories." In H. B. Clarke and M. Brennan, eds. Columbanus and Merovingian Monasticism, pp. 3–32. B.A.R. International Series 1113. Oxford: B.A.R., 1981.

Wortley, Raoul. *Connaissance religieuse et herméneutique chez Clément d'Alexandrie.* Leiden: Brill, 1973.

Wright, David F. "Homosexuals or Prostitutes? The Meaning of ΑΡΣΕΝΟΚΟΙΤΑΙ (1 Cor. 6:9, 1 Tim. 1:10)." *Vigiliae Christianae* (1984) 38:125–153.

Wrigley, E. A. "Fertility Strategy for the Individual and the Group." In C. Tilly, ed. *Historical Studies of Changing Fertility,* pp. 135–154. Princeton: Princeton University Press, 1978.

Wyrwa, Dietmar. *Die christliche Platonaneignung in den "Stromateis" des Clemens von Alexandrien.* Berlin, New York: de Gruyter, 1983.

Index